Pauline Fro

LONDON

SPEND LESS
SEE MORE ™

1st Edition

by Jason Cochran

Series Editor: Pauline Frommer

BICENTENNIAL
1807
WILEY
2007
BICENTENNIAL

Wiley Publishing, Inc.

Published by:

Wiley Publishing, Inc.

111 River St.
Hoboken, NJ 07030-5774

ISBN-13: 978-0-470-05228-0
ISBN-10: 0-470-05228-7

Editor: Jennifer Reilly
Production Editor: M. Faunette Johnston
Cartographer: Roberta Stockwell
Photo Editor: Richard Fox
Interior Design: Lissa Auciello-Brogan
Anniversary Logo Design: Richard Pacifico
Production by Wiley Indianapolis Composition Services

For information on our other products and services or to obtain technical support,
please contact our Customer Care Department within the U.S. at 800/762-2974,
outside the U.S. at 317/572-3993 or fax 317/572-4002.

Wiley also publishes its books in a variety of electronic formats. Some content that
appears in print may not be available in electronic formats.

Manufactured in the United States of America

5   4   3   2   1

Contents

List of Maps

About the Author

Jason Cochran has written for publications including  *Entertainment Weekly;* the *New York Times, Daily News,* and *Post; Travel + Leisure* and *T+L Family; Budget Travel; Newsweek; City; Inside.com; Marie Claire; Arthur Frommer's Smart Shopping; the South Florida Sun-Sentinel; Arena* (U.K.); *Who* (Australia); *Scanorama* and *Seasons* (Sweden). His writing has been awarded the Golden Pen by the Croatian government and was selected to appear in a permanent exhibit in the National Museum of Australia. He also devised questions for the first American season of *Who Wants to Be a Millionaire* (ABC) and before that, spent nearly 2 years backpacking solo around the world. As a commentator, he has appeared on *CNN, CNN Headline News, CNNfn, Australia.com, WOR, Outdoor Life Network,* and *MSNBC.com.* He is an alumnus of Northwestern University's Medill School of Journalism and New York University's Graduate Music Theatre Writing Program.

Thanks to my mother, Tracy O'Neal. If you hadn't sent me to London first, where would I be now?

Acknowledgments

Among the countless people who helped shape this book, several were particularly instrumental, including Zoe Shurgold from Visit London; Paul Chibeba and Andrew Weir from Visit Britain; Jessica Jacob of Friends of St. Paul's; David Landsel; my clever and patient editor Jennifer Reilly; and of course, my principled and vigilant series editor, Pauline Frommer, whose passion for even the most minor details is contagious. Thanks to all the people who stoked my love for London at the right moments, including Claire Kurtgis Hunter, Derek Ellwood, Alan Smith, and Lee Houck. The contributions of two witty Londoners transformed the book: Jennifer Jellicorse and Robin Oakley, whose bottomless well of appreciation gave me more ideas than I could use. Thanks to Holly Ambrose for doing it first and daring me to follow. Thanks also to Arthur Frommer for being a gracious teacher. A deep bow for Mark, who helped me get to know his home city better than he does, and to whom I'll always be grateful. I also can't express enough gratitude to my family and friends, who always strike the right balance of laissez-faire and cheerleading that makes everything easy—that includes Michael for his strings-free support, Julie for nursing me between battles, Curtis for touchstoning, and Jessica for minding the fort.

An Invitation to the Reader

In researching this book, we discovered many wonderful places—hotels, restaurants, shops, and more. We're sure you'll find others. Please tell us about them, so we can share the information with your fellow travelers in upcoming editions. If you were disappointed with a recommendation, we'd love to know that, too. Please write to:

Pauline Frommer's London, 1st Edition
Wiley Publishing, Inc. • 111 River St. • Hoboken, NJ 07030-5774

An Additional Note

Please be advised that travel information is subject to change at any time—and this is especially true of prices. We therefore suggest that you write or call ahead for confirmation when making your travel plans. The authors, editors, and publisher cannot be held responsible for the experiences of readers while traveling. Your safety is important to us, however, so we encourage you to stay alert and be aware of your surroundings. Keep a close eye on cameras, purses, and wallets, all favorite targets of thieves and pickpockets.

Star Ratings, Icons & Abbreviations

Every restaurant, hotel and attraction is rated with stars, indicating our opinion of that facility's desirability; this relates not to price, but to the value you receive for the price you pay. The stars mean:

No stars: Good
    ★ Very good
   ★★ Great
  ★★★ Outstanding! A must!

Accommodations within each neighborhood are listed in ascending order of cost, starting with the cheapest and increasing to the occasional "splurge." Each hotel review is preceded by one, two, three or four dollar signs, indicating the price range per double room. Restaurants work on a similar system, with dollar signs indicating the price range per three-course meal.

Accommodations	**Dining**
£ Up to £75/night	£ Main courses for £5 or less
££ £76–£7110	££ Main courses for £6–£8
£££ £111–£150	£££ Main courses for £9–£11
££££ More than £151	££££ Main courses for £12 and over

In addition, we've included a kids icon 🧒 to denote attractions, restaurants, and lodgings that are particularly child friendly.

Frommers.com

Now that you have this guidebook to help you plan a great trip, visit our website at **www. frommers.com** for additional travel information on more than 3,500 destinations. We update features regularly to give you instant access to the most current trip-planning information available. At Frommers.com, you'll find scoops on the best airfares, lodging rates, and car rental bargains. You can even book your travel online through our reliable travel booking partners. Other popular features include:

* Online updates of our most popular guidebooks
* Vacation sweepstakes and contest giveaways
* Newsletters highlighting the hottest travel trends
* Online travel message boards with featured travel discussions

A Note from Pauline

I STARTED TRAVELING WITH MY GUIDEBOOK-WRITING PARENTS, ARTHUR Frommer and Hope Arthur, when I was just four months old. To avoid lugging around a crib, they would simply swaddle me and stick me in an open drawer for the night. For half of my childhood, my home was a succession of hotels and B&B's throughout Europe, as we dashed around every year to update *Europe on $5 a Day* (and then $10 a day, and then $20...).

We always traveled on a budget, staying at the Mom-and-Pop joints Dad featured in the guide, getting around by public transportation, eating where the locals ate. And that's still the way I travel today, because I learned—from the master—that these types of vacations not only save you money, but give you a richer, deeper experience of the culture. You spend time in local neighborhoods and you meet and talk with the people who live there. For me, making friends and having meaningful exchanges is always the highlight of my trip—and the main reason I decided to become a travel writer and editor as well.

I conceived these books as budget guides for the next generation. They have all the outspoken commentary and detailed pricing information you've come to expect from the Frommer's guides, but they take bargain hunting into the 21st century, with more information on how you can effectively use the Internet and air/hotel packages to save money. Most importantly, we stress the availability of "alternative accommodations" not simply to save you money but to give you a more authentic experience in the places you visit. In this London book, for example, we'll tell you about a homestay in Virginia Woolf's childhood home, where you can lodge for just £79 a night (p. 31); perfectly comfortable rooms in a private home in southwest and central London where singles cost just £23 a night and doubles are £38, far less that what you'd pay to share your sleep space with 10 others in a hostel; and a family owned B&B that gives a new meaning to the term full English breakfast—not only is it delicious, but after eating, lunch becomes optional (p. 50).

The chapter on "The Other London" immerses you in the life that residents enjoy: The lectures they attend, the work they do, the pub parties they crowd. Page through this guide and you'll find information on how to attend the knock-down, drag-out, take-no-prisoners sessions of Parliament (p. 203); how to volunteer with the London Wildlife Trust for a day, working to protect the endangered species who call the city home and meeting terrific people along the way (p. 205); or how to attend a rollicking, joyous British pantomime (p. 215), among other experiences.

The result, I hope, is a valuable new addition to the world of guidebooks. Please let me know how we've done! I encourage you to e-mail me at editor@frommers.com or write me care of Frommer's, 111 River Street, Hoboken, NJ, 07030.

Happy Traveling!

Pauline Frommer

Pauline Frommer

London the Lionhearted

The best the city has to offer

WHETHER YOU REALIZE IT OR NOT, LONDON HAS AFFECTED YOUR DESTINY. There's hardly a quarter of the globe that it hasn't changed. The United States was founded in reaction to London's edicts. Australia was peopled with London's criminals and later, with settlers looking for a better life away from England's hardships. Modern Canada, South Africa, and New Zealand were cultivated from London. India's course was irrevocably changed by the aspirations of London businessmen, as were the lives of millions of Africans who were shipped around the world while Londoners lined their pockets with the profit. You're holding proof in your hands of London's pull: that you bought this very book, written in English somewhere other than in England, is evidence of London's reach across time and distance.

Although London is the world's city, it still has a distinct culture. Shopkeepers are respectfully standoffish and don't flatter their customers with effusive niceties. Strangers mind their own business, honoring the dearly held national mantra, "mustn't grumble." When you're in London, you know you're not home, yet it still feels strangely familiar. London never loses its sense of place or its livability. London is historical, but it's no inert museum.

London is inexhaustible. You could tour it for months and barely know it at all. Few cities are home to such a cross section of people living together in remarkable harmony. That diversity makes London like a cut diamond; approach it from a slightly different angle each day, and it takes on an entirely fresh shape and sheen.

> *Much as I hate to agree with that tedious old git Samuel Johnson, and despite the pompous imbecility of his famous remark about when a man is tired of London he is tired of life (an observation exceeded in fatuousness only by 'Let a smile be your umbrella'), I can't dispute it.*
>
> —Bill Bryson, *Notes from a Small Island*

That's the goal of this book: to encourage you to take one step sideways, off the beaten tourist track, and see the city from a different perspective. Don't see it only for its misty rains, its lilting accents, or its monumental buildings of stone. See it like a South Asian immigrant in East Ham, who spends Wednesday nights at the Bollywood movie house and worships in the largest Hindu temple outside of India. Or like the Jamaican-born Brixton resident who spends each morning shopping for exotic greens at a street market that's been running for well over a century. See it like a twenty-something whose weekly highlights are the quiz night at the local pub and the Saturday breakfast at the local caff. Step sideways and see another London. And then another.

After all, their London is your London.

THE SIGHTS YOU SIMPLY CAN'T MISS

For all the years during which London was the capital of a globe-spanning empire, treasures flowed into the city, so it possesses some of the finest collections of international art and antiquities on the planet. London deserves its reputation as an expensive city, but people overlook that its finest museums cost nothing to see: the relics of **The British Museum** (p. 134); the comprehensive holdings of **The National Gallery** (p. 143) and **The National Portrait Gallery** (p. 151); and the rare clothing, art, and decorative arts at the **Victoria and Albert Museum** (p. 148) are just four enormous collections, each of which could absorb you for an entire cost-free day.

London is also a nerve center for cutting-edge modern art, and the free display in the soaring industrial caverns of **The Tate Modern** (p. 145), on the bustling riverside promenade of Bankside, has quickly become a requisite stop during a visit. **The Saatchi Gallery** (p. 182), assembled by a renegade art fan, is a favorite for envelope-pushing ideas, and the world's top art aficionados convene on the many **galleries** (p. 182) and **auction houses** (p. 272 to augment their collections. Wealth has always created architectural showpieces: The distinctive two-level **Tower Bridge** (p. 184) over the River Thames was a great engineering feat of the Victorian era, and across town on the same water, the handsome observation wheel called the **London Eye** (p. 137) was embraced by the city quickly after its 1999 erection, proving that modern architecture can be just as iconic. The rounded tower at **30 St. Mary Axe,** nicknamed the Gherkin for its pickle-like profile, is the latest evolution on a skyline that, in recent years, has continuously reinvented itself.

As a magnet for the world's sophisticates, London has peerless **shopping areas** (including Oxford St., Regent St., Piccadilly, and King's Rd.), although given the power of the pound, you'll probably be more inclined to window-shop. London's **theaters** (p. 289) have been setting the aesthetic bar for more than 500 years. You won't have experienced the depth of London's culture without spending at least one night in front of one of its stages. You can also experience unique performances at **Shakespeare's Globe** (p. 296), a faithful re-creation of an Elizabethan theater, or at one of the city's many **comedy clubs** (p. 303), from which spring movie stars and household names. And, of course, the productions at the **Royal Opera House** (p. 301) are among the world's most acclaimed. To get around, take the city's **Underground** (p. 9), or Tube, parts of which opened as the world's first subway system in the 1860s; the Tube is a sight unto itself.

THE FINEST HISTORICAL SIGHTS

Fortified with enough maps and books, you could find true tales that happened on virtually every corner in London, and a long ramble through its jumbled streets, soaking up the places where history happened, is an essential experience. Since the city was built before cars and trains, it's a true walker's town.

London in a Nutshell

Population: 7.2 million (an eighth of the entire U.K. population)
Ethnicity: More than 25% ethnic, the largest non-white population of any European city
Languages spoken: More than 250
Annual salary, manual jobs: £21,000 (men), £19,000 (women)
Annual salary, non-manual jobs: £42,000 (men), £31,600 (women)
Area: 1,584 square kilometers/618 square miles (30% of that is parkland or open space)
Total English land area occupied by London: 1.2%
Source: Visit London

Many spots where bygone famous names conducted their business have been carefully preserved, and visiting some of these ancient sights, some of which are more than a millennium old, can boggle the mind and inspire the imagination. The world's most famous castle, **The Tower of London** (p. 140), has stood sentry on the Pool of London since 1068, and has been used as a keep, a prison, a zoo, and now as the repository for the legendary Crown Jewels. **Westminster Abbey** (p. 138) has been the location of every coronation since 1066, and is the final resting place of the bones of more than a dozen monarchs including the steely Elizabeth I. **St. Paul's Cathedral** (p. 150), in the oldest quarter of the city, has been a symbol of London since it was designed by the impossibly prolific Sir Christopher Wren in the late 1600s. Many royal homes are open for public inspection, including the ancient **Hampton Court Palace** (p. 160), **Windsor Castle** (p. 321), **Kensington Palace** (p. 159), and their junior sister, **Buckingham Palace** (p. 160).

The day-to-day operation of the United Kingdom is still undertaken around Whitehall, where the finely decorated **Houses of Parliament** (p. 186) are proclaimed by the clock tower containing the famous bell **Big Ben.** Nearby is the prime minister's home, **10 Downing Street** (p. 239), whose Georgian facade appears humble but actually masks a virtual citadel of power.

DREAM ACCOMMODATIONS

Many visitors put off their dream trips to London simply because they don't think they can afford to go. Hotel costs usually take the blame. Yet the reality is that the least expensive places to stay often yield the most exciting visits. Many London residents maintain spare homes or rooms expressly for international visitors. Most are located in the same areas where the most popular hotels are found (p. 28).

One of the least expensive but most rewarding accommodation options is to rent a room in family-owned B&Bs, which are usually located in historic Georgian or Victorian town houses, complete with sweeping staircases and basement-level kitchens where the owners prepare you a hot breakfast as part of the bargain. The meal and the advice dispensed by your hosts—just politely ask for what you need and let the friendship develop—will prepare you for the rigors of a day of touring. Three such home-grown inns are the **Jesmond Hotel** (p. 49), the **Alhambra Hotel** (p. 46), and **St. Margaret's Hotel** (p. 50), all within walking distance of the West End. Your rooms will be clean and simple, but affordable, leaving you money to spend on what you came to do—see London.

For more cash, smartly designed **B+B Belgravia** (p. 77), **Twenty Nevern Square** (p. 59), **Hotel La Place** (p. 64), and **Number Sixteen** (p. 60) heighten the B&B concept with fashion-sensitive style that bridges the gap between a guesthouse and a hotel. If more traditional hotels are your preference, it's possible to find a room within a sensible budget. **The Sanctuary House Hotel** (p. 80) and the **Southwark Rose** (p. 69) provide amenities you'd see in a more expensive corporate hotel but with more attentive management and for less money. A few chain hotel brands also provide comfortable rooms, spacious enough for families, at acceptable prices; if you stay at the **Premier Travel Inn London Southwark,** you'll take your breakfast overlooking the Thames.

DINING FOR EVERY TASTE

London's cuisine reflects its diversity. Asian cooking is particularly prevalent, having supplanted fish and chips as England's go-to casual meal. One of the best Indian meals of my life was served at the long-running **Punjab Restaurant** (p. 110) in Covent Garden, although I also appreciate the authentic Indian flavors of **Masala Zone** (p. 122). The all-you-can-eat vegetarian buffet at **Indian Veg Bhelpoori House** (p. 94) is one of the city's greatest bargains.

Contemporary Southeast Asian is also in vogue; the communal wooden tables at the many locations of Chef Alan Yau's **Wagamama** (p. 100) chain are terrific places to chat with strangers over a flavorful bowl of noodles, and Yau repeats the winning formula with his equally popular **Busaba Eathai** (p. 106). Hip Asian is also served in style at **Ping Pong** (dim sum, p. 107), and **Hare & Tortoise** (Malaysian, p. 89), two places where you'd be as happy to be seen as to be sated. Vegetarian dining is something carnivores and herbivores alike appreciate, and you'll always find a crowd at **Govinda's Restaurant** (p. 104), student hangout **Food for Thought** (p. 109), and the diner-like **Eat and Two Veg** (p. 100).

Of course, traditional meals are back in fashion, and you'll be hard-pressed to find a table where English cuisine's dowdy reputation is upheld. **S&M Café** (p. 114) celebrates sausage; **The Fryer's Delight** (p. 114) is perhaps the prototypical "chippie" making fish and chips. **Frontline** (p. 124), a hangout for foreign correspondents, typifies the current trend toward upscale versions of comfort food that a British mum might prepare. Combating the high price of sit-down meals, the **triangle sandwich** (p. 92) is the ubiquitous London lunch, consumed on the go by seemingly everyone. And the so-called "beigels" of Spitalfield's 24-hour **Beigel Bake** (p. 113) are the unique missing link between the Polish originals and the breadier "bagels" of North America.

THE BEST SPORTS & "OTHER" EXPERIENCES

Londoners revel in learning and in sharing experiences—call it another byproduct of a city raised on diversity. Be one of them. Take a chance and leap out of the tourist rut so that you can experience what London life is really like. Kibbutz with

East End salt of the earth at the Victorian steam baths of **York Hall Leisure Centre** (p. 218) or with Marylebone doyennes at the ritzy **Porchester Spa** (p. 218); delve into deep topics at a scientific discussion at **The Dana Centre** (p. 200); or dig around in the sediment of the river for buried treasure with **Thames21** (p. 205). Hear one of the world's great choirs at a service at **Westminster Cathedral** (p. 210) and one of the world's best organs at **Brompton Oratory** (p. 210). In a city full of ghosts, hold a séance for spirits in the creaky old town house owned by the **Spiritualist Association of Great Britain** (p. 212).

Britain exports its soccer players around the world, and there are fewer pursuits more integral to an Englishman's sporting life than attending a British **football match** (p. 228); or a **cricket match at the Oval** (p. 230). Some little-known museums live on the margins of your normal experience: Spend the evening in the **Dennis Severs House** (p. 164), a thoroughly authentic 19th-century town house whose sights, sounds, and smells trick visitors into believing they have gone back in time. Despite their reserved appearances, Londoners relish a bit of irreverent nose-tweaking, and you can join in on that, too: Dress up as a nun and talk back to the silver screen at the **Sing-a-Long-a** *The Sound of Music* (p. 216); give the universe a what for at **Speaker's Corner** (p. 202); drink away your Sunday with a British brew at one of the countless pub roasts (p. 214); or go on a graffiti safari for work by the maverick artist **Banksy** (p. 185).

2 The Lay of the Land

FEW GREAT MODERN CITIES ARE AS MULTILAYERED, INTRICATE, AND YES, *MESSY* as London, and that's because history was knitted into its very layout and never removed. Nearly half the housing in Paris was pulled down in the 1800s so Napoleon II could indulge his fantasy of wide avenues of parks. Manhattan ordered widespread destruction of most everything standing in order to implement its gridded street system. But London's modern makeup is mostly the haphazard product of blind evolution, which piled up over successive generations to produce the complicated metropolis that exists today. One could say that London simply happened.

As recently as the early 1800s, London—and by London, I mean what we now call the City, between St. Paul's and the Tower—was a compact, teeming monster where many lives, birth to death, were carried out within the same few blocks. Within that frenzied cluster, districts developed out of logic or bias—the smoke of industry was banished downwind, for example, and kings lived near the Thames for easy transportation. All around the City were dozens of villages, many of which retain their original names, and often, a whiff of their original personalities.

Quickly, London swelled to swallow much of its current territory. Yet because of ancient echoes, neighborhoods remain surprisingly small—many are just minutes across by foot, and all but the most crucial streets can change names several times within a few blocks. It's still possible to stroll along and, within a block, sense a sudden shift in energy and character. In many ways, London is still a complex system of hundreds of hamlets. It's one of the many delights that makes it so surprising. It also means it can take a lifetime to scratch its surface.

Your first purchase, which can be made at any newsstand or bookstore, should be a map. Don't bother with the simplified map your hotel might offer—the inferior maps leave off side streets. The most cherished variety is the **London A-Z** (www. a-zmaps.co.uk), first compiled by the indefatigable Phyllis Pearsall, who walked every mile of the city for the 1936 debut edition and commanded the resulting cartography empire until her death sixty years later. The *A-Z* includes every street, hospital, post office, and train station, no matter how obscure, and although it comes in many sizes, your prime concern should be that your hotel's street is somewhere in it. I prefer the ***AZ Mini London*** (£4.95), a booklet that fits into a jacket pocket and can be consulted discreetly; I find the company's other tourist-oriented publications too simplified and missing the best outlying areas. Just be sure to call it an "A to Zed" or you may get a funny look; in England, the last letter in the alphabet is, quite sensibly, pronounced to not rhyme with eight others.

Where Is It?—Use the Code

Every address in this book includes its postcode, which corresponds to the neighborhood in which you'll find it. Don't worry—you won't need to memorize these because each listing also includes the nearest Tube stop to help you quickly place locations on a map. Here are some of the most common postcodes, along with which areas they cover:

WC1 Bloomsbury

WC2 Covent Garden, Holborn, Strand

W1 Fitzrovia, Marylebone, Mayfair, Soho

W2 Bayswater

W6 Hammersmith

W8 Kensington

W11 Notting Hill

SW1 Belgravia, St. James's, Westminster

SW3 Chelsea

SW5 Earl's Court

SW7 Knightsbridge, SouthKensington

SE1 Southwark

SE10 Greenwich

EC1 Clerkenwell

EC2 Bank, Barbican, Liverpool Street

EC3 Tower Hill

EC4 Fleet Street, St. Paul's

E1 Spitalfields, Whitechapel

E2 Bethnal Green

E14 Canary Wharf/Isle of Dogs

N1 Islington

NW1 Camden Town

NW3 Hampstead

For mail delivery, London is chopped into geographic parcels, and you'll see those **postcodes** on street signs and hear them in conversation. The heart of the city, in postcode terms, is near the Chancery Lane Tube stop. From there, areas are given a compass direction (N for north, SW for southwest, etc.) and a number (but ignore that, since a number greater than 1 doesn't mean the area is in the boonies). In the very center of town, addresses get an extra C for "centre," as in WC1, which is where Covent Garden is located. These codes are useful in orienting yourself.

GETTING AROUND

There are three methods for getting around sprawling London: by Tube (historic and enchanting, but expensive), by bus (less expensive and less glamorous, but more edifying), and by foot (the best method, but not always possible). Taxis are priced at the deluxe level, and driving your own car is madness.

THE UNDERGROUND

More culture shock: It's not called a "subway." In England, when you see a sign for a "subway," the word just signifies a foot passageway under a busy street.

Instead, Londoners call their 405km (253-mile) metro system the Underground, its official name, or just as commonly, "the Tube." Its elegant, distinctive logo—a red "roundel" bisected by a blue bar—debuted in 1913 as one of the world's first corporate symbols, and it remains one of the city's most ubiquitous sights.

There's no older system on Earth—London's Metropolitan Railway was not only the first, which took no small leap of imagination and engineering, but it also gave the world the standard coinage for subway, "metro." The first section, running from Paddington to Farringdon, opened in 1863, 33 years ahead of the next European city (Budapest), 34 years before Boston, and 41 years before New York—the original snippet is still in use today. The Tube's most recent major addition, in 1999, was the £3.5-billion Jubilee Line extension from Westminster to Stratford. Now underway: extensions to the East London line.

The Tube is an attraction unto itself. I'm fascinated by Tube history, probably because so much of it remains visible, and seeking out vestiges of the early system (1907 tilework on the Piccadilly Line; the fake house facades built at 23-24 Leinster Gardens to hide exposed tracks; abandoned stations like the ones on Dover St. and at Strand and Surrey St.) is one of my favorite activities on a visit. If such "urban archaeology" fascinates you, visit the London's Transport Museum in Covent Garden, one of the city's family-friendly highlights.

Operating Schedule

The Tube shuts down nightly. Although exact times for first and final trains are posted in each station (using the simple 24-hr. clock), based on when they arrive in central London, the Tube generally operates Monday to Saturdays from 5:30am (0530) to just after midnight (0000), and Sundays 7:00am (0700) to 11:30pm (2330). To give clubbers more time to party, starting May 2007, trains will run until 1:00am (0100) on Friday and Saturdays, and start on 6:00am (0600) on Saturdays.

What happens if you miss the last train? Don't worry—you're not stranded, although your trip may take a little longer. Just turn to the city's network of 100 Night Bus routes (p. 15). Or, as a last resort, take a taxi (p. 16).

How the Tube Works

There are 12 named lines on the Tube network, plus a light rail (the Docklands Light Railway, or DLR, serving Docklands, Greenwich, and southeast London) and a tram line, which together serve 275 stations. On an average visit, you're likely to become familiar with a dozen or so stations. Lines are color-coded: the Piccadilly Line is a peacock purple, the Central is royal red, the Bakerloo could be considered Sherlock Holmes brown, and so on.

Untangling the Tube

Don't be daunted. The Tube operates a 24-hour information line that answers even the silliest questions: ☎ 020/7222-1234. Or visit www.tfl.gov.uk, which contains more maps, journey planners, and FAQs than a normal person can use.

As endearing as the Tube is, it is not a perfect system. You need to be prepared for a few things:

1. **Stairs.** Most stations are as intricate as anthills. Passengers are forever being corralled sadistically up staircases, around platforms, down more staircases, and through still more staircases. The Victorians must have had some sexy legs. Yours might hurt after a day of touring. Even stations equipped with extremely long escalators (Angel has the longest one in the system—59m/197 ft.) perversely require passengers to climb a final flight of stairs to reach the street. So if you bring luggage into the Tube, be able to hoist your stuff for at least 15 stairs at a time. (This is where backpacks make sense.) The only tourist-area stations in zone 1 or 2 that have lifts all the way to the street are at Earl's Court, Hammersmith, Brixton, and everything on the Jubilee Line from Westminster east. A sorry list. The entire DLR is accessible, though. If you need information on disabled facilities, contact **Transport for London Access & Mobility** (☎ 020/7941-4600; www.tfl.gov.uk).

2. **Delays.** When you enter a station, look for a sign with the names and colors of the Tube lines on it. Beside each line, you'll see a status bar reading "Good service," "Severe delays," or the like. Trust this sign—it's updated by staff every 10 minutes because lines close without warning. If you note "Minor delays," don't worry, because you probably won't even notice the extra wait (unless the situation degenerates after you're through the turnstiles). Not only are Londoners hypervigilant about reporting things like suspicious packages, which suspends service for unpredictable chunks of time, but also remember the Tube system is older than dirt, and it's kind of falling apart. It was left to languish in benign neglect for much of the twentieth century, and now engineers can't keep up with the endless breakdowns, signal failures, and track issues that keep cropping up. It doesn't help that many of the private companies contracted to maintain the system are widely denounced as corrupt and/or incompetent. Should your desired lines be out of commission, plan another route, using other lines, or by walking or taking the bus.

3. **Tough weekends.** London's system was experimental, so it had to be built on the cheap, which means each line gets one set of tracks per direction. When they need maintenance, they shut down. Weekends, by and large, are when this happens. Check with staff in the ticket hall to see what's shut down, because something will be, even if (fingers crossed) it may not affect you.

The rest is mostly foolproof. Riders look for signs pointing them to the color and name of the line they want. Pretty soon, more signs separate them according to the direction they want to go in, based on the Tube map. So if you know the name/color of the line you want, as well as which direction you need to take it in, the multitude of signs will march you, cattlelike, directly to the platform you need.

If you need to change trains (and you will, now and then), the follow-the-signs method repeats until it's time to look for the "Way Out," which is Undergroundese for "Exit." You'll shuffle through a warren of ancient cylindrical tunnels, many of them faced in custard-yellow tiles and overly full of silent commuters, and you'll scale alpine escalators lined with ads for West End musicals.

One of the groovier things about the Underground, in addition to the hodge-podge of eras, styles, designs, and people you'll encounter, is the electronic displays on every platform that tell you how long it'll be until the next train. Knowing how long you'll have to wait (it's never that long) takes a huge amount of frustration out of a commute.

Not all trains will travel to the end of the line; some end their runs a few stations early. The final destination of the train at hand will be shown in the overhead displays as it rolls into the station, or it will appear on the front of the first carriage. Luckily, none of this usually matters to most tourists, since trains rarely end their journeys within the center of the city.

The confusing line for tourists is the Northern Line (black on the maps), which takes two paths because it was cobbled together from several independent train lines. One travels through the City, and one travels through Bloomsbury. Both legs meet up at Euston, so you can switch between them there, or else you can use one of six other Tube lines to cross between the two paths. To make things more confusing, the Northern Line forks again north of Camden Town station; the western leg visits popular Hampstead, and the eastern leg goes via Highgate. Know which train you're getting on, or you'll have to backtrack to fix your mistake.

Owing mostly to the petty backbiting and poor planning of the Victorians who built it, the District Line, which serves many budget hotels in West London, can also be tricky—trains veer off on different branches to several final destinations. You can handle it. Final destinations are clearly noted.

If you ride the DLR (and you should—it provides a lovely rooftop-level glide through the brickwork of the old East End and the monolithic towers of Canary Wharf), note your train's final destination as you board it, since the system is rife with forks in the routes. (The system is also rife with opportunities to change for the right train, so don't be put off.) Most DLR stations are above ground, and thoughtfully, carriage doors don't open to let cold air in until a passenger needs to go through them. Push the button on the door to open it.

Fares

Oy. Here we go.

London Underground gives some 976 million rides a year, and seemingly every passenger pays a different fare. The LU system is so unnecessarily complicated that I can only assume its architects designed it that way on purpose to bewilder travelers into paying more than they have to. The fare guide is 56 pages long. Never mind. I'll walk you through it and make it as simple as I can.

Finding "Mind the Gap"

As you gloss through London's tackier souvenir stands, you'll often see a peculiar catch phrase reproduced on bumper stickers, shirts, and brass-plated key chains: MIND THE GAP. The phrase has nothing to do with brainwashing customers into an allegiance to a certain denim chain selling baggy clothes. It's what you hear on some London Underground trains when they pull into curved stations. Wherever a chasm of a few inches might appear between carriage and platform, a recorded admonition—enunciated by a stern male voice—is played. (Because in England, they'd never say "watch your step"—that would mean "look at your feet.") You'll hear "Mind the gap" around the system, but if you want to be sure to catch it (and gain street cred over the tourists who merely bought the T-shirt), try these stations:

* Aldgate
* Bank (Central Line—it's a newer version by a posh female voice that drivers call "Sonya" because, as they say, "It gets *onya* nerves.")
* Embankment (Northern Line)
* Monument
* Tower Hill
* Wapping
* Waterloo (Bakerloo Line)

Start with the concept of zones. The center of town—basically everything the Circle Line envelops, plus a wee bit of padding—is zone 1. Heading outside of town, in a concentric pattern like a target, come zones 2 through 6. Most tourists stick to zones 1 and 2; very few popular sights are outside those (Wimbledon, Hampton Court, and Kew being the main exceptions). Your fare is calculated by how many zones you go through, and the lower the zone number, the less you pay. Where the zones lie won't come as a surprise to you because every station lobby has a giant map showing the boundaries. If a station appears to be straddling two zones, you'll always pay the cheaper zone's price.

Keep your ticket handy because you'll need it to get back out through the turnstiles. (If you can't find it, you'll have to fork over the maximum rate.)

Astonishingly, **kids under 11 travel for free** when accompanied by an adult after 9:30am weekdays, and all day weekends. Adults must buy their own ticket and then ask the staff to wave Junior through the entry gate. Kids 12 to 16 can travel with an adult for £1 all day with a Child Day Travelcard.

There are essentially three ways for adults to pay for a trip, which they can do at automated machines or at ticket windows. Cash and credit cards both work. One-way tickets are called "singles" and round-trips are "return."

A) **Per ride.** Only fools (or tourists) buy per ride. Why? I'll put it in perspective: It costs about $6,500 to fly the 3,500 miles from London to New York

City in First Class on British Airways, or about $1.85 per mile. But to travel a mile in zone 1 on the London Underground, the cash fare stands at £4, or about $7.20. So it costs three times as much to go a mile on the Tube than it does to go a mile in transatlantic First Class. Only choose this method if you need to travel a single time on a single day. (For short trips, though, you may find sharing a cab costs just as much.) Otherwise pick option B.

B) **Via Travelcard.** This is an unlimited paper pass for 1, 3, or 7 days on the Tube, bus, and the DLR. There are "Peak" Travelcards good for all hours, but

---

The Tube Map Lies!

Although the Tube's handsome map, first seen in 1931, is a marvel of design elegance (its draughtsman, Harry Beck, is a demigod among graphic designers for his restrictive use of angles and color), it tells filthy lies. Tourists who take it at face value will, to their pocketbooks' peril, believe that some stations are miles apart and only accessible via circuitous journeys. In truth, many are extremely close. Leicester Square and Covent Garden are 255m (850 ft.) apart; Charing Cross and Embankment less than 300m (1,000 ft.). Do you wanna spend £3 on *that?* In many instances, two stops that appear to be on distant, inconvenient detours are actually neighbors. Don't waste time and money because the Tube map makes something look hard-to-reach. These surprising station pairs are 450m (1,500 ft.)—or less—from each other.

Tottenham Court Road—Covent Garden
Farringdon—Chancery Lane
Barbican—St. Paul's
St. Paul's—Blackfriars
Moorgate—Bank
Bank—Mansion House
Liverpool Street—Aldgate
Aldgate East—Tower Gateway
Waterloo—Lambeth North
Euston—King's Cross St. Pancras
Baker Street—Marylebone
Great Portland Street—Warren Street
Regent's Park—Great Portland Street
Paddington—Lancaster Gate
Bayswater—Queensway
Monument—Mansion House

the "Off-Peak" ones cost roughly 25% less (£4.90) for zones 1 and 2), with the only caveat being that they're good after 9:30am, after the morning rush clears out; they're still valid for the evening rush. You'll likely still be eating breakfast at 9:30am, so it's the better choice of the two types. The card is also good for stations on the Mainline railway network, which covers South London well. If you find you have to pop into a zone that isn't covered by your card, buy an extension from the ticket window before starting your journey; it's usually £1 to £1.80 more. If you're staying for more than five days, Option C will save you a little money.

C) **Via Oyster.** This credit card-sized pass offers the lowest fares, but it's hardest for tourists to use. Basically, it's encoded with what you've paid. You can put the equivalent of a weeklong Travelcard on it, or you can pre-pay rides with a wad of cash that debits from your account. Just wave it over the yellow plate at the turnstiles and keep moving. No matter how many times you ride the Tube (debited at £1.50 in zone 1), bus (debited as 80p after the morning rush), and DLR (£1.50), the maximum taken off your card in a single day will always be 50p less than what an equivalent Day Travelcard would cost (so, £4.40 for zones 1 and 2). Translation: Oyster day passes cost 50p less than a Travelcard. But getting an Oyster requires a £3 deposit unless you're buying rides for more than a week, and you won't get that money back (or any money you don't use up) because London Underground only mails deposit refunds to U.K. addresses (gee, thanks). For travel in zones 1 and 2, I put on exactly £4.40 per day—the maximum I'll be charged. Pre-paid Oysters don't cover Mainline rail stations; you have to pay a surcharge to get to those before starting your commute. Still, you can lend your card to someone else when you're not using it. If you're staying more than five days and riding the Tube and bus hard, Oyster's a pearl.

Whichever method you choose, the Tube's still an expensive proposition. I do everything I can to plan days during which I don't have to take it at all. Fortunately, that's not hard to do because the city's very walkable. Trains go so slowly (34kmph/21 mph is the *average* and has been for over 100 years); you can watch the tunnel walls creep by, and in the center of town, stations are often close together. In fact, if your journey is only going to take you two or three stations, you can often walk the distance in the same amount of time.

EARL'S COURT—WEST BROMPTON MAINLINE RAIL

These are the commuter rail lines (sometimes called National Rail or, if you hate admitting Maggie Thatcher is gone, BritRail) that aren't operated by the Underground but are still covered by Travelcards. They're particularly useful for reaching South London, where marshy soil (and politics) prevented Victorian engineers from tunneling traditional Tube lines. Tube trains don't serve Hampton Court, for example, so you may end up using National Rail at least once.

There are many termini, but you don't have to hunt for the right one by trial and error. No one carries timetables anymore. They just call the 24-hour operators at **National Rail Enquiries** (☎ 08457/48-49-50; www.nationalrail.co.uk). Alternatively, each station posts timetables. Schedules are listed by destination; find the place you're going, and the departures will be listed in military time.

Mainline stations accept discount cards for certain folks. Each card costs £20 for a year and requires proof of eligibility (i.e. passport, ISIC student I.D.), but since they can be used for trips to distant British cities, they pay for themselves quickly if you're doing lots of rail-riding. Get them at rail stations:

◆ The **Senior Railcard** (www.senior-railcard.co.uk) snares discounts of about 33 percent for those 60 or over.
◆ The **Young Persons Railcard** (www.youngpersons-railcard.co.uk) gets those 16 to 25, plus full-time students of any age, 33% discounts. It requires a passport size photo; many Tube stations have photo booths for this reason.
◆ The **Family Railcard** (www.family-railcard.co.uk) is for at least one adult and one child aged 5 to 15, with a maximum of three adults and four kids on one ticket; at least one child must travel at all times. It awards adults 33% off and kids 60% off. But know that two kids under the age of five can travel with an adult for free at all times, even without this card.

BUS

The buses in your city may not come very often, but London's are frequent (every 5 min. or so on weekdays), plentiful (99 routes in central London and 700 in the wider city), and surprisingly fast (many operate in dedicated bus lanes).

And let's admit it: Sitting on the second level of a candy-apple red double-decker, watching the scrolling landscape, is one of London's priceless pleasures. A few routes are truly world-class, linking legendary sights. With routes like these, you won't need to splurge on those tedious hop-on, hop-off tour buses:

◆ The **15 bus,** which crosses the city northwest to southeast, takes in Paddington Station, Oxford Street, Piccadilly Circus, Trafalgar Square, Fleet Street, St. Paul's Cathedral, and the Tower of London.
◆ The **12** links Notting Hill, Kensington Gardens, Regent Street, Trafalgar Square, Whitehall, Big Ben, the London Eye, and Waterloo Station.
◆ The **10** passes Royal Albert Hall, Kensington Gardens, Knightsbridge (a block north of Harrods), Hyde Park Corner, Marble Arch, Oxford Street, Goodge Street (for the British Museum), and King's Cross Station.
◆ The **14** is for the Victoria and Albert Museum, Harrods, Hyde Park Corner, the grand shops of Piccadilly, Piccadilly Circus, the theaters of Shaftesbury Avenue, and the northwest corner of the Covent Garden area.

Best of all, the bus is much cheaper than the Tube. An all-day pass costs £3.50, no matter the zone, and that's £8.90 less than what you'd pay for the same access on the Tube. Single trips cost £2 in cash. Travelcards and Oysters yield the best fares, but cash users can get a 33% savings if they buy "Bus Saver" booklets of six bus tickets for £6. If you can't find an automated ticket machine that sells them, duck into the nearest Tube station and buy them from the cashier there.

Some shelters have automated ticket machines (cash only, and don't expect change), but all have easy-to-read maps of the vicinity that tell you where to catch the bus going in your direction. Many shelters even have electronic boards that approximate (read: completely fabricate) the arrival time of the next bus. Board by the driver, who operates the ticket machine, and get off via the door at the middle. Press one of the yellow buttons on the handrails to request a halt at the next stop.

Crosswalk Cheat-Sheet

Central London's authorities are big on erecting waist-high fences along the sidewalk ("pavement") to corral pedestrians toward crosswalks ("crossings"). After you press the button at these so-called "pelican" (**pe**destrian **li**ght **con**trolled) crossings, the light can take so long to turn that it feels timed to match the tides. If that annoys you, be grateful for two true concessions made for pedestrians:

♦ "Zebra" crossings (pronounced ZEH-bra) are your best friend. They're marked by alternating white bars painted across the road and tall, flashing orange-yellow lamps (called Belisha beacons) on both pavements. Here, you have right-of-way, and if it can, all oncoming traffic must stop for you (which explains why the cover of the *Abbey Road* album doesn't show a pile of Beatles roadkill). Considering London's relentless traffic, they're worth detouring to use.

♦ You'll often see "Look Right" or "Look Left" painted on the street to tell you where the traffic's coming from. It's helpful unless you're like me, and you absent-mindedly read the *other* side of the street's upside-down message.

Routes that start with N are Night Buses, which tote the clubbers home after the Tube stops. Bus passes and Travelcards expire at 4:30am the day after you buy them, so they're usually good for the Night Buses; the cash fare is £2, as usual.

TAXI

Even Londoners think taxis are crazy expensive. Personally, I use them exactly twice on any trip: Once when I arrive from the train station and once when I leave. And that's only if my luggage is too heavy to lug into the Tube.

It's not the fault of the cabbies. They're the best in the world. Before they're given their wheels, every London taxi driver (there are some 24,000 of them) must go through a grueling training period so comprehensive that it's dubbed, simply, "The Information." They arrive inculcated with directions to every alley, mews, avenue, shortcut, and square in the city, and if they don't know, they'll find the answer so discreetly you won't catch the gaffe. And then there are those adorable vehicles: bulbous as Depression Era jalopies, purring like kittens, spacious as one-bedroom apartments, yet able to do complete U-turns within a single lane of traffic.

But for this admittedly peerless carriage, you'll pay a £2.20 minimum. Trips of up to a mile cost £4 to £5.60 during working hours; 3.2km (2-mile) trips are £6.20 to £8.80; 6.4km (4-mile) trips are £10 to £14, and trips of around 9.6km (6 miles) hit you for a painful £14 to £19. Rates rise when you're most likely to need a taxi: about 10% from 8pm to 10pm, and roughly another 10% from 10pm until dawn. Mercifully, there is no charge for extra passengers or for luggage.

Taxis are often called "black cabs," although in fact 12 colors are registered for them, including "thistle blue" and "nightfire red." If you need to call a cab, **One Number** (☎ 0871/871-8710) pools all the companies, with a surcharge of £2.

RENTING A CAR

Don't. Rare is the local who drives in central London, where there's a mandatory daily "congestion charge" of £8 (don't believe me? See www.cclondon.com), and where daily parking fees are several times that. Streets, many of which were cramped even back in medieval times, aren't much improved today, and are dogged with one-way rules. You'll go crazy and broke, so why do it?

LONDON'S NEIGHBORHOODS

The beauty of so many of London's neighborhoods is that they were laid out and named during a period of wagon and foot traffic, when districts were defined in much narrower terms than we define them today; indeed, in centuries when people often lived complete lives without ever seeing the other side of town.

Ironically, the Tube has done much to divide these districts from each other; since visitors are more likely to hop a train between them, they don't often realize how remarkably close together they really are. There's no reason someone staying in, say, King's Cross, couldn't traipse over to the West End or Marylebone, or why a person in South Kensington wouldn't amble blithely into Victoria.

Are these the only areas of interest? Not even close. Although I've stuffed as many neighborhoods into this section as the limits of the timber industry would sensibly allow, literally hundreds of fascinating village clusters abound, many with names as cherishable as Ponders End, Tooting, and The Wrythe. But I've chosen places where foreign visitors are likely to spend time, and a few more where I think they should.

BLOOMSBURY & FITZROVIA

Best for: Museums, affordable inns, residential streets, universities, homewares and electronics shops on Tottenham Court Road
What you won't find: Evening entertainment, nightclubs
It's important to remember two things about Bloomsbury: The British Museum and Gower Street. The former is London's most popular attraction, and the latter is one of the best avenues for low-cost accommodation, made even more desirable because it's within walking distance of the West End, Oxford Street's shopping, Covent Garden—and the British Museum.

Bloomsbury's dark-brick, white-sashed residential buildings and leafy squares date mostly from the Georgian period, when the district became the first in a chaotic city to be developed; in later epochs, Victoria, Chelsea, and Kensington took up the same dignified layout using a more ostentatious architectural language. Bloomsbury's refined air must have been like oxygen because it attracted the intelligencia nearly from the start, and its two universities are both nineteenth-century institutions. The first surgery to use anesthetics, a leg amputation that took 30 seconds, was conducted at University College in 1846.

Recently, Bloomsbury became a place of remembrance as the neighborhood that bore the brunt of the bombing attacks of July 7, 2005; of the 52 who died that day, 26 perished underground on a Piccadilly Line train between King's Cross and Russell Square stations, and 13 were killed on a double-decker bus passing through Tavistock Square, 2 blocks north of Russell Square. But Londoners are hardy and forward-looking, so you won't find much evidence of that dark day.

London Neighborhoods

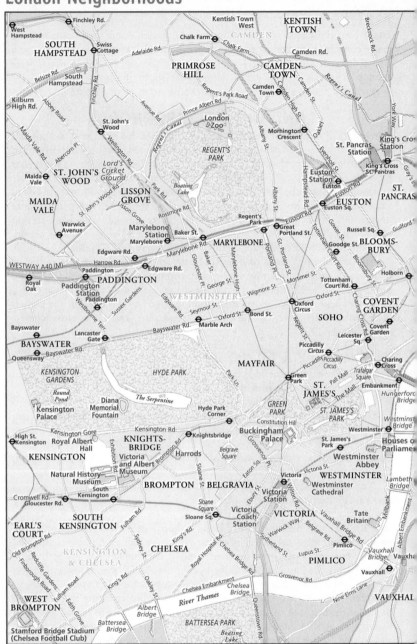

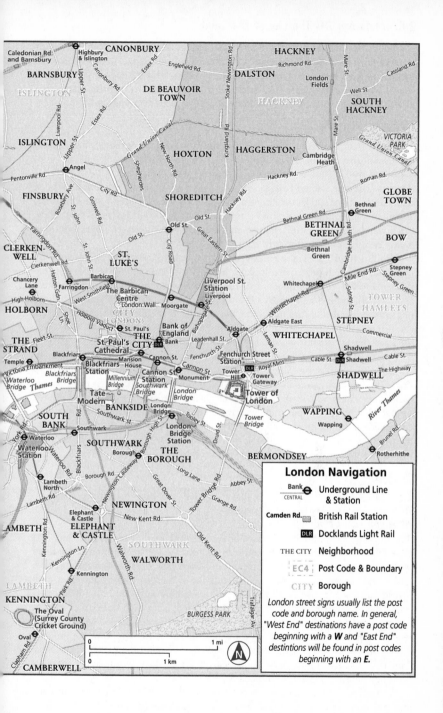

London Navigation

Bank CENTRAL ⊖	Underground Line & Station
Camden Rd. ▭	British Rail Station
DLR	Docklands Light Rail
THE CITY	Neighborhood
EC4	Post Code & Boundary
CITY	Borough

London street signs usually list the post code and borough name. In general, "West End" destinations have a post code beginning with a **W** and "East End" destinations will be found in post codes beginning with an **E**.

Bloomsbury's showier sister Fitzrovia, similar in character but devoid of major attractions, lies on the western side of Tottenham Court Road. Famous residents include George Bernard Shaw and Virginia Woolf, who both lived (at different times) at 29 Fitzroy Square. Charlotte Street, in the shadow of British Telecom's Tower is one of the West End's more happening places for restaurants.

KING'S CROSS

Best for: Budget hotels, trains heading north (and soon to Paris), alternative/down-and-dirty nightlife, student housing, take-away counters

What you won't find: Top-notch restaurants, parks, shopping

Recently, the area around King's Cross station was an unsavory tenderloin of porn stores and flophouses. Its turnaround, currently in play, has been just as dramatic, as millions of pounds are poured into its derelict industrial infrastructure. Now, brick warehouses built for produce and coal are more likely to house boutique media companies and after-dark dance clubs.

Until the mid-1800s, the area was known as Battle Bridge, after a Roman skirmish that occurred here. Stern-looking King's Cross station, which took its name from a short-lived monument to George IV, opened in 1852. Legend (surely apocryphal) says the Celtic queen Boudica rests somewhere near Platform 8. Fans of Harry Potter know that the young wizard boards the Hogwarts Express at the (fictitious) Platform 9¾; the movie versions have shot at Platforms 4 and 5 but used prettier St. Pancras station, right next door, as a stand-in facade.

By the time the Channel Tunnel Rail Link finally opens at St. Pancras in autumn 2007, replacing Waterloo as the starting point for Eurostar train trips to France and beyond, an estimated 50 million people will pass through King's Cross each year, and it will serve as both a city showcase and a prime bolt-hole for tourists. For now, it's appealingly scruffy and well located for access: Six Tube lines convene beneath its streets, and a few of the most stroll-worthy districts lie within 20 minutes' walk, including bookish Bloomsbury to the south, army-booted Camden Town to the north, and cafe-cultured Islington to the east.

MARYLEBONE & MAYFAIR

Best for: Shopping, hotels, restaurants, small museums, strolling, access to Regent's Park and Hyde Park, embassies

What you won't find: Historic sights

The middle-class hubbub of Oxford Street west of Regent Street divides high-hat Marylebone from its snobbish southern neighbor, Mayfair. Both areas are lined with warm 18th-century town houses, and both play host to upscale shopping and several fascinating, if overlooked, museums, but there the similarities end. World-famous Mayfair, typified by hyperluxe bauble shops and blue-blood heritage (the present Queen was born on Bruton St.), has a high opinion of itself as a starchy enclave of wealth and, aside from the eateries of Shepherd Market, it has less to offer the casual tourist—although admittedly, the window-shopping on New Bond Street may be the best on the planet. (Trivia to impress your friends: The title of the famous musical *My Fair Lady* is witty wordplay on how its Cockney heroine, Eliza, pronounced *Mayfair Lady.*)

Marylebone (MAR-le-bun), on the other hand, benefits from convenient Tube and bus connections, affordable hotels nestled in antique dwellings, and lively sidewalks crowded with evening celebrants, particularly around James Street. Also, thanks to a territorial local authority, its main shopping drag (Marylebone High St.) remains one of the last important streets in London that isn't awash with the same corporate chain stores that you'd find everywhere in the country. Miraculously, Marylebone retains a village atmosphere that has set it apart from central London for centuries.

They were cut from the same cloth, but one neighborhood turns its back on outsiders who press their faces to the glass while the other raises a glass with them.

SOHO, COVENT GARDEN, OXFORD STREET & CENTRAL WEST END

Best for: Shopping, restaurants, theater, cinema, nightlife, opera, free art (National Gallery and National Portrait Gallery), star sightings

What you won't find: Elbow room, hotel values, silence

London's undisputed center of nightlife, restaurants, theater, and swanky nightclubs, the West End seethes with tourists and merrymakers 24 hours a day, but the vibe changes hour by hour. The day shift comes for the bookstores of Charing Cross Road and Cecil Court; after work, the pubs and restaurants of Old Compton Street and Covent Garden (pronounced with the "o" sound of "covered") overflow with workers catching up with friends; by 7:30, the theaters and two opera houses are pulsing; by midnight, the action has moved into the dance halls of Leicester Square and lounges of Soho; and in the wee hours, you might find groups of partiers trawling Gerrard Street, in teeny Chinatown, hunting for snacks.

Oxford Street is the city's premier shopping street; the western half between Oxford Circus and Marble Arch is the classier end, with marquee department stores such as Selfridges, Debenhams, and Marks & Spencer, while the Oxford Circus-to-Tottenham Court Road end is more for knockoff luggage and mobile phones. A trot down Oxford Street on busy weekends quickly becomes a crawl.

Prim Trafalgar Square, presided over by the peerless National Gallery, has often been called London's focal point. On a sunny day, you'll find few places that exude such well-being and gratitude.

WESTMINSTER, INCLUDING ST. JAMES'S

Best for: Historic and government sights, river strolls, St. James's Park

What you won't find: Affordable hotels, a wide choice of restaurants

This is near the central West End, but its energy is markedly different. It's a district tourists mostly see by day. South of Trafalgar Square, you'll find regiments of robust government buildings but very little in the way of hotels or food.

You'd think this neighborhood would be stacked with hotels, because it's near the things visitors want to see (and hear), including Westminster Abbey, the Parliament House (and Big Ben), the Cabinet War Rooms, and Buckingham Palace. Yet it's more for government buildings, and has been since antiquity, when Whitehall was the location of (the now-lost) Whitehall Palace, the King's main residence, and Trafalgar Square was his stables. One of the few souls who dares to sleep here does so out of duty: The Prime Minister's home at 10 Downing Street is protected by a garrison of gun-toting bobbies behind impregnable gates.

Whitehall's severity doesn't spread far. Just a block east, its impenetrable character gives way to the proud riverside promenade of Victoria Embankment, overlooking the London Eye, and just a block west, to the greenery of St. James's Park, which is, in effect, the Queen's front yard. North of the park, the staid streets of St. James's are even more exclusive than Mayfair's, if that's possible, with few stores or restaurants to enjoy.

Whenever a state event is held at Westminster Abbey (coronations, funerals), the royal retinue usually emerges from the Palace, heads east up The Mall, detours through Horse Guards Parade (the de facto "front door" of the Palace), turns onto Whitehall, and proceeds south to the Abbey—the official processional route.

THE CITY

Best for: Old streets, the Tower of London, St. Paul's, financial concerns
What you won't find: Old buildings, nightlife or weekend life, affordable hotels
Technically, this is the only part of London that's London. Other bits, including the West End, are under the jurisdiction of different local governments, such as Westminster or Camden. Shocking as it is to realize that the Queen herself doesn't technically live in the City of London, the soothing reality is that the greater city is still considered to be London, no matter what the borough borders say.

The City, as it's called, is where most of London's history happened. It's where Romans cheered gladiators. It's where London Bridge—at least 12 of them—have touched shore. It's where the Great Fire raged. And, more recently, it's where the Deutsche Luftwaffe focused many of its nocturnal bombing raids, which is why you'll find so little evidence of the preceding two millennia of events. Eager to put the war behind it, the city threw up blocks of undistinguished office towers, turning the so-called "Square Mile," which until medieval times was protected by stone battlements, into a nine-to-six business-and-banking wilderness of plate glass, lobby security desks, and suits. Although 320,000 work here, scarcely 7,200 call it home. Outside of working hours, the main thing you'll see in the City is your own reflection in the facade of corporate offices on weekend lockdown.

Although this is where you'll find such priceless relics as the Tower of London, St. Paul's Cathedral, the Tower Bridge, the Bank of England, and the Monument, some of the most authentic remnants are underfoot, since much of the spiderweb of lanes and streets dates back to the Roman period. Buildings have come and gone, but the veins of the city have pumped in situ for thousands of years.

The district of Clerkenwell is northwest, and it hosts meat markets and media lofts by day and some of the city's cooler nightclubs and restaurants by night.

SOUTHWARK & BOROUGH

Best for: Museums, memorable pubs, strolls, gourmet groceries, and wines
What you won't find: Shopping, parks
Revisit your old textbooks and look up a map of London from four hundred, three hundred, or even ninety years ago. Southwark is barely there. Although it lay just a few hundred feet across the Thames from one of the world's most dynamic cities, Southwark was outside city walls and out of mind. The neighborhood, considered until the 19th century as part of Surrey, not London, was where respectable Londoners sojourned to misbehave—it was the place of Chaucer's pilgrims, Shakespeare's stages, bear-baiting amphitheaters, rowdy pubs and brothels,

and pleasure gardens for wayward couples. Eventually, grimy warehouses, breweries, and factories took over, and the district's unsavory character was cemented.

The devastation of World War II and the collapse of river-borne trade caused the city to take a new look. During Southwark's rehabilitation, a blighted power station became one of the world's greatest museums (the Tate Modern). A master playwright's theater was re-created (the Globe). An ambling riverfront path (the Jubilee Walk) replaced the coal lightermen's rotting piers with pleasing waterfront pubs, and a dramatic showpiece (the National Theatre) was erected. Now, the South Bank, which stretches from the London Eye east to Tower Bridge, has reclaimed its status as the city's pleasure garden, and the dank arches under its railway viaducts have been filled with wine bars, museums, and buzzy restaurants. It's gratifying to see that some things never change, though; Southwark Cathedral has risen above the changing scenes for 900 years, and Borough Market, which attracts gourmet foodies from around the world, is the direct descendent of the market that fed the denizens of that medieval skyscraper built over the water, London Bridge.

VICTORIA & CHELSEA

Best for: Boutiques, low-cost lodging, attractive town homes, wealthy neighbors
What you won't find: Transit options, street life, museums

Victoria as a name doesn't technically apply to the neighborhood around the eponymous train station—Belgravia (to the west) and Pimlico (south and east) take those honors—but generations of tourists have learned that some of the city's most affordable hotels are found within walking distance of Victoria station, and the shorthand stuck. Most of the area, which is residential, was developed starting in the 1820s in consistent patterns of white stucco terraced homes. Then, as now, it's a lovely place to spend the night, but it doesn't wake up much during the day.

Chelsea, though, has a history of well-heeled bohemianism—Oscar Wilde, James McNeill Whistler, the Rolling Stones, and the Beatles all lived here—although today it's known more as one of the most exclusive communities in the city, and a stroll past the boutiques and high-end furniture stores of the King's Road (sadly, turning ever-more corporate and indistinct) leaves little doubt about the elevated tax brackets of their intended patrons. Chelsea's exclusivity is guaranteed by the insulation that comes with being a 15-minute walk to the Tube.

> " London is on the whole the most possible form of life. . . . It is the biggest aggregation of human life— the most complete compendium of the world. The human race is better represented here than anywhere else, and if you learn to know your London you learn a great many things. "
>
> —Henry James

KENSINGTON, KNIGHTSBRIDGE & EARL'S COURT

Best for: Museums, shopping, French pastries, hotels, celebrities
What you won't find: Historic sights

If you want to spot England's most famous faces—the ones who appear at the business end of a paparazzo's lens in English gossip rags like *Heat* each week—hang out around Kensington. Here, one expensive neighborhood bleeds into another as they press against the soothing greenery of Hyde Park and Kensington Gardens. South Kensington and Brompton draw the most visitors with the Victoria & Albert, the Natural History Museum, Royal Albert Hall, and the Science Museum; and Knightsbridge, put succinctly, is home to Harrods and Harvey Nicks. Privilege has long had an address in Kensington—that's a reason those edifying institutions were located here to begin with, away from the grubby paws of the peasants. Kensington Palace, at the Gardens' western end, was where Princes William and Harry were raised by their mum, Diana.

The upscale character of each nook differs in marginal ways. South Kensington is notable for its contingent of French-speaking expats and when school lets out each afternoon, Kensington (often referred to by its Tube stop, High Street Kensington) morphs into the domain of football mums. The orphan among this opulence is Earl's Court, the only area deprived of a contingency to the park, and consequently a frumpy, slightly tattered zone good for cheap eats and sleeps.

BAYSWATER & PADDINGTON

Best for: Inexpensive lodging, ethnic food, well-preserved Victorian thoroughfares
What you won't find: Attractions, non-chain stores, street life

Its whitewashed, terraced houses were briefly the most fashionable in the city (Churchill and Dickens were residents), and they're as regimented and as elegant as the ones in Victoria or Chelsea, yet today, something is missing in Bayswater. Perhaps the fault lies with the sizable transient population, including tourists, that quickly passes through the neighborhood, depriving it of sustained energy. In recent decades, the area has borrowed some of its identity from new immigrant communities from Greece and Middle Eastern and Arab countries (Edgware Road is a magnet Halal cuisine). One exception to the muddle is Queensway, a popular shopping street crowned by Whiteleys, a gorgeous 1911 department store edifice converted into an urban shopping mall in 1989.

Although Paddington station is one of London's most beautiful train hubs (it was built by the legendary architect Isambard Kingdom Brunel in 1838), because of lame Tube links, it's also the most inconvenient. The disused 19th-century canal behind it is being revitalized for condos and shopping, so within a few years the area may rediscover a portion of its fashionable cachet.

DOCKLANDS

Best for: Gleaming developments, ancient warehouses, super-cheap chain hotels
What you won't find: Street life, nightlife

Most of East London along the Thames is ignobly called by a single, sweeping name: Docklands. Yet Captain Cook set off on his explorations from here, and its hand-dug basins once teemed with ships bearing goods from around the planet. In more ways than modern people bother to recognize, Docklands made colonial Britain successful—and thus America, Canada, Australia, and South Africa, too.

Adolf Hitler swept most of that away, and East London's hand-dug pools have been resettled by corporations in stacks of fluorescent-lit office cubes. If Tower

Bridge represents the apotheosis of Victorian British engineering ingenuity, surely the Canary Wharf area, which contains One Canada Square, the tallest building in Britain, symbolizes the heedless economic prowess of modern-day Britain. Even as you read this, developers are working to sweep the rest of the area's dilapidated relics away. Plenty of brick warehouses and drooping dockside pubs live on, if only you have the fortitude to battle the currents of car traffic and seek them out.

Away from the river, in salt-of-the-earth neighborhoods like Bethnal Green, Stratford, and West Ham, the city's Pakistani and Indian population flourishes (marvelous food, authentic shops), but sad to say, they have yet to be fully accepted and absorbed. Some things about East London are destined to be ignored, it seems.

OTHER GREAT LONDON NEIGHBORHOODS

Mostly because of iffy transit connections (for example, service by a single Tube line that, should it go on the blink, would derail your vacation), I haven't included these areas in my list of prime places to stay. But there's no doubt that they'll enrich your time abroad, and many count among my favorite places in the city.

Islington

Best for: Antiques, music shops, gastropubs, theater, street markets, cafes, strolls
What you won't find: Museums, hotels
Few neighborhoods retain such a healthy balance between feisty bohemianism and groomed prosperity, and almost none retain streetscapes as defiantly mid-century as Chapel Market. Its leafy byways are dotted with charming puppet theaters, antiques dealers, hoary pubs with backroom theater spaces, beer gardens, and most pleasingly on a sunny day, pedestrian towpaths overlooking Regent's Canal. Why more tourists don't flood Islington is a mystery—and a blessing.

Camden

Best for: Alternative music, massive street markets and food markets, punks, pubs
What you won't find: Refined company, hotels, upscale restaurants
Name a British tune that got under your skin, from Madness to the Clash, and chances are it received its first airing in the beer-soaked concert halls of Camden Town, the landscape of the seminal British comedy *Withnail & I*. The area's margin-pushing markets, which hawk touristy hokum in the former warehouses and stables serving Regent's Canal, are so thronged with weekend sightseers that the inadequate Tube station only serves one-way traffic on Sunday afternoons. The punks loitering along Camden High Street are wise to the tourist influx; they'll expect a few bob to pose for your photos. Watch for pickpockets, mate.

Greenwich

Best for: Museums, antiques and food markets, river views, strolls, pubs
What you won't find: Evening entertainment, hotels
More than any other place near central London, Greenwich, on the south bank across from the Canary Wharf development, retains the vibe of an untouched village; if you can't get into the countryside to sample England's little towns, a day

trip here (Sundays are good, for the markets) will more than satisfy. That's because the Tube (well, the DLR) didn't connect it to the greater city until 1999—all the more remarkable when you consider the town's illustrious pedigree as a royal get-away (it's got the oldest royal park in London), as a scientific citadel, and as one of the world's most crucial command centers. If it all sounds like a living museum, it is: On top of largely being a UNESCO World Heritage Site (Maritime Greenwich), the village is literally the center of time and space, since it inhabits the exact location of Greenwich Mean Time, and of longitude 0° 0' 0".

Whitechapel & Spitalfields

Best for: Nightclubs, live music, Indian food, art galleries, clothing and crafts
What you won't find: High-end restaurants, hotels

If Mayfair is London's champagne, Whitechapel has always been its hangover. For centuries it was an impoverished, squalid slum. When you think of obscene Dickensian depravity—of Jack the Ripper slashing or The Elephant Man suffering jibes—this is probably where it happened. That's all in the history books now. By the last century, the gallery-clogged area (which blends seamlessly with equally edgy Spitalfields (SPIT-all-fields), just north) settled into anonymity as a refuge for immigrants, first Jewish and then Pakistani and Indian—and Brick Lane is the city's most popular evening drag for curry meals. Prostitutes and orphans have been replaced by artists, musicians, fashion designers, and hipsters; its Whitechapel Art Gallery, founded 1901, is among Europe's best fringe modern art exhibition spaces; and Old Truman Brewery, once a smoke-stacked citadel of industrial gloom, has been remade into a complex of inviting cafes and stages.

Notting Hill

Best for: Markets, a village vibe, restaurants, pubs, touristy strolls, antiques
What you won't find: Well-priced shopping, museums, Hugh Grant

Thanks partly to Hollywood, this westerly nook of London, once known for its race riots, appears high on many visitors' checklists. Its Saturday Portobello Road market, the principal draw, is fiendishly crowded and the stuff for sale is cynically pitched to the gullible, but some authentic charmers can be uncovered, including the fabulous Electric Theatre, which dates to silent film but now seduces movie buffs with loveseats that have built-in wine buckets. The area, whose identity has been so conflated with neighboring Notting Hill Gate as to not bear separation, is hammocked between Bayswater to the east and Kensington to the south.

Brixton

Best for: Caribbean and Indian food, markets, nightclubs, decaying Victoriana
What you won't find: Upscale shopping, hotels

Once upon a time, when Victoria was Queen, Brixton was a sparkling new neighborhood of matching homes, and respectable families flocked to live near the incandescent lights of Electric Avenue, which in 1888 became one of London's first shopping streets lit by electricity. But within 100 years, hard times moved in. Although the grim days of the 1980s and 1990s (recession followed by riots) are buried in the past, Brixton remains rougher than other areas, which is perhaps why so many alternative music and dance clubs fit in comfortably here. By day, to explore the glazed awnings of Brixton's markets, with meat, fish, and exotic spices and herbs dazzling the nose, is to walk through a portal to Jamaica, India, or China, and to be reminded that London, like few others, is a truly worldly city.

Hampstead

Best for: Cafes, parks, pubs, historic homes, high-end shopping
What you won't find: Unique shops, hotels
In hilly North London, the rich come out to play on weekends. The little houses and hidden mews are adorable, but it all feels like a very wealthy, very insulated bubble, or at least like a party to which you weren't invited. Fortunately, Hampstead's green space, the Heath, is enough to make anyone forget the slight, and its stately brick homes impress.

Primrose Hill

Best for: Strolls, views of the city, cafes, bookstores
What you won't find: Easy transport links, shopping selection
Enviable town houses, winsome French-style cafes, prams stuffed with plump yuppie offspring, and frivolous, obedient dogs—Primrose Hill, which is secreted between Camden and the top end of Regent's Park, is the pseudo-suburban paradise to which recently moneyed Londoners aspire. One stroll down its hamlet-like streets, which are so endearing they could have been laid out by a film set designer or by a diabolical Valentine artist instead of by sensible Victorians, and you'll instantly wish you were a Londoner. A panorama of the city bows down like a servant from its eponymous hill, at the southern end of Regent's Park Road.

3 Accommodations, Both Standard & Not

In which you'll discover all the options, from spare cots in private apartments to comfy digs in boutique hotels

LET'S CUT TO THE CHASE: THE MOST EXPENSIVE PART OF YOUR TRIP IS going to be lodging. You're going to a pricey city carrying a currency that wilts like Earl Grey tea leaves in the steaming presence of the pound. You should admit it, you should embrace it, but you shouldn't let it stop you. Because although, yes, London is an expensive city, bargains can be found.

Part of the secret is understanding the culture you're walking into. When you know what qualifies as a good value in London, you'll know when you see one. The other half of the puzzle is actually finding those bargains. And for the next chapter, I'm going to throw as many lifelines your way as I can.

STAYING IN A PRIVATE APARTMENT

It's a tradition in the Pauline Frommer series to lead off with the most illuminating, most edifying, and most economical way to see any city in the world. Well, no, I'm not talking about staying with friends, although that's a really good idea, and if you can arrange that, you're way ahead of the game. Kindly skip this chapter.

I'm actually talking about renting an apartment, or a *flat*, as the British usually say. If you've stayed in a hotel lately, you'll know why I have such a high opinion of flat rentals. These days, when you check into even a middling hotel run by a well-known company, you start by paying a great deal for what amounts to a single smallish room. From then on, everything you do or say ends with a huge charge on your bill. Parking. Laundry. Lots of places even add "resort fees" for using the pool or the gym—the very perks that drew you to a hotel to begin with!

When you calculate the per-day cost, flats are often a fraction of the price of hotels. If you don't believe me, read on and do the math for yourself. Visit London, the official tourism organization for the city, recently quoted the average London hotel room rate as £110. Yet:

- The weekly rate for a simple, freshly renovated studio apartment in the Paddington area from Price Apartments is £365, or £52 a night. Split that between two, and you're paying just £26 a night to be in central London.
- The nightly price to stay in a B&B room in the same town house where Virginia Woolf grew up, and where she published some of her earliest writing (a household newsletter called *The Hyde Park Gate News*), is £79 for two,

or around £40 per person, including a breakfast prepared by a gourmet chef. That's through At Home in London.

♦ Six people sleeping on a luxury duplex houseboat on the Thames, rented by Coach House Rentals, would split a nightly bill of £205, or about £34 each. Even if two people hogged it for themselves, they would pay £103 each, which is still less than the average hotel rate.

♦ The value holds even at the top end of our scale. A penthouse apartment, with panoramic views, at Scala House in the West End costs £1,050 a week, or £150 a day per couple/£75 per person. But since they fit four, you can feasibly have

---

Where to Bunk: Basic Training

Because tourists are enamored of the Underground and tend to remain in its orbit, some of the least crowded, and consequently least expensive, accommodation is found in neighborhoods nearer to a Mainline or National commuter rail station than a Tube stop. Choosing one of those doesn't mean you'll have to take the equivalent of Amtrak to get to the heart of the city. British trains are still among the best in the world, and millions of Londoners rely on them daily in the same way North Americans rely on highways. Why some areas are better served by Tube and some are better served by Mainline stations is usually the product of complicated histories involving 19th-century railway company building rights and the engineering challenges of digging through South London's soft soil.

In truth, Mainline stations are only marginally less convenient than Tube stations, since trains are regular. And it doesn't make much difference in cost: When you buy a Travelcard for the Underground, you must always select which zones it's good in. That Travelcard will include all rides to *both* Tube and Mainline stations within the zones you choose, so you can use the same ticket to get from your local commuter-rail station to the Tube, ride the tube and buses all day, and come home by the same commuter station, all for the same price. (The trick doesn't work with Oyster cards, but I digress. The entire Tube system's fare structure is explained starting on p. 9.)

Before you sit down to sort through the options that these flat-rental and homestay companies throw at you, I strongly suggest that you visit the **London Underground's website** (www.tfl.gov.uk/tube/maps) and download the free "Tubes, Trams, and Trains" map. On it, all the stations and zones in both networks will appear on the same page, making it easy to know where your prospective flat will be and, if your agency hasn't already told you, which zone it's in. The website www.streetmap.co.uk will further help you pinpoint street locations. When you see how close to town some of those discounted flats really are, you'll be much more likely to pounce on one.

that penthouse for £38 a night. Amazingly, even hostels in the same neighborhood charge £35 for their bare private rooms. A penthouse view for £2.50 more than a hostel? Why are you even considering anything else?

All right, so flats can save you money. But there are more bonuses to flats in a city like London: First of all, you can cook. That's not a poke at British cuisine (hey, it's come a long way), but a reference to the city's dozens of markets that sell fresh meats, vegetables, and spices. You can't bring that stuff home—Customs won't let you—and so if you want a taste of it, let alone a crack at cooking something exotic for a change, you have to have a kitchen.

If you're traveling with kids, flats have doors that close on them when they give you a headache, or when you take a look at your spouse and realize a headache is the furthest thing from your mind.

Flats often have history. You might even find a place that was once a country cottage on a rustic village green before London's swelling sprawl caught up with it many years ago. Flats may have neighbors, too, who might be open to making friends and sharing the secrets of their neighborhood with you.

In short, flats give you more room to be yourself, as well as a vehicle for opening yourself up to local influences, which is presumably one of the reasons you travel.

The British love renting flats when they go on vacation and, culturally speaking, that's important, because it means they have lots of them available back home, and you have a long, long list of potential places to pick through.

There are actually two kinds of flats, and I give resources for each below.

HOSTED FLATS

In many places staying in a quaint private room usually corresponds with a huge uptick in price. But English B&Bs, or hosted flats, have been one of the world's great travel bargains for many lifetimes. Instead of being hosted by semiretired lawyers and marketing executives, like in some Vermont or northern California establishments, they're usually hosted by interesting working-class folks who'd like to make a few extra pounds where they can. It's an impressive cottage industry, one that makes up a significant slice of the accommodation culture.

One potential hidden advantage of this sort of stay comes if you've got a car—for example, if you're stopping in London during a drive round the island. Staying with a family in zone 3 or 4 may enable you to park your car cheaply. After all, driving into the city incurs a £8-per-day congestion surcharge (p. 17), and that's *before* parking fees. What's included? At the minimum, a bed-and-breakfast—yes, stays like these are how the term "B&B" got started. Everything else depends, since homestays are as unique as the hosts themselves. Your hosts may allow you to make free local calls, or they may ask that you use a prepaid card. They may have wireless Web access, or they may think toaster ovens are the latest word in technology. They probably won't clean your room; many of them are far too observant of privacy to do that. Since no industry standard exists, prepare a short list of what you think you'll need. Armed with a wish list, your broker should be able to pair you with suitable options. Just keep in mind: Even B&B agencies categorize their homes according to their amenities and their convenience, so every extra request might bump you into a higher nightly rate (though still not a rate that will break your bank). Don't make even a verbal agreement until you've found your best match.

The following agencies specialize in booking visitors in private homes—what used to be called bed-and-breakfasts. Most of these organizations inspect their inventory and vet every last one, and if that's not the case, I let you know. At any rate, the people who run the homes they represent are generally pleased to meet tourists (otherwise they wouldn't have opened their doors to them) and their continued good standing is dependent on their treatment of you.

Maggie Dobson has personally selected the homes that make it into the stable of **At Home in London** (☎ 020/8748-1943; www.athomeinlondon.co.uk) since 1986. "About 50% of my decision is based on the attitude of the hosts," she says. Her 80-odd properties are in the tourist areas of West London, near the Tube, and are priced accordingly: £59 (Fulham, Hammersmith) to £64 (South Kensington, Belgravia, Knightsbridge). A few of its most prime locations (Mayfair, Westminster) are priced closer to £90 a night for doubles. Thorparch Road in Vauxhall is owned by an opera singer, and goes for £74 for doubles, £50 for singles. Hyde Park Gate (£79 doubles, £65 singles) is the house where Virginia Woolf spent the first 18 years of her life; its owner, who happens to be a professional cook and prepares a colossal breakfast, will pull out the Woolf mementos for anyone who asks. Dobson, who makes an effort to set up tourists with compatible hosts, also aims to put the first-time homestay customer at ease: "Some people are concerned that they'll have to talk to the host too much, that the host will be intrusive, or that they'll have to be back at a certain time or risk annoying their host. Nobody does that anymore." She even puts out a free newsletter, to bring customers up to speed on how her service works and what's worth doing in London. Prices include service fees, taxes, and nearly always, breakfast.

Bulldog Club (☎ 020/7371-3202; www.bulldogclub.com), around since 1988, aims to provide a luxury experience in the kind of home you might see spotlighted in a decorators' magazine. Guests are greeted on arrival by their host, who'll have been vetted for their willingness to help visitors acclimate to the city. One double bedroom, located in a 160-year-old house near the famous Portobello Road market, comes with a claw-footed bathtub and a walk-in shower, plus access to a private roof terrace. It costs £85 for a single or £105 for a double room, including breakfast. Another, in the Limehouse section of the historic Docklands area, just east of the Tower of London, is in a private wing of an apartment that's been slotted into a spacious 19th-century shipping warehouse—think exposed brick and vaulted timber ceilings. In the morning, you can watch boats ply the Thames from your breakfast table. The cost is £116 a night. More properties are on offer, of course, at similar prices, and most have a 2-night minimum stay. All are non-smoking and come with a full English breakfast.

London Bed and Breakfast Agency (☎ 020/7586-2768; www.londonbb.com) is another agency that personally inspects all of its properties (Victorian, modern, Edwardian—about 40 at last count) and gives the heave-ho to hosts who don't pull their weight. One of its properties, in the chi-chi northern suburb of Hampstead, is hosted by a film actress well known in England. The three operators of this firm are women and because they frequently host single female travelers, they pay special attention to listing homestays in safe neighborhoods with hosts who have proved themselves trustworthy. Its price structure is based on how close to the center of London you want to stay. Category A homes are in zones 1 and 2 (the most central, most urban zones) and cost £70–£90 for doubles, £40–£60 for singles. B category homes are in zones 2 and 3, which is to say they're 20–30 minutes by Tube or bus from the center of town in average neighborhoods, and they're £52–£64 for doubles, depending on whether you get your own bathroom, and £32–£60 for singles. The C categories are situated in London's many bedroom communities: zones 3 and 4, where few tourists usually go. That's why they're £48 for doubles and £26 for singles. No kids under 5 are allowed (a good rule of thumb for any homestay, I'd say). A £5 fee is added to the total.

ROCK BOTTOM HOME STAYS OUT OF THE CENTER

The tradition of paying to stay in spare rooms goes back a long, long way in Britain. The following agencies see things the old way. That is, their main concern is placing you in a home at the price you can afford. I can't promise that your hosts will bend over backwards to acclimate you to the city (which may actually suit more private travelers), but I can promise low prices:

You can tell that **London Homestead Services** (☎ 020/7286-5115; www.lhs london.com), in business since 1985, is an old-fashioned place by taking a look at the landlords' monikers—all are referred to by their initials, as in Mr. and Mrs. R., who offer a £22 double room in their home at Wembley Central. The budget category is incredibly cheap (£20 is the average fee for both doubles and singles), but that's usually because they're located in commuter neighborhoods a good half-hour train ride from town, within small, traditional homes. Staying in one of these rooms feels a lot like visiting a distant relation whom you'll want desperately not to disturb, but on the other hand, you'll be spending what you would at a hostel for a dorm bed, in authentic London neighborhoods (old-fashioned grocers, markets, and so on) that few tourists bother to explore. Loosely speaking, the agency's "budget" properties are in smallish semidetached homes; its "standard" ones in slightly larger houses; and its "premier" options are in some of the largest homes (though they're still not palatial by suburban standards). Remember that you will have to pay a little more for trains to reach those neighborhoods, but if you stick to a weekly Oyster pass, adding a zone only costs a few extra quid. "Standard" rooms are generally £25, and "premier" class is typically £30–£35, although there's one flat, fitting six and including a kitchen, near Russell Square for £150/night.

Established in 1992, **Happy Homes** (☎ 020/1352-5121; www.happy-homes. com) specializes in rooms in central and southwest London, about a 25-minute commute to the West End. Its catalog also offers fairly typical, middle-class homes, which is why its rates can be stupendously low. Unfortunately, its clunky website means you have to call to hash out where you're going to stay. Two types of rooms are offered: Short Term (4–13 nights) and Long Term (2 weeks and over), plus a one-time fee of £15 per person. For short term, singles are £23 and doubles are £38. Long-term prices for a single room are £110 per week, with a £55 administrative fee, and for a double, it's £185 per room per week, with an £80 fee. If you pay with a credit card, you'll incur a surcharge of 3%.

If you're scraping the linty depths of your wallet, you'll do well to stay a bit farther out of town, such as in Wimbledon, Clapham, or Putney—all about 30 minutes away from the West End by Tube or train. For those subdued but

Pauline Frommer Says: Questions to Ask Your Potential B&B Host

Though most in-apartment B&B stays are fun, carefree holidays, some-times . . . well, things can go mighty wrong. It's extremely important to find out what sort of person you may be sharing your vacation with and what the apartment is like before you put down a deposit. Call your poten-tial host or the agency to go over any concerns you may have before committing to a hosted stay. You may want to ask your potential host or agency the following questions:

1. **What is the host's schedule?** Some hosts will be in the apartment for most of the day, while others work outside the home, meaning that you'll have the apartment to yourself for large chunks of time. Find out before you leave.

2. **Where does the host sleep in relation to the room you'll be using?** Another privacy issue: Will your host be in the room right next door, eavesdropping, intentionally or not, on your every sigh or snore? Or will there be a room or two between your two bedrooms? In some extremely rare cases, cash-crunched hosts have been known to rent out their own bedrooms and take the living room couch for a week. If the listing is for a one-bedroom, you may want to find out if this is the case, as that can be an uncomfortable situation, espe-cially if you have to walk through the living room to get to the bed-room or bathroom. (From what I understand, this is not a common scenario, but hey, it's better to ask.)

3. **Is the bathroom shared or private?**

4. **Are there pets in the house?**

5. **Are children welcome as guests?**

6. **Are there any rules the host has for his or her guests?** Whether or not guests can smoke in the apartment is obviously a common issue, as is the guest's use of the shared space (I once met a host who only allowed the guests she liked to venture into the living room). Most hosts do not allow guests to cook, except to reheat prepared foods, so if this is an issue for you, bring it up. And sometimes the rules can be even more unusual—I know of a Kosher hostess who requires guests to separate the plates used for dairy products and meat prod-ucts (not an easy task).

7. **What does the bedroom face?** Does the room get a lot of sun in the morning? Does it face a busy street, or a quiet back courtyard? For light sleepers these questions are key.

money-saving areas, try **Annscott Accommodation Service** (☎ 020/8540-7642, www.holidayhosts.free-online.co.uk). The price of a single room with shared bath arranged by Annscott (in business under one name or another since the early

1990s) goes as low as £17, topping out at £40. Doubles are £34–£65. Don't expect the red carpet—just someone's spare room done up nicely, as if they were expecting a visiting school chum. Homes closer to town (Chelsea, Knightsbridge, Belgravia) go for £36–£54 for singles and £58–£90 for doubles. The management personally inspects all homes, and a minimum stay of 2 nights is required. Rooms all come with breakfast, TV, and tea and coffee facilities.

SERVICED APARTMENTS

The following agencies specialize in renting someone's home or second home. Many of them come with homemade booklets telling you about the best shops and restaurants nearby, and you may encounter helpful neighbors keeping an eye on the place and on your welfare (at one property I know of, the owner herself pops round and pretends to be a helpful neighbor), which is an advantage if you want to learn more of the city's secrets. Many have minimum stays of 5 to 7 nights, but that varies by property; a few have no minimum stay at all.

Although it was initially set up in 1995 to help gay and lesbian travelers find safe temporary apartments, **Accommodation Outlet** (☎ 020/7287-4244; www. outlet4holidays.com) welcomes bookings from anyone. Be thankful they're inclusive—this company's flats are better located for tourists than perhaps any other firm's. Because the Outlet caters to gay folks, its locations are around the gay 'hood of Old Compton Street, above the thriving Soho cafe-and-club scene, smack in the West End. The properties are mostly owned and decorated by stylish, worldly professionals, who may only use them themselves for a month a year and rent them out the rest of the time. They're equipped with free Wi-Fi linens and towels, and they're given some pretty campy code names, such as Oprah, Bette, and Diana. Prices range from £54–£70 for Soho rooms. Make a note of when your international flight arrives, because there are £15–£20 fees for checking in outside of office hours or on Sundays. This is on top of a non-negotiable booking fee of about £15. Should trouble arise, each flat has its own property manager, and the company's office is in Soho, so you won't have far to go for assistance.

For a good range of homes from mid-range to fantasy, **Coach House Rentals** (☎ 020/8772-1939; www.chslondon.com) shines brightest in Chelsea, South Kensington, Millbank (east of Victoria) and in the bedroom communities southwest and west of town, such as Wandsworth. All flats are selected and approved by the bosses, Meena and Harley Nott, and are owned by Londoners who are out of town much of the time; calendars reflecting availability are posted online. The Notts supply every incoming guest with a starter pack for the first morning's breakfast plus a handbook detailing what's worth doing around their temporary home. The company's namesake is a converted carriage house tucked behind a home in Wandsworth that belongs to the Notts themselves. It's a detached building with its own entrance and an atmospheric beamed bedroom, and it fits up to five people. In the morning, you cross the garden to the main house, where breakfast—made fully organic for another £3—is served by Meena, who uses the time to coach you on how to fill your day. That room can book up six months in advance in high season, and is £100 for two and £120 for three, sliding to £165 for five (or just £33 per person). Other properties are simply furnished flat rentals and don't come with breakfast. Typical of what's available: The Vale, a smartly redecorated one-bedroom double in the cellar of a building by fashionable King's

Road in Chelsea for £120 a night (6 or fewer nights) or £105 (more than 6 nights). One of its swishier homes is an honest-to-goodness duplex luxury houseboat (original sculptures, central heating, four-posted bed, and use of a nearby pool and fitness center—the works) moored in the Thames; that's £205 a night, but it fits six. Many properties have a minimum stay of 5 nights, and many have high-speed broadband. Maid service is weekly, and most properties are nonsmoking.

OTHER OPTIONS WORTH A LOOK

Upscale **In the English Manner** (☎ 800/422-0799, www.english-manner.com) rents second homes in the tony areas of Chelsea, Knightsbridge, and Kensington; most sleep two or three, although a few sleep more. Its best deals (£565–£1,000 per week) are found in Chelsea, off the ultratrendy King's Road shopping street, which is slightly removed from the Tube system (10–15 min. walks) but close to the Thames. Even the lowest price level buys you a flat that's more than comfortable, complete with glassware, china, towels, sheets, TV, and washing machine. About half the properties have microwave ovens (which you don't always find in British homes). The minimum stay is usually a week in all but a few apartments, but if you stay beyond that, it'll prorate the nightly rate. There's always a duty manager on call, but no daily maid service (it's £10 an hr. if you request it). The agency requires refundable credit-card deposits of $400–$900 to protect against damage. It will gladly bill in dollars so that you won't get slammed if the exchange rate changes.

Holiday Serviced Apartments (☎ 01923/82-00-77; www.holidayapartments. co.uk) usually carries about 20 London properties divided between serviced apartments in hotel-like buildings (three-star studios start at £90 nightly in winter or £100 in summer) and unserviced private apartments in residential buildings (from £85 a night or £600 a week). Properties, which aren't luxe but are central, are organized by star level, from three to six, depending on location, amenities, and furnishings.

Price Apartments (33 Belcombe St., NW1; ☎ 020/8870-9234; www.priceapts. co.uk) started as a niche service for American professors in the 1950s and is now marketing to tourists in general. Its inventory is split among studios, one-bedrooms, and two-bedrooms (about 10 in each category, spread in convenient locales around town), plus a few three-bedrooms. Most offer daily rates (starting at £80 for studios and £125 for one-bedrooms), but a few require stays of at least a week. Price owns two buildings (on Balcombe St., near Baker St.) and acts as an agent for the rest of its inventory. Among its best deals is London House in Paddington, a town house of 36 basic, low-cost flats with kitchenettes; prices start at £430 a week for two in summer and drop to about £360 a week in low season. The least expensive of its one-bedrooms, which are either quite simple or located in zone 2, are £575–£700 a week. All apartments require a £200 deposit, and if you arrive after 10pm, you'll have to pay another £25 to get your keys.

The choice for someone who wants a business-traveler vibe, **Central London Apartments** (☎ 0845/644-2714; www.central-london-apartments.com) has some 300 units in town, many managed by other companies but rented by CLA. What rooms lack in personality, they often make up for in perks, such as (often) a stereo, VCR, and DVD player (one that usually only plays DVDs coded to Britain, though). The emphasis is on modern buildings where you won't have to talk to your neighbor. (Probably because he's in his flat trying to figure out why his DVD player won't work for his discs.) Prices start at around £93 a night for small flats in corporate hotels such as Ramada, and go up to around £145 for ones in tony neighborhoods like Mayfair. You're paying, basically, to be left alone.

BUILDINGS OF SELF-CATERING FLATS

Finally, London boasts some entire buildings that are dedicated to self-catering flats. Often, you have to book these directly with the property, which is why I've listed them separately (although you may find them represented through an agency, it's always cheaper to book directly). A little bit like hotels, they usually have a front desk offering standard hotel services (concierge, for example) and pretty much everyone staying there is a temporary resident. So choosing one is not a good way to meet locals. However, you'll have privacy, a kitchen, and more space than a normal hotel room provides. This class of lodging is popular with long-term travelers such as businessmen and West End actors, but short-term tourists are almost always accepted, too. In some cases, there's a minimum stay of a week.

The cream-colored town house of **Vancouver Studios** ★★★ (30 Prince's Square, W2; ☎ 020/7243-1270; www.vancouverstudios.co.uk; Tube: Bayswater or Queensway) is so crisp and homey inside, you instantly wonder why all low-cost lodgings in Bayswater can't rise to the same standard. Although flats aren't huge and have power showers but not bathtubs, they're well equipped with a microwave, toaster, two burners (or "hobs"), utensils and pans, crockery, wireless internet, TV and DVD player, membership to a nearby gym, and daily maid service. There's a private ivy-lined garden with a gentle fountain out back for guest use. The owners keep rooms ship-shape but are not afraid to be eccentric in the common spaces: Scented candles frequently permeate the lobby, and two friendly cats have the run of place. It's a happy environment. Singles cost £75, doubles are £99, (doubles with a mini balcony over the street are £125), and triples are £140. Extra beds are £18. The handsome stone **Astons Apartments** ★ (31 Rosary Gardens, SW7; ☎ 020/7590-6000; www.astons-apartments.com; Tube: Gloucester Road) is just south of the Gloucester Road Tube station, about 10 minutes west of the Victoria & Albert Museum, and is completely given over to self-contained flats with hotel-style furniture and decor, satellite TV, kitchenettes, and modern bathrooms. Its unremarkable furnishings, combined with the town-house-style building unfashionable among big-spending business travelers, makes it one of the better values in terms of flat buildings. Studios with shower and WC are £68 for singles, £94 for doubles, and £100 for twin beds. If you have more than two people, you're in the family apartment category, which costs £131 for three and £174 for four. Want an extra bed in there? That's £10 more. Weekly rates net a (weak) 5% discount.

About a 7-minute walk east from the Tower Hill Tube station (you skirt the Tower of London to get there), **Hamlet** (UK) ★★ (☎ 800/504-9851 or 01462/67-80-37; www.users.globalnet.co.uk/~hamlet_uk) rents a few one-bedroom apartments in 1970s apartment buildings. Rooms with twin beds are £580 per week in summer and £525 in the off season. Its two-bedroom apartments, sleeping up to six if you pull out the sofabed, are £760 a week during the summer, and £705 a week during off season. Some of its apartments have a view of the marina at St. Katherine's Docks, with the Tower Bridge in the distance.

The Gallic Alternative

The French-owned chain **Citadines** (www.citadines.com) is devoted to cheap, private, apartmentlike quarters (they call them "apart'hotels"), light on the service but often conveniently located. Nightly rates are set at one level for stays of 1 to 6 nights and generally drop about 10% for stays between 7 and 29 nights. You get a pull-out couch (in studio apartments, it's your bed, but the mattresses are thicker than on a standard pull-out couch), king-size bed (in apartments), desk, kitchen (with microwave, small fridge, hot water kettle), bathtub and shower, modem jack, HiFi (in most units), TV, private telephone number, safe, and at least two sockets. Extra beds are around £12, and laundry (wash and dry) is about £7 in a laundry room. Room cleaning is weekly but extra once-overs are £14, breakfast is £9, parking is £18 to £20 a day.

Found just up the block from the Tube, the French-run **Citadines London Barbican** ✸ (7-21 Goswell Rd., EC1; ☎ 020/7566-8000; www.cidatines.com; Tube: Barbican) is on an ugly, windswept street, which may account for its below-market rates, but it's near enough to the action to consider. It's located in a modern 129-unit building over The Coconut Lagoon, a riotously decorated Indian restaurant. Just west are the nightclubs and restaurants of hip Clerkenwell. Studios that fit two start at £103 and one-bedrooms that fit four start at £159.

Citadines London Holborn-Covent Garden ✸✸ (94-99 High Holborn, WC1; ☎ 020/7395-8800; www.citadines.com) boasts a terrific location near Covent Garden and on the Central Line. Of 192 units, 40 are one-bedrooms, and the rest are studios, which are perfectly adequate; imagine hotel rooms with kitchenettes. Those on the front face a noisy street, but also overlook the magnificently ornate facade of the Renaissance Chancery Court. Studios fitting two start at £118 and one-bedrooms fitting four start at £177.

The 92-room **Citadines London South Kensington** (35A Gloucester Rd, SW7; ☎ 020/7543-7878; www.citadines.com; Tube: Gloucester Road) is found farther from the West End than any other Citadines in London, but its advantage is that it's nearer to Kensington Gardens and Hyde Park than almost any other economy property in the museums quarter. Studios that fit two start at £111 and one-bedrooms that fit four start at £163.

The best-located Citadines property, **Citadines London Trafalgar Square** ✸✸ (18-21 Northumberland Ave., WC2; ☎ 020/7766-3700; www.citadines.com), with 187 units, is a quick trot toward the Thames from Trafalgar Square, in the heart of tourist's London. That's why its prices are the highest among the chain's London properties, but its sensationally easy Tube connections may make it worth the extra price, especially if you've got kids in tow. Studios that fit two start at £130, one-bedrooms sleeping four start at £203, and two-bedrooms fitting six start at £257.

The Pleasures (& Perils) of Packaged Hotels

What if I told you that you could spend 6 nights in London, airfare and all hotel nights included, for $399 plus tax from November through March? Or for around $699 in the spring and the fall? Even in summer, when airfare by itself can cost $850–$1,000 and many people put off visiting London because they can't afford hotel expenses on top of airfare, air-hotel packages can be $919—with air, hotel, and often a tour or two thrown in. With prices like that, it's as if the hotel stay is free.

I love air-hotel packages. There's often no cheaper way to get to London. And unlike escorted tours, with air-hotel packages you don't have to amble around the city on a bus full of tourists—you get your air ticket and your hotel voucher, and off you go to explore. The lowest prices leave from eastern American cities such as New York and Boston, but for a few dozen dollars more, you can leave from just about any other American city. You can also often extend the return airfare by as much as a month.

The king of affordable air-hotel deals is **Go-Today.com** (☎ 800/227-3235; www.go-today.com), which usually offers 6- and 4-night packages to London, often paired with other European destinations such as Paris or Amsterdam, including local flights between the cities. Other big brokers can share the same inventory, so options might be similar among them: **EuropeASAP** (www.europeASAP.com) has prices that are competitive with Go-Today, but it only accepts reservations online. **Virgin Vacations** (☎ 888/937-8474; www.virgin-vacations.com), the air-hotel wing of funky Virgin Atlantic Airways, does 3-, 4-, and 6-night deals. The best deals from **British Airways Holidays** (☎ 877/428-2228; www.baholidays.com) are its 3-night air-inclusive vacations, but some of its packages are priced higher than others on the air-hotel market. **Gate 1 Travel** (☎ 800/682-3333;

A bit more pricey but perhaps worth it for the centerstage location, the 32 two-bedroom/1½ bathroom apartments at **Scala House** ★★ (21 Tottenham St., W1; ☎ 020/7580-6644; www.scala-house.co.uk; Tube: Goodge Street), just west of the British Museum, cost £840 week in high season for one or two people, dropping to £665 the rest of the year. Additional people are £10 a night. Nightly rates, with a minimum of 2 nights, start about 20% higher, or £150 peak/£130 winter, sliding down to the weekly prices the longer you stay. That includes very well-equipped kitchens with a dishwasher and washer/dryer. Because of the 10-story height of this 1976 concrete apartment tower, the views are also among the best in the West End. The management, which pretty much controls the entire building and its security (and isn't too swift to bring its furniture up-to-date), will buy you a few groceries before check-in if you like (at an extra charge). For big spenders, there are also a couple of two-bedroom/2½ bath penthouse apartments which fit four and cost £1,225 weekly during peak season, or £1,050 weekly off season, which comes to £200/£180 nightly. Sure, the rates are higher than more

www.gate1travel.com) does 4-nighters, which it calls 6-day trips. **E.E.I. Travel** (☎ 800/927-3876; www.eeitravel.com) is Go-Today's corporate cousin, so deals are similar except that it offers fewer low-cost hotel options. **Auto Europe** (☎ 888/223-5555; www.autoeurope.com) sometimes adds London to its offers.

The small catch with package deals is this: Although all air-hotel deals give you a range of hotels to pick from, many of the least expensive ones ("budget" and "tourist") are pillow mills that have seen better days. Depressing but true. So what can you do about this? First of all, don't give up on air-hotel packages. The money you save could make or break your trip, and besides, you'll only endure even the worst hotel for a few minutes before you sleep and for an hour or two after you wake up. The rest of the time, you'll be unconscious or touring.

Unless you find that one of your potential hotels appears in this chapter, opt for a slightly more expensive "superior" or "deluxe" property, but that might negate the original savings. Another good idea: Hit Internet message boards and see what others have said. **TripAdvisor** (www.tripadvisor.com) has active London boards, as do **Frommers.com** and **Yahoo! Travel** (http://travel.yahoo.com).

The slate of budget and tourist hotels changes by the month, but there are options that I think are a little cleaner, friendlier, and more recently renovated than the others. No promises, because innkeepers can get lazy at any time, but the best are: Tria, My Place Hotel, Bayswater Inn, Holiday Villa London, Somerset hotels, Citadines hotels, Thistle hotels, Comfort Inn Kensington Hotel, and Queens Park Hotel.

remote apartments, but you'll find the cheap eateries and stores catering to students nearby. If you're smart, you can save on Tube tickets, since many of the city's best sights are within a half-hour's walk.

The building housing **Chelsea Cloisters** (Sloane Avenue, SW3; ☎ 020/7589-5100; www.chelsea-cloisters.co.uk; Tube: South Kensington) went up in the 1930s, and in the 1980s, it became one of London's first serviced apartment buildings, with some 600 units. Picture something renovated but faceless, a battery-hen apartment building with high guest turnover and a detached staff, but also with an enviable South Kensington location about 10 minutes by foot south of the big museums and 15 minutes southwest of Harrods. Studios are £505 a week and sleep two, while one-bedrooms, which also sleep two, supply an extra living room for £740 a week. The kitchens are better equipped than most, with plenty of cutlery, a fridge, microwave, toaster, kettle and hot plate, plus a washing machine and a dryer. All stays are subject to a £71 "tenancy agreement fee," whatever that is. Perhaps it pays for the 24-hour concierge you're probably not going to use.

ACADEMIC ROOMS
Wait, don't skip this section yet!

Staying in an empty dorm room is actually an ideal option. After all, given the size of London's hotel rooms—even the pricey ones—you're not going to get much more space than a college student, anyway. Besides, by summertime, when the dorms open to the public, the students are long gone and every square inch has been polished to a glare by custodial staff, so it's not like you're going to deal with student filth or sleep under posters of Pink.

Even though there are 24 universities and colleges in town with 350,000 students, it used to be a royal pain to book a dorm room in England. For years, you'd have to write away to the universities, wait weeks for a response, only to be told you'd missed out by *that* much. Now, the schools are savvy and they have mounted detailed websites on which you can book rooms. For summer, reservations are usually accepted starting in March or April.

At all of them, you should expect a wood-frame bed with linen, a desk, a dresser, an in-room sink, windows that open, nightstands, the possibility of an equipped kitchen (although it might be shared), an en suite bathroom (shared situations are noted), laundry facilities, breakfast (often at a reasonable charge), and phones in the room or in the hall. A few even have TV lounges. And all of them have round-the-clock security.

London School of Economics ★★★ (☎ 020/7955-7575, www.lsevacations.co.uk). Check these rooms out first. They're in terrific condition, with modern furnishings and the dignity that you'd expect of a school that trains the world's future power players in business. Generally, rooms rent cheaply for July, August, and the first chunk of September. School's not in session around Christmas, either, but LSE only opens Rosebery then. Some (in Carr-Saunders, Passfield, and Rosebery) are also available around Easter.

> **Grosvenor House Studios** (141-143 Drury Lane, WC2; Tube: Covent Garden): These rooms, which opened in July 2006, have in-room microwaves, grills, and hot water kettles. Singles run from £40–£50, twins run from £75–£85, and one-bedroom flats with full kitchens are £95. Disabled accessible.

> **High Holborn** (178 High Holborn, WC1; Tube: Holborn): £31 singles, £49 twins, £70 twins with en suite, £80 triple with en suite. Summers only. This is the only place on the list without phones in the room. Disabled accessible.

> **Carr-Saunders Hall** (18-24 Fitzroy St., W1; Tube: Warren Street): Singles: £28 around Easter/£30 in summer. Twins with shared bath: £44 /£48. Twins en suite: £46/£52.

> **Bankside House** (24 Summer St., SE1; Tube: Southwark): En suite rooms: £46 singles, £66 twins, £84 triples, £92 quads. Some singles share baths, and they're £37. This is the only spot on this list without kitchens. Disabled accessible.

> **Passfield Hall** (1-7 Endsleigh Pl., WC1; Tube: Euston Square): £27 singles, £48 twins, £62 triples. This is the only hall on this list without a laundry facility.

Rosebery Hall (90 Rosebery Ave., EC1; Tube: Farringdon): £31 singles, £50 twins, £62 triples. Some twins are en suite and cost £60. Disabled accessible. Shared bath.

Butler's Wharf (11 Gainsford St., SE1; Tube: Tower Hill): £30 singles, £48 twins, £130 nightly/£860 weekly for five, £155 nightly/£1025 weekly for six. This is the only hall on this list without breakfast and guaranteed en suite bathrooms.

Also ask about LSE's **Northumberland House** (Northumberland Avenue, WC2; Tube: Embankment). This one's got a better location than many hotels—in the middle of London between Strand and the Thames Embankment. Once it opens in July 2007, it's bound to be the most popular of LSE's options.

A few more options, ordered within each list from most central to least central:

City University London ✦ (☎ 020/7040-8037; www.city.ac.uk/ems): Two of its dorms open mid-June to the first week of September:

Finsbury Residences (15 Bastwick St., EC1; Tube: Barbican): Singles only (£21) with shared bathrooms and shared kitchen without utensils.

Peartree Court (15 Bastwick St., EC1; Tube: Barbican): Singles only (£25) with one bathroom per four to six people and kitchen without utensils.

These following two options have a higher standard and are mostly open year-round:

Francis Rowley Court (16 Briset St., EC1; Tube: Farringdon): Three singles conjoined with a kitchen and a bathroom (£36 per bed), with TV. Closed late August to mid-September and over the December holidays.

Walter Sickert Hall (29 Graham St., N1; Tube: Angel): Hotel-style en suite singles (£40) and twins (£60). No kitchens, but there is a cafeteria.

University College London ✦ (☎ 020/7631-8310; www.ucl.ac.uk/residences). Its dorms are less prestigious than LSE's, but they still fit the bill and aren't depressing. From mid-June to mid-September, its seven residences are available for public use, but four of them only accept groups. The three that accept both individuals and groups (act quickly) are:

Astor College (99 Charlotte St., W1; Tube: Goodge Street): Singles from £23 and twins from £44. Mostly singles, all with a small fridge. Shared bath.

Campbell House (5-10 Taviton St., WC1; Tube: Euston): Singles from £22 and twins from £43. There are 15 kitchens for 180 bedrooms. Shared bath.

Ifor Evans Hall (109 Camden Rd., NW1; Tube: Camden Town): Singles from £22 with kitchens or £27 with breakfast. Shared bath. Disabled accessible.

King's College (☎ 020/7836-5454; www.kcl.ac.uk/kcvb): Open July through mid-September. It opens four dorms, but only three are in central London (its King's Hall location is only accessible by commuter rail in the south-central area of Camberwell). The candidates, all with kitchens that lack tools of any kind (a disappointment that diminishes their utility), are:

> **Stamford Street Apartments** (127 Stamford St., SE1; Tube: Waterloo): All singles, en suite, with a small fridge (£35). Disabled accessible.

> **Great Dover Street Apartments** (165 Great Dover St., SE1; Tube: Borough): Mostly singles (£33), all en suite with small fridge. Disabled accessible.

> **Hampstead Campus** (Kidderpore Avenue, NW3; Tube: Hampstead): Mostly singles (£27), some twins (£45), all shared bath with continental breakfast.

> **King's College Hall** (Champion Hill, SE5; Mainline rail: Denmark Hill): All singles (£20), all shared bath with cooked breakfast.

International Students House ★★ (229 Great Portland St., W1; ☎ 020/ 7631-8300; www.ish.org.uk; Tube: Great Portland Street): Part dorm, part sub-dued hostel. £12–£19 in a dorm, £34 singles, £26 twin. Most of the year, it's full of students from around the world, but in summer, it has the space to admit short-stay visitors. Bathrooms are shared and some are co-ed but partitioned. The rooms boast modern furniture and are notably clean and safe.

If you're still stuck after plowing through this list, try contacting **Venuemasters** (☎ 0114/249-3090, www.venuemasters.co.uk), an organization that helps tourists locate and book academic accommodation in the U.K for free.

LONDON'S HOTELS

I understand that you might prefer to check into a hotel rather than an apartment or a homestay. Fortunately, because of London's long tradition of privately oper-ated B&B hotels, going the hotel route doesn't preclude you from having an authentic English experience. London has more than 100,000 rooms, but I've whittled down the choices for you considerably. Hotels are listed by neighbor-hood starting with the cheapest and moving upwards to end with an occasional big splurge.

London essentially has three varieties of hotel, from family-run inns that pro-vide B&B, to traditional hotels, to hostels. In case you were leaning against the family-run B&Bs, know that they're more private than you might think. Because times are hard for little businesses, it's now unusual for proprietors to live on-site. It's more economical to rent out the rooms that, in years past, the family would have occupied. There's also this: If you stay at a family-run B&B, you'll be privy to the owners' personal counsel about what's worth doing and what's not. These days, many higher-end hotel desk clerks are actually from continental Europe, and many of them know London only barely better than you do. But people who run family inns have usually been at it since their parents taught them how.

In many of the hotel write-ups, you'll read a range of prices. London's hotels are pretty good about sticking to their posted rates; in fact, every property is required by law to post them in the lobby. When you're quoted a price, rest assured it will never go higher. Hotels are permitted to charge more if there's a rare major event happening, such as the London Marathon (Apr) or a giant trade show, but even then, the increase will usually be limited to one or two neighborhoods.

Accommodation is subject to a Value Added Tax (VAT) of 17.5%. Happily, almost all small B&Bs include taxes in their rates, so you don't have to think about it for most of the places below. However, more expensive hotels (those around £150 or more) tend to leave it off their tariffs, which can result in a nasty surprise at checkout. It never hurts to ask about it before you commit.

Where are the luxury hotels? Trust me, London has some unforgettable ones. But I figured you don't want to spend £400 a night to hide out in a velvet box and that you'd rather use your funds to get underneath the skin of the city.

SOHO AND COVENT GARDEN

Let there be no doubt: This is the middle of modern London: The West End. The one that knows no closing hours. The one that offers everything you need right outside your door. The one that's not only within walking distance to just about everything, but the one that's also crawling with inebriated twenty-year-olds singing drinking shanties by the light of the moon as you press your pillow to your sleepless head. Hotels around here, by virtue of the prime location, can slide by with lesser quality than others in town, but frankly, you may not care. I wouldn't, because staying centrally can save on Tube fare more than it costs in shoe leather.

££–£££   Fans of the **Seven Dials Hotel** (7 Monmouth St., WC2; ☎ 020/7681-0791; AE, MC, V; Tube: Covent Garden) generally praise its top-drawer location and ignore its shortcomings, and if you can do the same, you'll think it's a fine, central choice. Rooms aren't big; a few have furniture and bathroom doors that appear to be duking it out for space. Still, there's usually enough storage space, a TV mounted on an armature, a writing desk, clean bathrooms, and firm beds. Forget all the ways it's average. Its situation on Monmouth Street, steps from dozens of pubs and bars clustering around Covent Garden, is peerless. You can pop out at any hour, no planning or public transportation required, and walk to many of the city's most important sights; everything from St. Paul's to Westminster will take you less than a half hour to reach. Few fancy, expensive hotels can match it. For that, I'd gladly pay £65 for singles and £75 for doubles (shared bath) or £75 for singles and £85 for doubles (en suite). The owners, who also run a few middling properties around King's Cross, don't maintain a website for the hotel, so you have to call. Because of its busy location, all guests must use the door buzzer to enter, no matter the time of day.

£–£££   No affordable hotel in the central Covent Garden area will offer much space, but we'd be in good shape if they all offered the throwaway charisma of **The Fielding Hotel** ★★ (4 Broad Court, Bow St., WC2; ☎ 020/7836-8305; www.the-fielding-hotel.co.uk; AE, MC, V; Tube: Covent Garden or Holborn), set in perhaps the most peaceful alley within a square mile. In this early-19th-century warren of tight staircases and fire doors, most of the 24 rooms face Crown Court and the blank building about 4.5m (15 ft.) across it. The management (at it for more than 40 years) has taken the unusually helpful step of posting local suggestions for restaurants, laundromats, and Internet cafes in every room. Very small singles (about the size of a double bed, and somewhat airless) are £80, appealingly cramped and creaky doubles and twins £100–£115 (for a slightly larger one). Room 10 (£130) is a double with a sitting area that catches lots of afternoon light

All in the Timing

To save money on hotels and inns, remember two simple rules:

1. **Off season is cheaper.** Many hostels and big hotels have two seasons: April through September and October through March. Prices will be 10% to 25% cheaper during the latter period. Interestingly, very few family-owned B&Bs and inns bother with this system.
2. **To save pounds, stay longer.** While researching this book, I don't think I found a single hotel that wasn't willing to lower its prices for anyone who stayed for 5 or 6 nights. Chances are, that applies to your vacation.

thanks to its corner position and copious windows. Everything's en suite (but shower only). The Fielding must be one of the last hotels in town to still use old-fashioned rod keys and traditionally-shaped keyholes. Trivia: Oscar Wilde was convicted of gross indecency in the Bow Street Magistrates' Court next door, which closed in July 2006 to await rebirth as—what else?—a high-end boutique hotel.

KING'S CROSS

While Victoria and Kensington/Earl's Court rule as the most popular areas for low-cost hotels, there's little debate that King's Cross is better situated, given that it's served by six important Tube lines and is closer to other interesting areas. The attractions of the West End are a 20-minute walk away, and the bohemian drags of Camden Town and antiques markets in Islington are also within strolling distance. But there's still the matter of the area's vanishing sleaze. Despite an ongoing rebirth, and despite the credibility that comes with the invasion of some popular low-cost chain hotels, too many inns surrounding King's Cross station are junky B&B catastrophes favored by construction workers who flock in from other parts of the country for short jobs in the district. That's why there are plenty of budget inns crowding the streets, but few options a tourist should accept. But when you do find a sensibly priced hotel here, the convenience makes any search worth it.

£   Proof positive that King's Cross is rising again to reclaim its 1960s crown as a viable budget traveler's hood, **Albion House Hotel** ★★★ (29 Argyle Square, WC1; ☎ 020/7837-0571; www.albionhousehotel.com; MC, V; Tube: King's Cross St. Pancras) may have only 13 rooms, but they're stylish, bright, and en suite. Owned by the same brother-and-sister team, Patrick and Cherie Parekh, who control the Excelsior Hotel on the west side of the same square, the Albion was given a design makeover a few years back. The result is a compact Georgian town house remade into an comfy B&B with perky orange accent walls and geometric rugs, asthmatic-friendly wood floors, beds with deep duvets, heated towel rails, radio alarm clocks, and a tiny but social breakfast room (serving an unexciting continental only) outfitted with custom-made tables. Are rooms small? Yes, but few other bargain hotels in town at this price are as clean, well-designed, and put together so

Oxford Circus to King's Cross Accommodations

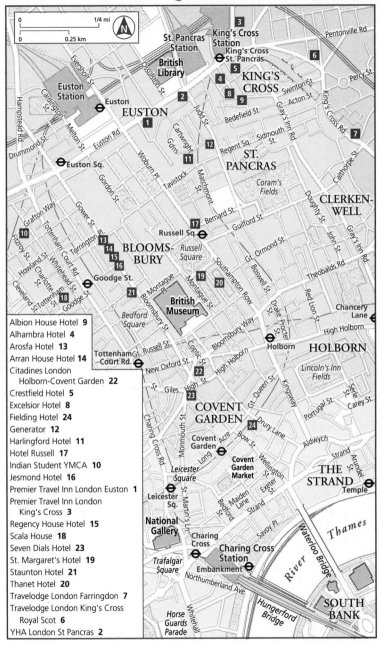

Albion House Hotel **9**
Alhambra Hotel **4**
Arosfa Hotel **13**
Arran House Hotel **14**
Citadines London
  Holborn-Covent Garden **22**
Crestfield Hotel **5**
Excelsior Hotel **8**
Fielding Hotel **24**
Generator **12**
Harlingford Hotel **11**
Hotel Russell **17**
Indian Student YMCA **10**
Jesmond Hotel **16**
Premier Travel Inn London Euston **1**
Premier Travel Inn London
  King's Cross **3**
Regency House Hotel **15**
Scala House **18**
Seven Dials Hotel **23**
St. Margaret's Hotel **19**
Staunton Hotel **21**
Thanet Hotel **20**
Travelodge London Farringdon **7**
Travelodge London King's Cross
  Royal Scot **6**
YHA London St Pancras **2**

snazzily. Rates run from £55 for singles, £75 for a double or twin (a "junior suite" comes with two single beds and a futon bed for £5 more), £90 for triples, and £ 130 for a quad. Be warned that the hotel office is at the Excelsior Hotel (see below), which makes solving problems time-consuming.

£   Argyle Square, located a block south of the castle-like St. Pancras station, used to be budget travel Purgatory, but like its sister hotel Albion House, on the south side of the square, **Excelsior Hotel** ★★★ (42 Argyle Square, WC1; ☎ 020/7837-0571; www.excelsiorhotel.co.uk; MC, V; Tube: King's Cross St. Pancras), on the western side, was recently rejuvenated. Even the ancient coal dust that still stains the rest of the square has been sandblasted from the facade, and with it, it seems, gloom was banished. The chief difference is that the Excelsior, which was renovated second, has superior amenities such as flat-screen TVs (instead of the Albion's tube sets) and free Wi-Fi access in the rooms (and no trouser presses, like the Albion has—but who uses those?). Even with those twists, rooms, which are as tiny as the London average, are no more expensive than at its sister property: singles are £60, doubles (most are convertible to twins) are £70, triples are £90, and quads are £150. Breakfast is taken at the Albion, which is annoying if it's raining. If only the rest of the dingy neighborhood would follow suit. The family's third Argyle Square property, the once-grim Melville, a door north, was being reshaped as this went to press; book via the Excelsior.

£   One of a dying breed, the well-kept **Alhambra Hotel** ★★ (17-19 Argyle St., WC1; ☎ 020/7837-9575; www.alhambrahotel.com; MC, V; Tube: King's Cross St. Pancras) can't claim to be stylish or modern, but there's no denying that it's a family-run inn with heart, and a top value. In fact, it dispels the myth that extremely affordable London B&Bs must also be in some way depressing. Its family proprietors work hard, and they keep the prices low. They also like Americans; when I last visited, they had just been to New York for a vacation. Picture basic rooms (TVs but no phones) squeezed into old spaces and freshened up with bright bedspreads, cream pinstripe wallpaper, and inviting new blue carpeting. Frank, the patriarch, does the cooking, and he dabbles in art, too; in the basement breakfast area, check out the pastel still life he drew to illustrate what's included in his generous full English breakfast. His Portuguese son-in-law, who used to work at Harrods, now handles the hotel's more arcane modernization, such as the addition of free Wi-Fi (his baby daughter has a role, too—she often entertains guests by the front desk). Its prices haven't budged since 2001, when 9/11 sucker-punched small-time hoteliers: If you share a bathroom, singles are £35, doubles and twins are £45, and triples are £65. Add £10 to singles and doubles if you want a shower but not a toilet, and add £20 to £25 if you want both a shower and a toilet. Using a credit card incurs a 3% surcharge, but come on, when prices are that low, will you notice? Although it's barely 90m (300 ft.) from the King's Cross Tube and seething Euston Road, it's remarkably quiet. The Argyle Hotel, located directly across the street, is operated by the same family and is much in the same vein; you can book via the Alhambra.

£   Southeast of King's Cross station (not at Farringdon, as the name implies), the chain hotel **Travelodge London Farringdon** (10-42 King's Cross Rd., WC1; ☎ 0870/191-1774; Tube: Farringdon or King's Cross St. Pancras) is the latest tenant of a gorgeous old stone building. Rooms on the front, which you can request but can't

The Deal with Those Economy Hotel Chains

Love them or hate them, chains are here to stay, and they're a viable accommodation option for folks who prefer some predictability in a topsy-turvy town. London's budget-hotel landscape has changed dramatically with the proliferation of several economy corporate brands, which are chipping away at the city's already-suffering B&Bs. At these cookie-cutter economy hotels, the desk will mostly be staffed by distracted young people from other European countries, so don't expect much local expertise or service. But rooms, while hardly oozing charm, are brightly designed, well cleaned, and reliable—there's not much difference between one Ibis room and another. All offer both smoking and nonsmoking options, all charge by the room and not per person (unless you squeeze in more people than the prescribed limit), and most also have up-sized family rooms for the same price. They all have cafes that can serve up sandwiches, soups, beer, and the like at odd hours. Because of Web deals, you're always best off booking online directly with each company instead of calling.

Premier Travel Inn (☎ 0870/242-8000; www.premiertravelinn.com; AE, MC, V): This is my favorite of London's economy brand hotels, not just because its rooms feel the most upbeat, but also because it constructs attractive buildings that fit in with their surroundings. Weekend rates (Fri–Sun) are almost always lower than weekday rates. You get a king-size bed, bathtub and shower, climate control, tea- and coffeemaking facilities, TV, phone, iron, paid Wi-Fi access, at least three outlets, and a desk. Full breakfast costs £7.50, continental £5.25, and up to four kids (under 10) eat free. Londontown.com often discounts rates a further £12.

Ibis Hotel (www.ibishotel.com; MC, V, AE): This French chain is distinguished by its trademark three-foot-square windows, its just-off-the-margins locations, and its bare-bones but cheerful decor. It's probably the simplest of the economy brands. You'll get a double bed, shower, climate control, tea- and coffeemaking facilities, TV, phone, paid Internet access, at least one outlet, and a desk. The breakfast charge varies per property, but food is usually served from 4am, making this a smart choice if you need to catch an early flight or train. The fresh-baked breakfast baguettes are delicious—hey, it's French.

Travelodge (☎ 0870/850-950; www.travelodge.co.uk; MC, V, AE): Rates here start at a head-slapping £10–£26 if you book many months ahead; in truth, those are very hard to snag. Expect king-size beds, bathtub and shower, tea- and coffeemaking facilities, TV and phone, paid dial-up Web access, paid in-room movies, at least one power point and a desk. "Family rooms" have a pull-out couch for two kids but cost the same as a double. A continental "Breakfast bag" to go is £4, while full English and table-served continental breakfast charges vary per property. It's nicer than the American Travelodge brand, which is a separate beast entirely, but service is spotty.

secure, have floor-to-ceiling windows. Because its historic breakfast room is protected by the city, cooking isn't allowed. That means, unlike other Travelodges, it only serves a continental breakfast (£5.25). Rooms run £65 a night. If that one's full, you might consider **Travelodge London King's Cross Royal Scot** (100 King's Cross Rd., WC1; ☎ 0870/191-1773; Tube: King's Cross St. Pancras). It isn't as appealing as the Farringdon location, but it does a cooked breakfast, and for £66, it's a fab deal. For a description of Travelodge amenities, see p. 47.

£–££   The 56-room **Crestfield Hotel** (2-4 Crestfield St., WC1; ☎ 020/7837-0500; www.crestfieldhotel.com; MC, V; Tube: King's Cross St. Pancras) stands out for holding itself to a higher standard than most of its neighbors. It may be on the basic side, but it's not grim; yes, it's an old guesthouse, but it boasts a lovely iron gate and genteel blue trim. Rooms are tiny, freshly painted in canary yellow and done up with lace curtains, have glass-topped bedside tables (a sign of trust for budget guests if ever there was one), and there are generous touches such as baskets of potpourri. Rooms also boast TVs (albeit teeny ones), but no phones. There's a back terrace where breakfast is served in nice weather; otherwise, you eat in the basement dining room. Bathrooms (most rooms have their own, with toilet) are essentially tiled cubicles with drains in the floor, but some have their own windows, which is unusual for town house hotels. Room 9, a double, is located on a landing facing the back, so it's even quieter than most. The licensed bar area proves that the owners are trying for a hotel, not a hostel, image. Singles are £45–£55, doubles and triples are £60–£65, and quads are £90–£110. If you're only staying on weekdays, ask for a special deal, because the hotel sees a lot of weekend trade. Although the owners are gradually adding private facilities to all rooms, some still share bathrooms; you'll pay £10–£15 less for those. Are there finer hotels in town? Sure. But if you don't need much, it's a strong value.

£–££   Opened in 2004 in a modernized brick building out the eastern side door of King's Cross station, **Premier Travel Inn London King's Cross** ★★ (26-30 York Way, N1; ☎ 0870/990-6414; Tube: King's Cross St. Pancras) has an open, glassy atrium that belies its budget rates. The cafes of Islington are a 15-minute walk east. Rooms are £85 weekdays and £75 weekends. The other Premier in the vicinity, **Premier Travel Inn London Euston** (1 Dukes Rd., WC1; ☎ 0870/238-3301; www.premiertravelinn.com; MC, V, AE; Tube: Euston), is in a drab office building rehab beside the infernal traffic of Euston Road. That said, you won't suffer noise, since windows are well buffered, and you won't want for Tube connections (six lines run nearby). Expect to pay £85 on weekdays and £75 on weekends. For a description of Premier Travel Inn amenities, see p. 47.

BLOOMSBURY

If King's Cross has the personality of a genial but uncouth warehouse worker, Bloomsbury is a clean-shaven college student. After all, the area's prime institutions are the British Museum and two universities, and much of its cultural pop history is literary. That doesn't mean the neighborhood is staid: Bloomsbury's chocolate-colored Georgian town houses lie within a 20-minute walk of Soho and Covent Garden. To be honest—and I don't want to spill a dirty secret here—these places are better located than many of London's most expensive hotels.

£   I confess a soft spot for the **Jesmond Hotel** ✪✪✪ (63 Gower St., WC1; ☎ 020/ 7636-3199; www.jesmondhotel.org.uk; MC, V; Tube: Goodge Street), because I stayed here when I was a young backpacker just getting to know London (I stayed in number 3, a cozy single on the rear landing—still there, still snug). Back then, the Beynon Family, who took over the Jesmond in 1979, had a young son Glyn. Today, Glyn is the man in charge, and he's doing a solid job of updating the family business far beyond the expectations of his tariff range. He recently had contractors build new bathrooms with all-new piping (accounting for the larger-than-average showers), he soundproofed the front windows to keep out the roar of Gower Street's bus traffic, and he converted the house's 18th-century coal chute into a kitchen where full English breakfasts are prepared and served in a cellar breakfast room that doubles as a day lounge—check out the free Internet and DVD player with movie library. The back garden now provides welcome respite from the city and is culti- vated with daffodils and a birdbath. He also converted the former parlor, with its antique (non-working) fireplace, into room 2, a spacious double. It's simple, it's friendly, it's clean, and it's still one of London's last "they're charging *how* much?" values. The prices vary by shared/en suite: singles are £40–£50 (most are on the top floor, where it's quietest), doubles are £60–£75, triples are £75–£85, quads are £90–£100. Pay for 6 nights, and you can stay for 7. Don't confuse this place with the Jesmond Dene, a decent B&B on mostly shabby Argyle Square in King's Cross—it's fine, but not as central as the Jesmond.

£   Another solid Gower Street value, **The Arosfa Hotel** ✪ (83 Gower St., WC1; ☎ 020/7636-2115; www.arosfalondon.com; MC, V; Tube: Goodge Street) is distin- guished by the antique lacquered sign out front that still advertises its old tele- phone exchange: "Museum 2115." Owners Mr. and Mrs. Dorta have run their nonsmoking inn since 1993, and they've put a lot into it: double-glazed windows, a garden for guest use, bright red carpet, powerful showers, English breakfasts, a book swap, lounge furniture that actually matches (not too common in the hand- me-down world of B&Bs), and a smattering of fabric flowers to enliven the mood. Prices haven't changed since 2002: Singles go for £45 and generally lie behind fire doors on the stairway landings, away from the other rooms. Doubles or twins are £66, triples are £79, the quads are £92 (like room 5, a family room that still has its rich-looking carved fireplace, now filled in). If there's a down side, even at this sensational price point, it's the prefabricated plastic bathrooms that were recently inserted into all the rooms in lieu of actual contractor-built booths. Directly across the street, you'll find one of the city's largest Waterstone's bookstores, patronized by students from neighboring University College London.

£   Gower Street's streak of admirable budget lodging continues at **Regency House Hotel** ✪ (71 Gower St., WC1; ☎ 020/7637-1804; www.regencyhouse-hotel.com; MC, V; Tube: Goodge Street). The interior doors are numbered with cheap hard- ware-store metal stickers, but don't let that fool you. Victor Gilbert, the proprietor since 1977, makes and fixes almost everything himself because, he laments, work- men are no longer willing to come into the city due to tolls. He's got good taste— the cornflower blue-striped wallpaper and golden embellishments go a long way to approximating (not replicating) this town house hotel's bygone glory days as a pri- vate home. Showers have doors, not curtains, plus rooms have matching bedside tables, two chairs for the desk (many places just supply one), and Gilbert also lays out plenty of towels. There are 14 rooms; number 17, a double, has an exceptionally large bathroom for a town house B&B, and number 5 boasts an intricately carved marble fireplace that has been insured for £10,000. You can enjoy it for £75, the price of a double room. Singles are £52, triples are £88, and full English breakfasts are included. In peak season, prices crawl upward £12. Rooms on the top floor are quieter but have smaller windows.

£–££   Whoever waved a magic wand over the once-dreary Gower Street B&Bs didn't neglect **Arran House Hotel** ✪✪ (77-79 Gower St., WC1; ☎ 020/7636-2186; www.arranhotel-london.com; MC, V; Tube: Goodge Street), which continues the street's streak of affordable, basic B&Bs. Here, prices are a notch higher than at its neighbors, but you're paying for perks like hair dryers, matching pillows and carpet, and—a rarity with inns—access to the money-saving kitchen. Flooring and much of the furniture are warm and wooden, done up in a sort of rustic country style unusual for London. The bathrooms are less heartwarming; the shared baths are covered in displeasing linoleum, and the private baths are mostly tiny molded fiberglass units. The exceptional beds make up for that—the thick white duvets have a nearly magnetic pull. The ground-floor lounge has a gas-powered fire in the winter, which is also rare. Laundry can be done for £5 a load, including detergent, and the English-style rose garden is open to guests. Shared bath rates are as follows: singles £45, doubles £72. En suite rooms are singles £55, doubles £95. Unusually, Arran House also offers a minidorm, in the cellar but at the front by the street (windows are soundproofed), with four bunks for £19 without breakfast or £24 with breakfast. There's free Wi-Fi if you're lucky enough to lodge in the basement or on the ground floor, and breakfast is full English (included in the non-dorm rate). The owners, who mostly leave the running of the place to a slate of businesslike young Europeans, love the theater and opera, so ask for viewing advice.

£–££   Another old-fashioned, thoroughly dowdy, but ultimately adorable budget option, **St. Margaret's Hotel** ✪✪✪ (26 Bedford Place, WC1; ☎ 020/7636-4277; www.stmargaretshotel.co.uk; MC, V; Tube: Russell Square) has been under the same family management for about half a century. If you want something no-frills but with an earnest staff, this is it. For every alienating attribute, such as fluorescent lighting in the perplexingly rambling hallways, there are ten endearing ones, like fresh daffodils in the bright, social breakfast room, the homey hodgepodge of slouching furniture throughout, or the plentiful afternoon light that back-facing rooms soak up. In fact, the whole back of the property is enlivened by the Duke of Bedford's private gardens—guests may steal his view for free. There's no doubt that the environment could use some updating—or even just a coherent look—but this is a by product more of expense than of laziness. Few other budget hoteliers put as much heart and energy into making sure guests are acclimated to London by answering questions, obliging special dietary requests, and filling bellies with a cooked breakfast that's so enormous (try the banana yogurt) that lunch might become optional. The warm-and-fuzzy reasons why St. Margaret's has a following don't come across in photos of the basic rooms, all of which at least have hand basins, a TV, a phone, and a sink. If you share a well scrubbed bathroom, your room will be a bit larger than if it had one of its own shoehorned in, and it'll cost you £54 for a single, £66 for a double or twin. Rooms with an en suite shower but a shared toilet are singles £74, doubles £82, and rooms with an en suite shower and toilet are singles £77, doubles £95. If you only stay a single night, they'll tack £2 onto the rate. Some rooms have DVD players, and the hotel boasts two ground-floor lounges, one with TV, and one without. Room 53, featuring a glass conservatory ceiling and a Jacuzzi, is a popular shoestring romance spot at £101/night.

£–££   Styled as an affordable boutique B&B, **Harlingford Hotel** ★ (61-63 Cartwright Gardens, ☎ 020/7387-1551; www.harlingfordhotel.com; MC, V, AE; Tube: Russell Square), with a facade that crawls with ivy in the summer months, succeeds on many levels. Its design takes a cue from its corporate logo: an easy chair with a pillow emblazoned with an H. All beds are piled with just such a pillow, and bedspreads match curtains in an array of purples, golds, and creams. It doesn't hit you over the head; it's simply all-around nice, as are the newly spruced-up bathrooms with seafoam-green tilework, slender spigots, and green-glass bowl sinks. Granted, all of this tastefulness is squeezed into typically small town-house-hotel rooms and bathrooms. The helpful staff, who serve a free full English breakfast in the ground-floor breakfast room, loans keys to the tranquil semicircular park out front. You're also within sight of one of the city's best (and last) fish and chip shops, North Sea Fish. For guests worried about security, the only way a crook could break into the place from behind would be to first pass through the London Transport police station out back. It's a contemporary twist on a traditional B&B experience, and prices, which are about £20 higher than nearby competitors with fewer sartorial gifts, reflect the envelope-pushing: singles are £79, doubles and twins are £99, triples are £110, and quads are £115. The owner's family has run this place for three generations.

£–££   The values of the owners of **Thanet Hotel** (8 Bedford Place, WC1; ☎ 020/7636-2869; www.thanethotel.co.uk; MC, V, AE; Tube: Russell Square) become evident when you observe the details: A classic blue awning distinguishes the building from the rest of the (quiet) street, bathrooms were recently renovated, and original architectural details such as transom fan windows and carved fireplaces are lovingly highlighted. It's a little hotel with the usual small rooms but friendly and run with care. Probably because its neighbors also command high rates, its prices are a little higher than similar hotels along Gower Street: singles are £74, doubles or twins £98, triples £108, quads £118. The location around the corner from the British Museum is choice, which accounts for the slight inflation. It's owned by Richard and Lynwen Orchard—she does all the decorating, and if she's responsible for the rather random collection of blandly pointless modern art prints decorating the walls, she's also to thank for the flowers decorating the lobby. Breakfast is full English and filling.

£–££   Though not as cheap as its Gower Street neighbors, which in my mind makes it a second-rung choice, the 17-room **Staunton Hotel** (13-15 Gower St., WC1; ☎ 020/7580-2740; www.stauntonhotel.com; MC, V, AE; Tube: Goodge Street) is an admirable, welcoming small hotel. Even though it's situated in a pair of 230-year-old town houses on the corner of two loud streets (Store and Gower), windows have been double-glazed and adorned with treatments, which tamps down a bit on aural

The Gist of "Listed" Hotels

Many town house B&Bs will proudly proclaim that they're "listed" build-ings. What does that mean, and why should you care? It means that the authorities have deemed the building to be of historical or architectural importance—it's a surviving example of a fine Georgian home, for exam-ple, or it occupies a stately Victorian terrace. To keep unsentimental devel-opers from knocking down a gem, "listed" buildings are protected by the government. Changing just about anything, down to the color of the paint, requires permission, and permission is tough to come by.

Why should you care? Because if you're staying in a listed place, your host inherited an aging building with traditions of its own. When first arriving in an ancient city like London, many tourists, used to new build-ings with lots of breathing room, must learn to let go of expectations and to embrace the historic peculiarities of their new temporary home:

Ceilings get lower as you go higher. Until the 20th century, the floors of fashionable London town houses usually served distinct functions. The cel-lar was for kitchens and coal storage (coal was delivered through a hole in the sidewalk). The ground floor was usually used for daily living rooms. The first and second floors were reserved for bedrooms, and the top floor was for servants and for the children's nursery, which accounts for the slightly lower ceilings up there. If you book a top-floor room, the experi-ence won't make you feel like Alice in Wonderland—ceilings are 2.1m or 2.4m (7 or 8 ft.) tall.

Rooms are small by American standards. Look up in almost any room of a town house B&B, especially on the lower floors, and you'll see vestiges of carved molding disappearing unsymmetrically into blank walls. Yes, those walls were added to subdivide large rooms after the house was built,

clutter. Rooms also have safes, satellite TV, firm beds, AC with remote control, modem ports, luggage racks, and strong showers. I imagine the owners are charging more for the slightly larger-than-usual quarters, as well as the formidable location within walking distance of the entire West End. Singles are £70, doubles are £110, "trebles" are £150. If you can, secure room 103—it's larger than a standard double.

££–££££   Hotel Russell ✮ (Russell Square, WC1; ☎ 020/7837-6470; www.principal-hotels.com; MC, V, AE; Tube: Russell Square), standing proud in its regal Victorian-era brick colossus, is just the sort of handsome, staircase-laden, marble-lined, chandelier-hung English hotel that you might have been fantasizing about; only unlike many of the others (Claridge's, the Lanesborough, the Goring), it's within an attainable price range. Still, it has a high self-regard and quotes extreme rack rates. Desk clerks will tell you singles go for £200 and doubles or twins for £230. Yet a check of its website yields rates a full £110 lower, especially for its

but no, the current owners had nothing to do with it. Most room subdivision was done in the mid–20th century to fill a housing gap after many of the city's big hotels were destroyed in the war, and now, even removing those unoriginal walls requires civic approval, which is nigh impossible. Here's a tip: The largest rooms in such B&Bs usually face the front.

Bathrooms are even smaller. In the old days, all guests shared bathrooms, but to suit changing tastes, landlords have slotted compact booths containing the staples (toilet, shower, sink) into rooms that weren't designed to have them (remember, they're not allowed to bash down any plaster), which naturally cuts down on floor space. Adding bath cubicles makes for smaller rooms, but it's one of the reasons why town house B&Bs are so much more affordable than standard hotels.

Don't expect an elevator, or "lift." It takes years of begging and a small fortune to convince the council to allow the destruction that elevator construction brings, so few hotels have them. Assume you're going to have to use the stairs. They may be narrower than you're used to, especially the ones leading to the cellar, but on the bright side, the banisters are pretty. The trade-off is that rooms on higher floors receive more light, less noise, and fewer patrons, so you'll get a better view and more privacy.

Not all windows are double-glazed. The councils enforce all sorts of arcane rules about changing windows, too, and in some buildings, adding a second layer of glass to keep out street noise is not feasible. You think it's loud now? Imagine how it must have sounded when horses and carriages were clattering up the cobbles at all hours. If you're a light sleeper and your chosen B&B doesn't have double-glazing, simply ask for a room at the back.

"classic decor" rooms, which are essentially the ones the hotel hasn't gotten around to renovating yet to look like its "luxurious decor" rooms (the amenities don't differ). The 373 rooms are modern, fully equipped, and comfortable, but not luxuriously so. Some guests complain that booking online yields bad rooms at the back, but I can't confirm that. Best rates are scored through packaged deals with airlines, which is why I've included it here. I wouldn't want you to pay rack rate to stay here as there are warmer hotels.

KENSINGTON, EARL'S COURT & SOUTH KENSINGTON

These family-oriented, generally well-to-do residential neighborhoods, which hug the southwest corner of Kensington Gardens, have been hallowed grounds for budgeters for generations. Reaching the energy of Piccadilly Circus may take about 20 minutes on the Underground from here, and that remove from the action has traditionally fueled the low-priced competition. Unfortunately, things are changing. As rents rise, fewer family-run hotels can afford to stay open in neighborhoods such as Earl's Court, while others can barely make ends meet. In the past year, more than 15 inns that were operating here finally became apartments. The area is still the right choice if you want to stay within walking distance of the park, and there are plenty of inexpensive dining options, but it's best used as a base for touring the rest of London.

£   The English know all about the cheap-and-basic ethic behind **easyHotel Kensington** ✪ (14 Lexham Gardens, W8; www.easyhotel.com; MC, V; Tube: Earl's Court or Gloucester Road), because its founder, Stelios Haji-Ioannou, has made himself a minor celebrity by creating budget brands (easyJet, easyCruise) that cost less when you book early and more if you book at the last minute. So it goes here, where reservations are accepted only over the Web, but typically cost £30–£45 for double rooms if you book five to six months ahead, and £50–£70 if you procrastinate. (You've got to act months in advance to beat other tourists to the lowest prices.) Stelios' other revelation: prefabricated room units in day-glow orange and white that differ only in how little floor space you're given. Beds, which are double-sized with white duvets, are near the ground on pedestals and rarely have an inch of space between mattress and wall. In "a very small room," (the hotel's terminology, not mine), you may find a long ledge on which to pop a travel alarm clock, but bathrooms aren't more than plastic cubicles combining a shower, toilet, and sink in one water-splashed closet. "Tiny" rooms won't have much space to turn around. Most rooms don't even have windows, and forget about hair dryers, baby cots, safes, phones, and laundry. Want to watch TV? You'll pay £5 for 24 hours (for seven channels including BBC News), but you'll get a remote control you can take home. Now that you know all that, you know what easyHotel is good for: clean, no-nonsense crash pods for someone who wants to pay hostel prices without putting up with hostel mayhem. It works. Shockingly, it's also one of the few truly disabled-friendly budget hotels in town; there are a few "special needs" rooms, there's a lift to get over the stoop, and Earl's Court station, its main Tube stop, is also accessible. There's a 10-night maximum, and no smoking is permitted. Very nearby, **easyHotel Earl's Court** (44-48 West Cromwell Rd., SW1; www.easyhotel.com; MC, V; Tube: Earl's Court) was, at press time, transforming the tired, 40-odd room TownHouse Hotel, into a 70-odd room easyHotel for a late 2006 opening. Given a choice, I'd pick the easyHotel Kensington, which is on a much more pleasant Victorian side street, and operated directly by Stelios' company (this one is a franchise). By the way, easyHotel will soon have some competition when another pod hotel franchise, **Yotel,** begins operating in London from £40 a night. As of press time, it was slated to cut the ribbon at Heathrow and Gatwick in spring 2007 and somewhere in central London in 2007. Visit www. Yotel.co.uk to see if it's making good on its stylish capsule-hotel promises yet.

£   You can say what you want about **The Mowbray Court Hotel** ✪✪ (28-32 Penywen Rd., SW5; ☎ 020/7370-2316; www.mowbraycourthotel.co.uk; AE, MC, V; Tube: Earl's Court). It's world-weary. It's not even slightly trendy. It needs not just a face-lift but a whole body lift. But it's also remarkably inexpensive and delightfully clean. And the Dooley family, which runs this basic "tourist class economy" choice, cares a great deal about making sure its guests are comfortable even though they don't pay a lot. The Dooleys' patriarch emigrated from Ireland in 1959 with £50 in his pocket, and the hotel is named for the road he raised his family on. His sons Peter and Tony now direct the show, providing Wi-Fi in the rooms (£3 an hr. or £15 a week, which is less than the big hotels charge for a single day), folding fresh towels in a playful origami style, and striving to keep the phone rates lower than calling card company charges. Singles are £55, doubles £69, triples £84—those are with facilities, but if you're willing to share, and if you don't need a TV, you'll dock about £9 off the price for a "standard" room. There's an honest-to-goodness lobby bar for draught beer (Boddingtons, Castlemaine), and Earl's Court Tube station, which links directly to Heathrow, is literally behind the hotel. The Mowbray, which consists of four former town houses with bright southern exposures on the back, is one of those struggling places doing what it can to update without much cash. I dread the inevitable day when, thanks to sky-rocketing rents, we no longer have rock-solid, no-frills, family-run bargains like this to rely upon.

£   As soon as you walk into the cavernous **Abbey House** (11 Vicarage Gate, W8; ☎ 020/7727-2694; www.abbeyhousekensington.com; no credit cards; Tube: High Street Kensington), which was constructed in 1860 on land once inhabited by royal attendants to nearby Kensington Palace (the hotel is essentially in its backyard), you can tell the Abbey House was a very palatial mansion. In fact, the owner, Albert Nayach, claims that Lord Shackleton, the Arctic pioneer, once called it home—a claim I can't confirm; given the towering ceilings, brass fittings, windows full of light, and heel-clicking Belgian marble checkerboard tiles reminiscent of an upper-class manse, it doesn't seem far-fetched. It's the sort of house from which Peter Pan might pluck you. The premises are so enormous, in fact, that most guests don't realize that Nayach lives on-site. It must be hard to fill such resounding spaces, so the 16 en suite rooms—their echoes of luxury tamped down by a puny TV, a teeny desk, and eyesore floral bedspreads—are bare and simple (when you check in, you'll find a folded towel topped by a naked bar of soap). Not a lot has been freshened up in two decades, but if you want something dead cheap and diligently scrubbed, you couldn't do better. The sweeping staircase, which winds around an atrium and past lovely antique paned windows, is breathtaking in more ways than one: Reaching the top floor supplies some incidental cardio training. All that space makes it less claustrophobic than many other inns, and suits it to families. Nayach only hires staff with service-industry backgrounds (waitresses, hotel workers), and he dresses them in striped aprons with white caps, an optimistic touch. No rooms have a private bath, but if there's availability, you can arrange to assign a bathroom solely to your room. Rates are singles £45, doubles £74, triples £90, and quads £100, including a full English breakfast, but in winter, those prices can drop by £20 or so. There's a small park in front, and lots of cheap food on nearby High Street Kensington.

£   An incredible find. The rates at the **Oakley Hotel** ★★ (73 Oakley St., SW3; ☎ 020/7352-5599; www.oakleyhotel.com; AE, MC, V; Tube: Sloane Square or South Kensington), like the homey vibe, channel a bygone era: £45 for singles and £59 for doubles or twins. But there's a trade-off: To reach the Tube, you must either walk 20 minutes northeast up King's Road to Sloane Square station (hardly

Kensington Accommodations

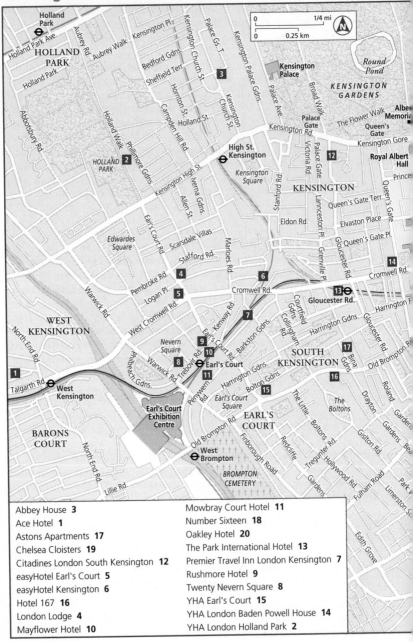

Abbey House **3**
Ace Hotel **1**
Astons Apartments **17**
Chelsea Cloisters **19**
Citadines London South Kensington **12**
easyHotel Earl's Court **5**
easyHotel Kensington **6**
Hotel 167 **16**
London Lodge **4**
Mayflower Hotel **10**

Mowbray Court Hotel **11**
Number Sixteen **18**
Oakley Hotel **20**
The Park International Hotel **13**
Premier Travel Inn London Kensington **7**
Rushmore Hotel **9**
Twenty Nevern Square **8**
YHA Earl's Court **15**
YHA London Baden Powell House **14**
YHA London Holland Park **2**

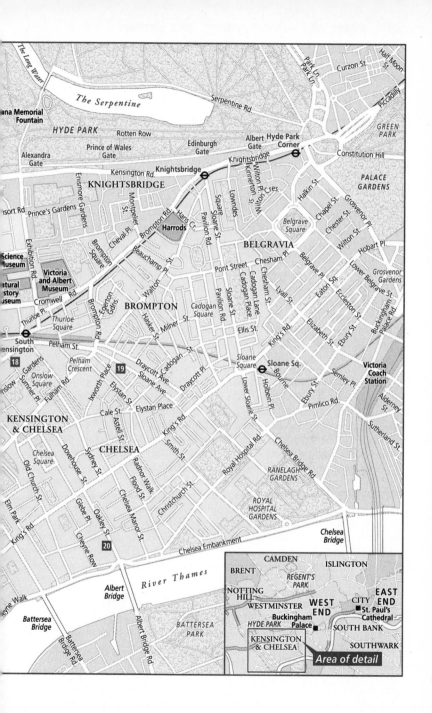

The Long Water

The Serpentine

Serpentine Rd.

Diana Memorial Fountain

HYDE PARK   Rotten Row

Prince of Wales Gate

Edinburgh Gate

Albert Gate   Hyde Park Corner

GREEN PARK

Alexandra Gate

Constitution Hill

Kensington Rd.   Knightsbridge

Knightsbridge

PALACE GARDENS

KNIGHTSBRIDGE

Enismore Gardens

Consort Rd.   Prince's Gardens

Montpelier St.

Brompton Rd.

Cheval Pl.

Sloane St.

Square

Lowndes

Wilton Pl.

Kinnerton St.

Wilton Cres.

Halkin St.

Halkin St.

Chapel St.

Chester St.

Grosvenor Pl.

Wilton St.

Belgrave Square

Hobart Pl.

Science Museum

Exhibition Rd.

Brompton Square

Beauchamp Pl.

Pavilion Rd.

Hans Cr.

Harrods

BELGRAVIA

Victoria and Albert Museum

Natural History Museum

Cromwell Rd.

Egerton Gdns.

Walton St.

Pont Street   Chesham Pl.

Cadogan Lane

Belgrave Pl.

Lyall St.

Chesham St.

Eaton Sq.

Eccleston St.

Lower Belgrave St.

Grosvenor Gardens

Buckingham Palace Rd.

Thurloe St.

Brompton Rd.

Hasker St.

Milner St.

BROMPTON   Cadogan Square

Sloane St.

Pavilion Rd.

Cadogan Place

Elizabeth St.

Ebury St.

Thurloe Square

Ellis St.

South Kensington

Pelham St.

Onslow Gardens

Summer Pl.

Pelham Crescent

Draycott Ave.

Sloane Ave.

Cadogan St.

Sloane Square

Draycott Pl.

Lower Sloane St.

Bourne

Sloane Sq.

Ebury St.

Semley Pl.

Victoria Coach Station

Onslow Square

18

Fulham Rd.

Ixworth Place

Elystan St.

19

Holbein Pl.

Pimlico Rd.

Alderney St.

Cale St.

Elystan Place

King's Rd.

Smith St.

Sutherland St.

KENSINGTON & CHELSEA

Astell St.

CHELSEA

Chelsea Square

Dovehouse St.

Sydney St.

Radnor Walk

Christchurch St.

Royal Hospital Rd.

Chelsea Bridge Rd.

RANELAGH GARDENS

Old Church St.

Elm Park

Glebe Pl.

Oakley St.

Flood St.

Chelsea Manor St.

ROYAL HOSPITAL GARDENS

King's Rd.

Cheyne Row

20

Chelsea Embankment

Chelsea Bridge

Cheyne Walk

River Thames

Albert Bridge

Battersea Bridge

Albert Bridge Rd.

Battersea Bridge Rd.

BATTERSEA PARK

CAMDEN

BRENT

ISLINGTON

REGENT'S PARK

NOTTING HILL

WESTMINSTER   WEST END   CITY   EAST END

St. Paul's Cathedral

HYDE PARK   Buckingham Palace   SOUTH BANK

KENSINGTON & CHELSEA   SOUTHWARK

Area of detail

a chore, considering how fashionable the shopping avenue is), or you can hop on the 239 bus from Victoria Station and be there in 8 minutes. Choose among twelve rooms, six of which have their own facilities (shower only), and six of which share bathrooms (although there are so many WCs that you won't have to wait even if everyone else has just consumed a pork vindaloo). No rooms have phones. The compact 1850s house, one of the oldest on a block that includes the former home of the poet Carlyle (now a museum), has seen grander days, and its rooms were subdivided for hotel use before our time, but since the mid-'80s, owner Brian Millen has kept the facilities in fine condition and built entire new areas with his own two hands. When I showed up for an unannounced inspection, he was covered with wood dust and paint from a guest room renovation, which is always a good sign. He's got some gorgeous furniture, much of it older than the house itself, and he's not stingy about letting you use it in the guest rooms. Although rooms on the front face noisy Oakley Road and have only single-glazed windows, almost all rooms are buffered by an extra fire door, which cuts down on internal noise. The double with a four-poster bed is £69, and it was a favorite of the late, dissolute football superstar George Best, who regularly stayed here, presumably on his London binges. Perhaps apropos of the discretion you'll find here, Mr. Millen (who calls his neighborhood "high class") declines to tell any tales. Guests can use the kitchen like it's their own, and about 90m (300 ft.) right outside the front door, you'll find the tranquility of the Thames River and, across the cast iron Albert Bridge, soothing Battersea Park.

£–££   An odd duck, **Rushmore Hotel** (11 Trebovir Rd. ☎ 020/7370-3839; www. rushmore-hotel.co.uk; AE, MC, V; Tube: Earl's Court) is a standard town house inn that was inflicted with an ill-advised makeover in classical themes. Corridors are adorned with murals of Mediterranean and Roman iconography (fig trees, anyone?), making the place feel like the butt of a design joke that the staff, friendly as they are, don't seem to be in on. But that kitschy art doesn't make staying here awkward because its 22 rooms are clean and meet expectations, done in a fading Regency style, and have their own shower and bath equipped with plugs for U.S. razors. The bright dining room, in a garden conservatory, boasts a much savvier tone involving blue glass, black metals, and cacti as tall as basketball players; sadly, only continental breakfast is served. All in all, it's reasonably priced and good enough on all counts, and just quirky enough to be someone's favorite. The prices run from singles £59–£69, doubles £79–£89, and a few triples and quads for £99–£129, with the usual concessions for low season and long stays. Although no elevator is present, someone is always on hand to do the heavy lifting.

£–££   Like its sister hotel, Twenty Nevern Square (see below), the 47-room **Mayflower Hotel** ✪✪✪ (26-28 Trebovir Rd., SW5; ☎ 020/7370-0991; www. mayflower-group.co.uk; MC, V, AE; Tube: Earl's Court) was transformed a few years back by tasteful, stylish renovations to become an economy town house property with exceptional value. The little touches, like something out of *The Jungle Book*, impart dignity and exotica to a stay, from antique doors mounted on the walls as art, to dark rattan furniture, to a silvery fountain behind the front desk, to rainbow-hued halogen accent lighting, to the open sensation of wood flooring throughout. Rooms come with TVs with 50 channels, CD players, marble desks, and a few complimentary magazines. There's also a lovely back garden. A quibble: Its bathrooms are marbled and sleek—they could use better ventilation, but that's also part of staying in a town house. Singles cost £60 to £69 (but are often upgraded to double rooms), doubles run £80 (regular double beds) to £99 (king-size beds), triples are £109, and the family room is £130. I like room 18, a deluxe double (£99), with a little outdoor terrace over the quiet street, its peaked carved headboard, and its farmhouse-style rafters overhead. There's a lift, albeit one the size of a shower stall, and a bar. The nearby Mayflower Apartments have studios for two, one-bedrooms for two, and a two-bedroom that sleeps up to six, all of which have fully equipped kitchens and washing machines.

££   Mazerati and Ferrari have dealerships just a few doors east of **Hotel 167** (167 Old Brompton Rd., SW5; ☎ 020/7373-3221; www.hotel167.com; MC, V, AE; Tube: Gloucester Road), but don't let that fool you into thinking you're on a haughty block. Staying here is a little like staying in your spinster aunt's cluttered spare bedroom—the nostalgic whiff of dusty memories hangs in the air. That's a compliment, although it may not be what you crave. Rooms are stuffed with 1930s furniture—tassels lamps, collectible desks—and combined with the metallic, splotchy modern art on the walls, the decor imparts a sense of bohemian eccentricity, if not of an outright split personality. Its ad hoc approach has already inspired a book (1993's *Hotel 167* by Jane Solomon, a disturbing yarn about a bulimic woman's sexual self-abuse) and a song by the Manic Street Preachers. Room 16, with its view of the redbrick houses of Gledhow Gardens curving into the distance, is a standout. All rooms have minifridges and face the street, but the windows are double-glazed. Doubles are £99, and the sole single room is £79. Thoughtfully, the owners post clippings of good restaurants by the front door, which is a 10-minute walk from the big Kensington museums. But uh-oh: After more than 35 years in the family, the hotel is on the market, which is a sure sign the family is losing interest. Rather than allow it to change, won't you buy it?

££   Hidden in a residential back street off noisy Cromwell Road, **Premier Travel Inn London Kensington** (11 Knaresborough Place, SW5; ☎ 0870/238-3304; Tube: Earl's Court) occupies an ugly '70s box distinguished by poo-brown panels and ample windows. It links via pedestrian bridge to a building shared with a Marriott charging £100 more. Neither annex is larger or quieter, but rooms on the southern sides get more sun (some also overlook Tube trains hurtling to and from Earl's Court station—they're not horribly noisy). Prices are £82 on weekdays and £75 on weekends. Londontown.com sometimes discounts those an additional £12. For a description of Premier Travel Inn amenities, see p. 47.

££   As soon as you step into **Twenty Nevern Square** ★★★ (20 Nevern Square, SW5; ☎ 020/7565-9555; www.twentynevernsquare.co.uk; AE, MC, V; Tube: Earl's Court), on the south side of the square of the same name, you can tell it's not your run-of-the-mill economy hotel. It may reside in an old English town house, but its heart is in colonial Malaysia. Lovebirds chirp in wooden cages. Bedrooms are warmly done in carved wood headboards, wood wardrobes, and richly colored window treatments. Gilchrist & Soames toiletries are concealed in mini chests in the marbled bathrooms. Each room has a CD player, and TVs are wide-screen. It's

telling that everyone receives a fresh apple upon checking in because there's something so romantic about the decor as to invite sin. Although all rooms feel cloistered and inviting, room 11, a double, may suit human lovebirds most, given that
it's on its own private landing and has windows on two sides. At the continental
breakfast, which is served beneath the cathedral-like rafters of the ground-floor
conservatory (also a bar), you can choose from 15 types of honey from around the
world. Considering all the amorous set dressing, the prices are even more heart-
swelling: singles are £79, doubles £99, quads £130, and the Pacha Suite, with a
king-size four-poster bed and a terrace overlooking the square, is £170. Rooms
have showers, bathtubs, or both, so if you have a preference, ask, and if you're a
light sleeper, request not to be placed in a basement room, which are privy to footsteps from the lobby's wood flooring. The same owners, originally South African,
also operate the Mayflower around the corner. There's a lift and a porter, and the
front desk has a key to the private gardens in the square.

££   For those who just want a cheap contemporary hotel, there's **The Park
International Hotel** (117-125 Cromwell Rd., SW7; ☎ 800/729-1736; www.park
internationalhotel.com; AE, MC, V; Tube: Gloucester Road), which is unremarkable
in most ways, but inoffensive in as many more. It takes up five interconnected
town houses, four stories high, just west of the big South Kensington museums.
Its rooms, lobby, and even the TVs are noticeably larger than the area average, but
the interior design smacks of *The Golden Girls*. The overworked staff, mostly
Eastern European transplants, do what they can to be professional but are mostly
too harried to be effective. Rooms are standard-issue and aging, if carefully serviced, and have air-conditioning, minifridges, and safes big enough for a laptop.
Wi-Fi is only available in one part of the hotel, so if you want it, ask, and keep in
mind that the nonsmoking rooms are on the higher floors. Singles are £75, doubles £85, although in summer, prices can pop up by £25 for doubles, £10 for singles; and if you snare an "early booker" deal online, doubles can sink to £70. Because
of its size (117 rooms), this hotel also crops up among air-hotel discounters.
Continental breakfast is a ridiculous £8, but you can get it thrown in for free if you
book directly, and besides, there's a Sainsbury's grocery store about 2 blocks away.
Honestly, guests only stay here because it's cheap, safe, and well located.

££–££££   Another admirable boutique hotel at the top end of our range is stylish **Number Sixteen** ★★★ (16 Sumner Place, SW7; 020/7589-5232; www.number
sixteenhotel.co.uk; AE, MC, V; Tube: South Kensington), belonging to the Firmdale
Hotels group, whose husband/wife designer/owners, Tim and Kit Kemp, are fixtures on the city scene. I count it as one of the loveliest B&B experiences in the
city. It's the least expensive of the brand's offerings in town, but it comes closest to
supplying a movie-star's pampering at less-than-Hollywood prices: Singles are
£100–£130, doubles £160–£195. The lowest prices are available in winter and
from late July to early September (when business travel drops off). For those prices,
expect all the trappings of a luxury hotel, only in a series of very well-refurbished
town houses in an updated English country style. Every available space is adorned
with changing displays of forward-thinking British art from the owners' personal
collection, and all rooms, which are individually designed and truly beautiful,
come with huge, come-hither beds (laid with more pillows, skirting, and spreads

Avoid the Tangled Web

You may be used to booking through sites such as Expedia.com or Travelocity. com for the best prices, but when it comes to London, think again. Many London hotels, particularly the most affordable ones, are privately owned, and many of them are represented on the Web by third-party travel agents and booking engines that pad the price with a few extra bucks, which they'll skim off for themselves as commission. So if you call the hotel directly for your bookings, you'll not only get the lowest price, but you'll also have the power of negotiation.

Of course, if you want to stay in a corporate hotel, all bets are off. Online searching works for those. These sites will help:

Mobissimo.com, Sidestep.com, Orbitz.com, and **Kayak.com** are three "aggregator" sites that scan dozens of sites for deals and pull them all together.

Visit London, the city's official tourism office, also has an area on its web-site (visitlondon.com) for discounted hotel bookings, although it's main-tained by an outside travel agent. The **British Hotel Reservation Centre** (www.bhrc.co.uk), also sports some discounts, as does **LondonTown.com**, where I've seen £85 rooms (mostly from chain hotels) marked down to £59.

Lastminute.co.uk is one of the most popular booking sights in the U.K., so you may find bargains there that you won't find on the American sites.

And **Priceline.co.uk** works just like its American counterpart; most of its hotels are corporate-owned. As with all bid-for-travel sites, you could end up with a deal, but you could get stuck with a lemon.

than most people have at home), safes, voice mail, a VCR, and ample polished-stone bathrooms (with bathtub and shower). On the ground floor, a library and a drawing room with an honor bar are at your disposal. At bedtime, instead of a mint, you're given lavender and grapefruit spray to apply to your pillow, and in the morning, sunlight pours into the conservatory where continental breakfast is served. In good weather, you can dine in the verdant back garden, accented by a soothing ornamental pond that spans the width of the hotel. There's a lift, a door-man, an attentive and friendly staff, and the location off restaurant-rich Old Brompton Road, steps from the South Kensington station and from the banner museums, ranks high for convenience. Don't use the in-room Internet though, since it costs more than any other London hotel I've stayed in: £20 a day!

£££–££££ Situated on a genuinely quiet, stately Victorian street, **London Lodge** ★ ★ (134-136 Lexham Gardens, W8; ☎ 020/7244-8444; www.londonlodge hotel.com; AE, MC, V; Tube: Earl's Court) is attentively run by partners Mandy and

Lea, who make a superhuman effort to personally greet everyone who sets foot in the lobby. Deservedly, their 28-room hotel attracts a lot of regulars, particularly Americans, who presumably appreciate the custom-made furniture (in a corny Louis style but not ostentatiously so), lift, air-conditioning and ceiling fans, and a service level that approaches luxury-level lodging, although prices don't. The management seems like it's forever trying to make life easier for guests: Even the glare of bathroom lights is thoughtfully shielded by wooden mirror frames. Cooked breakfast is served in the on-site Stephanie's bar, which also serves dinner if you're around. Singles are £125, and doubles are £161. Those prices are a smidge high, but considering the tranquility, the high-quality furnishings, and the eager management, it's a worthy splurge. The website often posts weekend discounts.

MARYLEBONE

For visitors who want a balance of central location and residential vibe, Marylebone's the place. A 10-minute walk takes you to the "smart" end of Oxford Street and Mayfair to the south, the wide-open fields of Regent's Park to the north, and the shops and cafes of Soho to the southeast. Add to that one of the most attractive shopping thoroughfares in the city (Marylebone High Street) and a cluster of affordable restaurants (on James Street), and you've got the makings for an ideal tourist stomping ground. Why bother with Earl's Court instead?

£   What can I say about the **Wyndham Hotel** ✯ (30 Wyndham St., W1; ☎ 020/ 7723-7204; www.wyndhamhotel.co.uk; AE, MC, V; Tube: Marylebone or Baker Street) except that it's wee and plain and sweet? Well, it's an old-fashioned inn in an old-fashioned neighborhood, and it's one of the most solid values that London has. All rooms have shared bathrooms, which is why it's so cheap: £49 for singles, £67 for doubles or twins, £79 for triples. You won't get much space to wiggle around the bed in a double room, and you won't see much that dates from before 1995. That said, I am utterly charmed by the Wyndham. The staff is young and attentive (how could they not be with just 10 rooms?), the level of cleanliness is peerless, and it's on a quiet, pretty residential street. I also love the neighborhood: It's five minutes' walk west of Baker Street, with its high street shopping, 10 minutes' walk from the Middle Eastern restaurants of Edgware Road, and 10 minutes' walk from Paddington Station.

£–££   Because it's been in the same family for years, the **Wigmore Court Hotel** (23 Gloucester Place, W1; ☎ 020/7935-0928; www.wigmore-court-hotel.co.uk; MC, V; Tube: Marble Arch) hasn't been renovated much. As you might imagine, that's both a boon and a warning. The decor doesn't dazzle. Think powder-blue rubberized wallpaper, mirrors bolted to the wall beneath yellowing fluorescent tubes, and a fair share of veneered wood and random cigarette burns. But along with the telltale signs of downmarket digs, plenty of vestiges of the house's glorious Regency past remain, including generally commodious rooms and bathrooms that make this inn a cut above its price competition. Over the double bed of room 1, a triple on the (noisy) front road, hangs a gold-colored crest of a classical maiden. The spacious room 2, a double on the (quiet) back, has an expansive curving back wall overlooking the garden; it's popular with elderly guests because no stairs separate it from the street. The fourth floor, which is normally a little shorter in buildings of this era, has been modified to boast higher ceilings. The staff is attentive and friendly—it even allows guests to use the kitchen—and it serves a devoted repeat clientele, a fact which is proudly trumpeted by a sign in the front window. Factoring in its convenient location, this place could certainly charge more for its 16 en suite rooms than £62 for singles, £89 for doubles or twins, £120 for triples, and £135 for a quad. There are just two rooms that share a bath: a single (£48) and a double (£55).

£–££ Andrew Bowden has been part of **Hart House Hotel** ★★ (51 Gloucester Place, W1; ☎ 020/7935-2288; www.harthouse.co.uk; MC, V; Tube: Marble Arch or Baker Street) since he was six years old, when his family took it over, so he knows his nonsmoking, fully en suite hotel—and his city—very well. He runs his perfectly lovely inn extremely professionally, with a consistency that you might expect of a posher place. He outfits chambermaids in black frocks with white trim, and stocks rooms with top-quality furniture, built to last. He's even thought to put power outlets near the desks. Showers tend to the tiny side (what else is new?), but towels are plentiful and the rooms themselves are well cared for, embellished with little sculptures, mild putty-colored paint schemes, and reading lights for each bed, which are being fitted with thick duvets instead of blankets. Singles cost £75; try for room 11 at the front (it has a four-foot-wide bed). Doubles and twins are £105, triples are £130 (room 9, on the back, comes with an enormous bathroom located in its own nook), quads £150.

££ As affordable inns go, **Lincoln House Hotel** ★★ (33 Gloucester Place, W1; ☎ 020/7486-7630; www.lincoln-house-hotel.co.uk; AE, MC, V; Tube: Marble Arch) is in extraordinarily good condition—or, as Londoners might say, "in good nick." Each of the 24 rooms has a private bathroom, so that's easy, but the rates are byzantine, subcategorized by bed size. For example, a single "budget" is £65 because it has a twin bed, but there's a "single plus" with a four-foot-wide bed that goes for £75. Doubles are "budget" (meaning they have a double mattress that won't suit basketball players) for £85, or "standard" (meaning they have a queen size mattress) for £95. Two twin beds are £105, and triples are £125. Forget all those prices now because the owners regularly lop off 25% if it's not busy or if you book months in advance. Half the fun of Lincoln House, which has been in the same family for more than 30 years, is the nautical theme, which recurs in unexpected ways (portholes as mirrors, antique barometers as art). Handmade paneling on the hallway walls adds warmth, and there's 24-hour security. Larger rooms are equipped with wardrobes and minifridges, and Wi-Fi is free. Four types of breakfasts are served: continental, full English, vegetarian, and refreshingly, Mediterranean. The one bummer is that the bathrooms are prefabricated fiberglass units, but if you've ever been on a cruise ship, you'll cope.

££–£££ When you want to check into **22 York Street** (22-24 York St., W1; ☎ 020/7224-2990; www.22yorkstreet.co.uk; AE, MC, V; Tube: Baker Street) you'd better know where you're going, because it's not marked. The persnickety owners, Michael and Liz Callis, discourage riff-raff by refraining from advertising. When I showed up unannounced and walked into the spacious kitchen, I thought at first that I'd knocked on the door of a private home of some wealthy doctor or lawyer.

Marylebone & Bayswater Accommodations

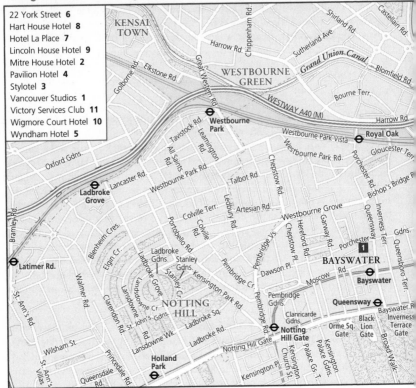

22 York Street **6**
Hart House Hotel **8**
Hotel La Place **7**
Lincoln House Hotel **9**
Mitre House Hotel **2**
Pavilion Hotel **4**
Stylotel **3**
Vancouver Studios **1**
Victory Services Club **11**
Wigmore Court Hotel **10**
Wyndham Hotel **5**

Inside, the couple is going for a farmhouse feel, with warm wooden floorboards, plenty of antiques and oriental rugs, and large bathrooms, almost all of which have tub/shower combinations. Guests get their own keys and are let loose to treat the premises as their own, which includes a drawing room with a grand piano and plenty of tea, coffee, and biscuits for munching. Adding to the home-away-from-home feel, guest rooms aren't numbered. Breakfasts are continental but, as Michael succinctly puts it, "quite substantial" and served in the kitchen at a country table. Singles are £89 and doubles are £120, although doubles sometimes run £100. The Callises also run a 1930s-styled villa in Cannes, France. That should tell you a lot about their tastes and what they're going for here. Although they're not explicitly banned, kids may not feel comfortable.

££–£££   Everything about **Hotel La Place** ★★★ (17 Nottingham Place, W1; ☎ 020/7486-2323; www.hotellaplace.com; AE, MC, V; Tube: Baker Street) is nicer than it has to be. It's run by Hal Jaffer and his French-born mom, who spent time in Tennessee and Texas learning hotel management. The Jaffers, who bought this town house building as a derelict dump in 1988 and shaped it into the mid- to upper-level property you see today, grasp the exacting demands of the American market. That means that, although it's priced a bit higher than standard budget

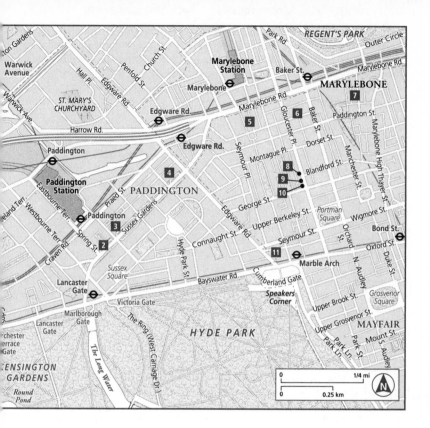

hotels (singles £99–£115, doubles £129–£145), you'll find a pile of extras that are more in keeping with chain hotels, starting with a proper full English breakfast, and including ice machines, double beds that are genuinely king size (rooms with smaller, five-foot-wide beds are £4 less), a cafe-cum-wine bar in the lobby offering 24-hour room service, free Wi-Fi, plenty of electrical outlets for charging stuff up, and even a lift. Beds are given particular attention, with orthopedic mattresses and testers (fabric canopies) that match the pillows and spreads. Bathrooms are done up in granite and marble, nearly every window is dressed, and rooms classified as doubles or higher boast air-conditioning. Room 102 (£160) is good for families, since it's got two side-by-side double beds, Holiday Inn-style. It's a block southeast of Madame Tussaud's, where the dummies spend *their* nights.

BAYSWATER

Although you may have heard that this neighborhood is prime ground, that news is old. As the budget hotel scene gravitates back to central London, you'll find fewer reasons to choose Bayswater aside from decent Underground connections. There are no tourist sights, save Hyde Park and Kensington Gardens, within reasonable walking distance. Worse, Sussex Gardens has been plagued by complaints of, shall we say, "working girls" prowling the streets at night. To be fair, it's perfectly safe, and the city is pouncing on the problem. Besides, strolling down street after street of regal, impossibly identical terraced houses does conjure up some serious *Mary Poppins* fantasies. Still, some visitors prefer to stay near Paddington merely out of a sense of tradition, perhaps, or merely because the Heathrow Express train alights there. Choose your hotel carefully, though, because there's plenty of fading flophouse chaff among the cut-price wheat.

£   Before brothers Barry and Paul Charalambous got hold of the family business, it was a forgettable inn, Ruddiman's. But now, those forward-looking chaps have given the old digs the *Star Trek* treatment, and by late 2005, **Stylotel** ★★ (160-162 Sussex Gardens, W2; ☎ 020/7723-1026; www.stylotel.com; AE, MC, V; Tube: Paddington or Lancaster Gate) was one of the city's wildest budget properties. Rooms are standard London sized, but they've been profoundly transformed with dimpled sheet-metal walls, blonde wood floors, pristine beds with duvets and royal blue padded-vinyl headboards, frosted lightboxes that double as side-tables, and ample slab mirrors to reflect back your hypermodernist room in all its angular, stainless-steel glory. The cellar breakfast room, with its military rows of jagged high-backed chairs creating a virtual blade garden, is perhaps Paul's masterpiece. I'll bet the Germans love it. Single "stylorooms" are £50, doubles or twins are £70, triples ("trios") are £87, and quads (er, "quatros") are just £105. The lobby bar also takes care not to hose guests, with soda priced at just 70p, and breakfast is selected from a 30-item cooked menu. It's easy to be grateful to the Charalambous boys (who also give top advice on London nightlife) for bringing some swagger and couture to the low-end of the lodging market.

£–££   Let's face it: In another decade, the interior of the family-friendly **Mitre House Hotel** (178-184 Sussex Gardens, W2; ☎ 020/7723-8040; www.mitrehouse hotel.com; AE, MC, V; Tube: Paddington or Lancaster Gate) could be included among the V&A museum's design artifacts, it's so rooted in the early '80s. We're talking walls and carpets in bleary rose-and-rust tones, hallways lamely gussied up with outdated theatrical posters, mismatched furniture in pressed wood and wicker, and a slouching bar in the lobby. But it's spotless, the owners are old hands at the value-hotel game, and there's a lift (although, weirdly, it's upholstered). Of the 69 rooms, singles are generally the equivalent size of a double bed, and cost £70, doubles and twins are much more generous and cost £80, and triples (here, called "trebles") are £90. You can combine rooms, such as 101 and 102, to form a "family suite" with a bathroom, for £100. Corner rooms such as 303 (a twin) have bigger bathrooms, lots of light, and views up and down Sussex Gardens. If you need a bathtub, request one, because not all rooms have one. A few "standard" rooms share bathrooms, and those are £60. All in all, it's a decent value, but not someplace you'll want to linger.

£–££   Like Stylotel, the 29-room **Pavilion Hotel** ★ (34-36 Sussex Gardens, W2; ☎ 020/7262-0905; www.pavilionhoteluk.com; AE, MC, V; Tube: Edgware Road) distinguishes itself from the grubby Sussex Gardens rabble through elaborately themed rooms, dreamed up by the owners, who've had the place since 1989. Casablanca Nights, one of the most popular and largest doubles, faces busy Sussex Gardens but compensates with a preposterous design of rich cobalt drapes, leopard-print fabric, and ostensibly Moroccan furniture. Other popular gag rooms,

Should I Wait to Book till I Get There?

In many European cities, you can pretty much roll off the train, waltz into the tourist's office, and book a room on the spot. Can you do that in London? Sure, but I wouldn't. Summertime (June–Sept) is extremely busy, and you might get shut out or totally hosed. It's also not very kind to turn up at a family-run hotel at 11pm just to browse rooms. But if you insist on booking last-minute, these resources work:

Britain & London Visitor Centre (1 Lower Regent St., south of Piccadilly Circus; ☎ 08701/56-63-66; www.visitlondon.com), the city's official tourism branch, has staff that will help you find a place according to your ideal price and your selected area, and it'll do it for free. You can also do it online at its website. It's open Mondays 9:30am to 6:30pm, Tuesday to Friday 9am to 6:30pm, and 10am to 4pm Saturdays and Sundays. In summer months, weekend hours are 9am to 5pm.

At Heathrow and Gatwick, stop by the **British Hotel Reservation Centre** (Heathrow: ☎ 020/8564-8808; Gatwick: 01293/50-24-33; www.bhrc.co.uk), which also books for free in person and online. It also has offices at Victoria, Paddington, and Waterloo stations. All are usually open until midnight.

Two websites proficient at last-minute bookings are Lastminute.co.uk and Laterooms.com, both light on the very cheapest options. It's better not to go online at the extreme last minute, though, lest your reservation fail to transmit to the front desk in time.

embellished with amusingly mismatched accoutrements are: War and Peace (military), Quiet Please (a library), and Solitaire (a single reimagined as a deck of cards). Of the doubles, Enter the Dragon (Asian themed) is a bit larger than its brothers, but disco-era Three's Company and Honky Tonk Afro are more requested. The gimmick enlivens an otherwise average B&B. Singles are £60, doubles £100, triples £120, and quads £130. Is all this silliness worth the extra £20 a couple will pay compared to others on the same street? Is it groovy or just a distraction? That depends on your sense of fun.

SOUTHWARK & WATERLOO

You won't find many hotels in this area, despite the sensational location. Since medieval times until about 15 years ago, "respectable" Londoners wanted nothing to do with this once-industrial area, which explains the proliferation of anonymous apartment blocks and the overabundance of railway viaducts. The same Londoners are wishing they'd bought property now. It's actually a terrific place to dwell in good weather, when the area comes alive with walkers, booksellers, pubgoers, and playgoers reveling in the nearby re-creation of Shakespeare's *Globe* theater.

££   If I had to pick one property from one chain to recommend, it would be the **Premier Travel Inn London Southwark** ★★★ (Anchor Bar, 34 Park St., SE1; ☎ 0870/990-6402; Tube: London Bridge). The neighborhood is atmospheric, cobbled, and historic (the walkabout on p. 244, passes right by it), and although the hotel structure is new, it blends seamlessly with the adjoining historic Anchor pub, where guests take breakfast overlooking the Thames. Rooms are £88 on weekdays and £84 on weekends, but book far in advance, because the secret's out. **Premier Travel Inn London County Hall** ★ (County Hall, Belvedere Road, SE1; ☎ 0870/238-3300; Tube: Waterloo) is also in the vicinity and commands a stellar location yards from the London Eye and shares a palatial building on the Thames with a high-end hotel. Although few of the sizable rooms offer the slightest glimpse of the river (in fact, most overlook a large air shaft), you can walk to many top sights. Since it's in tourist ground zero, you won't find many inexpensive

Diamonds Are a Churl's Best Friend

Several rating systems are in place in Britain—including stars for hotels and diamonds for guesthouses—but in practical terms, those official ratings aren't always useful. For example, the difference between a no-star inn and a one-star inn has nothing to do with the size of the shower or the age of the mattress or anything important like that. Stars instead depend on whether there's a bar and a place to eat dinner. Yes, that extra star is because you can get lit there. So you'll see quite a few places with a line of liquor bottles gathering dust in the corner of the lounge. When you also see how nebulously the guesthouse criteria are expressed by Visit Britain, the official national tourism aegis, you'll grasp how subjective and slippery the topic can be:

One-diamond guest accommodation: Clean and comfortable accommodation, providing breakfast, and helpful service.

Two-diamond guest accommodation: Good overall level of quality and comfort, with greater emphasis on guest care.

Three-diamond guest accommodation: Well maintained, practical decor, a good choice of breakfast dishes, a very good level of customer care.

Four-diamond guest accommodation: An even higher level of quality and comfort. Very good levels of customer care.

Five-diamond guest accommodation: Exceptional overall quality in furnishing and rooms and customer care, anticipating guests' needs. Exceptional level of quality.

All this is by way of saying that getting hung up in the star ratings won't get you very far; as long as the price is right and the place has everything you need, you'll be covered.

places to eat nearby, unless you count stuff like Starbucks. Prices are the highest for the chain: £92 a night, barring specials. For a description of Premier Travel Inn amenities, see p. 47

££–£££   A modern addition to one of London's oldest neighborhoods, the **Southwark Rose Hotel** ★★★ (43-47 Southwark Bridge Rd., SE1; ☎ 020/7015-1480; www.southwarkrosehotel.co.uk; AE, DISC, MC, V, Tube: London Bridge or Southwark) gets a lot right for a design hotel. First, it doesn't charge snob rates. You'll be told that doubles and twins cost £140, but online, you'll regularly find prices as low as £75 to £85 for Friday, Saturday, and Sunday, when the business folk go home, and rates about £115 on weekdays. Its six-story, 84-room, purpose-built home is entered via a garage-like lobby hung with cauldron-like lamps that doubles as an art gallery. When I was last there, the spotlight artist was a petulant Japanese photographer named Mayumi, whose work mined a provocative schoolgirl fetish. Upstairs, rooms are a bit smaller than the American hotel norm (tip: rooms ending with 06 are a touch larger), but well conceived for the price, with large, cushy white beds piled with pillows, backlit chair rails and headboards, motorized blackout curtains, and, behind a curving wall, a smartly designed bathroom (showers only) that maximizes minimal space with clever triangular sink spaces and plenty of mirroring. Safety is particularly well observed here, since key cards are required to use the elevators and room doors are extra-sturdy and have peepholes. The penthouse floor is devoted to a spacious bar/restaurant with a sunny western exposure.

££–£££   Another pub hotel that bills itself more as a borderline mainstream hotel, **Mad Hatter Hotel** ★★ (3-7 Stamford St., SE1; ☎ 020/7401-9222; www.fullershotels.co.uk; MC, V, AE; Tube: Southwark or Blackfriars) could easily seduce guests into lingering in its gorgeous Victorian-styled bar, part of the sizable Fuller's chain. But upstairs, soundproofed from the typically English frolic, the sizable rooms feel like they were lifted from a respectable Sheraton. Think decent-size bathrooms with tub/showers, rose-colored bedspreads matching painted accent walls, a lift, and ice machines—rare as diamonds in the U.K. The rack rate for its 30 rooms is £125, for singles or doubles, which I think is a bit high, but outside of busy summertime, you're more likely to be quoted £10 less than that online, and even less on the weekends (£95 isn't unusual). It's an ideal location for strolling the bank of the Thames, 2 blocks north, in good weather. Ask for a room facing the back—they're not only sunnier, since they face a churchyard, but they avoid the noise of the skyscraper construction going on across Stamford Street. Some rooms can be conjoined for families, or extra beds can be added for £12. The general manager here is married to the general manager of the Sanctuary House Hotel, which accounts for both hotels' noticeably high standards.

THE CITY

Because the so-called "square mile" essentially shuts down after work, tourists will find that amusements and family-run hotels are both in short supply. Although rooms in The City are often dramatically cheaper during the weekend and you'll be in the oldest part of London, come Saturday, you'll have to forage for a coffee like a Sioux hunting for buffalo. The exceptions are Clerkenwell (pronounced "CLARK-en-well"), a seat of hip hotels and nightclubs, and the artsy hoods of Spitalfields and Whitechapel east of Liverpool Street station.

Blue Light Specials at Blue-blood Hotels

When the briefcase brigade retreats home for the weekend (Fri–Sun nights), you'll find terrific values at expensive hotels. Sure, the downside of changing hotels for the weekend is that it undercuts your ability to negotiate lower prices for longer stays at privately owned hotels during the rest of the week. But the upside is that you can experience another part of town and kick back in an exclusive hotel for democratic rates. Just about every corporate hotel in The City or the Docklands will hack tariffs over the weekend, so play around on their websites to uncover the gold. To get you started, here are a few samples:

Apex City of London Hotel ★★★ (1 Seething Lane, EC3; ☎ 01316/66-51-24; www.apexhotels.co.uk; AE, MC, V; Tube: Tower Hill): During the weekend, when The City is deader than Old Marley (good luck even finding a sandwich outside of the hotel), the Apex becomes a peaceful urban retreat. It's handsomely designed by chic Scots, with huge rooms done in hardwood and walnut, and bathrooms larger than many B&Bs' guest rooms, including walk-in showers. It's literally steps from the Tower of London and the Tower Bridge. Weekday rate: £200 (City King room). Weekend rate: £80.

Swissôtel The Howard ★★ (Temple Place, WC2, ☎ 020/7836-3555; http://london.swissotel.com; AE, MC, V; Tube: Temple): Strangely, London has precious few hotels situated on the Thames. But here, above Temple Tube stop, many rooms boast the most flabbergasting views of the river imaginable—from St. Paul's dome all the way to Parliament and the

£–££   The newest Ibis property in town, **Ibis London City** (5 Commercial St., E1; ☎ 020/7422-8400; Tube: Aldgate East or Aldgate) is in an off-putting white block near the bohemian galleries, ethnic takeaways, and clubs of Whitechapel and Spitalfields. The hotel has 348 rooms, which means there's usually availability. Rooms are £83 for weekdays and £60 on weekends. For a description of Ibis amenities, see p. 47.

££   Hemmed in by modern office buildings near Liverpool Street station, the six-story **Travelodge London Liverpool Street** ★ (1 Harrow Place, E1; ☎ 08701/91-16-89; Tube: Liverpool Street) overlooks a sleepy but not-very-florid pocket park which means no traffic will keep you awake. The area is lifeless after work, although the happening Spitalfields is just 5 minutes northeast. The rate is £85, plus £6.50 for a breakfast buffet. No one can get in without swiping a key card. For a description of Travelodge amenities, see p. 47.

££–££££   The sort of place that has its own style magazine with articles extolling the merits of top-shelf tequila, the 97-room **Malmaison** ★★ (18-21 Charterhouse Square, EC1; ☎ 020/7012-3700; www.malmaison-london.com; AE,

London Eye. You won't want to close your eyes, and to help you, all rooms have their own Lavazza espresso machine for free unlimited use. Weekday rate: £210 (Swiss Advantage room with garden view). Weekend rate: £120.

Jury's Great Russell Street (16-22 Great Russell St., WC1; ☎ 020/7347-1000; www.jurys.com; AE, MC, V; Tube: Tottenham Court Road): The Jury's chain is known to British and Irish business travelers, but how many North Americans know its large business-class rooms go for a song during the weekend? Of its several large-roomed London properties (it's in Islington and Chelsea, too) this one is ideally located for British Museum and West End theater and clubbing. Weekday rate: £155. Weekend rate: £90. Last-minute specials are posted online.

By the same token, a few upscale hotels make a habit of filling rooms in the summer by offering the same rate in American dollars that's normally offered in pounds. So a £189 room becomes $189. That's still more than you have to pay to stay in London, but if getting a cut-rate deal on a posh place interests you, poke around these hotels and see if they're offering something: **Hazlitt's** (☎ 020/7434-1771; www.hazlittshotel.com; Tube: Tottenham Court Road); **The Rookery** (☎ 020/7336-0931; www.rookeryhotel.com; Tube: Farringdon); **The Gore** (☎ 020/7584-6601; www.gorehotel.com; Tube: South Kensington); **The Mandeville** (☎ 020/7935-5599; www.mandeville.co.uk; Tube: Bond Street); **The Athenaeum** (☎ 800/335-3300; www.athenaeumhotel.com; Tube: Hyde Park Corner).

MC, V; Tube: Barbican) is the sole London branch of a burgeoning British design chain. The lobby, accented by high-backed chairs the White Queen might enthrone herself in and flat-screen TVs replaying fashion runway shows, is so stage-managed with faint colored lighting that you'll fumble around in your bag for your passport when you check in. I think such theatrics are part of the fun, and, because it's not snooty, this full-service hotel has the right level of *Zoolander*-esque posturing. Rooms are equally hyperbolic in their heavy-handed but frivolous design (slender art lamps, earth tones and metallics, and machine-like lever handles on everything from the sinks to the doors), but the beds don't suffer from the same preening. They're giant, just soft enough, and inviting, and the modernist bathrooms have both showers and tubs along with sinks like oversize noodle bowls. All in all, it's refreshing to see a hotel that takes itself so seriously charge prices for customers with their feet on the ground. As a bonus, Charterhouse Square is a traffic-free oasis; in mid-day, you can hear school kids playing out front. There's a buzzing brasserie and bar in the basement, but you'll find plenty of equally stylish nightlife right out the door around Smithfield Market. Doubles go from £185 on paper, but cost £99 in reality, since the hotel routinely cuts deals, especially on weekends. There's a gym, too, plus a lift.

The City Accommodations

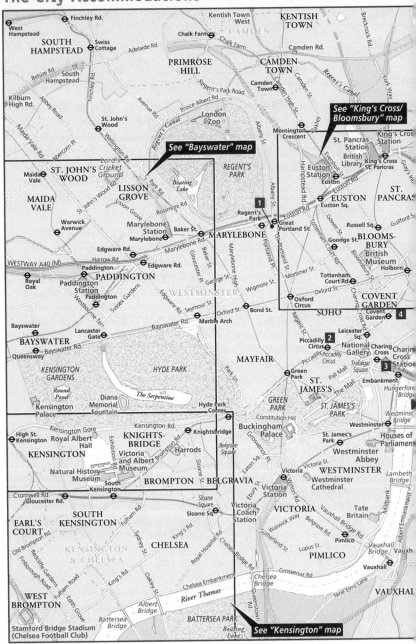

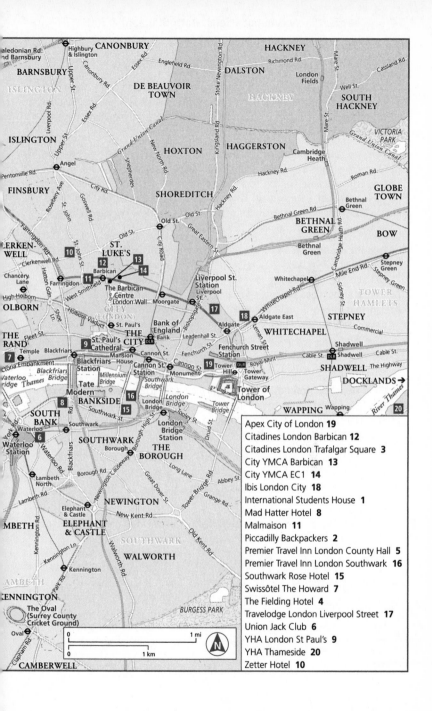

Apex City of London **19**
Citadines London Barbican **12**
Citadines London Trafalgar Square **3**
City YMCA Barbican **13**
City YMCA EC1 **14**
Ibis London City **18**
International Students House **1**
Mad Hatter Hotel **8**
Malmaison **11**
Piccadilly Backpackers **2**
Premier Travel Inn London County Hall **5**
Premier Travel Inn London Southwark **16**
Southwark Rose Hotel **15**
Swissôtel The Howard **7**
The Fielding Hotel **4**
Travelodge London Liverpool Street **17**
Union Jack Club **6**
YHA London St Paul's **9**
YHA Thameside **20**
Zetter Hotel **10**

A London Lodgings Glossary

When you're booking your bed, you're going to hear some terminology that you might not understand. Don't pretend like you know what they're talking about, because the English are too polite to presume that you need explanations. Here's a cheat sheet:

Twin vs. Double: Twin rooms have two single beds, like the ones the Cleavers might sleep in. A double room almost always has a big bed for two in it. Because London rooms are so often small, single rooms usually come with just a single bed. If you want to sleep alone in a double bed, you'll probably have to pay for a double room unless occupancy is light and you score a free upgrade. (Be nice. It happens.)

En suite vs. shared: En suite is just a fancy way of saying you'll have your own toilet, or "W.C." (which is "water closet," a polite British term for toilet) attached to the room. Shared (or "standard") rooms mean your toilet will be a short pad down the hallway. "Private" facilities may be down the hall, but they will only be used by you. Many old-fashioned rooms also have a sink in the room. Don't despair that you're in a dump if you have to share a W.C., because there's a long tradition of shared facilities in Europe. Even the Waldorf Hotel on Aldwych, one of the city's finest hotels, opened in 1908 with 176 bathrooms for 400 bedrooms.

First floor vs. ground floor: The English call street level the "ground floor" and start counting up from there, so the first floor is what many Americans might call the second floor. If you're lucky, there will be a "lift" (elevator) to it.

Pub hotel vs. guesthouse: "Pub hotels," which are located upstairs over a pub, are descended from inns of the past that supplied travelers with one-stop food and lodging. "Guesthouses" are usually the same as bed-and-breakfasts.

Full English vs. continental breakfast: "Continental" generally means breads (toast, croissant, muffin), maybe some yogurt and fruit. "Full English" is a plate of cooked food. Both will come with tea or coffee. If you find a place that does Full English for free (usually eggs, bacon, beans, mushrooms, cooked tomatoes), consider yourself lucky because most hotels are cutting back or throwing down a surcharge for it. And if you find something like tattie scones or black pudding on your plate, rejoice, because extras like those are rare indeed (although you may stop rejoicing when you're told that black pudding is actually blood sausage).

£££–££££ For those who have to hang with the in-crowd, the current hot bed-der is the 59-room **Zetter Hotel** ★ (86-88 Clerkenwell Rd., EC1; ☎ 020/7324-4444; www.thezetter.com; AE, MC, V; Tube: Farringdon), which opened in a for-mer warehouse on a noisy street in 2004. Its restaurant attracts scenesters with its DJ nights, readings, and mixers. Its visual gag is described by some as "punk-chintz." If you don't think that's funny, this place isn't for you, because it trans-lates into a quirky, sometimes overly angular symphony of sliding doors, wood shutters, Raindance shower heads, and butterfly stencils; you'll admire its chutz-pah but may find it a bit prickly. The building, noted for its five-story atrium, stands above the buried Fleet River, and it's from there that mineral water is drawn, purified, and sold for £7. On weekends, movies and Internet access are free, and in the winter, beds are adorned with hot water bottles and throws. The least expensive rooms (which is to say £140 in winter, £165 summer, £275 for a 2-night weekend) are on the lower floors, while the fifth floor is given over to deluxe penthouse suites, with panoramic terraces (£329), that you and I can only dream about. London certainly has better-value hotels but not many that are cooler.

VICTORIA, CHELSEA & WESTMINSTER

The streets around Victoria Station, lined with proud mid-19th-century houses as evenly spaced and white as a line of wedding cakes, were built for the rising mid-dle class but have long hosted good low-cost lodging. The area is slightly less bustling than Bloomsbury and King's Cross, appealing to visitors with a yen for peace. Deals tend to flower the farther southeast you walk from the station along Belgrave Road, but be warned that some of the hotels on this stretch are becom-ing as grotty and dim as the flophouses of Bayswater. (Except the ones I've cho-sen, of course.) I prefer the B&Bs along Ebury Street, which sprouts southwest of Victoria Coach Station because they're closer to the boutiques and cafes of Belgravia, such as along Elizabeth Street. Farther south, window-shopping with the wealthy on Chelsea's King's Road is a fine weekend pursuit, and because of its relative remove from the Tube system (but not the bus routes), hotels and flats come cheap.

£ More bare-bones beds: **easyHotel Victoria** (36-40 Belgrave Rd., SW1; www.easyhotel.com; MC, V; Tube: Victoria or Pimlico) was set to open its second London property, a new 78-room conversion carved into a 50-room budget hotel, in late 2006. That was too early for me to inspect it, but if there's one predictable brand, it's easyHotel, since the rooms are prefabricated. Prices also weren't set at press time, but expect something starting around £30 a night if you book early. Just like the original Kensington location (see p. 54 for how that place works), this joint isn't for everyone. Few rooms have windows or even space to properly prop up big luggage. But they're cheap, cheap, cheap, and if you're planning on being on the go during your trip, why pay more?

£–££ Because they started life as two separate hotels and were conjoined in the 1990s, you'll sometimes see the **Luna Simone Hotel** ★ (47-49 Belgrave Rd., SW1; ☎ 020/7834-5897; www.lunasimonehotel.com; MC, V; Tube: Victoria or Pimlico) called the Luna & Simone. Prices for rooms rise based on availability: Doubles go from £60–£85; triples from £80–£105; and the quad from £100–£120. The only category in which not every room is en suite is the single category (prices start at £35 for shared bath and cap at £60). Internet access is free in a booth off the lobby. Although it's a protected building with old metalwork on the banisters and oddly sized guest rooms, the owners have taken pains to modernize with fresh, inexpensive furniture and modernist prints by Rothko and Miró. Its two large morning rooms, done up like a diner, have a weird undulating blue ceiling that makes scooping your cereal feel a bit like doing the backstroke. Everything is in excellent condition, which is a bit of a surprise when you consider that the owners have been at it since 1969. No wonder it's popular.

£–££   Every time I visit **Morgan House** ★ (120 Ebury St., SW1; ☎ 020/7730-2384; www.morganhouse.co.uk; MC, V; Tube: Victoria), I'm amazed by how chirpy the guests look. They treat this cramped Georgian B&B like home, lingering over breakfast to swap travel tales, or hanging out on the staircase in the foyer to warn each other of the bad plays seen the night before. There must be something extra special about this place, or its owners, Ian Berry and Rachel Joplin, for it to attract such friendly devotees. Maybe it's the low prices: £46 for singles, £66 for doubles, and £86 for triples. It certainly can't be the rooms, which are tight but adequate; only four of them have their own bathrooms (add £30 to the bill for singles and £20 for doubles if you want one of those). But you get a full English breakfast), plus orthopedic mattresses and a peaceful communal garden with white iron furniture. With only nine rooms, there's no hubbub to contend with—indeed, breakfast is only available in a 90-minute window each morning. Over a stay, you almost get the sense of what it must have been like to live in a mid-20th-century boarding-house, from getting to know your neighbors to learning the pleasure of pausing for a mid-day cup of tea. This hotel is not to be confused with the Morgan Hotel, a perfectly nice, but doubly expensive, B&B/flat letter in the lee of the British Museum.

£–££   Actually two houses across the street from each other, the typically English **James & Cartref House** ★ (108 Ebury St. and 129 Ebury St., SW1; ☎ 020/7730-7338 and 020/7730-6176; www.jamesandcartref.co.uk; AE, MC, V; Tube: Victoria) are called home by Sharon and Derek James, second-generation hoteliers who raised their two kids here and clearly care about the direction of their 19-room business. "Cartref" means "home" in Welsh, although since they entertain an 85% American clientele, you won't feel put off by the language barrier. Rooms are light but done up simply in gentle lavender, with unadorned wood furniture, and wardrobes in some rooms (such as in #1). A "standard" room means it shares a bath, and those are £52 for singles, £70 for doubles, and £95 for triples. About three-quarters of the rooms have private (if slightly stuffy) bathrooms; for those add £10 for a single, and £15 for a double or triple. The quad only comes in the en suite variety, and that's £135. Rooms are basic but cheery for the price, and breakfast is taken in a handsome glass-ceiling conservatory. Prices dip in November, January, February, and March.

£–££   The good-value **Sidney Hotel** ★★ (68-76 Belgrave Rd., SW1; ☎ 020/7834-2738; www.sidneyhotel.com; AE, MC, V; Tube: Victoria or Pimlico), comprising four conjoined town houses, is assiduously cleaned by a tenacious army of

B+B Belgravia **3**
easyHotel Victoria **6**
James and Cartref House **2**
Luna Simone Hotel **7**
Morgan House **1**
Sanctuary House Hotel **4**
Sidney Hotel **8**
The Elizabeth **5**

mop-brandishing chambermaids. To cultivate a business traveler clientele, the hotel has invested in a few extra touches that lift it a level above many others of the price. All 81 rooms are en suite (albeit many have only tiny plastic cubicles), with new pine green carpets and pastel-hued bedspreads, flat-screen televisions, free Wi-Fi, and where space permits, two extra chairs and a desk. The professionalism of the staff makes the enterprise feel a bit impersonal but not slapped together. Singles start at £55 in winter and rise to £69 in summer, while doubles are £70–£89, triples are £85–£115, and the lone quad is £115–£135. There's also a quint (£135–£155). In the lobby, a cocktail bar crackles with three flat-screen TVs, making the joint feel as upscale as a business hotel. Its desk staff puts noticeable elbow grease into helping guests find their way around the city, and the kitchen staff cooks a full English breakfast. As a bonus, there's even a lift.

££   Until recently, **B+B Belgravia** ★★★ (64-66 Ebury St., SW1; ☎ 020/7823-4928; www.bb-belgravia.com; AE, MC, V; Tube: Victoria) was a cookie-cutter B&B with nothing to recommend it, but a group of forward-thinking investors gave the premises an extreme makeover and are now angling to export their newfangled brand of "sophisticated simplicity" to other properties around the city. I hope they succeed. Although it follows the form of a typical town house hotel (rooms of

Read This to Avoid Booking Blunders

Do you need to swap the date and month? In Europe, the month and date are usually written in the reverse order of how they're ordered in the U.S. So May 11, 2008 in America becomes 11 May 2008 when you're using a British booking engine, or 11/5/08. (Dates go from the smallest increment of time to the largest.) Check carefully or you may reserve for the wrong month!

Deals are better direct. In my experience, if you can find a room in a hotel for £100 through a discounter, you will always be able to find it for at least as little from the hotel itself—probably lower, since if you book directly with the hotel, you won't pay commission. This goes double for London, where so many hotels are run by families, not rule-bound companies.

Make sure you're sure. If you don't like your hotel, you can change, but empty rooms hit tiny family-run places in the purse. Check the property's cancellation policy before you book—for example, is there no backing out within 48 hours of your reservation? Even if you think the joint's a dump, if you've missed a cancellation deadline, you won't get a refund.

Remember the time difference! If you need to call England to make reservations, make sure you know what time it is there first. Many of the inns listed in this book are run by everyday folks who may not appreciate receiving a phone call at 2am.

various sizes, stairs instead of lifts), it dares to have a strong sense of style. An ocean of white paint has been applied to every surface, and a futuristic glass-floored bridge was constructed, no doubt at great expense, to link the ground-floor sitting area (enormous wall clock, free espresso machine) with the light-drenched kitchen and dining area. Once you've made your way to the kitchen, you get a high-end breakfast that includes French press coffee and Wilkin & Sons jam. Rooms are of standard London size, meaning barely big enough for you and your luggage, but the bathrooms, with cylinder sinks and pleasingly detailed tilework, bear little resemblance to the dated closets on offer at the competition. You won't spot a yard of chintz in its 17 rooms, although Ikea is well represented. Your TV is flat-screen, and if you have a laptop, Wi-Fi is free; you can also borrow the laptop in the lounge. Each night on your pillow, instead of chocolate you'll find a slice of "rock," a traditional British seaside treat. For this high-concept execution, catnip to penny-pinching business travelers and style mavens, the rates are £94 for singles (typically in a double room), doubles £99—not bad at all, and in winter, you can negotiate £10 or so lower.

££   You'll find better-priced places than **The Elizabeth** ★★ (37 Eccleston Square, SW1; ☎ 020/7828-6812; www.elizabethhotel.com; MC, V; Tube: Victoria), but few that deliver English charm by the syrupy gallon. The desk staff is decked out in topcoats and cravats, and the tangled town house hallways, a maze of doors and panels, are layered with gilt-framed mirrors and antiquarian prints (typically depicting a deceased monarch of some sort). Of the 42 rooms, most of which are occupied by tourists on group tours who probably weren't prepared for the shoe-box London-sized quarters, singles cost £79, and doubles or twins £108 (although one that even the owners admit is tiny costs £96). If you'll share a bath, subtract £21 from the single price and £17 from that lowest double price. Rounding out the rooms are triples (£120), quads (£130), quints (£140) and a two-bedroom apartment sleeping up to six (£205) that makes for a cozy self-contained flat, with

---

Do You Need It?

Mind the culture gap. Don't let these quirks take you by surprise:

Although all hotels include towels and linen, you'll find for the most part that travelers are expected to bring their own washcloths. I've never figured out if this is for hygienic reasons or if Brits are so economical they use towels to wipe everything. But you've been warned, so don't get cross with the proprietor if you don't find one.

Many beds have duvets but not top sheets. It's just a European style; locals would probably explain that the duvet cover *is* the top sheet. Many Americans, after riding through the initial sensation that they're in a naked bed, find the setup surprisingly comfortable.

You may find that your hotel makes your bed each morning but doesn't change the sheets. This, too, is normal, and it saves on water, electricity, and detergent. If you want them changed, simply request it.

Nearly all rooms in the budget category have phones and TVs these days, but not cable, so expect only four or five broadcast (or "terrestrial") channels (BBC 1 and 2, ITV, Channel 4). Within a few years, this will all change as the entire country migrates to mandatory digital technology.

Ask permission before using a hair dryer in the bathrooms because the electrical system in many buildings can't handle them.

Your family-run B&B probably can't employ a porter but rare is the place that doesn't have at least one strong person on call to tote your baggage upstairs. It's yet another incentive—beside massive airline penalties for overweight bags—to pack lightly.

Not every small hotel stocks irons, sometimes for safety reasons. If yours doesn't, steam your clothes using the hot water in the bathroom; at least there's one advantage to their puny size.

Most places don't have air-conditioning because during a normal summer, London doesn't get that hot. Even if it gets warm during the day, it almost always gets chilly again after sunset. If you do get hot, don't panic. Most town house hotels have windows that open, and they loan out table fans. A few also have ceiling fans. If all that fails, you could do worse than to retreat to the breezes of one of London's world-famous parks.

its own equipped kitchen. Rooms on the front look onto lovely Eccleston Square, which was also once home to Winston Churchill; his bulldoggy portrait glowers from various frames on the walls. There's an elevator that climbs, laboriously, to the doors to the flats. Breakfast skimps on nothing, and the front desk strives for concierge-level assistance. Check its website for regular discounts—if you have the page onscreen at the top of the hour, you can hear Big Ben chime.

££–£££   For a dreamy location straight down the block from Westminster Abbey's doorstep, **The Sanctuary House Hotel** ★★★ (33 Tothill St., SW1; ☎ 020/7799-4044; www.fullershotels.co.uk; AE, MC, V; Tube: St. James's Park) may be a pub hotel, but its vibe is more in keeping with a professional high-end bedder. It's also a splurge, but a guiltless one, because pretty much no other hotels in Westminster rate as highly in quality for such a good price. The Fuller's pub, which has a separate entrance, is a classy businessman's one, so it's usually quiet by bedtime, and it sends up room service to boot. The 34 rooms here have been recently renovated without much concern toward expense—doors open by key card, there's plenty of storage and sitting space, and the pleasing rust-and-tan color schemes imply wealth. Rooms are bigger than average and the bathrooms, many of which approach the size of the one you may have at home, are stocked with brand-name toiletries by Pascal Morabito. Several touches make the hotel seem more expensive than it is, including a lift, choice of synthetic or down pillows, big tubs, plugs for U.S. razors, satellite TV, and heated towel racks. Doubles are £150, although £99 weekend deals are the norm. The "superior" corner rooms (£175) have four-poster beds and a curving wall full of windows down Tothill

Staying Web Connected in Your Room

These days, even budget travelers are packing their laptops and keeping in touch with e-mail and free Internet-based phone calls such as Skype. (Hide those computers under your dirty socks, though, because most low-cost hotels don't have in-room safes.)

You can't judge Web availability by the room rate. About 30% of inns currently offer some kind of in-room high-speed Web access, almost always for free. Many more provide free service on terminals in their lobbies, and a few charge by the minute for lobby use. You should assume that if I don't mention Web access at a small hotel, then it hadn't been installed at press time; it's being added quickly these days at even the lowest-priced places, though, so ask when you're ready to reserve.

Your Web access at homestays and serviced apartments will depend on your host. Tell your reserving agency if it's important to you.

As for major hotels with more than 100 rooms, almost all of them have it, even if I don't say so. But unlike the little guys, they charge for it. The most expensive 24-hour access I found? A scalding £20 at mid-priced boutique Number Sixteen.

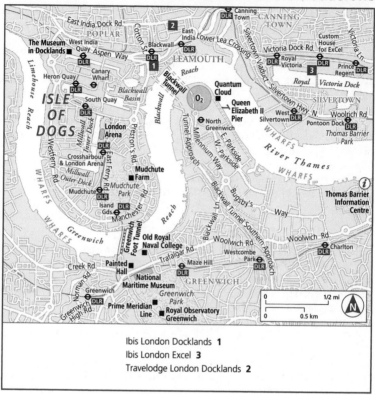

Ibis London Docklands **1**

Ibis London Excel **3**

Travelodge London Docklands **2**

Street toward Broadway; I like #203 because the painted pub sign is part of the view. Full English breakfasts cost £10, which is no bargain.

DOCKLANDS & GREENWICH

Docklands, the wide zone showcased in the TV show *Eastenders*, is a terrain of offices and some of the city's best-priced chain hotels. Even though it takes just as long to get to the City from Canary Wharf as it does from, say, High Street Kensington, the prices in Docklands are competitive since the area is off most tourists' radars. On the plus side: If you stay here, you'll mainly commute using the above-ground DLR train (entirely disabled accessible), which enables you to see a lot more than on the Tube. On the negative side: There aren't many places to eat outside of the Canary Wharf malls. In addition to lunch, you'll also have to pack your personality—these hotels don't have much of their own.

£ As part of modern redevelopment around the docks, **Travelodge London Docklands** (Coriander Ave., off East India Dock Rd.; ☎ 08701/91-16-91; Tube: East India DLR) can feel, like many Docklands chain hotels, a little windswept and lonely. Think of it as modernist northern European, and you'll feel better. It's close to the DLR station, though, and that 15-minute scoot into town can make the £56 room rate (£26 is often possible at this property if you book far ahead) worth it. For a description of Travelodge amenities, see p. 47.

£   A few steps south of the DLR station in a cul-de-sac haunted with cobbled vestiges of its dockworker past, **Ibis London Docklands** (1 Baffin Way, E14; ☎ 020/7517-1100; Tube: Blackwall DLR) is good for a crash pad, but there's not much to do nearby. Fortunately, the price compensates: £77 on weekdays and a scandalous £59 on weekends—surely worth taking a 15-minute ride to the city. Also in the area, the **Ibis London Excel** (Royal Victoria Dock, E16; ☎ 020/7055-2300; www.ibishotel.com; Tube: Custom House DLR or Royal Victoria DLR) sits in a Lego-like congregation of faceless hotels serving the ExCel Convention Center. When shows aren't on, rates plummet to £60 on weekdays, £50 on weekends. For those marvelous savings, you'll have to endure a 10-minute walk to the DLR and then a 25-minute ride into the city. For a description of Ibis amenities, see p. 47.

MILITARY HOTELS

A club hotel catering expressly to world servicemen, **Union Jack Club** ★★ (Sandell St., SE1; ☎ 020/7928-4813; www.ujclub.co.uk; AE, MC, V: Tube: Waterloo) was opened by King Edward VII in 1904 to shield soldiers from the wickedness of Edwardian London. Today, its vague modern furnishings and hotel-like amenities (restaurant, library, souvenir shop, bar) recall a much pricier hotel's. It's certainly as large as a goliath hotel: 330 rooms rest in the 1975 tower. In addition to American and Commonwealth servicemen and women, it accepts commissioned officers, firefighters, policemen, and ambulance workers, too—although it frowns upon accepting officers; after all, they have their own clubs. It costs £20 to gain membership and £10 for a year, which is prorated as the year wears on. If you don't feel like paying that but you still qualify, your accommodation rate will be about 15% higher than the standard rates, which start low (£31 single, £58 twin) and rise if you want a bathroom (£43 single, £79 double). Family rooms have bunk beds for kids and cost £99. Flats for four to six people, with kitchens, cost £945 a week or £135 a night.

The Victory Services Club ★ (63-79 Seymour St., W2; ☎ 020/7616-8335; www.vsc.co.uk; AE, MC, V; Tube: Marble Arch) was established in 1907 to ease the homecoming of veterans of Britain's many wars and is only for those who have served in the military. It's open to retired personnel of the Crown, Commonwealth, or Allied nations, including NATO personnel. Once the £20 annual membership is paid (in advance by mail), you can crash in one of the Club's 220 rooms, which are more basic than those at the Union Jack Club. Prices are comparable to other budget hotels, but mingling with former British and international servicemen is an interesting experience. Rooms in the Old Club House (dating to 1948) are simpler, with shared bath, while rooms in the newer Memorial Wing (1954) are en suite. Depending on if you're in the old wing or the new, and if you want your own bathroom, it's £39–£51 for singles and £75–£98 for doubles, including a cooked breakfast. Subtract about £6 if you don't want to eat. There's a cheap restaurant that gets playful on periodic theme nights (Curry Night, Best of British Night), and a lounge bar that segues from coffee to stronger stuff as the day wears on.

HOSTELS & LOW-COST SPECIALTY HOTELS

Not all hostels are created equal. The two major players are **YHA** (once called Youth Hostel Association, 8 properties in central London; www.yha.org.uk; MC, V) and independently owned properties. Independents have no standardized protocol, so they're operated pretty much as the desk staff—often, Australian visitors—see fit, and that includes dorms that sleep both sexes. Loosely speaking, hostels that are independently owned will attract a more social crowd and cost about a third less than those operated by the YHA network, but YHA properties, which usually divide guests into same-sex dorms, have standards that are reliably higher. (These are gross generalizations, I know. I've been in independents run with military accuracy and at YHAs where I've met lifelong friends, but use these guides as a rule of thumb.) If you don't have a YHA membership (it costs £16 a year, and you can buy one when you arrive into town), you're still welcome, but you'll pay £3 more per night. The more people you jam in your room, the less you pay. Ask ahead if small children are welcome because policies vary.

A third category is **Young Men's Christian Association** (YMCA, 6 properties in central London; ☎ 020/8520-5599; www.ymca.org.uk; AE, MC, V). Given that they're operated by a Christian charity, they have zero party potential, and sometimes barely more personality, but they're secure, tidy, gender-separated, and a top value, if occasionally a little lonely-feeling. You'll find a lot of long-term guests here, mostly foreign visitors who bunk down early and who may even hold down honest-to-goodness jobs or academic schedules.

£–££   An independent, fresh-faced hostel that's not as party-crazed as the city's others, **Ace Hotel** ★★ (16-22 Gunterstone Rd., W14; ☎ 020/7602-6600; www. ace-hotel.co.uk; MC, V; Tube: West Kensington or Barons Court) is a good 20-minute ride from the West End on the Tube, but that commute buys you a quiet, secure street inhabited by everyday Londoners. There's a garden patio that's heated in the winter and that hosts barbecues in the summer, plus a bar and an Internet cafe, and as a token of the easygoing social atmosphere they're trying to create, the owners recently added a hot tub (it closes at 8pm). It's noticeably cleaner than many London hostels, but that might be the result of considerate guests who come here to escape the drink-and-cruise insanity at some of its bigger competitors. A pallid breakfast (toast, coffee) comes free, but no self-catering kitchen

What to Bring—& Not to Bring—to a Hostel

The good news: Hostels requiring guests to do chores, bring bed linen, be under a certain age limit, or come home by a set time are pretty much banished to history. Still, you'll probably need to bring

- Earplugs (if you're a light sleeper)
- Your own padlock to secure your gear in lockers
- Toiletries and flip-flops for the shower
- Your own towel (although some hostels provide them)

facilities are offered. Dorms come in three-, four-, six-, and eight-bed flavors, with prices from £17 to £26 depending on how many you shack up with and whether you want an attached bathroom. Simple private twins are £48 with a shared bath and £53 with a private bath, and doubles with bathrooms are £80, which aren't worth it when you consider what some budget hotels are charging in the middle of town. November through March, prices drop £2 to £4 across the board. Book early because it's gaining in popularity.

£   YHA hostels have changed a lot in the past generation. Gone are the curfews, the parochial rules, and the antiseptic lounges that sent your mind reeling back to your middle-school scoliosis checks. Instead of operating like an institutional charity, YHA now runs like a professional discount lodging concern where a customer can comfortably kick back in between day tours and crash in a single-sex dorm. The YHA off Oxford Street is popular for its location, but I find it to be airless and noisy. Instead, seek out a hidden gem that's practically on the Thames: the **YHA Thameside** ★★ (20 Salter Rd., SE16; ☎ 0870/770-6010; www.yha.org. uk; MC, V; Tube: Rotherhithe or Canada Water), which is so well-built that a Holiday Inn or a Hampton Inn could move in tomorrow. Rooms are giant by hostel standards, and although designers took too much advantage of the extra space by triple-stacking the bunks, it's rarely full, which means you won't always be assigned roommates. There's a kitchen, a full English breakfast (included in the price), and you can buy a picnic lunch for a few quid. All rooms, mostly four- and six-bunkers (£17 a bed) have bathrooms, even if you have to share them with whomever's bunking with you. Ten private twin rooms (£51 a room) are also on hand. Another perk: The hotel is on a poplar signposted cycle network skirting the Thames (rentals are £1.50 an hour or £9.50 a day), and boasts a fully equipped bike workshop. What keeps this property from massive popularity is its location well east of town (convenient for Greenwich and the Tower of London), off the Rotherhithe Tube stop, which is on the little-used East London line. You can solve that problem by walking about 15 minutes to the Jubilee Line's Canada Water station, and you'll be in Oxford Circus in 15 more minutes. This hostel used to be known as YHA Rotherhithe, but that name proved about as alluring as YHA Middle of Nowhere.

£   One of least expensive YHAs in town is the 181-bed **YHA Earl's Court** ★★ (38 Bolton Gardens; ☎ 0870/770-5804; earlscourt@yha.org.uk; MC, V; Tube: Earl's Court). From the intricate tile flooring in the foyer to its sweeping staircase, it has settled inside a grand single-family home. (Beatrix Potter was born and spent her formative years, raised mostly by servants, in a neighboring house, 2 Bolton Gardens.) Choose between four-bed and seven-bed dorms for £20 adults and £17 for under-18s, or save a little by packing into a 10-bed dorm for £17. Small private rooms cost £54 for twins, £59 for triples, and £78 for quads and come with a free continental breakfast. There's laundry, a kitchen, TV lounge, bike hire (£1.50 an hour or £9.50 a day), and a simple back garden. The property sustained serious fire damage in the spring of 2006, a few days after I inspected it, and re-opens after massive renovation in April 2007, so expect things to be even fresher now. It's tricky to find because there are so many streets named Bolton; from Earl's Court Road, go down the one with Caffe Mokarabia on the corner, and you'll find the hostel on the right.

£ There's no question that the modern, nonsmoking **YHA London St. Pancras** (79-81 Euston Rd, NW1; ☎ 020/7388-6766; www.yha.org.uk; MC, V; Tube: King's Cross St. Pancras) is in a convenient spot: across from the British Library, and within quick reach of six Tube lines. But this hostel doesn't have much personality. Still, it books up early. Rooms, most of which are four-bedded, are bigger than the norm, with the added luxury of a table and a few chairs and lots of storage space, and although the road outside is busy, security is tight and windows are triple-glazed. It's a good place to crash if you're catching a morning train from King's Cross station. Beds are £26 if you're over 18, £21 if you're under 18; the price includes a full English breakfast, which is unusual. Twin-bunked private rooms are £56. "Premium rooms" come with either double beds or twin bunks and have a TV and bathroom (£62). There are also similarly priced "family bunk rooms" holding two to six bunks; most include a bathroom, but you must check in with at least one child under 18. The maximum stay is 10 nights. There's a kitchen, air-conditioning, and a lift.

£ If you're looking for a hostel where you can party all night, there's no bigger playground than the **Generator** ★★ (Compton Place, off 37 Tavistock Place, WC1; ☎ 020/7388-7655; www.generatorhostels.com; MC, V; Tube: Russell Square or Euston), discovered down a blink-and-you'll-miss-it cobbled lane on the opposite Kenton Street. By day, it appears like some kind of tanker ship stranded in the mews, and by night, when the socializing is in full swing, it's like the monkey house at the zoo. The Art Deco building was a police station in its younger years but a makeover of sheet metal and cobalt neon gave it a *Blade Runner* mood that's at distinct odds with the party-hearty playfulness of the clientele. You'll meet lots of young backpackers from Australia and continental Europe—with more than 800 beds, there's plenty of opportunity to make a new friend or 12. Management is unusually alert for a hostel, although it could stand to enforce the nonsmoking room on the dorm floors and apply a scrub brush to the bathrooms with more vigor. Guests get access to a microwave and a toaster, but not a full kitchen. The cafeteria, Fuel Stop, dishes up changing square meals like barbecue chicken and mixed vegetables for a paltry £3.50. The bar is open until 2am (happy hour, £1 pints), and for better or worse, many make heavy use of it. All rooms (standard metal bunks, nothing to shout about) have wash basins but share bathrooms. Everyone is assigned a backpack-size locker (bring your own lock), and there's a laundry, lift, and a lobby shop that sells everything from washing powder to discounted tours to Vegemite. Breakfast (cereal, toast, coffee or tea) is free. Private rooms are singles £35 daily/£245 weekly; twins (no double beds) £25 daily/£140 weekly per person; triples £20 daily/£126 weekly per person; quads £17 daily/£119 weekly per person. Prices for mixed-gender dorms are £17 in a four-bed, £15 in an eight-bed, and £13 in a room with either 12 or 14 beds. Some eight-bed dorms (£15) are female-only. No one under 18 is allowed in the dorms.

£ For a well-located hostel sans drunk Australians vomiting beside your bunk, try the no-nonsense **City YMCA Barbican** ★ (2 Fann St., EC2; ☎ 020/7628-0697; www.cityymca.org, MC, V; Tube: Barbican), which occupies a dull-as-dirt concrete 14-floor high-rise at the northwest corner of the plain but safe Barbican development. Because of its off-putting landscape, most tourists overlook Barbican, which is probably why the prices are so good: £212 for a week's stay in a single room, or £37 per night; and £182 for a week's stay per person in a twin room (no double beds), or £35 per night. That price includes a light breakfast daily and a cooked dinner, balanced but hardly gourmet, Monday through Friday. Rooms are cleaned daily (linens changed weekly), there's a TV lounge and lift, and all guests, many of whom stay for several months, are entitled to use the handy fitness center (weight training, cardio) for free. If you'd rather not look down on busy Aldersgate, ask to face eastward, over the garden. A supermarket is nearby, and so is the popular nightlife zone of Clerkenwell. You'll find identical prices at the nearby **City YMCA EC1** ✚ (8 Errol St., EC1; ☎ 020/7628-8832; www.cityymca.org; MC, V, AE; Tube: Barbican or Moorgate), a 2-minute jaunt east down Fann Street, but the Barbican is closer to transit.

£   Perhaps because visitors assume it only welcomes Indians, not much attention is paid to the **Indian Student YMCA** ✚✚ (41 Fitzroy Square, W1; ☎ 020/7387-0411; www.indianymca.org; AE, MC, V; Tube: Warren Street). That's their loss and your find. Although, it *is* popular with Indian students studying in London (in fact, it's operated by the National Council of YMCAs in India), you're welcome to stay here. Its lobby is as institutional as a 1950s airport lounge, but upstairs it's much more than advertised. Private rooms have blue carpet, thick red blankets, TVs, phones, and lamps that turn on and off with a tap. You could eat off the bathroom floor, but I don't know why you'd want to when the downstairs canteen, attended by staff in white uniforms and chef hats, serves some delicious authentic Indian food at all three mealtimes for next to nothing (onion bhajia £1!, veggie curry £1.35!). Four-bedded dorms are £22 per person, and private rooms come with a shared bath (singles £35, doubles £50) or an attached bath (singles £46, doubles £62). Those prices include both breakfast and dinner but not the £1 surcharge for nonmembers. There's a lift, and let's not ignore the location: On the southeast corner of a historic, pedestrianized square within walking distance of seven Tube lines, the British Museum, Oxford Street, and the West End.

£   The chief advantage of the 200-bed **YHA London Holland Park** ✚ (Holland Walk, Kensington, W8; ☎ 020/7376-0667; www.yha.org.uk; MC, V; Tube: Holland Park or High Street Kensington) is its location within a Jacobean former mansion in a wooded area of Holland Park, which is like a western annex of Kensington Gardens. The chief disadvantage, besides the place's popularity with unruly school groups, is that the idyllic-seeming location actually places it about 10 minutes from the nearest Tube station, and both of those are about another 15 minutes from the West End. Single female travelers may not feel comfortable walking to the hostel at night through the park. But the facilities are strong, with clean rooms, generous lockers, individual reading lights, park views, a cafe, bike hire (£1.50 an hour or £9.50 a day), a kitchen, laundry, and cheap restaurant. There are only dorms (8–20 beds) costing £22 adults, £19 under-18s. The similarly equipped, 178-bed **YHA London Baden Powell House** (65-67 Queen's Gate, SW7; ☎ 0870/770-6132; www.yha.org.uk; AE, MC, V; Tube: Gloucester Road) isn't all that much closer to the West End (it's one Underground stop nearer), but its prices are much higher: Adults pay £28 and under-18s pay £22, probably because all rooms are en suite and have TV; there's no kitchen, though. It's frequently booked out by groups.

£   A party hostel in the middle of the tourist universe, **Piccadilly Backpackers** (12 Sherwood St., W1; ☎ 020/7434-9009; www.piccadillyhotel.net; AE, MC, V; Tube: Piccadilly Circus) got some attention by unveiling its "pods" in February 2006. In truth, they're not so much sleek Japanese-style capsules as lines of bunk beds, each with a reading light, separated by flimsy wood partitions, but they still give a modicum of privacy that few other joints can claim. The place is popular, but for my money, it's too harried and basic and borderline grimy. What you gain by being in the middle of it all, you lose through slightly higher rates and cramped quarters: Some 600 beds are packed into four floors. Eight-ten bed dorms are £12; six-beds are £18; six-bed "pods" (maybe they should call them "coffins") are £21; four-beds are £19. Private doubles or twins are £58; singles are £39 (both with shared bath). Friday and Saturdays are £3 more, but booking online will often save you about £2. You get a small locker (some of which, annoyingly, won't fit a thick combination lock), and breakfast is a joke (toast and instant coffee). Verdict: You can find better hostels, but you won't find a better location.

Dining Choices
For all tastes & pocketbooks

IN 1957, ARTHUR FROMMER VISITED LONDON'S BEST RESTAURANTS DURING research for his seminal *Europe on $5 a Day*. His report was dispiriting: "With great despair, this book recommends that you eat in these inexpensive chains while in London and save your money for the better meals available in France and Italy. Cooking is a lost art in Great Britain; your meat pie with cabbage will turn out just as tasteless for 40¢ in a chain restaurant as it will for $2 in a posh hotel."

Thankfully, the English palette has caught up with the rest of the world, and the residents of London now rightfully pride themselves on their advanced and multicultural cuisine. Your food will almost certainly not be tasteless, and cabbage has been banished from the menus of most establishments. But eating in London is still a problem, and in many ways, the best choices are still dominated by chain restaurants—albeit chains that often don't exist outside of London.

The trouble is most kitchens here are shockingly pricey. That resurgence of British home cooking you've heard about—the rise of the gastropub—is a trend aimed at wealthy diners. (And considering the blistering exchange rate, few visitors can consider themselves "wealthy.") Once you get to London and see the menus, you'll be amazed (and appalled) at how comparatively expensive even basic food is. The affordable places are often Asian, part of a chain, or sandwich counters.

That may be because eating out, as a pastime, is still gaining cultural traction. Remember that this is a place that was, as recently as the 1950s, still living on rations. It's in their bones to cook for themselves. For most Britons of an average income, going out to eat is a treat, and usually something done to catch up with friends or on a special occasion. Ordering dinner for delivery is almost never done.

Here's another thing you won't find much of: fish and chips. In London (if less so than in the north of Britain), old fry-ups have been replaced, by and large, with Britain's new favorite comfort food, the curry shop. You also won't find many pubs serving the classic definition of English cuisine, such as steak-and-kidney pie or Yorkshire pudding. Most pubs have followed changing tastes and have reduced old-fashioned menu items to a few roast meats or unadventurous beef pies, in favor of ever-popular pizzas, sandwiches, and burgers.

THE AFFORDABLE RESTAURANTS OF LONDON

Most of these establishments also serve lunch, should you get sick of sandwiches or need to rest your legs for a spell, but since your hotel will surely serve breakfast, I won't waste space on morning eateries.

My focus is places charging under £10 for a main dish. Any more than that, and you'll be paying US$20 before you've added a starter, dessert, coffee, or tip—a full meal at those prices will hit you for £30. Do that twice daily, and you'll have lost more than US$100 a day to food alone! My price ratings are restrictive, but scaling it more liberally would mean this list would be a lot less useful to you.

The Five Rules for Finding Affordable Restaurants

If you want to find good, inexpensive places to eat (beyond the places that I list later in this chapter, that is), follow these rules:

* Sandwiches, sandwiches, sandwiches (see the "Save Your Bread at Sandwich Shops" box, below).
* The cheaper places are usually one road behind the busiest streets.
* Asian cuisine—Thai, Malaysian, Indian—is key.
* You'll find more interesting and more affordable choices in non-touristy areas.
* If all else fails, drop by Marks & Spencer for prepared meals (p. 117) or the nearest pub; their menus are cheapish and filling.

For each neighborhood, I list spots in order of cost so that it's easier for you to find something according to what you're willing to pay. When and if you find yourself ready to splash out, you will find no shortage of pricier options vying for your palette; a few of my favorites are included here for breadth:

BLOOMSBURY & FITZROVIA

£   One of the most spectacular buys in the city, the **YMCA Indian Students Hostel** ★ (41 Fitzroy Square, W1; ☎ 020/7387-0411; www.indianymca.org; AE, MC, V; Tube: Warren Street), on the southeast corner of Fitzroy Square, serves truly authentic Indian food, not a Pakistani hybrid; not surprisingly, its clientele consists mostly of Indian students. Apart from having the personality of an airport lounge, this buffet-style cafeteria is welcoming to anyone, resident or visitor. Pay the clerk, who'll give you a receipt that you show to the cook (who wears an immaculate, white chef's tunic), who in turn loads you up. Rices, chapatis, and fish curries make regular appearances, along with plenty of vegetarian options, many of them Punjabi. Get here right after noon, when it opens for lunch, or right after 7pm, when it re-opens for dinner, for the best pickings (but don't B.Y.O., since alcohol is not allowed). And the price? From £2 to £5. Amazing.

£–££   One of those secret cafes you have to have a friend tell you about, **Camera Café** (44 Museum St., WC1; ☎ 020/7831-1566; www.cameracafe.co.uk; MC, V; Tube: Tottenham Court Road or Holborn) is a coffee house tacked onto the back of Aperture Photographic, a small shop near the British Museum specializing in lenses and SLR cameras; the walls are decorated with shots taken by local artists. Food (£3.50–£6) takes its sweet time in coming (at least there are lots of coffee-table books on art and Britain to borrow, plus a vintage Scrabble set) but arrives in a big way; the huge chow mein noodle bowls could serve two. The free Wi-Fi, plus the brewed coffees and teas, mean boho patrons tend to relax for hours.

£–££   It does business in a hideous slug of a concrete fortress, but **Hare & Tortoise** (15-17 Brunswick Shopping Centre, WC1; ☎ 020/7278-4945; MC, V; Tube: Russell Square), peps up its surroundings with nonstop crowds of chatty young customers, who stream in until 11pm daily. It's always a good sign when a

London-wide Dining

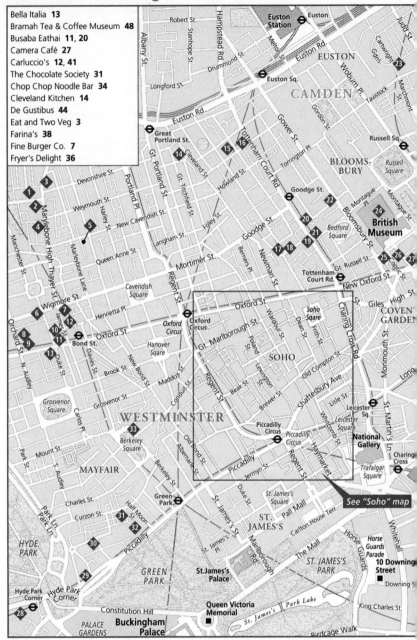

Bella Italia **13**
Bramah Tea & Coffee Museum **48**
Busaba Eathai **11, 20**
Camera Café **27**
Carluccio's **12, 41**
The Chocolate Society **31**
Chop Chop Noodle Bar **34**
Cleveland Kitchen **14**
De Gustibus **44**
Eat and Two Veg **3**
Farina's **38**
Fine Burger Co. **7**
Fryer's Delight **36**

See "Soho" map

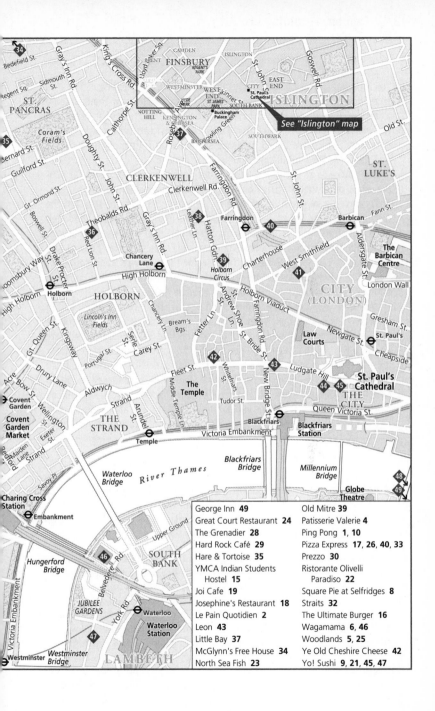

George Inn **49**	Old Mitre **39**
Great Court Restaurant **24**	Patisserie Valerie **4**
The Grenadier **28**	Ping Pong **1**, **10**
Hard Rock Café **29**	Pizza Express **17**, **26**, **40**, **33**
Hare & Tortoise **35**	Prezzo **30**
YMCA Indian Students Hostel **15**	Ristorante Olivelli Paradiso **22**
Joi Cafe **19**	Square Pie at Selfridges **8**
Josephine's Restaurant **18**	Straits **32**
Le Pain Quotidien **2**	The Ultimate Burger **16**
Leon **43**	Wagamama **6**, **46**
Little Bay **37**	Woodlands **5**, **25**
McGlynn's Free House **34**	Ye Old Cheshire Cheese **42**
North Sea Fish **23**	Yo! Sushi **9**, **21**, **45**, **47**

Save Your Bread at Sandwich Shops

You'll probably go all day without crossing paths with a police officer or a true Cockney in London, but you can barely walk 3 blocks without passing a sandwich shop. Sandwiches are a cultural institution in England: Anywhere people work, you'll find £2 to £4 sandwiches, soups, and "jacket potatoes," which are baked potatoes stuffed with fillings such as cheese and bacon or tuna salad (often called "tuna mayo").

My advice is to eat like the locals do. Save the splashy meals for supper. Most of London's attractions are only open from about 10am to 5pm. That doesn't give you a lot of time to see what you came to see, and the last thing you can afford is a marathon lunch. To dine like a true Londoner, have a big breakfast (your hotel probably serves it for free, so chow down), and at midday, grab a carb-laden bite (a sandwich, a jacket potato) and get on with your day. Dinner is the time for table service, long conversation, and adventurous cuisine—in fact, many sandwich places close in mid- to late-afternoon, dictating your choices for you.

You don't need my help finding sandwiches. They're everywhere, and in terms of flavor, well, they're sandwiches. But I will tell you that the cheapest of the sandwiches are what I call the **triangle sandwiches,** which are ready-made, sliced diagonally, and sealed into triangular plastic containers. The British don't usually call them triangle sandwiches—they just call them takeaway sandwiches, undistinguished from a sandwich made to order—but the nickname fits. Triangle sandwiches range from 99p (for an egg salad/"mayo" or other vegetarian selection) to about £3.50 (for triple-packs containing three sandwich halves with a variety of fillings).

place serving Asian cuisine is popular with native-born Asians. Its roasts are a good deal—duck, pork, or chicken served with rice, ramen, or lo mein for £4.30 to £4.50; a two-meat combo plate is just 20p more. Gyoza dumplings are £2.80, and main dishes (ramen soups, lo mein bowls) span £4.30 to £5.50—servings are big. Lunch can be so busy that you may feel rushed.

££   You'd never know it from the sleepy avenue it is today, but Cleveland Street, which runs a block west of Fitzroy Square, was once one of the city's most notorious red-light districts, where many a writer fell afoul of his unchecked libido. A little hedonism, in the form of sublime comfort food, lives on at **Cleveland Kitchen** ★★ (145 Cleveland St., W1; ☎ 020/7387-5966; AE, MC, V; Tube: Great Portland Street), a blink-and-miss-it, homespun hole in the wall beloved by its neighbors but untouched by tourism. It looks in passing like a greasy spoon, but in fact this cramped storefront knows its way around a plate. The menu (pan-fried cod, steak, with an emphasis on genuine Italian textures and flavors such as risottos and eggplant ravioli) changes according to the chef's moods and what's fresh,

Here are explanations of ingredients that I wish someone had given me:

- *Pickle* is a tangy vegetable spread that tastes a bit like steak sauce.
- *Cress* is slang for watercress.
- *Mayo* is like saying "salad," but "salad" listed as an ingredient usually denotes just a cursory pinch of lettuce.
- A *bap* is a round bread roll, and a "toastie" is a sandwich that's been cooked in a sandwich press.

A few ubiquitous chains catering to the triangle sandwich trade are:

Pret a Manger (www.pret.com): The highest-end sandwichier, with gourmet fixings in snazzy combinations, Pret is co-owned by McDonald's.

Eat (www.eat.co.uk): Its quality is right behind Pret, with a good selection of organics and whole grains.

Boots (www.boots.com): The cheapest triangle sandwiches on the High Street, and a wide selection.

Marks & Spencer (www.marksandspencer.com): Lots of cheap stuff.

Gregg's (www.greggs.co.uk): Its sandwiches are average in every way, but people also queue for its pies and hot meat rolls.

Benjy's (www.benjys-sandwiches.com): The lowest quality of the bunch; its bread tastes like grammar-school paste to me.

but ask about the specials, which cost £5 including an alcoholic drink (£6 if you eat pizza). Even better for couples, you can get two mains plus a starter for £10. Set lunches are generously programmed: you get a starter such as pappardelle with wild boar ragout, a main such as ribeye steak or sea bass, plus coffee, all for £11.

££ Unlikely as it seems, one of London's growing niche cuisines is the all-you-can-eat meatless Asian buffet. **Joi Café** (14 Percy St., W1; ☎ 020/7323-0981; no credit cards; Tube: Goodge Street or Tottenham Court Road) masters the genre with a pleasing steam table lined with constantly replenished lo meins, faux-beef stir fries, fried dumplings, and spicy Thai salads and curries, all for £5 at lunch or £6 Sundays and evenings. Stuff your face in the simple dining room for as long as you can stand it, or stuff a take-out box for £3. Partly because chefs furnish a hearty complement of spices and sauces, even die-hard carnivores have been known to appreciate this fare. It's located near the big campuses, so it's popular with students, and if you have a student ID, you get a free drink after 3pm.

When Restaurants Are Open

Lunch at family-owned restaurants is served from about 11am to 3pm, although a few may wind it up at 2:30pm. Dinner starts at around 5:30pm and goes to 10:30 or 11pm. I've noted exceptions in the reviews that follow. At an increasing number of places, including chains, serving hours don't stop in the afternoon, but you may find that kitchens start closing down about a half-hour before the posted closing time. In Britain, closing time often means the time staff clocks off, not the moment last orders are taken.

Most of London's restaurants aren't strict about defining their genres. You'll see pizza alongside noodles alongside sandwiches, and Thai fused with Chinese fused with Malaysian.

For sandwich shops, see p. 92; for pubs, see p. 126; and for caffs, see p. 119.

KING'S CROSS & ISLINGTON

£   It ought to be protected by the National Trust. Not only is the **Indian Veg Bhelpoori House** ✦✦✦ (92-93 Chapel Market, N1; ☎ 020/7833-1167; no credit cards; Tube: Angel) meat-free, but it's also probably the best meal value in London. You pay just £2.95 for a giant all-you-can-eat-buffet in a city where plain rice usually costs more—that's enough to make this off-the-beaten-track, multi-level restaurant inkworthy. You'll get a mix of spicy choices, conventional choices (onion bhajis, which go fast), and weird choices (like curried brussel sprouts). Its homey decor—the walls are coated in essays and dubious bar graphs extolling the virtues of vegetarianism—make it even more of a must-see. Many a penniless student has survived thanks to the long-running deals. It even serves booze.

£–££   A creative space to escape for a few hours, **Candid Café and Courtyard** (3 Torrens St., N1; ☎ 020/7837-4237; www.candidarts.com; AE, V; Tube: Angel) is on the second floor of Candid Arts Trust, a gallery-and-studio complex in a converted Victorian warehouse just east of the Angel Tube station. This time-warp cafe is a mellow, candle-filled hangout for reading, tea nursing, deep conversation, and, if you're so inclined, admiration of the Sapphic, psychedelic paintings on the walls. Sandwiches (from £2.80) come with upscale fillings like brie, avocado, and feta, and the changing cooked meals (£5–£10) usually include organic meat and a few vegetarian dishes such as lasagna or mixed veg in coconut sauce with couscous. Service isn't what you'd call sprightly; your waitress may have to set her own coffee down to fetch your food. Most customers just buy a slice of cake and a coffee and linger. In the summer, the idle pleasures spread to the courtyard out back.

£–££   On rainy days, the plate-glass windows of **Chop Chop Noodle Bar** (3 Euston Rd., N1; ☎ 020/7833-1773; Tube: King's Cross/St. Pancras; MC, V) fog up, concealing the crowds of students, commuters, and Asian tourists who favor this simple eating hall over the many banal fast food chains that clog King's Cross. The menu's huge (98 items: noodles, soups, rice dishes, and fresh juices), and since it's up to customers to fill out their own order card, it's easy to go crazy and order too

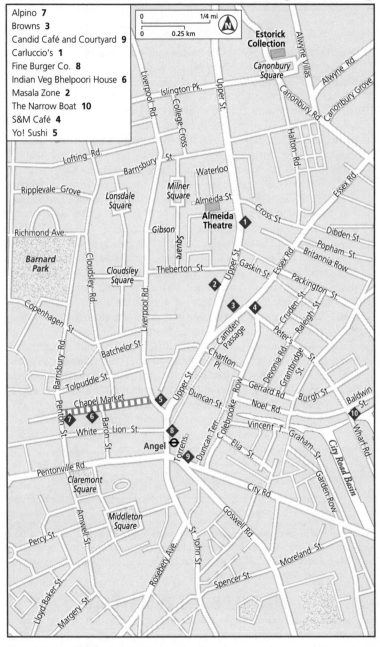

Islington Dining

Alpino **7**
Browns **3**
Candid Café and Courtyard **9**
Carluccio's **1**
Fine Burger Co. **8**
Indian Veg Bhelpoori House **6**
Masala Zone **2**
The Narrow Boat **10**
S&M Café **4**
Yo! Sushi **5**

The Cabman's Shelter

As you roam, keep an eye out for curious kelly-green shacks, no bigger than a horse and cart. Wooden, shingled, and peaked, fringed in simple ginger-bread latticework, topped by a wee cupola vent, they're as cute as a hob-bit's outhouse. Some balance in the median of an overcrowded avenue, some hunker like newsstands along the pavements. These are Cabman's Shelters, built by a charity between 1875 and 1914, when "respectable" classes were worried about cab drivers straying into the pubs on a working day. Inside, instead of a pint, horsemen could find hot soup, tea, and other wholesome refreshments. Of the 61 original shelters, barely more than a dozen survive, and a few of those, against the odds, still contain teeny greasy spoons where cab drivers can pull over for a cuppa. Not all of them court custom from tourists, but if you're friendly, outgoing, and not with a large group, you can hold your own with some garrulous cabbies at the counters. The conversation zings. Simple meals (cooked as if by miracle on little more than a burner and a microwave) can be had for unbelievably low prices: tea for 50p, sandwiches for £2, enormous English breakfasts for £4.95. Some shelters, such as the one on Temple Place, even do takeaway. (It also advertises "pie, mash + liquor!"—a lax policy that would scandalize its original land-lords). Some are closed for weeks on end, and hours are erratic, but when they're cooking, they're open from breakfast to mid-afternoon.

Chelsea Embankment, near Albert Bridge (Tube: South Kensington; Embankment Place at Northumberland Avenue (Tube: Embankment or Charing Cross); Grosvenor Gardens; west side (Tube: Victoria); Hanover Square, north side (Tube: Oxford Circus); Kensington Park Road, numbers 8-10 (Tube: Notting Hill Gate); Kensington Road, north side (Tube: South Kensington); Pont Street (Tube: Knightsbridge); Russell Square, west cor-ner (Tube: Russell Square); St. George's Square, north side (Tube: Pimlico); Temple Place (Tube: Temple); Thurloe Place, opposite the V&A (Tube: South Kensington); Warwick Avenue at Clifton Gardens (Tube: Warwick Avenue); Wellington Place at Wellington Road (Tube: St. John's Wood).

much. I'll guide you: the Singapore Laksa soup, big as a hot tub, strikes upon the ideal medley of creamy coconut, vermicelli, shrimp, and come-from-behind spici-ness. Most London noodle bars wimp out on the zing, but Chop Chop doesn't do bland. It also steams on until midnight.

MARYLEBONE & MAYFAIR

£   No one should leave Britain without having pie for lunch. The handheld, meat-stuffed pastry parcels occupy a vital cultural position as a quick, satisfying lunch or snack. A top choice for a well-stuffed one is **Square Pie** (Selfridges Food Hall, 400 Oxford St., W1; ☎ 020/7318-2460; www.squarepie.com; AE, MC, V; Tube: Bond Street or Marble Arch), in the rear, ground-floor food hall at Selfridges.

Speak the Right Tongue for the Right Flavor

Some people call dinner **tea.** If you need it to go, say it's for **takeaway.** To request your final check, ask for the **bill.** If you want an American-style appetizer, you want a **starter.** French fries are sometimes called **chips,** but decreasingly so. What North Americans call entrees are **mains.** Dessert might be called a **pudding,** even if it's cake. A packet (such as for sugar or ketchup) is a **sachet** ("sash-AY").

Finally, before we call the whole thing off, if you say "to-*may*-to," they say "to-*mah*-to." But save yourself chagrin: the same is not true for potatoes.

baked potato = **jacket potato**
beet = **beetroot**
chicory = **endive**
cookie = **biscuit**
cotton candy = **candy floss**
eggplant = **aubergine**
ground beef = **mince;** but pie filling of dried fruit, etc. = **mincemeat**
Jell-O = **jelly**
juice drink (not fresh-squeezed) = **squash**
lemon-flavored soda pop = **lemonade**
molasses = **treacle**
potato chips = **crisps**
sausages = **bangers**
shrimp = **prawn**
squash = **marrow**
string beans = **French beans**
yellow corn = **sweetcorn**
yellow raisin = **sultana**
zucchini = **courgette** or **baby marrow**

"Classic" pies weigh over half a pound and come in a dozen varieties including steak and cheese, steak and Guinness, jerk chicken and sweet potato, and the infallible steak and kidney (all are £4.50 to eat-in, £3.95 to go). To be truly authentic, pair your pie with mashed potatoes, beans, or mushy peas (95p–£1.15 each). Meal deals get you a pie plus mash, peas, and gravy for £6.50/£5.75. On Fridays, Fish Pie joins the lineup. There's a second store at 16 Horner Square, at Spitalfields Market (Tube: Liverpool Street); both are mobbed during lunch hour.

Lunch Make a Deal

Lots of expensive restaurants advertise lunch deals and pretheater menus. Some are prix fixe, and some are low-price offers for a la carte courses. These are ever-changing, but as an example, Café Fish, on Rupert Street near Shaftesbury Avenue, normally charges from £9 for a main. At lunch, it'll do two courses for £10; and Ebury Wine Bar, a refined bistro on Ebury Street south of Victoria station, charges around £13 for a main except at lunch, when £14 gets you two courses and £18 gets you three. Check menu boards around town for frequent offers.

££–£££   Local Filipinos favor **Josephine's Restaurant** (4 Charlotte St., W1; ☎ 020/7580-6551; AE, MC, V; Tube: Goodge Street or Tottenham Court Road), which is somewhat surprising when you take a gander at the tacky trappings (bamboo chairs, a slatted ceiling, basic canteen dishes). Then again, it is the only Filipino place in the West End. Food arrives via dumb waiter from the cellar kitchen; eschew the Chinese dishes (which aren't terrific) for the "traditional" Filipino choices (which are), such as *lechon kawali* (pork belly boiled in spices then drained and fried crisp), *chicken adobo* (tangy chicken with garlic; the Philippines' national dish) and crispy *pata* (deep-fried pork leg). At lunch, two courses cost £6.50, and three £8.50; dinner prices are reasonable, too. Try the cassava cake for dessert; it tastes like sweet potato with yam cream.

££–£££   **Pizza Express** ★★ (30 Coptic St., WC1; ☎ 020/7636-3232; www.pizzaexpress.com; AE, MC, V; Tube: Russell Square) is so ubiquitous—some 280 outlets in the U.K.—you could call it something of a British institution. In fact, since its rise, which began in 1965 (9 years before McDonald's first stuck its flag in English soil), it seems like half the casual restaurants in town have added knife-and-fork, thin-crust pizzas to their bills of fare. Money-saving tourists will certainly turn to pizzas at least once during their trip, and they would do well to dig in at this classy chain, where two dozen pizza varieties (£5.15–£8.25, but mostly around £7.50)—not too bready, well topped—rightfully keep the traffic coming. I favor La Reine (ham, olives, mushrooms, £6.95) and Veneziana (onions, capers, olives sultanas/raisins and pine nuts, £5.55), but there are 22 other varieties, plus six types of salad and six more of pasta. Service is

£–££   Considering its organic breads and lush-looking pastries, it's no wonder journal writers and book readers never seem to vacate **Le Pain Quotidien** (72-75 Marylebone High St., W1; ☎ 020/7486-6154; www.lepainquotidien.com; AE, MC, V; Tube: Baker Street). It functions as a patisserie or a cafe, depending on your mood. Selections are light but fresh, such as carrot and coriander soup (£3.20, with bread), juicy strawberry tarts (£2.75), and slices of pavlova (an Australian meringue, £3.50). The tartines (open-faced sandwiches) are more substantial; get one with aged Gruyère and three mustards (£5.50) or tuna salad, capers, and

almost always freakishly fast and cheerful. There are more than 70 branches in town. The location at 10 Dean St. is probably the best because its nightly jazz concerts sometimes book important names like Van Morrison and Jamie Cullum (Reservations: ☎ 020/7439-8722; Tube: Tottenham Court Road); and the one at 11-13 Knightsbridge is the current tenant of a 1907 ticket hall for the Piccadilly line, which runs underneath (Tube: Hyde Park Corner). Other handy branches include 133 Baker St., by Madame Tussaud's (Tube: Baker Street); 9 Bow St. (Tube: Covent Garden); 80-81 St. Martin's Lane (Tube: Leicester Square); 30 Millbank, by Tate Britain (Tube: Pimlico); 9 Charlotte St. in Fitzrovia (Tube: Goodge Street).

££–£££ Back in the day, this place was so well-known that the Marx Brothers chose to dine here during their only trip to Blighty. Today, **Ristorante Olivelli Paradiso** (35 Store St., WC1; ☎ 020/7255-2554; www.pizzaparadiso.co.uk; AE, MC, V; Tube: Goodge Street) is an unpretentious place for good Italian food. It deserves props for its homemade pastas (£7.25–£8.55), which are a notch more creative than other bistros at this level: gnocchi timoniere is savory with calamari, sundried tomatoes, garlic, and tomato sauce; and pappardelle al funghi porcini is a satisfyingly rich mix of wild mushrooms, garlic, white wine, and cream. Save by getting pasta as a slightly smaller starter for £1 less. The menu has nine types of pizza, from £5.55, plus a slate of meats (£10–£12).

££–££££ One of the last bastions of batter-fried fish and chips, **North Sea Fish** (7 Leigh St., WC1; ☎ 020/7242-4119; AE, MC, V; Tube: King's Cross St. Pancras or Russell Square) isn't a linoleum-lined chippie, but a classy fish market-cum-restaurant, hidden on a lost-in-time side street. Every hotel manager within a 2-mile radius recommends it. Portions are huge, and there's always a selection of fresh fish (bream, trout, skate, halibut, and so on). Always ask the price when ordering because it's easy to get hit with a high market price (haddock and cod tend to be cheaper). If you need a healthier option, you can also get your fish grilled. Try the terrific homemade vegetable soup (£3.45) or, for fans of little fishies, sample grilled sardines with salad (£3.50).

anchovies (£4.90). Or just grab a simple pain au chocolat (£1.20). A second outpost is at 9 Young St. (Tube: High Street Kensington).

££   The solid-value minichain **Carluccio's** ★ (St. Christopher's Place, W1; ☎ 020/7935-5927; www.carluccios.com; AE, MC, V; Tube: Bond Street) apparently fashions itself after an Italian grocery from Manhattan's Little Italy; you enter through a little shop selling pastas and sauces and then beg for attention from the harried staff (just like the real thing). Pastas, which reach beyond spaghetti into the zone of fresh

Keeping the Bill in Check

Bear in mind these cultural differences while ordering and you'll avoid some nasty dining pitfalls:

Avoid Coke: It often costs £1.50, and you'll probably just get a puny glassful.

Avoid rice dishes: It's customary to pay £1.50 to £3 for a side dish of plain rice, even if you order something you think should come with it.

Avoid eating in: Some counter-service establishments charge as much as 20% more if you decide to eat your purchases there.

Avoid water: Well, avoid bottled water. If you just order "water," many waiters will bring expensive sparking water, so if you want it for free, specify "tap water."

Avoid starters: Even at places where mains are £6, starters can be £3 to £5.

Avoid cocktails: These are luxury items. Mixed drinks can cost a dizzying £8 to £10. If you do drink, stick to beer (£2–£3 a pint) or wine (around £4 a glass).

---

tomatoes, saffron, and ravioli, are well made and cost mostly in the £6 to £7 range, but there are salads, meat plates, and focaccia sandwiches as well. The £10 "Massimo!" antipasto dish serves two. Polish off dinner with a £1.40 demitasse of cioccolate fiorentina drinking chocolate, but do resist ordering the "transporti": It's a £1,799 Vespa scooter. Carluccio's is genuinely popular with locals, and worthy of its repeat clientele. The upstairs dining room is brighter but noisier; the cellar rooms are cozier but darker. Plenty of other branches are scattered around town, but some of the most convenient include 8 Market Place, (Tube: Oxford Circus), 1 Old Brompton Rd. (Tube: South Kensington), 108 Westbourne Grove at Westbourne Corner (Tube: Notting Hill Gate or Bayswater).

££–£££   A cosmopolitan veggie place, **Eat and Two Veg** (50 Marylebone High St., W1; ☎ 020/7258-8585; no credit cards; Tube: Baker Street) somehow appeals to every taste with its juice-based cocktails, huge portions, and contemporary diner-inspired vibe. The food is serviceable, the wait staff less so, but the hangout quotient is through the roof—insist on one of its cavernous booths. The soy-based "Chykn" BLT sandwich comes with homemade coleslaw and fries (£7.95), and the Lancashire Hot Pot (a mix of soy, gravy, and veggies served with mashed potatoes or brown rice) packs enough energy to carry anyone through the night. The cocktails prove this is no fuddy-duddy greenie joint.

££   Its huge selection of pastas (13 recipes) and pizzas (12), all at prices that hold under the £8 ceiling, won't win it awards for creativity, but it does qualify **Prezzo** (17 Hertford St., W1; ☎ 020/7499-4690; www.prezzoplc.co.uk; AE, MC, V; Tube: Green Park) as one of Mayfair's rare bargains. Sure, it's a chain, but only in England, and because it makes an effort to purchase good-quality pizza toppings and to adorn its dining room with fresh-cut flowers, it's a cut above.

££   All hail **Wagamama** ★★ (101a Wigmore St., W1; ☎ 020/7409-0111; www.wagamama.com; AE, MC, V; Tube: Bond Street;)! It's impossible to overstate the addictive popularity of this sociable, stylish noodle bar. There are 22 locations in town, each one more packed than the other; this one is tucked behind Selfridges at Duke Street, perfect for Oxford Street shoppers. Diners are seated at long, communal wooden tables, so you'll have ample opportunity to meet your neighbor, and orders are transmitted by handheld tablets straight to the kitchen. Part of the appeal is the varied menu that includes ramen, kare noodles, teppan, and chilli men, served in deep white bowls, no skimping on the ingredients or the spice. Teens love it. Mains span £6.10 to £8.95, which pound-earning Londoners find marvelously cheap, but I think is high enough to be mostly a dinner option. Some of the best-located branches are at 4 Streatham St. (Tube: Tottenham Court Road); 1 Tavistock St., south of Covent Garden (Tube: Covent Garden); 8 Norris St. (Tube: Piccadilly Circus); Tower Place, next to the Tower of London (Tube: Tower Hill); at Harvey Nichols, 109-125 Knightsbridge (Tube: Knightsbridge); and Royal Festival Hall (Tube: Waterloo).

High Tea, Low £

Nowadays, with a Starbucks on every British corner, only tourists and matrons with ice in their veins partake of high tea. But I know, I know. That doesn't mean you wouldn't like to try it, especially since you're in London, right? The Thames Room at the Savoy Hotel and the English Tea Room at Brown's Hotel are lovely—if you want to part with £30 per person. You can save a little by choosing Fortnum & Mason, but is £22 for tea and teeny sandwiches really such a deal? Only your creditors think so. Instead, try these spots for afternoon tea, generally from 3pm to 6pm. It pays to reserve:

Bramah Tea and Coffee Museum (40 Southwark St., SE1; ☎ 020/7403-5650; www.bramahmuseum.co.uk; AE, MC, V; Tube: London Bridge) is run by passionate people who know their Assams from their Oolongs. So their afternoon teas (Cream Tea: £7 with scones and clotted cream; Afternoon Tea: £9 with sandwiches and cake) feature a properly chosen leaf, assiduously brewed. The setting is simple, but you can visit the adjoining museum afterward, and you might even learn something.

Great Court Restaurant at the British Museum (Great Russell Street; WC1; ☎ 020/7323-8990; www.thebritishmuseum.ac.uk; MC, V; Tube: Russell Square). Tea and a fruit scone with clotted cream and jam, and finger sandwiches are £8.95. Or do the whole lot, plus sparkling wine and cake, for £13.95—all under the dazzling glass-and-steel canopy in the museum's courtyard, overlooking the famed Reading Room. It's not the best tea in London, but who cares when the setting is so sterling.

Tea Palace (175 Westbourne Grove, W11; ☎ 020/7727-2600; www.tea palace.co.uk; AE, MC, V; Tube: Westbourne Park), at the top end of Notting Hill, was set up as an alternative to high-priced tourist traps; it delivers the same upper-class frippery for £12 (although a single pot, without extras, costs from £3.50). The tea is impeccably chosen, and it comes with plenty of scones, sandwiches, and organic jam.

££–£££   Mayfair is hardly crawling with restaurants that don't require second mortgages, but **Straits** (5 White Horse St., W1; ☎ 020/7493-3986; www.thestraits. co.uk; AE, MC, V; Tube: Green Park), a reasonable South Asian choice near Shepherd Market, is relaxed, tasty, and has a staff that senses how attentive you want them to be. The cuisine is based on flavors from Thailand, Malaysia, and Singapore, including greatest hits like *nasi goreng* (fried rice with eggs, chicken, king prawns, and vegetables, £8.95) and the *tahu goreng claypot* (fried bean curd and veggies, £7.95). Singapore laksa (£8.95) is bountiful and plenty spicy. Straits often trots out £6 two-course lunches.

£££–££££   I have little praise for **The Hard Rock Cafe** (150 Old Park Lane, W1; ☎ 020/7514-1700; www.hardrock.com; AE, MC, V; Tube: Hyde Park Corner), located since 1971 near Hyde Park Corner. You'll find one in every town from Key West to Kuwait, its burgers (though excellent and sizable) hover around an outrageous £9 to £10, much of the so-called memorabilia consists of instruments that big names played maybe once, and waiting up to 90 minutes for a table chews up time that could be used for more authentic touring. It's true that this Hard Rock was the world's first, but it's also true (and telling) that its corporate headquarters has moved to Orlando, Florida, and no rock star would be caught dead in there today (they're at The Ivy instead). About as hard-rockin' as Barry Manilow, it's strictly a milquetoast tourist joint, so let no one convince you that it's the thing to do in London. You can barely move for all the American tourists—there are so many that it accepts U.S. dollars. So why is it in this book? One, because some visitors demand to see it. Two, because rugrats often dig it. And three, its mini museum of rock lore, The Vault, is free and open to the public (see John Lennon's revisions to the lyrics of "Imagine" and Jimi Hendrix's guitar), and that I applaud, even if it's just a come-on to funnel tourists through its merchandise store.

SOHO, COVENT GARDEN & THE CENTRAL WEST END

Everyone ends up around here, the dining and entertainment hub of London, for at least a day or two of their London odyssey. Naturally, a miasma of dining also-rans has sprung up, from junky steam-table buffets to the usual fast-food culprits to overpriced bistros that cook up a glitzy image better than anything they serve.

Soho's southern fringe hosts a meager Chinatown in the neon-tinted 2-block section between Leicester Square and Shaftesbury Avenue. The district survives mostly as a tourist attraction, and I don't think many of its restaurants are distinguished enough to single out.

£   Italians settled Soho in the 1940s, and before they decamped for the suburbs, they bequeathed the district with a set of mod, gleaming coffee bars and caffs. The most vibrant is **Bar Italia** ★ (22 Frith St., W1; ☎ 020/7437-4520; AE, MC, V; Tube: Leicester Square), a haunt of slumming celebrities and artists, yet modest enough for the rest of us. While the place is busy all day—making simple sandwiches, delivering pastries—it swells with revelers after midnight. Even Rome doesn't have bars that steam, press, and shuffle cups of strong coffee with such

West End Dining

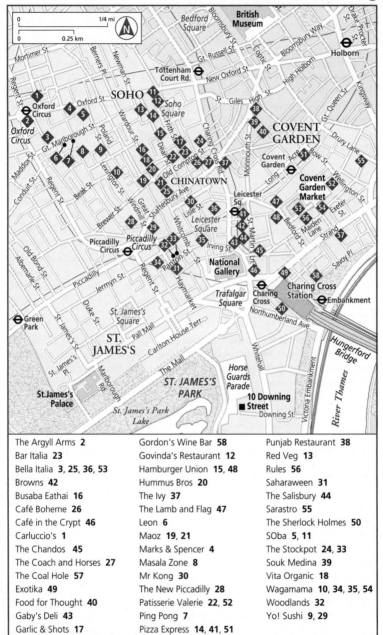

The Argyll Arms **2**	Gordon's Wine Bar **58**	Punjab Restaurant **38**
Bar Italia **23**	Govinda's Restaurant **12**	Red Veg **13**
Bella Italia **3**, **25**, **36**, **53**	Hamburger Union **15**, **48**	Rules **56**
Browns **42**	Hummus Bros **20**	Saharaween **31**
Busaba Eathai **16**	The Ivy **37**	The Salisbury **44**
Café Boheme **26**	The Lamb and Flag **47**	Sarastro **55**
Café in the Crypt **46**	Leon **6**	The Sherlock Holmes **50**
Carluccio's **1**	Maoz **19**, **21**	SOba **5**, **11**
The Chandos **45**	Marks & Spencer **4**	The Stockpot **24**, **33**
The Coach and Horses **27**	Masala Zone **8**	Souk Medina **39**
The Coal Hole **57**	Mr Kong **30**	Vita Organic **18**
Exotika **49**	The New Piccadilly **28**	Wagamama **10**, **34**, **35**, **54**
Food for Thought **40**	Patisserie Valerie **22**, **52**	Woodlands **32**
Gaby's Deli **43**	Ping Pong **7**	Yo! Sushi **9**, **29**
Garlic & Shots **17**	Pizza Express **14**, **41**, **51**	

gusto. "Like everything in this city that Londoners really enjoy, it reminds us of being abroad," quipped the *Guardian*. Whatever; it practically leaks hipness.

£ Strictly for quick bites—a common need if you're prowling the bars and clubs—**Maoz** (43 Old Compton St., W1; ☎ 020/7851-1586; www.maozveg.com; no credit cards; Tube: Piccadilly Circus; or 4 Brewer St.; ☎ 020/7734 9414; Tube: Piccadilly Circus) is a modern-looking, forward-thinking Dutch chain. Its two glassy Soho locations are within a falafel ball's toss from each other; the Old Compton Street spot, scarcely 100 paces east of its sister, has more indoor seating, but both are good for people-watching. Complete meals—falafel, fries, and a drink—cost from £3.80.

£ Although the communist theme is tasteless (what does the face of Che Guevara have to do with everything being "cooked to order?"), the food is anything but. **Red Veg** (95 Dean St., W1; ☎ 020/7437-3109; www.redveg.com; no credit cards; Tube: Tottenham Court Road), perhaps compensating for the bloodshed fostered by Guevara, serves no meat. Instead, you get inventive and remarkably flavorful tofu concoctions like the RedVeg burger (£2.85), the spicy ChilliVeg burger (£2.85), hickory smoked veg burger (£2.95), and vegwurst vegetarian hotdogs (£2.85). Falafel sandwiches (£3.85) and fries (from £1.05) round out the healthy-fast-food experiment. If you're keen, everything can be made vegan, but the seating isn't so accommodating; there's barely enough space to turn around in.

£ **The Stockpot** ★★ (18 Old Compton St., W1; ☎ 020/7287-1066; no credit cards; Tube: Leicester Square), high on function and low on glamour, could qualify as a founding member of London's Budget Hall of Fame. It's been indispensable to scrimping visitors and families for years and got me through many a lean day of backpacking. A perennial appearance is made by the country pâté, as wide as a fist. Other common cameos are made by vegetarian moussaka, omelettes, and beef stroganoff. No dish will set you back more than £5, though a two-course set menu is £5.30, and all portions overflow their plates. A glass of house wine is £1.95, and the whole bottle just £7.60. On one recent visit, a brief power outage interrupted my dinner. "Just like the food," my neighbor inveighed, "it has a certain Eastern Bloc flavor." There are two more locations: one a few blocks south at 38 Panton St. (Tube: Leicester Square), and one at 273 King's Rd. in Chelsea (Tube: South Kensington or Sloane Square).

£–££ The "pure vegetarian" **Govinda's Restaurant** (10 Soho St., W1; ☎ 020/7437-4928; www.iskcon-london.org/govindas; AE, MC, V; Closed Sun; Tube: Tottenham Court Road) is run by the Hare Krishna movement, which also operates the Radha Krishna Temple next door, so the staff is unsettlingly smiley—not all that common in mind-your-own-business Europe. The cooking style is "karma free" and Vedic, meaning no meat, onions, garlic, eggs, or mushrooms, which some diners mistake for unintentional blandness, and others cherish for its simplicity. Soho's vegetarian options have grown in number and in hipness since Govinda's first opened its doors, but its value has never changed. After 3pm but before the dinner rush, you can eat all you want for £5.95; during peak times, prices for a single plate are about a £1 less, and £2 less if you order for takeaway.

Chains of Love

In many places, restaurants run by corporations are the bane of authentic dining. But London is a different beast. Some of its best restaurant choices are part of local or British chains. Being part of one doesn't automatically mean the food is pre-frozen or machine-made. It often just means that a single restaurant became so popular that its owners decided to open more outlets in other parts of town.

In this guide, rather than duplicate a restaurant in every location where it's found, I've named each chain once followed by a list of other locations, organized by Tube stop. Below is a geographic rundown of the strongest chains in this chapter; where you see a name in italics, that chain's description is located in that neighborhood's section.

Bloomsbury and Fitzrovia: Ask, Busaba Eathai, *Pizza Express,* Wagamama

Marylebone and Mayfair: Ask, Bella Italia, Busaba Eathai, Browns, *Carluccio's, Le Pain Quotidien,* Patisserie Valerie, Ping Pong, Pizza Express, *Square Pie, Wagamama,* Woodlands, Yo! Sushi

Soho and Covent Garden: Bella Italia, *Browns, Busaba Eathai, Leon,* Masala Zone, *Patisserie Valerie, Ping Pong,* Pizza Express, *The Stockpot,* Wagamama, *Woodlands,* Yo! Sushi

The City: Carluccio's, Leon, *Little Bay,* Pizza Express, *S&M Café,* Square Pie, Wagamama, Yo! Sushi

Southwark and Borough: Pizza Express, Wagamama, *Yo! Sushi*

Victoria and Chelsea: *Ask,* Bella Italia, Pizza Express, The Stockpot, Wagamama, Yo! Sushi

Knightsbridge, Kensington, and Earl's Court: *Bella Italia,* Carluccio's, Le Pain Quotidien, Little Bay, *Masala Zone,* Patisserie Valerie, Pizza Express, Wagamama, Yo! Sushi

Paddington, Bayswater, and Notting Hill: Carluccio's, Ping Pong, Pizza Express, S&M Café

Islington: Browns, Carluccio's, Masala Zone, S&M Café, Wagamama, Yo! Sushi

If you have a religious issue with your dinner being offered to Lord Krishna before being served to you, skip this one. Also skip the desserts, since they're boring.

£–££   You'd think the last thing Soho needs is another healthy place, but the heaping bowls at finger-lickin' **Hummus Bros** ★ (88 Wardour St., W1; ☎ 020/7734-1311; www.hbros.co.uk; AE, MC, V; Tube: Piccadilly Circus or Tottenham Court Road) are so tasty, and the service so merry, that you'd be wrong. In a shared-table, airy eating hall, you pick your hummus bowl size (a regular, for £4.50–£6, comes with two pitas, a small costs £3.50–£5, with one pita) and then decide on the crowning pile of goodness: guacamole, mushroom (a portobello-button mix), chunky beef, chicken, or three other veggie options. The food arrives warm, accompanied by little dishes of chopped chillis and lemon juice, and you just scoop away with your pita. Save room for *malabi,* a light-tasting milk custard drizzled with date honey, for £2. Rich homemade brownies are £2. Everything is 50p to £1 cheaper before 4:30pm.

£–££   The meat-and-all options at **Leon** ★ (35-36 Great Marlborough St., W1; ☎ 020/7437-5280; AE, MC, V; Tube: Oxford Circus; or 12 Ludgate Circus, EC4; ☎ 020/7489-1580; www.leonrestaurants.co.uk; Tube: Blackfriars) are fashioned from a free trade/organic shopping list, and in 2005, true to the city's love affair with healthy eating, it was rated the best new restaurant in Britain. Its block wood tables and chairs are usually crammed with young office girls grabbing a healthy, casual meal. If it's full (a likelihood), pack your meal in one of the cute brown folding boxes and eat al fresco on Carnaby Street. The menu is seasonal, but the best recurring options include Moroccan meat balls in plenty of red sauce; grilled *halloumi;* a "superfood" salad combining energizing ingredients such as beans; and organic chocolate bars. Drinks are sweetened with natural fruit sugar instead of refined sugar. Other locations are about 10 minutes' walk west of St. Paul's Cathedral and at 136 Brompton Rd., near Harrods (Tube: Knightsbridge).

£–££   If you like fine pastry but your thighs like it more, you might want to keep your distance from **Patisserie Valerie** (44 Old Compton St., W1; ☎ 020/7437-3466; www.patisserie-valerie.co.uk; AE, MC, V; Tube: Leicester Square). Its picture-window frontage, a tempting ballet of pastry, croissants, mousses, marzipan novelties, and other lush confections, will do no favors for your pant size. If you'd rather avoid the buttery, fork-fed indulgences, know that you can also get fresh espressos and fruit juices. Valerie has five locations, but it was in Soho first, since 1926. The cafe also does light meals and savories (chicken and bacon salad, butterfly grilled prawns) for £6 to £8. Its upstairs 50-seat cafe churns out popular English breakfasts. There's a location across from Harrods at 215 Brompton Rd. (Tube: Knightsbridge), at 8 Russell St. (Tube: Covent Garden), and at 105 Marylebone High St. (Tube: Baker Street).

£–££   The industrial-chic noodle bar **SOba** (11-13 Soho St., W1; ☎ 020/7287-7300; www.soba.co.uk; AE, MC, V; Tube: Tottenham Court Road) has a deal worth noting: mains are £4.50 between 4 and 7pm Monday through Wednesday, noon to 5pm Saturday, and all day Sunday. Outside of then, they're a less thrilling £6 to £7, so time your visit. SOba's value-minded menu is dead-on Japanese, with 13 kinds of stir-fry noodles (seafood yaki udon, chicken yaki soba), 11 rice dishes (tofu black bean, chicken fried rice), and slightly more adventurous sides (salt and pepper squid, won tons). There's another branch a few blocks west at 38 Poland St. (Tube: Tottenham Court Road). The Soho Street location cooks until midnight.

££–£££   Founded by Alan Yau, the renegade who began the revolutionary Wagamama chain (p. 100), **Busaba Eathai** ★★ (106-110 Wardour St., W1; ☎ 020/7255-8686; AE, MC, V; Tube: Piccadilly Circus) duplicates its forebearer's formula: a high-design dining area, convivial tables shared with strangers, and a Thai-inspired menu that abandons curry-and-rice banality. I've yet to sample a dish I couldn't say something nice about, be it the wok-prepared ginger beef with spring onion (£6.90), the spicy *sen chan phad Thai* (noodles with prawn, peanut, green mango, and crab meat, £8.30), or the butternut pumpkin curry with cucumber relish (£6.40). This high-minded yet populist-priced supper has enchanted the masses, so you'll probably wait for a seat even though turnover is quick. Check out the signs for the toilet, which depict the position each gender must adopt in order to use the facilities. It's also at Marylebone (8-13 Bird St., W1; Tube: Bond Street) and Bloomsbury (22 Store St., WC1; Tube: Goodge Street).

££–£££   Open until 2:45am Monday through Saturday (till 11pm Sun), the agreeable, casual Parisian brasserie **Café Boheme** (13-17 Old Compton St., W1; ☎ 020/7734-0623; cafeboheme.co.uk; AE, MC, V; Tube: Leicester Square) is where you should go for an unpretentious, noisy late meal during a night out at the bars. Little plates (£5) include fried camembert and frog's legs, but I gravitate toward its substantial and decent sandwiches (chicken club with perfectly crispy pomme frites (£8), salads (goat's cheese with basic and olive tapenade, £6.50 small and £10.50 large), and soups (pea and ham, £4.50). Main plates are expensive for bistro fare (£10–£14), but the prix fixe, at £12 for two courses and £14 for two, works better. After midnight, options are restricted to a few breakfast items, burgers, salads, and meats (£5–£10), which is more than most cafes in the area offer. Many afternoons, the cafe hosts live jazz. The staff can be overworked.

££–£££   A chic fusion of Chinese dim sum and cocktail lounge, **Ping Pong** ★ (45 Great Marlborough St., W1; ☎ 020/7851-6969; www.pingpongdimsum.com; AE, MC, V; Tube: Oxford Circus) boasts such a cutting-edge, glass-and-steel design (tip: check out the space-age toilets) that it appears at first to be one of the West End's many overpriced clubhouses for young, upper-class toffs. Yet it's affordable, with a service staff willing to walk newbies through the process. Baskets of piping hot dumplings (£2.80 for four pieces) arrive almost as quickly as they're ordered, and they're stacked in towers on your table as a trophy of your progress. The cocktails bear repeating, too (I like the vanilla, lemon, and vodka, served in a huge milk glass, for £5.50). If you can't decide, go for the "Dumpling fix" (£10.90), which buys 10 various pieces, sticky rice, and two scoops of ice cream for dessert. The Jasmine tea, made with a huge flower suspended in a glass, is just £1.75. The brand began in 2005 and has spread to 10 Paddington St. (Tube: Baker Street), 29a James St. (Tube: Bond Street), and 74-76 Westbourne Grove (Tube: Bayswater).

££–£££   The latest fringe culinary trend to delight London is the subjective "superfood" movement, in which recipes are formulated according to how their ingredients react in the body once metabolized. The menu at Soho's vegetarian, carcinogen-free **Vita Organic** (74 Wardour St., WC1; ☎ 020/7734-8986; www. vitaorganic.co.uk; no credit cards; Tube: Piccadilly Circus) is annotated according to how each dish is thought to affect your chakras. At dinner, which is a crowded, slow-service affair conducted at communal tables under candlelight, three heaping buffet-style helpings (lots of bean-based casseroles, bakes, and salads) cost £5.50. Hearty soups—nine choices, including Orange Sweet Potato Dal and Parsnip Fennel Mushroom—cost £3.90.

£££–££££   I am repeatedly drawn to **Garlic & Shots** ★ (14 Frith St., W1; ☎ 020/7734-9505; www.garlicandshots.com; AE, MC, V; Tube: Leicester Square) despite its high prices. It's simply too much fun. Everything at this scruffy bar and restaurant, run by tattooed Swedes and frequented late at night by Scandinavian headbangers (it sounds like I'm making this up, doesn't it?) is infused with doses of garlic. Seriously—it's even floating in the beer. Mains (£9.10–£14.75) are mostly infused versions of American comfort food, such as "XXX-Hot Texas Chili in a Pan" (just what it says), spaghetti, and honey-roasted baby back ribs. The house clove even takes a final bow at dessert; the garlic honey ice cream is remarkably supple. As for the "shots," those are the 101 varieties of vodka shooters designed to put you (and your deadly breath) under the table, from the clever Bloodshot, a reduced Bloody Mary (vodka, tomato, garlic, chili), and the tummy-tangling Yellow Death (tequila, bananas, and rum). You'll be a social and sexual pariah for a while, and small children will flee on your approach—but you'll leave smiling.

COVENT GARDEN & LEICESTER SQUARE

While the streets of Soho are great for cafes and bars for quicker bites and after-hours noshes, the lanes around Covent Garden are best for sit-down establishments and destination restaurants where you'd be more likely to pass an evening.

£–££   You gotta love the **Café in the Crypt** ★ (Trafalgar Square, WC2; ☎ 020/7766-1158; www.stmartin-in-the-fields.org; MC, V; Tube: Charing Cross), the finest graveyard bistro I know. Under the sanctuary of the historic St Martin's in the Fields church, atop the gravestones of eighteenth-century Londoners, one of the West End's sharpest bargains is served each day. The menu at this dependable cafeteria changes daily, but the satisfying (if not quite gourmet) options always include a few hot meat mains, a vegetarian choice, soups, and a traditional English dessert such as bread and butter pudding or apple crumble. The soup-and-pudding deal is £5.25, and mains are £5.95 to £7.50, including three vegetables. Soup with bread is £2.75. As proof that this busy diner isn't stuffy (after all, it shares space with a gift shop and a brass rubbing center), it even serves wine for £2.95 a glass. Twice a month, it hosts evening jazz nights (£3–£5 entry) along with dinner.

£–££   Don't be put off by the dreadful name: **Exotika** (7 Villiers St., WC2; ☎ 020/7939-6133; www.exotika.co.uk; AE, MC, V; Tube: Charing Cross or Embankment), done up in sleek black-and-red geometrics, is actually one of the best values in the Trafalgar Square area. The food, like so much in London, is a wobbly fusion of Asian and European flavors, and everything's fairly healthy, often steam-cooked, and quickly served. Salads are a highlight; the Italian Parma has plenty of ham, tomatoes and red peppers with olives, pistachios, and spinach (£5.10). Cooked dishes are inventive for the price: The Moroccan chicken with apricot and pine nut couscous, a tangy blend of savory and sweet, comes to mind, as does the chicken tikka masala with basmati rice, which has a clean taste for such a traditionally heavy dish (£5.90). Takeaway is 30p to 70p cheaper.

£–££ A long-running vegetarian whole foods kitchen, **Food for Thought** (31 Neal St., WC2; ☎ 020/7836-0239; no credit cards; closes at 8:30pm Mon–Fri, 8pm Sat, and 4:30pm Sun; Tube: Covent Garden), feels like a commune, what with the mismatched plates, and a changing slate of three or four dinner items (casseroles, salads, stir-fries, bakes, couscous, etc.) that, often, run out after 6 or 7pm. The basement dining room is elbow-to-elbow—just eight tables. I find the offerings (spooned out in huge portions) to be heavy on the beans, and I make liberal use of the salt and pepper since the food is so "clean," but I also like the earthy, doing-right-by-my-body sensation I get after I wipe my plate here. There's no doubt the price is right, especially for the area. The fruity, sugary "scrunch" at dessert reverses some of the virtuous feelings. A full dinner tops out at £6.50, but most people will be satisfied with what £4.50 buys.

£–££ Strong in the pretheater eat-and-run department, the West End standby **Gaby's Deli** (30 Charing Cross Rd., WC2; ☎ 020/7836-4233; no credit cards; Tube: Leicester Square) makes a lame attempt at rustic decor—pinning ladles to the wall does not a design concept make—but it puts more effort into its singularly afford-able bites. Grab stuff a la carte (falafel for £3, salt beef sandwiches for £5) or spring for the day's special (a typical sample: giant stuffed peppers served with falafel balls or a starter of tuna salad, £6.50). The vegetable fritters (£3 with salad), big as saucers and stacked in the window, often stop passersby in their tracks.

££ One of the Chinatown rabble worth pausing for, the cramped **Mr. Kong** (21 Lisle St., WC2; ☎ 020/7437-7341; AE, MC, V; Tube: Leicester Square), across from the Prince Charles Cinema, works from a lengthy Chinese menu, and works it well. It's not much to look at, and its steely waiters treat patrons as little more than business transactions, but it's one of the few establishments to supplement Western-style Chinese dishes with daring ones (starring eel, soft-shell crab with chilies, and the like, mostly in the £6 zone). In addition to laying claim to a following of Asian-born devotees, who order razor clams and scallops by the bowl-ful, it's kid-friendly and open until 3am nightly.

££–£££ In London, there's a Browns for fashion, and a Brown's Hotel, but the spacious cafe **Browns** ★ (82-82 St. Martins Lane, WC2; ☎ 020/7497-5050; www. browns-restaurants.com; AE, MC, V; Tube: Leicester Square) is the only affordable one. Installed in the former Westminster County Courts, it serves updated English food and imported beer. The globe lanterns, enormous mirrors, and staff buttoned into crisp white oxford shirts impart the sense of a Gilded Age chop house. Expect lots of rich ingredients such as goat's cheese salad, haddock and chips battered with Leffe beer, and baked mushroom pudding with tomato au jus. Despite such indulgent aspirations, £5.95 lunch specials are always posted on the blackboards, and the pretheater menu gets you two courses for £11. Otherwise, many mains are under £10. There's another Brown's at 47 Maddox St. in Mayfair (Tube: Oxford Circus) and at 9 Islington Green (Tube: Angel).

££–£££ The victuals are barely more than steam-table chow, but the atmos-phere is peerless at **Gordon's Wine Bar** ★★★ (47 Villiers St., WC2; ☎ 020/7930-1408; www.gordonswinebar.com; AE, MC, V; Tube: Charing Cross or Embankment),

London's oldest wine bar. It was established in 1890 (when Rudyard Kipling lived upstairs) and, thank goodness, hasn't been significantly refurbished since. These crusty old cellars are wallpapered with important newspaper front pages from the 20th century—the Crystal Palace's destruction by fire, the death of King George VI—while ceiling fans threaten to come loose from their screws. Everything has been dyed a mustardy ochre from more than 42,000 evenings of tobacco smoke. It's so resistant to change that tables are still candlelit, and music is not played. Oddly, it only takes reservations during quieter times, so come down well before offices let out to secure seating in the tight, craggy cellars, which tunnel intimately beneath Viliers Street. Wine by the glass is £3.40 to £4.45, including Madeiras, dry sherries, and even bottles from India and Corsica; and eats include poached salmon with salad (£7.95) and homemade Scotch eggs, a favorite (£5.95). Sundays see a complete roast (meat, veggies, pudding) for £8.95.

££–£££   Ignore that it looks like every other curry shop sponging off the Covent Garden tourist trade. **The Punjab Restaurant** ★★★ (80 Neal St., WC2; ☎ 020/7836-9787; www.punjab.co.uk; AE, MC, V; Tube: Covent Garden) has been cooking since 1947—it proclaims itself the oldest North Indian restaurant in the U.K. Beneath its golden twill wallpaper, you could end up sitting next to an elderly fellow who has his lunch there five times a week, or by editors hashing out the layout of their new children's book. The common bond, of course, is superlative cooking, light on the oil and *ghee* (clarified butter). Meats (from £7.50) and tandoori (from £7.95) have been well marinated and so they arrive tender. But what I personally come back for, and dream about when I'm not in London, is the *anari gosht,* or pomegranate flavor lamb (£8.40). The flavors dovetail gorgeously with every bite, winding up with a slight spicy twang. The menu is cheeky, too: "If you have any erotic activities planned for after you leave us, perhaps you should resist this sensational garlic naan." (And no, you shouldn't.) I have been threatened with bodily harm for revealing this find, but to share such bliss, it's worth it.

££–£££   Unbeknownst to many tourists, an oasis of fun restaurants awaits on the street south of Leicester Square, and one of its most enjoyable is **Saharaween** ★ (3 Panton St., W1; ☎ 020/7930-2777; AE, MC, V; Tube: Leicester Square), which means "people of the Sahara." Relaxation sets in when you cross its threshold. In a dim, cool, two-level space, candles flicker behind lattices, fabric billows against the ceiling, and couples lounge on pillows eating off silver tables. (There are standard seats, too.) Start with the satisfying chorba soup (£4), a North African specialty as velvety as chili without meat. Move on to couscous with chicken (£9) or, more theatrically, to a tagine casbah (stew) of minced meat, garlic, coriander, and cumin prepared in a clay pot and topped with egg, for £10; when it arrives, the waitress lifts its lid, releasing a flourish of steam. The service is relaxed, so set aside at least an hour—longer if you'd like to puff on the hookah pipe.

££–£££   A 30-strong international vegetarian chain, **Woodlands** (37 Panton St., SW1; ☎ 020/7839-7258; www.woodlandsrestaurant.co.uk; AE, MC, V; Tube: Leicester Square) should be seen for what it is: a cheap place for reliable South

Meat the Newcomers

As much as it irks Londoners to admit they're adopting any aspect of American culture, it's true that the humble hamburger is becoming a staple of the British dining scene. Not only does every pub now serve them along with ales and lagers, but a few restaurants even specialize in replicating, to fine effect, that delicacy of the Texas plains. Here's how they stack up:

££ Fine Burger Co. (50 James St., W1; ☎ 020/7224-1890; www.fine burger.co.uk; Tube: Bond Street; or 330 Upper St., N1; ☎ 020/7359-3026; Tube: Angel; AE, MC, V). Regular: £5.25. With cheese: £6.25. Weirdest: Satay, with spicy peanut sauce, coriander, and sweet chili, £6.50. Guiltiest pleasure: Peanut butter and banana milkshake, £3.30.

£–££ Hamburger Union (2-4 Garrick St., WC2; ☎ 020/7379-0412; www.hamburgerunion.com; MC, V; Tube: Covent Garden; or 23-25 Dean St., W1; ☎ 020/7437-6004; Tube: Tottenham Court Road; or 341 Upper St., N1; ☎ 020/7359-4436; Tube: Angel). Regular: £3.95. With cheese: £4.50. Weirdest: "Protein style," between lettuce instead of a bun, same prices. Guiltiest pleasure: Crème de Menthe cocktail milkshake, £3.95.

££ The Ultimate Burger (34 New Oxford St., WC1; ☎ 020/7436-6641; www.ultimateburger.co.uk; AE, MC, V; Tube: Holborn; or 98 Tottenham Court Rd., W1; ☎ 020/7436-5355; Tube: Warren Street). Regular: £5.45. With cheese: £5.95. Weirdest: Surf and Turf, with deep-fried spicy prawns and Monterey Jack cheese, £6.95. Guiltiest pleasure: Chili fries, £2.95.

Indian food. It's decorated as if someone raided Crate & Barrel, and the recorded smooth jazz is just as bland. Woodlands does a range of dishes, though, including snack-worthy *chaat* (crispy pastry rounds you stuff with chutneys, £4.95), but its signature is the dosa, an enormous crepe made from soaked lentils and rice, formed into a cone, and stuffed with one of eight fillings. The onion *rava masala dosa,* my favorite, has a crepe flecked with sautéed green chilies and a filling of potatoes, onions, and peas. Of course, when a dosa arrives, your table suddenly looks like an old gramophone. Order a Kingfisher, an authentic Indian beer (slogan: "most thrilling chilled"). It's also at 77 Marylebone Lane (Tube: Bond Street).

£££–££££   Keep your eyes peeled for celebrities at **The Ivy** ✪ (1 West St,. WC1; ☎ 020/7836-4751; www.the-ivy.co.uk; AE, MC, V; Tube: Leicester Square or Covent Garden); Britain's biggest stars (Look! Hugh Grant! Ooh! Simon Cowell!) have been coming here for years and show no signs of abandoning its wood paneling and stained glass for greener pastures. The food is sumptuous, spanning

Britain to Thailand to Italy, and served by some of the city's most professional waiters. Try the slow-roasted pork belly (£15), something off the asparagus-only submenu, or a freshened-up view on fish and chips with deep-fried haddock served with minted pea puree and chips (£17). When it's in season, don't miss the stunner of a rhubarb pie. Its weekend lunch set meal, for around £22 for three courses, is a bargain for cooking of this level. The crowd-pleasing luster is diminished by the policy of allowing smoking—a fault that may soon be changed through legislation. Book way ahead—like, now.

£££–££££   What if Mozart went insane? He'd open the flamboyant **Sarastro** ★ (126 Drury Lane, WC2; ☎ 020/7836-0101; www.sarastro-restaurant.com; AE, MC, V; Tube: Covent Garden), an over-the-top paean to the opulence of opera. Sarastro's every cranny has been gilded, sheathed in shimmering fabric, or filled with erotic statuary (you can't miss the self-pleasuring Diablo). Along the walls, ten intimate opera boxes, reached up precarious stairs, have been hammered up. You'd think that all this hammy folderol would come with tourist-trap prices, but amazingly, a standard two-course meal clocks in at only around £14. The menu—like it matters amid such eye candy—is Mediterranean, and not half bad. The "chicken Princess," tender and savory with asparagus and red wine sauce, goes for £9.95, while the top-of-the-line seafood salad with a whole dressed crab is £17. On Sundays and on Monday evenings, opera singers serenade diners.

£££–££££   If you want a West End restaurant experience that's both cool and reasonably priced, **Souk Medina** ★★ (1a Shorts Gardens, WC2; ☎ 020/7240-1796; www.soukrestaurant.co.uk; AE, MC, V; Tube: Covent Garden) plays the lively Marrakech hideaway to the hilt—stairways are elaborately candlelit and winding; and romantic nooks are heaped with pillows and illuminated by silvery lamps. Cocktails (the aicha martini has vodka, watermelon, and vanilla), dispensed by fez-wearing bartenders, are priced below the London average (£5.95). Couscous with chicken or *merguez* (lamb sausage) starts at £9.95, and clay-pot stews called tagines start at £9.95 (I love the lamb with prune and almonds); plenty of vegetarian versions (£8.95) are also on hand. After dinner, share a potbellied, silver shisha pipe packed with mild, flavored tobacco, easy even for nonsmokers (from £7.50). The place is jumping on weekends, so reserve ahead. If you want a subtler Moroccan evening, try Saharaween on nearby Panton Street.

££££   For a high-end kitchen that takes British cuisine seriously, **Rules** (35 Maiden Lane, WC1; ☎ 020/7836-5314; www.rules.co.uk; AE, MC, V; Tube: Covent Garden) is an iconic choice. In fact, it's London's oldest restaurant, having been cooking since 1798. Being a major stop on the tourist trail has gone slightly to its head, and its view of a dining experience is steeped in its own hype; beer comes in a "silver tankard," for example, and the dining rooms are an overdressed mélange of yellowing etchings, antlers, and rich red fabrics. But what's on the plate, much of it English-reared meat like venison and pheasant, suits the lofty set pieces: steak and kidney pie with oyster pudding (£17), grilled calves liver and bacon (£18), and roast rack of West Devon lamb (£20). For a real taste of classic England, try a cool glass of Pimms No. 1 Cup (£7), an apertif of orange peel, Champagne, and the famous tonic made of herbs and quinine.

WESTMINSTER & ST. JAMES'S

I'll warn you now: Westminster may be where you find some of the city's top tourist attractions, but it's a dead zone for food.

££–£££   You'll thank me later for pointing you toward **Tevere Café Restaurant** (47 Great Peter St., SW1; ☎ 020/7222-4901; no credit cards; Mon–Fri 11:30am–3pm; Tube: Westminster) a family-run Italian cafeteria in a defiantly 1950s diner setting, complete with sailboat-themed transom glass. It's the sort of place where waitresses wear too much makeup and yell at the chef when he takes too long, and its clientele is mostly government workers from the surrounding buildings. Pair one of 7 pastas with one of 8 sauces (£7–£7.80), spring for one of 11 pizzas (£6.80–£7.80), or spring for the simple fish and chips (£7.50–£9). To get here from Westminster Abbey, take the Dean's Yard exit, turn left, and then veer left again down Great Smith Street until you reach the corner of Great Peter Street.

THE CITY, SPITALFIELDS & WHITECHAPEL

£   The city's most famous bakery, **Beigel Bake** ★★★ (159 Brick Lane, E1; ☎ 020/7729-0616; no credit cards; Tube: Liverpool Street) never closes but there's always a line. The queue moves quickly, though, and it snakes past the kitchen, where you can glimpse the bakers using strange contraptions and wooden planks. The patronage is a microcosm of London, ranging from bikers to hipsters to arrogant yuppies to the homeless. Its 15p beigels ("BI-gulls"), while Kosher, are not as puffy or as salty as the New York "bagel" variety. With smoked salmon, they're just £1.20, and they're 80p with cream cheese. Its pastries are gorgeous, too: The 60p

---

Brick Lane: 24-hour Playground

Central London has few thoroughfares that are associated with a single ethnic group or nationality, but Brick Lane (so named for its medieval status as a source for bricks) has become so strongly identified with immigrants from the Indian subcontinent that its name has transcended geography to become a sort of shorthand term for England's South Asian population. In the span of just a few blocks, most of which have signage in both English and Bengali, some 40 Indian restaurants jockey for business. No discerning Londoner would claim that any serve the city's best Indian cuisine—most of them are run by Bangladeshi or Pakistani entrepreneurs catering to the average Englishman's watered-down notion of curry—or even that there's much difference between them, but it's nonetheless a terrific place to stroll along, leverage competition, and shop for a bargain meal. (Bring your own wine, though, since most are run by Muslims who don't sell alcohol.) By night, the street morphs into a hipster habitat as a major street for music venues. On Sunday mornings, it hosts a market for vintage clothes, produce, books, and art (www.bricklanemarket.com). Reach Brick Lane via the Aldgate, Aldgate East, or Liverpool Street Tube.

chocolate fudge brownie could be nursed for hours. Watching the clerks slice juicy chunks of pink salt beef in the window, then slather it onto a beigel with mustard from a crusty jar (£2.30), is an attraction unto itself.

£–££ In the eclectic Old Truman Brewery complex, the inviting **Café 1001** (1 Dray Walk, E1; ☎ 020/7247-9679; www.cafe1001.co.uk; no credit cards; Tube: Aldgate East), strewn with cushions and lit by votive candles, has the same owner as nightlife hub 93 Feet East, and goes for the same aloof crowd. The food is simple but cheap: lasagna with salad for £3.95, stuffed jacket potatoes for £3.50, and smoked salmon on a cream cheese bagel for an astoundingly low £1.80. There are also £6 set meals (dishes change daily) that come with a free glass of wine. Upstairs, coffee drinkers hang out on low leather sofas beneath concrete walls covered with poetry. By night, it converts into a laid-back lounge, and it hosts free live jazz on Wednesdays from 7pm to midnight.

£–££ Don't visit St. Paul's Cathedral on an empty stomach because the options within sight of the dome are priced to exploit the business crowd. A refreshing exception is the counter-service **De Gustibus** (53-55 Carter Lane, EC4; ☎ 020/7236-0056; www.degustibus.co.uk; closed weekends; MC, V; Tube: St. Paul's), on a side street south of the cathedral's entrance. Under a veritable solar system of spherical white lamps, handmade European baked goods and sandwiches are produced, including croque monsieur (£2.95), couscous with roasted vegetables (£3.95), and the tortino, a focaccia filled with vegetables and fresh mozzarella (£2.95). Since eating at the tables costs another £1, enjoy your food on the benches a block east at Peter's Hill.

£–££ In this age, no one would dare name their takeaway something as hydrogenated as **The Fryer's Delight** ★★★ (19 Theobald's Rd., WC1; ☎ 020/7405-4114; no credit cards; closed Sun; Tube: Holborn or Chancery Lane). Fortunately, this takeaway is not of this age. It's a true old-world chippy, where the fish and chips are served crisp, the wooden booths date to the postwar days, and the men behind the counter gruffly demand to have your order. Prices are anachronistic, too: Of the six types of fish (I like the cod), nothing's more expensive than £4.20 (takeaway; eat-in prices are about £1 more), and most are around £3.50. Seamy? Not at all—it's just one of the last hangers-on from the lost fish-and-chips tradition, so get a taste while you still can. It's a 10-minute walk east of the British Museum.

£–££ England's country links rule **S&M Cafe** (48 Brushfield St., E1; ☎ 020/7247-2252; www.sandmcafe.co.uk; MC, V; Tube: Liverpool Street), also known as Sausage & Mash, opposite Spitalfields Market. Introduce yourself to the world of wieners at one of its diner-style tables, covered with classic red checkered plastic: Cumberlands are pork with "a touch of treacle;" Somersets are made with apples and cider; and the Glamorgan is a mix of leek and Caerphilly cheese (see, vegetarians aren't ignored). They make Oscar Meyer look like a clown. Don't forget the mushy peas—a lurid green, cherished British side. Full breakfasts are £4.95, all day. Two other outposts are well located for shoppers: 268 Portobello Rd. in Notting Hill (Tube: Ladbroke Grove), and 4-6 Essex Rd. in Islington (Tube: Angel). The Islington one is in a fine old cafeteria, once the long-standing Alfredo's, full of 50-year-old tilework, fittings, and signs ("Ices 3d. 4d. 6d.").

Grape Expectations

Many popular restaurants don't have licenses to serve alcohol, but they will allow you to bring your own ("B.Y.O."). Most places charge a £1 to £3 "corkage fee" for the privilege. Fortunately, the English don't tolerate a bad quaff, so even the cheapest bottles of store-bought stuff (£3–£6) are highly drinkable. You can pick up some excellent hooch on the go at the following common High Street chains:

Oddbins (www.oddbins.com)

Majestic Wine Warehouse (www.majestic.co.uk)

Marks and Spencer (www.marksandspencer.com)

Thresher (www.victoriawine.co.uk)

Sainsbury's (www.sainsburys.co.uk)

££   Of my favorite restaurant finds, **Little Bay** ✪✪✪ (171 Farringdon Rd., WC1; ☎ 020/7278-1234; www.little-bay.co.uk; MC, V; Tube: Farringdon) is a contender for first place. It's a tad out of the way (10 minutes' walk north of the Tube, opposite Vineyard Walk, or 15 minutes east of the British Museum), but that's why it's a find. The decor is beyond fab—a Romanesque fun house of plaster murals and gnarled chandeliers overseen by a massive mask of Zeus adorned with tendrils of metallic fabric. ("But he looks more like Jesus Christ with the Statue of Liberty's hat on," cracked my waitress one day.) Prices are simple: Starters are £1.99 from noon to 7pm, and £2.95 after that; mains are £5.95/£7.95 by the same clock; and sides are £1.95 all the time. Rarely has paying so little afforded such dignity: The menu changes, but on one visit, I received an astounding 22 mussels in my mussels marinier (shallots, garlic, and white wine) for my piddly £1.95—and yes, they were well sauced. Mains are just as generous. Possibilities include a duck and leek parcel with braised red cabbage and ginger and honey sauce; fillet of salmon with spicy coconut potatoes; and a confit of guinea fowl. It's a favorite of journalists from the *Guardian* offices nearby. Sunday is roast day: £5.95 including potatoes and vegetables.

SOUTHWARK & BOROUGH, INCLUDING AROUND WATERLOO STATION

£–££   One of those amazing discoveries, the **Southwark Cathedral Refectory** (London Bridge, SE1; ☎ 020/7407-5740; no credit cards; daily 10am–5pm; Tube: London Bridge) is on the Thames-facing side of the 900-year-old church. Wholesome as a church should be, it concentrates on freshly made soups (like coriander and carrot), sandwiches, quiche, and pasta and stir fry that's made-to-order (all £3–£6). This is no sloppy potluck; desserts are wickedly massive, and even the salads' honey-mustard dressing is made from the real stuff, not bottled junk. Try the elderflower presse, a typically English cordial. The Anglican Church, being modern, displays work by local artists, sells wine by the bottle, and even makes cute napkins with the church's logo on them.

££–££££   It's easy to go overboard at **Yo! Sushi** (Belvedere Rd., County Hall, SE1; ☎ 020/7928-8871; www.yosushi.com; MC, V; Tube: Westminster or Waterloo), on the street behind the London Eye box office, because it's one of those fun rotary sushi places—you know, you sit in front of a conveyor belt and grab what you want to eat off of it, and plates are colored according to how much they cost (the decent ones are £2–£5). Kids love it, but three plates make for a moderate lunch, and four could spell disaster for your day's spending. But the protein fix is refreshing for a bread- and noodle-obsessed city, and the fish is fresh. Just take some advice your meal should have heeded: Don't get hooked. Besides this location, there are ones at 5-14 St. Paul's Church Yard (Tube: St. Paul's), the Trocadero at 19 Rupert St. (Tube: Piccadilly Circus), Selfridge's at 400 Oxford St. (Tube: Bond Street), Harrods at 102-104 Brompton Rd. (Tube: Knightsbridge), Harvey Nichols at 102-125 Knightsbridge (Tube: Knightsbridge), among other spots.

Binging at Borough Market

Although about a dozen vendors at Southwark's **Borough Market** (8 Southwark St., SE1; ☎ 020/7407-1002; www.boroughmarket.org.uk; Tube: London Bridge) sell their countryside meats, cheeses, and vegetables all week long, make a point of dropping by on Friday noon to 6pm or Saturday from 9am to 4pm, when up to 50 additional vendors unpack and the awe-inspiring scene hits full swing. The best time to arrive is Friday ahead of the lunch crowds; Saturdays are plain nuts.

Work up an appetite at **Trethowan's Gorwydd Caerphilly,** which revitalized a nearly forgotten cheese variety—unpasteurized, consumed young, with a thick rind and a lemony taste—and now makes it on its 100-acre Welsh farm (around £1.50 per 100g). The **Northfield Farms** stall does organically raised beef and lamb burgers for £3.50, which attract quite a queue, but the most popular dish at the market is unquestionably the grilled chorizo sandwich at the **Brindisa** booth under the metal canopy; make sure you get yours with oil-drizzled piquillo peppers from Spain (£3). One stall over, at **Maria's Market Café,** the moon-faced proprietor slaves over a stove making fresh bubble (kind of a mushy version of home fries) that brings office workers from far and wide (it's £1 on a roll). Outside at 9 Stoney St., wash it down with whatever unusual brew is on tap this month (such as Park Star Brewing Company's espresso stout) at the **Market Porter,** which is known for daring microbrews. Put your feet up by its double-sided fireplace. Overhead by the Bedale Street market entrance, check out the hand-painted wooden panel listing the 90-year-old rent structure for stalls. **Dark Sugars** artisanal confectionary stall excels in mouthwatering bud-teasers such as extra bitter dark chocolate and Tia Maria truffle cake (£1.85–£2), and its delectable truffles (£5.50 for 100g) include chili, dry apple cider, and white chocolate with nutmeg. Got room left? Good—there are a few dozen more stalls to sample.

The M&S Break

If you're hungry and roaming a major shopping area, **Marks & Spencer** department stores are your stomach's salvation. Head straight to the basement of almost any outpost of the important British chain, where you'll find a spacious wonderland of ready-to-eat hot dishes, sandwiches, and soups, all usually well under the £5 notch. You'll find a large slate of seasonal food including wraps made with non-genetically modified ingredients, ice cream made with Channel Islands milk, fresh produce, fair-trade coffee . . . you get the idea. M&S's stand-alone **Simply Food** stores sell many of the same items. For B.Y.O. dinners, M&S sells inexpensive (under £5) but well-selected wines, too. Responding to the popularity of M&S's foods, grocery giant **Sainsbury's** now produces its own impressive line of prepared foods. M&S's largest store is at 458 Oxford St. (Tube: Marble Arch). Other handy branches include 173 Oxford St. (Tube: Oxford Street); 10 Cardinal Place, off Victoria Street (Tube: Victoria); and Simply Food at Euston, King's Cross, Liverpool Street, Marylebone, Paddington, Victoria, and Waterloo stations.

VICTORIA & CHELSEA

£–££   When the little metal bell above the door tinkles, another addict has fallen to the siren song of **The Chocolate Society** ✸ (36 Elizabeth St., SW1; ☎ 020/7259-9222; www.chocolate.co.uk; MC, V; closed Sunday; Tube: Victoria). They sit at one of the few small marble tables and indulge in handmade bonbons (like the Greta Laît: Soft hazelnut praline with a dusting of nuts, 60p) and ultra-rich brownies (£4, but a meal). The crowning dish is the Original Hot Chocolate (£4), made with organic milk and raw cane sugar, topped with shaved fresh chocolate that gradually melts into the milk foam, and served with a square of 70% pure dark chocolate. "I don't make sugar water," sniffed the chef on one recent visit. There's a second one in Mayfair (32-34 Shepherd Market, W1; Tube: Green Park).

££   I'm not a cheerleader of **Ask** (160-162 Victoria St., SW1; ☎ 020/7630-8288; www.askcentral.co.uk; AE, MC, V; Tube: Victoria). The chain's Italian output is quick—I'm usually served within 10 minutes—but not to my tastes; the pasta, which overcrowds the sauce, tastes freezer-burned to me. But countless Londoners insisted that I include it (there are 23 busy locations), and it's certainly cheap: the 17 types of pastas go for £5.60 to £7.95. The space is interesting, though, having originated as the Metropole Cinema in 1929.

££   The one-room, canteen-style **Jenny Lo's Tea House** (14 Eccleston St., SW1; ☎ 020/7259-0399; no credit cards; closed Sunday; Tube: Victoria) is one of the few low-priced restaurants among the budget hotels of the Ebury Street area, but it comes with a pedigree; the proprietor's late father operated the expensive Ken Lo's Memories of China around the corner. Jenny does Cantonese/Szechwan, and does it quickly, but with less spice than in China, and with more noodles and dumplings, to suit British taste. Soup noodles (like chicken, Chinese mushrooms, and cabbage,

Victoria Dining

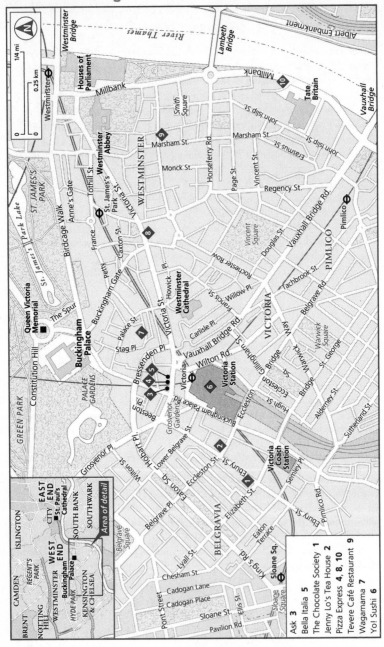

Ask **3**
Bella Italia **5**
The Chocolate Society **1**
Jenny Lo's Tea House **2**
Pizza Express **4, 8, 10**
Tevere Café Restaurant **9**
Wagamama **7**
Yo! Sushi **6**

In Praise of the Caff

The mid-century London cafeteria, like the fish-and-chip platters many restaurants once served, is quickly vanishing. These Jet Age–style, neighborhood diners, once as ubiquitous as the roundel of the Tube, are being swept into Formica heaven by fast-food joints, coffee bars, and triangle sandwich sellers. As Edwin Heathcote puts it in his elegiac 2004 book *London Caffs,* "the increasingly sparse network of surviving refuges represents the dying, but still steaming, breath of a particular moment in the city's history." The precious few left in central London, some garish, some plain, aren't gastronomic discoveries—they serve standards, well portioned—but in terms of interior design, they're as individual, elegant, and of their moment as Bakelite, Rolleiflexes, and Edsels. They're an excellent value, too, since not only does a pound spent here go into the pocket of the family that runs the place, but also because as longtime refuges for the working class, they're priced well (average mains £5, all-day breakfasts £4). Have a cup of tea while they're still steaming:

Alpino (97 Chapel Market, N1; ☎ 020/7837-8330; Tube: Angel)

Farina's (61 Leather Lane, EC1; ☎ 020/7405-4420; Tube: Farringdon or Chancery Lane, lunch only)

L. Rodi (16 Blackhorse Lane, E17; ☎ 020/8527-4541; Tube: Blackhorse Road)

The New Piccadilly (8 Denman St., W1; ☎ 020/7437-8530; Tube: Piccadilly Circus)

Regency Cafe (17-19 Regency St., SW1; ☎ 020/7821-6596; Tube: Pimlico)

River Cafe (1 Station Approach, SW6; ☎ 020/7736-6296; Tube: Putney Bridge)

£6.50) are large enough to perform as a complete meal. Jenny cares about her dishes, but she won't reshape your view of Chinese food. Mains are £6 to £10.

KENSINGTON, KNIGHTSBRIDGE & EARL'S COURT

£   Ideally situated to save tourists from the restaurant desert around the big museums, **Café Primo** (10-12 Old Brompton Rd., SW7; ☎ 020/7589-3555; no credit cards; Tube: South Kensington), a few steps south along Cromwell Place from the Natural History Museum, makes a few lovely sandwiches (grilled halloumi is my standing order), salads (the Niçoise is £5.25), and a wide selection of Illy coffees, all at prices (£2–£3) you'd just as soon pay for a slapped-together triangle sandwich at Boots or a latte at Starbucks. Sit awhile and watch the wealthy locals double-park their SUVs to buy fresh flowers from the florist in the traffic island.

Kensington Dining

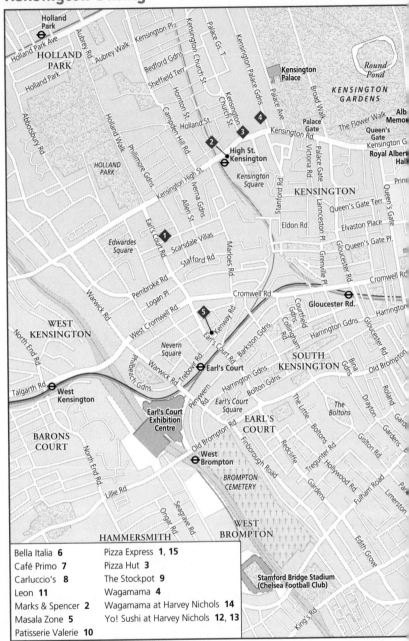

Bella Italia **6**	Pizza Express **1, 15**
Café Primo **7**	Pizza Hut **3**
Carluccio's **8**	The Stockpot **9**
Leon **11**	Wagamama **4**
Marks & Spencer **2**	Wagamama at Harvey Nichols **14**
Masala Zone **5**	Yo! Sushi at Harvey Nichols **12, 13**
Patisserie Valerie **10**	

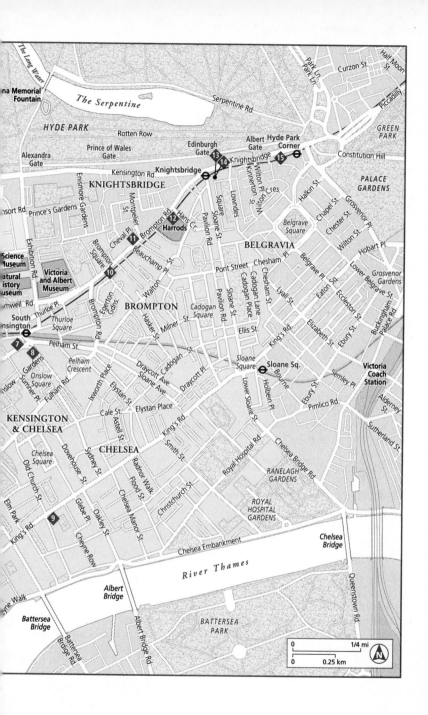

The Long Water

na Memorial Fountain

The Serpentine

Serpentine Rd.

HYDE PARK

Rotten Row

Prince of Wales Gate

Alexandra Gate

Edinburgh Gate ⑬

Albert Gate

Hyde Park Corner

Kensington Rd. Knightsbridge ⑭

GREEN PARK

Piccadilly

Constitution Hill

PALACE GARDENS

KNIGHTSBRIDGE

Ennismore Gardens

Prince's Gardens

Montpelier St.

Brompton Rd.

Cheval Pl. ⑪

⑫ Harrods

Hans Cr.

Sloane St.

Pavilion Rd.

Lowndes Square

Wilton Pl.

Knightsbridge ⑮

Kinnerton St.

Lowndes St.

Halkin St.

Chapel St.

Grosvenor Pl.

Chester St.

Wilton St.

Hobart Pl.

Belgrave Square

Grosvenor Gardens

Lower Belgrave St.

BELGRAVIA

Point Street

Chesham Pl.

Belgrave Pl.

Eaton Sq.

Eccleston St.

Ebury St.

Buckingham Palace Rd.

Science Museum

atural istory useum

Victoria and Albert Museum

Exhibition Rd.

Cromwell Rd.

Thurloe Pl.

Brompton Square

Egerton Gdns.

Walton St.

Beauchamp Pl.

⑩

BROMPTON

Thurloe Square

Brompton Rd.

Hasker St.

Milner St.

Cadogan Square

Pavilion Rd.

Sloane St.

Cadogan Lane

Cadogan Place

Chesham St.

Lyall St.

Eaton Sq.

South ensington ⑦

Pelham St.

Cadogan St.

Ellis St.

King's Rd.

Elizabeth St.

Sloane Square ⑧

Onslow Gardens

Sumner Pl.

Pelham Crescent

Ixworth Place

Draycott Ave.

Sloane Ave.

Draycott Pl.

Sloane Square

Sloane Sq. ⑯

Bourne

Semley Pl.

Ebury St.

Victoria Coach Station

nslow Gardens

Fulham Rd.

Elystan St.

Cale St.

Astell St.

Elystan Place

King's Rd.

Lower Sloane St.

Holbein Pl.

Pimlico Rd.

Alderney St.

Sutherland St.

KENSINGTON & CHELSEA

Chelsea Square

Dovehouse St.

Sydney St.

CHELSEA

Radnor Walk

Smith St.

Christchurch St.

Royal Hospital Rd.

Chelsea Bridge Rd.

RANELAGH GARDENS

Old Church St.

Glebe Pl.

Oakley St.

Flood St.

Chelsea Manor St.

ROYAL HOSPITAL GARDENS

Elm Park

⑨

King's Rd.

Cheyne Row

Chelsea Embankment

Chelsea Bridge

yne Walk

Albert Bridge

Battersea Bridge

Battersea Bridge Rd.

Albert Bridge Rd.

River Thames

BATTERSEA PARK

Queenstown Rd.

0   1/4 mi

0   0.25 km

N

£ I'm embarrassed to say this, so I'll say it quickly. The all-you-can-eat lunch buffet deals at **Pizza Hut** (2 Kensington Church St., W8; ☎ 020/7376-1800; www.pizzahut.co.uk; AE, MC, V; Tube: High Street Kensington) are a head-turning £3.99. Locations are spread out around the city. There, I said it.

££ Serving Indian food in a stylish environment of fire engine–red walls and clear glass, **Masala Zone** ★ (147 Earl's Court Rd., SW5; ☎ 020/7373-0200; www.realindianfood.com; MC, V; Tube: Earl's Court) is another affordable minichain. It's also smart enough not to sacrifice Indian authenticity or spice for a modern personality; its slogan is "real Indian food at unreal prices." Among the wholesome marquee items are the *thalis,* the working man's lunch of breads, stews, and sauces served on a large platter; and *masala dosa,* a cone-shaped bread sheaf stuffed with a potato-based filling—think of it as Bombay bubble. Locations are also at 80 Upper St. (Tube: Angel) and 9 Marshall St. (Tube: Oxford Circus).

££–£££ Some chains just do it better than others, and **Bella Italia** ★ (60 Old Brompton Rd., SW7; ☎ 020/7584-4028; www.bellapasta.co.uk; AE, MC, V; Tube: South Kensington), decorated in a mild, urban-Tuscan style, is one of the winners. It's the best Italian-style chain among the many vying for your attention. Flavors here simply strike the right balance. Roasted vegetables—a medley of courgettes, onions, peppers, squash, and sage—arrive neither too oily nor too hot. The pastas taste exactly as advertised; the Penne Diavola, for example, comes with fresh garlic and lots of pepperoni. Pastas are sensibly priced (£5.45 for penne pomodoro to £8.45 for spaghetti with tiger prawns). There are also a dozen personal pizzas (£5.35–£8.25) to choose from, all delicious. Although this location is near the big museums, there are plenty of others, including 1 Cranbourn St. (Tube: Leicester Square), 30 Henrietta St. (Tube: Covent Garden), 64-66 Duke St. (Tube: Bond Street), 25 Argyll St. (Tube: Oxford Circus), and 152 Victoria St. (Tube: Victoria).

BAYSWATER, PADDINGTON & NOTTING HILL

£ An insulin pick-me-up on a Portobello Road spree, **Hummingbird Bakery** (133 Portobello Rd., W11; ☎ 020/7229-6446; www.hummingbirdbakery.com; AE, MC, V; Tube: Notting Hill Gate) imports southern American baking. In a shoulder-to-shoulder setting that recalls an Alabama grandma's 1950s kitchen, crowds queue for cupcakes with caramel-filled hearts (£1.75), banana bread (£1.20 a slice), and the old standby, vanilla cupcakes slathered with icing (£1.45 with sprinkles).

£–££ When your kids get tired of tromping past the antiques stalls of Portobello Road, swing them into the whimsical **Lazy Daisy Café** (59a Portobello Rd., W11; ☎ 020/7221-8416; no credit cards; Tube: Notting Hill Gate) at the overlooked, southern end of the market road. Kids get their own menu (stuff like fish fingers and baked beans, £3–£4), but that's a formality, since the regular menu is full of British favorites that they won't turn up their nose at. Point them toward the box of toys in the corner, then indulge your grown-up tastes with specials such as sweet potato and coconut cream soup (£4), quiche lorraine (£5.50), and a slate of moist cakes (get the homemade cheesecake if it's on the menu). Unaccountably, it's one of the only cafes around where you stand a chance of finding a table on a Saturday afternoon.

£–££ Burmese cuisine isn't common even in the world's most multicultural cities. Another standout on Edgware Road, **Mandalay** ✮✮✮ (444 Edgware Rd., W2; ☎ 020/7258-3696; AE, MC, V; Tube: Edgware Road), barely 30 seats, big and deceptively plain, revels in the coconut milk, lemongrass, tumeric, and garlic that distinguishes much Asian cooking, but it replaces the cloying cloves and cardamom of Indian cooking with an array of dried prawns and fish sauces. Traditional dishes, all multilayered with flavor, include *ohn-no khaukswe* (turmeric-yellow soup with noodles, veggies, and prawns) and the *laksa-esque sett-na-myo-hin-cho,* called "dozen ingredient" soup on the menu (£2.90). Ask for some *balachaung* (£2.90), which is a blend of onion, dried prawns, garlic, and chili, fried together and applied as a condiment or spice to just about everything. The twice-cooked fish curry (£6.50) is a customer favorite, as are the calabash fritters (£2.40 for two). The owners are proud of their cuisine, so if you show an interest, you'll be rewarded with a whistle-stop tour of their country's best plates. Book ahead.

£–££ Ideal for a quick bite when you're Notting Hill way, **Manzara** (24 Pembridge Rd., W11; ☎ 020/7727-3062; AE, MC, V; Tube: Notting Hill Gate) is oft overlooked as another storefront kebab house by the hordes that pass it on their way to Portobello Road. Inside, it's not much more attractive, with a shiny interior more appropriate to a fast-food joint than a place serving palatable grub. Get past that, though, and you'll taste a wide range of well-seasoned Turkish and Mediterranean dishes, including many vegetarian options. The marinated chicken and lamb with rice uses top-quality meat, and the spicy aubergine dip has a kick stronger than striker Michael Owen's. My favorite is its long, rectangular Turkish pizza, or "pide." You'll pay a £5 minimum to eat in, but considering that the minced lamb and spinach and feta are both £6.95, that's not hard to manage.

££–£££ For unique, exotic cuisine served by friendly, family-run restaurants, Edgware Road is about as good as it gets near the center of London. **Kandoo** (458 Edgware Rd., W2; ☎ 020/7724-2428; AE, MC, V; Tube: Edgware Road) is an unassuming little bit of Iran, proudly embellished by its owners with homey touches like a jerry-rigged jug fountain and a little dining garden out back. Breads are baked in a handmade, tiled oven in the front window, while the many dishes, mostly lamb-, chicken- and salmon-based, come out of the back kitchen. Mains (around the £10 mark) are cleanly flavored and suffused with just the right amount of garlic, mint, saffron, or tarragon; a few are sprinkled, compellingly, with barberries, a lightly sour fruit common in Persian dishes. The chance to taste Iranian cuisine, let alone stuff this carefully and cheaply done, makes it worth the shuffle up Edgware Road.

££–£££ Forgive its cheesy interior, tarted up like an old piazza. It's the cheesy pizza you want at trattoria **Luna Rossa** (190-192 Kensington Park Rd., W11; ☎ 020/7229-0482; MC, V; Tube: Ladbroke Grove). It's baked in rectangular sheets and arrives on ridiculously long wooden planks that, once they're placed precariously across your table and between your chairs, will have everyone in your party diving for new positions like a Romance version of *Twister.* This regressive bit of fun appeals to young residents of Notting Hill, to say nothing of their kids (who are treated like gold by the wait staff), but if you don't want pizza, plenty of

Bayswater & Notting Hill Dining

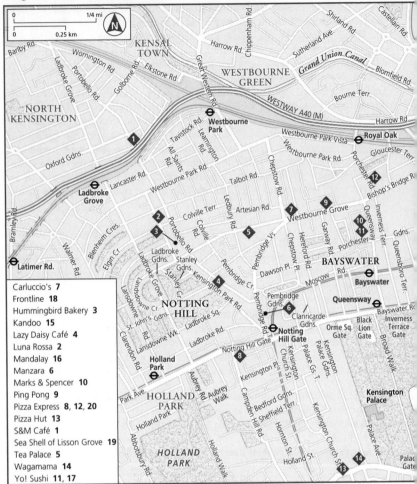

Carluccio's **7**
Frontline **18**
Hummingbird Bakery **3**
Kandoo **15**
Lazy Daisy Café **4**
Luna Rossa **2**
Mandalay **16**
Manzara **6**
Marks & Spencer **10**
Ping Pong **9**
Pizza Express **8, 12, 20**
Pizza Hut **13**
S&M Café **1**
Sea Shell of Lisson Grove **19**
Tea Palace **5**
Wagamama **14**
Yo! Sushi **11, 17**

pastas are on the menu, too. The wine list is pricy, and things get noisy, but it's a good time.

£££–££££ **Frontline** ★★★ (13 Nolfolk Place, W2; ☎ 020/7479-8960; www.thefrontlineclub.com; AE, MC; closed Sunday; Tube: Paddington) functions as a base for war correspondents, so its walls are adorned with emotional still images from more than 60 years of international events, and proceeds go toward fostering fair independent journalism. But it's not like people eat here out of charity. Frontline maintains the warm, airy vibe of a place that could charge twice what it does, with leather banquettes, oversize hanging lampshades, and white tablecloths. The knockout dishes are smart, with a modern British flair and seasonal variations: leek and potato soup; fish pie; parsnip, sage, and onion tart; and pear

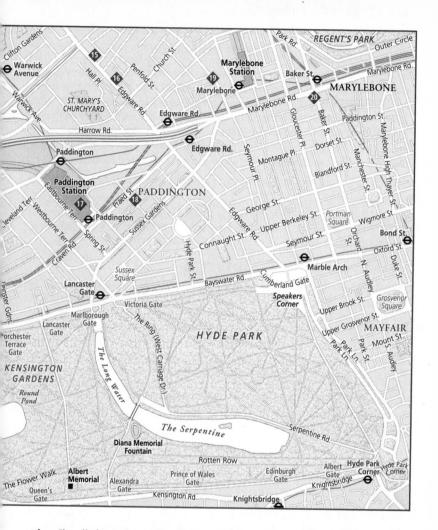

sorbet. I'm all about the shepherd's pie with buttered spinach (£11) with a side of creamed leeks (£2.50). The owners also price their excellent wine list about as low as you'd find it at the wine shops, a touch that doesn't go unnoticed. Mains are £10 to £16, making this a splurge, but the quality of the cooking and the aspirations of the club make it a splurge well spent. Its club room programs lectures on modern news issues.

£££–££££ It charges way more than it ought to, but **Sea Shell of Lisson Grove** (49-51 Lisson Grove, NW1; ☎ 020/7224-9000; www.seashellrestaurant.co.uk; AE, MC, V; closed Sunday; Tube: Marylebone), which looks like an upscale pub, is highly rated by connoisseurs of fish and chips. Even if it's a splurge, it's worth dining here because you'll get fried haddock, cod, or plaice the way it's meant to

A State of Vegetation

Don't like meat? London's greenie culture is far more entrenched than in nearly any other Western city, and in addition to supporting a huge number of meat-free establishments that are considered cool by carnivores and herbivores alike, virtually every menu will have at least three or four—usually more—items for vegetarians to eat. The situation for vegans isn't quite as flexible, although most servers understand vegan dietary requirements and are likely to know which dishes comply. In short, good news for both human plant-eaters and farm animals.

taste (£12–£14 a plate). Fish also comes grilled for £14 to £20. Desserts are just like Mum's: *spotted dick* (steamed suet pudding with currants), served with custard and treacle sponge are among the tasty options (£3.50 each).

BRIXTON

££   Because of its colonial past, London hosts huge numbers of settlers from the islands. For some of its best Jamaican food, try the cheek-by-jowl **Bamboula** ★ (12 Acre Lane, SW2; ☎ 020/7737-6633; www.walkerswood.com; MC, V; Tube: Brixton). The fare here is curated by Jamaican-born Virginia Burke, author of the cookbook *Eat Caribbean.* Standouts include curried goat, red pea soup, stir-fried callaloo (a spinach-like leaf), and of course, jerk chicken served with a mountain of beans, rice, and sweet plantain. Among its surprises is Guinness Punch, an egg-noggy sipper made with nutmeg, milk, and Irish stout. Reserve ahead or squeeze in before 12:30pm for lunch and by 7pm for dinner. Also, the wait staff is on island time, so don't expect to get in and out in a hurry. Bamboula is opposite Lambeth Town Hall, a 2-minute walk south of the Tube.

FIFTEEN PUBS YOU'LL LOVE

Pubs are the beating heart of British life, and they have been for centuries. Hundreds are scattered throughout the city, but you might be shocked to learn that many of the oldest premises have been so well-loved (or so well-bombed) that most of their original features are gone. Many other pubs, particularly in the suburbs, are what's called "locals"—places that cater to a neighborhood, not tourist, clientele.

The following pubs will do you right, however. Be they truly ancient, stunningly beautiful, happily situated, or simply charming, they're all authentic and unlikely to let you down. All of them serve food of some kind (burgers, meat pies, and the like) and commonly charge under £3 for a pint.

Few pubs meld abundant history with an enviable location as perfectly as the three-story **Anchor Bankside** (34 Park St., SE1; ☎ 020/7407-1577; MC, V; Tube: London Bridge), whose Thameside patio in sight of St. Paul's dome is perhaps the most agreeable (and popular) spot in London at which to sit a spell with a fresh-pulled pint. There's been a tavern here at least since the 1500s, when Londoners ferried to Southwark by the hundreds to experience bear baiting, gardens, brothels, and Shakespeare (the playwright surely would have known the place). Diarist and royal confidant Samuel Pepys is said to have watched London burn to the ground from the safety of this bank in 1666, and another Samuel, this one Johnson, may have kept a room here while he compiled the first English dictionary. The industrial Anchor brewery that subsumed it for 200 years was cleared away in the 1980s, a spacious (but always crowded) riverside terrace was added, and the pub building was thoughtfully restored to the maze of creaking rooms that captivates punters and river walkers today. If you're staying at the budget hotel Premier Travel Inn London Southwark (p. 68), your breakfast is taken upstairs at the Anchor.

Having a beer in **The Argyll Arms** (18 Argyll St., W1; ☎ 020/7734-6117; MC, V; Tube: Oxford Circus) can feel like drinking in a bejeweled, red velvet box. That's thanks to the many acid-etched glass screens that subdivide the space into dignified drinking areas. Originally installed in 1895 to prevent brawls between the working and middle classes, the screens somehow survived the 20th century and now serve to hide Oxford Street shoppers as they wait for their well-swiped credit cards to cool down. It's one of the prettiest pubs in London, and its location southeast of Oxford Circus (by several of the Tube's exits), makes it an easy stop.

A laid-back, wood-lined, and easy-to-find pub situated east across the road from the entrance to the National Portrait Gallery, **The Chandos** (29 St. Martin's Lane, WC2; ☎ 020/7836-1401; AE, MC, V; Tube: Leicester Square or Charing Cross) has an upper-floor Opera Room that's popular with staff and patrons of the English National Opera, a few doors north. Big and relaxed, it looks older than it is (it was renovated in early 2006), but it's heavy on charm and surprisingly light on tourists.

The simple corner beerhouse **The Coach and Horses** (29 Greek St., W1; ☎ 020/7437-5920; MC, V; Tube: Leicester Square), in the thick of Soho's tourist crowd at Romilly Street, dates to the mid-1800s, and although several pubs in London bear its name, few others share its history as a hangout for inebriated journalists.

A onetime haunt of actor Edmund Kean, who drank himself to an early curtain, **The Coal Hole** (91 Strand, WC2; ☎ 020/7379-9883; MC, V; Tube: Charing Cross or Embankment), rebuilt in 1904 in the Arts and Crafts style, is still a hangout for performers at the adjoining Savoy Theatre. Use the entrance in back, by the stage door, to access the clubbier lower level.

The 17th-century charmer **The Dove** (19 Upper Mall, W6; ☎ 020/8748-5405; AE, MC, V; Tube: Ravenscourt Park) houses many legends: that Charles II would cheat on his queen by sneaking off with Nell Gwynne here (probably false); that the composer of "Rule Britannia" lived, and died prematurely, upstairs (true); that dissolute artists Graham Greene, Ernest Hemingway, and Richard Burton all got wasted here (so very true, along with many other imbibers commemorated on the walls). It's a prototypical English pub with character, down to the low ceiling crossed by dark oak beams, brick facade, and open fire. But it's the terraced Thameside situation that makes it endure. Sitting outside and watching the river, you'll understand why Hammersmith was a favored retreat from the city for so many centuries. Arrive early on weekends to snare a seat.

Unquestionably one of the most important ancient pubs still standing, **The George Inn** (77 Borough High St., SE1; ☎ 020/7407-2056; MC, V; Tube: London Bridge) traces its lineage to at least 1542, when a map of Southwark first depicted it; the Tabard Inn, from where Chaucer's pilgrims left in *Canterbury Tales,* was a few doors south (it's gone now). The oldest part of the current structure, a galleried wood-and-brick longhouse, dates to 1677, after a horrific fire swept the district. It later functioned as an 18th-century transit hub, and its courtyard was encircled on three sides with a tavern, a hotel, stables, wagon repair bays, and warehouses. Shakespeare knew it, and Dickens memorialized it in *Little Dorrit,* but the rise of a railway nearly saw it destroyed, and only one side of the former complex survives. The National Trust now protects it. Sip an ale in the low-ceilinged timber-and-plaster chambers, or sit in the cobbled courtyard and soak up the echoes of history.

You're going to hear a lot of stories about the Duke of Wellington when you're in this part of town (it was his 'hood), so you might as well be drinking when you do. **The Grenadier** (18 Wilton Row, SW1; ☎ 020/7235-3074; AE, MC, V; Tube: Hyde Park Corner), it's said, was his local bar and the unofficial clubhouse for his regiment, hence the battlefield artifacts on display, from old trumpets to lanterns. This tiny plank-floored pub, pretty as a picture in a cobbled mews, comes off like a boozer in some tiny upcountry village, with only 15 places at its island bar, part of which is still faced with its original pewter top. It's less known for its resident ghost (a soldier) than for its freshly mixed bloody marys, nicely tart with a giant celery stalk (£5). Find this secret place by heading down Grosvenor Crescent from Hyde Park Corner station, hanging a hard right upon arriving at Belgrave Square onto Wilton Crescent, and taking your first right on Wilton Row.

Too tiny and thronged to give tourists much respite, **The Lamb and Flag** (33 Rose St., WC2; ☎ 020/7497-0504; Tube: Covent Garden or Leicester Square), is nonetheless the epitome of a city pub, tucked as it is down an atmospheric brick alley and blessed with an original fireplace. It has been known throughout its 375 years as both the Coopers Arms and The Bucket of Blood, and its building is said to be Tudor in origin. No one can prove it, since it was heavily rebuilt in the 1890s. You'll find it on a lane just east of the intersection of Floral and Garrick streets. But you probably won't find a place to sit unless you start drinking after lunch.

McGlynn's Free House (1-5 Whidborne St, WC1; ☎ 020/7916-9816; AE, MC, V; Tube: Russell Square or King's Cross St. Pancras) isn't hundreds of years old, or even important, but it fulfills the image of a "local" where the neighborhood folks hang out in peace and the landlord welcomes new faces. Its coal-blackened brick corner building, painted in old-fashioned green and red trim, is hard to find (it's southwest of Argyle Square in King's Cross), which accounts for some of its appeal. Its street is so quiet that, unlike at most London pubs, you'd actually consider loitering at one of its outdoor picnic tables in summer. It's the sort of place with a giant juke box (100 CDs), a few "pokie" gambling machines jangling in the corner, and a rugby or football game on the TV every afternoon. The food's retro, too, starting with prices: £3.95 burgers, £4.95 lasagna. Because it's a "free house," it can serve a range of lagers and stouts from a variety of brewers.

The enchanting **Old Mitre** (1 Ely Court, off Ely Place, EC1; ☎ 020/7405-4751; AE, MC, V; closed weekends; Tube: Farringdon or Chancery Lane), suspended between streets and seemingly between centuries, was once part of a great palace mentioned by Shakespeare in *Richard II* and *Richard III.* The medieval St.

Etheldreda's Chapel, the palace's surviving place of worship, stands just outside. As further proof that it's a straggler from another society, this extremely tiny pub (established in 1546 but built in its present form in 1772) has two entrances that feed either side of the bar. The one on the left grants you access to "the Closet," a fine example of a semiprivate sitting area called a "snug." The one on the right brings you face-to-face with a blackened stump said to be part of a cherry-tree maypole that Elizabeth I danced around. (Yeah, right, drink another one.) Suck down one of the house specialties: pickled eggs, for 60p. To locate it, seek a little alley among the jewelry stores on eastern Hatton Garden between Holborn Circus and Greville Street.

There's no pretending that **The Narrow Boat** (119 St. Peters St., N1; ☎ 020/7288-0572; MC, V; Tube: Angel) is historically significant. It's simply a smashing place to pass a few hours on a pretty day. Picture windows overlook an attractive basin of the Regent's Canal, where you can watch barges, ducks, and wealthy folks in their waterfront loft conversions. Combine a visit with a stroll along the canal's footpath, and you've got one of the most romantic afternoons London has to offer.

The Covent Garden/Leicester Square location is unbeatable, and the ornate exterior and interior of **The Salisbury** (90 St. Martin's Lane, WC2; ☎ 020/7836-5863; AE, MC, V; Tube: Leicester Square) is unmistakably Victorian—ostentatious, just-how-much-did-the-designer-drink Victorian, to be precise. Thrill to the Grecian urns in brilliant-cut glass, the pressed-copper tables, and the nymphs entwined in the bronze lamps. Long a haunt of the city's theatrical community, it's now a suitable pit stop for any West End exploration. The plate meals run the gamut of international offerings—baked asparagus tarts; chicken tikka with pappadum; sausage and mash—and they're £5.45 to £7.45. On Sundays, you can get Yorkshire pudding with gravy, plus lots of meat, during its roast (£7.45).

The facade of **The Sherlock Holmes** (10-11 Northumberland St., WC2; ☎020/7930-2644; AE, MC, V; Tube: Charing Cross or Embankment) is a valentine to Victoriana, its interior subdued, and its stock of Holmsian memorabilia (assembled a half century ago as a tourist gag) will save you a trip to the similar attractions at the Holmes museum on Baker Street. Note that it's not on busy Northumberland Avenue, but on the street of the same name, which runs just north.

Just the sort of rambling, low-ceilinged tavern you imagine London is full of (and was, once), **Ye Olde Cheshire Cheese** (Wine Office Court off 145 Fleet St., ☎ 020/7353-6170; AE, MC, V; Tube: Blackfriars, Temple, or Chancery Lane) was built behind Fleet Street in the wake of the Great Fire in 1666, and because of steady log fires and regularly strewn sawdust, it still smells like history hasn't finished passing it by. In later generations, it played regular host to Dr. Samuel Johnson (who lived behind on Gough Square), Charles Dickens (who referred to it in *A Tale of Two Cities*), Yeats, Wilde, and Thackeray. You can get pretty well thackered yourself today: There are six drinking rooms (some in a courtyard converted for the purpose in our day), but the cozy front bar is the most magical. Ask to see the Chop Room's oak paneling and furniture or, if you're free-spending, to sample a steak dinner. Don't confuse this place with the Victorian Cheshire Cheese pub at nearby Temple.

Why You're Here: The Sights of London

What's worth seeing, what isn't

LONDON IS INFURIATING! HOW ELSE CAN YOU DESCRIBE A CITY WITH SO much to see? Unless you have the time and the money to hang out for months, you're simply not going to be able to see even a smidge of a sliver of the amazing things on offer. Even with the best planning, when it comes time to leave, you're going to be hungry for more.

Put simply: England has been a top dog for the past 500 years, and London is where it keeps its bark. For centuries, many of the world's finest treasures came here and never left. Most cities store their best goodies in one or two brand-name museums. In London, riches are everywhere. You can walk into a place you've never heard of before and see something priceless.

London's brand-name attractions could by themselves occupy several days of deep contemplation. But the sheer abundance of history and wealth—layer upon layer of it—means that London boasts dozens of exciting smaller sights, too. Even if you daydreamed in high school history, you'll be fired up when face-to-face with the underground bunker where Britain fought for its life in World War II, or the jewel-encrusted crown worn by the country's kings and queens back to 1661.

There's lot of other good stuff to do in the city besides sidle past important relics at a museum desk, though. Also check out my chapters on London's world-renowned parks (p. 219), nightlife (p. 288), theater scene (p. 289), and those little-known, "under-the-skin" activities that help you meet, play, and learn with real Londoners—I call it "the Other London" (p. 199).

HOW TO BEST USE YOUR TIME

If you have just 1 day in London: First of all, what were you thinking? If you're in town on a layover, didn't you know that most airlines will allow you to stick around for a few days at no charge? Never mind. What's done is done. Eat a huge breakfast and make your way to **The Tower of London** (p. 140) because it opens an hour earlier (9am) than most attractions. Spend about 2 hours there, making stops at the **Crown Jewels** and the **White Tower,** and snap that requisite photo of the **Tower Bridge** (p. 184) from the quay outside. Grab a triangle sandwich for lunch (the quintessential London midday meal) and Tube it to Westminster **Westminster Abbey** (p. 138; allot 2 hours). Then walk up Whitehall, passing the **Houses of Parliament** (p. 186) and **No. 10 Downing Street.** If you like art, breathe in the atmosphere of **Trafalgar Square** (p. 242), one of the symbolic hearts of the city, before popping into **The National Gallery** (p. 143) for an hour or two. If you don't care much for art, head back to the Thames for a ride on the **London Eye** (p. 137), where you can watch the sun go down on the Clock Tower where **Big Ben** (p. 186) rings. **West End shows** start around 7:30pm (p. 294), and when the curtain comes down, head to the nearest **pub** and raise a glass to a city you've barely scratched the surface of (see p. 126 for pub suggestions).

If you have just 2 days in London: You're going to have to move incredibly fast, but you'll be able to see a good amount of London in 2 days. Start at **The Tower of London,** as on the 1-day tour, but stay until lunch—it's still not enough time to see everything, but we're crunched here. Then take the Tube to Mansion House or Blackfriars, where you can hastily appreciate the underside of the Dome of **St. Paul's Cathedral** (p. 150) before crossing the Thames on the Millennium Bridge to binge on modern art at the **Tate Modern** (p. 145). If it's summer, you can catch an evening show at **Shakespeare's Globe** (p. 189), just a few yards east; in winter, any West End theater will show you what modern British performance is all about. Wind up your day with a beer overlooking the Thames at the **Anchor** pub, or at the wooden-galleried **George Inn** (see p. 127 for both).

Start your second day with a pilgrimage to **Westminster Abbey.** After you leave, walk along **St. James's Park** (p. 221) to behold the front of **Buckingham Palace** (p. 160), before heading across **Green Park** (p. 221) to browse the incredible shops of **Piccadilly,** including **Fortnum and Mason** (p. 268). Next take the Tube or a bus to Russell Square, where you'll spend the afternoon roaming, but barely getting to know, **The British Museum** (p. 134). Maybe you'll even want afternoon cream tea at its cafe (p. 101). Wind up the afternoon on the **London Eye** or with a stroll past the shops of **Oxford Street, Regent Street,** and **Carnaby Street** (p. 259). Grab dinner at a West End restaurant of your choice, and afterward, stroll through the neon lights of **Piccadilly Circus,** where you can catch the Tube back to your hotel.

If you have 3 days in London: Follow the itinerary for 2 days in London, but add in one of the city's South Kensington museums, preferably the **Victoria & Albert** (p. 148), and follow that with a walk through **Hyde Park** (p. 219), possibly to see the Diana, Princess of Wales Fountain, and to tour Diana's former home, **Kensington Palace** (p. 159), in Kensington Gardens. Take the Tube or a bus to Westminster, and dive into the time capsule of the **Churchill Museum and Cabinet War Rooms** (p. 154). Dine in Islington or Marylebone, and follow that up with a long stroll through those neighborhoods.

If you have 4, 5, 6, or 7 days in London: Go through this chapter and place a check mark next to all the attractions that interest you. Put a circle around the ones I've just named above. If you schedule one or two circled check marks per day, you can sprinkle one or two more uncircled checks in the hours surrounding them. Provided the places you choose for each day are located within five or seven Tube stops' distance apart, the commute between them shouldn't chew up your time. Just remember: Attractions are generally open from 10am to 5 or 6pm—to maximize efficiency do daytime things (museums, attractions) during the day, and evening activities (entertainment, long meals) during the evening.

London Attractions

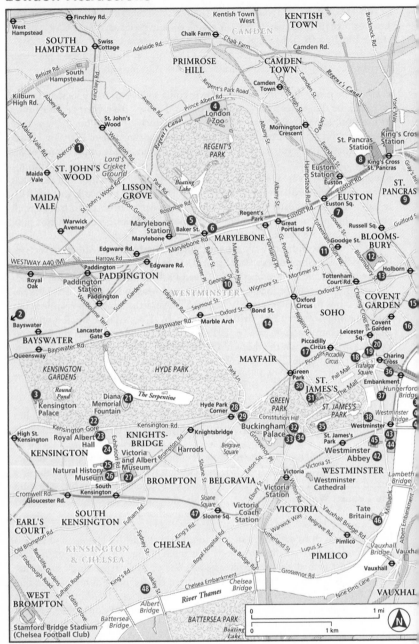

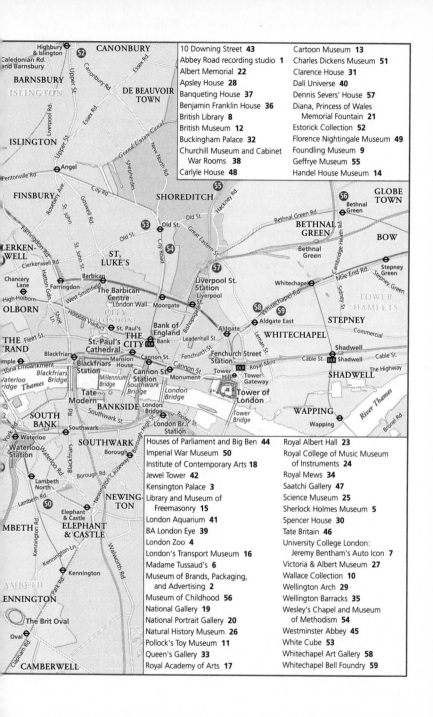

10 Downing Street **43**	Cartoon Museum **13**
Abbey Road recording studio **1**	Charles Dickens Museum **51**
Albert Memorial **22**	Clarence House **31**
Apsley House **28**	Dalí Universe **40**
Banqueting House **37**	Dennis Severs' House **57**
Benjamin Franklin House **36**	Diana, Princess of Wales
British Library **8**	Memorial Fountain **21**
British Museum **12**	Estorick Collection **52**
Buckingham Palace **32**	Florence Nightingale Museum **49**
Churchill Museum and Cabinet	Foundling Museum **9**
War Rooms **38**	Geffrye Museum **55**
Carlyle House **48**	Handel House Museum **14**

Houses of Parliament and Big Ben **44**	Royal Albert Hall **23**
Imperial War Museum **50**	Royal College of Music Museum
Institute of Contemporary Arts **18**	of Instruments **24**
Jewel Tower **42**	Royal Mews **34**
Kensington Palace **3**	Saatchi Gallery **47**
Library and Museum of	Science Museum **25**
Freemasonry **15**	Sherlock Holmes Museum **5**
London Aquarium **41**	Spencer House **30**
BA London Eye **39**	Tate Britain **46**
London Zoo **4**	University College London:
London's Transport Museum **16**	Jeremy Bentham's Auto Icon **7**
Madame Tussaud's **6**	Victoria & Albert Museum **27**
Museum of Brands, Packaging,	Wallace Collection **10**
and Advertising **2**	Wellington Arch **29**
Museum of Childhood **56**	Wellington Barracks **35**
National Gallery **19**	Wesley's Chapel and Museum
National Portrait Gallery **20**	of Methodism **54**
Natural History Museum **26**	Westminster Abbey **45**
Pollock's Toy Museum **11**	White Cube **53**
Queen's Gallery **33**	Whitechapel Art Gallery **58**
Royal Academy of Arts **17**	Whitechapel Bell Foundry **59**

The Rules of Attraction(s)

- Attractions are closed December 24 to 26, and New Year's Day; many are also closed on Good Friday.
- Unless noted, if your kids are under 6, their tickets are free.
- Many attractions offer Family Tickets offering discounted admission for parents with children, including single parents; ask about them.
- I call it "The 10-Minute Rule": Security guards will turf you out 10 minutes before the posted closing time, so schedule accordingly.
- Most museums don't allow photography, not just to protect the works from flashes, but also to boost the bottom line in souvenirs.

THE TEN BEST: LONDON'S ICONIC SIGHTS

London has no shortage of wonders, but these are the don't-miss attractions that have kept visitors buzzing for years. If you're not keen on seeing some of them—few children would stamp their feet and beg to be taken to the Tate Britain, for example—replace them with something from one of the other categories in this chapter, such as "Attractions that Ought to Be More Famous" (p. 153) or "Attractions with Niche Appeal" (p. 171).

The British Museum ✸✸✸ (Great Russell Street, WC1; ☎ 020/7323-8299; www.thebritishmuseum.ac.uk; free admission; Sat–Wed 10am–5:30pm and Thurs–Fri 10am–8:30pm, closed New Year's Day, Good Friday, and December 24–26; Tube: Tottenham Court Road or Holborn or Russell Square), founded in 1753 and first opened in 1759 in a converted mansion, may be the museum to beat all museums. In fact, it's the top tourist attraction in the country. Those with an interest in classical crafts and antiquities could spend days here, combing the cases for stimulation. Put on your walking shoes because it's huge.

In many ways, the British Museum is a monument as much to great craftsmanship as it is to the artistic piracy carried out by 18th- and 19th-century wealthy Englishmen, who, on their trips abroad, grabbed whatever goodies they could find—usually objets d'art from the classical period—and then told the bereft that the thievery was for their own good. Yet the good taste of these English collectors is unquestionable.

Holdings are grouped in numbered rooms by geography, with an emphasis on the Greek and Roman Empires, Europe, and Britain. It's impossible to choose the *most* priceless item in a welter of priceless items, but if you have only a few hours to see the most famous and instructive selections, you should see the following:

Dominating the center of the Great Court like a drum in a box, the cream-and-gold **Reading Room,** completed in 1857 but closed to the general public until 2000, was once part of the British Library, which shared the site with the museum until 1998. Famous patrons here included Lenin and Karl Marx, who developed their political theories in the room; George Bernard Shaw; Charles Dickens; and Virginia Woolf. On the southern wall (through which you enter),

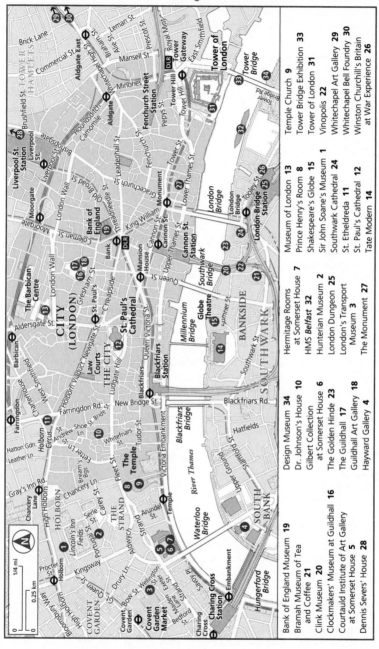

Bank of England Museum **19**
Bramah Museum of Tea
 and Coffee **21**
Clink Museum **20**
Clockmakers' Museum at Guildhall **16**
Courtauld Institute of Art Gallery
 at Somerset House **5**
Dennis Severs' House **28**

Design Museum **34**
Dr. Johnson's House **10**
Gilbert Collection
 at Somerset House **6**
The Golden Hinde **23**
The Guildhall **17**
Guildhall Art Gallery **18**
Hayward Gallery **4**

Hermitage Rooms
 at Somerset House **7**
HMS *Belfast* **32**
Hunterian Museum **2**
London Dungeon **25**
London's Transport
 Museum **3**
The Monument **27**

Museum of London **13**
Prince Henry's Room **8**
Shakespeare's Globe **15**
Sir John Soane's Museum **1**
Southwark Cathedral **24**
St. Etheldreda **11**
St. Paul's Cathedral **12**
Tate Modern **14**

Temple Church **9**
Tower Bridge Exhibition **33**
Tower of London **31**
Vinopolis **22**
Whitechapel Art Gallery **29**
Whitechapel Bell Foundry **30**
Winston Churchill's Britain
 at War Experience **26**

you can read panels on the museum's history. The Reading Room, which still houses some 25,000 books pertaining to the Museum's stash, is open from 10am to 5:30pm.

The museum's most famous, and most controversial, possessions are probably the so-called **Elgin Marbles,** which the museum gingerly refers to as **The Sculptures of the Parthenon** (rooms 18 and 19) to disguise their imperialist provenance: They were looted from Greece by Lord Elgin in the early 1800s. These slab sculptures (called friezes and Metopes), plus some life-size weathered statuary, once lined the pediment of the Parthenon atop Athens' Acropolis but were defaced (literally—the faces were hacked off) by invading vandals in the 500s. They suffered further indignities in a 1687 gunpowder explosion. They're laid out in the gallery in the approximate position in which they appeared on the Parthenon, only facing inward. The government of Greece has lobbied for years for their return, but the British have argued that they're better cared for in London. If you've ever seen the smog-burnt portions left behind in Athens, it's easy to see their point, which makes a muddy political issue murkier.

Fragments of **sculptures from The Mausoleum at Halikarnassos,** one of the lost Seven Wonders of the Ancient World, loom in rooms 21, 77, and 81. So colossal are these chunks—a lion carved from a single block of stone, a horse's head that measures some 7 feet long—that they call into question everything we assume about the ancient peoples' limited technology and culture.

The pivotal **Rosetta Stone** (196 B.C.), in room 4, is what helped linguists crack the code of hieroglyphics, and its importance to anthropology can't be exaggerated. Napoleon's soldiers found it while enlarging their fort in Egypt in 1799, but it was nabbed in 1801 by the British. Consider it his first Waterloo.

The grisly array of **Egyptian Mummies** in rooms 62, 63, and 64 have petrified children for years, and on your visit, they'll probably be thronged with school groups as usual. In addition to the wizened, raisin-like corpses, there are painted coffins; the hair and lung of the scribe Sutimose, dating to 1100 B.C.; and scarabs galore. In room 64, check out the body from 3400 B.C., found in a fetal position without a coffin, which was preserved by dry sand. Beside it is another body, 400 years younger, that rotted to bones and soil because it was laid to rest in a basket.

Kids should also love the leather-faced **Lindow Man** in room 50; he was discovered, throat slit, in a Cheshire bog nearly 2,000 years after his brutal demise. Preserved down to his hair and fingernails, he looks like he could spring to life and pound the glass of his case. Nearby is the **Mildenhall Treasure,** a hoard of silver Roman tableware unearthed by Gordon Butcher, a Suffolk farmer, as he plowed his fields in 1942; the saga of how Butcher was cheated of his unexpected fortune was chronicled by children's author Roald Dahl.

The **Enlightenment Gallery,** at the east of the ground floor, is the museum's oldest room (1823), from the Greek Revival edifice that replaced the converted mansion and was gradually subsumed by the massive building that exists today. Its towering walls, lined with wood-and-glass cases and stuffed with knickknacks from around the world, give you a sense for how rarified the museum must have felt in the glory days of British conquest and discovery. Case 22 is full of stuff brought back from **Captain James Cook's voyages** to the South Pacific, when the region was still relatively uninfluenced by Europeans.

Navigating the British Museum

With more than 250 years of collecting behind it, the British Museum possesses a mind-boggling number of artifacts, and aimlessly trundling from
room to room can quickly numb the brain. Free admission forces directors
to coax money from your pocket in other ways, such as charging you £2
for a **map.** Get around that fee by printing the floor plans from the website; these don't pinpoint the location of the highlights but will at least
keep you from getting lost in the labyrinth of exhibitions.

Be sure to stop at the Info Desk (at the left of the 2-acre Great Court,
under a dazzling glass-and-steel canopy installed as part of a £100 million
renovation in 2000) as the museum is always humming with talks, tours,
and special exhibitions, some of which will require timed tickets. I particularly recommend looking into the excellent (and free) **"Hands On"**
demonstrations, at which visitors are permitted to handle and inspect artifacts from the collection with an informed curator. **Guided tours** of the
museum's highlights are a steep £8, three times a day. Considering the
price, you're better off perusing the place on your own armed with information gleaned from the books in the gift shops. Even better are the free
EyeOpeners tours, which take about 45 minutes and focus on a single
room or theme; they run about 10 times a day. Audio tours come in four
varieties, each £3.50. The Reading Room loans free kids' materials, including activities backpacks, scavenger trail maps, and event guides.

Room 70, on the upper floor holds three remarkable holdings: **The Portland
Vase,** a black, cameo-glass jug that's very difficult to make even today; the bronze
head of Roman Emperor Augustus, found in the Sudan and lifelike to an unsettling degree (it still has its painted eyeballs, as most statues of the time did); and
The Warren Cup, a First Century silver chalice graphically depicting homosex-
ual sex in relief. The Warren Cup's acquisition in 1999 for £1.8 million caused
some juvenile titters; the discomfort of some guests is made all the keener by the
fact they have to bend over to inspect its indecorous decorations.

Eighty-two pieces from the medieval **Lewis Chessmen** set, room 42, were
carved from walrus ivory and whale teeth but apparently never used. The Norse
toys were discovered in a Scottish sand dune in 1831. Have a close look at their
whimsical, cleverly carved faces—they make for a refreshing spot of folly among
the Museum's portentous, solemn-eyed icons and statues.

Of the several **gift shops** in the Great Court, the one at the back, under the
sky bridge and easily missed, has the best selection. There's a **restaurant** above the
Reading Room which serves a lovely afternoon tea (p. 101).

The **British Airways London Eye** 👶 ★ (Riverside Building, County Hall, SE1;
☎ 0870/500-0600; www.ba-londoneye.com; adults £13, seniors £10, children 5–15
£6.50, under 5 free; Oct–May 10am–8 pm, June–Sept 10am-9pm; closed for maintenance in the first week of January; Tube: Waterloo or Westminster) was erected in

1999 as the Millennium Wheel, and like many observational wheels of the past, it became such a sensation—and a money-minter—that it was never taken down. The London skyline will never be the same. It rises above everything in this part of the city (at 135m/443 ft. high, it's the sixth-tallest structure in London, and 1½ times taller than the Statue of Liberty). The 30-minute ride above the Thames affords an unmatched perspective on the prime tourist territory. On a clear day, you can see to Windsor, but even on an average day, the entire West End bows down before you. That's why you should either go as soon as you arrive in the city, to orient yourself, or (my choice), on your last day in town, when you can appreciate what you're seeing and what you've seen. It's pricey, but satisfying.

Each of the 32 enclosed capsules, which accommodate up to 25 people, is climate-controlled and rotates so gradually that it's easy to forget you've left the ground—which means it's safe for anyone except the desperately height-averse. Best of all, capsules are fixed to the outside of the wheel, so by the time you reach the top, you'll have true 360-degree views unobstructed by the support frame, although you can see into adjacent pods. The ticket queue often looks positively wicked, but in fact, it moves fairly quickly, processing up to 15,000 riders a day. *Tip:* Booking on the Web saves waiting in the boarding queues, and it gives two other advantages: You can pick your time (I like going up 15 minutes before sunset, when the city turns from sun-orange to twilight-blue), and you'll save 10% off the price listed above. Sometimes there are discounts on Lastminute.com.

At peak times (weekend afternoons and summer), you'll ride with 24 new friends, but if you prefer less company, try immediately after opening, before the school groups descend, or after dark. For a stirring view for £4 less, you can always climb to the Stone Gallery of St. Paul's Cathedral, which surveys The City.

If you had to pick one church in London to see, pick **Westminster Abbey** ★★★ (Broad Sanctuary, SW1; ☎ 020/7654-4900; www.westminster-abbey.org; £10 adults, children 11–17, seniors, and students £6; Mon–Tues and Thurs–Sat 9:30am–3:45 pm, Wed 9:30am–7 pm, closed Sun and occasionally for special events; Tube: Westminster). Heck, even if you had to pick one church in the world, it's hard to do better. The echoes of history here—the current building dates from the 1200s, but it was part of a monastery dating to at least 960—are simply mind-blowing: Every English monarch since 1066 has been crowned here (with three minor exceptions: Edward V, Edward VIII, and possibly Mary I). Seventeen monarchs are interred here (their deaths date from 1066 to 1760), as are dozens of great writers and artists. Even if England's tumultuous history or the thought of bodies lying underfoot don't pluck the strings of your imagination, the interior—in places, as delicate and as intricate as lace—will earn your appreciation. A full visit should take about 3 hours.

Unlike St. Paul's Cathedral, which boasts a stately beauty, the much smaller Westminster is more like time's attic, packed with artifacts, memorials, tombs, and virtuosic shrines. It's easy to feel overloaded after just a few minutes; by the time you've pocketed the change from your admission ticket, you're already treading on the final resting place of poor William Bradford (died 1728 at age 32). It only gets busier from there. Take your time and don't get swept along in the current of visitors. There are dozens of stories to be told in every square meter of this place.

Inside the sanctuary, tourists are corralled clockwise from the North Transept. The royal tombs are clustered in the first half of the route, in the region of the

High Altar, where coronations and funerals are conducted. Hard to believe as it is, but some of the most famous rulers of all time are *here*—not in story, but in body, just behind marble slabs. Some are stashed in cozy side chapels (which once held medieval shrines before Cromwellians bashed them to pieces during the Reformation; some vandalism is still visible), but the oldest are on the sanctuary side of the ambulatory (aisle). The executed **Mary Queen of Scots** was belatedly given a crypt of equal stature to her rival, **Elizabeth I,** by Mary's son **James I,** who gave himself only a marker for his own tomb beneath **Henry VII**'s elaborate resting place. James I's infant daughter Sophia, who died after 3 days, was given a vividly creepy bassinet sarcophagus in the Lady Chapel.

Only tombs are labeled, so it helps to have an audio guide. Rentals stop by early afternoon. If you have questions, approach anyone in a red robe; they're "vergers," or officers who attend to the church. They also lead 90-minute tours at least once daily (usually at 11am, for £4). If your question stumps even them, you may win an invitation to the atmospheric Library, a creaking loft that smells of medieval vellum and dust, where an archivist can answer you.

The South Transept is **Poet's Corner,** where Britain's great writers are honored. You'll see many plaques, but most (Shakespeare, Austen, Carroll, Wilde, the Brontes) are merely memorials. The biggest names who truly lie underfoot are Robert Browning, Geoffrey Chaucer (he was placed here first, starting the trend), Charles Dickens, Thomas Hardy (buried without his heart), John Gay, Rudyard Kipling, Dr. Samuel Johnson, Laurence Olivier, Edmund Spenser, and Alfred Lord Tennyson. Ben Jonson is commemorated here but is actually buried in the Nave near Isaac Newton and Charles Darwin.

Now for a few Abbey secrets:

- That oak seat between the Sanctuary and the Confessors' Chapel, near the tomb of Henry V, is the **Coronation Chair.** Unbelievably, every English monarch since 1308 has been crowned on this excruciating-looking throne. The slot under the seat is for the 336-pound Stone of Scone, said to be used as a pillow by the Bible's Jacob, and a central part of Irish, Scottish, and English coronations since at least 700 B.C. After spending seven centuries in the Abbey (except for when Scottish nationalists stole it for 4 months in late 1950), the Stone was returned to Scotland in 1996, where it's on view at Edinburgh Castle. It will return to its slot for every future coronation.

- **Oliver Cromwell,** who overthrew the monarchy and ran England as a republic, was buried with honors behind the High Altar in 1658. Three years later, after the monarchy was restored, his corpse was dug up, dragged to Tyburn (by the modern-day Marble Arch), hanged, decapitated, the body tossed into a common grave, and its head put on display outside the Abbey. The joke was on the Royalists—he was already dead. Today his much-abused cranium is at Sidney Sussex College in Cambridge. Cromwell's daughter, who died young, was mercifully allowed to remain buried in the Abbey.

- The **Quire** is where the choir sings the daily services; it comprises about 12 men and 22 boys who are educated at the adjoining Westminster Choir School, the last of its type in the world. The wooden stalls, in the Gothic style, are Victorian, and are so delicate they have to be dusted using vacuum cleaners. (Considering how many royal Henrys are buried here, it's fitting that Henry brand machines are used.)

◆ *The Da Vinci Code*'s climax took place in the octagonal **Chapter House,** but the movie was shot elsewhere. From 1250, the graceful room still has its original floor of handmade tiles and its mural depicting the Apocalypse, considered the most extensive and best-preserved of its type in the country. Its southwestern stained glass windows, the last ones before the exit, were blown out during World War II; look closely for the single replacement pane depicting bombs falling and buildings burning.

The Abbey's oft-overlooked **Museum,** beside the Pyx Chamber, contains some amazing treasures, including **Edward III's death mask** (thought to be the oldest of its kind in Europe; it's made of walnut and doesn't ignore his facial droop, which resulted from a stroke), **ancient jewelry** "found in graves" (we know what that means—pried from skeletons), the **fake Crown Jewels** used for coronation rehearsals, 14th-century leather shoes and Roman tiles unearthed on the grounds, and the fateful **Essex Ring,** which Elizabeth I gave to her brilliant confidant Robert Devereux, telling him to return it if he needed her. He tried to, but his enemies intercepted it, and he was beheaded at the Tower of London in 1601. Oops.

Time seems suspended in the **Cloister,** or courtyard. But better gardens are hidden away. At the Museum, head for the corridor to the left and you'll find the fragrant and fountained **Little Cloister Garden,** blackened by 19th-century coal dust, and beyond that to the right, the wide **College Garden,** a tempting courtyard with daffodil beds, green lawns, and five plane trees dating to 1850. The garden has been continuously planted for 900 years, when it grew herbs for an adjacent hospital. Westminster School, started by the abbey's monks in the 1300s, stands nearby. (Incidentally, there haven't been monks in Westminster Abby for 550 years, yet Londoners persist in calling it an "Abbey"; the formal name is The Collegiate Church of St. Peter, Westminster.)

The Tower of London ★★★ (Tower Hill, EC3; ☎ 0870/756-6060; www.hrp. org.uk; adults £15, children 5–16 £9.50, students/seniors £12, family of up to 5 £43; Nov–Feb Tues–Sat 9am–5pm, Sun–Mon 10am–5pm, and Mar–Oct Tues–Sat 9am–6pm and Sun–Mon 10am–6pm, last admission an hr. before closing; Tube: Tower Hill or Tower Gateway DLR) is the most famous castle in the world, a UNESCO World Heritage Site and a symbol of not just London, but also of a millennium of English history. Less a tower than a fortified minitown of stone and timber, its history could fill this book. Suffice it to say that its oldest building, the four-cornered White Tower, went up in 1078 and the compound that grew around it has served as a palace, prison, treasury, mint, armory, zoo, and now, a lovingly maintained tourist attraction that no visitor should neglect. It's at the very heart of English history, and exploring its sprawl should take between 3 and 5 hours.

Tickets are sold outside the battlements. Hit the Welcome Centre, just past the Ticket Office, and grab a copy of the "Daily Programme," which runs down the times and places of all the free talks, temporary exhibitions, and miniperformances. Plenty are offered—the Tower at times feels more like a theme park than a living museum with 1,000 years of history behind it. The prime excursion is the **Yeoman Warder's Tour,** led with theatrical aplomb by one of the Beefeaters who live in the Tower (there are about 100 residents, including families) and lovingly maintain it. Those leave every 10 minutes from just inside the portcullis in the Middle Tower. They're engaging, but juvenile—expect bellowing and histrionics,

I'll Pass, Thanks

You'll hear occasional recommendations for the **London Travel Card** (www.londontravelpass.com), good for unlimited travel on the Tube and bus system, which comes in 1-, 3-, and 7-day varieties. You won't hear one from me. The **Off-Peak Travelcards** that you can purchase in London are not only substantially less expensive (about 25% less, as long as you begin your Tube trips after 9:30am—which most tourists do), but they also don't require shipping. Why spend $10 to have something shipped to you if you can buy it in person for less at any London Tube station? No reason, unless you love parting with your savings.

I only bring up the **London Pass** (www.londonpass.com), which gets you into some 55 attractions, with deep reservations. It ranges from £30 for 1 day to £72 for 6 days, which is a huge amount of money. Few of the attractions it covers cost so much that they justify the price. The Tower of London, one of the most expensive attractions in England, is still only £15 for adults, or half the 1-day price of the pass. So to break even on your card, you'd have to race around to at least two more attractions in the same day—which is not realistic given opening hours that usually span 10am to 5pm. Besides, many of London's greatest museums are free. Anyone considering the London Pass should know, before purchasing, which attractions they'd use it on and then ensure that it would pay for itself.

If you're a "palace person," however, there is one pass (really a membership) that I would recommend. **Historic Royal Palaces** manages five major sites in London: The Tower of London, Kensington Palace, Hampton Court, Kew Palace, and the Banqueting House. If you're going to several, you might save money by purchasing an annual membership to HRP, which costs £35 per person or £69 for a family of up to five people. But do the math using the admission prices in this book before you commit, remembering that two of the five must be seen on day trips from the center city. Passes, on sale at all five sites, are good for unlimited visits to all.

plus a gleeful fetish for yarns about beheadings and torture. (In truth, you can count the people executed inside the Tower on your fingers and toes; it was considered an honor to be killed here, since it was private.) For reasons I'm about to explain, I suggest you double back and join the tour later in the day. If you'd like your history delivered without vaudevillian shenanigans, head to the gift shop on the right after Middle Tower and grab an audio tour (£3.50, but do it early; headsets run out). The official guidebooks (£3.95) here are also a good value.

The key to touring the Tower is to arrive close to opening. Make a beeline for the two star attractions since intimidating queues form there by lunch: the Crown Jewels, housed in the Waterloo Block at the north wall (farthest from the Thames) and the White Tower, in the center of the grounds. As you enter the **Crown Jewels** exhibition, you'll see archival film of the last time most of the jewels were

Caw! Caw!

Ravens probably first visited the Tower in the 1200s to feast on the dripping corpses of the executed, who were taken from Tower Hill (the public execution ground, near the present-day Tube stop) and hung outside the battlements as a warning. You've heard the legend that if the ravens ever leave the Tower, England will fall—so where are the ravens? Their cages, north of Wakefield Tower, are empty. Not to worry: In February of 2006, they were given temporary digs in the Brick Tower (behind the Crown Jewels) to protect them from avian flu. You can't see them, but England's safe. It's just as well. They bite, anyway.

officially used, at the coronation of Queen Elizabeth in 1952. After passing into a vault, visitors glide via people-movers past cases of glittering, downlit crowns, scepters, and orbs worn by generations of British monarchs. Check out the legendary 105-carat Koh-I-Noor diamond, once the largest in the world, which is fixed to the temple of the **Queen Mother's Crown** (1937), along with 2,000 other diamonds; the Indian government has been begging to get the stone back. The 530-carat Cullinan I, the world's largest cut diamond, tops the Sovereign's **Sceptre with the Cross** (1661). The **Imperial State Crown,** ringed with emeralds, sapphires, and diamonds aplenty, is the one used in the annual State Opening of Parliament. After those come trumpets, swords, and candlesticks that could support the roof of your house, plus the inevitable traffic jam around the **Grand Punch Bowl** (1829), a supremely elaborate riot of lions, cherubs, and unicorns that shows what it would look like if punch bowls could go insane. Since Oliver Cromwell liquidated every royal artifact he could get his hands on, everything dates to after the Restoration (the 1660s or later). Clearly, the monarchy has more than made up for the loss.

Touring the four levels of the cavernous **White Tower** requires much stair-climbing but takes in a wide span of history, including a fine stone chapel, Norman-era fireplaces and toilets, the gleaming collection of the Royal Armoury (even small children can't help but notice the exaggerated codpiece of King Henry VIII's intricately etched suit from 1540), and some models depicting the Tower's evolution (it's been much altered, but the six smallest arched windows on the White Tower's south side are original to the 11th century). After you're finished in here, you'll have an excellent overview of how the whole complex worked.

Once you've got those under your belt, take your time exploring the rest. You could easily spend all day here. I suggest a stop in the brick **Beauchamp Tower** (pronounced "BEECH-um," 1280), where important political prisoners were held and where you can still glimpse graffiti testifying to their suffering. In front of it on Tower Green is the circular glass memorial designating the **Scaffold Site,** where the unlucky few (including sitting queens Anne Boleyn and Lady Jane Grey) lost their heads. The **St. Thomas's Tower,** from the 13th century, is closest to the Thames and re-creates King Edward's bedchamber with authentic materials. Beneath it, **Traitor's Gate,** once called Water Gate, originally was used to ferry prisoners in secret from the Thames. Torture was never a part of English law, but it happened here, anyway, and the **Bloody Tower** was where some of the worst stuff went down. Don't forget to climb the ramparts for that classic photo of the Tower Bridge. But save the extra quid and skip the Royal Fusiliers Regimental Museum, a dreary hodgepodge of military memorabilia. Daily at 11:30am on the Tower Green, a Royal Guard mounts and performs a short ceremony with 21 men. On Sundays, your admission ticket allows you to attend services at the **Chapel Royal of St. Peter ad Vincula,** the Tower's church, at 9:15 or 11am (call ☎ 08707/51-51-77 for info); otherwise, the only way to get in, and to see the marble slab beneath which Boleyn and Grey's decapitated bodies were entombed, is with a Yeoman Warder's Tour.

When the bells of St. Martin in the Fields peal each morning at 10, the doors promptly open to **The National Gallery ★★★** (Trafalgar Square, WC2; ☎ 020/ 7747-2885; www.nationalgallery.org.uk; free admission; Thurs–Tues 10am–6pm and Wed 10am–9pm; Tube: Charing Cross or Leicester Square). Don't miss this. It's as relentless as a fireworks show—each famous picture follows an equally famous picture. "Oh, I know *that* one!" you'll hear yourself repeating.

The National Gallery boasts the strongest, widest collection of paintings in the world—a painting of every important style is on display, and it's almost always the best in that genre. The Uffizi in Florence focuses mostly on Italian art, and the Louvre in Paris rambles on with too many second-rate works. If a painter isn't here, though, he isn't worth knowing. There are 2,300 western European works— mostly royal-owned, originally—which is plenty to divert you for as long as you can manage. The building was built in 1835; Trafalgar Square was selected because it was considered central, and therefore reachable by poor Londoners who had to travel on foot. Even today, crowds swell around lunchtime as working Londoners pop in for a free art infusion. As you enter via the main Portico Entrance, gallery areas imperceptibly surge through time in a clockwise arrangement, from 1500 to 1600 paintings, to 1600 to 1700 paintings, to 1700 to 1900 paintings. The sleek Sainsbury Wing, opened in 1991 to house the early Renaissance collection from 1250 to 1500 can only be reached through room 9 (inside 1500 to 1600) or from the street. Be warned that this section is plagued by surly staff that has been known to close galleries without warning.

The rooms jumble together, so grab a free "Gallery Plan." The best course is to start in the Sainsbury Wing and backtrack, which will order your viewings more or less chronologically. Among the museum's many noteworthy holdings:

SAINSBURY WING

- Piero della Francesca, one of the most sought-after Renaissance painters (there's only one of his works on display in the entire United States), is represented by *The Baptism of Christ* (1450s, room 66) with its advanced use of light and foreshortening. The faces of its subjects verge on bemusement, and the dove, representing the Holy Spirit, seems to fly into viewers' faces.
- In his later years, Sandro Botticelli fell under the spell of the hardline reformer Savonarola. He burned many of his finest paintings in the Bonfire of the Vanities and changed to an inferior style, so his best works are rare; *Venus and Mars* (1485, room 58), depicting the lovers reclining, is one of them, and it's in a room full of others.

THE MAIN BUILDING

* The Gallery has four Michelangelos. *The Entombment* (around 1500, room 8) is unfinished but one of the most powerful. The feminine figure in the red gown is now thought to be St. John, but it's hard to know for sure, since the artist favored strong masculine traits.

* Kids love Holbein's *The Ambassadors* (1533, room 4), full of symbolic riddles and famous for a stretched image of a skull that can only be viewed in proper perspective from the right of the painting; and the hideous, porcine old lady in *A Grotesque Old Woman* (1525-30), thought to be a satire on ladies who try to look younger than they are.

* Nearby is Hans Holbein The Younger's oil-on-oak portrait of *Christina of Denmark, Duchess of Milan* (1538), painted for King Henry VIII when he was wife-shopping. She declined to marry him, and as a happy consequence, survived to 1590.

* The Gallery is rich in Peter Paul Rubens, with some 25 works attributed to him. His *Samson and Delilah* (1609-10, room 29) is known for Samson's muscular back and Delilah's crimson robe, but it's his disturbing *The Massacre of the Innocents* (1611-12, room 29), depicting the emotional and structural complexity of the slaughter of newborn boys by Herod's soldiers, that leaves a lasting impression. Mislaid in 1767, the painting was thought lost until its reappearance in 2001.

* Edouard Manet's *The Execution of Maximilian* (1867-8, room 43) was sliced into five sections after the artist's death, but Edgar Degas reassembled what he could; the missing sections lend the firing-squad scene further tension.

My list of recommendations could continue: George Seurat's almost pointillist *Bathers at Asnieres* (1884, room 44), van Gogh's *Sunflowers* (room 45), Leonardo da Vinci's *The Virgin on the Rocks* (room 2), Jan van Eyck's *The Arnolfini Portrait* (Sainsbury Wing, room 56), a mysterious but fabulously skillful depiction of light that dates to 1434, years ahead of its time. **Rembrandts. Cézannes. Uccellos.** There's so much art here that you may want to go twice during your visit, and the Gallery is so centrally located that you can.

Hear the Masterpieces at the National Gallery

The National Gallery's audio tour is free (they hold your I.D. as collateral), but doesn't offer much more information than you could read on the signs, which are awfully straightlaced. Your visit would be best illuminated by some expert input. Check the info desk for daily events, such as the "Ten Minute Talks" about a single work; hour-long 1pm talks devoted to a specific work or artist; storytelling for kids; or the few guided tours (often at 11:30am and 2:30pm). The displays are usually supplemented by temporary exhibitions, one free and one paid (around £8).

The opening of the **Tate Modern** ✦✦✦ (Bankside, SE1; ☎ 020/7887-8888; www.tate.org.uk/modern; free admission; Sun–Thurs 10am–6pm and Fri–Sat 10am–10pm, last admission 45 minutes before closing; Tube: Southwark) in 2000 redefined the recreational landscape. Seemingly overnight, Southwark went from an inhospitable no-man's-land, mocked and avoided, to one of the city's artistic hearts. Bankside's chief eyesore, a mammoth power station—steely and cavernous, a cathedral to industry—became as integral to London as the Quire of Westminster Abbey or the Dome of St. Paul's. The gigantic Turbine Hall, cleared of machinery to form a meadow-like expanse of smooth concrete, hosts changing works specially created by major-league artists, and art hounds of every background recline there as if it were a city park. Even if you don't care for modern art, the building is still a star.

The flow through the galleries, stacked from floors three to six on the river side of the building (the Turbine Hall is alongside them, and can be surveyed from balconies), is sensibly directed, so you won't need much help. Holdings, which focus on art made since 1900, are divided into four areas of thought, loose enough that you never know what sort of witty article waits behind any corner: On Level 3, you'll see *Material Gestures* (about abstract expressionism) and *Poetry and Dream* (for surrealism, probably the most arresting wing); and on Level 5, *States of Flux* (for cubism and futurism) and *Idea and Object* (for minimalism and pop art). Level 4 hosts two changing exhibitions, which require tickets (£7–£10; check online for what's showing). The Tate website allows you to locate works on an interactive map and, cleverly, build your own tour based on your favorites.

The formidable collection, one of the world's best for approachability and breadth, suffers from over-representation of old-school works and a relative dearth of truly progressive stuff, but it includes some seminal items by Picasso, Léger, Braque, and Rivera—and that's just in one room (number 2, in *States of Flux*). In room 2 of *Poetry and Dream,* the hits are just as thick: Miró, Man Ray, and a clutch of surrealist Magrittes. There's a smattering of 1930s urban photography (room 4, *Poetry and Dream*), from Alfred Stieglitz, Berenice Abbott, and Lewis W. Hine. True, the descriptions ramble too often about the incestuous culture of the art world, but fortunately, the daring of the pieces themselves speak louder than the curators' self-satisfied descriptions. Who can say which pieces of modern art are the most important? It's a matter of taste, since reputations haven't been cemented by time. But you might recognize the following heavy hitters:

◆ Salvador Dalí's **Lobster Telephone** (1936, room 2, *Poetry and Dream*), a surrealist piece that tops a phone's handset with a realist sculpture of an orange, apparently boiled lobster. Another unconventional sculpture of an everyday object, Marcel Duchamp's **Fountain** (1917, room 8, *Idea and Object*), an earthenware urinal tipped on its back, is a 1964 replica approved by the artist; the original was lost. A clone in Paris has twice been attacked by an elderly vandal; here's hoping he doesn't know about Eurostar. Across the room is Andy Warhol's **Brillo** box (also 1964).

◆ A contemplative series by **Mark Rothko** (room 3, *Material Gestures*) in rusty brown and dirty greys that were originally commissioned for the Four Seasons restaurant in New York City, then withdrawn and given to the Tate.

Ensconced in their own room, they make for a moody getaway from the shifting crowds in the main galleries.

◆ Monet's hypnotizing **Water-Lillies** (after 1916, room 7, *Material Gestures*), in which depictions of light patterns on water take on virtually an abstract character—but not enough to ruffle a classicist's feathers. Still, the painting was called a harbinger of abstract expressionism by mid-century critics.

◆ One of my favorite pieces at the Tate is Juan Munoz's **Towards the Corner** (room 7), a tickling (yet weirdly unsettling) tableau of seven identical, diminutive men on a pair of benches, frozen in mid-giggle.

Keep an eye out for the free Audio Points, low pedestal-like kiosks fitted with headphones. They play up to 10 chapters with art historians and archival interviews explicating an important work nearby, such as Jackson Pollock's 19-foot-long **Summertime** (room 7, *Material Gestures*) or Joseph Beuys' haphazard-seeming installation **Lightning with Stag in its Glare** (room 6, *Poetry and Dream*). The supply of collapsible stools, interspersed around the galleries on wall-mounted racks, are another excellent touch for those who like to sketch artwork. And when your feet begin to ache, head to the Level 3 Reading Room, where you can read coffee-table books on art as you rest on leather benches and overlook the Turbine Hall. Level 4 has a Thames-facing espresso bar, plus a balcony with a postcard view. There are two free daily guided tours of the general collection, usually at 11am and 3pm; ask at the ground floor information desk to find out where they meet. The free kids' activities, called Start, are centered at a desk on Level 3. Only the sit-down restaurant on Level 7 is inhospitable, and that's due to high prices—its panorama of St. Paul's and the Thames is primo.

Some advice: The glass panels rimming the roof like a movie marquee announce the names of the artists currently showing exhibitions. The shop, on the bottom floor by the west entrance, is epic. Try to enter the Tate Modern via the doors at its narrow end, facing the west (not the riverside entrance), because that's the most dramatic way to absorb the powerful negative space of the Turbine Hall. The Tate is planning a major expansion for the 2012 Olympics, so there may be construction going on.

Tourists often wonder what the difference is between the Tate Modern and its sister located upstream on the Thames, the **Tate Britain** ✖ (Millbank, SW1; ☎ 020/7887-8888; www.tate.org.uk/britain; free admission; daily 10am–5:50pm, until 9pm on the first Friday of the month; Tube: Pimlico). Well, the Modern is for modern art of any origin, and the Britain is exclusive to British-made art. Not to diminish the quality of the peerless work on display here, but you won't spot many recognizable masterpieces. Britain has a historic knack for collecting international art, not so much for creating it, so a lot of the work on display is rich with historic relevance but highly imitative of classical or Renaissance styles. Although the oldest portion of the collection, full of documentary or moralist works by William Hogarth and Joshua Reynolds, illustrate what everyday British life was like centuries ago, it's hard to shake the feeling that, artistically speaking, Britain was playing catch-up. That changes when the galleries progress chronologically into the modern era, and works by visionaries such as Francis Bacon and James Abbott McNeill Whistler (granted, not English, but an American who lived in England) reveal the originality and ebullient colors that were latent in the national mind.

The presentation of these galleries is nowhere near as friendly as it is at the Modern. Descriptions are often didactic and pretentious (works are described, emptily, to be "questioning" or "explorations") and many paintings are placed at such high levels that glare makes them inscrutable.

But the Tate Britain isn't without sass. Room 17, for example, is populated mostly by Victorian paintings of naked boys. In the lobby at the Millbank entrance, pick up a handful of the museum's free, brilliantly written in-house pamphlets, which point out works themed to every visitor's need, including "The I'm Hungover Collection" (works about sin, soothing pastorals); "The I'm in a Hurry Collection" (just one painting, John Constable's *Flatford Mill* in room 10, which redefined landscape painting); and "The I Like Yellow Collection." Those are for sport, but there are also definite must-sees, such as:

◆ John Everett Millais' sublime ***Ophelia*** (room 14), is a delicately painted image (1851-2) of Hamlet's lover drowning herself in a brook as she sings herself to death. Check out the astonishing detail work on the leaves and moss, as well as in the refraction effect of the water on her body.

◆ John Singleton Copley's smoke-filled ***The Death of Major Peirson*** (1783, room 9) was the Duke of Wellington's favorite painting; it figures, since it shows men in uniform. Below it, JMW Turner's trenchant ***The Field of Waterloo,*** was painted in 1818 three years after the battle; its gloomy piles of corpses, and of bereaved family members searching them, makes the text-book battle suddenly vivid and touching. Better than any war painting I can name, it reminds me that real families suffered mightily because of long-forgotten battles.

◆ The oil-on-canvas ***Carnation, Lily, Lily, Rose*** (room 15) depicts children holding paper lanterns so luminous that visitors often halt in their tracks as they pass it. John Singer Sargent (another American who settled in London) is the genius responsible.

◆ A series of abstract eye-catchers are in rooms 21 and 22: The polished, fluid ***Mother and Child*** (room 22), by one of the country's most important sculptors, Barbara Hepworth; nearby is Henry Moore's undulating, semitangled ***Recumbent Figure*** (1938, room 21) of a female. In a duel between abstract prostrate women, Hepworth's diffident grace wins—even though her work was completed four years earlier.

◆ The crowning attraction here is the **Turner Galleries,** with its expansive collection of JMW Turners. Turner (1775-1851), the son of a Covent Garden barber, was a master of landscapes lit by misty, perpetual sunrise, and the dozens of paintings and sketchbooks on display testify to his undying popularity. Turner's work is lovely, if sleepy, but the mania for him is a bit beyond me (in April 2006, one of his works set a record at auction, fetching £20.5 million). Just don't sully his name in these halls; even his crusty paint box and his fishing rod are dotingly preserved.

A word of advice: Weekends are a smart time to drop by, when the schedule of activities—the appearance of the Art Trolley activity center for kids, free 15-minute gallery talks by curators, and themed tours (such as of the Turner rooms)—is in full swing. It's possible to see the entire collection online before you come.

The Tate-to-Tate Boat

The best way to get between the Tates is not via Tube (a circuitous route) but via the **Tate Boat** (☎ 020/7887-8888; www.tate.org.uk/tatetotate; singles £4.30 for adults, £2.15 for children under 16, unless you have a valid London Transport Travelcard, which reduces singles to £2.85 adults, £1.45 children), a 220-seat catamaran that zips along the Thames every 40 minutes from 10am to 4:40pm (5:15pm on weekends) between the docks in front of the Tate Britain and the Tate Modern. Along the way, it stops by the London Eye and also supplies the only view of Big Ben and the Houses of Parliament that isn't spoiled by angular fences and gun-fondling guards. For hop-on, hop-off service all day, including additional services from the Tate Modern to the Tower of London and Canary Wharf, buy a River Roamer pass for £7.30 adults/£3.65 children (£4.90/£2.45 with a Travelcard); family tickets are available. Its decor is by art bad boy Damien Hirst, who fortunately abandoned his famous formaldehyde-dipped sharks for a conservative polka-dot theme. Tate's entertainment!

As a decorative arts repository, The Victoria and Albert Museum, usually called the **V&A** ★★★ 🅺 (Cromwell Road, SW7; ☎ 020/7942-2000; www.vam.ac.uk; free admission; daily 10am–5:45pm, Wed and the last Fri of the month 10am–10pm; Tube: South Kensington) is about eye candy. This means that although the museum occupies a portentous High Victorian edifice more suited to a courthouse or a capitol, it celebrates beauty and style, not politics or history. If it's good-looking, fabulously well-designed, or might look smart on your wall, it'll be here.

The ground floor, a grid of hard-to-navigate rooms, has lots of good stuff, but lots more bric-a-brac (Korean pots, 1,000-year-old Egyptian jugs of rock crystal) that you'll probably walk past with polite but hasty appreciation. The second, third, and fourth levels have less floor space and therefore are more manageable. The second floor is where the special exhibitions, which require paid tickets, are held.

Rooms are arranged by country of origin or by medium (ironwork, tapestries, etc.) but you'll want to see the **20th Century** (room 72-74, level 3), which surprises by including objects you may have once kept in your home (a Dyson vacuum cleaner, Tinkertoys); **Architecture** (rooms 127-128a, level 4), for a nautilus-like preconstruction model of the Sydney Opera House; and endless slices of **medieval stained glass** (rooms 83-84, level 3). Wherever you go, you may use the little stools hanging from pegs on the wall, and if you see a drawer beneath a display case, open it, because many treasures are stored out of the light.

The V&A, which, tellingly, was endowed by the proceeds from the first world's fair (the Great Exhibition of 1851), is very much about fine objects from everyday life, so wandering around the premises, discovering whatever catches the eye, is half the point. Just don't neglect these highlights:

◆ The seven **Raphael Cartoons** (room 48a), dating from 1515, are probably the most priceless items in the house. These giant paper paintings—yes, paper—were created by the hand of Raphael as templates for the weavers of his ten tapestries for the Sistine Chapel. Before Queen Victoria moved them here, they hung for around 175 years in the purpose-built Cartoon Gallery at Hampton Court Palace. The colors are fugitive, meaning they're fading: Christ's red robe, painted with plant-based madder lake, has turned white—his reflection in the water, painted with a different pigment, is still red.

◆ None of the sculptures in the sky-lit **Cast Court** (rooms 46 and 46b) are original. They're all casts of the greatest hits in Renaissance art, and they crowd the room like a yard sale. They were put here in 1873 as a sort of World's Fair for the poor, who could never hope to travel and see the real articles for themselves. Like much of the V&A, it was set up for learning, which is why there are so many significant works, such as Ghiberti's doors to the baptistery at Florence's San Giovanni, whose design essentially kicked off the artistic revolution of the Renaissance. Michelangelo's *David,* floppy puppy feet and all, looks down from his pedestal; an optional fig leaf, fitted during Victorian royal visits, hangs behind him. Amazingly, many of these replicas are now in better shape than the originals, thanks to the deleterious effects of acid rain and vandalism.

◆ It's not just that **Margaret Laton's jacket** (room 56) is a gorgeous garment. Its silver-thread embroidery and trim cut will leave you agog, and the survival of such an everyday piece of clothing is highly rare. But what's truly astonishing about the jacket is that it's displayed alongside a 1620 oil portrait of Margaret Laton herself—wearing the same jacket. The odds against both items surviving and being reunited in the same case are astronomical. Every time I come, I visit the jacket and imagine the long-departed woman who once filled those empty sleeves.

◆ **Tippoo's Tiger** (room 41) 🧒 is a macabre wooden sculpture commissioned by an Indian sultan in the 1790s. Depicting a life-size tiger in the act of devouring a hapless European, it's rigged with clockworks that cause the tiger to growl and its victim to moan plaintively and weakly bat his arm. It's been a crowd favorite since 1808, when it was part of the East India Company's house museum. Kids will leave either awed or freaked out.

◆ **The Great Bed of Ware** (room 57), a vast four-poster of carved oak that dates to about 1590, was apparently once a tourist attraction at a country inn, renowned enough for Shakespeare to mention it in *Twelfth Night*: "big enough for the bed of Ware." As you admire it, consider that in those days, bed canopies were installed to protect sleepers from insects that might tumble out of their thatched roofs and into their mouths. Canopied beds, a mark of luxury today, were a sign of a humble home then.

◆ The **Ardabil carpet,** the world's oldest dated carpet (copies have appeared on the floors of 10 Downing Street and Hitler's Berlin office alike), is part of a £5.4 million Islamic arts gallery, opened in 2006.

The bulk of family events here fall on weekends, including the availability of "Back-Packs," which contain activity sets for kids that engage them in some of the museum's most eye-catching holdings.

Be warned that for the next few years, various sections of the V&A are closing for renovation, but a majority of the collection will be on view. More of its holdings are exhibited at the Museum of Childhood (p. 190). Make a side visit to the museum's western exterior near Cromwell Road. Scarred during the bombing raids of The Blitz, the stonework was left damaged as a memorial. If the damage was this bad in Kensington, just imagine how bad it was in the German's main target, East London.

The magnificent spire of **St. Paul's Cathedral** ★★★ (St. Paul's Churchyard, EC4; ☎ 020/7236-4128; www.stpauls.co.uk; £9 adults, £3.50 children 7–16; £8 seniors and students; Mon–Sat 8:30am–5pm; open for worship only on Sundays, Whispering Gallery and Dome cleared and last admission at 4pm; Tube: St. Paul's) was a London landmark and part of Old St. Paul's, which stood on this site for nearly 600 years before it was claimed by 1666's Great Fire. So when Sir Christopher Wren was commissioned to rebuild London's greatest house of worship, he devoted 40 years to the project, and decided to go one further and give the city a mighty dome—highly unusual for the time. My, how people talked.

St. Paul's cost £750,000 to build, an astronomical sum in 1697, when the first section opened for worship, and now, it costs £3 million a year to run. Wren overspent so much that decoration was curtailed; the mosaics weren't added until Queen Victoria thought the place needed gussying up. Stained glass is still missing, which allows the sweep and arch of Wren's design to shine cleanly through. Many foreigners were introduced to the sanctuary during the wedding of Prince Charles and Lady Diana Spencer in 1981, but the cathedral also saw a sermon by Martin Luther King in 1964 and Churchill's funeral the following year.

The **High Altar** has a canopy supported by single tree trunks that were hollowed out and carved, and its 15th-century crucifix and candlesticks take two men to lift. (They're nailed down, anyway. As one docent, a 46-year veteran of Cathedral tours, lamented, "You'd be surprised what people try to steal.") Behind it is the **American Memorial Chapel** to the 28,000 American soldiers who died while based in England in Word War II. In a glass case, one leaf of a 500-page book containing their names is turned each day. The **organ**, with 7,000 pipes, was regularly played by Mendelssohn and Handel, and the lectern is original. The **Great West Doors,** largely unused, are 90 feet high and on their original hinges; they're so well-hung that even an old lady can swing them open. In 2005, the Cathedral completed a £10.8 million cleaning program; a stone panel beside the doors was left filthy to show just how bad things were.

Most people are familiar with the famous 1940 photograph of the **Dome,** lit purely by firelight during the Blitz, which has come to symbolize London's fortitude during Word War II. What most people don't know is that St. Paul's *was* hit, many times—a bomb blasted the floor of the North Transept (photos of the devastation are in the Crypt), and another obliterated the east end. So many people were assigned to stamp out incendiary bombs before they could melt through the Cathedral's lead-lined roof that huge areas of the City were left unmanned—much of London was lost so that St. Paul's could be saved, a bittersweet fact.

Eight central pillars here support the entire weight of the wood-frame Dome; Wren filled them with loose rubble. In 1925, engineers broke them open to find the debris had settled to the bottom, and they filled them with liquid concrete. If you're fit, you can mount the 259 steps (each an awkward 5 inches tall, with benches on many landings) to the **Whispering Gallery,** 30m/99 ft. above the floor. Famously, its acoustics are so fine you can turn your head and mutter something that can be understood on the opposite side. That's in theory; so many

Taking a St. Paul's Tour

Ninety-minute tours by volunteers, called "supers," cost £3 at most, and leave at 11 and 11:30am and 1:30 and 2pm. Take one of these instead of an audio tour, which costs about the same, because the supers are the elder statesmen of the Cathedral; many have been associated with it for decades, going back to the 1940s. Just don't ask them if they know the "Feed the Birds" Lady from *Mary Poppins*—that was shot in Burbank, California. You can also worship here; see p. 150 for information.

tourists are usually blabbing to each other that you won't hear a thing, although it is a transcendent place to listen to choir rehearsal on a mid-afternoon. Climb higher (you've gone 378 steps now) to the **Stone Gallery,** an outdoor terrace just beneath the Dome, and catch your breath, if you choose, for the final 152-step push to the **Golden Gallery,** which requires you to scale the inner skin of the Dome, past ancient oriel windows and along tight metal stairs. It's safe, but it's not for those with vertigo or claustrophobia. The spectacular 360-degree city view from the top (85m/280 ft. up), at the base of the Ball and Lantern (you can't go up farther), is so beautiful that it defies full appreciation. For more than 250 years, this was the tallest structure in London, and therefore the top of the world.

If you miss the **Crypt,** you'll have missed a lot. In addition to many memorials to the famous dead (such as Florence Nightingale and plenty of obscure war heroes), you'll find the tombs of two of Britain's greatest military demigods: **Admiral Horatio Nelson** (whose body was preserved for the trip from the battlefield by soaking it in brandy and wine; the 72,000-ton weight of the Dome is borne by the walls of this small chamber), and **Arthur Duke of Wellington** (flanked by flags captured on the field of battle; they will hang there until they disintegrate). To the right of the OBE Chapel, in **Artists Corner,** there's a monument to poet **John Donne** that still bears the scorch marks it suffered in Old St. Paul's during the Great Fire (they're on its urn, and it was the only thing that survived the conflagration), and you'll find the graves of the artists **JMW Turner** and **Henry Moore,** plus **Christopher Wren** himself, who rests beneath his masterpiece. "I build for eternity," he once said, and so far, so good: In 2010, the cathedral will celebrate 300 years since its completion. If you're hungry, scope out the cafe, since it's one of the cheaper options in this neighborhood.

The National Portrait Gallery (kids) ★ (St. Martin's Place, WC2; ☎ 020/7312-2463; www.npg.org.uk; free admission; Sat–Wed 10am–6pm, Thurs–Fri 10am-9pm, last admission 45 min. before closing; Tube: Leicester Square) could be considered the documentary companion to the National Gallery; everything inside depicts a famous Brit. On paper, that concept sounds like Field Trip Hell. But actually, you'll be surprised how the best works capture the sparkle of life that made their subjects such charismatic history-shapers. Quickly, a name from your high school textbook can flower into a flesh-and-blood human. The longer you stare, the more life they seem to have.

I find the ancient kings and queens have the most heft, partly because it's hard to wrap my brain around the fact that in many cases, the actual people posed in the same room as these very canvases. One of the most instantly recognizable paintings is the **Ditchley portrait of Elizabeth I,** in which the queen's jeweled gown spreads out like wings and Her Majesty firmly glares at the viewer under stormy skies. Right away, it becomes clear that many artists are slyly commenting on the disposition of their sitters. The troublesome **Henry VIII** is shown in several likenesses. One is an especially delicate paper cartoon, by Hans Holbein the Younger (for a mural at Whitehall—a rare survivor from that palace), in which the king suspiciously peers out with flinty grey eyes—hinting at a shiftiness that His Majesty probably couldn't recognize in his own likeness, but that all who knew him caught. One painting of **King Edward VI,** painted when he was nine, is executed in a distorted perspective (called anamorphosis) that requires it to be viewed from a hole on the right side of its case. You'll also find no fewer than six **George Washington**s (he was born an Englishman, after all), and one of the only authoritative images of **Captain James Cook,** painted in Cape Town by a Swiss draughtsman on the explorer's fatal voyage.

Fortunately, the portraits don't stop when people started snapping photos. The 1982 oil-on-canvas image of **Margaret Thatcher,** as viewed from below her gun-ship-grey podium at the Conservative Party Conference in Brighton, is a fearsome and not-very-fond representation of the Iron Lady. In contrast, a 1950 sitting-room portrait of **Queen Elizabeth II** with her parents, **King George VI** and the **Queen Mum,** mines Rockwell-esque, just-us-folks imagery (Mum's about to pour tea, Dad's smoking) to make the Royal Family seem as normal and as middle-class as The Cleavers, while an odd 3-D diorama of **J.K. Rowling** eating hard-boiled eggs and toast says more about the peculiarity of the artist than the sitter. Some portraits are actually films, such as the 67-minute digital voyeurism of toothsome football star **David Beckham** sleeping in Madrid—a rare moment of true intimacy for such a frequently photographed icon.

See everything by taking the escalator to the top floor and then working your way down over about 2 hours. The oldest works (Tudors, Jacobeans, Elizabethans) will come first, and you'll progress forward in time—adding photography when canvas fatigue sets in. Frankly, it helps to have a little historical knowledge so that these pictures ring some bells, so consider visiting near the end of your trip, when many of these names will be fresh in your mind from your tours.

Bring along kids; the front desk loans free rucksack tours (pick Tudors, Victorians, or 20th-century) for kids aged 5 to 11. The Portrait Gallery isn't the sort of place where you'll spend half your day, but it's a sleeper favorite.

Finding the Best of Any Museum

Overwhelmed by some of London's giant museums? Have limited time but not sure what exhibits you'd most enjoy seeing? Make a trip to the gift shop first. Not to make a purchase (at least, not yet), but to check out the posters and postcards. They always picture the museum's highlights.

ATTRACTIONS THAT OUGHT TO BE MORE FAMOUS

Housing far and away one of the most precious collections of books, maps, and manuscripts in the world, the permanent "Treasures of the British Library" exhibition at **The British Library** ★★★ (96 Euston Rd., NW1; ☎ 020/7412-7332; www.bl.uk; free admission; Mon and Wed–Fri 9:30am–6pm, Tues 9:30am–8pm, Sat 9:30am–5 pm, Sun 11am–5pm; Tube: King's Cross St. Pancras), displayed in a dim, climate-controlled suite of black cases and rich purple carpeting, is a dazzler. I think it's the most incredible museum in town, and I make a point of going during every visit, if I can. I will never understand why it isn't always mobbed.

The library holds approximately 150 million items, and adds 3 million each year, so when it puts the cream of its collection on display, prepare to be floored. On a recent visit, I encountered a dejected-looking visitor staring into space from an upholstered bench. His wife came over and asked what was wrong. "There's too many things to see," he said. Indeed—a small portion of the trove includes:

- Two of the four known copies of the Magna Carta from 1215.
- The Beatles' first lyric doodles for the songs that became "Yesterday," "A Ticket to Ride," and "I Wanna Hold Your Hand" (containing an early line, happily revised: "let me hold your thing").
- The Diamond Sutra, the oldest known printed book, which was found in a cave in 1907 and estimated to have been made in China by woodblock nearly 600 years before Europeans developed similar technology.
- Fragments of the book of Genesis, on cotton, from the 5th or 6th centuries.
- A Mozart score for the glass armonica, and Chopin's *Barcarolle in F Sharp Major* (you can listen to the final works on headphones, too).
- Lady Jane Grey's prayer book (1554) with handwritten notes; that's next to a letter by Queen Elizabeth I, The Virgin Queen, about whether she would get married; and beside that, Sir Thomas More's last letter to Henry VIII.
- An early-11th-century copy of *Beowulf* on vellum, in Old English, the only surviving manuscript copy.

Touch-screen "Turning the Pages" displays allow you to thumb through some of the prettiest specimens as if they were open in front of you. Leaf through the Sultan Baybars' Qur'an, written in gold; take a peek at Leonardo da Vinci's sketches of musical instruments; browse Lewis Carroll's complete hand-drawn copy of *Alice in Wonderland* that was presented to the girl herself; and read the 15th-century *Golf Book,* each page a major illuminated work of art.

You can't handle books unless you're an accredited scholar, but the Library encourages anyone to hang out in its public spaces, regardless of credentials. In addition to the treasures, rotating and permanent exhibitions are on display. For example, the hall off the cafe contains the huge **Philatelic Collection,** 500 vertical drawers containing thousands of stamps from around the world.

Head to the info desk to pick up a free guide and events info; the librarians schedule frequent talks and occasions to inspect unique items from the stacks (including, oddly, non-bibliophilic objects such as locks of Napoleon's hair and the ashes of the poet Shelley). Audio tours of the cache are £3.50, and so are architectural audio tours of the building itself, narrated by its architect, Sir Colin St. John Wilson. The cafe on the ground floor is one of the city's best-kept secrets, considered by those in the know to serve the best cappuccino in town.

I find most war-related attractions to be stiff and barely related to the drama of the events they purport to address. So because I recommend it highly, you can appreciate how fascinating the **Churchill Museum and Cabinet War Rooms** ✹✹✹ (Clive Steps, King Charles St., SW1; ☎ 020/7930-6961; www.iwm.org.uk; £11 adults, free for children under 16, £8.50 seniors/students; daily 9:30am–6pm, last admission 5pm; Tube: Westminster) must be. This was the secret command center used by Winston Churchill and his cabinet during the most harrowing moments of Word War II, when it was looking like England would soon become German. We may regard the period with nostalgia now, but the abject terror of life then cannot be exaggerated; a staggering 30,000 civilians were killed by some 18,000 tons of bombs in London alone and more than 65,000 innocent people were killed in Britain as a whole. Here, in the cellar of the Treasury building, practically next door to 10 Downing Street and Parliament, the core of the British government hunkered down in secret.

When the war ended, the bunker was abandoned but stayed a secret, in case hostilities flared up again. In the 1970s, historians found everything left just as it was in August 1945—from pushpins tracing troop movements on yellowed world maps to rationed sugar cubes hidden in the back of a clerk's desk. Although the hideout functioned like a small town, with sleeping quarters for the Churchills and 526 others, kitchens, radio rooms, and other facilities that would enable leaders to live undetected for months on end, it feels a lot more like your old elementary school, with its painted brick, linoleum walls, and round clocks.

If the Cabinet War Rooms are old-school, the connecting **Churchill Museum,** opened by the Queen in 2005 after an expense of £6 million, is surely the most cutting-edge biographical museum open at this moment. Exhaustively displaying every conceivable rarity (Churchill's bowtie, his bowler hat, and even the original front door to 10 Downing Street), it covers the exalted statesman's life from entitled birth (interestingly, his mother was an American blue-blood) through his antics as a journalist in South Africa (where he escaped a kidnapping and became a national hero), to, of course, his years as prime minister. Although the entire museum is atwitter with multimedia displays, movies, and archival sounds, the centerpiece will blow you away: a 50-foot-long Lifeline Interactive table, illuminated by projections, that looks like a long file cabinet and covers every month of Churchill's life. Touch a date, and the file "opens" with 4,600 pages of rare documents, photos, or, for critical dates in history, surprise animations that temporarily consume the entire table (select the days for the Hiroshima bombing or the Titanic sinking to see what I mean). It's a breathtaking design that injects learning with play. It's too bad the addition of the Churchill Museum has caused admission to soar more than 50% in the past 5 years, but the expense is worth it.

The history of London is the history of the Western world, so the miraculous cache of rarities from everyday life in the **Museum of London** ✹✹ (London Wall, EC2; ☎ 020/7600-3699; www.museumoflondon.org.uk; free admission; Mon–Sat 10am–5:50pm, Sun noon–5:50pm, last admission 5:30pm; Tube: Barbican or St. Paul's) wouldn't be out of place in the greatest national museums of any land. But here, they're cataloged in a museum that most tourists, judging by the name, might assume will be lame. Well, it's not. This huge storehouse, smartly and sleekly presented, contains so many forehead-smackingly rare items that by the time you're two-thirds through it, you'll start to lose track of all the goodies you've seen. When it comes to the history of this patch we call London, no stone has been left unturned—literally—because exhibits start with archaeological finds (including elephant vertebrae and a lion skull) before continuing to 3,500-year-old spearheads and swords found in the muck of the Thames. Voices from the past come alive again in chronological order: There's a first-century oak ladder that was discovered preserved in a well, painted wall plaster from a Roman bath, loaded gambling dice made of bone in the 1400s, a leather bucket used in vain to fight the Great Fire of 1666, and far, far more. The biggest drawback here is that you need to budget a few hours; otherwise, you'll end up in a mad rush through the entire lower floor covering the Great Fire to now, which means you'll miss the Victorian Walk, a kid-friendly re-creation of city streets, shops and all, from the 1800s (grab a card at its entrance so you'll know what you're seeing). You can't miss the Lord Mayor's state coach, carved in 1757, which garages here all year awaiting its annual airing at the Lord Mayor's Show in November (p. 339). The museum, which overlooks a Roman wall fragment outside, is easy to combine with a visit to St. Paul's. Its shop is one of the better places in town for books on city history.

If you dig the Museum of London, the **Museum in Docklands** ★★ 🎒 (West India Quay, Canary Wharf, E14; ☎ 0870/444-3857; www.museumindocklands. org.uk; £5 adults, free for children under 16, £3 seniors/students; daily 10am–6pm, last admission 5:30pm; Tube: West Indian Quay DLR) gives a similarly lush, ultimately redeeming treatment to life on the river in London's East End. Many of the city's other museums would have you believe that London was always a genteel bastion of graceful gentlemen. This place tells the real story of the working men who sweat to put the teacups into more privileged, manicured hands. The history of the Docklands is one of grubby boatmen, unsavory profiteering from the slave trade, and relentless Word War II bombings, so studying it has only recently come into vogue. This is unfair because the labors of this area, honeycombed with derelict ship basins now redeveloped with skyscrapers and al fresco cafes, made London a world power. Housed in a brick rum-and-coffee warehouse from 1804, the three-floor museum, strong on plain-speaking explanations, traces the history of working on the Thames starting with Anglo-Saxon times. You'll learn that Victoria River Gardens, the riverside park alongside Embankment Tube station, was the Saxon river edge. You can inspect an intricate model of the medieval London Bridge, which like the Florentine Ponte Vecchio was stacked with homes and businesses but clogged the river's flow so dramatically that it was a threat to life. You'll also see "Sailortown," a dark warren of quayside alleys, all sawdust and shanties, meant to evoke the area's early-19th-century underworld. Finally, the spotlight shifts to the harrowing 1940s, when the whole area was obliterated by fire from the sky and forced to reinvent itself as a corporate citadel. The whole circuit takes several hours. There's also a play area for kids, Mudlarks, themed after Docklands landmarks, and a ticket here is good for unlimited repeat visits all year.

Although it looks like a kingly mansion on the Thames, **Somerset House** (Strand, WC2; Tube: Temple), at the river south of Covent Garden, is actually a aggregation of civil buildings in a palatial costume; Londoners used to troop here to register births, deaths, and to research family histories. Now, it's open to the public as a trio of museums. The masses don't visit it, but art historians consider **The Courtauld Institute of Art Gallery** ★★ (☎ 020/7848-2526; www. courtauld.ac.uk; £5 adults, £4 children/seniors/students, free admission Mondays 10am–2pm; daily 10am–6pm, last admission 5:15pm) one of the most prestigious

Altar Your Plans: These Churches Are Worth It

I know, I know—in Europe, where so many historic sights are ecclesiastical, it doesn't take long before Church Fatigue sets in. But don't give up on God yet. Some of these houses of worship have been altered by well-meaning preservationists, falling bombs, or the ravages of time, but all possess dense histories that set them apart.

Southwark Cathedral ✸ (London Bridge, SE1; ☎ 020/7367-6700; www.southwark.anglican.org/cathedral; free admission; Mon–Fri 8am–6pm, Sat–Sun 9am–6 pm; Tube: London Bridge). Pick up an antique panoramic map of London and look next to old London Bridge on the southern bank. See that church with the square Early English tower? The one flying a pinnacle, and tending to the poor river men? It still stands. Called St. Saviour's until its elevation to an Anglican cathedral in 1905, the retro-choir, choir, and choir-aisles, dating to the 1200s, constitute the earliest surviving Gothic building in London, but the roof and nave were rebuilt in the mid-1800s. Its Refectory (p. 115) is a choice place to grab an affordable lunch. It's included in the walking tour on p. 253.

Temple Church ✸ (Temple, EC4; ☎ 020/7353-3470; www.templechurch.com; free admission; hours vary, so call ahead, but opening days are Wed–Sun; Tube: Temple or Chancery Lane). A well-kept secret until a decoy plot twist in *The Da Vinci Code* launched it onto the tourist circuit, the Temple Church was consecrated in 1185 by the Knights Templar, who were Crusaders, and it was designed to evoke the circular Church of the Holy Sepulchre in Jerusalem. Famous for its life-size effigies of knights, it was bombed in 1940 and rebuilt, but that's not why the marble columns are leaning. The originals did, too. The church stands in the Middle and Inner

collections on earth. Its small two-level selection is supreme, with several masterpieces you will instantly recognize. Among the winners are Manet's scandalous *Le Déjeuner sur l'herbe*, depicting a naked woman picnicking with two clothed men and the artist's *A Bar at the Folies-Bergère*, showing a melancholy barmaid standing in front of her disproportionate reflection. There are multiple Cézannes, Toulouse-Lautrecs, and Tahitian Gauguins. Degas' *Two Dancers on a Stage* is popular, as is van Gogh's *Self-Portrait with Bandaged Ear*. Especially rare is a completed Seurat, *Young Woman Powdering Herself,* which depicts his mistress in the act of dressing and initially included his own face in the frame on the wall—he painted over it with a vase of flowers to avoid ridicule. Two other galleries in Somerset House are ticketed separately: Less rewarding are the **Hermitage Rooms** (☎ 020/7845-4630; www.hermitagerooms.org.uk; £5 adults, £4 children/seniors/students, includes free audio guide; daily 10am–6pm, last admission 5:15pm), dedicated to temporary exhibitions from St. Petersburg's famous museum, as well as random other shows. Whether it's good depends entirely on what's on, but I usually find it too small to warrant the admission fee. Lastly, the

Temples, and lawyers' chambers surround it like a little litigious village. Organ recitals are held Wednesdays at 1:15pm.

St. Etheldreda (14 Ely Place, off Charterhouse St., EC1; ☎ 020/7405-1061; www.stetheldreda.com; free admission; daily 8:30am–7pm; Tube: Farringdon or Chancery Lane). Britain's oldest Catholic church, built from 1250–1290, would have baked in the Great Fire were it not for a sudden shift in weather. In *Richard III*, Shakespeare mentioned the succulent strawberries that once grew in its garden. Today, to gain access to the sanc-tuary (the jeweled cask to the right of the high altar contains a piece of the hand of Etheldreda, a 7th-century saint), you must head down the hallway at the left of the building, up the stairs, and into the doors at the right. Beneath the hall is an undercroft that in the 1500s doubled as a tavern; the singing and brawling used to disrupt the services upstairs. Around back is the sublime Mitre House Tavern pub, a perfect mid-day hideaway.

Wesley's Chapel (49 City Rd., WC1; ☎ 020/7253-2262; www.wesleys chapel.org.uk; free admission; Mon–Sat 10am–4pm, Sun noon–1:45pm, last admission 30 min. before closing; Tube: Old Street). John Wesley, the 18th-century founding father of Methodism, constructed this chapel as his London base in 1778 on a plot St. Paul's Cathedral was using as a dump. It's one of the few city churches to come through the War virtually unscathed. Wesley's final home, pulpit, and resting places are all here, as is a small **Museum of Methodism** in the crypt. Across the street in Bunhill Fields is a nonconformist cemetery containing the earthly remains of Daniel Defoe, William Blake, and John Bunyan.

Gilbert Collection (☎ 020/7420-9400; www.gilbert-collection.org.uk; £5 adults, £4 children/seniors/students; daily 10am–6pm, last admission 5:15pm) collects impossibly fine decorative arts: jewel boxes, cameos, silver, fine mosaics, and the like. The V&A shows similar treasures, except it's free. If you plan to see two or three of the collections on a single day (although I think the Courtauld alone will do most people), ask about a discounted joint ticket. That way, you can tour two collections for £8/£7 or all three for £12/£11. The central courtyard, beneath which lie the foundations of a Tudor palace that once stood here, has a walk-in fountain that delights small children, and it's the scene of popular summer con-certs (www.somersethousesummer.org.uk). The terrace overlooking the Thames (from across the street) can be enjoyed for free. Wander around because some-times a few other galleries pertaining to the building's history are open, including the King's Barge House, on the river side, which was where visiting boats were once able to moor inside the building, before the embankment landlocked it.

It's hard to imagine London without its wheeled icons: the red double-decker bus, the black taxi, and the Tube. The **London's Transport Museum** ★★ 🧒

(Covent Garden, WC2; ☎ 020/7565-7299; www.ltmuseum.co.uk; £6 adults, free for children under 16; Sat–Thurs 10am–6pm, Fri 11am–6pm [last admission 5:15pm]); Tube: Covent Garden) is the best transport museum in the world, popular with visitors who are enchanted by the trappings of the Underground system, now as much a part of London lore as its kings and queens. In this soaring Victorian-era hall, which takes about 2 hours to tour, the development and evolution of the Tube and bus systems, including plenty of old cars and vehicles, are traced. There's also a gallery including some of the system's famous Edwardian and Art Deco posters, as well as background on Johnston, the distinctive typeface created by Frank Pick in 1916 for the Underground system. Along the way, you'll learn a great deal about the shifts in everyday London life. Although the museum pleases trainspotters to no end (especially its book shop, overloaded with resources on track gauges and rolling stock), it's just as interesting for little kids, who get to try their hands at operating simulator buses and trains. (It's not that easy even for those of us with driver's licenses.) As of this writing, the museum was in the throes of an extensive, £18.6 million makeover, set to open in the summer of 2007 with new admission fees and entrance times, so call ahead.

Hard-core train nuts should venture to the storage facility of the London Transport Museum (p. 157) at the **Museum Depot** (118-129 Gunnersbury Lane, W3; ☎ 020/7379-6344; www.ltmuseum.co.uk; £10 adults, £8.50 children/seniors/students; visits by tour only on Fri and Sat; Tube: Acton Town), a good 45 minutes by Tube west, which displays hundreds of carriages, signs, and hardware that wouldn't fit (or interest average tourists) at Covent Garden. You must call ahead to book a tour.

Small but devastating, **The Foundling Museum** ★★ (40 Brunswick Square, WC1; ☎ 020/7841-3600; www.foundlingmuseum.org.uk; £5 adults, free for children under 16, £3 seniors/students; Tues–Sat 10am–6pm, Sun noon–6pm; Tube:

It's Free!

All of the following attractions charge no admission fees. Not a shabby lineup! If you can't fill a week out of the free admission at these incredible places, I can't help you:

Free all the time:

The Bank of England Museum, The British Library, The British Museum, Guildhall including the Clockmakers' Museum, The Hunterian Museum, Kenwood House, Library and Museum of Freemasonry, Museum of Childhood, Museum of London, The National Gallery, The National Maritime Museum, The National Portrait Gallery, The Natural History Museum, The Old Naval College, Greenwich, Prince Henry's Room, The Queen's House, The Science Museum, Sir John Soane's Museum, The Tate Britain, The Tate Modern, The V&A, The Wallace Collection

Free part-time:

Courtauld Institute of Art Gallery (Mondays, 10am–2pm), Guildhall Art Gallery (every day after 3:30pm, Fridays all day)

Russell Square) tracks the history of the Foundling Hospital, which took in thousands of London's orphans between 1739 and 1953. This was a period in which few people cared about kids: In 1802, a law was passed limiting the time children could work in mills—to 12 hours a day. By that measure, it's clear that the benefactors, who seem needlessly harsh today, were truly helping kids by locking them in this borderline prison. Don't miss the heartbreaking cases of tokens that mothers left at the doorstep with their babies; these tiny objects, into which a lifetime of hopes were imbued, never made it to their children's hands lest they compromise a mother's anonymity. Also take the time to listen to the oral histories by some of the last kids to be raised by the hospital; at the time of recording, they were elderly but still obviously quite shaken. Upstairs is the hospital's modest but solid collection of 18th-century English works (Hogarth, Reynolds, Gainsborough), which believe it or not was one of the first permanent art exhibitions in the world. The museum arranges absorbing events, such as concerts, tastings of old beer recipes, and meetings with former pupils of the hospital. The exercise grounds are now a kids-only park called Coram's Fields; see p. 220 for more info.

ELEVEN AMAZING HOUSES

These palaces and mansions are noteworthy for their architecture and design. For houses that function more like museums to the notables who lived in them, such as Handel or Dickens, look in the "Attractions for Niche Appeal" section (p. 171).

Although modern people know **Kensington Palace** ★ (Kensington Gardens, W8; ☎ 08707/51-51-70; www.hrp.org.uk; £12 adults, £7.50 children 5–15; £9 seniors/students including a free audio tour; Mar–Oct daily 10am–6pm, Nov–Feb daily 10am–5pm, last admission 1 hr. before closing; Tube: High Street Kensington) as the place where Lady Diana raised Princes William and Henry with husband Charles from 1984 to 1996, it's been a royal domicile since 1689, when William III and Mary II took control of an existing home (then in the country, far from town, which inflamed William's asthma) and made it their palace. Handsome and haughty, with none of the logical symmetry that defined later English architectural tastes, the redbrick palace has little of the ostentatious grandeur you might expect of the place where Queen Victoria was born and raised.

The main tour, a walk-through of important palace rooms, starts off with a few rooms showcasing ceremonial dress and royal outfits (the Queen's 1957 Norman Hartnell gown, embroidered with Napoleonic bees and French wildflowers in pearls, defies reason). Then it's on to the State Rooms, including the Red Saloon, through which 140,000 people passed in the fortnight after Diana's 1997 death. The walk-through includes the magnificent King's Staircase, lined with delicate canvas panels whose perimeters are rigged with tissue paper slivers designed to tear as a warning of shifting or swelling. The staircase is considered so precious that it was only opened to the public in 2004, 105 years after the rest of the palace first accepted sightseers.

Queen Victoria is well memorialized here: Take a peek at the Cupola Room in which she was christened; cases of her toys, including a wax doll that was beheaded and repaired in a childhood incident in 1828 (surely the last time a British sovereign caused a decapitation); and the bedroom where she learned of her ascension, at age 18, in 1837. Near the tour's end, over the fireplace in the Gallery, is a working Anemoscope, which has told the outside wind direction since 1694, and a map of the world as known in that year; face it, and you're facing north.

At press time, the tour included a walk through the apartment of Queen Elizabeth's sister Princess Margaret, who lived here, raising orchids and collecting seashells in a plainly decorated apartment (the poor thing), from 1960 until her death in 2002. You won't see the apartments in which Diana lived, nor will you see the room in which Victoria was born. Parts of the palace (the parts you won't see) are "grace and favor" flats (loaned for free by the Crown in thanks for past services), and it's for their privacy that some windows remain shaded. Within a decade, it's estimated, the entire palace will be opened to visitors.

I'll be honest. If you were to fall asleep tonight and wake up inside one of the State Rooms of **Buckingham Palace** ✦ (Buckingham Palace Rd., ☎ 020/7766-7300; www.royalcollection.org.uk; £14 adults, £8 children 5–16, £13 seniors/students; open late July to late September daily 9:45am–6pm, last admission at 3:45pm; Tube: Victoria), you'd think you were in any number of sumptuous old mansions. Is it opulent? No question. But if ever gilding, teardrop chandeliers, 18th-century portraits, and ceremonial halls could be considered standard-issue, Buckingham Palace is your basic palace. Queen Elizabeth's mild taste in decor—call it "respectable decadence" of yellows and creams and pleasant floral arrangements, thank you very much—is partly the reason. Remember, too, that much of this palace was built or remodeled in the 1800s—not so long ago in the grand scheme of things—and that the Queen considers Windsor Castle to be her real home. All tickets are timed and include an audio tour that rushes you around too quickly. The route threads through the public and ceremonial rooms (nowhere the Royal Family spends personal time, and besides, the Palace is open only two months a year, when they're in Scotland) at the back of the palace. Highlights include the 50m- (164-ft.) long Picture Gallery filled mostly with works amassed by George IV, an obsessive collector; the 14m- (46-ft.) tall Ballroom, where the Queen confers knighthoods; the parquet-floored Music Room, unaltered since John Nash decorated it in 1831, where the Queen's three eldest children were baptized in water brought from the River Jordan; and a stroll through the thick Garden in the backyard. It's definitely worth seeing—how often can you toodle around the spare rooms in a queen's house, inspecting artwork given as gifts by some of history's most prominent names? But it's no Versailles.

Since the Palace is only open in high summer, it's smart to book ahead by phone, but doing so adds £1.25 per ticket. If you're in London any time other than August or September and spot the Union Jack flying above, you'll at least know the Queen is home. So near, yet so far.

If I had to pick just one palace to visit in London, I'd select **Hampton Court** ✦✦✦ (East Molesey, Surrey; ☎ 0870/752-7777; www.hrp.org.uk; £12 adults, £8 children 5–15, £10 seniors/students; Apr–Oct, daily 10am–6pm and Nov–Feb daily 10am–4:30pm, last admission 1 hr. before closing; Mainline rail: Hampton Court) because it makes for such a complete day out. It looks like the ideal palace because it defined the ideal: The redbrick mansion was a center for royal life from 1525 to 1737, and its forest of chimneys still stands regally in 24 hectares (60 acres) of achingly pretty riverside gardens, painstakingly restored to their 1702 appearance, which you can see without the palace for £4. The Crown still stocks many of the 70 public rooms with rare art. Visitors come looking for vibrations left by Henry VIII during the 811 days he spent here (yes, that's all; he had more than 60 houses), and the curators try not to disappoint: Costumed docents wander the courtyards, answering questions, and there are often well-conceived events such as Tudor-style cookoffs in the old kitchens, Shakespeare plays in the hammer-beamed Great Hall, and horse-drawn carriage rides in spring and fall (£11 for 20 min.). Such corny but satisfying perks help rekindle some of the history that was snuffed out by successive remodeling—styles seem to change from room to room, starting out Tudor and ending up Queen Anne, but the decor is always over-the-top. A 1986 fire consumed Hampton's King's Apartments (now restored), as desperate volunteers hustled priceless furniture and tapestries out of the building. Whatever you do, don't neglect to head into the gardens and lose yourself in the Northern Gardens' shrubbery Maze, installed by William III; kids should love to giggle their way through to the middle of this leafy labyrinth. There are metal rods in the hedges to prevent you from cheating. The well-mannered South Garden has the Great Vine, the oldest vine in the world, planted in 1768; its grapes are sold in the gift shop at the end of August.

Transportation: From April to September daily, you can take **London River Services** (☎ 020/7930-2062; www.tfl.gov.uk/river or www.wpsa.co.uk) all the way from Westminster pier in central London, the way Henry VIII did on his barges, but it's a round-trip commitment of £11 single/£17 return, and tides sometimes prevent the first 3-hour trip of the day from landing at Hampton Court until 3pm, too late to see much. Consider taking the train out and the boat back. Otherwise, trains leave twice an hour from Waterloo station, take 35 minutes, and let you off right across the river from the Palace.

The great palace of Whitehall was home to some of England's flashiest characters, including Henry VIII. In a wrenching loss for art and architecture—to say nothing of bowling history, since Henry had an alley installed—it burned down in 1698. But if you had to pick just one room from the glorious palace to survive, it would have been the one that did: **The Banqueting House** ✦ (Whitehall at Horseguards Avenue, SW1; ☎ 0870/751-5185; www.hrp.org.uk; £4.50 adults, £3 children under 16, £3.50 seniors/students, including free audio tour; Mon–Sat 10am–5pm; Tube: Charing Cross or Westminster). The house was designed with Italianate Renaissance assurance (in a city made of timber and brick) by Inigo Jones and completed in 1622, which means Henry never set foot in it, but another fateful king set his *last* foot in it: In 1649, Charles I walked onto the scaffold from a window that stood in the present-day staircase, and met his doom under an axe wielded by Cromwell's republicans. The nine grandiose ceiling murals by Peter Paul Rubens, in which the king is portrayed as a god, give you a clue as to why the rabble would want to see His Highness brought low. Curators provide mirrors so visitors can inspect the ceiling without craning their heads to behold why Charles lost his. The remarkable building blends in inconspicuously, if that's the word, among the portentous state edifices along Whitehall.

The Queen dictates who in her family lives at which palace, and she herself lived at the four-story **Clarence House** (Stableyard Rd., SW1; ☎ 020/7766-7303; www.royalcollection.org.uk; £7.50 adults, £4 children 5–16; £6.50 seniors/students; Aug–early Oct daily 10am–5:30pm, last admission 4:30pm; Tube: Green Park), part of St. James's Palace, just before she took the throne. Her mother dwelled here for nearly half a century until her 2002 death at age 101, and now it's chez Charles and Camilla. Prince Charles, having a keener sense of public relations than perhaps any royal before him, recently decided to open the house,

Two Hybrid Galleries/Historic Homes

Upon entering **Sir John Soane's Museum** ✸ (12 Lincoln's Inn Fields, WC2; ☎ 020/7405-2107; www.soane.org; free admission; Tues–Sat 10am–5pm, the first Tues of the month 6pm–9pm; Tube: Holborn), a doorman will politely ask you to hold your bags to your chest. With good reason: These two town houses on the north side of Lincoln's Inn Fields are so overloaded with furniture, paintings, architectural decoration, and sculpture, that navigation is a challenge. The Georgian architect, noted for his bombastic neoclassical buildings (the Bank of England) as much as for his aesthetic materialism, bequeathed his home and its contents as a museum for "amateurs and students," and so it has been, looking much like this, since 1837. It's as if the well-connected eccentric has just ducked out to purloin another Greek pilaster, leaving you roam his creaking wood floors, sussing out the *objets d'art* from the certifiable treasures. His oddball abode is so cramped that precious Canalettos, which often fetch $10 million at auction, are banished to the gift shop. Ask to join a guided tour of the Picture Room, built in an 1823 expansion, so you can watch its hidden recesses be opened, revealing layer upon buried layer of works (such as William Hogarth's 8-painting *The Rake's Progress* series), filed inside false walls. You have to wonder how Soane could legally acquire antiquities such as the sarcophagus of Seti I, carved from translucent limestone, much less what kind of damage is being caused to it by parking it in a packed cellar crypt with barely more notice of its priceless status than a terse descriptive sign (which is more than most works receive here). Mostly, a visit reminds you of the unseemly way in which wealthy Englishmen used to stuff their homes with classical art as a way of stocking up on a sense of righteousness.

If Soane's museum is the life's work of a pack rat, its upper-class analog **The Wallace Collection** ✸✸ (Hertford House, Manchester Square, W1; ☎ 020/7563-9500; www.wallacecollection.org; free admission; daily

where royals have lived since 1827, to tourists during the summer months when the family is in Scotland. You won't get to poke around the Prince's medicine cabinet on your hour tour, since you can only tour the ground-floor public rooms, which still feel like an old lady's house despite being recently renovated. It feels much more like a grand town house than a mansion fit for a future king and reflects the Windsors' homey, cluttered decorating style, heavy on paintings of horses and light on the gilding and glitter. You'll find it about a third of the way east down the Mall from Buckingham Palace.

Most kings and queens don't have modern-day followings, but eccentric King George III comes close. He's the ruler who, during his reign from 1760 to 1820, lost his American colonies and gradually went crazy from suspected porphyria: See

10am–5pm; Tube: Bond Street), in Marylebone, showcases the fruit of an absurdly rich family's unerring tastes. Yet it's got the dignity of a boutique museum. A little bit V&A (decorative arts and furniture), a little bit National Gallery (paintings and portraits), but with a French flair, the Wallace celebrates fine living in an extravagant 19th-century city mansion, the former Hertford House. Rooms drip with chandeliers, clocks, suits of armor, and furniture, usually of royal provenance, and there's not a clunker among the paintings. While other museums were stocking up on Renaissance works, the Wallaces, visionaries of sorts, were buying 17th-century and 18th-century artists for cheap. You might recognize Jean-Honoré Fragonard's *The Swing*, showing a maiden kicking her slipper to her suitor below. Peter Paul Rubens' *The Rainbow Landscape* is also here; its sister painting, *Het Steen,* is at the National Gallery. Thomas Gainsborough's *Mrs. Robinson 'Perdita'* depicts the sloe-eyed actress in mid-affair with the Prince of Wales; she holds a token of his love, a miniature portrait, in her right hand. If she seems a little suspicious, it's for good reason—the Prince dumped her before the paint was dry. At the Ritblat Conservation Gallery, in the cellar, you can try on a replica suit of armor to test its weight. Also check out the room to the right of the foyer at the top of the hour, when a mid-18th-century musical clock, festooned in a golden starburst, chimes one of 14 tunes.

The museum asks for £2 donations, but you could put the money to buying a guide instead. The £3 audio guide highlights the same paintings as the meaty £7 printed guide; don't buy the £5 guide, since it's written like a picture book. Kids should grab a free "Monster Trail" guide, which leads them to the most attention-holding works. I don't usually point out museum cafes because they're a dime a dozen, but Café Bagatelle, in the covered courtyard, has an exemplary atmosphere. The Wallace makes for a gentle break from an Oxford Street shopathon—and let's face it, the place puts on a *real* display of power shopping.

the movie *The Madness of King George* for the tragic tale. **Kew Palace and Queen Charlotte's Cottage** (Royal Botanic Gardens, Kew, Richmond; ☎ 020/8332-5655; www.hrp.org.uk; To get onto the grounds, admission to Kew Gardens is required: £12 adults, children under 17 free, £8.75 seniors/students; admission to the house is an extra £5 adults, £3 children 5–16, £4 seniors and students; Kew Palace: Tues–Sun 10am–6pm, last admission 5pm, closed Nov–Mar; Cottage: June–Sept Sat–Sun 10am–4pm; Tube: Kew Gardens) was where he lived. Well, sort of. He lived in this smallish red house, 10km (6 miles) southwest of London, while his dream home, the Castellated Palace, was being built just to the east. His son hated that never-finished building so much (critics said it looked like a French prison) he blew it up with gunpowder as soon as he could, but the getaway he built for himself in

The Time-Machine Museum

My personal favorite home tour, the one I'll do again and again without tiring, is **Dennis Severs' House** ★★★ (18 Folgate St., E1; ☎ 020/7247-4013; www.dennissevershouse.co.uk; reservations required only on Monday evenings (£12), open the first and third Sundays of the month 2–5pm (£8) and 12–2pm on the Monday following the first and third Sundays (£5); Tube: Liverpool Street). The opening schedule is complicated, but I'll clean it up for you: Go on Monday nights for "the Experience!" As you approach this humble-looking town house on a dark street in Spitalfields, the shutters are closed and a gas jet burns. You're admitted by a manservant who speaks very little. He only motions you to explore the premises, room by room, silently and at your own pace. Suddenly, you're in the parlor of a reasonably prosperous merchant in the 1700s, and the owners have just left the room ahead of you. Candles burn, a real fire pops in the hearth, the smell of food wafts in the air, and a cat sleeps contently in the corner. Out on the street, you hear footsteps and hooves. Room by dusky room, without ropes or rules, you explore every corner overflowing with the implements of everyday life of the age. Wherever you go, it's as if the residents were just there, leaving behind toys on the stairs, beds unmade, tobacco in bowls, spilled mulled wine, buttered toast and tea growing cold on the table, and cosmetics half-applied. The effect gives you an incredibly strong sense for the period. As you go, you catch the tail ends of quiet, unseen conversations and pleasant smells continue to linger, while printed signs encourage you to assemble the clues in front of you and envision the residents. By the last of ten rooms, the attic, you'll have accompanied the house and its changing occupants through its decay into a terrifying slum.

In reality, this house survived in a declining neighborhood until the late 1970s, when an eccentric American named Dennis Severs purchased it for a pittance, dressed it with antiques, and invented this imagination odyssey—he called it "Still Life Drama" and a "game." Other museums are half-empty and unrealistically neat, but the Severs House is intentionally unlike any museum in the world, designed to make the past come alive through the power of suggestion and imagination. It reassembles life as a messy reality, not as a pretty picture created by researchers and hermetically sealed from further interaction. As the curators put it, *"Whether you see it or you don't, the house's ten rooms harbour ten 'spells' that engage the visitor's imagination in moods . . . Your senses are your guide."* Reservations are required, and visitors are spaced far enough apart so that they don't often run into each other and spoil the illusion of time travel. The house's daytime hours have much less of the brain-teasing magic that makes Monday's "Experience" one of London's most invigorating evenings, particularly for incurable romantics.

Brighton, an Indian folly, was even weirder. But this secondary crash pad near the Thames, where George III's wife Queen Charlotte died, survives, although it's really only the size of a standard manor house. It reopened in April 2006 after a decade-long restoration, carried out with scientific exactitude, and takes about an hour to tour. The little Queen Charlotte's Cottage, an imitation of a humble village home, was probably built for a zookeeper of a long-gone menagerie. Even if you have a Historic Royal Palaces pass (p. 141), you still must pay entrance to the Gardens (p. 186), making this one expensive time capsule.

This is how you'd be rewarded if you became a national war hero: **Apsley House** ★ (149 Piccadilly; ☎ 020/7499-5676; www.english-heritage.org.uk; £5.10 adults, £2.60 children, £3.80 seniors/students, including an out-of-date audio tour; Apr–Oct Tues–Sun 10am–5pm, Nov–March 10am–4pm; Tube: Hyde Park Corner), with Hyde Park as a backyard and Buckingham Palace Gardens as a front yard, was the home of Arthur Wellesley, who in 1815 defeated Napoleon and became the Duke of Wellington and later, Prime Minister. The mansion, still in the family (they live part-time in private rooms), was filled with splendid gifts showered upon him by grateful nations, but he never seemed to get his nemesis off his mind. One dining room table centerpiece, 72m (22 ft.) long in the form of an Egyptian temple, is beyond fabulous, and it was once Napoleon's. Aspley's art stash, which was largely looted by the French from the Spanish royal family and never went home, includes a few Jan Bruegel the Elders; Diego Velazques' virtuosic *The Waterseller of Seville* (I can understand why it was the artist's favorite work, since just looking at its execution makes me thirsty); and Correggio's *The Agony in the Garden,* in a case fitted with a keyhole so the Duke could open it and polish it with a silk hanky. In the grand staircase stands a colossal nude Napoleon that the little emperor despised; the Duke got hold of it, too, as yet another token of victory. The whiff of faded masculine glory pervades the place like cigar smoke, both fascinating and sad. The Duke and his best friend lived here together after their wives died, and in the cellar, you can see the Duke's own death mask, together with that of his most bitter rival, Napoleon Bonaparte. I get the feeling that in other circumstances, they would have been buddies. If you're also visiting Wellington Arch across the street, a joint ticket will save you £1.65.

A home so lush that its current tenants are the Rothschilds, who host diplomatic and corporate events here that make the world go round, **Spencer House** ★ (27 St. James's Place, SW1; ☎ 020/7499-8620; www.spencerhouse.co.uk; £9 adults, £7 children under 16/students/seniors, no reservations accepted; Sun 10:30am–5:45pm, closed Jan and Aug; Tube: Green Park) is the only surviving London mansion with an intact 18th-century interior. Tours of the ground floor and a portion of the first floor are on Sundays only, conducted by very proper guides employed by the Rothschild banking group, who are prone to peering down their noses at weekend sightseers. The home was begun in 1756 as a love nest by Diana Spencer's ancestors (and, by extension, the future king's), and the lavish gilt and carved decor repeatedly invoke the symbols of fidelity and virility. War damage spooked the Spencer clan, who moved out in the 1920s, and since then, they've gradually transferred the most precious elements to their estate at Althorp, 120 miles north of the city, and replaced them with equally fantastic facsimiles—the fireplace library, for instance, took 4,000 hours to carve. Expect your jaw to drop: three Benjamin West paintings are on loan from the Queen, a chair in the Palm

Home, Sumptuous Home: More Mega Mansions

I think the stately homes mentioned above are the best in town, and after you've seen them, there's a limit to how much more gilding, "Do Not Sit Here" signs, and velvet ropes you can take. But these lesser houses are gorgeous and recommended too, even if they aren't in quite as ideal condition or as well located as my main choices.

In Northwest London: Kenwood House ★ (Hampstead Lane, NW3; ☎ 020/8348-2528; www.english-heritage.org.uk; free admission; Apr–Oct daily 11am–5pm, Nov–Mar 11am–4pm; Tube: Hampstead or Highgate) is a neoclassical villa from 1640 full of paintings by Reynolds, Turner, Gainsborough, and Vermeer (*The Guitar Player*). Its exterior was used in *Notting Hill* for the scene when Hugh Grant drops in on Julia Roberts' film shoot. The views of London are ideal.

In Southeast London: Eltham Palace (off Court Rd., Greenwich SE9; ☎ 020/8294-2548; www.english-heritage.org.uk; £7.60 adults, £3.80 children, £5.70 seniors/students; Apr–Oct Sun–Wed 10am–5pm, Nov–Dec 20 and early Feb–Mar Sun–Wed 10am–4pm; Mainline rail: Eltham), pronounced "EL-tam" from 1936, mixes Art Deco, ocean liner style, and Swedish design. The 8 hectares (19 acres) of gardens, crawling with wisteria, are popular with picnickers and nappers.

In West London: Chiswick House (Burlington Lane, Chiswick, W4; ☎ 020/8995-0508; www.english-heritage.org.uk; £4 adults, £2 children, £3 seniors/students; Apr–Oct Wed–Sun 10am–5pm; Tube: Turnham Green) was built by the Earl of Burlington (1694-1753), who was so into Italy that he commissioned a Palladian home to evoke the villas and gardens of Rome's suburbs. The interior has been restored, and the Italianate gardens are specked with classical statues of lions and the like.

In Southwest London: The family of the Duke of Northumberland has owned **Syon** ★ (Syon Park, Brentford; ☎ 020/8560-0881; www.syonpark. co.uk; £7.50 adults, £6.50 children 5–16/seniors/students; late Mar–Oct Wed, Thurs, and Sun 11am–5pm; Tube: Gunnersby, then 237 or 267 bus to Brentlea Gate), boasting Robert Adam interiors, for over 4 centuries. In addition to gorgeous interiors, its 1826 Great Conservatory, built from gunmetal, Bath stone, and lots of glass, was a landmark in architecture. It's just across the river from Kew, but you'll feel like you're in the middle of the country.

Room has a companion in the Museum of Fine Arts in Boston, and the original Painted Room suite was once at the V&A. If this jewel box of a mansion were any sweeter, it would be made of gingerbread.

Death Takes a Holiday

If you're a major musical star, stay away from London! It seems a dispro-portionate number of singers have met untimely ends here. These houses aren't open to the public, but their grim pasts make them infamous:

June 22, 1969, 4 Cadogan Lane, Belgravia; Tube: Sloane Square
Judy Garland overdosed on barbituates and expired in the bathroom of the two-room flat here. The public outpouring of grief, and its suppression by police, resulted in riots in New York City and started the gay rights movement as we know it today.

September 18, 1970, 22 Lansdowne Crescent,
Notting Hill; Tube Notting Hill Gate
In a basement flat of the Samarkand Hotel, **Jimi Hendrix** washed down nine Vesperax sleeping pills with alcohol. An ambulance was summoned from St. Mary Abbots Hospital, Kensington, but arrived too late for the virtuoso guitar player. The plot thickened 26 years later, when the last per-son to see him alive, girlfriend Monika Dannemann, was found asphyxiated in a car in Seaford, East Sussex, not long after being accused in court of keeping secrets about Hendrix's final moments.

July 29, 1974, 12 Curzon Place, Mayfair; Tube: Hyde Park Corner
"Mama" Cass Elliot of The Mamas and the Papas was found dead in between solo performances at the London Palladium in a flat owned by Grammy-winning songwriter Harry Nilsson, who wasn't home. Contrary to lore, she did not die from choking on a ham sandwich, but from a heart attack, brought on by morbid obesity (she was 5'5" and weighed 238 pounds).

September 7, 1978, 12 Curzon Place, Mayfair;
Tube: Hyde Park Corner
Four years after Elliot's death, **Keith Moon,** drummer of The Who, died in the same flat. His undoing: chlormethiazole edisylate, a prescribed anti-alcohol drug. Horrified that two of his friends should die while borrowing his apartment, Nilsson quickly sold the flat to Moon's bandmate Pete Townshend.

ATTRACTIONS WHERE LONDONERS
TAKE THEIR FAMILIES

Many major cities have their own equivalent of the **The Natural History Museum** 🧒 ★ (Cromwell Rd., SW7; ☎ 020/7942-5000; www.nhm.ac.uk; free admission; Mon–Sat 10am–5:50pm, Sun 11am–5:50pm; Tube: South Kensington). You know: A hall filled with dinosaur bones, countless cases of colorful rocks, a taxidermist's menagerie of stuffed wild animals, and endless, depressing reminders of just how many animals are on their way to being snuffed out for eternity. The

Maritime Greenwich: History's Theme Park

While you're in Greenwich, about 30 minutes east of Central London, take in the few other attractions that comprise **Maritime Greenwich** (www. greenwichwhs.org.uk; Tube: Cutty Sark DLR), a UNESCO World Heritage Site. Situated on a picturesque slope of the south bank of the Thames, Greenwich once was home to the Greenwich Palace, where the Old Royal Naval College stands, and it was where both Henry VIII and Elizabeth I were born. The last part of the palace to be constructed, The Queen's House (1616, Inigo Jones), still stands, but most of it was rebuilt in the late Georgian period as the equally palatial Royal Hospital, a convalescence ground for disabled and veteran sailors. So many of these treasures are owned by the state that many entrance fees are waived; you can play the whole day without paying more than a few pounds. Stop by the Visitor Centre, alongside the *Cutty Sark*, for background information.

Cutty Sark ★ (King William Walk, SE10; ☎ 020/8858-3445; www. cuttysark.org.uk; £5 adults, £3.70 children under 16, £3.90 seniors/students; daily 10am–5pm, last admission 4:30pm, free guided tours before 3:30 weekdays; DLR: Cutty Sark). This handsome wooden ship, launched in 1869, is the only tea clipper left in the world, and the symbol of a trade that gave England its muscle. Against the odds, she still has nearly all of her fabric and riggings. But call ahead to make sure enough of her will be open; she's getting a massive, gradual restoration that will last into 2008.

Old Royal Naval College ★ (Greenwich, SE10; ☎ 020/8269-4747; www.oldroyalnavalcollege.org; free admission; grounds open daily 8am–6pm, buildings open daily 10am–5pm, Royal Chapel open Sun at 11am for worship and from 12:30pm–5pm for visits; DLR: Cutty Sark). This 1696 neoclassical complex, the work of Wren, offers two main sights: the

commodious NHM, good for several hours' wander, has all that, of course, and more. Organization is a cut above, since pathways through exhibits are clearly marked and plenty of plain-speaking signs for kids are placed at their eye level. Even the dinosaur bones are supplemented by scary robotic estimations of how they sounded and moved. The mock-up of an average middle-class kitchen infested with various vermin is a visitor favorite, as are *The Earth Galleries,* a multimedia display that evolved from the Geological Museum, absorbed in the 1970s. A welcome new addition is the **Darwin Centre** (☎ 020/7942-5011; free admission; Mon–Sat 10am–5:50pm, Sun 11am–5:50pm; 45-min. tour; ages 9 or older), named after Charles Darwin, who bequeathed his specimens here. Seen only by tour, its goal is to bring visitors face-to-face with the army of scientists working behind the scenes at the museum; book a place to see some of the 22 million archived specimens (including those that came back on the *Beagle,* mostly bottled in vials of preservative) on 27km/17 miles of shelves.

Painted Hall and the Chapel. The Painted Hall has incredible paintings by James Thornhill that took nearly 2 decades to complete. It was the setting for the funeral of Admiral Nelson—check out the electrified diorama of the event in a side room. The Chapel, in the Greek Revival style, is the work of James Stuart. Tours by accredited guides run daily (☎ 020/8269-4791; 90 minutes; £4 adults, free admission for children).

The Queen's House (Romney Rd., SE10; ☎ 020/8312-6565; www.nmm.ac.uk; free admission; daily 10am–5pm; DLR: Cutty Sark) is connected to the **National Maritime Museum** (p. 170) by a colonnade. This Palladian home, elegantly decorated, was a pet project for Inigo Jones, who took 22 years (1616–38) to complete his commission. Its nautilus-shaped Tulip staircase, and other rooms, are considered to be haunted by an unknown spectre, so have a camera ready.

The Royal Observatory and Planetarium ✦ (Greenwich Park, SE10; ☎ 020/8312-6565; www.rog.nmm.ac.uk; free admission; daily 10am–5pm; DLR: Cutty Sark), yet another creation of Christopher Wren (from 1675), was the Empire's most important house for celestial observation, and it still houses significant relics of star-peeping. The Prime Meridian, located at precisely 0° longitude, crosses through the grounds (the Equator is 0° latitude), enabling you to have a foot in two hemispheres at once. In 2007, the attraction will open Time and Space, a state-of-the-art planetarium.

The Fan Museum (12 Crooms Hill, SE10; ☎ 020/8305-1441; www.fan-museum.org; £4 adults, £3 children/seniors/students, includes free audio guide; Tues–Sat 11am–5pm, Sun noon–5pm; Tube: Greenwich), is the only museum in the world devoted to the art of hand fans, going back 900 years. The 3,000 exhibits, most handmade, are spread through two Georgian town houses.

Even if you don't give a hooey about remedial ecology, the 1880 Victorian building that houses the museum is a landmark. It crawls with carved monkeys whimsically clinging to the terra cotta and plants growing across ceiling panels. The western wing depicts living animals, and the eastern side showcases extinct creatures. Rent a nifty handheld architecture tour that plays both audio and video (sketches, pictures) for £3.50 at the Life Galleries desk. Kids under 7 can borrow free explorer backpacks with pith helmets, binoculars, activities, and drawing materials themed to monsters, primates, birds, oceans, or mammals; they tend to run out early on weekends (call ☎ 020/7942-5555 for kid info). Kids 4 to 16 can grab Discovery activity guides for 40p to 80p; and those 7 to 14 should look for the free Investigate hands-on lab in the basement. So many family-oriented activities and demonstrations, many free, take place here that it takes a 20-page guide every 3 months to publicize them all; events are also touted online.

Around the corner from the Natural History Museum and across the street from the V&A, the mammoth **Science Museum** 🧒 ★ (Exhibition Rd., SW7; ☎ 0870/870-4868; www.sciencemuseum.org.uk; free admission; daily 10am–6pm; Tube: South Kensington) is really two museums, one old-style and one far-out, that have been grafted together. So many interesting exhibitions are on display here that I always seem to run out of time. The old-school section, split over six levels (four huge, two small), is an embarrassment of riches from the history of science and technology. Exhibits are similar to what lots of science museums have, but in almost every case, they display the most original or most rare specimen available: 1969's *Apollo 10* command module; "Puffing Billy," the world's oldest surviving steam engine; a 1950 computer pioneered by Alan Turing; and one of the V2 missiles that terrorized London in the waning months of Word War II. The quieter upper floors are full of subjects like model ships and early computers (second floor), a history of veterinary medicine (fifth floor), and aviation (including the *Vickers Vimy*, the first plane to cross the Atlantic without stopping, third floor).

The high-concept Wellcome Wing is easy to miss, in a separate area buried in the back of the ground floor, but seek it out. A hyper-cool, cobalt-blue, humming, multileveled cavern dedicated to interactive games and displays, the Wellcome Wing bears little relation to the mothballed museum you just crossed through. The *Antenna* exhibition (ground floor) is exceptionally cutting-edge, and updated regularly with the latest breakthroughs; past topics have included biodegradable cell phones implanted with seeds and robots controlled by a lamprey fish's brain signals. Kids can buy sassy themed "trail" booklets (space, medicine, etc.) in the bookshop for £1. Science-lovin' adults should check out the events at the Dana Centre, the museum's sleek venue for talks and discussions (p. 200).

The museum doesn't always score. BP sponsors a fawning section on energy, and the gift shop (mostly mall-style toys) and guidebook disappoint. I also don't recommend spending £7.50 on its gimmicky (and unspecial) IMAX 3D cinema or £4 on its SimEx motion simulator rides.

You might be put off by the name, however, **The National Maritime Museum** ★★ (Romney Rd., Greenwich, SE10; ☎ 020/8858-4422; www.nmm.ac.uk; free admission; daily 10am–5pm, last admission 4:30pm; Tube: Cutty Sark DLR) actually isn't as, ahem, dry as most would expect. Since so much of Britain's history from the 17th to 20th century was transacted via the high seas, this place, the largest maritime museum in the world, isn't just about boats and knots. The facility has an endless supply of Smithsonian-worthy artifacts that would do any museum proud. Highlights include a pocket watch of a *Titanic* passenger, stopped at 3:07am; the *Rainbow Warrior*'s binnacle; a bottle, half full of port, from the wreck of the *Royal George*, which killed 900 people in 1782; and, most ghoulishly, the bloodstained breeches and bullet-punctured topcoat that Admiral Lord Nelson wore on the day he took his fatal shot. It's a museum so complete it even has the North Pole itself—the Arctic location shifts magnetically from year to year, and the museum has the first, obsolete one, planted in 1831 by Captain James Clark Ross. The pole is on exhibit near relics from Sir John Franklin's ill-fated 1848 Arctic expedition, including lead-lined food tins that likely caused the explorers to go mad and resulted in their deaths. It's not all so gloomy, though; you'll spot figureheads, old ships, antique instruments, and a section on the heyday of the oceangoing liner. Weekends are full of free kids' events (storytelling, treasure hunts) that bring suburban London families pouring into the gates.

> ## Lifting the Veil on History
>
> From time to time, you'll come across museum cases that are shrouded in dark fabric. That's not to keep you from touching them. It's to protect their contents from light. Feel free to lift the material and have a look at the precious artifacts underneath—just make sure to cover them again.

ATTRACTIONS WITH NICHE APPEAL

ARCHITECTURE

Back in 1677, it was the tallest thing (61m/202 ft.) in this part of town and therefore a world wonder. **The Monument** ★ (Monument St. at Fish St. Hill, WC4; ☎ 020/7626-2717; www.towerbridge.org.uk; £2 adults, £1 children; daily 9:30am–5pm; Tube: Monument or Bank) was erected to commemorate the destruction of the city by the Great Fire in 1666. Its 61m (202 ft.) height is also the distance from its base to the site of Thomas Farynor's bakery in Pudding Lane to the east, where the conflagration began. Today, there's only one thing to do in this fluted column of Portland stone: Climb it. The spiral staircase of 6-inch steps, which has no landings, gradually narrows as it ascends to the graffiti-stained, outdoor observation platform—a popular suicide spot until 1842, when a cage was installed. They'll tell you it's 311 steps to the top, including on the certificate of achievement you receive upon leaving, but they're lying. It's 313 if you count the two before the box office. Go on a pleasant day unless you'd like a good wind-whipping. Check out the metal band snaking down the north side; it's a lightning rod, and it crosses along an inscription, in Latin, that blamed Catholics for starting the fire (the insult was chiseled off in 1831). If you plan to visit this and the Tower Bridge Exhibition, a combo ticket will save £1.

The city opens it so briefly each day that I hesitate to mention it, but **Prince Henry's Room** ★ (17 Fleet St., first floor, EC4; free admission; Mon–Fri 11am–2pm; Tube: Blackfriars) is too cool to ignore. Though housed in one of the only London buildings that dates to before the Great Fire of 1666, the room's interior is contemporary. The building's half-timbered facade is original to the 1600s, and the room itself has one of the finest (and last) remaining Jacobean enriched plaster ceilings in London. It's thought that the room was once part of a tavern. It shelters a small exhibition about Samuel Pepys (pronounced "Peeps"), whose diary entries are one of the texts historicists read for understanding its era.

Wellington Arch (Hyde Park Corner, Apsley Way, W1; ☎ 020/7930-2726; www.english-heritage.org.uk; £3 adults, £1.50 children 5–15, £2.30 seniors/students; Apr–Oct Wed–Sun 10am–5pm, Nov–Mar Wed–Sun 10am–4pm; Tube: Hyde Park Corner), built between 1826 and 1830, was intended as a triumphal entry to Buckingham Palace and stood some meters northwest, in the vicinity of the grassy patch east across the street from the Lanesborough Hotel. Tales of its relocation and the switch from Wellington's original statue on top to a smaller statue (*Peace Descending Upon War*, the largest bronze sculpture in Europe) are told in the little museum inside, which also discusses the period when the Arch served as the city's smallest police station. If you buy a joint ticket with the Duke

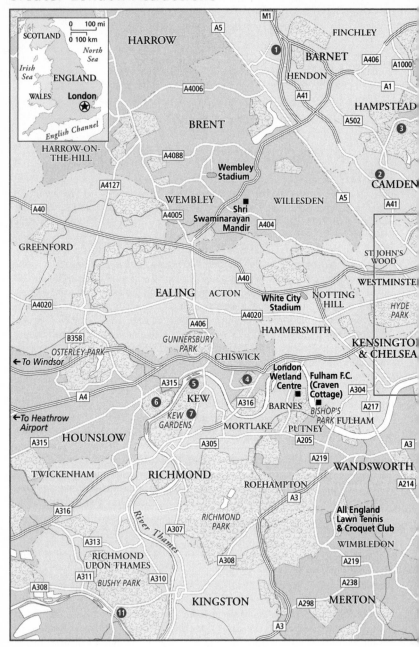

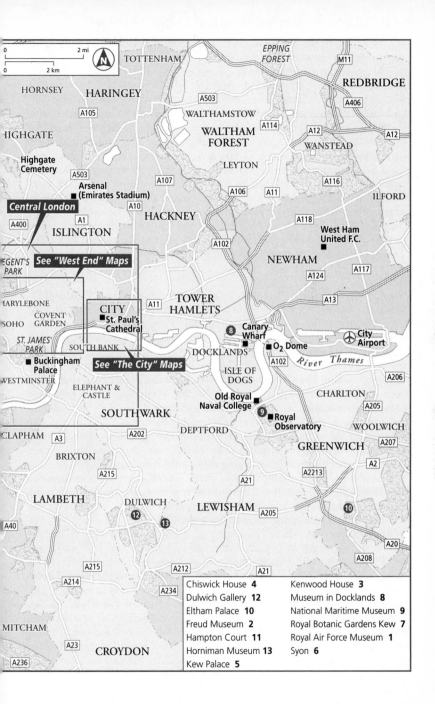

Chiswick House **4**	Kenwood House **3**
Dulwich Gallery **12**	Museum in Docklands **8**
Eltham Palace **10**	National Maritime Museum **9**
Freud Museum **2**	Royal Botanic Gardens Kew **7**
Hampton Court **11**	Royal Air Force Museum **1**
Horniman Museum **13**	Syon **6**
Kew Palace **5**	

of Wellington's Apsley House, across Piccadilly, you'll save about £1.65; you can take an elevator up with the admission price.

The quiet, minor **Jewel Tower** (Abingdon St., SW1; ☎ 020/7222-2219; www.english-heritage.org.uk; £2.70 adults, £1.40 children 5–15, £2 seniors/students; Apr–Oct daily 10am–5pm, Nov–Mar daily 10am–4pm; Tube: Westminster), built circa 1365, is one of only remnants left over from the 1834 fire that ravaged the Royal Palace of Westminster (the Abbey is another). This stone three-level tower, once a moatside storehouse for the king's treasures, has walls so thick it was later considered an ideal setting for taking accurate measurements. Curators now use it for displays about Parliament, across the street, and weights-and-measures standards. The medieval architecture has character: winding stone stairs, wooden foundations, and a ground floor with a 14th-century ribbed vaulted ceiling under which tourist trinkets and hot tea are dispensed to the few who wander in. Check the glass case by the window, which halfheartedly lays out incredible relics dug up nearby (a 1,200-year-old-sword, a 16th-century wine bottle stamped Royal Oak Tavern) as if they're about to go out with the next day's trash.

ART

Dulwich Picture Gallery ✦ (Gallery Road, Dulwich Village, SE21; ☎ 020/8693-5254; www.dulwichpicturegallery.org.uk; £4 adults, free for children, £3 seniors/students; Tues–Fri 10am–5pm, Sat–Sun 11am–5pm; Mainline rail: West Dulwich Station) would be more famous were it not for one fact: Reaching it requires a 15-minute train ride from Victoria station and a 15-minute walk from the local station. Fortunately, such effort lands you in a pretty villagelike enclave of South London. The Gallery, which keeps one of the world's most vital collections of Old Master paintings of the 1600s and 1700s, was once a household name. Magnanimous collectors bequeathed it to become England's first public art gallery (opened 1817), designed with a surplus of space and light by Sir John Soane (who left us his own cramped, dark museum; p. 162). A visit is almost indescribably graceful and serene, and its old-fashioned display method—frames hang from wires suspended from ceiling rails—imbues the bestilled air with a lost-in-time illusion. Soane's skylight system was so novel that it more or less invented the private-gallery genre—you'll see shades of it in the Getty Museum in Malibu, California—and the collection was so well assembled that after it opened, Britain wasted little time in creating its own National Gallery.

Royal Academy of Arts (Burlington House, Piccadilly, W1; ☎ 020/7300-8000; www.royalacademy.org.uk; free admission; Sat–Thurs 10am–6pm, Fri 10am–10pm, last admission 30 min. before closing; Tube: Piccadilly Circus or Green Park), Britain's first art school, was founded in 1768 and relocated to Burlington House, a Palladian-style city mansion, in Victorian times. Only a few of its restored 18th-century rooms, the six John Madejski Fine Rooms (Tues–Fri 1–4:30pm, Sat–Sun 10am–6pm; free tours Tues–Fri at 1pm) can be toured without an admission fee, but what's displayed there is worth a half-hour: John Singer Sargents, Thomas Gainsboroughs, Stanley Spencers, and even Winston Churchills (the old bulldog was good at everything). The paintings change regularly, but they're always strong. Charles Darwin's *Origin of the Species* papers were delivered for the first time in the Reynolds Room on July 1, 1858; the space now displays 20th-century paintings. Beyond those, you'll pay £7–£10 for whatever exhibition is on. The museum's biggest event is the annual **Summer Exhibition,** which since the late 1700s has displayed the best public works, submitted anonymously; careers have been made by it.

Extend your Guildhall visit by popping next door into the **Guildhall Art Gallery** (Guildhall, EC2; ☎ 020/7332-3700; www.cityoflondon.gov.uk; £2.50 adults, £1 children/seniors/students, Fri and after 3:30pm, free admission; Mon–Sat 10am–5pm, Sun noon–4pm, last admission 30 min. before closing; Tube: Bank), an unpatronized collection of about 250 pieces of British art (think war paintings and cityscapes). I'd classify most exhibits here as ephemera: The art was talked about in its time, but it's hardly compelling today. The main draw is the access to the ruins of the Roman Amphitheatre, built around the year 70, abandoned in the 4th century, but discovered by accident in 1988 deep under the courtyard in front of the Guildhall. The complex's **Guildhall Library Bookshop** (Aldermanbury, EC2; ☎ 020/7332-1858; www.cityoflondon.gov.uk/corporation/shop; Mon–Fri 9:30am–4:45pm) is one of the city's better sources for London history books.

BIOGRAPHY

The Benjamin Franklin House ★ (36 Craven St., WC2; ☎ 020/7930-6601; www.benjaminfranklinhouse.org; tours (required) cost adults £9, children/students/seniors £6; reservations are required; there are ten tours daily, plus two more on Fri evenings, which cost £4 more for adults, £3 more for everyone else; Oct–May Wed–Sun 10am–5pm; June–Sept also open Mon; Tube: Embankment or Charing Cross), the only residence of the portly politico left standing in the world, opened as a sort of architectural preserve in 2006. Astonishingly, Franklin lived here, in a boarding house by the Thames, without his family, for 16 years—much longer than many Americans realize—and it was only the Revolution that forced him to pack up and move back to the Colonies. For much of his life Franklin was a fervent loyalist and British imperialist who, even as late as 1775, felt that the differences between Britain and the Colonies could be settled in "half an hour." Tours are conducted by a young actress playing Polly Hewson, the daughter of Ben's landlady, who tells wistful tales as recordings chime in with other voices from her memory. The rewards of a tour are mixed. On the one hand, you can't ask questions, exhibits are sparse (one exception is the ghoulish deposit of human bones in the backyard, likely left over from dissections by Franklin's doctor neighbor), and there are no kid's activities. But on the other hand, it's rare for a famous home of this age to have survived into our lifetimes. It's also humbling to see how this legendary man made do with much smaller quarters than we might accept; his study is no larger than the smallest London hotel rooms. The worn back wooden staircase, on which the Founding Father got his exercise when French trollopes weren't available, is so well preserved it feels ghostly. On my visit, I couldn't help moving through the mushroom-colored, wood-paneled, empty rooms and remarking that "Ben Franklin touched *this actual door* and stoked *this actual stove*"—a rare sensation even in London, where such vestiges have usually been combed-over, bombed, burned, or "restored" into oblivion. If you like showier stuff, you might leave hungry.

The former home (from 1834 to 1881) of writer Thomas Carlyle and his exacting wife Jane, **Carlyle House** (24 Cheyne Row, SW3; ☎ 020/7352-7087; www.nationaltrust.org.uk; £4.20 adults, £2.10 kids; late Mar–late Oct Wed–Fri

2–5pm, Sat–Sun 11am–5pm; Tube: Sloane Square, then bus 11, 19, 22, or 211) has been converted into a shrine, with his letters, books, and writing chair all on display. The modest home, which has a walled garden and is an excellent vestige of the middle-class Victorian lifestyle, was a salon of sorts for Dickens' era scribes like Dickens, Thackeray, Tennyson, and Browning. Because it was opened to the public just 14 years after the writer's death, it feels as forgotten and forlorn as the set of a play after the final curtain. It's a short walk from here to comfortable Battersea Park (p. 224), which eases the long trip to Chelsea somewhat.

Although Dickens moved around a lot, **The Charles Dickens Museum** ★★ (48 Doughty St., WC1; ☎ 020/7405-2127; www.dickensmuseum.com; £5 adults, £3 children, £4 seniors/students; Mon–Sat 10am–5pm, Sun 11am–5pm; Tube: Chancery Lane or Russell Square) is his last London home still standing. A museum since 1925, these four floors don't exude many vibes from the old guy; after all, he departed in 1839 after staying less than 2 years here. It could be anyone's humble home. Still, his celebrity got a kick-start while he lived here: *Oliver Twist* and *Nicholas Nickleby*, arguably his biggest hits, were written while he was in residence, a short stroll from the Foundling Hospital for orphans. As you watch the half-hour biographical video and inspect the dusty spreads of his desks, his podium, and installments of his biggest books, an unpleasant realization sets in: Charles Dickens was a compelling character but kind of a jerk. Tough on his kids and unfaithful to his wife, his greatest possession seems to have been his ego. Ironically, his audience still feeds it, nearly 150 years after his death.

A rare surviving middle-class home from the 18th century (c. 1700) in The City of London, this slouching and brick-faced abode happens to be that of the famous sage and lexicographer: **Dr. Johnson's House** ★ (17 Gough Square; ☎ 020/7353-3745; www.drjohnsonshouse.org; £4.50 adults, £1.50 children, £3.50 seniors/students; May–Sept Mon–Sat 11am–5:30pm, and Oct–Apr Mon–Sat 11am–5pm; Tube: Blackfriars). He lived here from 1748 to 1759. If you're hoping to learn a lot about the man, you'll have to spring for a book in the gift shop. Little substance is provided in the house itself, which fortunately merits some interest on its own terms (the corkscrew latch on the front door, which prevented lock-picking from above, is an example). The rooftop garret in which Johnson and his six helpers toiled to create the first English dictionary was burned out in the Blitz, ironically, by a barrel of burning ink which flew out of a bombed warehouse; you can still see some scorch marks on the ceiling timbers.

In a hilly Hampstead neighborhood of spacious brick-faced homes, Sigmund Freud, having just fled the Nazis, spent the last year of his life. His daughter Anna, herself a noted figure in psychoanalysis, lived on in the same house until her own death in 1982, after which **The Freud Museum** (20 Maresfield Gardens, NW3; ☎ 020/7435-2002; www.freud.org.uk; £5 adults, free for children under 12, £3 seniors/students; Wed–Sun noon–5pm; Tube: Hampstead) was established. The eight rooms of the house and their contents, though original and passionately preserved by Anna (Elektra complex, indeed), are not well explained, so don't expect to learn much about the Freuds' pioneering methods. Still, the house is authentic, and if nothing else, you'll be struck by what a lovely place it must have been for winding down a notable life. Sigmund's study and library, which came from the doctors' famed offices at Berggasse 19, Vienna, were left precisely as they were on the day he died—which he did on a couch, of course.

Body of Work: Jeremy Bentham's "Auto Icon"

Like England's own Ben Franklin, Jeremy Bentham (1748–1832) was a renaissance man, a philosopher, a utilitarian, and a subversive. Bentham's progressive worldview helped shape civilized England. Prison reformer, supporter of suffrage and the decriminalization of homosexuality, educator, and pen pal of U.S. president James Madison, Bentham worked tirelessly to enable all citizens equal access to courts and schools. He coined the words international, maximize, and codification.

He was so ahead of his time, his head still refuses to stay in the past. Bentham was obsessed with furnishing eternal access to his corpse—the gift that keeps on giving, really—and he stipulated it in his will. Starting years before his death, he purportedly carried around a pair of glass eyes that were intended for his future "Auto Icon," as he called it (auto=self, icon=image), which would represent him forever. Once he expired, his body was dissected during medical lectures. A colleague dressed Bentham's remains in his earthly garments and propped them in a wooden case at University College London in 1850. Bentham's severed head was placed between his own feet. Unfortunately, his shriveled noggin wasn't preserved with much skill, and kids from rival colleges kept swiping it (in 1975, some hooligans from King's College held it for a £10 ransom); so today, to keep it from completely falling apart, it's stashed in the vaults, along with his long-pocketed eyeballs.

Anyone can see Bentham's Auto Icon in the lobby of UCL's South Cloisters. His skeleton is hidden by his clothing and gloves, but his doughy wax head, which sagely observes the current scholarly crop at UCL from beneath an old straw hat, is freakishly lifelike. (A digital image of his preserved head is in on a bulletin board to the left.) You'll find it on the east side of Gower Street between University Street and Grafton Way, opposite the castle-like, redbrick Cruciform Building. Go in the gates, veer right around the flank of the grand portico, and enter the door marked South Cloisters. Once inside, hang a right and head for the stone lions (Tube: Euston Square). Then clear your head, and your own eyeballs, with a visit to the changing exhibitions at **Strang Print Room** (South Cloisters; ☎ 020/7679-2540; www.ucl.ac.uk; Mon–Fri 1–5pm; free admission), UCL's collection of rare drawings and prints by masters including Whistler, Rembrandt, and Dürer.

Florence Nightingale Museum (p. 177) is too expensive to appeal far beyond those interested in nursing or the headstrong, 19th-century lamplighter for sanitary hospital conditions. It preserves many of Nightingale's letters and souvenirs, as well as leftovers from the mostly forgotten Crimean War (1854-56), and it tells the story of how Nightingale helped establish nursing as a respected discipline.

Diana, Princess of Wales Memorial Fountain

In July 2004, the Queen came to Hyde Park to open a beautiful fountain designed to conjure the memory of the mother of her grandchildren and a longtime thorn in her side, Princess Diana. As designed by American architect Kathryn Gustafson, this graceful o-shaped **Diana, Princess of Wales Memorial Fountain** (between West Carriage Dr., Rotten Row, and The Serpentine, Hyde Park; free admission; Oct–Feb daily 10am–4pm, Mar daily 10am–6pm, Apr–Aug daily 10am–8pm, Sept daily 10am–7pm; Tube: South Kensington) undulates down a gentle slope, sending two flumes of water rushing and bubbling into a calm collecting pool. At three points, bridges bring you to the center of the space.

Shortly after opening, the trouble began. A day later, it clogged with leaves, flooding the surrounding grass. As originally conceived, visitors would be able to splash in the waters, but that ended when the first three guests slipped and fell—the planners hadn't planned for algae growth. So for 5 months in 2005, it closed while an asphalt-like path was laid around it, spoiling lawsuits and the effect alike. After it re-opened, hairline cracks were found in its 545 blocks of Cornish granite. The bill so far? £5.2 million. Londoners have decided they don't miss Di *that* much. A House of Commons committee declared it "ill-conceived and ill-executed." I admit that rather than putting me in a state of remembrance, it puts me into a state of wishing I had an inner tube. But for all that, the Fountain, which is gated and switches off exactly on time (so don't bother coming outside of its opening hours), makes lovely sounds and is one of the city's most popular new tourist sights, with some 800,000 visitors in the 10 months after its re-opening. You can reach it most quickly from the Alexandra Gate at Kensington Gore, Knightsbridge, up Exhibition Road from the trio of great South Kensington museums.

Mildly interesting for fans of the *Messiah* composer, **The Handel House Museum** (25 Brook St., W1; ☎ 020/7495-1685; www.handelhouse.org; £5 adults, £2 kids except Sat (free), £4.50 seniors/students; Tues–Wed and Fri–Sat 10am–6pm, Thurs 10am–8pm, Sun noon–6pm; Tube: Bond Street) doesn't have much in the way of artifacts. This Mayfair building, the German-born composer's home from 1723 (he was its first tenant) to his death in 1759, has lived many lives—before the museum's 2001 opening, conservators chipped 28 layers of paint off the interior walls to uncover the original grey color. You'll see a 15-minute video on Handel's life, and then move on, often attended by old dears serving as volunteers, to see the few humble rooms, furnished with period furniture that wasn't his. There's a small alcove where kids can try on period costumes and grown-ups can listen to Handel's greatest works. You're best off coming during one of the house's many concerts, held every 3 or 4 days in a plain recital room (£7–£8.50 depending on performance). Handel fans should also investigate the composer's collection at the Foundling Museum (p. 158).

CARTOONS

The Cartoon Museum (35 Little Russell St., WC1; ☎ 020/7580-8155; www.cartoonmuseum.org; £3 adults, free for children under 18, £2 seniors/students; Tues–Sat 10:30am–5:30pm, Sun noon–5:30pm; Tube: Tottenham Court Road or Holborn), a small but well-put-together suite of rooms, puts an emphasis on British artists, particularly political ones. Its 750-odd original illustrations, going from Victorian (Cruikshank) right up to contemporary satirists (Simon Bond's *101 Uses for a Dead Cat*), also has a few faces from the funny papers, including Andy Capp and Dick Tracy.

CLOCK MAKING

Through the western entrance of the Guildhall complex, now City of London offices, you'll find a small **Clockmakers' Museum** (Guildhall Library, EC2; ☎ 020/7332-1868; www.clockmakers.org; free admission; Mon–Sat 9:30am–4:30pm; Tube: Bank), rich with centuries-old examples of the craft. The Rolling Ball Clock is powered by a metal ball that rolls back and forth across a pivoting table; the ball travels 4060km (2,522 miles) in a year. Too bad this place is so neglected by the city that not even a minor burglary several years ago has encouraged the government to employ an on-site watchman (so to speak).

DESIGN

If it weren't such a pain to reach, it might be more celebrated. As it stands, the charming **Geffrye Museum** ★★ (Kingsland Rd., E2; ☎ 020/7739-9893; www.geffrye-museum.org.uk; free admission, including audio tour; Tues–Sat 10am–5pm, Sun noon–5pm; Tube: Old Street, then bus 243 or a 20-minute walk), founded in 1914 as a resource for the furniture industry, is beloved by local families and design students. Especially on fine days from April to October, you'll spot these folks relaxing in the excellent garden here. (The walled herb garden encourages touch, to release scents, and its period plots are historically accurate, cultivated with plants used in several eras, including Elizabethan and Victorian times.) The entire complex, a U-shaped line of dignified brick almshouses built in 1714 for ironworkers, feels removed from the rush of the East End. Inside is a walk through time: re-creations of typical middle-class London homes from the 1600s to the late 20th century, artfully arranged to appear lived-in, and complete with explanations of each item on display, including illuminating information about which pieces were necessary and which were merely trendy. To some, they're rooms full of furniture. To others, the Geffrye is a chance to understand how people of the past lived. You know which person you are.

One building here is a restored almshouse; you can book timed tours to see how charity cases lived back in the day (the first Saturday and first and third Wednesdays of the month; £2 adults, free for children under 16). On weekends, curators plan many discussions, lectures, and kid-oriented crafts workshops, which gives the place much more energy than you'd expect from a design-based attraction.

The Design Museum (Shad Thames, SE1; ☎ 0870/833-9955; www.designmuseum.org; last admission 5:15pm; £7 adults, £4 seniors/students; daily 10am–5:45pm; Tube: London Bridge or Tower Hill), just east of the Tower Bridge on the southern bank of the Thames, is strictly for contemporary top-drawer talent—the cool kids of style. To me, that makes it more of a gallery than a

Public Sculpture

In London's heyday, celebrities weren't rewarded with advertising contracts or reality TV shows. They were carved in stone. A slew of important statues dots the city—so many that you'll stop noticing them within a day or so. For example, did you know that there's a 6m (20-ft.) metal replica of the Houses of Parliament's Clock Tower, called Little Ben, on a traffic island in front of Victoria station? Keep your eyes peeled for these other notable works, five of hundreds:

Albert Memorial, Kensington Gardens (Tube: South Kensington): Albert, Queen Victoria's German-born husband (and first cousin), was a passionate supporter of the arts who piloted Britain from one dazzling artistic and architectural triumph to another. But when he died suddenly of typhoid in 1861 at age 42, the devastated Queen abruptly withdrew from the gaiety and remained in seclusion and mourning until her death in 1901, shaping the Victorian mentality. The bereaved Queen arranged for this astounding spire—part bombast, part elegy—to be erected opposite the concert hall Albert spearheaded. Some of the spire's nearly 200 figures, represent the continents and the sciences, and some, higher up, represent angels and virtues. At the center, as if on an altar, is Albert himself, sheathed in gold. The Royal Parks recently completed a restoration that has the memorial gleaming as brightly as it did on its dedication day in 1872. Tours of the interior go at 2 and 3pm on the first Sunday of each month, March to December (no reservations required; £4.50).

"Eros," Piccadilly Circus (Tube: Piccadilly Circus): Every guide book will tell you that the fleet-footed, winged lad atop the Shaftesbury Monument in Piccadilly Circus is Eros, the Greek god of sex, erected in 1893 by Alfred Gilbert and one of the first to be cast in aluminum. Except they're wrong. The statue is based on Anteros, Eros' brother, the god of selfless love. In fact, the work, which tops a fountain dedicated to a Victorian philanthropist, is officially called *The Angel of Christian Charity*. But Anteros, gallant deity that he is, lets Eros cop all the glory. Until World War II, when he was moved, his arrow pointed up Shaftesbury Avenue; now he aims down Lower Regent Street.

museum. The high fee also means it's best for devotees of high design, not for average sightseers. Shows by the latest hot names, as well as haughty explorations of random topics (race cars, furniture), are less than approachable, but at least they're thought-provoking. Each spring, the museum hosts its prestigious Designer of the Year competition, and mounts exhibitions by each nominee. The gift shop (www.designmuseumshop.com) stocks some wild, strange gifts such as artist-conceived housewares, dolls, and office supplies—how about a USB drive embedded in a rubber duckie?

Cleopatra's Needle, Victoria Embankment (Tube: Embankment): London and New York are sister cities in many ways. They share the same theatrical shows (*The Lion King, Mamma Mia!, Mary Poppins*). They share hot restaurants and clubs (Nobu, Bungalow 8). They even share priceless relics. The romantically named Cleopatra's Needles—which Cleopatra had nothing to do with—were originally erected in Heliopolis, Egypt around 1450 B.C., and their inscriptions were added 200 years later. The Romans moved the granite spires to Alexandria, where they were later toppled and buried in the sand, preserving them until Egypt gave them away in the early 1800s. New York's Cleopatra's Needle was installed in Central Park in 1881. London's was erected in 1878. The ship designed to carry it to England was flawed, and it capsized and nearly sank on the way, but the obelisk finally made it to the side of the Thames, where two sphinx were installed to guard it (some say backwards, since they face the sculpture, not away from it). In 1917, damage from the little-remembered first bout of German bombings, in World War I, scarred the southern sphinx, and the damage was left as a testament. There's a third needle in Paris.

Traffic Light Tree, Heron Quays, Isle of Dogs (Tube: Heron Quays DLR): Paris-born artist Pierre Vivant conceived this sly electrified work, which clusters 75 traffic lights—each one relentlessly and independently cycling through red, yellow, green, red—atop a stalk, in imitation of a bushy tree. In 1998, the 7.8m (26-ft.) -tall sculpture replaced a living plane tree that suffocated from the mounting traffic around Canary Wharf. It's at the intersection of Westferry, Marsh Wall, and Heron Quay. The surrounding roundabout doesn't make it easy to see up close; be careful if you go.

Quantum Cloud, O_2 Dome, North Greenwich (Tube: North Greenwich): Mathematics as art. Antony Gormley worked with an engineering firm, which itself puzzled over fractals and physics, to design the colossal (nearly 30m/100-ft.-tall) mass of 3,500 four-sided, 1.5m (5-ft.) -long "tetrahedral units" that appear at first like a random "cloud" of metal rods but, when viewed from the right angle, reveal the ghostly outline of a standing figure within. The 1999 work stands on cast-iron caissons in the Thames, to the east of the Dome.

Although many of the products it covers are British in origin—Bovril, Cadbury, and so on—the **Museum of Brands, Packaging, and Advertising** (2 Colville Mews, Lonsdale Rd., W11; ☎ 020/7908-0880; www.museumofbrands.com; £5.80 adults, £2 children 7 to 16, £3.50 seniors/students; Tues–Sat 10am–6pm, Sun 11am–4pm, last admission 1 hr. before closing; Tube: Notting Hill Gate) still makes for an interesting overview of the history of product art and logos, and there's no denying that many of its Victorian and Jet Age specimens—the sum of a 4-decade-long collecting binge by one man—are marvels of design. It's a testament to the unheralded

London's Galleries

In case its top-notch selection of museums hasn't clued you in to the fact, I'll start by saying that London is a world capital for art. No other city in the world has such a breadth of art on display. You won't just find antique fine art; some of today's most exciting, high-priced, and controversial artists live or work in London, including Damien Hirst (he of the animal corpses in formaldehyde), Tracey Emin (she of the unmade bed as art installation), sculptors Ron Mueck and Rachel Whiteread, and architect Zaha Hadid. The city plays such an important role in modern art that a term, Britart, has even been coined to describe some of the more experimental work emerging from the country.

Dozens of galleries are sprinkled around town—with concentrations in Mayfair and Whitechapel—and most of them will have something interesting on display. *Time Out* lists many of them in its Art section; another good resource is the booster organization **New Exhibitions of Contemporary Art** (www.newexhibitions.com), which lists events online.

The most celebrated (or, depending on your viewpoint, reviled) collection of Britart, ranging from self-sculpture in frozen blood to immovable hyper-realistic sculptures of homeless people, belongs to adman Charles Saatchi, who displayed works at his popular gallery near the London Eye until 2005, when landlord disputes drove him out. The collection moves in summer 2007 to the new **Saatchi Gallery** (Duke of York Square, SW3; www.saatchi-gallery.co.uk; Tube: Sloane Square) at the 4,645-square-meter (50,000-sq.-ft.) former Royal Military Asylum building (1801) in Chelsea, complete with a cafe, bookshop, and massive exhibition halls. It conducts guided tours on Mondays at noon and 3pm. Prices weren't set by press time, but expect them to be around £10.

Another important player on the Britart scene is the **White Cube** (48 Hoxton Square, N1; ☎ 020/7930-5373; www.whitecube.com; free admission; Tues–Sat 10am-6pm; Tube: Old Street), a free gallery with many rotating exhibitions. This influential gallery was set up to provide an unfussy, small, focused space for works.

The Hayward Gallery (South Bank Centre, Belvedere Rd., SE1; ☎ 020/7921-0813; www.hayward.org.uk; adults £7.50, children £4; Mon, Thurs, Sat–Sun 10am-6pm; Tues–Wed 10am-8pm; Fri 10am-9pm; Tube: Waterloo) is the principal exhibition space of the inhospitable, concrete South Bank Centre, and its prices are equally hostile, although Mondays are half-priced. Still, there's no denying that the space hosts some pretty terrific blockbuster shows, usually 3 months long, which have included

Ansel Adams, Roy Lichtenstein, 1920s Surrealism, and a 60-artist panorama of modern African art. The Hayward also plans about two talks a month, which are free with your ticket.

Following are some notable **free galleries.** They are generally open 10am to 6pm weekdays, 11am to 6pm Saturday, and noon to 5pm on Sunday:

The **Institute of Contemporary Arts** (The Mall, SW1; ☎ 020/7930-3647; www.ica.org.uk; Tube: Charing Cross), is a cutting-edge booster of art, films, performance, and evening talks followed by "club nights" with a D.J.; tickets range from £6.50 to £11. There's always something challenging or intellectual on display here. **South London Gallery** (65 Peckham Rd., SE5; ☎ 020/7703-6120; www.southlondongallery.org; closed Mon; Tube: Elephant and Castle or Oval), or SLG, has also been pushing the envelope in one form or another since 1868 with abstract pieces, performance art, and plenty of talks. **The Wapping Project** (Wapping Hydraulic Power Station, Wapping Wall, E1; ☎ 020/7680-2080; www.thewappingproject.com; Tube: Wapping), in a disused hydraulic power station, makes for an awesome setting, and its installations and performances, which can be "artsy" in that pretentious way, clearly find inspiration from the impressive space. The **Whitechapel Art Gallery** (80-82 Whitehapel High St., E1; ☎ 020/7522-7888; www.whitechapel. org; closed Mon; Tube: Aldgate East) is one of the city's preeminent contemporary galleries, having been active since 1901 and given the first European airings to names as important as Kahlo, Pollack, and Rothko—the East End is home to more artists than any other neighborhood in Europe, and many of them congregate here at its exhibitions, talks, films, and evening events with DJs, (tickets £6–£9).

For photography, **The Association of Photographers** (81 Leonard St., EC2; ☎ 020/7739-6669; www.the-aop.org; Tube: Old Street) highlights photojournalism in its gallery; **The Photographers' Gallery** (5 and 8 Great Newport St., WC2; ☎ 020/7831-1772; www.photonet.org.uk; Tube: Leicester Square) established in 1971, is very popular, hosting as many as 500,000 visitors a year, and operates a bookshop and cafe; **Proud Galleries** (Buckingham St. at John Adam St., WC2; ☎ 020/7839-4942; Tube: Charing Cross or Embankment; or at The Gin House, The Stables Market, Chalk Farm Rd., Camden, NW1; ☎ 020/7482-3867; www.proud. co.uk; Tube: Camden Town) mostly shows high-end vintage shots of rock stars and celebrities.

beauty of all the tins, boxes, and tubes that our mothers have thoughtlessly thrown away over the ages.

ENGINEERING

In the late 1800s, there was no bolder display of a country's technological prowess than to build a spectacular bridge. Consider The Brooklyn Bridge or the Firth of Forth Bridge. The **Tower Bridge Exhibition** ✠ (Tower Bridge near the Tower of London, SE1; ☎ 020/7403-3761; www.towerbridge.org.uk; £5.50 adults, £3 children, £4.25 seniors/students; Apr–Oct daily 10am–5:30pm, Nov–Mar daily 9:30am–5pm; Tube: Tower Hill or Tower Gateway DLR), winding through the twin-towered bridge often mistaken for the humdrum London Bridge to the west, was one such triumph. The museum dedicated to it (once the insipid Tower Bridge Experience but now revised) is like two attractions in one. The first satisfies sight-seers who have dreamed of going up in the neo-Gothic towers and crossing their high-level observation walkways. For them, it's a close encounter with a world icon. The second aspect of the museum, delving into the steam-driven mechanics that so impressed the world in 1894, will hook the mechanically inclined. The bridge's mighty original bascule-raising equipment, representing the largest use of hydraulic power at the time, remains in beautifully kept condition despite being retired in favor of electricity in 1976. Why did such a proud monument survive the Blitz when everything around it got flattened? Answer: The Luftwaffe needed to use it as a landmark. For a joint ticket that will also get you up The Monument (p. 171), adults can pay another £1, kids another 50p, and seniors/students 25p.

Although the engineering contributions of Marc Brunel and his son Isambard Kingdom Brunel are largely taken for granted, they're given their due in the small **Brunel Engine House** (Railway Ave., SE16; ☎ 020/7231-3840; www.brunelenginehouse.org.uk; £2 adults, £1 children/seniors/students; Thurs–Sun 1–5pm; Tube: Rotherhithe). With the help of a shield system they invented, these pioneers executed the first tunnel to be built under a navigable river, but London's soft earth didn't make it easy. It took from 1825 to 1843, and the redbrick home of the museum, marked by a chimney, was where steam engines pumped the seeping water out of the Thames Tunnel as diggers toiled. The museum sometimes runs floodlit tours of the tunnel, which was a failure at the time but is now used every few minutes by the Underground's East London line.

FINANCE

At the surprisingly complete **Bank of England Museum** ✠ (Threadneedle St., EC2; ☎ 020/7601-5545; www.bankofengland.co.uk/education/museum; free admission; Mon–Fri 10am–5pm; Tube: Bank), the intermittently compelling history of the B of E and its trustees is recounted in laborious but generous detail, accompanied by plenty of very old papers and antiques from the vaults. That's fine if you understand finance, but most people lose the plot pretty quickly. Along the way are some fun oddities, including a million-pound note, printed in the early 19th century for internal accounting. There's lots of expensive swag, such as an iron chest from 1700, heaps of silver treasures dating to the silver standard, and a gold bar so pure (1 part in 10,000 impure) that it was given to Queen Elizabeth as a coronation gift. (Why is it here? I would have kept it.) It's also fun to watch Her Majesty age on the money over the years. The most popular exhibit is probably a standard gold bar, locked in a clear plastic box, that you're invited to lift.

FOOD

A labor of love by a tea aficionado, **The Bramah Museum of Tea and Coffee** ★★ (40 Southwark St., SE1; ☎ 020/7403-5650; www.bramahmuseum.co.uk; £4 adults, £2.50 children/seniors/students; daily 10am–6pm; Tube: London Bridge), pays respect to the two imports that held the greatest sway over London's economic history, especially in Southwark, where the homegrown museum is located. Covering everything from ancient China to modern times and from teapots to teabags, the museum showcases a hodgepodge of holdings—the various pots, cups, and grinders on display are particularly eye-catching. The facilities aren't fancy—signs are Xeroxed—but the exhibits are well-written and fact-packed. The afternoon cream teas in the adjoining shop are some of the most affordable, yet best, in the city. The museum's owner and curator, Edward Bramah, had a former career as a tea planter in Malawi, and he has written a walking-tour guide book on Southwark's tea and coffee heritage. He's frequently on the premises answering questions and steering his cafe customers to the best flavors.

FREEMASONRY

The Library and Museum of Freemasonry (60 Great Queen St., WC2; ☎ 020/7395-9257; www.freemasonry.london.museum; free admission; Mon–Fri 10am–5pm; Tube: Holborn), stashed in the magnificent but ultimately not-terribly-historic 1933 Freemasons' Hall near Covent Garden, has one of the world's best collections of Masonic material, including archives and artifacts once owned by Winston Churchill and Edward VII. Although Freemasonry was founded in this neighborhood, and it had an incalculable effect on the men who founded the United States, these stoic collections will likely bore everyone except Masons. Free tours of the building depart hourly from 11am to 4pm, excepting 1 pm.

Banksy: Graffiti or Genius?

In the shadowy lanes of The City and the East End, a secret avenger lurks. His name is Banksy, and he takes on corporate greed, government surveillance, the death of beauty, and war. No, Banksy isn't a super-hero. He's a graffiti artist and London institution, and he tackles his topics with the acerbic aplomb of a political cartoonist. He has hung his own work, unnoticed and without damage, at museums in Paris and New York. He painted "We're bored of fish" over the penguin enclosure at the London Zoo. He even painted Israel's West Bank barrier with tropical beach scenes and mountain landscapes. Who is he? Many people would love to know, not so they can bring him up on vandalism charges, but so they can shake his hand. Banksy's satire, identified by its stencil design and often by anthropomorphic rats, has garnered such esteem that after he strikes, local councils don't always rush to remove his work. Wherever Banksy's guerrilla art unexpectedly appears, a new temporary art attraction is born. Track the latest installations at www.banksy.co.uk and www.artofthestate.co.uk/Banksy/banksy.htm, and then go on an art safari.

GOVERNMENT

The Houses of Parliament (Bridge St. and Parliament Square, SW1; ☎ 08709/06-37-73; www.parliament.uk; free admission; check website for hours; Tube: Westminster) are a virtual modern-day castle dedicated to government. Throughout the Middle Ages, this was considered one of the monarch's main homes, only to burn down in 1512 and again in 1834, when it was rebuilt into the Gothic palace now used for the day-to-day running of the Empire. It's roughly divided into three areas: those for the House of Lords (whose members inherit seats, done in rose), the House of Commons (by far the most powerful, elected by the people, seats of blue-green), and a few Royal sitting rooms and dressing rooms, which the Queen flits through when she shows up once a year to kick off sessions.

Frustratingly, The Clock Tower above the Houses (it contains the 13.5-ton bell known as Big Ben), is only open to tours for U.K. residents. But visiting the rest of the complex is a possibility. Citing security concerns, the government has said that foreign visitors may show up and take a tour only in summer (Aug 1 to Sept 30), when the government is not in session. Booking ahead is advisable, but you can try your luck for last-minute openings at the ticket office, which opens from mid-July on Abingdon Green, across the street from Parliament. Foreigners still might be able to tour the building at other times of the year; they must pre-arrange a "card of introduction" by writing their country's Embassy or High Commission in the United Kingdom many months ahead of time (find yours via www.embassyworld.com). Even then, they're usually only admitted late in the afternoon, when the politicians are out of session. If you haven't managed to obtain a card from your government's bureaucrats, you can always queue up outside the St. Stephen's Entrance of Parliament in the hopes of taking the spot of a prior visitor who has left for the day. A 2-hour wait is not uncommon. Fridays, when hardly anything is in session, is a good day to try. To learn how to attend a debate (it isn't easy), see p. 203.

HORTICULTURE

The 300-acre **Royal Botanic Gardens, Kew** ✯ (www.kew.org; ☎ 020/8332-5655; Daily 9:30am; closes at 4:15pm in winter and 7:30pm in summer; Admission £12 adults, free for children under 17, £8.75 seniors/students, Tube: Kew Gardens) would be a delightful place to stroll were it not for the painful entrance fee. It's not that the gardens and glasshouses aren't impressive—there are plants from around the world, many descended from specimens collected in the earliest days of international sea trade, and all are beautifully maintained to satisfy the upper-class ladies who lunch here. Of the seven conservatories, the domed Palm House, built from 1844-48, is probably the world's most recognizable greenhouse, while the Temperate House (which contains the world's largest indoor plant, the 16m/48-ft.-tall Chilean wine-palm) is the largest surviving Victorian glass structure. The gardeners are the best in the world; in 1986, they coaxed a bloom from a portea that hadn't flowered in 160 years. Kew's contributions to botanical science, ongoing since 1759, earned it a spot on the UNESCO list of World Heritage Sites in 2003. I just can't get past the crazy price, or how long it takes to get here, some 10km/6 miles from the city. Worse, many of the park's outdoor attractions shut down in winter (including Kew Palace, p. 163), so this is mostly a summer attraction.

Set in the former graveyard of St. Mary-at-Lambeth, the **Museum of Garden History** ★ (Lambeth Palace Road, SE1; ☎ 020/7401-8865; www.museumgarden history.org; £3 adults, £2.50 children/seniors/students; daily 10:30am–5pm; Tube: Lambeth North) was the world's first gardening museum, and today it's a reasonably priced alternative to Kew. Its 17th-century knot garden, in which woody herbs are clipped to make low hedges, contains plants popular in that period, and a special emphasis is given to topiary and to the tastes of John Tradescant and his son, the gardeners to Charles I and II. The distinctive gardens were planted in the disused graveyard of a derelict parish church that served for 900 years before its 1972 deconsecration. Of the estimated 26,000 graves here, including Captain William Bligh of *The Bounty* and Elizabeth I's grandmother, virtually no memorials survive, making the place more poignant.

ITALIAN ART

Some might argue that it's worth more than a half-hour, but for most people, that's enough for the genteel, little-known **Estorick Collection** ★ (39a Canonbury Square, N1; ☎ 020/7704-9522; www.estorickcollection.com; £3.50 adults, £2.50 children/seniors/students; Wed–Sat 11am–6pm, Sun noon–5pm; Tube: Highbury & Islington), memorable for its tranquil ambience in a Georgian house on one of the city's most pleasing residential squares. The narrow collection—modern Italian art, especially Futurism—was established by an American political scientist and art dealer, and its walled garden is a blissful place to enjoy a coffee in fair weather—you don't even need to pay admission to do that.

MARITIME

See also the National Maritime Museum (p. 170) and the *Cutty Sark* (p. 168).

Tucked into one of the few remaining slips that enabled ships to unload in Southwark (another is Hay's Galleria, downstream by the HMS *Belfast*, now converted to a boutique shopping area), **The *Golden Hinde*** 🧒 (St. Mary Overie Dock, Cathedral St., SE1; ☎ 0870/011-8700; www.goldenhinde.org; £5.50 adults, £5 children/seniors/students; daily 10am–6pm, closed for some special events; Tube: London Bridge) is a 1:1 replica of Sir Frances' Drake's square rigged galleon, which circumnavigated the world from 1577–80. This 1973 version, which is so tiny you will forever be in awe of what those old explorers could do, made its own circumnavigation in 1980. Self-guided and guided tours are available daily, but it also hosts Pirate Academy afternoons (£12) for kids as well as sleepovers (£40) during which kids can dress in period clothes, hear tales from costumed actors, and help with shipboard tasks on an imaginary voyage.

If you have a physical limitation that keeps you from climbing ladders, stay ashore and admire **HMS *Belfast*** ★ (Morgan's Lane, Tooley St., SE1; ☎ 020/7940-6300; http://hmsbelfast.iwm.org.uk; £8.50 adults, free for children under 16, £5.25 seniors/students; Mar–Oct daily 10am–6pm, Nov–Feb daily 10am–5pm; Tube: London Bridge) from afar. It's as if the powerful old warship, upon being retired from service in 1965, was simply motored to the dock and instantly opened as an attraction. Nearly everything, down to the grey-and-red checked flooring and decaying cables, is exactly as it was (although I imagine those mannequins with the bad toupees might have been added), making the boat a fascinating snapshot of mid-century maritime technology. The authenticity also makes it a devil to navigate. Getting around her various decks, engine rooms, and hatches requires dexterity and a well-calibrated inner compass. You can roam more or less as you wish, visiting every cubby of the ship from kitchen to bridge, all the while being thankful that it wasn't you who was chasing German cruisers (the *Belfast* sank the *Scharnhorst*) and backing up the D-Day invasion in this tough tin can. Kids receive a free, thorough activity book that helps them locate and understand the most interesting bits.

MEDICINE

A treat among London museums—but don't eat first—**Hunterian Museum** ✫ (35-43 Lincoln's Inn Fields (south side), WC2; ☎ 020/7869-6560; www.rcseng. ac.uk/museums; free admission; Tues–Sat 10am–5pm; Tube: Holborn), at the Royal College of Surgeons, chronicles the life's work of John Hunter (1728-1793), who elevated surgery from something your barber dabbled in to something a saw-wielding "scientist" would, ahem, undertake. It's a ghoulish scene, crowded with thousands of specimens, all tastefully presented in a gleaming two-level hall. See Napoleon III's bladder stone and Winston Churchill's gold dentures, designed to fix his childhood lisp. Most of your time will be spent squeamishly perusing some 3,000 black-lidded jars of human and animal pathology and anatomy (many originally obtained by grave-robbers, the common practice then), plus a bone-grinding collection of crude surgical instruments that could chill even the steeliest physician. Check out Hunter's dissection table, still bearing his knife scars, and the cross section of a chicken's head that he grafted with a human tooth. Such Frankenstein projects funded his school of anatomy. Cluckers got no respect from Dr Hunter: He also proved that bones grow from the ends by firing a lead shot into the center of a chicken's bone, measuring its location, sewing the poor bird up, and killing it later on for dissection. Upstairs, as part of a history of surgery, you'll find an ill-conceived amputation buzzsaw. In its first use, it became slick with blood, slipped, and lopped off a nurse's hand; both patient and nurse were killed by subsequent infection. Ask the staff questions, since they have a good sense of humor about their catalog, or else catch the weekly free guided tour, Wednesdays at 1pm (book ahead). Afterward, you may need to take a breather in lovely Lincoln's Inn Fields square, laid out by Inigo Jones, right out the front door.

A disturbing snapshot of treatment in the early 1800s, **The Old Operating Theatre** (9a St. Thomas St., SE1; ☎ 020/7188-2679; www.thegarret.org.uk; £4.95 adults, £2.95 children under 16, £3.95 seniors/students; daily 10:30am–5pm; Tube: London Bridge) was a space built by St. Thomas's Hospital in which surgeries, mostly amputations and other quick-hit procedures, could be conducted under the eyes of students and other observers. When the hospital moved in 1862, it was abandoned and sealed away. It was considered lost until 1956, when an enterprising historian thought to look in the attic space above a church that adjoined the old hospital, and he found the secret surgical space, original plaster and all. It's now the centerpiece of a modest museum delving into medical methods of the early 1800s.

MILITARY HISTORY

I classify the **Imperial War Museum** ✫✫ (Lambeth Rd., SE1; ☎ 020/7416-5320; www.iwm.org.uk; free admission; daily 10am–6pm; Tube: Lambeth North or

Elephant & Castle) as one of London's unexpectedly great museums, in the same unjustly overlooked category as the National Maritime Museum and the Cabinet War Rooms. There's plenty to do here, and not just for military buffs. Instead of showcasing obsolete implements of death, the IWM, the latest tenant of the commodious former mental hospital known as Bedlam, takes great care to help visitors understand the sensations, feelings, and moods of soldiers and civilians caught in a variety of past conflicts. In addition to giving visitors an easy-to-grasp background on major wars, the museum has plenty of authentic artifacts and well-maintained displays like The Trench, a walk-through mock-up of a muddy fortification in Somme, 1916; The Blitz Experience, a rousing re-creation of an air raid shelter under aural assault; a gallery of artworks about the Great War and Word War II; and an exceptionally thoughtful Holocaust exhibition. Sure, there are tanks and guns, too, but, the museum is much less about the toys of war than about the people who found themselves mired in battle.

In North London, on the site of the old Hendon Aerodrome, you'll find the **Royal Air Force Museum London** ✈ (Grahame Park Way, NW9; ☎ 020/8205-2266; www.rafmuseum.org; free admission; daily 10am–6pm; Tube: Colindale). It's in a part of town where there's not much to see, but for students of aircraft history and military strategy, this giant collection is deeply satisfying: More than 100 aircraft are on display in five hangers. Like many of Britain's military museums, the RAF also receives enough money to keep it modern, clean, and interactive—this is no rusting pile of flightless wings.

THEATER & MUSIC

A painstaking re-creation of an outdoor Elizabethan theater, **Shakespeare's Globe** ✪✪ (21 New Globe Walk, SE1; ☎ 020/7902-1500; www.shakespeares-globe.org; £9 adults, £6.50 children 5–15, £7.50 seniors/students; daily Oct–Apr 10am–5pm, May to Sept 9am–5pm; Tube: London Bridge) tends to bewitch fans of history and theater, but it can put all others to sleep. Arrive early in the day, since timed tours fill up, and you'll be stuck waiting for far too long in the UnderGlobe, its well-crafted but exhausting exhibition about Elizabethan theater. Also avoid matinee days, since tours don't run during performances. The open-air theater above was made without power tools, using Elizabethan technology such as oak framing, pegs, and plaster panels mixed with goat's hair (the original recipe called for cow's hair, but the breed they needed is now extinct). The first Globe burned down, aged just 14, when a cannon fired during a performance caused its thatched roof to catch fire. It took a special act of Parliament, plus plenty of hidden sprinkler systems, to permit the construction of this, the first thatched roof in London since the Great Fire. The original theater was the same size (and stood 180km/600 ft. to the southeast), but it crammed in 3,000 luckless souls. Today, just 1,600 are admitted. In summer, the Globe also conducts tours of the foundation of the Rose, a second Shakespearean theater that was located nearby. Who cares if the scene is touristy? It supplies an immediate entrée into the long-lost Elizabethan world. For information on attending shows here, see p. 296.

Horniman Museum (100 London Rd., Forest Hill; ☎ 020/8699-1872; www.horniman.ac.uk; free admission; daily 10:30am–5:30pm; Mainline rail: Forest Hill), the legacy of a dilettante tea trader that first opened in 1901, is a hike into South London. But it has a cherished collection of 7,000 musical instruments, plus noted stores of items regarding anthropology (masks, puppets, folk art) and natural history (i.e., stuffed animals galore), and a modest aquarium. Trains from London Bridge take about 15 minutes, but you'll be unlikely to take the journey unless it's for the instruments.

Music aficionados should follow a tour with a visit to the little-known **Royal College of Music Museum of Instruments** (Prince Consort Rd., SW7; ☎ 020/7591-4346; www.cph.rcm.ac.uk; free admission; Wed–Thurs 2–4:30pm (closed July–Aug); Tube: South Kensington), just across the street from Royal Albert Hall. The Museum holds more than 800 instruments, mostly European ones dating back to 1480, including Handel's spinet and Haydn's clavichord (gesundheit!), plus about a dozen Stradivarius violins.

In addition to being a great concert venue, **Royal Albert Hall** ✸✸ (Kensington Gore, SW7; ☎ 020/7838-3105; www.royalalberthall.com; tours vary; admission £7.50 for tours; Tube: South Kensington) is also one of London's great landmarks, so you don't need a seat to enjoy it. Tours run daily from 10:30am to 2pm. Conceived by Queen Victoria's husband Albert and opened in 1871, a decade after his death from typhoid (Vicky was still so distraught that she didn't speak at the opening ceremonies), the hall contains such oddities as Britain's longest single-weave carpet (in the corridors), the Queen's Box (still leased to the monarchy), and a spectacular glass dome (41m/135 ft. high and supported only at its rim). I'll warn you now: You don't go backstage; some 320 performances a year are presented, many with less than 24 hours' set-up time, and sightseers would be in the way.

TOYS

When you're in the neighborhood of the Geffrye, it's a 20-minute walk east to the **Museum of Childhood** 🧸 ✸✸ (Cambridge Heath Rd., E2; ☎ 020/8983-5200; www.vam.ac.uk/moc; free admission; Sat–Thurs 10am–5:50pm; Tube: Bethnal Green), run by the awesome V&A Museum, which pulls from its considerable collection of toys, kids' clothing, dolls and dollhouses, books, teddy bears, and games to chronicle kiddom through the ages. As of this writing, the 130-year-old Victorian building and its galleries were in the midst of a massive, £4.7-million overhaul, which should be open by the time you read this. The MoC's glass-and-steel building has an interesting history; it began its life in South Kensington as the home of the nascent V&A collection but was re-erected here in the 1860s. This place has rightly been a family favorite since 1974, and there's no chance that's going to change much. As you can imagine, there are free children's programs galore—up to five a day.

For lots more antique toys, visit **Pollock's Toy Museum** (1 Scala St., W1; ☎ 020/7636-3452; www.pollockstoymuseum.com; £3 adults, £1.50 children; Mon–Sat 10am–5pm, last admission 4:30pm; Tube: Goodge Street). A few mildewed old apartments were barely altered before being fitted with cases of vintage toys, and, as you thread through the creaking rooms, you might wonder whether you're going into Sweeney Todd's shop to be murdered. It doesn't help that wax-headed dolls stare at you wherever you turn. The collection is exhausting, if not exhaustive: Mechanical cast-iron banks, 1950s rocket toys, puppets, Gollywogs, wax dolls, the 1921 forerunner to G.I. Joe (Swiss Action Man), doll's houses, a board game based on the Falkland Islands invasion that was banned for being in poor taste. Even if you don't care to gaze at dusty dolls, its ground-floor shop, free to enter, has some terrific, hard-to-find toys that don't cost much, including reproduction tins, lots of handmade items, and cardboard theaters—the museum takes its name from the last great printer of toy theaters.

WORLD WAR II

What an odd, homegrown attraction is **Winston Churchill's Britain at War Experience** ★ (64-66 Tooley St., SE1; ☎ 020/7403-3171; www.britainatwar. co.uk; £9.50 adults, £4.85 children 5–15, £5.75 seniors/students; the website often posts coupons for £1.50 off; daily Apr–Sept 10am–5pm, daily Oct–Mar 10am–4pm; Tube: London Bridge). At first blush, because it begins with one of those "you are there" gimmicks—a simulated lift ride to a re-created Tube station shelter—I suspected it might be a tourist trap. But in between its full-color films of London during Word War II and the cases of quirky relics such as a Rent-a-Cake, a cardboard wedding cake couples could borrow during rationing (it had a tiny drawer for a morsel of real cake), I was hooked. I find this reassuringly amateurish place, and its frozen-faced mannequins, deeply affecting. Something about this attraction's earnest, let's-put-on-a-museum ethic—as if half of London cleaned their attics of wartime memorabilia just to share the story—rhymes with the improvised efforts that got Britain through the war. Still an interest in The Blitz will help you see past the place's ragged seams. The creepy windowless atmosphere includes an Anderson Shelter piped with the disturbing sounds of bombs in flight and climaxes in a two-story walk-through of the bombing of a city block, complete with smoke and gushing water. Kids might be bored by the ration coupons, but that part gets their attention. If you have to make a Blitz-related choice, though, the Cabinet War Rooms are still the best.

OVERRATED ATTRACTIONS YOU CAN SKIP

Why list attractions in this book at all if they're overrated? Because you're going to be exposed to ads and brochures touting these places, and some of them are unjustly staples on the tourist circuit. Besides, I'm aware that if you have bored kids in tow, some of the more inauthentic sights might be just the tonic to jolt them back into a good mood.

The Queen inherited one momma of a priceless art collection—7,000 paintings, 30,000 watercolors, and half a million prints, to say nothing of sculpture, furniture, and jewelry—and she shows a tiny bit at **The Queen's Gallery** (Buckingham Palace Rd., SW1; ☎ 020/7766-7301; www.royalcollection.org.uk; £7.50 adults, £4 children 5–16, £6.50 seniors/students; late Sept–late July daily 10am–5:30pm, late July–late Sept 9:30am–5pm, last admission 1 hr. before closing; Tube: Victoria). Unfortunately, even though the collection is held "in trust for the nation," the Queen keeps most of the goodies to herself. The few works that are on display (in a side building at the southwest of Buckingham Palace; budget an hr.) are undoubtedly exceptional (one of the world's few Vermeers, a Rubens' self-portrait given to Charles I, glittering ephemera by Fabergé), but they're not the cream of what she owns. Those who adore and appreciate fine art and furniture might extract enjoyment from the Queen's stuffy gallery, but you can see an equally good representation of the Royal Collection by touring Buckingham Palace, and there's more exciting stuff to be had for free at the National Gallery.

Next door to the Queen's Gallery is **The Royal Mews** (Buckingham Palace Rd., SW1; ☎ 020/7766-7302; www.royalcollection.org.uk; late Mar–late July and late Sept–late Oct Mon–Thurs and Sat–Sun 11am–4pm, and late July–late Sept daily 10am–5pm, last admission 45 min. before closing; Tube: Victoria). Most visitors pop in and out of what amounts to the Queen's garage in about 15 minutes. The highlight among many gorgeous carriages is the Gold State Coach used since every coronation since 1821, covered in sea deities and tritons, which makes Cinderella's look like a Chevy. But you'll also see stables (fit for a you-know-who; they barely smell at all), and Her Majesty's Rolls-Royces (many of which, at Prince Charles' behest, have been converted to run on green fuels to counter pollution). As with everything to do with the Crown, the rituals are beyond fussy, and you'll overdose on learning about regulations for when this set of harnesses may be used and when that leather must be polished. Is it all worth the price? Not for me, although equine- and engine-heads may disagree. Both the Gallery and the Mews can be seen on a joint ticket (£12 adults, £6.50 children 5 to 16, £10 seniors/ students). It takes 45 minutes.

Avoid it like the plague. **The London Dungeon** (Tooley St., SE1; ☎ 020/7403-7221; www.thedungeons.com; £20 adults, £14 children 5–15, £16 seniors/ students, discounts on www.lastminute.com; daily 10am–5:30pm; Tube: London Bridge) is a chain attraction with sister outposts in Hamburg, York, Edinburgh, and Amsterdam, and it survives not by its merits but by booking groups, hence its never-ending lines. Ostensibly a gruesome history of the city, the dungeon is mostly a sophomoric setup to gross you out. Costumed actors bark and bray at visitors as they lead them through mist and darkness from set to set, each representing another period of English history as a 13-year-old boy might define them. Plague-ridden rubber corpses "sneeze" on passersby, fake organs squirt "blood" during an autopsy, mannequins re-enact truly horrible tortures, and cutthroat barber Sweeney Todd gleefully commands you to sit in his chair. If you're nervous in haunted houses, or if you're one of those people who dreads being picked on by a stand-up comic, you're going to hate this place.

I don't want to carp, but *carp*? That's the kind of fish you see at **The London Aquarium** (County Hall, Westminster Bridge Rd., SE1; ☎ 020/7967-8000; www.londonaquarium.co.uk; £12 adults, £8.25 children 3–14, £9.50 seniors/ students; daily 10am–6pm; Tube: Waterloo or Westminster). There's nothing here that you can't see at other, swankier fish zoos. Displays on the Amazon rainforests, Thames wildlife, and jellyfish are fine but not interactive. What can you say for an aquarium that counts robotic fish, created by engineers, among its most popular and promoted displays? Spend your time seeing the sights in London that can't be repeated back home.

In the same building, also dependant on not-so-discerning passersby, is the **Dalí Universe** (County Hall Gallery, SE1; ☎ 08707/44-74-85; www.daliuniverse. com; £11 adults, £6.50 children 8–16, £5 children 4–7, £9.50 seniors/students; daily 10am–5:30pm; Tube: Waterloo or Westminster). Unless you're a mad fan of the surrealist artist, this museum is way too costly for what you get—a few notable originals. Besides, there's enough free Dalí at the Tate Modern and the V&A.

The concept is Victorian in nature: Set up a house as if it were really the home of a fictional character, and then charge people to see it. That's the scheme behind

Ritual Abuse

I'm only telling you this because I love you: the **Changing of the Guard** (Buckingham Palace; ☎ 020/7321-2233; www.royal.gov.uk; free admission; 11:30am daily in July, and every other day in other months, cancelled in heavy rain; Tube: St. James's Park, Victoria, or Green Park), sometimes called Guard Mounting, is well known, but it's an underwhelming use of 40 minutes of your time. Arrive at Buckingham Palace at least 45 minutes ahead if you don't want to end up facing the backs of other tourists. A marching band advances from Birdcage Walk (often, playing themes from *Star Wars*, *West Side Story*, or ABBA, which comes as a rude shock), then members of the Queen's Life Guard—two if the Queen's away, three or four if she's in—do a ritual change around their sentry boxes in the forecourt. And that's more or less it, give or take some additional prancing for the chattering cameras. It has more in common with a halftime show at a football game than with sanctified tradition. Your friends at home will ask you if you saw it, but a Londoner never will.

If you must see goose-stepping young men in elaborate redcoats and bearskin hats, guards patrol all day at both Buckingham Palace and at Horse Guards Arch on Whitehall (which does its own, uncrowded change at 11am, 10am Sun). Or park yourself in front of the yard of the **Wellington Barracks,** a few minutes' walk east of the Palace along Birdcage Walk, by 11am, and catch the Inspection of the Guard that happens before the same guards march over to the Palace for the main event. Then run off and use the day's golden hours for something less touristy.

Ceremony of the Keys (Tower of London; ☎ 020/7488-5741; www.hrp.org.uk; free admission; 9:53pm nightly; Tube: Tower Hill or Tower Gateway DLR), held every night as the Yeomen lock up the Tower of London, has been a nightly routine for more than 700 years—not even German bombs cancelled it. But it's an awful lot of work for not much payoff: You need to enter the Tower at 9:30 (several hours after closing time, so you can't combine it with a day's visit) and won't leave until around 10:05pm, even though the whole show takes less than 7 minutes—plus, photos aren't allowed. As for the show, the Chief Yeoman Warder approaches the heavy wooden gate with keys and a lantern, is asked "Halt, who comes there?.," passes muster, and locks up the gates to a bugle call. The gates can't be that secure, or else how would the tourists get back out? If you still want to try it, apply for tickets with a minimum of two International Reply Coupons (the equivalent of an SASE, available at your post office) to Ceremony of the Keys Office, Tower of London, London, EC3N 4AB, Great Britain; include the names of all attendees, two possible dates that are at least 2 months in advance (3 for summer, when there's a group maximum of six).

The Sherlock Holmes Museum (221b Baker St., NW1; ☎ 020/7935-8866; www. sherlock-holmes.co.uk; £6 adults, £4 children; daily 9:30am–6pm; Tube: Baker Street), and it has worked for years, even though it's embarrassingly threadbare, and most visitors have never read a Holmes story in their lives. If you have, and if you're a huge fan, you might grasp the references, but most people come simply to check this off their shopping list of attractions. It's fun to pick up a calabash pipe, sit in an easy chair, and have your photo taken, but little of what you see is explained, and the shabby waxworks of characters from the stories, found on the top floor, are just plain scary. There are worthier uses for your precious time.

The London Zoo (Outer Circle Rd., Regent's Park, NW1; ☎ 020/7722-3333; www.londonzoo.co.uk; £15 adults, £12 children 3–15, £13 seniors/students, buy online for a 10% discount; daily 10am–4 or 5:30pm, depending on time of year, last admission 1 hr. before closing; Tube: Camden Town, then 274 bus) makes a soothing, if pricey, addition to a day out in Regent's Park, but it is just a zoo, and a smallish one at that, with few large animals. So it's not what I would call one of the city's most illustrious attractions, despite a long history and a few attractive old buildings that date nearly to its opening in 1828 as a menagerie open only to members of the Zoological Society of London. Some of the most popular habitats include the penguins (feeding time, 2:30–3pm), the aviary along Regent's Canal, and the gorillas. But is it worth nearly the same price as the irreplaceable Tower of London? Not a chance.

Aggressively marketed as a "wine tasting attraction," **Vinopolis** (1 Bank End, SE1; ☎ 0870/241-4040; www.vinopolis.co.uk; £15 including five tastings and a gin cocktail; Mon, Fri, Sat noon–9pm, Tues–Thurs, Sun noon–6pm, last admission 2 hr. before closing; Tube: London Bridge) is too general and expensive to be of much use to neophytes and too pleased with itself to satisfy most wine fans. Exhibits are expensive-looking but vacuous, and many of them appear to be paid for by external interests, such as a video on the Australian polymer cork industry, and a room that gratuitously hawks Bombay Sapphire gin (although its cocktails *are* delicious). If you have questions, it's best to ask the people who pour samples (mostly of the cheap stuff, £8 a bottle), since they seem to be in the know. There are plenty of special tastings (wine, whisky, champagne), but they'll hit you for £35 and up. The gift shop (free to browse) is full of interesting quaffs, though, including absinthe, which is banned in many other countries.

From the outside, **The Clink Museum** (1 Clink St., SE1; ☎ 020/7403-0900; www.clink.co.uk; £5 adults, £3.50 children under 16, £3.50 seniors/students; Mon–Fri 10am–6pm, Sat, Sun, 10am–9pm; Tube: London Bridge) looks like fun. A place devoted to the prison that gave all prisons their nickname! Tapes of monks singing! Cool! Except that prison is long gone, having been destroyed in the Gordon Riots of 1780, and this small place actually occupies the cellar of an old warehouse. It exists mostly to exploit the weird obsession with torture that tourists are encouraged to nurture in London. You'll find plenty of information cards about the hugely atmospheric environs, but they're poorly written and lack a clear timeline, and the museum lapses into amateurish, filthy displays of dummies being throttled by random devices. The TV show *Most Haunted Live!* recently spent the night looking for ghosts. They didn't find anything worthwhile here, either.

Have you ever heard of Davina McCall? Amitabh Bachchan? Ant and Dec? If your answer is no, you're not going to get much joy out of the ferociously priced

Cross Abbey Road—Off Your List

The famous zebra crossing immortalized by the Beatles on the cover of *Abbey Road* is located at the intersection of Grove End Road and Abbey Road (just southwest of the St. John's Wood Tube station). Getting your picture taken there is certainly good holiday-card fodder, but it's not all it's cracked up to be. First, it's a pretty long trip here from town (about 30 min. each way from Leicester Square by Tube) for a snapshot. Second, the spot swarms with cars that come speeding from behind a curve, so you won't have more than a couple of nerve wracking seconds to get your picture taken. Third, the white stripes have been rearranged and repainted since 1969, so it won't even look the same. Fourth, the locals have despised sightseers ever since they started vandalizing a nearby wall with graffiti. Last, although EMI-owned Abbey Road Studios at 3 Abbey Rd. is still around, they don't have any facilities for tourists—unless you count scowling receptionists.

Madame Tussaud's (Marylebone Road, W1; ☎ 0870/999-0046; www.madame-tussauds.co.uk; pricing is complicated based on time of year and time of day, but it peaks at £22 adults, £18 children, £19 seniors, prices drop about 40% for entries after 3pm in winter and 5pm in summer; daily 9am–6pm; Tube: Baker Street). The execution of their wax doppelgangers, which you can usually touch (Will and Harry are behind ropes, girls), is superb. But the focus of this world-famous waxworks is on British and international celebrities, so you're not going to be consistently engaged. The Blush room covers celebs and Hollywood names, and the Hall of World Leaders, many of whom sat for their own figures, is embedded with whimsy (Jiang Zemin stares down George Bush from behind; De Klerk looms behind Mandela). Madame Tussaud, born Marie Grosholtz, began her career by reluctantly making copies of those slaughtered in the French Revolution, but that heritage is done a disservice by being retold as a fleeting house of horrors—you briefly see the actual guillotine blade that killed Marie Antoinette, whose likeness is speared on a pike, and then it's back to the movie stars. You can waste an extra £2 on Chamber Live, a 4-minute haunted house. A 5-minute, Disney-esque ride, "The Spirit of London," in which you ride a slow-moving "black cab" from room to room, invokes every conceivable stereotype, from the Artful Dodger to plague victims. All in all, with all the coach tours and the school groups, it's hard to get close to the likenesses, which makes you wonder who the real dummies are.

WALKING TOURS

London is a walker's city, one where history is accumulated on every block. You could carry a stack of reference books around wherever you go but isn't taking a walking tour a much better idea? There are so many guides to choose from that you could fill an entire week with walking tours alone. In addition to the tours listed below, you'll find operators who are sometimes open to walk-up trade. Check the "Around Town" section of *Time Out* magazine to hook up with one-off tours.

The list of **London Walks** (☎ 020/7624-3978; www.walks.com) is daunting. On weekdays, there are often 13 choices, and on weekends, nearly 25, which means that if you ever find yourself with a few hours to kill, you can always leaf through one of the organization's white timetables (dispensed at every tourist haunt in quantity) and find instant occupation. Every tour departs from a Tube stop, and most are £6, which makes arrangements easy. The marquee tour is probably "Jack the Ripper Haunts," which heads out to the streets of Whitechapel after sunset and, in the pursuit of ghoulish entertainment, deploys considerably more grotesquerie than uncontested facts. I find many of the group's other walks to be more informative, including "The Blitz," "Old Westminster," and "Behind Closed Doors," which includes a visit to the Royal Courts of Justice, guided by a barrister. The group also conducts tours of sightseeing staples such as the British Museum and Westminster Abbey, as well as cheap (£12) "Explorer Days" of Bath, Brighton, Cambridge, Oxford, and other favorites (you pay your own transit and entry fees). If there's any fault with London Walks, it's that some groups swell to untenable sizes, and many of the guides, although proven knowledgeable when pressed, rely too commonly on canned performance schtick. The best way to remedy both problems is to pick a tour with narrower appeal; you'll have a better chance to ask your guide questions. Check the website for schedules.

Actor, rock-and-roller, and lecturer Peter Powell, who has lived in Islington since the early 1970s, has led his **Angel Weekend Walks** (☎ 020/7226-8333; www.angelwalks.co.uk; adults £5, children £4; Tube: Angel) since 1985. He knows the hood's history well; he's the chairman of the local History and Archaeology Society and lives (enviably) on Canonbury Square next door to a flat famously inhabited by George Orwell. Orwell himself was so depressed by Islington's post-war blight that he was inspired to write *1984* (he also finished *Animal Farm* while living here). The area is so leafy and inviting today that it's hard to envision it being downtrodden, although Powell's performances bring you close. Saturday at 11:15am is "Charles Dickens and Islington," a literary tour; Saturday at 2:15pm, is "Islington's Murder Mile," touted as a "catalogue of foul deeds" touching on the hacking death of playwright Joe Orton and the notorious Kray twins. Sunday at 11:15am, "George Orwell's Islington" brings back the miserable days in which the district endured a series of brutal body blows by the Luftwaffe. All tours meet at Angel Tube station, but spots must be booked.

Richard Porter, a Beatles nut and extensive writer on the Fab Four, has led his **London Beatles Walks** (☎ 020/8960-2092; www.beatlesinlondon.com) for more than 15 years; the most regular are the "Magical Mystery Tour" (important landmarks in the development of the band; Sundays, Wednesdays, and Thursdays) and "In My Life" (important landmarks in the members' personal lives; Tuesdays and Saturdays). Both are £6, last 2 hours, and require a 1-day Zone 1 and 2 Travelcard since they involve short Tube rides. You don't have to book ahead, but check in advance for the times and meeting places (usually, a Tube stop).

The Greenwich Tourist Information Centre carefully vets the guides of its **Greenwich Guided Walks** (☎ 020/8858-6169; www.greenwichtours.co.uk; £4, free for children under 14), so they know what they're talking about. Tours last about 90 minutes. Although the company rolls out themed tours with high demand, there are usually two basic tours daily; the 12:15 one takes in the main sights plus the Royal Observatory and the Meridian Line, where Mean Time is measured, while the 2:15pm tour omits those in favor of a trip into The Painted Hall and The Naval Chapel, two stunningly decorated 17th-century rooms in Maritime Greenwich.

The 2012 Olympics are going to be here sooner than you think, and in the run-up, it seems like every square inch of East London is being plowed over and redeveloped. Go East London, run by accredited guides, runs an all-day **Olympic 2012 Routemaster Tour** (☎ 020/8883-4169; www.goeastlondon.co.uk; £18) of all the major locations of the future games, so that when you finally see them on TV, you'll know where everything is. They include tons of Docklands, East End, and Greenwich history—topics otherwise neglected by many guides—and to effectively bridge past with present, the tours are conducted in the once-ubiquitous double-decker Routemaster buses (the ones with the rear exit), retired by London Transport in 2005. Go East's other tours (£6–£20) include Old Jewish East End, the Pirates Pilgrims and Penthouse wander through the Limehouse docks, and runs through the former almshouses of Whitechapel and Mile End.

HOP-ON, HOP-OFF COACH TOURS

I don't recommend those hop-on, hop-off bus tours. First, they're expensive (£16–£20). Second, after 10 minutes of rolling down the streets in these, everything you've seen will blend into one miasma of antiquity, and you'll feel hopelessly turned around, not oriented. London is a walker's city, and you're much better off seeing the big stuff either on foot or, if you really want to ride, from a window seat on a real double-decker bus, which costs £3.50 for the whole day. Sightseeing buses make you wait up to 20 minutes at a time to catch your next leg. But if you insist, these companies are the respected players, and you can buy tickets at any marked bus stop:

The Original Tour London Sightseeing (☎ 020/8877-1722; www.theoriginal tour.com; £18 adults, £12 children, including a river cruise; daily 8:30am–7:30pm), conducted on open-top coaches, has five different routes, all of which are covered for 24 hours with a ticket. Online booking saves £1.50. You can catch the bus at any stop on its route, but most people get on at Marble Arch, Piccadilly Circus, Charing Cross Road north of Trafalgar Square, or outside Madame Tussaud's.

The Big Bus Company (www.bigbustours.com; £20 adults, £10 children 5–15; daily 8:30am–7:30pm), also on open-top buses, has two routes. This is the better of the coach tour companies, and its guiding has won several tourism awards. Tickets are good for 24 hours. Online booking saves £2 off adult tickets. You can catch this coach at any stop, but most people get on at Marble Arch, Regent Street south of Piccadilly Circus, Charing Cross Road north of Trafalgar Square, or under the South Bank Lion at Westminster Bridge.

The one touristy excursion that I *might* come close to suggesting, with my heart in my mouth, is the touristy **London Ducktours** (kids) (55 York Rd., SE1; ☎ 020/7928-3132; www.ducktours.co.uk; £17.50 adults, £12 children 12 and under, £14 seniors/students; daily 10am to late afternoon; Tube: Waterloo). Like their forebears that have plied the Wisconsin Dells for decades, these 75-minute tours are conducted in American-made DUKW amphibious vehicles, which roll down streets like buses and then plow into the Thames and motor along briefly as boats. Roofed and mostly splashless, these vehicles were developed as Word War II transports. You may end up riding one used to ferry boys to the bloodbath of D-Day. You can't hop off, the narration is spotty, and you only see Westminster and Vauxhall, but if you have kids to amuse, it's a dumbed-down option.

THE THAMES BY FERRY

It's hard to imagine a time when the Thames was a jumble of ferries and delivery boats and when there was just one crossing, the London Bridge, but that was the case just a few hundred years ago. It's still possible to travel by boat, and on a beautiful day, there's not a prouder way to go, even if the Tube and buses are always cheaper. Don't make the mistake of taking the boat between piers that are close enough to walk between, such as Waterloo and Bankside. To see the most, sail as far as you dare, such as clear to Greenwich. Just keep an eye on the schedule, since unlike the Underground, ferries depart at rigid times.

Piers are served by a variety of boating concerns, and many are convenient to major tourist sights. There are 10 piers between the Tate Britain (Milbank Millennium) and the Tower of London/Tower Bridge (Tower Millennium). Other important stops include Westminster Millennium (for Westminster Abbey, the Cabinet War Rooms), Waterloo Millennium (for the London Eye), Bankside (for the Tate Modern, Shakespeare's Globe, Bramah Tea and Coffee Museum), Blackfriars (for St. Paul's Cathedral), and Greenwich (for Maritime Greenwich). One-way from Waterloo to Tower takes about 30 minutes, and trips to Greenwich, which pass the spectacular Canary Wharf developments, take almost an hour. It also runs intermittent service to Kew and Hampton Court, although, because of tides, a one-way trip usually must be combined with a Tube ride there or back.

London River Services (☎ 020/7222-1234; www.tfl.gov.uk/river; day passes £9 adults, £4.50 kids) is a branch of London Transport, so fares are integrated with those on buses and the Tube. Typical singles are £3 for short hops, £5.60 for crosstown hops, and £6.80 from Westminster to Greenwich; round-trip fares are only about 25% more. If you've put a Travelcard on your Oyster, you get a third off. You can pick up schedules (about seven runs each way daily) at Tube stations.

Catamaran Cruisers (☎ 020/7987-1185; www.bateauxlondon.com; day passes £9 adults, £4.50 kids) is hop-on, hop-off and covers five of the piers that London River does (Embankment, Waterloo, Bankside, the Tower of London, and Greenwich). It's comparable in every way to LRS.

6 The "Other" London

Be a local for a day—play how Londoners play, learn how they learn

- Spending an afternoon watching the borderline brawl that is a session of Parliament.
- Showing up at a pub on a Sunday afternoon to attend the weekly "roast," and taking part in what could best be called a public dinner party.
- Building a burrow for hedgehogs and working alongside other eager volunteers as you learn about the surprising array of English wildlife.

DON'T BE DAUNTED BY LONDON'S SIZE AND SWELL. IT'S EASY TO GET A glimpse of the "real" London. And by taking part in these activities (and others, see below) you'll discover a hidden perk: In London, it's refreshingly easy to mingle with the locals. The city boasts many local haunts where you'll be welcomed, even as a so-called outsider, and where you'll be brought immeasurably closer to understanding how Londoners live, play, and grow—and why they rightly claim that their city is among the coolest in the world. I call these places the "other" London primarily because most tourists, stuck in the same tourist circuit, miss seeing them. It's their loss—they're missing out on the London locals live every day.

Dive into two or three of these activities in addition to the standard tourist plans you already have. Once you get a taste of how Londoners live here, you'll probably wish you could be one of them forever.

HOW LONDONERS LEARN

Londoners seem to adore making themselves smarter. Edifying conversation is truly part of the culture here, and locals' seemingly boundless inquisitive nature has given the city a deserved reputation for intelligent pursuits. As Oscar Wilde, no slouch of a wag, once put it, "The man who can dominate a London dinner-table can dominate the world." Together with a long-running tradition of free lectures and one-night seminars—instituted for the improvement of the lower classes, but now a standard night out for everyone—this affection for discourse translates into dozens of stimulating, expert-led events every night of the week.

Besides getting educated, you'll reap another benefit when you attend a talk, and that's the chance to interact with normally reserved locals. The same Englishman who sits silently on the Tube or hews to the same corner of his pub every evening may in the context of a political discussion grow animated, impassioned, and eventually display the acquisitive vigor that fueled his country's rise to worldwide dominance.

TALKS

London has a long history of associations dedicated to viewing society from a critical distance. The Fabian Society, for example, whose members included George Bernard Shaw, suffragette Annie Besant, and children's writer Edith Nesbit (a co-founder), played a crucial role in the formation of today's Labour Party. The South Place Ethical Society, another such idealistic organization, was founded in 1793 as a salon for free thought and artistic advancement. In 1929, it opened its own lecture space, **Conway Hall** (25 Red Lion Square, WC1; ☎ 020/7242-8032; Tube: Holborn), which today attracts some 130,000 people a year to a steady bill of talks by authors and politicians, as well as concerts (music by the London Chamber Music Society, classical songbooks, and experimental compositions). Concerts are held almost every Sunday evening from October to April (usually £8), and many other free events are put on during the week. Sundays also see line-ups of free lectures, usually on political or agnostic themes, and often with question-and-answer periods that allow for interaction with thoughtful locals interested in social improvement. It's located off the northeast corner of Red Lion Square, about 10 minutes' walk east of the British Museum. **The Dana Centre** (Science Museum, Exhibition Road, SW7; ☎ 020/7942-4040; www.danacentre. org.uk; Tube: South Kensington) is a deeply stimulating find, devoted to casually discussing science, culture, medicine, and technology—and how those issues relate to current events. It's not as dusty as it might sound—events are consciously irreverent, punky, and often, laugh-out-loud funny. For instance, in the fall of '06, the subject was carnival thrill rides and participants spent half their time being spun, flipped, and jiggled in special machines, afterwards holding serious (if woozy) discussions on the physics of g-forces, and the sociology behind the exhilaration of these rides. Sponsored partly by the British Association for the Advancement of Science and a brain-research group, this endeavor throws a few events a week (usually Tues–Thurs) in a purpose-built cafe at the back of the Science Museum. Most events are free but require reservations.

The **Royal Geographic Society** (☎ 020/7591-3030; www.rgs.org; Mon–Fri 10am–5pm; Tube: South Kensington), a holdover from Britain's bygone days of global dominance, performs a similar service as the Dana Centre, except it deals with the subjects of geography and travel. What's it like to roam China's Silk Road or take a dog trek through the Russian Far East? Intrepid explorers appear to report on their adventures, slides in hand, as do authors who have recently written works on, say Shackleton's doomed expedition, early human habitation in Britain, or the history of Libya. The general public sometimes gets last pick of tickets to the most popular events, but those events are still worth trying for. A few times a year, it sponsors a "Discovering People" event, in which a travel luminary (such as Jan Morris, Michael Palin, or Sir David Attenborough) is interviewed. Events are mostly free but sometimes cost up to £15. Schedules of future events are downloadable via its website.

Let it not be forgotten that it was in that reformist period (at the British Museum, in fact) that Karl Marx studied and developed the political theories that would sweep the planet and shape much of the 20th century. Lenin spent about a year here, too. In the spring and the autumn, the **Marx Memorial Library** (37a Clerkenwell Green, EC1; ☎ 020/7253-1485; www.marxlibrary.net; Mon, Tues,

A Note About Opening Hours

In addition to keeping the regular business hours listed in this chapter, many places will stay open late into the evening on the days when they have special events scheduled. If you want to use standard facilities such as libraries or exhibitions, go during regular hours, because only a few rooms may be open during talks and events.

Thurs 1pm–6pm, Wed 1pm–8pm, Sat 10am–1 pm, closed Fri, Sun; Tube: Farringdon), fittingly, sponsors thought-provoking lectures on socialism and history that even the proletariat could afford: It's £1 per edifying session.

Catering to Brixton's diverse cultural mix, the **Black Cultural Archives** (1 Othello Close, SE11; ☎ 020/7582-8516; www.bcaheritage.org.uk; closed Sundays; Tube: Oval) is a fascinating source of information about the history of black people in Europe, stretching all the way back to the year 208 A.D., and for documentation of modern black history in Britain, including Caribbean and direct African influences. It plans plenty of art and photography exhibitions and talks year-round, but things get really busy around October, which is Black History Month. It's in a temporary space in Kennington while its new Brixton home is being fashioned; call for hours.

Here are a few more places, besides museums, to find glorified gab: **The London Review Bookshop** (14 Bury Place, WC1; ☎ 020/7269-9030; www.lrb.co.uk; Mon–Sat 1pm–6:30pm, Sun noon–6pm; Tube: Tottenham Court Road or Holborn), the retail wing of the literary publication, packs its schedule with author talks, mostly free, and its location in the British Museum's front yard makes a visit here a worthy companion to a day spent browsing antiquities. The **Institut de Français** (17 Queensbery Place, SW7; ☎ 020/7073-1350; www.institut-francais.org.uk; Mon–Fri 8:30am–10pm, Sat 10am–10pm; Tube: South Kensington), the country's official French cultural center, is for francophiles, and often, francophones, but French-only talks are flagged as such ahead of time. Not to be left out, the Germans run their own **Goethe-Institut** (50 Princes Gate, Exhibition Road, SW7; ☎ 020/7596-4000; www.goethe.de; Mon–Fri 8:30am–8pm, Sat 8:30am–5pm; Tube: South Kensington), and the Spanish have their **Instituto Cervantes Londres** (102 Eaton Square, SW1; ☎ 020/7235-0353; http://londres.cervantes.es; Mon–Thurs noon–7:30pm, Fri noon–6:30pm, Sat 9:30am–2pm; Tube: Sloane Square), though many of its talks are in English. Also consult the **Egyptian Cultural Centre** (4 Chesterfield Gardens, W1; ☎ 020/7491-7720; www.egyptculture.org.uk; Tube: Hyde Park Corner), in Mayfair, which organizes frequent talks on archaeology, Egyptology, as well as the occasional Sufi dance performance.

And, of course, there's the reigning seat of London gab. Near the northeast corner of Hyde Park, where Edgware Road meets Bayswater Road, generations of Londoners congregated to participate in grisly public executions. Such displays gradually fell out of favor, and by the early 1800s, the gathered crowds were jeering hangings instead of cheering them, and the locale's reputation for public outcry became entrenched. An Act of Parliament in 1872 finally legitimized

Talk Is Cheap (In Fact, It's Free)

I can't stress this strongly enough: London museums aren't just repositories for artifacts. They're also community centers. Above and beyond their usual exhibitions, nearly every museum and charitable foundation offers free talks at least a few times a month—by professors, authors, noted archaeologists, you name it. Plenty of post-talk time is allotted for you to ask questions of the curators and experts present. And the programs are creative: For example, Shakespeare's *Globe* recently interviewed an American who was pardoned from Death Row about his impressions of *Coriolanus*.

It's possible to program an entire week of evening entertainment from museum talks alone. Many of them are listed in the weekly *Time Out* magazine in the indispensable "Around Town" section. A few more (usually with small admission charges) are advertised in the "What's On" section of VisitLondon.com. Many more are promoted internally at the institutions that host them. If a particular topic interests you—Raphaelite art, for instance—check the website of the museum that might exhibit on the subject. Don't be afraid to ask at the front desk of any institution if free events are forthcoming, since they're simply part of the culture here.

Speakers' Corner (Tube: Marble Arch, exits 4, 5, 8, or 9) as a place of free speech, and its tradition of well-intentioned blathering has since evolved into one of the city's quirkier attractions. A century ago, it was where laborers and suffragettes fomented massive social change, but these days, you're more likely to encounter a rogues' gallery of kooks and idealists. Anyone can show up on Sunday mornings with a soapbox (or, these days, a stepladder) and orate about anything they want, from the Iraq War to Muslim relations to the superiority of 1970s disco—but if they don't have the wit or the facts to appease the crowd, they stand a good chance of being jibed, or at the very least vigorously challenged. In true British style, most speakers refrain from profanity and, while audience participation at this scholarly circus can be heated, it's usually based on facts rather than emotion. Even the heckling is usually polite. I wouldn't say it's worth rearranging your schedule to attend, since it's a true grab-bag of gab, but it's a dearly held tradition—and one of the only things to do in the city on Sunday morning, anyway.

For a schedule of additional talks, consult **The Lecture List** (www.lecturelist. org), the "Around Town" section of *Time Out* magazine, and the "What's On" section of VisitLondon.com.

AUCTION HOUSE EXHIBITIONS

London and New York City are the world's most important centers for the buying and selling of art and antiquities. But unlike in New York, in London the auctioneers assume every joe off the street could be a potential millionaire and an elite collector, so it's easy to view the lots that are about to go on sale at its two principal auction houses, **Sotheby's** and **Christie's**. Think of them as museums with very short exhibitions. Check both houses' websites for the opening hours of viewings, which are free and usually last between 2 and 5 days. Depending on your luck, you could see the Duchess of Windsor's jewelry, Old Masters paintings, a rare copy of Shakespeare's First Folio, antique teddy bears, or just an array of Roman clay pots. Most of the items will pass into private hands within a week and won't resurface again for many years, if ever. **Sotheby's** (34-35 New Bond St., W1; ☎ 020/7293-5000; www.sothebys.com; Tube: Bond Street or Oxford Circus; or Hammersmith Road, W14; ☎ 020/7293-5555; Tube: Kensington Olympia or Hammersmith) has two locations, but its Bond Street flagship tends to showcase the most newsworthy material. **Christie's** also has two showrooms, but displays the higher-profile lots at its King Street location in St. James's (8 King St., SW1; ☎ 020/7839-9060; www.christies.com; Tube: Green Park; or 85 Old Brompton Rd., SW7; ☎ 020/7930-6074; Tube: South Kensington). Although it's not an auction house, **Agnew's** (43 Old Bond St., W1; ☎ 020/7290-9250; www.agnews gallery.com; Mon–Fri 9:30am–5:30pm; Tube: Green Park) works closely with them in valuing Old Masters, Pre-Raphaelite paintings, and select 20th-century works, all of which it regularly displays.

HOW LONDONERS WORK

While you're gallivanting around the city on your vacation, Londoners are working for the man. See how they earn their pay packets—and how it differs from the way you do it back home—by tagging along at their workplaces for a few hours. Just be prepared to feel jealous if you compare vacations with them, too—the British receive 4 weeks of paid leave a year.

GOVERNING THE REALM

If you enjoy drama, and have a taste for a good knockout war of words, you'll get a rise out of watching the debates in the **Houses of Parliament** (☎ 0870/906-3773; www.parliament.uk; Tube: Westminster). It's as if someone tried to throw a professional wrestling match, but legislation broke out instead. If you are so lucky as to get inside the House of Commons for the **Prime Minister's Questions** (or "Question Time;" Wed at 2:30pm, 30 min.), you'll be seated mostly with British observers in the Strangers' Gallery (one level above, looking down, and well divided from the politicians by bulletproof glass). There, you'll witness the cantankerous inquisition of the prime minister (or his seconds) by his political opponents—supposed English gentlemen—whose every contemptuous verbal volley, thinly dressed in a veneer of deferent grammar, is cheered or jeered by all in attendance. Yet you're expected to be on your best behavior if you don't want to be hustled away for a little unofficial questioning of your own. Question Times attended by lesser bureaucrats than the PM are held Mondays and Tuesdays at 2:30pm, and Thursdays at 11am; Fridays, when there's not much going on in the Houses, is an easy day to get in for standard debate. The House of Commons, where members fight tooth and nail to get elected, is more raucous than the House of Lords, where representatives inherit their seats. Some Select and Standing Committee meetings may open to the public from Monday to Thursday when they are taking evidence, but they're plodding and nonconfrontational, hence their unpopularity with visitors.

Parliament sessions are wholly separate from tours of the Houses of Parliament, covered on p. 186. You can visit either house while they are in session (generally mid-Oct to mid-July, minus holidays)—you'll know when the Union Jack flies from the southernmost tower of the complex. Although it's not easy getting in, and trying to do so will eat up much of a day's schedule, it's worth attempting. To gain entry, foreigners must apply for a card of introduction from their Embassy or High Commission in the United Kingdom (searchable at www.embassyworld.com), and each country only has four cards per day to give, so long planning is advised. Even if you have a card, because priority is given to U.K. residents and security checks are laborious, you may not get into the building until 3:30pm or so, after the best stuff is over. Get there as early as you can, but if you still miss the Prime Minister's Questions, know that you can always tune in on TV.

LAW & ORDER

If Question Time has whetted your appetite for blood-and-guts government drama, then your venue of choice is the **Old Bailey** (Newgate St., EC4; ☎ 020/7248-3277; www.cityoflondon.gov.uk; Mon–Fri 10:30–1pm and 2–4pm; Tube: St Paul's) also called the Central Criminal Court, where white-wigged barristers strut and perform as they prove their cases for wizened, crusty judges. You're more likely to be privy to the brutal details of criminal cases at this court, although spectators are asked to leave before the most salacious details are disclosed. Judges enter proceedings carrying a flower—a tradition that began when the notorious Newgate Prison was on this site and men of law, as they visited to defend the accused, needed to disguise the stench of rotting corpses. The current building, topped by a landmark dome and statue of justice, dates from 1907; justice has come a long way from the days when people were simply executed in the street outside. The public galleries are similar to the balconies in a small theater, and cameras, mobile phones, large bags, or children under 14 aren't allowed. Given that the courthouse works with a foreign system with odd traditions (like the judge's posse), it helps to have a guide. For £5 a person, a tour outfit called **Old Bailey Insight** (☎ 01206/513-919; www.old-bailey.com), run by a former court reporter, will brief you on the court's history and then guide you to the best events of the day among the 18 courts; reservations are required.

Civil cases are tried at the **Royal Courts of Justice** (Strand, WC2; ☎ 020/7947-6000; Mon–Fri 9am–4:30pm; Tube: Temple), which strains to impress in the style of some Gothic sanctuary, but in fact is an 1882 hodgepodge of 88 courtrooms wherein the country's most important civil cases—the ones too serious to deal with in the counties—are conducted. The interior, with some 5.6km (3½ miles) of corridors and more than 1,000 rooms, is in many ways as ornate as the exterior, although it's possible the trials (mostly libel, appeals, divorce, and other crimes of paperwork), which you can watch from the back two rows of the benches, may not captivate you as thoroughly as the architecture. Pick up a crucial £1 packet of background information and trivia from the ladies in the lobby check-in booth; it explains the process, who's who in the courtroom, and even which company fabricates the barristers' white wigs—they're made of horsehair. As at the Old Bailey, cameras, phones, large bags, and kids are forbidden, so if you're planning on dropping by in between other sightseeing, you'll need to travel lightly that day.

Tourists are curious about **Scotland Yard** (10 Broadway, SW1; Tube: St. James's Park), the bland headquarters of the city police, and many pose in front of its twirling sign the way news correspondents do. The Yard doesn't give tours; its ghoulish Crime Museum has been open since 1875, but selfishly, it only permits officers to visit.

VOLUNTEER WORK

Few activities are as satisfying or make it so easy to meet locals as volunteering—even if you have only a day to spare for it. This is a messy city with lots of people who could use your help, yet unfortunately, few places in the city allow foreigners to legally pitch in. (You can blame that ubiquitous bugaboo which you will hear cited time and again when someone thinks something is too dangerous: "Health and Safety" rules. While other countries let you show up at a soup kitchen and grab a ladle, the U.K. requires preliminary labor training first, making it impossible for short-term tourists to help out, no matter how harmless the activity might seem.)

The following agencies, however, **do** accept short-term help from foreigners:

GO London (☎ 020/643-1341; www.csv.org.uk/Volunteer/Part-time/GO) organizes about 50 unregulated weekend events a year, such as mural painting, garden planting, and playground cleanups. **Thames21** (☎ 020/7248-7171; www.thames21.org.uk), an environmental charity, focuses energy on beautifying the waterway, and it hosts about a dozen litter-picking days throughout the year. That sounds kill-me-now dull, but in truth, a river sweep can be a bit like accidental archaeology; at low tide, it's not uncommon to find items in the muddy bed that were left there generations ago. The Museum of London should know; many of the Roman swords in its collection were retrieved from the river, since that's where people once left precious offerings for the gods. You'll be treading old stone stairs and slopes that were laid by people in the days of the great sailing ships. Few tourists think to experience the river in this way, so you'll find yourself grooming the sand with genuine London families. Should you rather not get your clothes muddy on vacation (I can't blame you), in the summer, Thames21 schedules Tightlines, free 4-hr. angling coaching sessions, at different points in the river's course, each of which attracts local kids and families from that area. You don't have to release what you catch, but most people do; after all, this is a love-the-river organization. Equipment is provided.

Another group, **Thames Explorer Trust** (☎ 020/8742-0057; www.thames-explorer.org.uk), organizes about a half-dozen clean-up events in the summer and participates in the odd kid-friendly fair, such as mid-September's Mayor's Thames Festival (p. 338); check its site, too.

Another prime source of one-day volunteering events such as building burrows for hedgehogs and unique animal viewings (such as Batwatches, which are evening safaris for bat colonies held in the summer) across the city is the **London Wildlife Trust** (☎ 020/7261-0447; www.wildlondon.org.uk), which works to protect animals, insects, and trees that call the city home. The free "Going Wild in London" pamphlet, which lists the upcoming schedule, can be downloaded from its website. Most of its activities require that you make contact with the individual volunteer who's organizing it, which guarantees you interaction with a like-minded local and possibly a new friendship too. On summer weekends, two or three events are often held, ranging from hands-on (path clearing and weeding in Waltham Forest, bird-watching in a little-known parks beside the disused King's Cross gasworks) to educational (lessons on composting, nature walks). Its website also lists contact numbers for the many neighborhood branches of Wildlife Watch (www.wildlifewatch.org.uk), the wing of

> ❝ It is not the walls that make the city, but the people who live within them. The walls of London may be battered, but the spirit of the Londoner stands resolute and undismayed. ❞
>
> —King George VI, 1940

the Wildlife Trust geared to kids aged 8 to 14, each of which can hook you up with the next kid-friendly event such as birdfeeder building or "pond dipping" (plumbing fresh waters for samples of what lives in them). You may need to bring helper items such as heavy boots or binoculars, but your contact can tell you where to find them, and besides, the events themselves are free.

Of course, lots of groups might be able to accept your temporary services on a strictly unofficial basis. Your chances of finding temporary occupation increase greatly if you can find a task that doesn't involve contact with food, money, or other people, such as stuffing envelopes. If you run across a place where you'd like to donate some time, it doesn't hurt to ask, but expect to be politely rebuffed.

THEATER TOURS

A number of historic, working theaters bring members of the public into their private spaces on tours. The most popular one, run daily, is at **Theatre Royal, Drury Lane** (Catherine St., WC2; ☎ 020/7494-5091; Mon, Tues, Thurs, Fri 2:15pm and 4:45 pm, Wed, Sat 10:15am, Sun at noon by prior arrangement; £9 adults, £7 children; Tube: Covent Garden), whose history, from decent to depraved, reaches back to 1663 (although the present building, one of the city's pre-eminent houses for musicals, dates to 1812). Its 75-minute tour is led by a troupe of costumed actors—apparently hired for their ability to amuse children as they imitate characters from the house's history—and it takes in the backstage, front-of-house, two royal boxes, and the under-stage hydraulics system. You'll also see the sealed entrances to tunnels that once snaked all the way to the river so that sailors, the original scenery riggers, could commute from the ropes of their ships to the ones in the fly space (which gave rise to the superstition about never whistling in a theater—it conflicted with the sailors' communication method). Whether you spot one of the storied ghosts is a matter of luck.

The **National Theatre** (☎ 020/7452-3400; www.nt-online.org; £5 adults, £4 children; up to five daytime tours daily Mon–Sat 10:15am–5:30pm; Tube: Waterloo), dating only to the 1950s, is more suited to fans of state-of-the-art theatrics than to people seeking atmosphere. For 75 minutes, it shows off the scene shops and backstage areas of this respected, three-house complex where every British thespian appears at least once in their careers.

Ninety-minute tours of **The Royal Opera House** (☎ 020/7304-4000; www.roh.org.uk; £9 adults, £7 children; up to three tours Mon–Fri 10:30am–2:30 pm, up to four tours Sat 10:30am–1:30 pm; Tube: Covent Garden) focus on the theater's illustrious history and tales of the two houses that stood on this plot first (this one's from 1858). Don't expect snooze-inducing stories of plump divas; in 1809, there was a run of civil disobedience here by mobs who were furious at pricing that excluded the poor. I also got the feeling, from the fulsome praise paid to the recent radical restoration (completed in 2000), that lip service was also being paid to its donors.

Two other 20th-century West End theaters also run tours for theater fans: The **Prince Edward Theatre** (Old Compton St, W1; ☎ 0870/850-9191; www.delfont mackintosh.co.uk; £5; Tube: Leicester Square), an established home for musicals including the original productions of *Evita, Chess,* and *Mary Poppins,* offers tours Thursdays at 11am, which include design details about the set for whatever show happens to be playing; and **The Prince of Wales** (Coventry St., W1; ☎ 0870/850-0393; www.delfontmackintosh.co.uk; adults £5; Tube: Piccadilly Circus), currently home to *Mamma Mia!* but at times trod by Barbra Streisand and Mae West, helps tourists appreciate its recently restored Art Deco features on Fridays at 2pm. Since these are all working theaters with changing situations, book in advance.

BREWERY TOURS

When in France, you take in the wineries. In London, ale's the word. Reserve ahead for 90-minute tours of **Fullers Griffin Brewery** (Chiswick Lane South, W4; ☎ 020/8996-2063; www.fullers.co.uk; Tube: Turnham Green), which begin at the brewery-owned Mawson Arms pub and culminate at a tasting of its well-loved London Pride quaff, plus other seasonal ales, inside its 200-year-old Hock Cellar. Records indicate that beer has been made on this site for more than 350 years, so the brewery claims (not uncontested) to be the city's oldest. Tours run Monday, Wednesday, Thursday, and Friday hourly from 11am to 2pm and cost £6 adults, £4.50 children 14 to 18 (they don't get a tasting). Kids under 14 aren't allowed. It's six Underground stops west of Earl's Court.

Young's Ram Brewery (Brewery Tap Visitor Centre, 68 High St., Wandsworth, SW18; ☎ 020/8875-7005; www.youngs.co.uk; £3.50 adults, £2 children 14–18. Mainline rail: Wandsworth Town), whose live drayhorses, which still deliver beers to pubs in the area, make it seem like a parcel of misplaced countryside, brews draught quaffs including its Special London Ale. Two steam engines, the oldest of their kind, were used until the 1980s and now stand alongside modern equipment. The brewery runs tours every day except Sunday at noon and 2pm; book at least 2 weeks ahead.

FOUNDRY TOURS

America's Liberty Bell. Montreal Cathedral's Great Bell. Big Ben himself. Name an important chimer from Western history, and chances are **Whitechapel Bell Foundry** (32-34 Whitechapel Rd., E1; ☎ 020/7247-2599; www.whitechapelbell foundry.co.uk; Tube: Aldgate East) cast it. Sure, the Liberty Bell cracked, by which time it was too late to return it, but the foundry's craftsmanship is not in question—Guinness verified it as Britain's oldest manufacturing company, established in 1570, with lineage traceable to 1420. Although Big Ben is still the largest job it's ever done (a cross section of a copy is mounted perilously over the doorway), it's still making and repairing bells in the East End, where foulsome industry such as metalworking used to be found. The foundry conducts tours on one or two Saturdays a month (always when founders are off duty, because flying sparks and molten metal equal unwinnable lawsuits) at 10am and 2pm for £8 adults, with a minimum age of 14. There's also a small museum and shop, which don't require tickets; it's open Monday to Friday.

TV STUDIO TOURS

The storied Pinewood and Shepperton movie studios in West London, the settings for the James Bond and Harry Potter films, among many other classics, don't allow tours. The same goes for Elstree Film and Television Studios in northwest London, which since 1914 has hosted *The Muppet Show, Raiders of the Lost Ark,* and many Hitchcock films. Entertainment buffs mustn't despair, as, an alternative, small studio tour exists: **BBC Television Centre Tour** (Wood Lane, W12; ☎ 0870/603-0304; www.bbc.co.uk/tours; Tube: White City). It's true that unless you're a regular viewer of BBC-made programming, you won't recognize many of the faces on the tour of these studios in West London, but you will get a fascinating behind-the-scenes glimpse of the country's principal entertainment factory—control rooms, sets, the newsroom (usually standing idle), Studio 8 (once of *Fawlty Towers*), and other trappings of technical production. Britain's studios are less precious than Hollywood's about controlling access to stars, so you may even get to see some live filming.

Since it's a working studio, tours change daily, but they usually last about 2 hours. Hours change, so reservations are strongly suggested. Tickets are £8.95 for adults, £6.50 for children over 9, or £25 for families of two adults and two or three kids. For kids under 10 but over 6, there's a kids' version, the CBBC Tour, which includes the set of British children's shows *Blue Peter* (beloved in Britain, mostly unknown outside it) as well as a visit to an educational TV studio; it costs the same as the main tour. The center also has a gift shop for souvenirs, books, and plenty of Britcom and miniseries DVDs. Another BBC Shop is on Aldwych in central London (Bush House, Strand, WC2; ☎ 020/7557-2576; www.bbc shop.com; Mon–Fri 10am–6pm, Sat 10am–5:30pm, Sun 12:30pm–5:30pm; Tube: Temple).

TICKETS TO TV TAPINGS

Of course, there's no better way to understand the singular culture of British TV than seeing a show being made. British production seasons are relatively short—often just a couple of months at a time—so what you'll see depends greatly on when you visit. To cater to regional differences, programs are produced all around the United Kingdom—for example, *Countdown,* the beloved daily game show, is shot in Leeds, and *The Jeremy Kyle Show,* like Jerry Springer with heart, is taped in Manchester. But London hosts the lion's share of the popular shows, particularly if they require the participation of major celebrities. Although tickets to pretty much every TV show are free, most studios require that audience members be at least 16 years old. The process of taping a show isn't much different from what it is in other major production centers such as Hollywood or New York City; audiences (which are notably more subdued than American or Australian crowds) are invited mostly for their willingness to applaud or laugh vigorously and on cue. Situation comedies and many game shows tend to stop and start, so a half-hour show may translate into a 4-hour commitment, but chat shows are usually in-and-out affairs. Don't expect free gifts or money for your presence—that's pure Oprah.

Many **BBC** tapings, particularly those with star power, book up months in advance, but it's still usually possible to snag free tickets to something interesting. Call ☎ 020/8576-1227 for recorded information or visit www.bbc.co.uk/tickets.

The other major British networks, which are hipper than the government-subsidized BBC channels, require potential audience members to arrange for tickets through the individual production companies responsible for each show. Each network's website will help you find the right place to make your request. **ITV** (www.itv.com/tickets) hosts regular TV tapings including *Parkinson* (a long-running talk show that books all the Hollywood stars) and *Who Wants to Be a Millionaire?*. **Channel 4** (www.channel4.com/tickets), broadcasts the edgiest material of the major networks, as well as the hottest American imports. Its most sensational shows, like *Big Brother*, aren't worth attempting since producers often distribute more tickets than they have seats for. Also check this important producer of multiple shows: **Granada Entertainment** (www.tickets.granadamedia.com). Many TV production companies place classified notices of upcoming tapings in *Time Out* magazine.

A few services broker tickets on behalf of producers, and they're good places to check and to register your e-mail address in advance of a trip: **The Applause Store** (☎ 0870/024-1000; www.applausestore.com), **Clappers Limited** (☎ 020/8532-2771/2770; www.clappers-tickets.co.uk), **Lost in TV** (☎ 020/8530-8100; www.lostintv.com), **Powerhouse Film & TV** (☎ 020/7240-2828), and **SRO Audiences** (☎ 020/8684-3333; www.sroaudiences.com). Some brokers will entice you with premium memberships promising advance word of popular shows, but as a tourist, the expense of subscribing isn't worth it. You shouldn't have to pay for tickets.

Radio is still huge in Britain, so free tickets are often available for concerts, interviews, and even radio plays that go out on the BBC's many stations. Contact the **BBC Radio Ticket Unit** (☎ 020/8576-1227; radio.ticket.unit@bbc.co.uk).

HOW LONDONERS PRAY

If you can't afford to pay the hefty entrance charges for the city's most visited churches, you can always get in free by attending a service there. That method won't afford you a look at its historic artifacts or exhibitions, but it will give you meditation time in the main sanctuary, ear time with some unbelievable organs and choirs, and the chance to mingle with a host of native Londoners who regard these world-famous sanctuaries as their spiritual homes. If you think about it, you'll be seeing the following churches the way they were intended to be seen: from the pews, in prayer.

All of London's most historic edifices are part of the Church of England (a kissin' cousin to the American Episcopalian), and most have no sermon, or else very short ones; simply put, they're light on the fire and brimstone. **St. Paul's Cathedral** (St. Paul's Churchyard, EC4; ☎ 020/7236-4128; www.stpauls.org.uk; Tube: St. Paul's) provides four to six opportunities for worship every day, including Mattins (7:30am weekdays, 10:15am Sun), Holy Communion (8am daily, plus 12:30 Mon–Sat), Sung Eucharist (11:30am Sun), Evensong (5pm daily), and an evening service (5 or 6 pm daily). Its organ can send music lovers into near euphoria. The main sanctuary of the Anglican **Westminster Abbey** (Broad Sanctuary, SW1; ☎ 020/7222-5152; www.westminster-abbey.org; Tube:

Lunchtime Concerts

On every working day at around 1pm, at centuries-old churches across the city, you'll find an array of free musical shows known as Lunchtime Concerts. Considered part of these houses' ministry to the public, the offerings range from chamber orchestras, to organists, to soloists, to singers, and are usually quite good. The concerts don't come with strings attached or with heavy-handed evangelism. Even better, they're all free, though many request (rightfully) a donation of a few pounds, which goes mostly to the upkeep of these ancient and crumbling sanctuaries.

Check the outdoor notice boards at any church to see what's lined up, but some notable or historic churches that get in on the act include the prolific **St. Martin-in-the-Fields** (Trafalgar Square, W1; ☎ 020/7839-8362; www.stmartin-in-the-fields.org; concerts almost daily; Tube: Charing Cross), which is famous for its musical prowess; Sir Christopher Wren's **St. James's Church Piccadilly** (197 Piccadilly, W1; ☎ 020/7734-4511; www.st-james-piccadilly.org; concerts generally fall on Mon, Wed, or Fri—on Tues, it hosts an antiques flea market; Tube: Piccadilly Circus); **St. Andrew Holborn** (5 St. Andrew St., EC4; ☎ 020/7583-7394; www.st andrewholborn.org.uk; Tube: Holborn); **All Souls Langham Place** (2 All Souls Place, W1; ☎ 020/7580-3522; www.allsouls.org; big on organ recitals; Tube: Oxford Circus); **St. Mary le Bow** (Cheapside, EC2; ☎ 020/7248-5139; www.stmarylebow.co.uk; Thurs; Tube St. Paul); and **St. Mary Le Strand** (Strand, WC2; ☎ 01296/74-88-27; www.stmarylestrand.org; Wed organ recitals; Tube: Temple), the central church of the Royal Air

Westminster) hosts evening prayer at 5pm weekdays and Sung Eucharist Sundays at 11:15am, plus a Sunday evening service at 6:30pm (but check ahead, since services are sometimes shuffled to smaller, but equally historic, chapels).

Good news! Catholics are no longer executed in England. They can freely attend the towering, Byzantine-style **Westminster Cathedral** (42 Francis St., SW1; ☎ 020/7798-9055; www.westminstercathedral.org.uk; Tube: Victoria), the largest Roman Catholic church in England and Wales and 18m/60 ft. taller than Westminster Abbey farther east down Victoria Street. It's a handsome historic building from 1903 but isn't popular with tourists, so it has the elbow room to plan a fuller slate of Masses: six weekdays and Sunday, four on Saturday. Best of all, its choir is considered one of the world's best. Notice that I said *one* of the best: **Brompton Oratory** (Brompton Rd., SW7; ☎ 020/7808-0900; www.brompton oratory.com; Tube: South Kensington) is recognized as having the U.K.'s best Catholic church choir, and its 1964 organ has been called the finest built in the postwar period. Mass with choir is held on Sundays at 9am. For a defiantly contemporary service that typifies the progressive form of Christianity sweeping England, head to the Vinopolis, the "theme park for wine" on Sunday afternoons, because that's the unlikely meeting place for **ChristChurch** (1 Bank End, SE1;

Force. Many of these churches also host a huge range of evening concerts, which cost £5–£10.

A few nonsanctified locales also get in on the act. Slip into the foyer of the **South Bank Centre** (Belvedere Rd., SE1; ☎ 0870/380-4300; www.rfh.org.uk; Tube: Waterloo), which hosts free musical entertainment from jazz bands to solo instrumentalists weekdays from 12:30pm to 2pm.

The **London Organ Concerts Guide** (☎ 01992/58-72-85; www.london organ.co.uk) keeps track of upcoming events. In the winter, the **City Music Society** (☎ 020/8542-0950; www.citymusicsociety.org) sets up a range of concerts at churches and halls across town, both at lunchtime and in the evening.

St. Paul's Cathedral (St. Paul's Churchyard, EC4; ☎ 020/7236-4128; www.stpauls.org.uk; last admission at 4pm; Tube: St. Paul's) isn't big on free concerts, but on many afternoons (from 3–6pm), your regular tour may be atmospherically accompanied by orchestral or choir rehearsals; it's a small comfort if you come to the Dome and find that it closes around 4:30. **Westminster Abbey** (Broad Sanctuary, SW1; ☎ 020/7222-5152; www.westminster-abbey.org; Tube: Westminster) hosts even fewer concerts; instead, its overlooked and plainer sister sitting in its yard, St. Margaret's Church (same contact info as the Abbey), sometimes puts on late afternoon or evening concerts (mostly £7) by professional musicians or recitals by students at its all-boy Choir School.

☎ 020/8560-0922; www.christchurchlondon.org; Tube: London Bridge). Despite the grape-centric locale, this church is traditional enough to stick to serving coffee after the service.

One of the city's most interesting Jewish houses of worship is the little-known **Westminster Synagogue** (Kent House, Rutland Gardens, SW7; ☎ 020/7584-3741; Tube: Knightsbridge), which took residence in an otherwise unobtrusive Belgravia town house in 1963. Today it's a repository for some priceless Czech Torah scrolls rescued from the Nazis; the curator lives upstairs. The 4,000-member **West London Synagogue** (34 Upper Berkeley St., W1; ☎ 020/7224-8258; www.wls. org.uk; Tube: Marble Arch) was founded in 1840 as the first Reform synagogue in Britain and is welcoming to outsiders. Men are asked to wear yarmulkes during services.

London boasts a sizable Muslim community, but the majority of its houses of worship are not yet established as casual attractions, so sightseers might feel uncomfortable. Muslims who would like to pray with locals would do well to visit the **London Central Mosque** (146 Park Rd., NW8; ☎ 020/7724-3363; www.icclcm. org; Tube: Marylebone or Baker Street), which accommodates 1,800 worshipers and has established itself as a progressive leader in the city. (Its one-time theological rival, the so-called Finsbury Park Mosque, was once a nest of radicalism that counted Richard Reid, Zacarias Moussaoui and Chechen rebels among its attendees but, following a 2003 raid by police, has been reclaimed by peaceful elders.)

Among London Hindus, the Swaminarayan movement claims the most adherents; the breathtakingly gorgeous, many-pinnacled **Mandir** (105-119 Brentfield Rd., NW10; ☎ 020/8965-2651; www.mandir.org; Tube: Neasden, then 112 or 232 bus) in northwest London is the largest Hindu temple outside of India, completed in 1995. Some 5,500 tons of Italian Carrara marble and Bulgarian limestone were carved in India and shipped here, where they were assembled by volunteers—its dome was built without using steel or lead. A visit to its delicately carved interior, as complicated and as white as a doily, is a must even for people generally unimpressed by such virtuosity, and tourists are warmly encouraged by the presence of a 279-sq.-m (3,000-sq.-ft.) exhibition entitled **"Understanding Hinduism"** (daily 9am–6pm; adults £2, children £1.50), which explains in the plainest terms possible how the religion works and how this spectacular house of worship was constructed. *Note:* If you're entering either the mosque or the Mandir, your shorts must not fall higher than the knee (although ankle-length is preferable and sarongs are available to borrow); all visitors must also remove their shoes before entering.

America may have invented and popularized the 19th-century spiritualist movement, but London still embraces it. **The Spiritualist Association of Great Britain** (33 Belgrave Square, SW1; ☎ 020/7235-3351; www.spiritualistassociation. org.uk; Tube: Hyde Park Corner), which has catered to clairvoyants and mediums since 1872, owns a humdrum Victorian town house in tony Knightsbridge, where it holds workshops on the psychic arts. Private sittings are £30, but for just £5, you can attend one of the "daily demonstrations," in which a medium stands at the front of the room and reports on the ghosts and psychic vibrations swirling around members of the audience. You won't get quivering tables or milky crystal balls; in truth, the plain meeting area is about as spooky as the function room of a midwestern Presbyterian church, and some guests will be relieved to know that most leaders acknowledge God during their sessions. Still, on more than one occasion, I have seen an idle evening here suddenly take an eerily thought-provoking turn when the audience starts getting emotional about what the mediums pick out of the ether. Demonstrations take place some afternoons at 3:30pm and most weekday evenings at 7pm, Saturdays at 4pm, and Sundays at 6pm. It's one of the most electrifying cheap nights out in town. The house is on the southeast side of the square; combine a visit with a drink at The Grenadier pub (p. 128) off the square's opposite side—an appropriate choice, since the pub is said to be haunted.

The **London Buddhist Centre** (51 Roman Rd., E2; ☎ 0845/458-4716; www. lbc.org.uk; Tube: Bethnal Green), open since 1978 in a disused fire station in the East End, is in a mini-community that includes Buddhist-run vegetarian restaurants, organic remedies shops, and gift shops. As with many Buddhist organizations, it's friendly to newcomers and has set aside large chunks of its schedule to helping them learn the ropes. It conducts meditation classes for beginners every weekday from 1 to 2pm (£1), and on Saturdays at the same time (£5) at 8 Hop Gardens, off St. Martin's Lane in Covent Garden. From Tuesday to Thursday starting at 7:15pm, it hosts drop-in sessions (£7) where you can learn to meditate

Pearly Kings & Queens

One of the most iconic symbols of London life is that of the Pearly King and Queen. You've seen pictures: grinning folks in suits outrageously embroidered with white buttons and baubles. The tradition began in the Victorian markets, when traders trumpeted their status by decorating their seams with smoke pearl buttons. A poor street sweeper named Henry Croft evolved this esoteric nomenclature into fully embellished outfits, weighing up to 30 pounds and worn to attract charitable donations. Soon the idea spread to a whole league of approved wearers, each with their own suit representing a different borough of London. Finding a "Pearly" these days isn't easy. Like the bowler hat and the London fog, they're not very common anymore. The tradition is dying out, and costumes are increasingly more likely to be found hanging in a museum than on the back of rightful owners. But these whimsical garments do come out of their closets for special occasions such as funerals, race days, and charity parties. The most important appearance on the annual Pearly calendar is probably the Harvest Festival in early October, when dozens gather for a thanksgiving prayer service (the location changes). Some of those appearances are announced on the official site of **The London Pearly Kings and Queens Society** (www.pearlysociety.co.uk), but you can also find them in the third weekend of every month at Jubilee Market Hall, Covent Garden, from 10:30am to 3:30pm. These figureheads exist to shake hands and spread goodwill, so get in there and ask them some questions. As for Harry Croft, his statue can be seen every day in the crypt at St. Martins in the Fields, Trafalgar Square. Now he looks as if he's made of pearl itself.

and get advice from experienced Buddhists. There's also an on-site bookshop selling cards, incense, and meditation cushions, plus a secondhand shop, Sudana (☎ 020/8981-1225).

Every Monday, Wednesday, and Friday at 12:30pm, **The College of Psychic Studies** (16 Queensberry Place, SW7; ☎ 020/7589-3292; www.collegeofpsychic studies.co.uk; Tube: South Kensington), set up in 1884 to foster an understanding of human consciousness, opens its doors for free meditation sessions, led by the same experts who normally charge £30 per course. The yogis belonging to the **Sri Chinmoy Centre** (www.srichinmoycentre.org) also offer free classes, although you have to e-mail ahead to be included.

HOW LONDONERS AMUSE THEMSELVES

Contrary to their undeserved reputations, Londoners do like a good-natured mix-it-up—more, perhaps, than other Englishmen. Although you'll find them to be mum and near-catatonic on their morning commutes, when the workday's over, they loosen their ties at events like the following.

SUNDAY PARTIES

Sunday afternoon parties, like Sunday roasts (see below), are a long-held tradition here. They're often programmed like a party on a weekend night—with DJs, maybe, or dancing—but Sunday parties are more inclusive and cosmopolitan, they cost less, and, because some attendees have been raging all weekend, their vibe is more anything-goes. Sunday's a great day to kick back with the locals, put your feet up, and watch the day trickle by. (Also see The Church, p. 314.)

Spun off from the popular Big Chill music-and-multimedia summer festivals held in the countryside, the laid-back **Big Chill Bar** (Dray Walk, E1; ☎ 020/7392-9180; www.bigchill.net; no cover; Sun–Thurs noon–midnight, Fri–Sat noon–1am; Tube: Aldgate East or Liverpool Street) is for young people who have outgrown dance music but not its languid disposition. In the Old Truman Brewery, Sundays are about loafing on fat sofas, making friends at communal dining tables, and grooving to DJs who, as they navigate a range of styles, would rather see you veg than pop.

The city's best names in thumping drum and bass hold court downstairs at **Grace** (Herbal, 12-14 Kingsland Rd., E2; ☎ 020/7613-4462; £6 before 10:30pm, £8 after; daily 9pm–2am; Tube: Old Street). For those who want their Sabbath filled with funk and jungle rhythm, the host, Grooverider, is a fixture on the club scene. Upstairs, the dominant mode is hip-hop.

More of a breezy, modern pub than a club, **The Lock Tavern** (35 Chalk Farm Rd., NW1; ☎ 020/7482-7163; www.lock-tavern.co.uk; no cover; Tube: Camden Town or Chalk Farm) calls itself "a tarted-up boozer." In fact, it's the panacea to the overcrowded Camden Lock Market just across the street. A wide range of DJs spinning on two floors carry the flag of its true indie spirit; there's a busy roof terrace and a garden doing their year-round impression of a summer party, and as if that weren't enough, a traditional Sunday roast is served. The good times start around lunchtime and end around 10:30pm.

QUIZ NIGHTS

The British aren't satisfied with confining the sharing of useless knowledge to Trivial Pursuit. They get beer involved and throw informal **quiz nights** at their local pubs. Contestants, who pay a nominal entry fee such as £1 per person, are generally grouped into teams of two to four. Some pubs award prizes for the best name, so try to come up with a witty one. Over many drinks, which complicates

The Roast with the Most

Eel pie? Um, maybe not. Beheading childless wives? No, thanks. But there's one English tradition worth upholding: the Sunday Roast. Rare is the truly popular pub that doesn't offer a spread including meats with the trimmings, Yorkshire pudding (a pastry-like shell), and veggies, washed down with copious amounts of beer. A standard starting price is £8.95. Find a pub with an inviting garden or back room, bring a stack of Sunday papers, and hang out until you're ready for Monday.

the recall process, teams write down the answers to a list of questions. After judging by a Quiz Master (who, in many cases, performs nightly around town for a living), the winning team is named and awarded with prizes ranging from free food to £100. Foreigners who win should expect to receive some good-natured ribbing from the regulars, which depending on your charms can easily be parlayed into some free pints. If you think you have what it takes—and mind you, you'll have to leap some tricky culture gaps in the sports, local politics, and TV categories—check the blackboard at any pub to see if one is scheduled. Should you need to recruit extra players on the spot for your team (which I recommend, since it will round out your knowledge base), you'll make some new English friends— after all, nothing bonds strangers together like useless trivia. They generally fall on Monday through Thursday evenings, when pubs are less full. One of the flashier quiz nights, complete with picture-only rounds and movie clips, is held the first Tuesday of the month (unusually, it can be booked in advance) at the upscale bar **AKA** (18 West Central St., WC1; ☎ 020/7836-0110; www.akalondon.com; Tube: Holborn or Tottenham Court Road) located in southern Bloomsbury. Another popular one is held at the rock 'n' roll bar **The Boogaloo** (312 Archway Rd., N6; ☎ 020/8340-2928; www.theboogaloo.co.uk; Tube: Highgate); check its schedule because it slots both monthly movie quiz nights (called "You're Gonna Need a Bigger Boat," the first Wed evening of the month; www.film-quiz.com) and general-knowledge nights (called "Who Killed Bambi?" usually Tues evenings).

PANTOMIME

If you're in Britain between late November and early January, absolutely do not miss partaking of the peculiar entertainment known as pantomime, more commonly called *panto.* A direct outgrowth of *commedia dell-arte* theatrical tradition that arrived in England in the Middle Ages, panto refers not to limber, black-clad mimes but to slapstick musical romps, drenched in mild innuendo, that enraptures children and titillates their more knowing parents. Many theater companies fund their entire seasons based on the success of these cash cows, which is one reason entertainment titans such as Clear Channel have recently gotten into producing them. Some pantos are performed in standard West End theaters, but the most rewarding ones are almost always mounted in gorgeous turn-of-the-century music halls located in old, multicultural London neighborhoods, giving tourists a two-for-one sightseeing experience. One house with a strong panto track record is the **Hackney Empire** (291 Mare St., E8; ☎ 020/8985-2424; www.hackney empire.co.uk; Mainline rail: Hackney Central), built as a variety house in 1901, where both Charlie Chaplin and Stan Laurel cut their teeth before decamping to Hollywood. **Theatre Royal Stratford East** (Gerry Raffles Square, E15; ☎ 020/8534-8381; www.stratfordeast.com; Tube: Stratford), a living theatrical museum (1884), is also respected for putting on a crowd-pleasing, traditional panto; it's easy to reach by Tube. **The Richmond Theatre** (The Green, Richmond; ☎ 0870/060-6651; www.richmondtheatre.net; Tube: Richmond), from 1899, has been known to hire well-known actors such as Simon Callow and Patsy Kensit. **The Old Vic** (The Cut, ☎ 0870/060-6628; www.oldvictheatre.com; Tube: Waterloo) scored a coup in 2005 by retaining Ian McKellen for its Widow Twankey in *Aladdin* (quipped the *Guardian,* clearly in the spirit: "We can tell our grandchildren that we saw McKellen's Twankey and it was huge."); as a serious company, the Old Vic

Oh, Yes You Can: The Panto Lingo

Attending your first pantomime performance can be as bewildering and alienating as going to your first interactive *Rocky Horror Picture Show*. It seems like everyone in the audience, including the infants, knows exactly when to yell and what to say. Don't worry—the whole point is to have fun, so your neighbors won't judge you. But you'll certainly impress them if you come in with a little foreknowledge:

- Most pantos pick from a list of about a dozen stories including "Jack and the Beanstalk," "Cinderella," "Aladdin," and "Snow White." The tale of Dick Whittington, about a poor boy (and his cat) who seeks and finds his fortune in London, is one panto you won't see much of outside the city. Each company tinkers with the plot to suit the talents of that year's cast.
- The leading man, also called "principal boy," is played by a woman pretending to be a man, usually by wearing revealing shorts or tights.
- The leading lady, or "dame," is a man dressed as a woman, and the campy double entendres fly. The fame of the actor retained for the role is the mark of a high-profile panto, although most of the time, you'll see a C-list TV celebrity. As you can imagine, it's where many comics' careers go to die.
- The villain should be hissed and booed.
- Whenever one character is being stalked by another, the audience must shout "It's behind you!"
- Whenever the good guy argues with the bad guy (or "the baddie"), the audience takes the side of the good guy and shouts along with the row. The exchange will be along the lines of "Oh, no, he isn't, and "oh, yes he is!"
- Invariably, two actors in a single costume will portray a horse or a cow.

doesn't do panto every year, although it probably should to line its coffers. Tickets for all shows, which tend to last a little over 2 hours to appease restless kids, usually cost between £10 and £25.

THE SING-A-LONG *SOUND OF MUSIC*

The family-friendly "Sing-a-Long-a" *The Sound of Music*, a giddy participatory screening of the 1965 classic, was born at the **Prince Charles Cinema** (7 Leicester Place; ☎ 0870/906-3864 or 020/7494-3654; www.princecharlescinema.com; £14; Tube: Leicester Square) in 1999 and swept the world. A documentary on the phenomenon even made it onto the 40th anniversary DVD re-release of the Rodgers and Hammerstein musical in 2005. Participants—some of whom arrive dressed as Nazis and nuns, without regard to gender—receive a "magic moment" bag with edelweiss, curtain swatches, and a party popper to deploy at the moment of Maria and the Captain's kiss. Unlike midnight *Rocky Horror* screenings, newbies aren't tortured with initiation rituals; all are welcome at this goofy lovefest, which includes a pre-show warm-up with an optional costume contest, on-screen lyrics, and an intermission. It's an absolute blast—though at times the frolic gets a bit too risque for the very young—and is held on most Fridays at 7:30pm. Now and then, the Prince Charles throws other "sing-a-long-a" versions, showcasing the hits of ABBA and *Rocky Horror*. While you're on the street and in a cinematic mode, duck into **Notre Dame de France** (5 Leicester Place, WC2; ☎ 020/7437-9363; www.notredamechurch.co.uk; Tube: Leicester Square) next door, where there's a series of dazzling 1960 murals by writer/director Jean Cocteau in one of its side chapels.

SNOOKER CLUBS

Snooker, a close cousin of American-style billiards, is played at "clubs" where gentlemen (as it happens, but not by requirement) can also buy drinks, snacks, and watch TV. An annual membership, which gets you in the door, costs around £10, and rental of a table goes from £4 to about £14 on a weekday or weeknight. Some central clubs include the **Centrepoint Snooker Club** (New Oxford St., WC1; ☎ 020/7240-6886; 11am–6pm daily; Tube: Tottenham Court Road), located in the basement of the Centre Point tower, and the **King's Cross Snooker and Social Club** (Pentonville Rd, N1; ☎ 020/7278-7079; Tube: King's Cross/St. Pancras), which never closes. Some clubs take themselves awfully seriously, and each one has its own rules for claiming a table—observe the ritual before diving in. Clubs also sometimes insist that non-members arrive with members, which is next to an impossibility for tourists, but they're more likely to be lax about the rules during quiet times, such as on midweek afternoons and evenings. The rarified snooker culture can be daunting, but for a looser vibe, opt for a casual pool hall such as **The Elbow Room** (103 Westbourne Grove, W2; ☎ 020/7221-5211; www.elbow-room.co.uk; tables £6–£9 per hour; Mon-Sat noon–11pm, Sun noon–10:30pm; and 89-91 Chapel Market, N1; ☎ 020/7278-3244; Mon 5pm–2am, Tues–Thurs noon–2am, Fri–Sat noon–3am, Sun noon–midnight), dimly lit but intentionally kitschy and patronized by dilettantes like students and young businessmen, not by sharks and hustlers.

For info on other sporting activities in London, see Chapter 7.

FAMILY DANCE CLASSES

The fabulous, crumbling 1930s city hall that has been given new life by the **Greenwich Dance Agency** (The Borough Hall, Royal Hill, SE10; ☎ 020/8293-9741; www.greenwichdance.org.uk; Tube: Greenwich DLR) throbs with activity year-round as moms of every income bracket and color drop their kids off for the many cheap dance classes here. The lessons are as multicultural as the clientele (numbering over 4,500 a year), with disciplines such as Irish step, capoeira, yoga, and salsa. Some courses require a multi-week commitment, but there is at least one drop-in class a day, too (check ahead), taught by professionals and costing around £4 for 90 minutes. In the spring, Saturday afternoons are reserved for Spring Tea Dances (£4), ballroom dancing mixers where tea and cake are served.

BATHS

In the old days, few Londoners had running water of their own, so neighborhood baths became a vital necessity. That necessity evolved into a Victorian vogue for Turkish-style baths, the precursor to the modern gym. They're now just an indulgent tradition, priced low enough to encourage continued civic use and often crawling with local characters who have spent their whole lives soaking in the same tubs. Unlike at haughty day spas, socializing is encouraged at these old-fashioned baths. In fact, each one has lounges or small cafes where, once clad in just a towel, people from every walk of life meet on equal footing. **Ironmonger Row Baths** (1-11 Ironmonger Row, EC1; ☎ 020/7253-4011; www.aquaterra.org/islington; Mon–Fri 6:30am–9pm, Sat 9am–6pm, Sun 10am–6pm; Tube: Old Street), an urban escape of low light, dark woods, and quietly gossiping senior citizens, has two pools (£3.40 adults, £1.50 children), but they're not the star attraction. The real draw is the astoundingly cheap subterranean Turkish Bath facilities, which include a steam room, three hot rooms, plenty of marble slabs for vigorous rubdowns from on-site licensed therapists, nap rooms, and a cold plunge pool. That's just £7.20 for 3 hours on weekday mornings starting at 6:30am, rising to £12 after noon and on weekends; those prices include access to the main pools. It's men only Tuesday, Thursday, Saturday; women only Wednesday, Friday, and Sunday; and mixed on Monday afternoons.

More ornate, but also more expensive, is **The Porchester Spa** (The Porchester Centre, Queensway, W2; ☎ 020/7792-3980; Mon–Fri 7am–10pm, Sat–Sun 8am–8pm; Tube: Royal Oak), an Art Deco facility with many of its original period details (high ceilings, green and white tiles, 1920s fixtures) intact. It boasts two Russian steam rooms, three Turkish hot rooms, a small Finnish sauna, and lots of beds in its rest area. Three hours cost £20 here, and a massage or a facial is £32 —high, but the environment is transporting. Call ahead for forewarning of its upcoming gender-separated days as well as to arrange treatments.

For a neighborhood feeling, **York Hall Leisure Centre** (5-15 Old Ford Rd., E2; ☎ 020/8980-2243; www.gll.org; Tube: Bethnal Green) is an East London landmark, hold the frills. I mean, its cafe serves fry-ups. Locals hang out all day playing cards, nodding off, and swapping stories. Of all the central London baths, it probably sees the fewest tourists, which means that outgoing foreigners are likely to be quite the novelty among the regulars, many of whom are deeply proud of East End institutions such as York Hall. But the Russian and Turkish baths (there are three hot rooms) are among the hottest in town, and following a petition by adoring locals, it's finally enjoying some long-awaited investment. The boxing ring was where pugilists Lennox Lewis and Audley Harrison learned their punches, and there are two swimming pools. A late 2006 renovation had prices in flux, so call ahead for those, and its schedule.

7 Outdoor London

Where to go in a city known for green spaces

YOU SHOULDN'T SPEND ALL OF YOUR TIME IN LONDON GAWKING AT masterpieces in museums or learning about old mansions from the talky end of an audio guide. Britain is an outdoorsy country, and its mild weather and topography tempt locals nearly year-round. Many of the things that make British culture famous—its emerald parkland, its invigorating sporting events, and even its picturesque meandering rivers—can only be enjoyed in the fresh air. Inside, you'll find the refined world of the pinkie-lifting, tea-sipping gentry, but under changeable British skies, chased by clouds, rain, and sunshine (often in the same hour), you'll find the England of the everyman.

PARKS

Parks are a significant part of everyday London life, so if you miss loitering in one, you'll miss one of the central pleasures of the city. You'll also have missed sampling the city's oft-overlooked ecology, animals, and the smells of its flowers and trees. There's a reason that English plants have been exported the world over and why English gardens are the envy of every horticulturalist—they're soothing, and they'll help bring you the relaxation you presumably are vacationing to find.

So what's the best park in town? Ask 10 Londoners, and you'll get 20 answers. Like pubs, parks have neighborhood devotees. But there's one given: On any day when the sun pokes even a few warm rays through the clouds, half of Londoners flock to the city's green spaces to lounge on benches, stroll the classical pathways, and lie (usually in full, long-sleeve dress) on the grass. Eight of the city's great parks, the Royal Parks (www.royalparks.co.uk) were originally owned by the monarchy for private use and, counted together, they comprise some 5,500 acres—which ranks London among the greenest cities on Earth.

Nearly every park posts a detailed map at every entrance, so it's never hard to pinpoint landmarks. (My advice: If you have a digital camera, snap a picture of the map as you enter—you can refer to it onscreen for the rest of your visit.)

FOR RESPITE IN THE CITY CENTER   **Hyde Park** (Tube: Hyde Park Corner, Marble Arch, or Lancaster Gate), bordered by Mayfair, Bayswater, and Kensington, is the largest park in the middle of the city. It's the tourist favorite, mostly because of its location and rolling landscape (136 hectares/340 acres) that recalls the English ideal. London itself identifies with the park, since it's home to the famous Speakers Corner (Tube: Marble Arch, p. 202), a meandering lake called the Serpentine, and the Diana, Princess of Wales Memorial Fountain (Tube: South Kensington, p. 178). The most famous promenade is Rotten Row, probably a corruption of "Route de Roi," or King's Way, which was laid out by William III as his private road to town; it runs along the southern edge of the park from Hyde

The Orphan Park

Coram's Fields (95 Guilford St., WC1; ☎ 020/7837-6138; Tube: Russell Square), was set aside in 1739 in Bloomsbury for the Foundling Hospital, a home for orphans. Ringed with impenetrable gates and overseen by pious benefactors, it took in some 1,000 "foundlings" a year and raised them, on little food and even less personal contact, until they were old enough to be shipped off as apprentices or soldiers elsewhere. In an era where 75% of London kids died before age five, even such a loveless upbringing was considered a blessing. George Frideric Handel counted himself as a benefactor and served as its governor, and his *Messiah* became a seasonal chestnut through its annual benefit performances for the hospital. Its southern stone gate, iron bars now clipped to nubs, is where countless desperate mothers once abandoned their unwanted babies along with a few small mementoes that, because of policy, the children never saw. The extent of the long yard, still lined with its original colonnade, was where generations of "foundlings" marched for their daily exercise. In 1936, it was converted to happier usage as a safe space devoted to kids; today, no adult may enter unless accompanied by a child. Coram's Fields is now the scene of joy between parents and children, with a playground, ball fields, a padding pool, sandboxes, a petting zoo with sheep, goats, and other animals—and toilets for kids, a lifesaver in central London. You'll find it, ghosts long gone, a few blocks east of Russell Square, not far northeast of the British Museum. The poignant Foundling Museum (p. 158) at the back of the park is dedicated to the Hospital.

Park Corner. Hyde Park is where many historic open-air concerts, such as Live 8 and shows by the Rolling Stones and Queen, were held, and it's where television screens are erected for overflow crowds during critical national events, such as Princess Diana's funeral.

FOR THAT COUNTRY MANOR FEEL   To the west across West Carriage Drive, so close that it might as well be one with Hyde Park, is the more formal **Kensington Gardens** (Tube: Lancaster Gate, Queensway, Notting Hill Gate, High Street Kensington, or Bayswater), which started as the front yard of Kensington Palace (Tube: High Street Kensington, p. 159). It only opened to plebes like us in 1851, and it hasn't yet shed its hemmed-in, snooty quality. Calming but a bit too busy for perfect peace, it's where you'll see George Frampton's famous statue of Peter Pan playing the pipes, snapped by tourists who think it sweet but dissed by locals as twee (Tube: Lancaster Gate). You'll also find the **Serpentine Gallery** (west of West Carriage Drive and north of Alexandra Gate; ☎ 020/7402-6075; www.serpentinegallery.org; Tube: South Kensington), a popular venue for modern art exhibitions sponsored by heavy-hitting corporations and art patrons. Each year, a leading architect is assigned the task of creating and building a fanciful summer pavilion there; in 2006, it was a giant egg-shaped canopy. Volunteers sometimes run guided tours of the park's lesser-known design quirks and statuary; check the bulletin boards at each park entrance to see if one's upcoming.

FOR FLOWER-GAZING AND QUEEN-SPOTTING The **Green Park** (Tube: Green Park), south of Mayfair between Hyde Park and St. James's Park, was once a burial ground for lepers, but now is a simple expanse of meadows and light copses of trees. It doesn't have much to offer except pastoral views, and most visitors find themselves crossing it instead of dawdling in it, although its springtime flower beds (which bloom brightest in Mar and Apr) are marvelous. **St. James's Park** (Tube: St. James's Park), the easternmost segment of the contiguous quartet of parks that runs east from Kensington Gardens, is bounded by Whitehall to the east and Piccadilly to the north. Its little pond, St. James's Park Lake, hosts ducks and other waterfowl. The Russian ambassador made a gift of pelicans to the park in the 1600s, and five (one from Louisiana, four from eastern Europe) still call it home; they're fed their 28 pounds of whiting daily at 3pm at the Duck Island Cottage. The park has a fine view of Buckingham Palace's front facade. It could best be described as royal—but the real draw is people-watching, since a cross section of all London passes through here on an average day. Not a place for picnics or ball-throwing, there's little in the way of amenities or activities, unless you count voyeurism, and I do.

FOR ENJOYING THE WEATHER WITH LOCALS Because its wide spaces make it feel miles away from the city, and because it borders some bohemian neighborhoods, I consider **Regent's Park** to be the people's park, best for sunning, Frisbee-throwing, and strolling long expanses. Once a hunting ground, it was very nearly turned into a development for the buddies of Prince Regent (later King

A Poignant Pocket Park

Little-known **Postman's Park** (west side of St. Martin's-Le-Grand between St. Paul's Cathedral and the Barbican Centre; open 8am–dusk; Tube: St. Paul's or Barbican), is beloved by those lucky enough to have stumbled across it. Hemmed in between buildings, its central feature is the moving **Watts Memorial,** a collection of plaques dedicated to ordinary people who died in acts of "heroic self sacrifice." Have a seat on a bench and ponder John Clinton, 10, "who was drowned near London Bridge in trying to save a companion younger than himself" in July 1894. In 1893, William Freer Lucas tantalizingly "risked poison for himself rather than lessen any chance of saving a child's life and died." The commemorations ceased in Edwardian times, making these forgotten faces seem forgotten once again. Playwright Patrick Marber extended the short life of at least one of the fallen; a character in his *Closer* took her name from Alice Ayres, who in 1885 saved three children from a burning house "at the cost of her own young life." On the silver screen, she got to sleep with Jude Law.

The Hidden Park

Sure, everybody knows about London's famous green spaces, but there's one recreation area, which stretches from London's northwest to its east through gentrified lanes and industrial wasteland alike, that few tourists are told about. It's the Regent's Canal, which threads from Paddington through Camden, Islington, and East London before joining with the Thames (26m/86 ft. lower) just before Canary Wharf. It was completed in 1820 to link with canals all the way to Birmingham and feed the city's massive seagoing trade. In those days, barges were animal-drawn and the districts along the waterway were rat-infested and perilous, but today, it's a frontier for development; many of the horse tracks are leafy promenades and an increasing number of the shadowy old warehouses have become affluent loft condos. Few tourists even know this ribbon of water is here to explore, but locals favor it for biking and walking (some come here to drink strong beer, too—just smile and nod at them). Along the way, you'll even pass some docks where houseboat barges tie up during their trips through England's canals; their owners can often be found hanging out topside, making conversation with passersby in the way intrepid travelers do. Even without a boat, the canal makes for a lovely backdrop for a stroll; the most popular segment is probably the crescent just north of the London Zoo at Regent's Park; the zoo's Snowdown Aviary abuts the water.

Several companies operate ferry service and tours on the leg between Paddington's "Little Venice" system of basins and Camden's popular lock market, among them the glass-sided **London Waterbus Company** (☎ 020/7482-2660; www.londonwaterbus.com; £5.80 one-way and £7.50 return); the slightly more luxe **Jason's Canal Boat Trip** (☎ 020/7286-3428; www.jasons.co.uk; £7.50); and the *Jenny Wren* (☎ 020/7485-4433; www.walkersquay.com; £7.50 return). Return trips take about 90

George IV), but only a few of the private terrace homes were built; Winfield House, on 5 hectares (12 acres) near the western border of the park, has the largest garden in London, after the Queen. The American ambassador lives there—surprised? In addition to boasting huge amounts of space (195 hectares/487 acres), the park also has an **Open-Air Theatre** (☎ 0870/0601-1811; www.openairtheatre. org; tickets from £10; Tube: Baker Street) for summer productions by the New Shakespeare Company, comedians, an annual musical, and children's theater; fine Italian and English gardens at the southeast corner; and the **London Zoo** (Outer Circle, NW1; ☎ 020/7722-3333; www.londonzoo.co.uk; Tube: Camden Town or Regent's Park), which is no great shakes as zoos go but still doesn't skimp on the cool creatures, including gorillas and giraffes. Because there's so much to do and so much space to do it in—it can easily take a half-hour to walk from one end to the other—this is my favorite of the parks in central London. In the center of the park, off the Broadwalk, you'll find an inexpensive, homey little cafe,

minutes and service is heaviest in the summer, when boats leave about hourly, and lightest in winter, when service is usually restricted to the weekends. The **London Canal Museum** (12-13 New Wharf Rd., N1; ☎ 020/7713-0836; www.canalmuseum.org.uk; £3; Tues–Sat 10am–4:30pm; Tube: King's Cross St. Pancras), in a former icehouse, is devoted to the waterway. It operates walking tours of its towpath and, in summer, a 1-hour. Sunday boat tour (£6.50) of the system's Islington Tunnel, which stretches for three quarters of a mile under the streets of London.

Along the way, keep an eye out for some unusual floating attractions, such as the **Puppet Barge** ^{kids} (box office only: 78 Middleton Rd., E8; ☎ 020/7249-6876; www.puppetbarge.com), which in winter and spring is moored opposite 35-40 Blomfield Rd., Little Venice (Tube: Warwick Ave.), but spends the other months floating around the system entertaining families for £7 to £9.50 a show. In summer, a variety of floating restaurants and cafes also waylay pedestrians; the most striking, the Fen Shang Princess floating Chinese restaurant, is too pricey to commit to, but its pagoda-like presence on the waters at the northeast boundary of Regent's Park makes for a jarring sight. Catch a glimpse of MTV Europe's futurist/modern studio, on the canal at Hawley Crescent in Camden, before putting your feet up a block west with a beer at one of the cafes around Camden Lock Market (at Chalk Farm Rd.; Tube: Camden Town), where you can watch the narrowboat skipper operate the old locks, still functioning after all these years. The industrial swath of canal between Islington and the Docklands is still gentrifying, so it calls more to enthusiasts than to idle walkers.

The Honest Sausage (☎ 020/7224-3872; www.honestsausage.com; Tube: Regent's Park or Great Portland Street), that feels like it flew on its own accord from the pastoral British hinterland; its sausages and bacon come from a family-run business in Gloucestershire, and its cake slices are truly generous. It's possible to find local tennis players for a pickup match at the sports center near the park's southwest corner. The most breathtaking way to enter the park is from the south through John Nash's elegant Park Crescent development, by the Regent's Park and Great Portland Street Tube stations (Tube: Regent's Park, Great Portland Street, Baker Street, or Camden Town). North of the park, just over the Regent's Canal and Prince Albert Road, **Primrose Hill Park** (Tube: Chalk Farm or Camden Town) affords a panorama of the city from its 62m (206-ft.) high top. On weekends, the summit can seem as busy as Oxford Street, and some badly dated signboards help you know what you're looking at, or more accurately, how much the skyline has changed in twenty years. In *101 Dalmatians*, Pongo barks at the sky from the park.

FOR PLAYING ROBIN HOOD   Northeast London has some of the most untrampled parks. Mostly because its soil is unsuitable for farming, **Epping Forest** (☎ 020/8508-0028; www.cityoflondon.co.uk; Mainline rail: Chingford) has for a millennium remained a semivirgin woodland, so it's the best place to get a feel for what Britain felt like before humans reshaped and denuded its land. It's the largest public space around, 19km (12 miles) long by 4km (2½ miles) wide, and containing a universe of diversion—650 plant species, 80 ponds where waterfowl splash, and even some 1,500 species of fungi (but don't eat any of them unless you know what you're doing). Getting lost in the woods is feasible, but not likely, since it stretches in a single direction. Henry VII built a timber-framed hunting lodge in 1542 that was inherited by his daughter Elizabeth and, astoundingly, still stands, now as a museum: **Queen Elizabeth's Hunting Lodge** (Rangers Rd., Chingford, E4; ☎ 020/8529-6681; www.cityoflondon.gov.uk; free admission; Wed–Sun 1pm–4pm. Mainline rail: Chingford.). Epping Forest links to the south with Wanstead's network of parks (Tube: Snaresbrook or Wood Street Walthamstow Mainline rail).

FOR GHOSTS   Haunting **Wanstead Park** (Tube: Wanstead) was, from the time of Henry VII to the early 1800s, the site of a grand, 70m-long (260 ft.) manor house, but when its ruling family ran into hard times, the house fell into disrepair and was razed. What's left are a few bizarre outbuildings and the remains of its formal gardens, including abandoned ornamental ponds with names like Shoulder of Mutton, which date to the early 1700s. It's a lilting park, and one of London's least crowded. Any local who meets you wandering this peculiar patch will be fascinated to hear how you, as a tourist, came across this ghostly bit of turf.

FOR SCIENCE NERDS   In southeast London, feeling more like an open space near a village than a city park, **Greenwich Park** (www.royalparks.gov.uk; Tube: Cutty Sark DLR) is 73 hectares/183 acres, and was once a deer preserve maintained for royal amusement; a herd of them still have 5 hectares/13 acres at their disposal. On top of its clean-swept main hill are found marvelous city views, and the world-famous **Royal Greenwich Observatory** (☎ 020/8312-6565; www.rog.nmm. ac.uk. Tube: Cutty Sark DLR) commissioned in 1675 by Charles II, which serves as the intersection point for the Prime Meridian as well as the center of Greenwich Mean Time; it's now a free museum. Most people combine a visit with the many other museums of Greenwich on weekends, when the markets are hopping. See p. 169 for more info.

FOR KIDS AND RIVER-WATCHERS   South London's **Battersea Park** (www.batterseapark.org; Mainline rail: Battersea Park or Tube: Sloane Square then 137 bus), a Victorian innovation, is popular for its elaborate children's playground, which is overseen by a youth group from the local government. I love it for its wacky variety: **The Pump House Gallery** (☎ 020/7350-0523; www. wandsworth.gov.uk; Wed–Thurs and Sun 11am–5pm, Fri–Sat 11am–4pm) has free exhibitions; the adorable **children's zoo** (☎ 020/7924-5826; www.batterseapark zoo.co.uk; £5.95 adults, £4.50 children; daily 10am–5pm) boasts monkeys, otters, and strange Australian animals; and its prancing Fountains Display, the Bellagio

FOR VIEWS & BREWS

Frolic with the rich in the 320-hectare (800-acre) **Hampstead Heath** (www.cityoflondon.gov.uk; Tube: Hampstead), in northwest London. Thickly wooded and easy to get lost in, the Heath is a perennial locale for aimless strolls and (it must be said) furtive trysts. If you venture onto the Heath, make an adventure of it, since it boasts several sublime places to rest your legs, including **Kenwood House** (Hampstead Lane, NW3; ☎ 020/8348-2528; www.english-heritage.org.uk; Tube: Hampstead or Highgate), a sumptuous neoclassical home from 1640 adorned with miles of gold leaf and important paintings by Reynolds, Turner, Gainsborough, and Vermeer (*The Guitar Player*); and **Spaniards Inn** (Spaniards Rd. at Spaniards End, NW3; ☎ 020/8731-6571; Tube: Hampstead), a garden pub dating to 1585 that has a pistol ball, said to be fired by the legendary outlaw Dick Turpin, framed above the bar. The Heath's hilltop is another favored lookout point. Despite all that, it isn't thought of as a park by most locals, but as a green space. I've never grasped the difference, but since the Heath was referenced as far back as 1086 in the Domesday Book, I can understand if its posh neighbors don't want to inflict such a venerable idyll with a mundane, civic label like "park." I have a friend who tripped in a mud bog here and came up with scarlet fever, which given the place's history, shouldn't surprise me. Even its diseases are old-fashioned.

on the Thames, runs from March to November. It's one of my favorite parks near town because it's the only park that's right on the river; sitting near its Peace Pagoda, watching the flow, is an easy way to while away time. Since the Tube doesn't stop here (another source of its quiet appeal), it's a good idea to combine a visit with a shopping trip down Chelsea's King's Road, and then cross to the park via Oakley Street and the handsome suspension Albert Bridge. As you go, look for the signs, dating to the 1870s, asking soldiers to break step as they cross it lest their vibrations damage the structure. Battersea Park has an active events calendar, so check its website for potential diversions.

FOR GREEN THUMBS   Not a park per se, but a rewarding oasis nonetheless, the walled **Chelsea Physic Garden** (66 Royal Hospital Rd., SW3; ☎ 020/7352-5646; www.chelseaphysicgarden.co.uk; £6.50 adults and £3.50 children 5–15; Apr–Oct Wed noon–5pm, Sun 2–6pm; Tube: Sloane Square) is a 1.6-hectare/4-acre plot founded in 1673 by the Society of Apothecaries as a garden for healing herbs, which makes it England's second-oldest botanical garden. Strike up a conversation with a gardener here, and you'll learn more about plantings than a professor could teach. The western side is arranged like a living timeline, with plants normally cultivated in the 17th century followed by ones more common to the 18th century. Described by some as "melancholy," this peaceful hideaway is only open Wednesdays and Sundays from April to October, with the addition of Tuesdays and Thursdays from mid-July to early September. That's not enough!

FOR FORGETTING THE CITY In southwest London, **Richmond Park** (www.royalparks.gov.uk; Tube: Richmond) is the largest open space in the city, at 944 hectares (2,360 acres). Charles I designated it as a hunting park, and to this day, it's home to free-roaming deer (they're testy when they're in heat, so mind the signs as you enter the gates). The Pen Ponds, in the center, are inhabited by waterfowl. The park adjoins **Wimbledon Common,** itself more spacious than the more central parks, and near the tennis tournament grounds. Unfortunately, it takes a lot of work to reach them all: It's a ride to the end of the Tube line plus a 15-minute walk before you see a blade of grass.

STROLLING THE BANKS OF THE THAMES

Until right after World War II, the Thames was a working river, teeming with coal boats, ships, dockworkers, and the stinking effluvia of the city's residents. It would regularly flood, too, sweeping away hapless children and inundating riverside property—a problem not wholly solved until the late 20th century. It's a lot more placid these days, and a lot cleaner, but it's still the city's spine, and it's the very reason the first settlers chose this particular spot in the otherwise marshy

---

Park as Natural History

For a strong sense for what London's topography used to be like, a visit to the **London Wetland Centre** (Queen Elizabeth's Walk, Barnes, SW13; ☎ 020/8409-4400; www.wwt.org.uk; £7.25 adults, £4.50 children; daily 9:30am–6:30pm, until 5pm in winter; Tube: Hammersmith or Barnes Mainline rail) is a tonic against the hyper-urban atmosphere surrounding it. Most people take for granted that the Thames sticks to its circuitous route, but it wasn't always that way. In fact, the river, which has been heavily embanked, was originally much wider, shallower, and subject to tidal whims. Ancient London was so marshy that only part of it was settled, which is why the Thames' north shore is built up and why Southwark, once a wetland, contains so few important old buildings. The waters were only tamed by brute force, and the paths of its countless tributaries are now literally set in stone under steel and concrete. So even though it was only converted from a disused waterworks in 2000, this 40-hectare (99-acre) preserve, seen on paths, in bird hides, and from a glass-enclosed observatory, didn't have to work hard to coax native animals back into its marshes. The south-bank site already welcomes 180 wild bird species, including Peregrine Falcons, the rare avocet (which recently returned to Britain after a 60-year absence), and a breeding colony for Sand Martins.

morass. Experiencing a bit of the Thames can bring you in touch with the city's past. And heady talk aside, it's just pretty.

A not-at-all taxing way to see the river is on the **Thames Path** (www.national trail.co.uk/thamespath), a walking route that follows the river for 296km (184 miles) from its source in the Cotswolds to the North Sea. The bits in town wind through some fascinating brown-brick areas that, more than any other parts of central London, recall the river's heyday as a center for trade and industry. Much of the route feels unofficial and is sometimes deserted, so bring along a map if you decide to sample a portion.

The innovation that made rampant river flooding a memory is the colossal Thames Barrier, east on the river south of Beckton, whose gates can be raised when the water rises, sparing the city from an influx. The barrier's multiple towers, shaped like a string of Sydney Opera Houses, makes for a singular sight, but acquiring that sight is a massive headache. The Docklands' new 22-acre **Thames Barrier Park** (☎ 020/7511-4111; www.thamesbarrierpark.org.uk; Tube: Pontoon Dock DLR) affords magnificent views of the engineering marvel from the north bank, but planners weren't clever enough to build its museum on the same side of the river. Reaching the modest **Thames Barrier Learning and Information Centre** (Unity Way, Woolwich, SE18; ☎ 020/8305-4188; £1.50 adults, 75p children; Apr–Sept 10:30am–4pm, Oct–Mar 11am–3:30pm; Mainline rail: Charlton then bus 177 or 180) is an ordeal, which is why few people go: You have to return to The City and take a Mainline train for the southern bank. Neither location permits access to the Barrier itself.

URBAN FARMS

England's roots as a farming country go back thousands of years, and it must be hard to break Englishmen of the habit, because the city still maintains a number of urban farms. The main product being churned out these days isn't milk or meat, but memories—city families come to let their kids pet the sheep, stare down the cows, and chill out in a field of green surrounded by sprawl. Because of Mad Cow disease, your Customs department now frowns upon visits to British farms in the countryside, so city farms (free of the disease) are your best bet for getting nose-to-snout with Britain's famous agrarian culture.

The most popular urban farm is the free, 12-hectare (31-acre) **Mudchute Park and Farm** (Lower Isle of Dogs, ☎ 020/7515-0749; www.mudchute.org; daily 9:30am–4:30pm; free admission; Tube: Mudchute DLR) which, within the incongruous sight of Canary Wharf's skyscrapers, stocks pigs, horses, cows, ducks, dogs, geese, and llamas; there's also a short nature trail. This slice of bucolic life may seem like the city grew up around it, but in fact, the land dates only to the mid-1800s, when dirt was moved here during the building of a nearby dock, and the animals weren't added until 1977. An hour's horse ride is £20 for adults and £17 for children; book ahead (the stables are closed Monday).

Another popular farm, which sees some 50,000 visitors a year, is the nearby **Newham City Farm** (Stansfield Rd., East Ham, E6; ☎ 020/7474-4960; www. newham.gov.uk/services/cityfarm; daily 10am–4pm in winter and 10am–5pm in summer; free admission; Tube: Prince Regent DLR), which was also established on fallow Docklands land in 1977. The free farm sells some of the things it produces, including chicken and duck eggs, honey, and herbs.

The free **Spitalfields City Farm** (Weaver St. at Pedley St., E1; ☎ 020/7247-8762; www.spitalfieldscityfarm.org; Oct–Mar Tues–Sun 10am–4pm, Apr–Sept Tues–Sun 10am–4:30pm; free admission; Tube: Liverpool Street or Aldgate East), another late-'70s creation, is on a former railway depot right behind Brick Lane, and developers have been salivating over the land for years. It's very small but still manages fur-to-face time with Ursula Goat, Bayleaf the donkey, a Shetland pony named Tilley, plus a mess of guinea pigs, hens, rabbits, sheep, and ferrets. Farms can get muddy, so wear closed-toe shoes. Petting chickens makes for a queer pairing with the many funky art galleries in the same area, but in a way, it makes sense—both attractions were outgrowths of a poor district with cheap land values. That is changing quickly in hip Spitalfields.

SPORTING EVENTS & ACTIVITIES

When faced with the electricity of a sporting match, the English lose all reserve. And all fashion sense—many red-blooded British men would sooner die than be caught in something other than their team's colors, a sartorial preference that marks them as faithful fanatics both in and out of the stadium. See these untamed creatures in their natural habitats, but be warned: Do not tease the animals.

FOOTBALL (AKA SOCCER)

There's no disputing that London is football mad—not unless you want a beer bottle to the skull. It hosts 13 professional soccer teams, more than any other city on earth. Six of the 20 clubs in the Premiership (or primary league) are based in London, and during the season, from mid-August to mid-May, there's barely a pub in town that doesn't get packed during match broadcasts. In the stadiums, grown men sing and cry, crowds by the thousand mock referees, and children are imprinted at a very early age with the team support considered appropriate in their house. As at many professional sporting events, tempers can run high and emotions can fray, but the club owners work very hard to maintain a family-friendly atmosphere, even if they charge prices that could put the average Mum and Dad in the poorhouse. Football is Britain's favorite sport, and it's London leisure at its most essential. Locals will be only too happy to persuade you to their side. Given the ferocious intensity with which many Englishmen regard their favorite team, it would be wise not to appear to favor one side of the match over another. The 2005 and 2006 champions, **Chelsea** (Stamford Bridge Ground, Fulham Rd., SW6; ☎ 020/7385-5545; www.chelseafc.com; Tube: Fulham Broadway) is currently enjoying a resurgence in popularity. It even offers daily **tours** (☎ 020/7957-8278; £13 adults, £7 children; museum only £5 adults, £3 children) through its stadium and its museum, although unless you've got some background knowledge about the team, it may not get your heart pumping. Across town in a brand-new (2006) 60,000-seat stadium, there's the 1998 and 2004 winners and 2005's runner-up, **Arsenal** (Emirates Stadium, Ashburton Grove, N5; ☎ 020/7704-4040; www.arsenal.com; Tube: Arsenal). For a less frothy fan experience, try **Fulham** (Craven Cottage, Stevenage Rd., SW6; ☎ 0870/442-1234; www.fulhamfc.com; Tube: Putney Bridge), which despite having played for over 130 years, never seems to place very high or low in the rankings and thus attracts a milder rabble. The *ne plus ultra* of traditional London footie is probably **West Ham United** (Boleyn Ground, Green St., Upton Park, E13; ☎ 0870/112-2700; www.whufc.com; Tube:

In the Swim

Although there are few days hot enough for most foreigners to crave an open-air swim in London, you don't have to get wet to appreciate the few remaining public outdoor swimming pools, or lidos, sprinkled around town. Many were constructed in the 1920s and '30s, before the dominion of the automobile, to give city families somewhere to cool off on warm days. Most of these Art Deco playgrounds limped, unloved, through several generations in which they lay fallow and suffered demolition, but a few lucky survivors are being embraced again by their communities. For a few pounds (typically £5, plus small charges for lockers), you can spend a summer day with crowds of Londoners. Bring your sunglasses—not because of the British sun, but to shield your eyes from all the alabaster skin. Hours vary, so call ahead.

Among the city's most famous lidos is the **Brockwell Lido** (Dulwich Rd., Herne Hill, SE24; ☎ 020/7274-3088; www.thelido.co.uk; Tube: Brixton), which attracts a wide variety of people—Caribbean to gay to old dears—and where you can supplement a dip with a class in Ashtanga yoga or Tai Chi—a separate club, the Brockwell Users Group (☎ 020/7738-6633; www.brockwelllido.com), posts schedules for those activities (usually £8 a session) online. The Lido's summer Whippersnappers kids' program (☎ 020/7738-6633; www.whippersnappers.org) entertains the neighborhood's multicultural kids with a Jamaican and English blend of music classes, workshops, and street dancing, all at the pool (£6.50 per event). **Hampstead Ponds** (Hampstead Heath at Gordon House Rd.; ☎ 020/7485-3873; Mainline rail: Gospel Oak or Tube: Kentish Town), is fed by the River Fleet, which is otherwise buried under the city, and was originally dug as reservoirs in the 1700s. From June through early September, you're actually permitted to swim in a marked-off area of the **Serpentine** (☎ 020/7706-3422; www.serpentinelido.com; Tube: South Kensington) in Hyde Park. Lounge chairs can also be rented. It's on the southern bank of the pond, just north of the middle stretch of Rotten Row. One of the few outdoor (and heated) pools open year-round is at the **Oasis Sports Centre** (32 Endell St., WC2; ☎ 020/7831-1804; www.camden.gov.uk/sport; Tube: Covent Garden or Tottenham Court Rd.), which is not particularly historic but, astonishingly, is hidden behind one of the city's busiest central intersections: High Holborn and Shaftesbury Avenue, making it hugely convenient for tourists. There's also an indoor pool; the complex opens at 6:30am daily. For more locations, consult the principal lidos preservation association, **London Pools Campaign** (www.londonpoolscampaign.com).

Upton Park), whose fans are rabidly devoted despite their team's status as a perpetual also-ran. Its stadium is in a middle-class South Asian neighborhood that affords good postgame meals at its authentic curry restaurants. Kickoff for any game falls between 3 and 7:45pm. For all clubs, match tickets starting prices range from £25 (Fulham) to £35 (Arsenal) for adults for nosebleed seats (you'll pay £60 to be close enough to catch the players' sweat), although for oversold games, Fulham opens some restricted-view seats for £20 adults/£5 children. For sparsely attended matches, West Ham offers a "kid for a quid" deal for which children pay just £1. All clubs make an effort to welcome seniors and children by granting discounts of about £20.

CRICKET

Filling the gap from April to September when the football players kick back in the Mediterranean, cricket is the quintessential colonial British sport. Half the reason to attend a match is to convince fellow spectators to attempt to explain it to you. (It's a little like baseball—and a lot like watching grass grow.) You'll have plenty of time; some games ("test matches"), played by men in white dressed more like sous-chefs than professional athletes, sprawl languidly over five days. For a more manageable time commitment, attend an "over match," which takes but a single day. The most prestigious games are played at **Marylebone Cricket Club Lord's Cricket Ground** (St. Johns Wood; ☎ 020/7432-1000; www.lords.org; Tube: St. John's Wood), considered the high church of the sport. If cricket has tides, Lord's would be their moon; the official Laws and Spirit, rulebooks that together serve as the Bible of the sport, are enshrined on its manicured grounds, as is the 1882 trophy known as The Ashes, a potent symbol of the ongoing rivalry between the Australian and English teams. Lord's one-day prices start at around £20 for adults, £5 for children under 16; if you know the lingo already, consider a tour of the **pavilion** (☎ 020/7616-8595; tours@mcc.org.uk; £8 adults, £5 children). Another important venue, **Surrey County Cricket Club** (Kennington Oval, SE11; ☎ 020/7582-6660; www.surreycricket.com; Tube: Oval), also called The Brit Oval, has an enviable situation very close to central London and stages England's final test match of the summer, plus a bunch of one-day games with international teams; those in the Twenty20 series last 3 hours—ideal for dabbling tourists. Tickets to an average match go as low as £10. The look on your face as you puzzle out wickets, googlies, silly points, and leg byes? Worth multiples of that.

GREYHOUND RACING

Wanna bet the British love wagering? The big gaming shops take wagers on everything from the outcome of current events to the winner of game shows. I don't suggest tourists sink their hard-earned vacation money into such risky pursuits, but for a good taste of the gaming culture, I do suggest hitting the track. Grandstand seats cost as little as £5, beer is plentiful, and betting isn't required. Nights, which attract plenty of working-class and middle-class revelers, usually go from about 7:45pm (gates open an hour ahead) to 10:30pm and include a dozen races. The best venue for historical value and local color is the East End's family-run **Walthamstow Stadium** (Chingford Rd., E4; ☎ 020/8498-3300; www.ws

greyhound.co.uk; Tube: Walthamstow, then bus 97, 357, or 215 north), in the game since 1933 and with a Deco neon marquee to show for it. Bookie William Hill, after whom the nationwide betting franchise is named, got his start taking wagers at the rails here. On Tuesday, Thursday, and Saturday, seats are £6 , and Monday at 1:15pm and Friday at 10:30am are free, but check its website for discounted packages. On the other side of town, in the southwest, try **Wimbledon Greyhound Stadium** (☎ 0870/840-8905; www.wimbledonstadium.co.uk; Mainline rail: Haydons Rd.). Its Punters' Pack, available online, buys two £2 betting vouchers and two drink vouchers for £5; if your willpower keeps you from wagering any more, you'll automatically come out ahead.

ICE SKATING
From late November through January, the noble courtyard at **Somerset House** (p. 155) is transformed into a public ice skating rink. Lit by torches and warmed by a cafe serving mulled wine and hot chocolate, this is where skaters from around London come to mingle and slide. Before dark, prices are around £10 adults, £6 children for an hour, and after dark they're £11/£6, including skate rental (Strand, WC2; ☎ 0870/166-0423; www.somerset-house.org.uk; generally 10am–10pm during winter; Tube: Temple).

ROWING
Each year on a Sunday afternoon in late March or early April, Oxford and Cambridge universities duke it out with their good-natured rowing **Boat Race** (www.theboatrace.org) on the River Thames. This is no goofy college rivalry; the big day attracts around 250,000 spectators, plus 7.2 million more who cheer the live TV coverage. It's been held since 1829, and since 1845 in London. The 6.8km (4¼-mile) curvy course runs upstream (westbound) from Putney (Tube: Putney Bridge) to Chiswick Bridge at Mortlake (Mainline rail: Mortlake). The race, which only takes about 19 minutes—Cambridge claims slightly more wins, incidentally—is more or less ridiculous, but it makes for an excellent excuse for a quarter million people to get merry and drunk at the many riverside pubs around Hammersmith.

RUGBY
Rugby is a great English sport, but it's played mostly in the North. The few clubs that play in town are more upperclass than in the northern league, and they don't stoke the fires of Londoners' hearts the way football teams do. The top place to catch an international match, from September through April, is **Twickenham Rugby Football Ground** (Whitton Rd., Twickenham; ☎ 020/8744-3111; www.rfu.com; Mainline rail: Twickenham). Games sell out, so reserve ahead by calling the ticket office at ☎ 0870/143-1111. Tickets are generally £10 to £40, but happily, many of the cheaper seats are covered in case of rain. The stadium also has a Museum of Rugby, but at £10 a head, it's only for die-hards. Tickets (around £20–£40) are easier to score for two local teams: the **London Wasps** (Twyford Ave., Acton, W3; ☎ 0870/414-1515; www.wasps.co.uk; Tube: Ealing Common) and the **Harlequins** (The Twickenham Stoop, Craneford Way, Twickenham; ☎ 020/8410-6000; www.quins.co.uk; Mainline rail: Twickenham).

TENNIS

It's easy watching the **Wimbledon Championships** (Church Rd., SW19; ☎ 020/
8971-2473; www.wimbledon.org; Tube: Wimbledon Park) on TV for 2 weeks in late
June and early July, but seeing it in person is a trickier matter. Because tickets for
the final matches go to VIPs, you're more likely to catch famous players during
the early rounds, when the club's 19 grass courts are all in use. Roaming access to
all but three of those (surcharges of £34–£83 are levied for Centre, No. 1, and
No. 2 courts, and tickets are distributed by lottery the previous summer) can be
had for the price of a "ground pass" (which cost, at most, £17). Around 6,000
ground passes are distributed each morning starting at 9:30am, and if you snag
one, you'll probably be inside by noon, when matches begin. Another clever way
to get in is to bum tickets off people as they get tired and leave for the day (just
don't offer money—the organizers hate that). A few more ground passes are resold
after 3pm for £5 to benefit charity. On weekdays and rainy days, your chances of
getting unfilled seats for the best courts are better, since people are working or
huddling indoors. And after 5pm, ground-pass rates dip to, at most, £11, which
isn't such a bad deal since matches continue until 9pm. If you aren't around for
the tournament, the **Wimbledon Lawn Tennis Museum** (Church Rd., SW19; ☎ 020/
8946-6131; £7.50 adults, £4.75 children; Tube: Wimbledon Park), which was
revamped in 2006, is open to the public the rest of the year. It's sort of like a Hall
of Fame with an emphasis, of course, on Wimbledon.

Walkabouts

Enjoy a unique curbside view of the city's life and history

PAYING FOR A SIGHTSEEING TOUR SEEMS SMART IN PRINCIPLE. YOU GLIMPSE monuments, briefly, and you hear one or two eye-glazing facts about them as you whiz past. But no coach tour, no hokey sightseeing boat, goes at your speed. None lets you spend as much time as you want, chewing over the vibe of what's before you, or allows you to stop for a few minutes and breathe in the atmosphere.

For that, you should be your own leader. With my self-guided walking tours, there's no "hurry up," and you can break away at any moment to chase whatever catches your interest. I supply commentary and point you toward adventure. You get to enjoy the rest.

My walking tours are packed with tales and tidbits, and they're loosely themed—choose the stomping grounds of kings (tour 1), dingy Dickensian back alleys (tour 2), or the London where modern-day trendsetters like Mick Jagger gathered no moss (tour 3). Each one passes important attractions and pubs that you're free to enter as you go, and they all start and end near Tube stations so that the going is easy.

I guarantee you'll go from not knowing much about parts of London to wanting to know more. You'll understand how the city fits together much better than people who sit idling at red lights on coach tours. All without paying a penny.

Walking Tour 1: Westminster, Whitehall & Trafalgar Square

Start:	Westminster Tube station
Finish:	Trafalgar Square
Time:	Allow approximately 60 minutes, not including time spent in attractions
Best time:	Be at the starting line just before noon to hear Big Ben deliver its longest chime of the day
Worst time:	After working hours, when energy drains out of the area

When most people hear the word "London," this is the area they immediately picture: the Houses of Parliament, the wash of the Thames, the gong of Big Ben, the humble facade of Number 10 Downing Street, and the imperial government buildings of Whitehall. Kings and queens, prime ministers and executioners, scoundrels and assassins—this is where they converged to shape a millennium of world events, at the command center for England and the British Empire. History fans, lace up.

❶ Westminster Tube Station

The best train to take here is the Jubilee Line, which was added at great expense in 1999. The station's concrete-grey, 36m (120-ft.) -deep cavern, ascended by escalators from the Jubilee's platforms, is one of the city's finest new spaces, providing a modern-day analog to the majestic space of Westminster Abbey nearby. Portcullis House, where many MPs (Members of Parliament) keep offices, is overhead.

Find your way to the Westminster Underground station, Exit 1, and walk outside.

❷ Victoria Embankment at Westminster Bridge

Once you're outside, you'll see the River Thames in front of you. If you stood here in 1858, in the midst of what came to be known as The Great Stink, you'd have choked on the fumes rising from the fetid effluvia floating in the river below. Until then, the city had no sewers to speak of—only pipes that dumped into the water. The solution was the Victoria Embankment, a daring engineering project, completed in 1870, that saved engineers from having to dig up the whole city. They simply built a new riverbank, laid sewers along it, paired that with new Underground railway tracks, and topped the unattractive additions with a garden and a new road. Destructive, but effective—how Victorian.

Today, the embankments' benches are raised to allow a good view of the water, the lampposts are rococo, and it's dotted with triumphant statuary like Boudicca in her bladed chariot, which you can also see from here. This tribal queen rose up against the Romans; she failed politically but succeeded aesthetically, becoming a potent symbol for English independence.

The bridge in front of you is the iron Westminster Bridge, from 1862, now the oldest bridge in the city. When the first one went up, in 1739, the builders had to contend with sabotage by river ferrymen, who didn't want to see their business wrecked. The final result wobbled anyway—like the Millennium Bridge in 2000—and made people nervous, prolonging the demise of the river ferry. The London Eye had its own tricky birth in 1999; it was constructed lying flat over the river, resting on pontoons, and then it was laboriously hoisted upright and into place. The mock-baroque building across the river is County Hall—it looks old, but it only dates to the early 20th century, and was once the seat of the London government.

At the bridge's opposite landing, you can see my favorite sculpture in the city, the South Bank Lion. Weighing 14 tons, 3.6m (12 ft.) tall, and eager-eyed and floppy-pawed as a puppy, he was carved in 1837 by the Coade Stone Factory, which once stood behind him, where County Hall stands today. Made

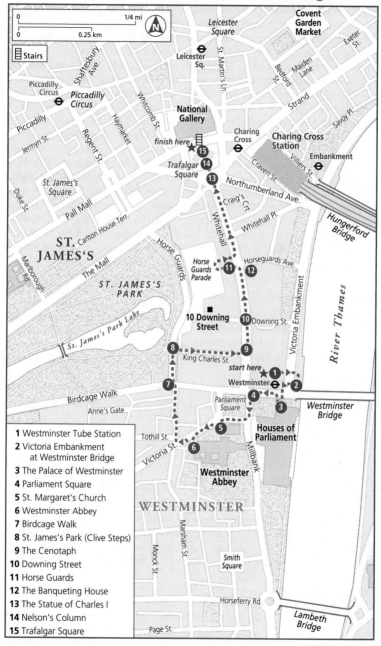

0   1/4 mi

0   0.25 km

N

Stairs

Leicester Square

Covent Garden Market

Exeter St.

Leicester Sq.

St. Martin's Ln.

Bedford St.

Maiden Lane

Piccadilly Circus

Piccadilly Circus

Shaftesbury Ave.

Whitcomb St.

National Gallery

Strand

Savoy Pl.

Piccadilly

Regent St.

Haymarket

finish here ★

15

Charing Cross

Charing Cross Station

Embankment

Jermyn St.

Trafalgar Square

14

13

Craven St.

Villiers St.

Duke St.

St. James's Square

Pall Mall

Carlton House Terr.

Northumberland Ave.

Whitehall

Craig's Crt.

Whitehall Pl.

Hungerford Bridge

ST. JAMES'S

Marlborough Rd.

The Mall

Horse Guards

ST. JAMES'S PARK

Horse Guards Parade

11

Horseguards Ave.

12

River Thames

St. James's Park Lake

10 Downing Street

10

Downing St.

Victoria Embankment

8

9

King Charles St.

start here ★

1

Westminster

2

7

4

Parliament Square

3

Westminster Bridge

Birdcage Walk

Anne's Gate

5

Houses of Parliament

Tothill St.

6

Victoria St.

Millbank

Westminster Abbey

WESTMINSTER

Marsham St.

Monck St.

Smith Square

Horseferry Rd.

Lambeth Bridge

Page St.

1 Westminster Tube Station
2 Victoria Embankment at Westminster Bridge
3 The Palace of Westminster
4 Parliament Square
5 St. Margaret's Church
6 Westminster Abbey
7 Birdcage Walk
8 St. James's Park (Clive Steps)
9 The Cenotaph
10 Downing Street
11 Horse Guards
12 The Banqueting House
13 The Statue of Charles I
14 Nelson's Column
15 Trafalgar Square

of a durable, synthetic ceramic stone formulated by a mother-daughter team, the lion stood proudly for over a century, painted red, atop the Red Lion Brewery that was located to the left of the London Eye. Blitz bomb damage destroyed his claim, but at the request of King George VI, he was saved and placed just feet from his birthplace.

If you want, you can run up to the top of the stairs here and grab a cheap sausage from the ever-present cart that feeds the tourist flocks. The view of Big Ben's Clock Tower here is particularly striking. Because of crowd control fencing, it's not easy or advisable to cross the street to see the Houses of Parliament up close, but hang on—at the next stop, I'll have you nose-to-nose with it.

Go back into Westminster station, head down the corridor, and turn left before the set of four stairs. Leave the station via Exit 3, marked Houses of Parliament. Climb the stairs to

❸ The Palace of Westminster

You're now standing directly underneath the mighty Clock Tower of the Houses of Parliament. Except you aren't, technically. If you want to be precise, you're under St. Stephen's Tower (the name of Big Ben's perch) at the Palace of Westminster (the aged name of the government buildings here). This is as close as you can get to it, so have a good look at the assorted crowns, kings, and crests carved into the facade. These buildings may look like they're from the Gothic period, but in fact they date to 1859, when they rose from the ashes of the old Parliament House, destroyed by a nightmarish fire in 1834. Big Ben, the name of the largest of four bells inside (2.7m/9 ft. in diameter, 13 tons), was named for the portly commissioner of

works who oversaw its installation, but there is a bigger bell in town: Great Paul at St. Paul's is two tons heavier. Each side of the Clock Tower's four faces is 6.9m (23 ft.) long. Since 1923, the very earliest days of wireless, BBC has broadcast the sixteen-note prelude (called "Westminster Quarters" and replicated in doorbells around the world) of Big Ben before its six o'clock news summaries using a microphone installed in the turrets. Thanks to a crack that developed in the 1860s, the bell is now slightly off from its original note: E above middle C, but you'd probably need perfect pitch to tell.

This plot of land has been used by royal residents since 1050, when Edward the Confessor built a palace here, away from the hubbub of the walled city. This is therefore one of the oldest sections of London outside The City. Kings ceased living at Westminster as of the reign of Henry VIII, when nearby Whitehall Palace became the main London home, followed by St. James's Palace and currently, Buckingham Palace—but since this land is still government owned, Westminster technically remains a palace.

Head away from the river along the side of the Houses of Parliament until you reach

❹ Parliament Square

The heavy metal bars on the spiked fence that distances you from this building are not there out of mere paranoia; as far back as the thwarted Gunpowder Plot of 1605, the Houses of Parliament have been a target for would-be revolutionaries. Prime Minister Spencer Perceval was fatally shot on the steps of the House of Commons by a former convict on May 11, 1812, and in the Blitz, the buildings were smashed on more than a dozen occasions, including one (May 10, 1941) that caused the near-total destruction of the House of Commons. Watch the security guards sweep the undercarriages of incoming cars with mirrors, and check out the formidable bollards that rise from the ground to prevent unauthorized vehicles from invading the government's seat.

Look across at Parliament Square; a group of protesters is always present, even though their government representatives usually hustle obliviously past them in bulletproofed sedans. Parliament is so embarrassed by the protests against the Iraq War (as of this writing, one man, Brian Haw, has appeared daily since 2001—look for a man in a bucket fishing cap) that it changed the free speech laws to require all citizens who wish to protest within a kilometer of Parliament to obtain permission from the police first.

The section of the Houses that juts into the yards, behind the statue of Oliver Cromwell, is Westminster Hall, from 1097, one of the only survivors from the 1834 fire. Charles I, Sir Thomas More, and Guy Fawkes were all condemned to death in the Hall.

Turn left and walk in front of the Houses of Parliament. Use the first crosswalk to your right, heading toward the church. Once at the far side of the church, enter the gate to see the front of

⑤ St. Margaret's Church

The little side church by Westminster Abbey (p. 138), the one with the four sundials on its tower, is the Church of Saint Margaret, dating to the early 1500s and much changed over the years. Sir Walter Raleigh, who was executed outside the Palace of Westminster, is buried inside, and both the poet Milton and Winston Churchill married their wives here.

You can see the statues of Parliament Square better from here. Probably the most famous one is that of American president Abraham Lincoln, at the western end; it's a copy of one in Chicago by Augustus Saint-Gauden. The statue of Winston Churchill received a temporary Mohawk made of grassy turf during the anticapitalist protests of 2000.

Follow the footpath to the front of

⑥ Westminster Abbey

The lawn beside the abbey—yes, the one you just walked across—is in fact a disused graveyard. In a city this old, you simply can't avoid treading on the final resting places of forgotten people. There are an unknown number of plague pits scattered through the city, into which thousands of victims were hastily and unceremoniously dumped to avoid the spread of disease, and several city parks likely had the germ of their beginnings, so to speak, as potter's fields—group graves for paupers.

Although most of the abbey is in the Early English style, the stern western towers above you now were the 18th-century work of Nicholas Hawksmoor, a protégé of Christopher Wren. Hawksmoor's designs are famous for emphasizing the forbidding, angry side of God. Some critics accuse him of using architecture to frighten people into piety. If you're interested, there's a gift shop at the front of the Abbey that you can enter from here, but most of the time the people who use this main entrance in an official capacity do so in either a crown or a coffin. The column in front of the abbey is a war memorial for Westminster School students who perished in the Crimean War—their loss was deeply felt at the time but, sadly, is now mostly forgotten. If you peer down Broad Sanctuary, which becomes Victoria Street, you can see the Italianate tower of Westminster Cathedral, the primary Catholic cathedral of England.

Cross the street to your right (Broad Sanctuary), and cross again at the next zebra crossing. You should be a block west of Parliament Square on Storey's Gate now. Walk straight for about 3 minutes until you find yourself at the corner of St. James's Park. You're at

⑦ Birdcage Walk

You've just walked past a variety of European Union offices; the proximity to the Houses of Parliament has attracted paper-pushers to take up tenancy around here for centuries. The military has a presence here, too. The road that heads to the left is Birdcage Walk, which leads to the front of Buckingham Palace. Halfway down, you'll find the Wellington Barracks, the headquarters of the Guards Division, where a battalion of one of the Queen's five regiments of foot guards (Grenadier, Coldstream, Scots, Irish, and Welsh) bunks down. There's also a small, curio-packed Guards Museum (☎ 020/7930-4466; 10am–4pm, £2) on the grounds, where you learn that their tall "busby" helmets are made of Canadian brown bearskin. Who knew?

Storey's Gate, which you just walked, was named for the keeper of Charles II's aviary. Birdcage Walk, the street you have now encountered, was named after a royal aviary that was in St. James's Park; until 1928, only the Hereditary Royal Falconer was permitted to drive on Birdcage Walk. The park continues its tradition of hosting bird menageries; the pond is a haven for ducks and geese, and a small flock of pelicans has been in residence since the 1600s. If you do detour down there, just come back to this spot to resume your tour.

Cross the street and walk 1 block, passing the Treasury Building on your right, until you reach Clive Steps at King Charles Street on the right. Peek into

⑧ St. James's Park

See if you can spot the lake in the park. The body of water was originally a formal canal belonging to St. James's Palace, the official royal residence from the burning of Whitehall in 1698 to the time Victoria moved into Buckingham Palace in 1837. The old canal was prim and straight in the French style and outfitted with gondolas, a gift of the Doge of Venice. In winter, Samuel Pepys wrote in the 1600s, it would freeze over, and people would frolic upon it using skates made of bone. It was later sculpted into something calculated to appear more random and thus more English. St. James's Palace, which is not open to the public (except for Clarence House, in summers, p. 161), is located on the north (far) side of the park. St. James's Park is essentially the front yard of the palace, and you're standing at its back gate. You might be able to make out a rustic-looking shack just inside the park. That's Duck Island Cottage, built in 1840 as a dwelling for the bird keeper. Not shabby for a servant's quarters.

You'd think that if London were under attack from flying bombers that you'd be much safer if you were a little farther from the Houses of Parliament. Yet in the basement of the sturdy 1907 Treasury Building, Britain's leaders orchestrated their country's "finest hour." Unbeknownst to the world, it was the hideout of Winston Churchill and his cabinet. Famously, but hardly wisely, that daredevil Churchill once went out onto the roof of the building so he could watch one of Goering's air raids slam the city. The cellar, preserved down to its typing pool and pushpins, is now the Cabinet War Rooms, an evocative tourist attraction and a superlative museum paying homage to the bulldoggy prime minister (p. 154).

The imposing building to the left of Clive Steps is the Foreign Office, an important civil office. So who is Robert Clive, the cutlass-wielding subject of this statue on the steps? He was the general who helped the East India Company conquer India and Bengal, partly through a series of underhanded bribes, thus delivering the region into the control of the British Empire for nearly 2 centuries. Don't be too hard on him; the opium-addicted fellow committed suicide by stabbing himself with a penknife.

Walk down King Charles Street and through the arches at the end. You should now be on Parliament Street. Look left, into the center of it. The somber stone column in the traffic island is

⑨ The Cenotaph

The Cenotaph (from the Greek words for "empty" and "tomb"), is a simple but elegiac memorial to those killed in the two World Wars. A 1919 plaster parade prop that was made permanent in stone by Edwin Lutyens the next year, it was executed with inconceivable restraint when you consider that nearly a million British men died in the Great War alone. Its inscription to the "Glorious Dead," coined by Rudyard Kipling, is repeated on other memorials in Commonwealth nations; the Cenotaphs in Auckland, New Zealand, and in London, Canada, are replicas. Uniformed service men and women will always salute it as they pass, and on the Sunday closest to November 11, Britain's Remembrance Day, the sovereign lays the first wreath while other members of the Royal Family observe from the balcony of the Foreign Office. You may see flowers around it, or possibly silk poppies (red flowers with black centers), the national symbol of remembrance.

Walk left up Parliament Street, which soon is renamed Whitehall. In about 30m (100 ft.) on the left, you will reach a black fence with glass lanterns. Stop there and look inside the gates. This is:

⑩ Downing Street

On the right, by the tree and tough to make out, is Number 10, the official home of the prime minister. It's famous for its lion's head knocker—although to be frank, if you have to knock, you won't be welcome. You used to be able to walk around in there, but Margaret Thatcher had many enemies and sealed the street, so you'll have to make do with peering down the lane. Such security was a long time coming. In 1842, a lunatic shot and killed the secretary to the prime minister, mistaking him for the big man; and in 1912, suffragette Emmeline Pankhurst and friends pelted the house with stones, breaking four windows, in one of many acts of civil disobedience in the fight for voting rights for women. If policemen are preventing you from even approaching the gates, then the prime minister is probably on the move. I've stood on the sidewalks of Whitehall, waiting to be permitted to pass, when suddenly the black gates have burst open, spewed forth an armada of police cars, and the prime minister's Jaguar has blasted onto Whitehall and sped toward the Houses of Parliament as if he'd just robbed a bank.

The lane was laid out by George Downing, the second man to graduate from Harvard University in America and by all accounts a shady individual, a turncoat, and a slumlord. He's one of history's great scoundrels; his underhanded dealings resulted in Dutch-held Manhattan being swiped by the British and the slave trade multiplying in the Colonies. Strange that the most important street in British politics should bear his name.

Downing built Number 10 (then, Number 5) as part of a row of terraced houses in the late 1600s, fully intending for it to fall apart after a few years (instead of actually laying bricks, he just painted on lines with mortar). Yet George II had his eye on the house, and he kicked out a man named Mr. Chicken—further information about him, tantalizingly, is lost to the mists of time—to give it as a gift to the first prime minister, Robert Walpole, in 1730. Instead of taking it as graft, as Downing might have done, Walpole insisted that the house be used by future First Lords of the Treasury, his official capacity. He also connected it to a grand home behind it on Horse Guards, now nicknamed The House at the Back—so now, this deceptive Georgian facade actually conceals 160 rooms. Number 10 is also connected with numbers 11 and 12, and it's even linked to Buckingham Palace and Q-Whitehall, a sprawling war bunker, by long underground tunnels. Many prime ministers elected to live in their own homes, using Number 10 for meetings, but not William Pitt, who moved in upon becoming prime minister at the virtually pubescent age of 24 in 1783. He lived here for more than 20 years, longer than any other prime minister, until his death at 46. Whitehall became a slum in the mid-1800s, and the house fell out of fashion, but once it served as the nerve center for the two World Wars, it became indispensable to the British spirit. You can see the original front door, now replaced by a stronger one, on display at the Churchill Museum at the Cabinet War Rooms (p. 154), two stops back.

A little up Whitehall from Downing Street, look for the bronze monument to "The Women of World War II," which depicts no women, but rather their uniforms and hats, which hang on pegs as if they've been put away after a job well done. The implication of this 6.6m (22-ft.) -tall tableau is, of course, that the women went back to the kitchen after briefly filling a more robust societal role. This sly bit of statuary-as-commentary was unveiled by the Queen in 2005. Some 80% of the cost of the memorial was raised by a baroness who won money on ITV's *Who Wants to Be a Millionaire?*.

Continue up Whitehall, past the monumental government buildings that line it. In about 60m (200 ft.), you will reach another black gate broken by two stone guard houses. Head inside the yard to view

⓫ Horse Guards

Built in the Palladian style between 1750 and 1758 on a former jousting field of Whitehall Palace, the Horse Guards is the official (but little-used) entrance to the grounds of St. James's Palace and Buckingham Palace. Two mounted cavalry troops are posted in the guardhouses every day from 10am to 4pm, and they're changed hourly. At 11am daily and 10am. Sundays, the guard on duty is relieved by a dozen men who march in from The Mall behind, accompanied (when the Queen is in town) by a trumpeter, a standard bearer, and an officer. Don't make the same mistake of some feckless tourists and try to force the guards to crack up at your shenanigans. It makes you look silly and rude—and they still won't react.

If you think the clock tower arch looks small, you're right. Its designer made it that way so that its proportions would match the rest of the building. You can walk through the clock tower arch (but you can't drive through—only members of the Royal Family can do that) to reach the graveled Horse Guards Parade, the city's largest non-park gathering space. The Parade was once a segment of the canal that's now the lake in St. James's Park, but it was filled in, providing an excellent terrain for state rituals such as Trooping the Colour.

Come back out of the yard onto Whitehall. Across the street you'll see

⑫ The Banqueting House

Built by Inigo Jones, this is the last remaining portion of the great Whitehall Palace (p. 161). One past director of the Museum of London has called it "the most important and most unassuming building" on this street, and a "slice of genius." Inside is a bombastic ceiling by Rubens depicting the king as a god. That vainglorious posture, and the king's grabs for more power, led to the gory event that happened on this spot on January 30, 1649. If you were standing here then, you would have been in the crowd that watched King Charles I mount the scaffold (wearing two shirts so that he wouldn't shiver—he was no true god, after all), place his head on the block, and be decapitated, handing the reins of the country to a military dictatorship led by Oliver Cromwell. When the executioner held the head aloft, one witness said there was a queasy silence,

followed by "such a groan by the thousands then present, as I never heard before and I desire I may never hear again." Charles I was buried privately at Windsor, not at Westminster Abbey, because his deposers (who wanted to rule the country without kings) didn't care to encourage a public scene that could lead to an uprising. If you want to see what poor Charles looked like, hang on for the next stop. The regicide was mostly for naught; by 1660, the country grew weary of its leadership and Charles I's son, the hedonistic spendthrift Charles II, was back on daddy's throne. In revenge, the second Charles chose the Banqueting House as the site for his restoration party, and showed up late. England was royal again, and how.

Turn left up Whitehall. As you go, look right as you pass Whitehall Place, and you'll catch a glimpse of the dome of St. Paul's Cathedral.

Take a break

The oldest part of the Silver Cross (25-33 Whitehall), the epitome of an everyday pub, has operated as an inn (pub) since 1674. It was recently lavished with a giant expansion, so you shouldn't have trouble finding a seat. The Cross attracts government secretaries and clerks (called "civil servants" round these parts) who nip in for a quick pint. Find it on the corner of Craig's Court, named for the family that owned the establishment for 135 years.

When you reach the square, cross the street twice so that you're on the traffic island, standing under

⑬ The Statue of Charles I

That this bronze statue stands here is a miracle. It's of Charles I, pre-headectomy, and is a precious Carolinian original from 1633. When the king was beheaded, the Royal Family was deposed (permanently, so most people thought) and all their trappings were melted down and broken up for profit. The owner of this statue was commanded to destroy it, but he was clever enough to bury it instead. After the Restoration, it was dug up and placed here in about 1675. That was even before Trafalgar Square existed (the zone was, as an equestrian statue might suggest, used as stables). Charles wasn't a very tall man, and saddling him on a horse goes some way toward making the luckless fellow seem imposing. Someone stole his first sword in 1867, and he went into hiding again during The Blitz, but otherwise, this is one of the oldest things in this part of London that remains in its original place. Its pedestal, unloved and weathered, could use some restoration itself.

This is a good spot, free of traffic and obstructions, to survey your surroundings and take some photos. Look back down Whitehall, from where you just came, and you'll see Big Ben's tower. To the right, the vista through Admiralty Arch concludes in the distance with the grand Victoria Memorial at Buckingham Palace. Important embassy buildings of two Commonwealth nations stand astride Trafalgar Square: Canada House to the left (west) and South Africa House to the right (east; its country's name is inscribed in Afrikaans as Suid-Afrika).

Cross again so that you're on the south side of

⑭ Nelson's Column & Trafalgar Square

Not long after Charles's statue lost its sword, lightning struck Lord Nelson, who is exposed at the top of his column, and damaged his left arm. The city finally got around to eliminating the bronze bands that held him together in 2006, using the same Craigleith sandstone with which he was constructed in 1843. Since the quarry had closed in the 1940s, craftsmen had to find stone left over from the restoration of a school in Edinburgh. During the work, surveying revealed that the monument is actually 4.8m (16 ft.) shorter than guide books have been claiming—it's 51m (169 ft.), not 56m (185 ft.), from the street to the crown of his hat. The man himself is 32m (18 ft.) tall. Why is Nelson so revered? The Admiral sacrificed his life in 1805 to defeat Napoleon Bonaparte's naval aspirations, which secured Britain's dominance over the oceans—and thus pumped untold wealth into London. The column's base is lined with four bronze reliefs that were said to be cast using metal from French cannon captured at the battle that each one depicts. All is guarded by four reclining lions (1867), which serve as mascots of the square.

In the southeast corner of the square, you'll see a stone booth big enough for a single person; that's the city's smallest police station, built in 1926. Once a closet for a phone that was used to summon backup, now it's used mostly to store chemicals for the fountains.

Lutyens, who did the Cenotaph, also designed the two fountains (from 1845 originals), which were ostensibly for beautification but also prevented mobs from gathering in dangerous numbers. Trafalgar Square has long been the setting for demonstrations that turned from protest to unrest, such as infamous riots over poll taxes and unemployment. The English gather here for good things, too, as they did for the announcement of V-E Day (May 8, 1945), and as they still do for free summer performances.

You may have heard about Trafalgar's Square's famous pigeons. So where are they? Banished, mostly, for overactive excretion. Until the early 1990s, the square swarmed with them—the fluttering flock was estimated to peak at 35,000—and vendors made a living from selling bird feed to tourists. Eventually, the GLC, London's government, grew tired of shoveling streaky poop off the statues and decided to return the square to its original function as a great public space. They began feeding the pigeons themselves first thing in the morning, and then hired a team of six hawks, tended by a leather-gloved keeper, to patrol the square from 10am to 4pm. The pigeons quickly learned to chow down and then clear out for the day.

Head to the other side of the fountains to

⑮ North Trafalgar Square

The GLC made a few other radical changes to the square in 2003, including closing the street to the north, which runs in front of the National Gallery (p. 143), to vehicular traffic. That gave the square a new elevated terrace, from which the views down Whitehall are sublime, particularly at night when landmarks are picked out by spotlights. The GLC also cut a new set of stairs to the Gallery—before then, the square's north side was a grim wall—and beneath the terrace it added the cheap Café on the Square. Suddenly, people really did start hanging out here, and not just to complain.

Most of the statues dotting the square are of forgotten military and noble men; James II is finely crafted, but he looks ridiculous in those Roman robes. The northwestern plinth of Trafalgar Square was designed for an equestrian statue of its own, but money ran out and it stood empty from 1841. More than 150 years later, the naked spot was named The Fourth Plinth (www.fourthplinth.co.uk) and filled by works commissioned from various artists. Sculptures show for 18 months at a time, and so far they've gotten the city talking. Rachel Whiteread mounted a mirror image of the plinth atop itself in luminous plastic. Marc Quinn's marble *Alison Lapper Pregnant* depicted a snow-white, nude woman born with limb deformities and heavy with child. In April 2007, Thomas Schutte's translucent, Perspex architectural model *Hotel for the Birds* begins tempting the square's confounded pigeons.

Along the north terrace, by the Café on the Square, look for the Imperial Standards of Length, which were set into the wall in 1876 and moved in 2003 when the central stairs were installed. They are the literal yardsticks against which all other British yardsticks are measured, showing inches, feet, and yards, plus mostly obsolete measures like links, chains, perches, and poles.

And now, you can reward yourself with a visit to the loo, left of the stairs, and a spot of tea in the cafe. Or, if you crave some more substantial victuals, head over to the street east of the square to St. Martin in the Fields church, finished in 1724. Its combination of spire and classical portico were controversial at the time, but today, it pleases people of all persuasions with its excellent Café in the Crypt (p. 108).

Walking Tour 2: St. Paul's & Southwark

Start: St. Paul's Tube station

Finish: The George Inn, near London Bridge Tube station

Time: Two hours, not including restaurant breaks or attractions

Best times: Weekend days in good weather, when the area is abuzz

Worst times: After dark, when some of the narrow, medieval streets are too dark to see well

It was the best of advertisements, it was the worst of advertisements. Charles Dickens' novels, largely social protests wearing the cloak of entertainment, made readers feel like they had traveled to London when they never left their own armchairs. Trouble is, the city that Dickens has primed visitors to expect—the foggy, coal-smudged metropolis teeming with pickpockets and virtuous orphans—is nowhere to be found. Have the librarians of the world fallen victims to one of the world's most successful smear campaigns? Not at all. Partly thanks to Dickens' work, London simply changed. On this tour, you'll explore what's left of its darker side—from the libertine London of Shakespeare's day to the desperate one Dickens sought to solve with his pen. Along the way, you'll enjoy gourmet food, cutting-edge design, and a beer by the Thames, which conceals a body count of its own.

❶ St. Paul's Tube Station

If you just took the Central Line here, you rode what was once called the Central Railway. In the first 75 years of the Underground, train lines were independently owned, and separate tickets were required each time a passenger changed trains. Fares were cumbersome, calculated according to the distance traveled and the class of carriage chosen. When the Central Railway held its grand opening in 1900, in the presence of American wit Mark Twain (who lived in London at the time), it soared above its competitors by dint of several innovations, the most important of which was that anyone could ride as far as they wanted on a flat fare.

The so-called "Twopenny Tube," which had one class of carriage like today's Tube trains, was a sensation. Gilbert and Sullivan, swept along, amended a line in their operetta *Patience* from a reference to the threepenny bus to "the very delectable, highly respectable Twopenny Tube." The Central Railway helped democratize public transit and accelerated expansion into the suburbs—even if authorities eventually went back to the old format of charging passengers by distance, not by ride. The St. Paul's station opened on July 30, 1900 as Post Office station—the city's main Post Office was then located across the street on St. Martins-le-Grand (hence the name of Postman's Park, p. 221, just north).

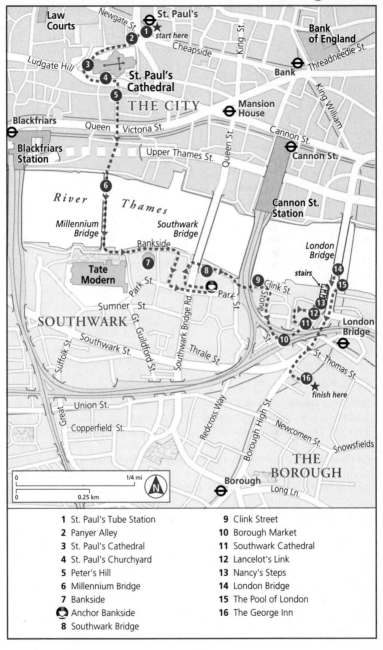

1 St. Paul's Tube Station
2 Panyer Alley
3 St. Paul's Cathedral
4 St. Paul's Churchyard
5 Peter's Hill
6 Millennium Bridge
7 Bankside
   Anchor Bankside
8 Southwark Bridge

9 Clink Street
10 Borough Market
11 Southwark Cathedral
12 Lancelot's Link
13 Nancy's Steps
14 London Bridge
15 The Pool of London
16 The George Inn

Exit the St. Paul's Underground station and turn left, toward

② Panyer Alley

Panyer Alley, where you're standing, was named for the basketmakers, or panyers, who once traded here. Look for a plaque on the wall depicting a child sitting on a basket. This plaque, the so-called Panyer Stone, is dated "August the 27, 1688," and reads, "When you have sought / the citty round / yet still this is / the highest ground." The artists behind this stone surely knew that Ludgate is not the highest point in the City; that's Cornhill, which is about 30cm higher. But it's been here so long that it would quite literally be a crime to take it down.

Head left, toward St. Paul's Cathedral, and make a right through the pedestrian alley, Paternoster Row, to Paternoster Square. Go through the ornate arch at the left and veer right to the front of

③ St. Paul's Cathedral

The area you've just walked through ranks among the most sacred in London. There have been major houses of worship on the plot of St. Paul's as far back as 604, and for centuries, these narrow surrounding streets have teemed with ecclesiastical scribes and clergy, as well as with untold hordes of desperate supplicants desperate for a handout from the merciful church. By the 1800s, Paternoster Row was known as the center of literary London, first for its publishers—who replaced the scribes—and later for its book market. Yet what you'll see today is an indistinct set of office buildings staffed with financial workers. Even its 23m (52 ft.-) tall column was created only a few years ago to appear older than it is. Why would planners permit the wholesale demolition of such a rich heritage? They didn't. This was Ground Zero of the Blitz. The area was annihilated during bombing raids in 1940. The Germans, recognizing that the destruction of St. Paul's would demoralize a nation that held it as a totem, focused their power on it. Every able-bodied firefighter was called to help preserve the church, saving it at the expense of just about everything else.

The stone archway that you passed through, however, is a true antique, although it didn't originally stand here. It's Temple Gate, one of eight ancient gateways to The City of London, which stood where Strand becomes Fleet Street from 1672. It was demolished in 1878 and was destined for a dump somewhere when a visionary stepped in and brought the stones home. After spending more than a century in the hinterland of his family's Hertfordshire estate, the gate, possibly designed by Christopher Wren, was restored and re-erected here in November 2004. The seven other gates, including Aldgate and Moorgate, were all lost more than 200 years ago.

A statue of Queen Anne, who ruled England when St. Paul's was completed, looks down Ludgate Hill, the street that approaches the cathedral from the west. In attendance are ladies symbolizing England, France, Ireland, and North America, which she considered her subjects. The statue is an 1886 copy of the 1712 original, which (like Temple Gate once did) now resides, in scabby condition, on a country estate.

Herbert Mason's iconic photograph of St. Paul's dome, snapped during the mighty conflagration that engulfed London after air raids on December 29th and 30th, 1940, was taken from Ludgate Hill. Next time you see that picture, note that it's lit entirely by firelight.

Skirt the right side of the cathedral along the busy street called

④ St. Paul's Churchyard

As they pass the southern yard of St. Paul's, most people notice the agonized statue of Saint Thomas Becket in mid-assassination, designed in 1973 by Edward Bainbridge Copal. But few have a look at the remains of the low stone walls that once encircled the cathedral, or of the metal lumps left behind when the iron fence posts were clipped off. At the end of the building of St. Paul's, Wren complained bitterly to Queen Anne that the construction of the fence around the churchyard was being executed without his consultation, and that its size was out of proportion with his design. Weary of his involvement, she paid him his fee, criticized his work, and sent him on his way. The fence stayed—for a century or two, anyway.

At the crossing, go over the street and head toward the round building. Now's a good time to duck into The City of London Information Centre (☎ 020/7332-1456), located inside the round building, and stock up on free tourist brochures and timetables.

If you don't need information, turn left. If you do use the information office, when you come out again, turn right. After the patch of grass, turn right again. You should be able to see down Peter's Hill all the way to a white pedestrian bridge over the river. Stroll down

⑤ Peter's Hill

On the right is the Firefighters National Memorial, which depicts a young man gesturing wildly toward St. Paul's as two others grapple desperately with a hose. It's impossible to exaggerate the devastation caused by the Blitz, both in property and in lives. The superheated firestorms created damage greater in area than those of the Great Fire of 1666. More than 20,000 people were killed, and 1,400,000 left homeless. The names of some 1,000 victims, all volunteer firefighters defeated by the wild blaze and collapsing buildings, are inscribed on the octagonal base. Winston Churchill dubbed this monument "The Heroes with Grimy Faces." For their families, the survival of St. Paul's Cathedral amidst utter devastation remains a testament to their sacrifice. Continue walking straight. After you cross Queen Victoria Street, the glassy building on the left, erected in 2004, is the Salvation Army, which has commanded its members across the world from this spot since 1881. Keep going toward the river.

Go onto the

⑥ Millennium Bridge

You're now on the steel Millennium Bridge, the central city's first new crossing over the Thames since the Tower Bridge in 1894. Its design, which features side-located suspension cables that sag about six times shallower than a conventional suspension bridge's supports do, was a little too advanced for its own good. When it opened, in 2000, and the structure admitted its first pedestrians, it was discovered that their shifting weight caused the bridge to sway. Alarmed pedestrians had to grasp the side rails for support. Engineers closed the 325m (1066 ft.) span, poured in another £5.2 million to solve the issue, and reopened it in 2002. Londoners initially derided it as "The Wobbly Bridge," one of several turn-of-the-century commemorative boondoggles, although they're warming to it now. It's still not perfect—it's plagued by yuppie joggers with little regard for idle strollers—but crossing the river here, in view of many of the city's landmarks, young and old, makes for some stirring photos.

Straight across the bridge is the monumental Tate Modern museum (p. 145), signaled by its factory-like "campanile" smokestack, which from 1952 to 1981 belched exhaust from the Bankside Power Station. Energy has been a fundamental part of the district's character for generations. The Tate's power station replaced an earlier one that dusted everything near it with a coating of grime, and that plant, too, supplanted a foul gasworks that once fed gas to much of the city. Before that, the district was the domain of a legion of coal merchants who shuttled their filthy wares around town in shallow boats. These "lightermen" worked from docks that lined the entire southern shore, where land was cheaper than it was in The City on the northern side. In a way, the building you see before you—only recently transformed into a gallery—is a direct descendant of the way of life that prevailed on the bank back in the 1700s.

How deep is the Thames? The river fluctuates greatly with the tides (which makes it dangerous for swimming), but depending on when you measure, it's generally 8.9m (29 ft.) deep at its highest tide and 1.8m (6 ft.) at low tide. The Thames' moodiness is the main reason Southwark, the side of the river where the Tate Modern sits, was for many centuries not even considered to be worth annexing into the city. Until medieval times, the low-lying southern bank was flood-prone and boggy and was instead thought of as an independent borough in Surrey, the county south of London. Londoners made use of the waterlogged land by turning it into gardens, fish farms (the Pike Garden, or Pye Garden, stood pretty much in front of you around the Tate's eastern flank), and romantic nooks you could sneak off to with a lover, but it wasn't until the latter part of the 1700s that people figured out how to drain the water adequately enough to settle the area fully. Simply put, Southwark was where you took a ferry to have a good time. Theaters, bear-baiting pits, brothels, betting halls, and other impure diversions were located there, out of the city's jurisdiction—that is, until the Puritans quashed the fun in 1642, starting the area's next chapter as an industrial center.

Before you completely cross the river, turn back for a stupendous view of St. Paul's dome symmetrically rising from the center of the bridge.

Once you're on the opposite bank, with the river in front of you, turn right. Stand midway between the cluster of town houses and the building with the thatched roof. The path you're on is

❼ Bankside

You're now walking along my favorite promenade in the city. It actually continues west, past the Tate Modern, to the London Eye and the Houses of Parliament. When Hugh Grant told Andie MacDowell he loved her by way of David Cassidy in *Four Weddings and a Funeral,* he did it farther along this walkway by the National Film Theatre. On a summer's evening, there's no better place to stroll, people-watch, and appreciate the sweep of the city. I've had many bouts of gratitude here.

As late as the 1960s, the path you're on, which at this place is called Bankside, was a vehicular street bearing two-way traffic, as it had been since the 1600s. Each building on the street owned rights to the docks or water-stairs on the river opposite it, so their tenants were usually people who needed access to the water, such as ferrymen or sailors. The four-story, white house at the left of the blind Cardinal Cap Alley, number 49, was one of them. The house was built around 1710 on the foundations of a pub, the Cardinal's Cap, which itself went up in 1547 to entertain the people who came to Southwark to carouse. Number 49 was home to successive generations of coal merchants, and in the 1930s to the actress Anna Lee (Lila on the U.S. soap *General Hospital*), but not, as the plaque on its front purports, to Sir Christopher Wren as he built St. Paul's. Wren did live nearby, but in a building that was torn down when the power station needed land—this plaque, which hung on that vanished home, was appropriated by a D.I.Y. revisionist in the mid–20th century. Number 49 is just one of countless houses that once lined the river for an unbroken mile along this bank, but it's now one of the last three or four left standing, and it's the only one that has received its own biography, *The House by the Thames* by Gillian Tindall, which recounts the structure's 300-year saga.

To the left of that small cluster of homes, which are stragglers from another era, is the open-air Shakespeare's Globe theater, which made a premature exit in its own era, only to be rebuilt in ours. The circular Globe's stage is even at the same compass point as the 1599 original's. You can learn how it was reconstructed on one of its excellent tours (p. 189).

Southwark may be famous for Shakespeare, but interestingly, the city's theatrical life was only centered here from about 1587 to 1642, while it was illegal to operate a theater in The City proper. Once the laws relaxed, the entertainment venues moved back into town, where they've been ever since.

Southwark was the Elizabethan version of a multiplex, where you could find any amusement to suit you, and the biggest blockbuster was bear-baiting—several bear-baiting arenas were in the area. Even King Henry VIII and Elizabeth I were huge fans; he had a bear pit installed at Whitehall Palace, and she barred Parliament from banning the pursuit on Sundays. One short block past the Globe, between the Pizza Express and The Real Greek restaurants, is a lane called Bear Gardens. Three quarters of the way down this atmospheric, crumbling alley of 19th-century warehouses, you'll find a small courtyard where the Globe Education Centre is today. That's the former location of the Davies Amphitheatre, one of the most popular bear pits, where masses came to enjoy the spectacle of vicious dogs let loose upon tethered bears. Samuel Pepys wrote in his diary in 1666 of attending one such slaughter where he "saw some good sport of the bull's tossing the dogs—one into the very boxes. But it is a very rude and nasty pleasure." Within a month, the north bank of London had burned to the ground in the Great Fire, but Southwark, buffered by the river, was spared that one. (It suffered its own fire 10 years later.)

Under a modern office building in the next street, Rose Alley, lie the foundations of another theater known to have premiered plays by Shakespeare, the Rose. It lasted from 1587 to about 1606. The Swan stood nearby, too, although we may never know exactly where. Ironically, this missing theater gave modern architects their biggest clues about what Elizabethan theaters looked like—they studied sketches made of it by a Dutch tourist in 1596.

Historians think they know where the original Globe stood, and the site, which is now partly covered by protected Georgian homes and Southwark Bridge Road, is marked by a semicircular set of black paving stones. If you'd like to see it, head down Bear Gardens 1 block to Park Street, turn left and go under the bridge, and just after it, past the buildings on the right, you'll find the arc of stones. Not very suggestive, is it? In 1949, it was even drearier. It lay behind the locked gate of the decrepit Anchor Brewery, and when American actor Sam Wanamaker (father of Zoë, who played Madam Hooch in the Harry Potter movies) dropped by to pay pilgrimage to the Bard, the indignity of the meager plaque (still there) so enraged him that he resolved to campaign to rebuild the Globe as a living home for England's great theatrical tradition. Which is what came to pass, albeit 4 years after his 1993 death.

Retrace your steps to the riverside. On the water at Bear Gardens, look for a stone seat embedded in the wall of Riverside House. It's said to be the last remaining Wherryman's Seat, dozens of which once lined the Thames. Boatmen, the taxi drivers of their day, would lounge in these perches—this one is fifteenth century—until someone came along and hired them for a trip across the water. Ferrymen would also court business by shouting destinations to crowds of theatergoers after their plays: "Eastward ho!" or "Westward ho!"

Continue along the river, keeping it to your left. You'll go through a pedestrian tunnel under

8 Southwark Bridge

On the walls of the tunnel, you'll see illustrations of skaters and revelers at the bygone "Frost Fairs" that, starting in 1564, were regularly held on the icy Thames. No matter how many winters you spend in London, you'll almost never see the Thames freeze over. But back then, they had the London Bridge, a few hundred yards downstream. Its 19 arches were so narrow, and its supports so thick, that the river's flow became sluggish, allowing water (and the outhouse filth that churned within it) to freeze. By contrast, during outgoing tides the rush of water through its spans was so fierce that boats frequently capsized, and passengers (few of whom knew how to swim in those days) often drowned. When the bridge was dismantled in 1814, the Frost Fairs melted into history.

Walk past the two modern buildings and take a look underneath Southwark Bridge where it meets the shore. You can still discern the remains of some water-stairs, dating to before the construction of the first bridge here in 1819. These ghostly stairs were once used to convey people and goods to and from the ferries that zipped around the river at all hours. The shoreline once supported dozens of these landings, but gradually, drainage works and fortification of the embankment all but erased most of them. This bridge is the second, dating to 1912, when its central 72m (240-foot) span was the largest ever attempted in cast iron. The drab hunk of a building to your right is the headquarters of the *Financial Times,* the internationally distributed, orange-hued newspaper nicknamed the *FT.*

Take a break

If you need a breather, few pubs in the city are more idyllic than the **Anchor** (p. 126), which is located here, just before Bankside meets the railway viaduct coming over the river from Cannon Street station. The riverside patio is open in good weather; otherwise, the interior of the pub is charming. This pub was once controlled, as nearly all pubs once were, by a brewery; in this case, it was Barclay Perkins, located just behind it from 1790 until about 1980. Even before brewery ownership, it was a Bankside fixture; in 1666, Samuel Pepys watched the Great Fire rage from here before coming to his senses and hurrying across the river to rescue his possessions from his home in Seething Lane, near the Tower of London. The pub was declared a slum and nearly cleared after World War Two, but preservationists rightly clamored against the move, and it was saved. It has since been respectfully rehabilitated, and it now presents much the same character as it did many years ago, give or take the iPod-rigged bikers who relax here on a summer's day.

After the Anchor, the path jogs inland. Take the first left onto

⑨ Clink Street

Pass under the railway arch. In a few moments, you've gone from Elizabethan Southwark (theaters, bear-baiting) to Georgian Southwark (coal merchants, breweries). Now you're enveloped by Victorian Southwark, a claustrophobic world teeming with fetid-smelling industry and river rats. You can almost hear the reverberations on this narrow wharfside street. One might even call the sensation Dickensian, and you wouldn't be

wrong, since when the writer was 12 years old, his father was thrown into a debtor's prison very near where you're standing, off the Borough High Street.

Prisons were something of a cottage industry for the area; the Clink Street Prison stood here from 1127, when the Bishop of Winchester built it as a lockup for his Winchester Palace, until 1780, when the anti-Catholic Gordon riots saw the dismal hole destroyed. Although the Clink gave its name as slang to all prisons that came after it; no one knows for sure how it got the name itself—Flemish or Middle English words for latch are likely the origin. Suffice to say it was pretty awful. And so is the museum (p. 194) here that purports to tell its story.

In the 1800s, warehousing goods instead of people became this street's stock-in-trade. Look overhead, and you'll see the remains of a pedestrian skyway that once connected the building containing the Clink Museum with a building abutting the Thames; its I-beam was amputated. All around, you'll see hints of the street's past maritime uses, from wooden loft doors to cranes used to hoist crates into upper floors. Today, these spaces house media companies and architects. During the week, you'll see them in their fashionable clothes, staggering across the cobbles in their Italian shoes on their way to mid-afternoon cocktails.

The latter Bishops of Winchester were not nice guys. Henry II (1133–1189) gave them control of this neighborhood, and because it was outside of the jurisdiction of the city, they could pretty much get away with whatever they wanted. Principally, they cultivated countless brothels and skimmed the profits for themselves—which is how Southwark got its rap as a den of vice. Anyone who annoyed them (heretics, troublemakers) wound up in the Clink, where no one was likely to find them again. Continue down Clink Street. Just before that beveled brick building on the right, you'll see all that's left of the Bishops' palace. This unique geometric rose window, dating to the 1300s when it lit the great hall, was hidden behind a wall until a warehouse fire exposed it again. The three doors below it originally led to kitchens. Double back to Stoney Street.

Turn down Stoney Street and walk under the railway arch. Just past it, on your left, you'll see

⑩ Borough Market

Stop at the frilly grey portico.

The mood of the neighborhood has changed drastically again. To your left, behind the portico, is Borough Market, a fantasy for the tongue (described in gastronomic detail on p. 116) and the oldest fruit and vegetable market in the city. A market has been held around here since A.D. 43, when Roman soldiers noted passing a market on their way to sack The City. More reliable records date it to 1014, when it served the denizens on the old London Bridge, the city's only river crossing, The market, which hopped around the neighborhood over the centuries, fed from the locus of all the main roads to London from southern England and Europe, so its wares were the best and most exotic in the city. The cream-grey portico is not original to this place; it's the cast iron Flower Hall of Covent Garden, rescued when the Royal Opera House was renovated and moved here in 2003. If it seems to blend seamlessly with its surroundings, it's probably

because it was made around the same time as the rest of the Borough Market structure (1859–60).

The Market still sells grocery staples, but it's best known as a font of gourmet supplies. London's most famous gourmands, including Jamie Oliver and Ainsley Harriott, are often seen milling about the stalls here. The shops across Stoney Street include some of the city's most celebrated coffee suppliers (Monmouth Coffee Company, p. 277) and bakers (Konditor & Cook, p. 277). Park Street, which runs into Stoney Street, looks as quaint as a movie-set version of old England; in fact, it was used in *Harry Potter and the Prisoner of Azkaban*. The Market itself has appeared in films including *Howard's End* and *Bridget Jones's Diary*.

Enter the market. Take your time to explore the 1.6-plus hectares (4-plus acres) of gated stalls and to read the whimsical signs like "Last Christmas, we made 2½ miles of chipolatas!" Astoundingly, this delectable scene is under threat from the advance of a commuter rail plan, Thameslink 2000, that would have part of this glorious building demolished. Railway suits have been lobbying to destroy chunks of the handsome glass-and-steel roof since 1987. Partly because Southwark was never seen as being worth as much as The City, railways have been given license to deface this area since their invention. In fact, the city's first railway, a 6.4km (4-mile) run to Greenwich, plowed its route a .8km (half-mile) east of here in 1836. Even after tunneling technology improved, railway men thought nothing of slicing massive brick viaducts through thriving neighborhoods, cutting them off from each other and creating slums. On your tour, you have crossed under a number of railway viaducts built that way, and shortly, you'll see how narrowly one of England's most historic churches averted its own destruction.

Cross the next street and enter the brick arch marked Green Market. Head straight into the grounds of

⑪ Southwark Cathedral

(If for some reason the Green Market arch is closed, just turn left down Bedale Street (it's not marked) and follow it until you see a church appear on your right.)

Before you stands the oldest Gothic church in the city, and the oldest building in Southwark. You'll see its tower appear in nearly every old drawing of the city. In Roman times, it was the site of a villa. Its Christian chapter was begun by the daughter of a ferryman in the 7th century; it was rebuilt in the 850s and again 300 years later. There were once a monastery and a chapel in this yard, where office workers now lunch on gourmet items from Borough Market, but those came and went, too. By the early 1800s, Southwark was crawling with the poor, with factory workers, and with grubby rivermen—people the industrialists didn't have much use for. This place, which by then was limping along as a humble parish church called St. Saviour's, dissolved into dilapidation—it was even roofless for a while—and we're lucky it wasn't removed completely, because in those days, progress, and not God, was king. The re-routing of London Bridge Road sheared away several small chapels, and in 1863, the railway forced its way alongside the yard—the filth and rumble of the early locomotives must have disturbed worshipers. But by 1905, its fortunes reversed when it was elevated to a cathedral, which now serves 2.5 million across southern London, and in 2000, it was given a lavish cleaning—so much of one that it's hard to discern the true age and sordid past of the place.

The cathedral's entrance is to the left. Go in, go straight across the sanctuary, through the glass doors opposite, up a short flight of stairs, and turn right to the end of the glass-roofed corridor, which traces the line of an alley that was called

⑫ Lancelot's Link

Nelson Mandela opened this building in 2001. Have a look at the display here, which preserves surprising discoveries made in this small area during a 1999 renovation. Look down into the well on the far right, and you'll see the original paving stones from the Roman road that cut through this space in the 1st century. You crossed over this same road several times already today; you were standing above it when you entered Borough Market. Other relics that were found here, piled on top of each other, include a stone coffin, probably from the 1200s, with a carved slot for the head; the foundations of the Norman priory that stood here; a kiln from the 1600s, soot marks intact (the Delftware it made has been found as far away as Williamsburg, Virginia); a lead pipe from the 1800s; and overhead in the wall, an apse and arch surviving from the 1200s. Any one of these items would alone be enough to spark the imagination, but seeing them sandwiched in one tight bunch is truly difficult to wrap your head around. It reminds you that the present really does clothe the bones of the past, and in a city as old as London, history is literally piled, forgotten, under every footstep.

As writer Geoff Ryman puts it, "silent as settling snow, experience falls on prepared ground." There's no telling what treasures have yet to be uncovered.

The cathedral has some beautiful painted monuments, including one of the oldest wooden effigies (1280) in England, and is worth a longer visit if you have time. Shakespeare's brother Edmond was buried here in 1607, as was Philip Henslowe, who built the Rose, in an unmarked grave. John Harvard, the founder of Harvard University in Cambridge, Massachusetts, was born the son of a butcher who owned a (long-gone) shop just northeast of the cathedral, and he was baptized here; the Harvard Chapel, off the North Transept, is named for him, and contains the oldest masonry in the building, from the Norman period. Other worthwhile sights include Edwardian stained glass tributes to the Bard's plays, and some of the original ceiling bosses, carved in 1469 and saved when things got bad. How bad? Here's a glimpse: During Elizabeth I's reign, the retrochoir (the part behind the altar) was walled off and rented to a baker. Later on, vestrymen discovered the baker was also raising swine in there.

Halfway back down the hallway, exit the cathedral. Go through the yard into the little lane (it's not marked here, but it's Montague Close; the Thames should be in front of you). Turn right, and just before you reach the overpass, look left for a set of stone steps labeled

🅫 Nancy's Steps

These are popularly held to be the location, in the Dickens novel *Oliver Twist*, where Noah Claypool eavesdrops on a conversation that leads to Nancy's

murder by Bill Sykes. In fact, those steps faced the Thames, but these steps are indeed a rare surviving remnant of the same New London Bridge, built here in 1821 as a replacement for the 600-year-old, hopelessly overcrowded London Bridge. The steps that Dickens wrote about were sold in 1968 to an American oilman who had most of it shipped, stone by stone, to Lake Havasu, Arizona, where it remains today. These steps were left behind and attached to this featureless 1973 replacement.

Just so you know, the existing London Bridge was not the source of the nursery rhyme "London Bridge is Falling Down"—that either referred to the burning of a wooden version in 1013, during a skirmish between Danes and Norwegians; or to Henry III's "fair lady" Queen Eleanor, who skimmed the tolls of the medieval bridge for her own purse, leaving its maintenance in a parlous state.

Climb the stairs to the road above. You're now on

🅮 London Bridge

At the top of the stairs, you'll see a pedestal topped by a dragon, the symbol of the city, holding London's crest. You'll see these dragons at several of the city's medieval borders. Three hundred and twenty-eight meters (100 ft.) east of here, under modern buildings, is where you would have entered the Stone Gateway, the entry to the disaster-prone medieval London Bridge. For more than 3 centuries, tar-dipped heads of executed criminals were impaled on pikes and stuck atop the Gateway as a vivid warning to would-be ne'er-do-wells.

Turn to the right to use the crosswalk. Go to the opposite side of the street and walk onto London Bridge, over the river. Don't cross the river—just enjoy the view of the

⑮ Pool of London

This section of the Thames, between London Bridge and the Tower of London (you can see it to the left of the Tower Bridge) is known as the Pool of London. It may be quiet now, but for nearly 2,000 years, it was the busiest stretch of water in town, and the heart of international trade. So many goods passed through here that warehouses along the southern bank became known as "London's Larder." During the industrial revolution, ships finally became so large that they had to unload downstream, closer to the sea. The section of river in front of you, parallel to this bridge, is where the medieval London Bridge stood.

Across the river from the Tower, you'll just make out an egg-shaped glass building in a grassy expanse. That's the City Hall (2002), designed for use by the Greater London Authority by Norman Foster (who also designed the Millennium Bridge) to be ergonomic and energy efficient, with a huge spiral staircase curling around its atrium and "smart" windows that open on hot days. Just like a politician, it has no discernible edge, and you can't tell if it's coming or going. London mayor Ken Livingstone, a man not known for tact or restraint, called it "a glass testicle." Anyone can have a ball in its public spaces (include a few small exhibitions) from 8am to 8pm, Monday to Friday (www.london.gov.uk).

Turn around and follow London Bridge inland, keeping on this (the left) side of the road. This street becomes Borough High Street. You will pass under another railway arch. Just after you pass a major street forking off to the right (Southwark Street), look for "The George" sign on your side of the street. It marks a passageway to

⑯ The George Inn

Because the London Bridge was the only crossing to the city from the south for so many centuries, this area became the equivalent of a train depot, and it was dotted with inns, stables, coach yards, and pubs. Everyone going to or coming from southern England or Europe stopped here, often spending the night before pushing into the shoulder-to-shoulder crowds of London Bridge. If you've ever read *The Canterbury Tales*, you'll recall that in 1386, the pilgrims began their journey to the shrine of Thomas á Becket from the Tabard Inn, which was located a short walk farther down Borough High Street, on the left. The George, described on p. 127, is the last survivor from this bustling coaching era. Although the wooden building, which once encircled the entire yard, dates to 1677, the inn was here for at least another 130 years before that, if not longer. We know it was typical of the time because John Stow, in *A Survey of London* (1598), termed it "a common hostelry for travelers." The National Trust took control of it in the 1930s, so it's no longer in danger of being replaced by some disposable office hive. Its outdoor tables are set up in good weather, and a drink here makes a fitting end to your journey through time. People have been drinking beer here for nearly half a millennium—but as you've seen today, the history of inhabited Southwark stretches back many times longer.

Walking Tour 3: Shopping, Soho & *Gimme Shelter*

Start: Oxford Circus Tube station

Finish: Goodge Street Tube station

Time: Two hours, not including shopping or restaurant breaks

Best times: Weekdays, when Berwick Street's market is on and Oxford Street is slightly less crowded

Worst times: After dark, when stores and markets close

All churched out? London is more than stories about dead queens and bloody uprisings. It's always been cosmopolitan, too, and the flash point for trends that ripple out to the rest of the world. Songs first sung at the clubs of Soho soon caused toes to tap on the other side of the planet, and fashion trends born on Carnaby Street remain internationally iconic 40 years later. Bring along your credit cards as we roam some of the city's best shopping streets—packed with stores geared at you, not at some Sloane Square socialite—and then touch upon a few leftovers from London's recent past, including forgotten air-raid shelters and the settings for some good, old-fashioned sexual scandals. This is the London you found out about from the radio and the runways, not from your social studies teacher.

① Oxford Circus

Leave the Oxford Circus Underground station using Exit 2. The sidewalks will certainly be busy, so position yourself between the Tube stairs and the balustrade so that you're out of the fray.

You are in the thick of the mile-long Regent Street, which to the right is punctuated by the witches-hat steeple of All Souls Church and to the left curves toward Piccadilly Circus. When the Prince Regent, later George IV, was planning his new pet project, Regent's Park, he decided he also wanted a road to connect his house directly with it. He chose this particular location because, in his mind, it would provide a suitable demarcation line between the gentry of Mayfair, to the west, and the rabble of the traders who lived in Soho, to the east. George tapped John Nash to do the job, completed in 1825. Originally, the sidewalks were covered by stone colonnades, but when those attracted prostitutes, they were removed, and most of the original buildings were later rebuilt—the only Nash original is now All Souls. Even if most of the facades you see now mask more modern buildings, few streets in London impart such a sweeping, uplifting feeling, though few are also as congested with dawdlers from the middle and working classes, folk George wouldn't have preferred.

The other avenue intersecting before you is Oxford Street, following the same line as a Roman road. George's class-centered definition of the landscape has more or less held: The exclusive shops of Oxford Street still lie west of Regent Street, and the downmarket stores tend to be east of it. Look west, left, and you'll spot some of the city's most famous department stores: John Lewis (p. 269), Debenhams,

New Cavendish St.
New Cavendish St.
Foley St.
Cleveland St.
Tottenham St.
Goodge
St.
finish here
Chenies St.
15
Store St.
Montague Pl.
British Museum
Gt. Titchfield St.
Langham St.
Charlotte St.
Whitehead St.
16
Tottenham Court Rd.
Bedford Square
Bloomsbury St.
Goodge St.
Rathbone St.
Windmill St.
Percy St.
Bedford Ave.
Mortimer St.
Wells St.
Berners Mews
Newman St.
Rathbone Pl.
Gt. Russell St.
Margaret St.
Berners St.
14
Hanway St.
Tottenham Court Rd.
New Oxford St.
Regent St.
Eastcastle St.
Oxford St.
SOHO
13
St. Giles High St.
Oxford Circus
1
2
12 Soho Square
Charing Cross Rd.
Oxford Circus
start here
Ramillies Pl.
3
Poland St.
Berwick St.
Wardour St.
Frith St.
Dean St.
Greek St.
11
Maddox St.
Gt. Marlborough St.
4
Marshall
5
Broadwick St.
7
8
Peter St.
Old Compton St.
Kingly St.
6
Lexington St.
9
10
Conduit St.
Carnaby St.
Beak St.
Shaftesbury Ave.
Gerrard St.
Lisle St.
Leicester Sq.
Savile Row
Regent St.
Golden Square
Brewer St.
Gt. Windmill St.
Whitcomb St.
CHINATOWN
Bond St.
Glasshouse St.
Leicester Square
Irving St.
Vigo St.
Albemarle St.
Piccadilly Circus
Piccadilly Circus
National Gallery
Piccadilly
Regent St.
Panton St.
Haymarket
Jermyn St.
Trafalgar Square

0 — 1/8 mile
0 — 100 meters

1 Oxford Circus
2 Marks & Spencer
3 Great Marlborough Street
  Magistrate's Court
4 Foubert's Court
5 Carnaby Street
6 Kingly Court
7 Berwick Street
8 Berwick Street Market
9 Brewer Street
10 Old Compton Street
11 Frith Street
12 Soho Square
13 St. Giles Circus
14 Tottenham Court Road
15 The Goodge Street Deep Level Shelter
16 Goodge Street Tube station

and in the distance, the wedding cake of Selfridges (p. 270). Having a presence on Oxford Circus is considered crucial for brands with mass appeal. On the corner opposite is the smart Swedish clothier H&M (p. 275) and opposite Regent Street is Niketown. Beside it is Topshop (p. 274), another fashion-forward discount chain, which bills itself as the world's largest clothing store—I know of none larger. It's so busy that it refreshes its stock twice a day.

Head right, east on Oxford Street. You will pass Argyll Street on the right. Stroll down Oxford Street. When you pass Ramillies Street, prepare to stop in front of

❷ Marks & Spencer

London has a love-hate relationship with Oxford Street. People come here to shop by the thousands, but they often despair of the crush of the experience. Charles Dickens Jr. described the street thusly in 1888: "It ought to be the finest thoroughfare in the world. As a matter of fact it is not by any means, and though it is, like all the other thoroughfares, improving, it still contains many houses which even in a third-rate street would be considered mean." We're only going to walk down a sample of Oxford Street. It's usually so crowded, it's all you can probably handle if you're keeping one eye on this book. Keep the other eye out for people propping up day-glo signs reading GOLF SALE. These unlucky individuals are an Oxford Street institution. They're trying to draw foot traffic to off-street bargain stores selling cut-rate (and cut-quality) sporting goods.

Marks & Spencer (p. 270), or M&S, dates to 1894 and is the favored British department store for the masses, although it's been taking hits from warehouse stores like Tesco. Perhaps proof of its appeal is that the chain can afford to run two giant frontages on Oxford Street; its flagship store is remarkably near here, between Bond Street and Marble Arch Tube stations. For a long time, M&S made a point of dealing in British-made goods, but the pressures of a global market ended that, although it still touts its buying ethics. The store has also been working to replace its stodgy image with one that will attract more style-conscious customers. Its Food Halls (at this store, in the cellar) are well known as an ideal place to pick up prepared foods, sandwiches, and inexpensive but well-selected wines. Across the street from M&S is the flagship store of music seller HMV. Use a crosswalk if you cross; buses roar along Oxford Street. HMV promotes its latest markdowns (CDs for £4–£6) in the lobby.

Turn right at Poland Street, walk 1 block, and turn right again onto Great Marlborough Street. Walk straight. Soon on your right, at 19-21, you'll see a stout white building that looks like it could repel a tank. That's the former

❸ Great Marlborough Street Magistrate's Court

Charles Dickens worked here as a reporter just before hitting it big as a novelist, and a variety of other big names appeared before the judges here, including the Marquess of Queensbury (defending himself from Oscar Wilde's libel charge) and Christine Keeler (the sex kitten depicted in the movie *Scandal*). When this neighborhood turned bohemian in the Swinging '60s, it began trying a string of drugs charges against the likes of Mick Jagger, Johnny Rotten, Keith Richards, Francis Bacon, and, curiously (and coming full circle), the guy who wrote the musical *Oliver!*, Lionel Bart. It's now a stylish luxury hotel by Kempinski, and rates start around £150, putting it out of our price range, but I suggest you go inside briefly, because much of the old judicial fittings were left intact. You can have a cocktail in one of the old jail cells—now converted into private booths, with Zen stones filling the old toilets—or even peek into Silk, a restaurant slotted into the authoritative Number One court, which still has its witness stand, bench, wood paneling, and vaulted glass ceiling.

Beyond the Courthouse Hotel on the left, you'll see a Tudor-style building of black beams and white plaster. This is Liberty (p. 270), famous for its haute fabrics. It's also famous for its building—it was made in 1924 using wood recycled from junked ships. Liberty's wares are alternately mocked and celebrated, and rarely cheap, but they're usually interesting at the least.

Great Marlborough Street runs into Regent Street. Turn left there and walk the short distance to

④ Foubert's Court

Times have been better on Regent Street. Wal-Mart-style box stores in the suburbs have put the screws on the destination shops of the city, and over the past few years, this avenue has seen a few long-termers lose their sizzle and die. Dickins & Jones, a department store at the corner you just turned, closed its doors in early 2006 after nearly 170 years of history, having been unprofitable for 4 years. Other upscale frontages, such as the Apple Store, have moved in, but the future personality of Regent Street remains in question.

Two doors farther from Foubert's Court, though, at 188-196, is a well-loved holdover from the street's glory days. It's Hamleys (p. 284), one of the largest toy stores in the world. Some five million customers pour through its doors every year, but since the sales force is famous for putting on a non-stop show on every floor, it's understandable if many of those customers come to gawp and not to buy. If you go into Hamleys, when and if you come out again, turn right and go back to Foubert's Court.

Walk down the very short Foubert's Court for 1 block; you'll see "Carnaby" on a metal arch. Go under it and head 1 block further. Go right, and now you'll see a much larger arch on

⑤ Carnaby Street

Yes, those obnoxious arches proclaim your location with a clarion call that proves this street is no longer the mod, super-cool, forward-trending shopping street of the kids in the know. It's more of a mall with an edge. A few names sell products here that are hard to find elsewhere—Ben Sherman, Puma, and All Saints maintain huge stores here—but the days of Swinging London, when men would cruise from store to store trying on hip-hugging black trousers and frilly shirts, are behind it. *Time* magazine spilled the secret of Carnaby Street in 1966, and by the early 1970s, it was pedestrianized as a shopping street, making its hipness a matter of history.

Just after you cross Ganton Street, where Broadwick Street hits Carnaby Street, duck into the passageway on the right:

❻ Kingly Court

Clever entrepreneurs are reviving Carnaby Street's mod appeal with this positive development, a retail experiment inhabiting a former timber warehouse. A few niche chains (Vans, Cult) are present, but the stores here are mostly boutiques pushing young designers, which is increasingly rare for London. Now and then, the mini mall produces a new label or product that catches some buzz in the fashion glossies.

Slip out the back door of Kingly Court, opposite its front door, and hang a left on Kingly Street. Three doors in, at number 8, is the Oliver J Benjamin haberdashery. In the 1960s, it was the fiercely hip Bag 'O Nails pub, where future Wings-mates Paul McCartney and Linda Eastman first clapped eyes on each other. The pub, which saw club performances from the likes of Jimi Hendrix, was also where Fleetwood Mac's John McVie proposed to Christine. Return to Kingly Court.

Retrace your steps out of Kingly Court, cross Carnaby Street, and head straight down Broadwick Street. You'll stop around

❼ Berwick Street

A hundred and sixty years ago, this block was a foul slum. French, Greek and Italian immigrants fled hard times and revolutions by cramming into these tight streets, and by the 1850s, cholera was storming through the overstuffed city. An 1854 outbreak killed 500 people in barely 10 days. Common wisdom at the time held that the disease was spread through the air—a reasonable conclusion, given how terrible the sewage-smeared city smelled—but a local anesthetist, John Snow, suspected polluted water was the cause.

He got permission to inspect the public pump at Broad Street, now Broadwick Street—it's on the sidewalk in the block before Berwick Street—and he found that it was being contaminated with sewage leaking from Number 40 nearby, proving his theory.

Take a break

How grateful were Dr. Snow's neighbors for saving them? Incalculably: They named their pub for him, albeit a century later. It stands at number 39, at Lexington Street, on the site of his practice, and was built as the Newcastle-upon-Tyne in 1867. Raise a pint in his honor here, or if you need caffeine, by Stop 10 we'll be on a prime cafe street.

When you reach Berwick Street, look left. The road here ought to ring a bell for rock fans. Think of this location as the modern-day Abbey Road. It's where, in 1995, Oasis photographed the cover of (*What's the Story) Morning Glory*, one of the seminal CDs of the age. The photographer shot from farther down the street, aiming south, toward where you're standing. (Noel Gallagher, with characteristic eloquence, said he thought the album cover was "s**t.")

And here's another slice of rock history: One miniblock farther down Broadwick Street at number 7, the corner shop covered in striking rust-colored tiles (now Sounds of the Universe record store), was the famous Bricklayers Arms pub. Brian Jones auditioned The Rolling Stones here in 1962, and they held their formative rehearsals upstairs. Across the road at number 6, is Agent Provocateur, a noted lingerie shop. The word "Soho" is probably derived from a hunting cry used when this area was parkland—it's nice to see that some folks around here are still on the hunt.

Turn south on Berwick Street. Walk down it to

⑧ Berwick Street Market

This is the last great market in the center of the city, and it has been in operation since the 1840s, although vestry records indicate some illicit trading was going on as far back as 1778. London's first publicly available grapefruit was sold here in 1890. Even though many shoppers have migrated to fluorescent-lit grocery stores, you can still buy all manner of fruit, veggies, and everyday staples every day except Sunday. Buy a snack here; these hard-working vendors, many of whom speak fluent Cockney, could use your support. They have been known to cut deals on perishables in late afternoon. Along the storefronts are some interesting punk shops and used music stores, plus a few of the city's last vinyl record shops, which polish up the street's jumble-sale personality.

Pass over Peter Street and under Maurice House, going under the crossover and winding up on

⑨ Brewer Street

From the late 1700s to the 1950s, Soho was the capital of London sin; it was impossible for a single gentleman to pass unpropositioned from one end of the neighborhood to the other. A 1959 act chased the open salesmanship indoors, to be replaced by drinking joints where men could buy lap time with a lady, and by the 1970s, even those establishments were forced to seek a lower profile or close altogether. By law, today's window displays are not permitted to offer much in the way of titillation, complying with the British reputation (inaccurate in my book) for sexual modesty.

It was in this fleshly carnival that Laura Henderson bought a theater, named it the Windmill, and got around indecency laws, which banned nude dancers, by ensuring that the performers in her naughty entertainment, "the Revudeville," never moved a muscle. Famously (she was the topic of *Mrs. Henderson Presents* as well as *Tonight and Every Night* starring Rita Hayworth), the Windmill never closed, not even during the Blitz. The building now houses a common strip joint at Great Windmill and Archer streets, on the other side of the block that's across the street and to the right—don't detour unless you really want to because the tour resumes from here.

When you walked through Walker's Court, you probably felt a change in the character of the businesses. This part of Soho is known for its gay-oriented pubs, cafes, and stores, starting with Prowler, a bookshop and video store that's on the corner opposite.

Go left to Wardour Street, make a right and then a quick left. You'll be at the head of

⑩ Old Compton Street

There are a few interesting things to note here. First is the church of St. Anne's, a few yards farther down Wardour Street, on the left. The church was built in 1685, possibly by Wren (then again, which ones weren't?), but everything, save the clock tower, was creamed by the Germans. At night, the fence in front of it is illuminated in the colors of the rainbow flag—a sure sign of the inclusive beliefs of England's progressive clergy. Also, take a look at the far side of the building on the right-hand corner of Old Compton; embedded in its upper floor is the word CHEMIST—the British word for pharmacist—spelled in tile. Like the Berwick Street Market, it's an aging, endangered reminder that, although Soho is now a vivacious district of cafes, clubs, and media companies, for many years it was a workaday neighborhood.

Walk down Old Compton Street, Soho's de facto main street, which is busy 'round the clock. Number 54 is the Admiral Duncan. Dylan Thomas once drank there (then again, where didn't he?), but more recently it has become an important gay pub, and it was here, in 1999, that Nazi sympathizer David Copeland planted a bomb stuffed with 500 nails. When it exploded, it killed three people and injured many more. A sculpted brass chandelier marks the spot. Copeland, an obvious lunatic, also bombed the South Asian population of Brick Lane and blacks in Brixton, but his only fatalities were here. The street's gay clientele has, understandably, been on edge since then, but the street is nonetheless more popular than ever.

On the corner of Dean Street, look right. Down the block on the left, at number 49, is the French House, more commonly called the French Pub. During World War Two, it was the drinking haunt of Charles de Gaulle, and it was where the exiled leader formed the Free French government and army. The street beyond the French House is Shaftesbury Avenue, the famous theatrical thoroughfare; many of the side streets between Old Compton and Shaftesbury contain the stage doors for the major playhouses, where you can often sneak autographs from famous actors reporting to work. Now look left, north up Dean Street. In the attic of number 28, Karl Marx dwelled in abject poverty with his wife and several kids, with no running water or toilet. Three of his kids died while he was in residence in Soho in the early 1850s. No wonder he thought communism would be better.

Turn left at
⓫ Frith Street

Bar Italia, the stylish cafe at number 22, is a nightlife landmark of its own (p. 102). But history doesn't stop at the ground floor. Upstairs is where, in October 1925, John Logie Baird privately tested a homemade invention he called "noctovision," using a local office boy as a test subject. In January of the next year, he unveiled an improved model for the science nerds of the Royal Institution upstairs in this building. Baird's mechanical system, which used a spinning disc, was eventually discarded, but it debuted ahead of American Philo T. Farnsworth's more famous electronic version by 18 months. Within a decade, the BBC was broadcasting "television"—its new name—regularly. In the 1940s, Baird invented the first color picture tube.

Walk up three doors. For 10 months starting in September 1764, the 8-year-old Mozart lived with his father and sister at a house located at number 20 (the building was replaced in 1858). While he was in London, the prodigy amused King George III with his abilities, wrote his first two symphonies, and befriended fellow composer Bach. Another talent of the age, essayist William Hazlitt, lived at number 6; he died in a back room on the third floor. The premises are now an eccentric, enchanting luxury hotel, Hazlitt's, furnished with antiques and heavy fabrics, where breakfast in bed is served every morning of a stay.

Use the gate to head into
⓬ Soho Square

Laid out in 1681, Soho Square was, early on, the fashionable, mansion-lined home of both Charles II's son and the daughter of his grandfather's nemesis, Oliver Cromwell. Later it became the center of the ambassadorial and scientific cliques. Sir Joseph Banks, who made his name collecting exotic specimens as a tagalong on Captain Cook's voyages, moved here in 1777, and in 1799 the square was the scene of the first annual meeting of the Royal Institution, which is now the world's oldest research body. These days, Soho is a center for the music and film industries. Twentieth Century House, the British HQ of 20th Century Fox, is on the southwestern corner. The British Board of Film Classification, which assigns ratings to movies and video games, is also on the square.

In the center of the square, which is technically a private garden even though it's been open to the public for half a century, is a cottage you'd swear was Tudor in origin. In fact, it's an 1895 pastiche made to hide an electrical transformer. Beneath the lawns lie empty air-raid shelters.

Exit the opposite side of the square and go straight down Soho Street. You'll soon hit Oxford Street again. Turn right and head for the next major intersection. Head toward the entrance to the Tottenham Court Road Underground station, which serves the crossing officially called

⑬ St. Giles Circus

We're not too far east along Oxford Street from where we started, but you can see how much less illustrious the shopping is at this end. That's fine if you want a cell phone, knockoff suitcase, or CD (a Virgin Megastore, p. 281, is ahead on the left), but this shabby end is not a browser's paradise.

We're approaching the part of town that used to be called "the rookery of St. Giles." It was a notorious slum, a haven for lepers and a source of the plague, which was only cleared through an aggressive program of demolition.

Look across the next major street, and you'll see the 35-story Centre Point development. Built in 1964 with heavy government concessions, it was kept empty for years by its unscrupulous owner, partly to hold out for astronomical rents and partly because doing so would get him off the tax hook, even as the city struggled through a homeless crisis. The charity Centrepoint, which started in the basement of St. Anne's church in Soho and grew into a powerful force in housing issues, derisively took its name from the waste. Critics have assailed Centre Point as an eyesore, and as an emblem of poor urban planning—its inadequate sidewalk has a way of pushing pedestrians in front of buses. Still, it's indisputably one of the landmarks of the London skyline, identifiable from miles away.

You may end the tour here, at the Tube station, which contains some tile mosaics by the great artist Eduardo Paolozzi. Or, if you like, turn right to explore the bookstores on Charing Cross Road. If you want to extend the tour by another 15 minutes, take a final jaunt left, up Tottenham Court Road, partly to explore its excellent home design shops, and partly to see the remains of a World War Two air-raid shelter.

Turn left and head up

⑭ Tottenham Court Road

I have to admit this blandly developed avenue lacks character, and it isn't my favorite stretch in London, although I seem to find myself walking down it quite a lot. Fans of Andrew Lloyd Webber (anyone?), or at least of T.S. Eliot, will recall that this is the "grimy road" roamed by Grizabella, the "glamour cat" who sings "Memory."

A few spotty points of interest: On the corner, The Dominion Theatre was where, in 1957, Bill Haley and the

Comets were the first American rock act to play Britain. Farther down the same side of the street, the indispensable city guide, *Time Out,* has its offices at number 251. This is also known as the city's main district for electronics, but prices here won't be cheaper than they are at home. Soon, on your left, you will see Goodge Street, whose pubs and charity shops are frequented by students who attend the several universities in this area.

Duck into Chenies Street, on your right. At the curving side alley of North Circle, look for the red-striped, rounded buildings on the left, at

⓯ The Goodge Street Deep Level Shelter

In 1939, planners decided to build an express train line beneath the existing Northern Line platforms of Goodge Street. War intervened. In 1942, the unfinished tunnel was allocated to the Americans, and it was under the ground here where General (later President) Dwight D. Eisenhower orchestrated D-Day and announced it to the world, in 1944. There were eight deep-level shelters, and five were open to bomb-shocked civilians; this is one of the most central and best-kept. It retains its ground-level entry blocks, one pillbox and one octagonal, connected by a brick building—thousands of Londoners pass it daily but don't know their original purpose. Since the Cold War, the onetime shelters, now

innocuously painted cream with red stripes and named The Eisenhower Centre, have been used for storage. The shelter at Chancery Lane was converted to a telephone exchange, and the one at Stockwell has been decorated, turning it into an improvised war memorial.

Double back onto Tottenham Court Road. Across the street on your right will be.

⓰ Goodge Street Tube station

Before you end your tour at the Tube station opposite, turn right. This block hosts two of the city's most celebrated furniture stores, Heal's (p. 279) and Habitat (p. 279), both of which, decades before IKEA, provided high-design homewares for affordable prices. Drop into one or both (Habitat is cheaper); you'll be jealous of what British decorators can get for their pound.

The Goodge Street Deep Level Shelter could originally be accessed from a second point on the west of Tottenham Court Road opposite Torrington Place; some abandoned brick-and-concrete structures and vents linger. Goodge Street Underground station, opened in 1907 and still sporting much of its original tilework, is one of the few in the system that uses elevators, not escalators, to transfer passengers to and from platforms. You can always use the 136 steps, too—that is, if you still have the juice after your walking tour.

9

London's Best Shopping

The city's most distinctive stores—in the bag

BLAME ELIZABETH I. SURE, THE OLD GIRL LOVED HER BAUBLES AND GOLD-embroidered bodices (for a glimpse at some Renaissance bling, check out the Ditchley portrait of her at the National Portrait Gallery), but her biggest contribution to English consumerism was probably defeating the Spanish Armada. You see, that established England as the dominant player on the high seas, which in turn opened up channels of international trade never before seen in the West. Ever since the Thames was more jammed with bounty than the parking lot at the mall on Christmas Eve, London has had a hankering for the finer things. Make that an addiction—and not an affordable one, since the richest of the rich flock here to outspend each other. To make matters worse, many of London's stores have been around for hundreds of years, so they're particularly skilled at coaxing cash out of visitors. So before you make a pilgrimage to these shrines to credit, put your window-shopping glasses within easier reach than your pocketbook.

TEN GREAT SHOPPING STREETS

Appropriately for a city obsessed with class, London's prime shopping streets aren't usually defined so much by what they sell as by how much you'll spend to bring home their booty.

New Bond Street (Tube: Bond Street or Green Park): The ultimate high-end purchasing pantheon runs from Oxford Street to Piccadilly, partly as Old Bond Street. Every account-draining trinket maker has a presence, including Lalique, Tiffany & Co., Harry Winston, De Beers, Cartier, Chopard, Boucheron, and Wartski. Asprey's, at 165-169, sells adornments few can afford, but its Victorian facade is a visual treat for all incomes. Sloane Street, in Kensington, has many of the same brands, but Bond Street is still the granddaddy of spendy streets.

The Arcades of Piccadilly and Old Bond Street (Tube: Green Park): Also in the area are several iron-framed, skylighted "arcades" (closed Sun), built by 19th-century blue bloods for shopping in any weather. The best include Burlington Arcade, parallel to Old Bond Street at Piccadilly (silverware, cashmere, objets d'art); the Royal Arcade, south of Burlington Gardens (antiques, art, chocolates); and Piccadilly Arcade, across from Burlington Arcade (men's tailoring; it leads to Jermyn St., once the heart of haberdashery).

Store Hours

Stores across the city generally open at 9 or 10am daily and close at 7 or 8pm, although the department stores and Oxford Street shops are often open as late as 8pm. On Sundays, relatively new terrain for British shopping, 11am or noon to 6pm hours are more common; very few places will stay open past then. Expect crowds on weekends, when people pour into town from the countryside.

Kensington High Street (Tube: High Street Kensington): London's coolest shopping street in the '60s, it's now a hodgepodge of brand names and boutiques.

Oxford Street (Tube: Marble Arch, Bond Street, or Oxford Circus): The king of London shopping streets supports the biggest names, including Topshop, H&M, and a few lollapalooza department stores like Selfridges, John Lewis, and Marks & Spencer. Boy, does it get crowded. Visit www.oxfordstreet.co.uk for info.

Carnaby Street (Tube: Oxford Circus or Piccadilly Circus): This used to be for the mod crowd, but today such hyperalternative shopping is mostly found on Memory Lane. Instead, expect mainstream choices and a few one-off boutiques. Don't miss Kingly Court, a former timber warehouse converted into a minimall for upcoming designers. Visit carnaby.co.uk for info.

King's Road (Tube: Sloane Square or South Kensington): The Chelsea avenue where affluent "Sloaneys" spend is where you go to dream. Peruse posh shops like Daisy & Tom (at 181, toys and kids' clothes) and Steinberg and Tolkien (193, vintage acquisitions like flapper dresses). It's getting increasingly corporate.

Floral Street (Tube: Covent Garden): Every lane around Covent Garden (Long Acre, Henrietta Street) is an obvious shopping drag, but they're full of the usual brands. This side street gives respite from the same old tourist tat. Duck in when you want to browse some originals. Visit www.coventgarden.uk.com for info.

> " Our primary cultural activity in London was changing money. We had to do this a lot because the dollar is very weak. Europeans use the dollar primarily to apply shoe polish. So every day we'd go to one of the money-changing places . . . and then we'd look for something to eat that had been invented in this century, such as pizza, and we'd buy three slices for what we later realized was $247.50, and then we'd change some money again. Meanwhile, the Japanese tourists were exchanging their money for items such as Westminster Abbey. "
>
> —Dave Barry

Upper Street (Tube: Angel): Islington's chief avenue is emerging as a low-key location for boutiques, vintage outfits, and kitchen-sink junk shops, all pleasantly spelled by unpretentious pubs and cafes. While you're southeast of the Green, explore the sidewalks of Camden Passage, known for antiques and bric-a-brac.

Tottenham Court Road (Tube: Tottenham Court Road or Goodge Street): Locals sniff, but the street's lower half, between Oxford and Store streets, is their only drag for cut-rate electronics (including voltage converters). North to Torrington Place, pickings shift to brilliantly designed homewares and furnishings at Habitat (191) and London's grande dame of smart styling, Heal's (199).

Cecil Court (Tube: Leicester Square): Distinguished by glazed-tile buildings, matching green-and-white shop signs, and a refreshing lack of cars, this block is a holdout of the antiquarian book trade that once dominated Charing Cross Road, its western anchor. My favorite is Marchpane, at 16, a trove of vintage children's literature. Visit www.cecilcourt.co.uk for info.

OUTLETS, SALVAGE & SALE SHOPS

Many world-famous designers maintain shops in London, and when, at the start of each fashion season, their newest line comes in, they ship the older items to little-known "sale shops" where they're unloaded for a song. Most are temporary; for advance word on those, sign up for a free email from the London edition of **Daily Candy** (www.dailycandy.com) a few weeks before your departure. But some sale shops pump out deals year-round; a few of the best are listed below. You never know what you're going to find, so check items carefully for hidden damage:

While consumers outside the U.K. view Burberry as a dignified brand, in London, thanks to years of plaid overdose by the "wrong" crowd, its primary clientele is mocked as trashy. So the **Burberry Factory Outlet** (29-53 Chatham Place, E9; ☎ 020/8985-3344; www.burberry.com; Mainline rail: Hackney Central or Tube: Bethnal Green) is in the "wrong" part of town, with a grumpy staff to boot, but nobody back home will know that when you turn up wearing £10 shirts.

The facilities for the **French Connection/Nicole Farhi Outlet Shop** ★ (3 Hancock Rd., E3; ☎ 020/7399-7125; closed Sun and Mon; Tube: Bromley-by-Bow) aren't many notches over a woodshed's, but then again, prices aren't much higher than a charity shop's. Discounts for men and women start at 25% off.

For sharp suits at dulled-down prices, try your luck at **Joseph Clearance Shop** ★ (53 King's Rd., SW3; ☎ 020/7730-7562; Tube: Sloane Square). The smart clothes that end up here—lots of grey, lots of updates on classical profiles—were dumped from the menswear chain's lines this season for minor stylistic reasons that probably won't bother you. You'll still look chic for up to 70% less.

If you're a fan of cutie-pie tee-shirts, then you'll want to raid the **Paul Smith Sale Shop** ★★ (23 Avery Row, W1; ☎ 020/7493-1287; Tube: Bond Street), where last season's tees, trousers, and accessories are marked down from £55 to £25, shoes from £110 to £55, jeans from £30 to £19, and hats from £115 to £50.

If you're renovating your home or you want to, you'll find few better sources for interesting architectural items than London, an antique city on a redecorating binge. Buying salvage requires a hardy budget, specific measurements, tedious

An Outlet Mall Daytrip

The region's one true outlet mall, **Bicester Village** ("BIS-ter") (50 Pingle Dr., Oxon; ☎ 01869/32-32-00; www.bicestervillage.com), is 90 minutes west of town, about 24km (15 miles) from the city of Oxford. Jigsaw, the popular High Street clothier, has an outlet here and nowhere else, and DKNY, Nicole Farhi, and Benetton are among the 80-odd luxury names that send their designer castoffs here to be snapped up at 30% to 60% off. As with many outlet malls, finds can be spotty, although they do exist. Considering that almost everything for sale here started life at luxury prices, even a modest spree can wallop the bank account. The easiest way to get here is to take a 1-hour train to Bicester North Station from London Marylebone station, which departs about every 30 minutes (£20–£22 round-trip). From the station, you can walk or take a connecting bus Thursday to Sunday (about £1 each way). It's an outdoor mall, which is tough considering some of the best deals fall in January.

shipping arrangements, and determination, but your reward can be incredible finds—ones that will remind you of your trip for the rest of your life. You can also find rare conversation pieces at one of many regular auctions (p. 272).

When developers knock down classic old buildings, their fireplaces are salvaged by **Blue Mantle** ★ (The Old Fire Station, 306-312 Old Kent Rd., SE1; ☎ 020/7703-7437; www.bluemantle.co.uk: Tube: Borough). Here, at the largest antique fireplace showroom in the world, hundreds await their next homes.

You'll get an incredible selection of fittings and furniture rescued from museums, churches, pubs, and homes at **LASSCo (The London Architectural Salvage and Supply Company)** ★★ (St. Michael's, Mark St. off Paul St., EC2; ☎ 020/7749-9944; www.lassco.co.uk; Tube: Old Street; or Brunswick House, 30 Wandsworth Rd., SW8; ☎ 020/7394-2100; closed Sun; Tube: Vauxhall), from stained glass to paneling and faucets to wood flooring.

THE SHOPPING PALACES

So venerable is **Fortnum & Mason** ★★★ (181 Piccadilly, W1; ☎ 020/7734-8040; www.fortnumandmason.co.uk; Tube: Green Park or Piccadilly Circus), which began life in 1707 as the candlemaker to Queen Anne, that in 1922 archaeologist Howard Carter used empty F&M boxes to tote home the treasures of King Tut's tomb. The *veddy British* department store, which has a special focus on gourmet foods, is renowned for its glamorous hampers, which were first distributed in the days before World War I, when soldiers' families were responsible for feeding their men on the field. Such picnic sets now come with bone china and cost £235, and the tables of its ground floor food hall are immoderately piled with a cornucopia of such tongue-teasing triumphs as Thai green curry crickets ("oven baked, not fried!"; £2.40); Scottish heather honey (£4.15 for 8 oz.); and fresh Blue Stilton cheese in crockery pots from £16. Even the bread rolls cost a scalding 50p (albeit in high-rent flavors like Parmesan). Content yourself, as most do, with a wander through the hushed upper-floor departments, which are lit by chandelier, accented by wooden cases, and illuminated by a lotus-like atrium skylight. The second floor (fragrances), smells like a rose garden. High tea, taken in the top-floor St. James's tearooms, is no bargain (£22) but is among the city's most sumptuous.

Under the steerage of its widely reviled owner, the ostentatious Mohamed al-Fayed, **Harrods** ★ (87-135 Brompton Rd., SW1; ☎ 020/7730-1234; www.harrods.com; Tube: Knightsbridge), a miraculous holdover from the golden age of shopping, has been reshaped into a vertical mall appealing to free-spending, not-too-discerning visitors. Still, based on its prior reputation (or maybe because it's become such a bombastic parody of itself), many visitors prioritize a visit right behind Westminster Abbey or the Tower. Its seven thronged Food Hall rooms are still a glut of exorbitantly priced meats and cheeses, its ornate facade is still emblazoned like a Christmas tree after dark, its endless upper floors are still spiked with racks of gowns and blinding jewelry, but much floor space is devoted to brands you'd find for a third the price at your local mall (HMV, Krispy Kreme, Starbucks, Coach). The whole artificial environment, from clerks wearing straw hats to the giant "emporium" devoted to the sale of souvenirs (£12 for small gusset bags; £15 umbrellas; teddies aplenty), would be more authentic on Main Street at Disneyland than anywhere in the London of old. Of the many escalator banks, the most interesting is the uproarious Egyptian-themed one at the store's center. At its base is a tacky brass fountain memorial to al-Fayed's son Dodi and Princess Diana, who died together in Paris in 1997; a wine glass, preserved from the couple's final tryst, is preserved under glass along with a ring with which al-Fayed claims his son intended to propose to Diana. All in all, if you crave a real British department store experience, visit Fortnum & Mason or Selfridges; if you want to be flabbergasted by the excesses of the jet-set, Harrods is the overly shellacked circus for you.

It speaks volumes that *Absolutely Fabulous* antiheroines Patsy and Edina spoke of **Harvey Nichols** ★ (109-125 Knightsbridge, SW1; ☎ 020/7235-5000; www.harveynichols.com; Tube: Knightsbridge) with the same breathless reverence most people reserve for deities. You'll need the income of a god to afford a single thread of Harvey Nick's women's and men's fashion, and although the store isn't as popular as it used to be, a stroll through this spendthrift's heaven is entertaining. In addition to the lunching ladies on display in the fifth-floor cafe—think of it as a zoo for old money—there's a smart juice bar, Fushi.

Every Englishman knows that if you want a sound deal, you go to **John Lewis** ★★★ (Oxford St. at Holles St.; ☎ 020/7629-7711; www.johnlewis.com/oxfordstreet; Tube: Oxford Circus), which has a price guarantee; it employs an army of people to scout for the lowest prices in the area, which it matches. That may sound like the gimmick of a low-rent wannabe, but John Lewis, established in 1864, is in fact a respected, 20-department cooperative owned by its employees, and their interest in its success shows in their attentive service and seemingly limitless product line. It also has some exceptional buyers; you'll find things here no other store carries (the bedding department is renowned). Art fans shouldn't miss the building's eastern face, upon which is mounted an abstract cast-aluminum sculpture, *The Winged Figure* (1960), by one of the most important British artists of the twentieth century, Dame Barbara Hepworth.

It's Cheaper in England

Believe it or not, even though the pound packs a wallop, some items are still inexplicably less expensive if you pick them up in London.

- **High-quality bedsheets.** £30 to £40 a set.
- **Holiday cards.** £3 a pack. But who's that "Father Christmas" dude?
- **Breakfast cereal.** £1 to £3. Bring an empty suitcase if you're weird.
- **Re-released recordings.** Entertainment becomes public domain after 50 years in the U.K.
- **Beer.** A pint of strong ale can set you back as little as £2. Cheers!

Liberty (210-220 Regent St., W1; ☎ 020/7734-1234; www.liberty.co.uk; Tube: Oxford Circus), founded in 1875, made its name (and earned much mockery) as an importer of Asian art and as a major proponent of Art Nouveau style. The timber-and-plaster wing looks Tudor, but is actually a 1924 revival constructed from the salvaged timbers of two ships, HMS *Impregnable* and HMS *Hindustan;* the length of the latter ship equals the building's length along Great Marlborough Street. The store's scarf selection is celebrated, as is its selection of fabrics, many of which are designed in-house. Finding your way around saps time but little patience, since the soft wooden spaces are creaky and seductive.

Although its 400-odd locations have been limping along with a deficit of respect from the English people, **Marks & Spencer** ✦✦ (Flagship: 458 Oxford St., W1; ☎ 020/7935-7954; www.marksandspencer.co.uk; Tube: Marble Arch) is in fact a solid High Street store with solid bargains. Its own-brand clothing, once shoddy and ill-fitting, has been re-envisioned as affordable riffs on well-tailored fashions, and customers are drifting back to enjoy the good buys. One such deal: three pairs of men's underwear for £5. But M&S's crowning achievement is its giant **Food Halls** ✦✦✦ (usually tucked underneath the store but sometimes a stand-alone shop called Simply Food), which sell an astonishing array of prepared foods, soups and sandwiches, and well-selected yet inexpensive wines. M&S is a national treasure, and it's about time the English realized it, too.

Aside from Harrods' olive drab sacks, no shopping bag brags louder about your shopping preferences than a canary yellow screamer from **Selfridges** ✦✦✦ (400 Oxford St., W1; ☎ 0870/837-7377; www.selfridges.com; Tube: Bond Street or Marble Arch). It's unquestionably the better of the two stores, since it's not merely a sprawling sensory treat, but it also sells items you'd actually want (unlike Harrods, it stocks both major brands and young designers). Since its 1909 opening by an American marketing executive from Marshall Field's in Chicago, Selfridges has pioneered standard department store practices, including placing the perfumes near the front door and inventing the phrase "the customer is always right." Some one million products are for sale, and the beauty department is Europe's largest. The thicket of food counters is mobbed at lunchtime, and the rest of the store is just as popular at other times; some 17 million visits are recorded each year. Given the size of the place, a percentage may still be finding their way out again. Selfridges has traded in history, too; the first public demonstration of television was held on the first floor in 1925, and 3 years later, the store sold the world's first set. During much of the Blitz, Churchill's transatlantic conversations with FDR were encoded via a scrambler stashed in the cellar.

SPECIALTY SHOPS

Although you can find just about anything you want at the palace stores, considering the city is bristling with such excellent smaller shops, why would you want to? You'll run across dozens of winning boutiques as you stroll along, but the following stores count among the city's most interesting and most historic.

ANTIQUES

More like an upscale junk shop, **After Noah** ★ (121 Upper St., N1; ☎ 020/7359-4281; www.afternoah.com; Tube: Angel) makes its name on vintage toys, crockery, bathroom fittings, cheerful celluloid jewelry, and wooden desks and bedsteads, sadly too large to get home. Its refurbished mid-century telephones are particularly sought-after. There's another location at 261 King's Rd. (Tube: South Kensington), and a small booth on the fourth floor of Harvey Nichols.

The earlier you come, the more you'll find at **Bermondsey Market** ★★ (Bermondsey Street at Long Lane, SE1; ☎ 020/7969-1500; Tube: London Bridge), a weekly event that yields some of the city's broadest inventory (a trove of Edwardian and Victorian ephemera) and most flexible prices. It kicks off before Mother Nature herself rises, at 4am Fridays, and is history by 2pm.

Military buffs should know about **Blunderbuss Antiques** (29 Thayer St., W1; ☎ 020/7486-2444; www.blunderbuss-antiques.co.uk; closed Sun and Mon; Tube: Bond Street), which has been redistributing war mementos since 1968. Sample steals: bugles encrusted with the Empire's lion and the unicorn for £42, and World War II gas masks from £35. You can even put together a uniform like the ones at the Changing of the Guard.

Plenty of tourists swing through the booths clustering in **Camden Passage** (off Upper Street, N1; ☎ 020/7359-0190; Wed and Sat only; Tube: Angel), so bargains aren't always very easy to come by. Still, shimmering examples of china, silverware, cocktail shakers, military medals, coins, and countless other hand-me-downs overflow the cases. Despite the name, it's in Islington.

Reasonable but still responsive to sharp bartering skills, **Past Caring** ★ (76 Essex Rd., N1; ☎ unlisted; closed Sun; Tube: Angel) is a co-op known for its modern-era oddities, like freaky '60s ashtrays and kooky mirrors; recently, locals gave directions to it by pointing visitors to the foosball tables on its front sidewalk.

BOOKS

Few bookstores are as idealistically realized as **Daunt Books** ★★★ (83-84 Marylebone High St., W1; ☎ 020/7224-2295; www.dauntbooks.co.uk; Tube: Baker Street), which is lined with oak galleries and lit by a long, central skylight. It prides itself on its travel collection, which is located down a groaning wooden staircase. Everything is arranged by the country it's about—Third Reich histories under Germany, Tolstoy under Russia. It's no slouch in the general interest categories, either. Clerks seem to know what will interest the vaguest browser.

For scripts, acting guides, theatrical histories, and performers' biographies, **French's Theatre Bookshop** (52 Fitzroy St., W1; ☎ 020/7255-4300; www.samuel

Auctions

In Britain, auctions attract customers from all walks of life—they don't rely on cat-stroking Russian mobsters like in some James Bond movie. Most houses, which are located in suburban London, do a heavy business in personal items (as opposed to old office equipment or farm stock), require a deposit of £10 to £50 before bidding (returnable if you buy something), and skim off 10 to 20% of your total, but if you're the only person interested in an item for bid, you could still walk away with a steal. Make sure you attend the free property viewings, which precede the auctions by a few hours or days. All of the houses below sell antiques, art, furniture, jewelry, bric-a-brac, and a steady stream of unexpected finds. Always call ahead or go online to get a sense for the house's character, viewing schedule, rules, and auction times.

Greenwich Auctions Partnership ★★ (47 Old Woolwich Rd., SE10; ☎ 020/8853-2121; www.greenwichauctions.co.uk; Tube: Cutty Sark DLR): High-volume house (700 items every week) in Greenwich, good for items sold without a reserve. Viewings Fridays and Saturday mornings; auctions Saturdays at 11am.

North London Auctions (9-17 Lodge Lane, N12; ☎ 020/8445-9000; www.northlondonauctions.com; Tube: Woodside Park): Between 400 to 700 tasteful items, once installed in lovely homes, go weekly. Viewings Sunday mornings and Mondays; auctions Monday afternoons.

R. F. Greasby (211 Longley Rd., SW17; ☎ 020/8672-2972; www.greasbys.co.uk; Tube: Tooting Broadway, or Mainline rail: Tooting). A mixed bag, it pawns stuff seized by police and Customs, like bikes and cameras. Viewings Monday afternoons; auctions Tuesday mornings.

Southgate Auction Rooms ★ (55 High St., N14; ☎ 020/8886-7888; www.southgateauctionrooms.co.uk; Tube: Southgate). Good for items culled from suburban homes. Viewings Saturday mornings and all day Mondays; auctions Mondays at 4pm.

french-london.co.uk; Tube: Warren Street), north of lovely Fitzroy Square, is the city's most reliable supplier.

Labyrinthine **Foyle's** ★★ (113-115 Charing Cross Rd., WC2; ☎ 020/7437-5660; www.foyles.co.uk; Tube: Tottenham Court Road) is the last major family-owned bookshop on CXR (Charing Cross Road) to survive the late-20th-century onslaught of high rents and low readership. After the death of its owner, the store caught up with modernity just in time to avoid closure; among other tweaks, it installed a cafe. Although two more large bookstores, **Borders** (part of the international chain) and **Blackwell's** (good for academic publications), are right across the street, Marks & Co., memorialized in Helene Hanff's epistle story *84 Charing Cross Road,* is now the site of the All Bar One cafe.

The librarian leviathan **Borders** (203 Oxford St., W1; ☎ 020/7292-1600; www.bordersstores.co.uk; Tube: Oxford Circus) controls several London shops as well as the common Books etc. chain, but this is its flagship, carrying some 250,000 volumes. As well as offering plenty of 3-for-2 deals on the latest paperbacks—compare the offers here with the other High Street shops because titles differ between stores—it runs a cafe ideal for caffeine infusions and skimming potential purchases. It's active in the author-appearance circuit, too.

Although the Duke of Wellington and the Queen herself are counted in the rolls of its customers, **Hatchards** ★★ (187 Piccadilly, W1; ☎ 020/7439-9921; www.hatchards.co.uk; Tube: Piccadilly Circus), the oldest bookseller in the city (1797), is also noted for its famous shoplifters: An 18-year-old Noël Coward was apprehended as he stuffed a suitcase full of books. (Characteristically, he talked his way out of trouble.) It has been trading since 1801 at its current location, which means it was selling books before Hardy, Dickens, or the Brontes were writing them. Hatchards is strong for non-fiction and gardening tomes, and it carries a wide selection of inscribed copies, since all the important authors sign here.

The quintessential secondhand bookstore, cavelike **Keith Fawkes** (103 Flask Walk, NW3; ☎ 020/7435-0614; Tube: Hampstead), down a side alley off Hampstead High Street, is so crammed it's barely possible to navigate. Those who enter should be prepared to leave, much later, bearing a few unusual discoveries and smelling of yellowed paper. Unlike the filing system, prices are sane.

With no insult to Daunt Books, the world's most comprehensive travel book shop has to be **Stanfords** ★★★ (12-14 Long Acre; ☎ 020/7836-1321; www.stanfords.co.uk; Tube: Covent Garden), which since 1901 has comprised these three floors of globe-trotting goodness, from guides to narratives to fiction with a worldview. Should you accidentally leave your map in your hotel room, beeline to the basement; its floor is covered with an oversized reproduction of the London A-Z map. There's also shelf after shelf of maps for purchase, for London or anywhere in Britain. You'll find plenty of 3-for-2 deals on the lobby tables.

Built in 1936 as Simpson's clothiers, the Art Deco model for Grace Brothers in the saucy Britcom *Are You Being Served?,* **Waterstone's** ★★★ (203 Piccadilly; ☎ 020/7851-2400; www.waterstones.com; Tube: Piccadilly Circus) is Europe's largest bookshop. Even if Waterstone's is the McDonald's of bookselling, it handles the stewardship of that dubious title with dignity; there are five sweeping floors, an enormous London section, and plenty of easy chairs for browsers and freeloaders. The lobby on the Piccadilly side, lined with beautiful curved plate glass, is where the bulk of bargain books are kept, including the chain's prolific 3-for-2 deals on recent releases. The top floor's panoramic cafe, 5th View, hops after work and into the evening. There are free restrooms on each stairway landing. In Bloomsbury, a rambling wood-lined branch is at 82 Gower Street (☎ 020/7636-1577; Tube: Goodge Street), which operated from 1936 until the late '90s as Dillon's and serves the students of the nearby universities.

Modest, inviting **Primrose Hill Books** (134 Regent's Park Rd., NW1; ☎ 020/7586-2027; www.primrosehillbooks.com; Tube: Chalk Farm) isn't what you'd call a destination store, and yet many shoppers linger inside as if it was, waylaid by its towering shelves and genial family-run service. It's the sort of typical, lovely London bookshop that makes you want to open your own.

The Royal Warrant

When you're snooping around the stuffy shops of St. James's or Mayfair, keep an eye out for a royal crest near the store's sign or in the window. That insignia is a seal of approval from someone in the royal family—its presence means that the store counts them as a customer and has done so for at least 5 years. To earn Prince Charles' plumed crest, stores have to do even more, and prove they abide by a sustainable environmental policy. Once a store wins a warrant, it's extraordinarily rare to see it withdrawn, but to its public humiliation, Harrods lost its seal from Prince Philip in 2000. But don't ask what goodies these businesses are delivering to the palace; shopkeepers aren't permitted to tattle. To learn which companies supply the Windsors—say, where the Queen buys her corgis' dog food—search the current warrant holders at www.royalwarrant.org.

CLOTHING

Dover Street Market ✦ (17-18 Dover St., W1; ☎ 020/7518-0680; www.dover streetmarket.com; Tube: Green Park) is a trendy multidesigner concept, heavy on alienating industrial architecture, that fuses haute couture (Comme des Garçons, Boudicca) with multimedia art installations and a DJ in a plywood booth, all in a six-story department store–like space with an organic cafe on the top floor. It's pretentious eye candy, sure, but with flashes of brilliance.

One of the first boutiques to move into Upper Street, **Diverse** (286 and 294 Upper St., N1; ☎ 020/7359-8877; Tube: Angel) keeps stock changing even as it spotlights white-hot labels such as Marc Jacobs and Paper Denim and Cloth. The clothes are funky, which is to say interesting but not always irresistible.

A secondhand shop that isn't mobbed with clothes vultures who pick the racks clean before the rest of us can have a gander, intimate **Dress for Less** ✦ (391 St. John St., EC1; ☎ 020/7713-5591; Tube: Angel) is good for designer duds, clothes, and accessories, particularly for women.

Only a die-hard clotheshorse would brave the 30-minute commuter train trip to bland Croydon, but for those who dare, the finds at **Fashion Enter** ✦ (Unit 2, Centrale Shopping Mall, 21 North End, Croydon; ☎ 020/3132-2433; www.fashion-enter.com; Mainline rail: West Croydon or East Croydon) may be worth it. Fledgling designers who aren't yet famous enough to charge much are given space to hawk their threads in the organization's retail space.

Clothing samples come off the catwalk and land on the racks of **Frockbrokers** ✦✦ (115 Commercial St., E1; ☎ 020/7247-4222; www.frockbrokers. biz; Tube: Liverpool Street), which specializes in eclectic day-to-evening wear, one-offs, and a few vintage pieces. This single-room boutique (shopped by both Uma Thurman and Angelica Huston) also sells maternity clothes up to size 24.

Because it's been cool for longer than many of its competitors have been in business, **Rokit** (42 Shelton St., WC2; ☎ 020/7836-6547; www.rokit.co.uk; Tube: Covent Garden) has a strong following. Probably the largest collection in the city, Rokit sells retro and vintage threads that are funky and hipster-prone, from 1950s industrial uniforms to camouflage to tracksuits. The two other locations aren't as well-stocked: **Spitalfields** (101-107 Brick Lane, E1; ☎ 020/7375-3864; Tube: Aldgate East) and **Camden** (225 Camden High St., NW1; ☎ 020/7267-3046; Tube: Camden Town).

Don't laugh: For some reason, in Europe, **The Gap** ★★ (223 Oxford St., W1; ☎ 020/7734-3312; Tube: Oxford Street) is a viable source of truly good-looking, season-aware styles. Its inventory is almost completely different from the baggy stuff it offers in other places on the globe. It fits better, has smarter fashion sense, and doesn't make an endless fetish of the brand's cowboy past. It's definitely worth a look. There's a Gap Kids nearby at 315-321 Oxford Street.

As it spreads, the Swedish chain **H&M** ★★★ (261-171 Oxford St., W1; ☎ 020/7493-4004; www.hm.com; Tube: Oxford Street) is becoming an international byword for flashy and cutting-edge clothing bargains. It's where the fashion conscious can find astoundingly cheap outfits—they won't last more than a season or two, but they will turn heads while they do. Some of the chain's biggest European stores are in London. This main store, on the northwest corner of Oxford Street and Regent Street has the widest selection, including men's; the outpost a few blocks east at 174-176 Oxford Street only stocks women's and kids'; and the one at Covent Garden (27-29 Long Acre) is small but has a good inventory.

Barry Laden, the force behind **The Laden Showroom** ★★ (103 Brick Lane, E1; ☎ 020/7247-2431; www.laden.co.uk; Tube: Whitechapel), takes chances on eager, young designers when no one else will. Since 1999, this lifelong Whitechapel resident has given counsel and space—a shelf here, a cubicle there—to newbie designers, about 40 at a time. You'll find one-of-a-kind leather handbags (£20–£30), topcoats (£50), and clothes (skirts from £25). Most items, but not all, are for women.

New Look ★★ (175-179 Oxford St., W1; ☎ 020/7534-2005; www.newlook. co.uk; Tube: Oxford Circus), is another reliable High Street chain that does casual wear simply, somewhat fashionably, and always cheaply (tops £15–25, jeans £15–20). Its specialty is women's clothes, but it does a few men's.

I say, old chap, what happened to all the tweed coats and bowler hats the British men were famous for wearing? They're gathering dust at **Old Hat** ★ (66 Fulham High St., SW6; ☎ 020/7610-6558; Tube: Putney Bridge), where classic British fashion, if that's the term, can be found for cheap (suits from £100).

Tucked into an alley east of Liverpool Street station, no-frills **Therapy** (119-121 Middlesex St., E1; ☎ 020/7377-1838; Tube: Liverpool Street) does men's designer clothes and basics at discount prices, such as Calvin Klein jeans for £15, Converse sneakers (called "trainers" in England) for £20, and Levis for £20.

After a visit to **Topshop** ★★★ (214 Oxford St., W1; ☎ 020/7636-7700; www. topshop.com; Tube: Oxford Street), you'll no doubt find yourself laden with bags but also in a foul mood—because you'll be furious that they don't have shops like this at home. Here, at an 8,361-square-meter (90,000-sq.-ft.) store, some 1,000 employees at a time are on hand, many charged expressly with helping shoppers put together a smashing new outfit. The range of accessories is dizzying. Designs are always at the vanguard of youth fashion, yet the prices are defiantly low, which makes this forward-thinking, blockbuster store a primary stop on any London shopping tour.

Saving Money, Saving Lives

One gratifying way to shop in the United Kingdom is to peruse charity shops, which are secondhand stores—priced like flea markets—whose proceeds go to charity. Because their merchandise is ever-changing, any charity shop at any moment could contain your future favorite outfit or that out-of-print CD you've been hunting for years. For more such shops, visit the Association of Charity Shops (www.charityshops.org.uk):

Cancer Research U.K. (24 Marylebone High St., W1; ☎ 020/7487-4986; www.cancerresearch.org.uk; Tube: Baker Street) puts an emphasis on quality goods, both new and old, and prices are accordingly higher.

Crusaid (19 Churton St., SW1; ☎ 020/7233-8736; Tube: Victoria or Pimlico) sells clothes, music, and household goods, and benefits from its upscale neighbors' castoffs. Its focus is HIV/AIDS concerns.

FARA (841 Fulham Rd., SW6; ☎ 020/7313-0744; www.faracharityshops. org; Tube: Parsons Green) is eclectic and devoted to Romanian orphans. At nearby number 662, it operates a kids' shop.

Notting Hill Housing Trust (59 Notting Hill Gate, W11; ☎ 020/7229-1476; www.nottinghillhousing.org.uk; Tube: Notting Hill Gate; or 24 Goodge St., W1; ☎ 020/7636-4201; Tube: Goodge Street) stocks casual wear, greeting cards, and novelties, benefiting abused and homeless people.

Oxfam Original (22 Earlham St,. WC2; ☎ 020/7836-9666; www.oxfam. org.uk; Tube: Covent Garden) is the trendy arm of the traditional Oxfam store. Designer and retro clothes are skimmed from area Oxfams and deposited here, where they appeal to club kids and deal spotters.

Red Cross (67 Old Church St., SW3; ☎ 020/7351-3206; www.redcross.org. uk; Tube: South Kensington) is near the wealthy and capricious ladies of Chelsea, who keep it stocked with lush pickings.

Salvation Army Charity Shop (284 Upper St., N1; ☎ 020/7359-9865; www.salvationarmy.org.uk; Tube: Angel) re-sells the same outfits that were first sold by the high-end boutiques that surround it in chic Islington.

For a few years in the 1970s, Vivienne Westwood's **World's End** ★ (430 King's Rd., SW10; ☎ 020/7352-6551; www.viviennewestwood.com; Tube: Fulham Broadway) was the coolest place on the entire planet. The clock at this guerilla boutique still runs backwards, but London's punk heyday is long over, and Westwood went from rebel to royalty. Never mind the bargains—her Anglomania label is a living museum, but it's not cheap. Still, the fanciful couture inventions, flowing with fabric, are outlandish enough to enchant.

A Spanish chain delivering sophisticated looks for below-market prices, **Zara** ✹✹ (333 Oxford St., W1; ☎ 020/7318-2700; www.zara.com; Tube: Bond Street) is a smart stop on any hip shopping spree. Together with Topshop and H&M, Zara is part of a Holy Trinity of budget clothiers who can sell you an entire outfit—one right out of this month's fashion pages—for £60 or less. It sells for men, women, and kids. The locations at 242-248 Oxford St. (Tube: Oxford Circus) and 118 Regent St. (Tube: Oxford Circus) don't sell for kids.

FOOD

Also take a gander at the markets in the city, listed at the end of this chapter.

English food has been the punchline of international jokes for so long that the British were starting to believe the reputation. Enter **A Gold** ✹✹ (42 Brushfield St., E1; ☎ 020/7247-2487; www.agold.co.uk; Tube: Liverpool Street), which looks longstanding because of its vintage fittings but is actually a newcomer. It unapologetically peddles country comfort food that, it turns out, you can't even find at the English supermarkets anymore, such as Cornish sated sardine filets, Lancashire Eccles cakes, and Yorkshire brack—a kind of fruitcake. Okay, I admit, those names haven't helped the PR, have they?

Have a hankering for jerky made of beef, ostrich, or kudu (a type of antelope)? **African Enterprises** (Unit 3, The Arches, Villiers St., WC2; ☎ 020/7839-5707; www.africanenterprises.com; Tube: Embankment or Charing Cross) specializes in the stuff, called *biltong*, which is eaten like potato chips in South African towns. You can also try unusual African candy bars, groceries, and sodas. The store is hidden under the railway arches leading to Craven Street.

Pure powdered cocoa, delectable hand-rolled bonbons suffused with hazelnut, hot chocolate as thick as hollandaise . . . what's not to adore about **The Chocolate Society** ✹✹✹ (36 Elizabeth St., SW1; ☎ 020/7259-9222; www.chocolate society.co.uk; Tube: Victoria; or 32-34 Shepherd Market, W1; ☎ 020/7495-0302; Tube: Green Park)? I once had to put my name on a waiting list for its rich, moist brownies. It was so worth it.

Responsible for bloating many waistlines, the artisan bakers at **Konditor & Cook** ✹✹ (22 Cornwall Rd., SE1; ☎ 020/7261-0456; www.konditorandcook.com; Tube: Waterloo; or 10 Stoney St., SE1; ☎ 020/7407-5100; Tube: London Bridge; or 46 Grays Inn Rd., WC1; ☎ 020/7404-6300; Tube: Chancery Lane; or Curzon Soho Café, 99 Shaftesbury Ave., W1; ☎ 020/7292-1684; Tube: Piccadilly Circus) do a brisk business around holidays, when their brownies, chocolate, and adorable hand-decorated cakelets (made with free-range eggs) fly off the shelves and into lovers' mouths. They do lunches (soups, sandwiches), too.

The principles of **Monmouth Coffee Company** ✹✹ (27 Monmouth St., WC2; ☎ 020/7379-3516; www.monmouthcoffee.co.uk; Tube: Covent Garden) are high—only beans from single farms and co-operatives are used, and the owners often venture to South America to check conditions. So the coffee quality is high, too. Each winter, Monmouth sells a batch of new chocolate made by French artisan Francois Pralus, who selects his cacao in much the same way (it's so popular, it sells out by spring). A second location is at Park and Stoney Streets at Borough Market (Tube: London Bridge). Yep, you can take coffee through Customs.

Let it be remembered that the common cheddar cheese, before it was blanded down by industrial cheesemakers, was the piquant star of Cheddar, England.

What Can I Bring Home?

On the subject of food, although you should always technically claim edibles when you pass through Customs, very few things will be confiscated. Most stuff, including baked goods, honeys, vinegars, condiments, roasted coffee, teas, candy bars, crisps, pickles, and homemade dishes, are good to go. But these things may make the inspector dog's nose twitch:

- Meat and anything containing meat, be it dried, canned, or bouillon.
- Fresh fruit and vegetables.
- Runny cheeses, but not firm ones, which make up most cheeses (rule of thumb: If you have to keep it chilled, leave it behind).
- Rice. As if you would import rice.
- Plants, soil, wood, and seeds (non-edible). Ask the nursery whether you need paperwork because many varieties are permitted. Be warned that officers in Australia respond to wood like it's kryptonite.

Farmhouse cheeses from across the British Isles are given their due at **Neal's Yard Dairy** ★★ (17 Short's Gardens, WC2; ☎ 020/7240-5700; Tube: Covent Garden), an upstanding, pure-as-milk cheese wheeler-dealer. Tastings are free.

At its shop in the city's legal district, **Twinings & Co.** ★ (216 The Strand, WC2; ☎ 020/7353-3511; www.twinings.co.uk; Tube: Temple) deals in specialty teas, herbal infusions, and coffee blends. There's a tiny museum dedicated to tea. Proof it's old-fashioned: It closes at 4:30pm daily and stays shut on weekends.

HEALTH & BEAUTY

Do I dare to suggest you patronize the ubiquitous High Street brand that has devoured all other drugstores, **Boots** ★★★ (multiple locations, www.boots.co.uk)? Yes, I certainly do. Something like 80% of fragrance sales in the U.K. are conducted over Boots' counters, and the chain's endless 3-for-2 promotions almost always include something worth taking home, be it soaps, razors, or other toiletries. The company is steering itself away from the chemical-drenched drugstore rabble, too, with its popular Botanics line, Shapers low-calorie drinks and food, and Detox body purifying products. Its sandwiches are some of the city's cheapest, and they're tasty, too.

You'll catch its fragrance a block away. **Lush** ★★ (Unit 11, The Piazza, Covent Garden, WC2; ☎ 020/7240-4570; www.lush.co.uk; Tube: Covent Garden), part of a growing international chain, slices fresh soap the way farmhouses cut cheese wheels. If you've come to London with someone you love, its fizzy "bath bombs," which turn even the plainest hotel tub into a fragrant pool, are as effective as Cupid's arrow. Other locations include 40 Carnaby St. (Tube: Oxford Circus); 96 High St. (Tube: High Street Kensington); and along the western platforms of Victoria station (Tube: Victoria).

At the forefront of Britain's powerful environmental movement, **Neal's Yard Remedies** ★★★ (15 Neal's Yard, WC2; ☎ 020/7379-7222; www.nealsyard

remedies.com; Tube: Covent Garden) supplies beauty aids, holistic treatments, massage oils, and even make-your-own-cosmetics ingredients, all cruelty-free, clear of toxins, and naturally formulated. Its product—London's answer to the New York beauty boutique Kiehl's—are well-respected for their quality as well as for their ethical standards. Neal's Yard is squirreled away between Monmouth Street and Shorts Gardens, just northeast of Seven Dials.

I don't really want to picture Prince Charles lighting a Bluebell Classic candle and anointing his body with a blend of roses, lavender, and jasmine, but the cold fact is that **Penhaligon's** ★ (41 Wellington St., WC2; ☎ 020/7836-2150; www.penhaligons.co.uk; Tube: Covent Garden), established in 1870, is listed as an official supplier to the Prince of Wales. It hand-squeezes and custom designs its own fragrances for both men and women—generally floral-based and gentle—and sidelines in luxury shaving and grooming products. A picturesque location is at 16 Burlington Arcade, just east of Old Bond Street (Tube: Green Park).

HOMEWARES

Its sleek couches and shapely tables are too big to bring back on the plane, but consider **Habitat** ★★★ (196-199 Tottenham Court Rd., W1; ☎ 020/7631-3880; www.habitat.co.uk; Tube: Goodge Street) for its cheerful linens, kitchen tools, and bath fabrics. In pursuit of the department store's mandate (set by founder Sir Terence Conran) to bring high design to the masses at affordable prices, A-list artists (Tracey Emin, Tom Dixon, Manolo Blahnik) are regularly recruited to contribute temporary sale items. Although this store is Habitat's showpiece, nice-size outposts are at 208 King's Rd. in Chelsea (Tube: Sloane Square or South Kensington); 26-40 Kensington High St. (Tube: High Street Kensington); and 121-123 Regent St. (Tube: Piccadilly Circus).

A stalwart of Tottenham Court Road since 1840, **Heal's** ★★ (196 Tottenham Court Rd., W1; ☎ 020/7636-1666; www.heals.co.uk; Tube: Goodge Street) was instrumental in forwarding the Arts and Crafts movement in England, and its furniture and homewares, which are usually defined by chic shapes, have proven so influential that in 1978, it donated its archive to the Victoria & Albert museum. The kitchen department is popular. It's now the corporate brother of Habitat, another high-design leader, with whom it shares a building.

MUSIC & MOVIES

One of the last pocket record stores left, **Disque** ★ (11 Chapel Market, N1; ☎ 020/7833-1104; www.disque.co.uk; Tube: Angel) might as well have been the inspiration for Nick Hornby's novel *High Fidelity;* think vinyl, listening stations, and a passionate, friendly staff. Out front, flyers promote upcoming gigs you might not otherwise have known about. Check the three for £20 CD deals.

The city's only store devoted to musical theater and standards vocalists, **Dress Circle** ★ (57-59 Momouth St., WC2; ☎ 020/7907-7000; www.dresscircle.co.uk; closed Sun; Tube: Covent Garden) also does a brisk trade in karaoke recordings and theatrical souvenirs. Because recordings become public domain in Britain 50 years after being released (much sooner than in most countries), you'll find re-released CDs of classic Broadway musicals from the 1950s and earlier for next to nothing: £3, although new releases are easily £10 more. The staff can be crotchety, and perversely, it closes at 6:30pm, an hour before the nightly curtain, making it impossible to shop on the way to a show.

The Great Museum Shops

Not all museum stores were created equally. The British Museum's stalls don't have enough space to get truly interesting, and the Science Museum is mostly interested in sending kids home with trinkets. But these exhibitors carry items you won't find anywhere else, and you don't have to spring for an admission ticket to peruse them.

London history: The Museum of London (p. 154) has not just the mainstream history books but also heaps of vanity pressings, specific to a neighborhood or an era, put together by passionate amateur historians. Running a close second is London's Transport Museum (p. 157), which in addition to more tomes on the Underground than you thought possible, carries a busload of gift items themed to the Tube's world-famous logo and catch phrases.

The arts: It may be a design museum, but the Victoria & Albert (p. 148) sells stuff that spans art, history, and design, and it's not picked over. I've found books for £18 that Amazon.co.uk listed for £80. And the National Gallery's (p. 143) Print on Demand kiosk, in the Sainsbury Wing, lets you pull up just about any of its masterpieces and print your own high-resolution poster of it on semi-gloss paper (£10–£25)).

Coffee table books: The Tate Modern's (p. 145) shop, long as a football field, tries to be all things to all art lovers, and it largely succeeds.

World War II: The Cabinet War Rooms' (p. 154) shelves of non-fiction are overshadowed only by its wall of postcards based on propaganda posters.

High design: The Design Museum's (p. 179) envelope-pushing ethic is embodied by its sometimes haughty, always eye-catching library.

Wine: The attached museum is worthless, but the shop of Vinopolis (p. 194) sells wine, whisky—even absinthe, the widely banned "green fairy" tipple.

Another eccentric Islington gem, **Flashback** (50 Essex Rd., N1; ☎ 020/7354-9356; www.flashback.co.uk; Tube: Angel) is a cramped shop that, happily, doesn't favor one style of music over another—as long as it's old, it's in.

The independent, Glasgow-born chain **Fopp** ★★ (1 Earlham St., WC2; ☎ 020/7379-0883; www.fopp.co.uk; Tube: Covent Garden), on a busy corner across from the Palace Theatre, is gathering a following for discounting new releases and employing staff that have a clue.

At first glance, **Steve's Sounds** ★★★ (20 Newport Court, WC2; ☎ 020/7437-4638; Tube: Leicester Square) is just another used CD jumble shop. But look deeper: Music journalists and DJs unload their promotional copies here, so you can find new releases and uncirculated pressings for under-single-digit prices.

Don't Let the DVD Code Crack You

In their aggressive drive to ensure they extract the maximum amount of cash from every economy, Hollywood studios release most DVDs with "region codes." American and Canadian players will only play Region 1 discs, and Australia and South America are zoned Region 4, but the DVDs you buy in the U.K. will be coded Region 2. This is annoying, to put it politely, because many DVDs for sale in Britain—TV shows, documentaries, and so forth—simply aren't available anywhere else. Some experts have warned that region coding is probably a violation of the WTO's free trade agreements. The only legal solutions for now: Buy DVDs marked "All Regions," (sometimes noted as Region 0) or, back home, pick up a "multizone" DVD player that accepts discs from any region. Those are often sold in neighborhoods where recent immigrants have settled.

Much like its siblings in countless world cities, the **Virgin Megastore** ★★ (14-16 Oxford St., W1; ☎ 020/7631-1234; www.virginmegastores.co.uk; Tube: Tottenham Court Road) is a cacophonous catch-all for the latest in DVDs, CDs, and video games. Granted, this is Virgin's home city, so the racks are curated with pride. The current markdowns are relegated to the Oxford Street entrance. The Piccadilly Circus frontage once occupied by Tower Records (1 Piccadilly, W1; ☎ 020/7439-2500; Tube: Piccadilly Circus) is also well stocked. Both stores host celebrity appearances and minigigs, which are well publicized on-site, although attendance may require free wristbands (obtainable ahead of time). The selection and vibe here are much better than at the overly mall-ified HMV stores.

SHOES

When a shoe hits it big on the runways, it soon appears, priced small, at **Faith** ★★ (192-194 Oxford St., W1; ☎ 020/7580-9561; www.faith.co.uk; Tube: Oxford Circus). Styles, all current and wearable, go for £40 to £60, and it also does retro designs and purses.

The H&M of footwear, **Office** ★★★ (61 St. Martin's Lane, WC2; ☎ 020/7497-0390; www.officeholdings.co.uk; Tube: Leicester Square) rips off designer styles cheaply but effectively, and its permanent sales shop is smack in the West End, opposite the Noël Coward Theatre. Top shoe labels are sold for peanuts, such as Postes for £15. You'll find lots of women's stuff, less so men's. The company's nearest non-sale shop is at 57 Neal St. (Tube: Covent Garden).

Canadian **Patrick Cox** ★ (129 Sloane St., SW1; ☎ 020/7730-8886; www.patrickcox.co.uk; Tube: Sloane Square) didn't become a confidant of England's rich and famous—he's one of Liz Hurley's best friends—by making flimsy footwear. No, this cobbler-cum-designer makes the kind of classically inspired shoes (big buckles, interesting patterns, from £120), for both men and women, that speak volumes about the wearer's refined tastes.

Chockers (1-3 The Strand, WC2; ☎ 020/7839-5293; Tube: Charing Cross) lacks glamour, and its saleswomen look bored, but prices are low: £15 espadrilles, £10 calf-high boots, and £15 sequined pumps. The store faces Trafalgar Square.

Know Your High Street Brands: A Primer

In England, a town's Main Street is usually called its "High Street," so when you hear someone referring to High Street prices or shops, it just means they're talking about the major names that exist everywhere. They could also be speaking in backhanded code, since between 2001 and 2005, these corporate brands squeezed out some 7,000 family-owned local businesses nationwide and consequently much traditional character has been lost forever. The situation is so dire that one London newspaper, the *Evening Standard*, launched an aggressive "Save our Small Shops" campaign, to lend political clout to independent shops. Wherever you go in Britain, whether it's London, Penzance, or John O'Groats, these are 31 major players you'll see, so you might as well say how d'you do:

Accessorize: Accessory giant associated with Monsoon (see below)

Argos: Electronics, toys, and furniture, selected by catalog in the store's lobby

Asda: Wal-Mart's British representative

Boots: See "Health & Beauty," p. 278

BHS: Department store known for lighting and bridal wear

Caffè Nero: Italian-style coffeehouse with light meals and seating

Carphone Warehouse: Despite its obsolete name, deals in standard mobile phones

Clinton Cards: Cards, gifts, and calendars featuring hot footballers

Coffee Republic: Coffees and teas; smoother flavor than Starbucks

Flight Centre: Travel agent and holiday booker, based in Australia

HMV: Flashy superstore for CDs, DVDs, and video games

...instore: Pompous new name of the old Poundstretcher chain, the equivalent of a dollar store

Jigsaw: Mid-price clothing for women and children

STATIONERY

One of my first shopping stops is always **Muji** ★★★ (187 Oxford Street, W1; ☎ 020/7437-7503; www.muji.co.uk; Tube: Oxford Circus) a Japan-based chain that sells an incredible array of nifty, sleekly designed gadgets (futuristic alarm clocks), stationery (gel pens in rainbow colors, slim pocket-size pads) and containers (clear Acrylic Stacking Pot tubes for vitamins and pills). Much of this book was collated using its E.V.A. Zip Pockets. It even sells cosmetics and clothing. Muji's witty "London in a Bag," an assortment of wooden blocks shaped like the major landmarks, is a great souvenir for kids (£5). Other locations include 41 Carnaby St. (Tube: Oxford Circus); 135 Long Acre (Tube: Covent Garden); Whiteleys

Majestic Wine Warehouse: Nicer (but not cheaper) than Oddbins

Mango: Funky throwaway outfits for under-25s

Mark One: Flimsy but trendy clothes that cost next to nothing

Marks & Spencer: See "The Shopping Palaces," p. 268

Monsoon: Mid-price clothing for women, men, and children

Next: Safe selection of clothing (men, women, kids) and homewares

Oddbins: Affordable wines

Odeon: The U.K.'s largest cinema chain, founded in 1930

Paperchase: See "Stationery," p. 282

Ryman: See "Stationery," p. 282

Sainsbury's: Massive supermarket chain; Lord Sainsbury, active in politics and science, is worth some £2 billion

Shelly's: Mainstream shoes

Superdrug: Low-cost pharmacy

Tesco: The world's largest supermarket chain builds more than one store a day

Thomson: Travel agency that ate the melodiously named Lunn Poly in 2004; now dying like all travel agencies

TK Maxx: English version of cut-rate clothes warehouse TJ Maxx

WH Smith: Magazines, books, newspapers, and snacks; ubiquitous at transit hubs

Waitrose: Co-op supermarket chain run by the John Lewis Partnership

William Hill: Long-lived betting shop taking odds on horse races, football matches—even *Big Brother*

Shopping Centre (Tube: Queensway); and 6-17 Tottenham Court Road (Tube: Tottenham Court Road).

   Paperchase ★★★ (213-215 Tottenham Court Rd., W1; ☎ 020/7467-6200; www.paperchase.co.uk; Tube: Goodge Street) does for stationery what Habitat does for chairs and tables: imbues them with infectious style, bold colors, and wit. Starting in summer, stock up on holiday cards, since they're not only much cheaper in the U.K. than abroad (about £3 for 8) but also because some proceeds go to charity. There are many so-so branches in this chain, but this three-floor flagship is a big paper cut above.

   If you're into office supplies (admit it—it's time to come out of the supply closet), the ubiquitous **Ryman the Stationer** ★ (multiple locations; www.ryman.

co.uk) chain, which makes an appearance on almost every busy shopping street, is a good place to stock up on hard-to-find stuff like A4 paper, envelopes, and convenient "box files" (strangely absent from many countries' stationers), which are available in a spectrum of sprightly colors.

The racks of **Scribbler** ★ (15 Shorts Gardens, WC2; ☎ 020/7836-9600; www.scribbler.co.uk; Tube: Covent Garden) are devoted expressly to greeting cards, and you'll never see its selections anywhere else. It's a great place to stock up on random, trendy cards none of your other friends will send.

The cotton-fiber content of the paper at **Smythson of Bond Street** ★ (40 New Bond St., W1; ☎ 020/7318-1515; www.smythson.com; Tube: Bond Street) is probably higher than in your bedsheets. The Queen, a one-woman thank-you note industry, buys her paper here.

TOYS

I like to think of **Daisy & Tom** ★★ (181 King's Rd., SW3; ☎ 020/7352-5000; www.daisyandtom.com; Tube: South Kensington or Sloane Square) as Hamley's for bookish kids. The usual dazzling gimmickry, such as a small in-store carousel, is here, but the merchandise veers toward unusual or cutting-edge toys, books, crafts, clothing, and shoes. The puppet theater, in the upstairs clothing department, puts on a Peter and the Wolf show every 30 minutes.

A dream of a toy store, **Hamleys** ★★★ (189-196 Regent St., W1; ☎ 0870/333-2455; www.hamleys.com; Tube: Oxford Circus), is so festive and colorful, it's likely to send your kid into sensory overload. It's one of the world's few department stores devoted just to children. The employees, themselves kids at heart, are having a grand time, and their ebullient demonstrations of the latest play technology, conducted spontaneously throughout the store's seven floors, are part of the fun of a visit. There's a cafe on the top floor, next to the action figures.

LONDON'S GREATEST MARKETS

Unfortunately, with the inexorable spread of megastores like Tesco, Sainsbury's, and the Wal-Mart-owned Asda, outdoor markets that have been feeding Londoners since the Dark Ages are finding themselves extinguished. The following markets solider on, providing a huge range of produce, meats, and cheeses straight from English farms, as well as cheap clothing, music, and even kinky underwear. Even if you aren't keen to buy any of that, a stroll down one of the city's market lanes, where stallkeepers bark in Cockney accents and the city's immigrant population gathers to resupply, is like a front-row seat to the ongoing opera of everyday London life. It's London as it was—and hopefully will continue to be.

Berwick Street Market (Berwick St. around Broadwick St.; daily except Sun; Tube: Piccadilly Circus)

Good for: Fruit and vegetables and basic wares; it's small, but it's the last daily street market in the West End, dating to the 1840s.

Also check out: Interesting punk clothing and record shops along the route.

Market Hours

Unless otherwise noted, markets generally kick off at around 8 or 9am in the morning and start packing up at around 3pm.

Borough Market (Southwark St. at Stoney St., Fri and Sat; Tube: London Bridge)
   Good for: Organic and farm-raised meats, cheeses, rare beers, fine produce—the market dates at least to Roman times; stalls have an upper-class tilt but excited saliva glands know no budget.
   Also check out: The artisanal food for sale in the stores along Stoney Street.

Brick Lane Market (Brick Lane between Bethnal Green Rd. and Buxton St.; Sun dawn–2pm; Tube: Aldgate East)
   Good for: Secondhand clothes, bike parts that might be stolen—more appealing are the trendy boutiques in the overlooking buildings.
   Also check out: Beigel Bake (159 Brick Lane), maker of the city's most beloved bagels (and also of a mean brownie); the artists selling handmade bags, shoes, and cards along Dray Walk, south on Brick Lane; the Indian spices and herbs on offer at **Whitechapel Market,** a 10-minute walk southeast by the Whitechapel Tube stop, daily except Sundays.

Brixton Market (Electric Ave. at Pope's Rd., daily except Fri and Sun. Tube: Brixton)
   Good for: Exotic produce, spices, halal meats, sold to reggae and hip-hop.
   Also check out: Brixton Village, stalls selling African and Caribbean clothes, foods, and homewares; Ritzy's Art Fayre, a designer market, every Saturday.

Camden Lock Market and Camden Canal Market (Camden High St. at Buck St.; daily [but weekends are best]; Tube: Camden Town)
   Good for: Cheap fashions, sunglasses, music mixes, fresh-made foods in a dockside setting favored by tourists.
   Also check out: Market Hall, behind the canal, contains three floors of artsy boutiques; Stables Market, off Chalk Farm Road, sells vintage clothes, antiques, and pop culture knickknacks; Electric Market is an indoor fair of cool tee-shirts, fake furs, and goth wear, Saturday and Sunday.

Chapel Market (Islington; daily except Sun; Tube: Angel)
   Good for: Cheese, dumplings, meat pies, toiletries—it's a real catch-all working-class market on a street that still looks the way it did 25 years ago.
   Also check out: The antithesis of a market, the gleaming N1 Islington mall, dominates the eastern end of the street; it's New London versus Old London.

Hacking the Tax Attack

First, the good news. When you see a price in England, that's the full price. Tax is always included.

Now, the bad news. That tax is usually charged at a rate of 17.5%. It's called VAT (Value-Added Tax), and it goes to enviable programs such as national health care, so that any British citizen who needs emergency care doesn't have to go into debt to get it.

Now, more good news. Tourists can often get that 17.5% back. As long as the store you're patronizing participates in the "VAT Retail Export Scheme" (not all of them do) and you get all the paperwork from them while you're making your purchase (stores have varying minimum-purchase requirements), you can apply for a refund, minus a chunk for administrative fees. The only purchases it doesn't work for are vehicles, unmounted gemstones, and anything (except antiques) requiring an export license.

To get your money back, you must:

- Be a non-European Community visitor to the U.K.
- Complete the valid tax refund document you got from the retailer.
- Present that document to Customs at the airport the day you leave Britain. You must also have the goods on hand, which means a) you must put them in your carry-on or b) you must pack the goods in your baggage but first check in at your airline to pick up your travel documents, then bring your yet-to-be checked baggage to Customs, and then re-submit your baggage at the airline counter once Customs is finished. This process can take anywhere from 5 minutes to 45 minutes, so plan ahead.

Some information is available at http://customs.hmrc.gov.uk, or you can request a copy of "The Retail Export Scheme for Overseas Visitors: V.A.T. Refunds," by sending a stamped, self-addressed business-size envelope to British Information Services, 845 Third Avenue, New York, N.Y. 10022.

Greenwich Markets (11A Greenwich Market; Thurs–Sun, but best weekends; Tube: Cutty Sark DLR)

Good for: Antiques, flea market items, crafts, honeys, breads, cakes.

Also check out: The cafes lining the covered Craft Market; take lots of photos because the entire area is in the clutches of developers.

Leather Lane Market (Leather Lane between Clerkenwell Rd. and Greville St.; weekdays from 10:30am–2:30pm; Tube: Farringdon)

Good for: Hot and ready-to-eat food, be it Jewish (latkes, salt beef), Mexican (burritos), or universal (salads); sweatsuits and skirts, juices, shoes, jeans.

Also check out: The classic sandwich shops and "caffs" (diners) on the street.

Portobello Road Market (daily except Sun; Tube: Notting Hill Gate or Westbourne Park)

Good for: Antiques, hot foods, jewelry, clothes, tourist crap by the ton.

Also check out: The packed pubs along the route; the galleries and antiques shops in the storefronts, where prices can be better than at the stalls.

Queen's Market (Green St. at Queen's Rd.; Tues and Thurs–Sat; Tube: Upton Park)

Good for: 80 stalls and 60 local stores for gourmands and world travelers, with ingredients from Asia, Africa, Russia, the Caribbean, and elsewhere; international clothes and rugs. Although it's been going for over 100 years, the town's council wants to sell the site to a Wal-Mart-run hyperstore

Also check out: Its defenders' website, www.friendsofqueensmarket.org.uk, which argues their market is 53% cheaper than what's for sale at Wal-Mart.

Riverside Walk Market (on Southwark under the Waterloo Bridge; noon–7pm in good weather; Tube: Waterloo)

Good for: Tables of used books, maps, lithographs, and wood engravings.

Also check out: Lower Marsh Market on Lower Marsh between Westminster Bridge and Baylis roads (south of Waterloo station), for a classic produce market.

Spitalfields Market (Commercial St. between Brushfield St. and Lamb St.; daily except Sat; Tube: Liverpool Street)

Good for: Up-and-coming designers and artists, prepared world food, handmade homewares, jewelry, vintage cinema posters.

Also check out: The market's theme days, including food (Wed), antiques (Thurs), and fashion (Fri).

Walthamstow Market (Walthamstow Market St.; daily except Sun; Tube: Walthamstow)

Good for: 450 stalls selling everything, from knockoff clothes to food to Chinese-made batteries—it's the longest market street in Europe.

Also check out: Nearby Walthamstow Stadium (www.wsgreyhound.co.uk), which has run live greyhound races since the sport's heyday in 1933. Tuesday, Thursday, and Saturday (£6) and Monday and Friday lunchtime (free).

10 London After Dark

Do Londoners ever just stay at home at night? Would you?

LET NO ONE TELL YOU THAT LONDON TUCKS ITSELF INTO BED EARLY. Perhaps that was true in your grandfather's day, but nowadays, the U.K. rocks all night. The Tube may shut down after midnight, but the entertainment rollicks until dawn. It's even true of the working sector: In the 1960s, you'd be lucky to find a place to buy a carton of milk after suppertime. Now, some 7 million people work during the night in the United Kingdom, and that figure is expected to double by 2016.

London, simply put, is an entertainment hub. With hundreds of theaters, comedy clubs, and nightclubs, London has more to offer on a single night than many cities can muster in an entire year. Whether your tastes run toward cinema or just plain sin, the city caters to everyone.

That said, London's nights aren't perfect. The city's prevailing liquor laws, to say nothing of a Tube system that often closes after midnight, force even top clubs to sometimes unceremoniously dump their clientele on the streets in mid-toast. Whereas in Spain, Greece, and New York, the night rarely begins before 1am, that's usually when the DJ packs up at many of London's top clubs. Recent changes to the law have only added an extra hour to a few clubs' operations. That can put a crimp in plans since it forces those who can't afford taxis to choose just one or two activities in a single night: dinner, theater, or club. The Night Bus system (p. 16) assuages some of the financial pain, but it's a buzzkiller to follow a festive night out with bus stop curb-gazing.

GETTING THE SCOOP: The best way to know what's going on is to do what the locals do: Hit the newsstand. Londoners turn to their newspapers for announcements of the latest to see, hear, and do. The most complete listings information for entertainment are published on Saturday. Start with these resources:

- *Time Out* **magazine,** £2.50: The original publication of what's now an international brand, *Time Out*'s 200-odd weekly pages constitute the most comprehensive listing of goings-on, hands down. It should be your first purchase upon landing. New issues come out on Tuesdays.
- **Visit London:** The "What's On" section of its website (www.visitlondon.com) is assiduously updated and, even better, it's free.
- The *Evening Standard:* Sold by countless hawkers on pavements around town (40p)—just make sure to pick up the free accompanying magazine section, such as *ES* on Fridays; it's usually in a nearby stack.

◆ *Metro:* Distributed for free in marked racks at Tube stations citywide, most copies are gone by mid-morning, but commuters leave copies behind on the trains, so look around; it's not considered weird to pick up a used newpaper.

GOING TO THE THEATER

If you leave London without seeing at least one stage show, then you'll have missed one of this city's most glittering attractions. No city in the world has influenced artistic culture more than London has. This is where Shakespeare defined great writing and Gilbert and Sullivan shaped modern musical theater. It's where David Garrick, Laurence Olivier, and countless other luminaries earned their enduring reputations as actors. London's influence isn't just in antiquity; the great work continues to this day, and if you doubt it, look at the lists of Oscar, Emmy, and Tony winners from the past decade—nearly every year includes at least a few London exports. Appearing on the hallowed boards of London's great theaters and concert halls has made stars of mere performers, and legends of mere stars. Every year, movie and TV stars from around the world happily book runs in the West End, where, unlike on Broadway, the performing seasons are usually so robust that a negative critical review won't close the show.

Whenever you hear the phrase "West End" in relation to shows, think of the term as describing the top tier of theaters in the middle of town. The well-known, open-ended runs usually dominate the 60-odd West End houses that rent themselves out to anyone with the cash, and they are where you catch most of the major tours and the big names. These are the shows that most tourists flock to see, but that doesn't mean they're always the best shows in town—the West End is increasingly clogged with mediocre dramas propped up by Hollywood names and by so-called "jukebox" musicals that are the intellectual equivalent of bubble gum. Look to the smaller houses, often called off–West End, or fringe, for the real innovative fare at much more affordable prices—often, the best fringe material ends up courting larger audiences on the West End, anyway.

THEATER TICKETS FOR LESS

If you want to see a specific show, book tickets before you leave home. Check with **The Society of London Theatre** (www.officiallondontheatre.co.uk), the trade association for theater owners and producers (established in 1908), for a key to what's playing, as well as for a direct link for online purchase. Keep in mind that while most shows will direct you to ticket sellers such as Ticketmaster or First Call, those agencies will charge you a premium of as much as 20% for your booking. Only use that method if you'd be heartbroken to miss a particular show. Instead, look for what's discounted. Given a lead time of a few weeks, the established website **LastMinute.com** sells many shows for half price, as does the London Theatre Club's **LoveTheatre.com** site (click "Offers"). The fan site **Theatre.com** also sometimes advertises slight discounts. And the website **BroadwayBox** (www.broadway box.com/london) posts a helpful, exhaustive listing of all the known discount codes for the West End shows.

Saving on the Stage

Apart from using TKTS, how can you save on a show? Try these ideas:

- Matinees are sometimes cheaper than evening shows. (Unfortunately, they also cut into your available daylight touring time.)
- Ask about standing room tickets. Not all theaters have them, but the Donmar, the National, and the Old Vic, to take three examples, do, and they sell for under a tenner (£10). These are only released once everything else has been sold, so you can't count on them.
- Buy directly from the box office to avoid paying telephone booking fees and surcharges.
- Seats at the tippy top of the back of the theater can cost a quarter to a third of what the seats in the stalls do—but bring opera glasses.
- In one of the older theaters, you can often settle for a restricted-view seat. You may have to crane your neck at times to see around the edge of the balcony or a pillar, but you'll be in the room. They cost about a third what top-price seats do.
- If you're a student, some box offices (but not TKTS) may offer you discounts of 20% to 40%. After 2pm, students can call the Student Theatre Line, which is periodically updated with shows offering discounts that night (☎ 020/7379-8900). Make sure you have a recognized I.D. card with you—see p. 358 about that.

Soho, Leicester Square, and Piccadilly Circus are dotted with closet-sized stalls hawking tickets to major shows and concerts. You'll see lazy tourists queue up at some, but my advice is strong and simple: Don't deal with them. Whatever you buy from them will inevitably cost more than if you'd bought it direct from the box office. And I shouldn't have to warn you about scalpers, called **touts** here, because they often issue counterfeit tickets or abscond with your cash before forking over anything at all. Some passes, like the London Pass (p. 141), also brag about discounts, but they don't save you much—around £10 off the top price.

Once you get to London, grab a copy of *The Official London Theatre Guide*, dispensed for free in nearly every West End theater's lobby and at all tourist's offices; it tells you what's playing, where, for how much and how long, and the location of each theater. Unless you buy tickets for full price directly from the box office of the theater (which, unlike Ticketmaster and its ilk, don't slap you with huge extra fees), there's only one intelligent place to get tickets: **TKTS** (www.tkts.co.uk; booth on south side of Leicester Square; Mon–Sat 10am–7pm, Sun noon–3pm; MC, V or cash for tickets, up to £2.50 per ticket service charge), operated by

Curtain Time & Pre-Show Wine

- Standard curtain times range from 7:30 to 8pm for evening shows, and matinees start anywhere between 2 and 4pm. Every theater is different, so check your ticket. Nearly all theaters are closed, or "dark," on Sundays.
- Rare is the theater that doesn't sport some kind of bar or cafe facilities—a cultural requirement for pub-raised Londoners—making it easy to make a night of a show. West End theaters, rented out by producers, tend to stick to booze, but theater companies with their own buildings (such as the Almeida, the Old Vic, and the Menier Chocolate Factory) often run their own mid- to high-end restaurants.

the Society of London Theatre. It sells same-day seats at mostly half-price for all the major houses. While the white-hot shows won't be represented here, about 80% of West End shows are. A board of laminated cards lets you know which shows are available (a list on its website is also updated daily), and when it comes time to make a purchase, there's a window for matinees and one for evening shows. Musicals range from half price (£25) to full price (around £50); dance performances are around £18; and plays cost £20–£23. Come armed with a magazine or a newspaper that lists what the shows are about because TKTS offers no descriptions. TKTS operates a second, no-cash booth at Canary Wharf (on platforms 4 and 5 at the Canary Warf DLR station; Mon–Sat 10am–3:30pm), but it's handier for business workers than tourists.

BEYOND THE USUAL WEST END FARE

The main West End theaters—the ones you'll see advertised in brochures and on the sides of double-decker buses—are mostly commercial ventures. They tend to show stuff that producers think will yield big audiences. That doesn't mean that the slate is comprised entirely of Vegas-style schlock or unadventurous revivals because the West End is still where you find some of the world's most acclaimed talent. But it does mean the shows there are generally the most crowd-pleasing, and enjoy all the positive and negative associations that come with mass appeal.

For challenging work mounted by producers intent on taking artistic risks, look to the many theater companies found elsewhere around town. Many of them have designed and built their own facilities expressly for pumping out fresh shows, and each of them has a devoted following of fans and donors that most tourists, because of the circles they travel in, don't hear about. Because these fringe companies put such a premium on developing quality material, you're just as likely to find a winner off–West End as you are on it. In fact, many West End shows began life as sold-out runs in these smaller houses. What's more, you're just as likely to catch the stars of tomorrow—all at prices that are half what you'd shell out for a West End megamusical that was created by committee.

Soho, Covent Garden & Trafalgar Square

Also see The Barbican Centre (p. 294).

You can't often snag a last-minute ticket to the 250-seat **Donmar Warehouse** ★★★ (41 Earlham St., WC2; ☎ 020/8544-7412; www.donmarwarehouse. com; Tube: Covent Garden) without standing in line for returns. Its productions, mostly limited runs of vividly reconceived revivals, are simply too hip and buzzy. Past coups for this comfortably converted brewery warehouse include the *Cabaret* revival that swept Broadway and appearances by world-class performers such as Ian McKellan, Nicole Kidman, and highly regarded British actors like Adrian Lester, Simon Russell Beale, and Jennifer Ehle. For edgy productions that are just palatable enough to be popular, it's top of the list.

For cultural thrills, try **The Drill Hall** ★ (16 Chenies St., WC1; ☎ 020/7307-5060; www.drillhall.co.uk; Tube: Goodge Street), a theater-and-cabaret venue with two houses that swing with adventurous works concerning sex, gender, and politics. A two-woman version of *The Marriage of Figaro*? Check. A play about an angry lesbian who fakes a stigmata to get back at the Catholic church? Sure. Regular appearances by lightly clad performance artist Tim Miller? Yup. Expect short, experimental runs, and even more frisson. Tickets usually cost £8.

Most of the best stuff mounted by the vaunted **Royal Shakespeare Company** ★★ (☎ 01789/403-444; www.rsc.org.uk) happens at its 5.6-hectare (14-acre) site (currently being rebuilt) up in Stratford-upon-Avon, but it does maintain a presence in London: principally, the Novello Theatre on Aldwych (Tube: Temple or Covent Garden), where you'll find a repertory of classic plays put on by some of the industry's most esteemed actors. Where Shakespeare's Globe has built a reputation for approaching old texts with trailblazing new ideas, the RSC is best described as supplying definitive versions of The Bard's work (albeit with some digressions made by splashy directors). The RSC also cultivates the youth market by selling £5 seats, including some of the best in the house, to those 16 to 25.

The well-heeled **Soho Theatre** ★ (21 Dean St., W1; ☎ 020/7478-0100; www. sohotheatre.com; Tube: Tottenham Court Road), which functions like an ongoing one-building arts festival, doesn't linger over any of its triumphs or its failures for long. With lightning-quick changeover (just a few weeks for most shows), it casts a wide net in looking for the latest voices in theater, comedy, cabaret, and wacky stunts (such as young writers given 300 min. to write a play about their youth). There's always something unusual going on. Tickets can be dead cheap; as low as £5. Check its website for discounted performances.

Another promising potpourri on the arts scene is **Trafalgar Studios** ★ (14 Whitehall, SW1; ☎ 0870/060-6632; www.theambassadors.com/trafalgarstudios; Tube: Charing Cross), with two spaces (in the gorgeous ebony-and-silver former Whitehall Theatre, located just south of Trafalgar Square) cultivating productions chosen more for their contemporary commercial potential than for their artiness. The menu is new plays, carefully chosen revivals, and small-scale comic performances that, it's hoped, will graduate to long runs in other West End houses. Among its recent attractions were shows with Alan Cumming and Antony Sher, and a revival of *Sweeney Todd* that later swept Broadway. On many Wednesdays at 10pm, it mounts Late Night Comedy (£5).

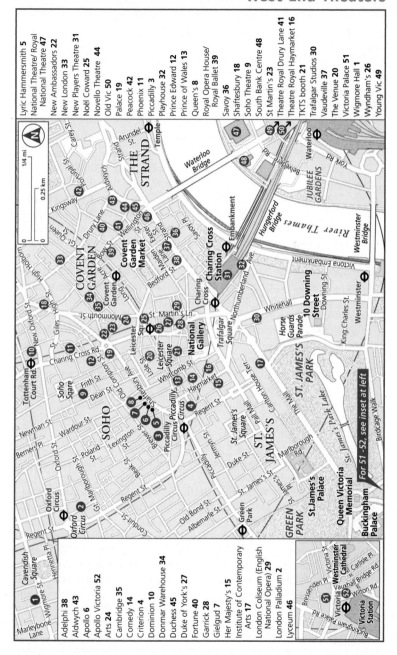

Lyric Hammersmith **5**
National Theatre Royal
National Theatre **47**
New Ambassadors **22**
New London **33**
New Players Theatre **31**
Noël Coward **25**
Novello Theatre **44**
Old Vic **50**
Palace **19**
Peacock **42**
Phoenix **11**
Piccadilly **3**
Playhouse **32**
Prince Edward **12**
Prince of Wales **13**
Queen's **8**
Royal Opera House/
Royal Ballet **39**
Savoy **36**
Shaftesbury **18**
Soho Theatre **9**
South Bank Centre **48**
St Martin's **23**
Theatre Royal Drury Lane **41**
Theatre Royal Haymarket **16**
TKTS booth **21**
Trafalgar Studios **30**
Vaudeville **37**
The Venue **20**
Victoria Palace **51**
Wigmore Hall **1**
Wyndham's **26**
Young Vic **49**

Adelphi **38**
Aldwych **43**
Apollo **6**
Apollo Victoria **52**
Arts **24**
Cambridge **35**
Comedy **14**
Criterion **4**
Dominion **10**
Donmar Warehouse **34**
Duchess **45**
Duke of York's **27**
Fortune **40**
Garrick **28**
Gielgud **7**
Her Majesty's **15**
Institute of Contemporary
Arts **17**
London Coliseum (English
National Opera) **29**
London Palladium **2**
Lyceum **46**

293

The Do-It-All Venues

In London, the arts are well-funded and well-patronized. These three arts complexes hum year-round with some of the best entertainment not just in town, but from traveling companies from around the world, which consider London a crucial stop on the arts circuit.

The Barbican Centre ✹ (Silk St., EC2; ☎ 020/7638-8891; www.barbican.org.uk; Tube: Barbican) was built in the 1950s, when earnest but misguided city fathers turned their attentions toward redeveloping a bombed-out crater. The end result was a preposterously forbidding, mixed-use luxury residential/business complex that took more than 20 years to finish. They optimistically planned for lively crowds by adding Europe's largest arts and conference center, too, with a concert hall, two theaters, three cinemas, and two galleries.

You can't always find something going on in all of its venues, and even when things are rocking full-tilt, the bunkered Barbican still feels so windswept it makes *Blade Runner* look like Candy Land, but what does play here is rarely dull. It hosted the first English-language run of the musical *Les Misérables* in 1985, and today is the home of the celebrated theater company Cheek By Jowl (www.cheekbyjowl.com), which often re-envisions classic texts to critical praise. It's nearly impossible to classify the Barbican's fare, since it receives a wide range of the world's great orchestras, singers, and composers, plus a handful of banner festivals each year, particularly in the realm of contemporary music and experimental theater. Its cinemas often screen features fresh from major film festival triumphs, and the loftily titled Young Genius program commissions new work from hot names. When you check out its website (tickets are cheaper if you book online), don't neglect the "Education" section, which lists family events (like sing-alongs) and talks by famous directors and (ironically, I think) architects. There are often free exhibitions in the Concourse Gallery, as well as in the foyer galleries.

To reach the main entrance from the Barbican Tube stop, head east on Beech Street, then turn right on Whitecross. Have a wander around this drab concrete carbuncle for a lesson in the dangers of hyperactive urban planning. On the grounds are the Guildhall School of Music and Drama (famous graduates: Ewan McGregor, Joseph Fiennes, and Orlando Bloom), a lake that buffers the noise from the Circle Line running underneath, the superlative Museum of London, and by the roundabout at London Wall,

Southwark

Also see the South Bank Centre (p. 295).

In an intimate setting among exposed beams and cast iron columns, **Menier Chocolate Factory** ✹✹ (51-53 Southwark St., SE1; ☎ 020/7907-7060; www.

ruins from old Roman fortifications. Interestingly, those stones are a link to the Barbican's performance history; in Elizabethan times, the area lay just outside the walled city, where theater was illegal, and it therefore was one of the few places you could catch a show. A forlorn artistic outsider: That's been the Barbican for 400 years.

Sadler's Wells (Rosebery Ave., EC1; ☎ 020/7863-8198; www.sadler-swells.com; Tube: Angel) has been a part of the fabric of London life for so long (since 1683) that its current two-house home, dating to 1998, is actually the sixth. Today, you can turn to this Islington establishment to catch some of the world's greatest companies in movement- or rhythm-based performances that transcend language. Its specialties are ballet (Matthew Bourne is a frequent guest artist), contemporary dance, and opera, with plenty of deserving international companies (the Ballet National de Cuba, as an example) and themed festivals (Brazilian samba, Indian theater) rounding out its boisterous, high-minded, multicultural seasons. The company also runs the Peacock Theatre on Kingsway east of the Covent Garden district (Tube: Holborn).

Like the Barbican, **South Bank Centre** (Belvedere Rd., SE1; ☎ 020/7960-4242; www.rfh.org.uk; Tube: Waterloo), a bleak canvas-colored slab, was conceived as a postwar pick-me-up, but age has not been kind; despite a peerless riverside location (once the site of the Lion Brewery), it's got a reputation as a forbidding architectural scowl that looks more like a pile of sidewalk curbs than an artistic capitol. It's perkier on the inside. Hit its website before visiting, because it's chockablock with listings for free and family-oriented events; some 1,000 events go down here at its three concert venues. Dance, classical and contemporary music, the London Jazz Festival, and films fill the bill, but by no means define it—you'll also find readings of new fiction, film, the Hayward Gallery for art (p. 182), the Poetry Library (Britain's largest collection of 20th-century poetry, with 90,000 volumes), and the classical music Mecca called the Royal Festival Hall. At concerts where the onstage choir seats aren't in use, you can often buy them for £6. The whole complex re-opens in June 2007 after 2 years of rotating renovation. Whether that will turn it from a godforsaken skateboarders' haunt to a vibrant magnet for people who linger more than 2 minutes past the final curtain? That's yet to be seen.

menierchocolatefactory.com; Tube: London Bridge), a converted you-know-what from the 1870s, is where some of the city's hottest shows have been mounted recently. In 2006, its *Sunday in the Park with George* transferred to the West End, and it produced the U.K. premiere of Jason Robert Brown's chamber musical *The*

Last Five Years. Ask about its top-value "meal deal" (£27.50), which combines a two-course dinner at its modern English restaurant with a ticket to the show.

American star Kevin Spacey moved to London to run the **Old Vic** ★ (The Cut at Waterloo Rd., SE1; ☎ 0870/060-6628; www.oldvictheatre.com; Tube: Waterloo or Southwark), and although the fruits of his stewardship have been mixed and he grabs the limelight as an actor here a little more than an artistic director probably should, his choices (generally mountings of talky, meat-and-potatoes drama—stuff actors love to sink their teeth into) have been mostly decent, if not barnstorming. And there's little doubt that under his steerage, the 200-year-old building is pulling bigger crowds than it did before. Those under 25 can snare a limited number of £12 tickets; otherwise, nosebleed seats usually start at £15.

Beside the Thames near the London Eye, the government-subsidized **Royal National Theatre** ★★★ (South Bank, SE1; ☎ 020/7452-3000; www.national theatre.org.uk; Tube: Waterloo), often simply called The National, is perhaps the country's most noted showpiece for top-flight drama and acting, and the frequent home of the city's hottest tickets. Every London-based theater nut ends up enjoying a show here at least a few times a year. Nicholas Hytner (*The History Boys*, *The Crucible*), its director, is one of the theater world's luminaries, and he plans a diverse repertoire for its three theaters that runs from envelope-pushing musicals (*Jerry Springer: The Opera*) to classic revivals (the Hugh Jackman *Oklahoma!*) to a huge range of dramas, including world premieres by famous writers cast with household names. Actors consider it a privilege to tread the boards at this modern theatrical complex, and the season runs year-round. Two-thirds of the tickets for every performance in its Travelex season, which usually includes about four plays, are just £10; the rest are £28. Check out its Platforms series, which features talks and performances by visiting artists and entertainment legends for £3.50. In the summer, its outdoor spaces host free screenings and performances; look into its Watch This Space series for what's up.

American actor and director Sam Wanamaker came to London in the 1950s and saw what locals didn't: The city had nowhere to see plays the way they were presented in the heyday of Elizabethan theater. He spent the next few decades struggling to re-create one of the principal houses of the early 1600s, and for its location, he naturally chose Southwark, where, back then, the city's performing halls were temporarily relegated. The new **Shakespeare's Globe** ★★★ (21 New Globe Walk, Bankside, SE1; ☎ 020/7902-1400; www.shakespeares-globe.com; Tube: London Bridge or Cannon Street), constructed using the old timber-and-plaster method, finally opened, 180m (600 ft.) northwest of its first location, with a few concessions to modern design (fire sprinklers, for one) in 1997; by 2011, it will already have outlasted the original. The best way to enjoy this open-air theater, located on the southern bank of the Thames, is to attend a play. Shows—so inventively conceived that the Globe has been called "the most free place in the country"—are performed in repertory from May to October. Seats are £15 to £26 in the gallery of this "wooden O," but you get the most immediacy as a "groundling" in the "Yard" in front of the thrust stage. Standing room is just £5, and although I can't believe I'm saying it, it's surprising how easy it is to be on your feet during a show—particularly here, where audience participation, in the form of cheers, hisses, and clapping—is as encouraged today as it was 400 years ago. (During a production of *The Merchant of Venice* in its inaugural season, I attended with a friend who cheered Shylock, normally the "villain," in support of his counterculture attitude—and no one blinked.) The quality of the performances, most critics agree, is very high, and productions strive not to talk over the heads of the audience. In addition to an exhibition and guided tours of the replica theater, the theater, which puts an emphasis on education, sponsors these regular events:

♦ In the free "Talking Theatre" series, audiences may talk with company members directly after many Wednesday and Saturday matinees.

♦ After some Tuesday night shows, Shakespeare scholars hold forth in the "Setting the Scene" talks series. (Adults £5, students £3.)

♦ In the "Read Not Dead and Rarely Played" series, which happens every couple of weeks in the summer, largely forgotten plays by Shakespeare's contemporaries are dusted off for staged readings. (Adults £10, students £6.)

♦ The "Childsplay" program for kids 8 to 11 is like a babysitting service. While parents see the show, kids participate in a workshop about the same play, and then they're brought into the theater as groundlings to see about 20 minutes of the performance. (£10 per child.)

As if all that weren't enough, the theater also has an exhibition space and regular tours; check the "Attractions" chapter for information (p. 189).

A rare children's theater that caters to kids without suffering from over-precious programming or a depressing lack of funding, **The Unicorn Theatre** 👶 ★ (147 Tooley St., SE1; ☎ 020/7645-0500; www.unicorntheatre.com; Tube: London Bridge) is operating on a high note, having opened its very own state-of-the-art facility near the theater cluster of Bankside in 2005. At least two productions, one for each of its theater spaces, run at a time; some are script-based and some sensory-based for younger kids and kids with autism. Many shows are designed to expose kids to other cultures, places, and classic stories for the first time. Everything is carefully classified according to the age for which it's appropriate. If only every city had a kids' facility as lush as this one.

Spry and in fighting form following the complete rebuilding of its theater-and-cafe complex, completed in late 2006, the **Young Vic** 👶 ★ (66 The Cut, SE1; ☎ 020/7928-6363; www.youngvic.org; Tube: Waterloo or Southwark) makes a habit of pairing new, unknown talent with established directors and actors, stepping back, and hoping for frisson. It often achieves it, and if it fails, it doesn't dally long, since it has three theaters (seating 500, 160, and 80) to fill. Odd musicals, plays from other countries, experimental (but approachable) drama—the programming is limber. Around the holidays, it mounts original family shows. It often furnishes discount tickets for students.

North London, Including Islington & Camden

Also see Sadler's Wells (p. 295).

One of the nice things about the **Almeida Theatre** ★★ (Almeida St. off Upper St., N1; ☎ 020/7359-4404; www.almeida.co.uk; Tube: Angel) is the way it sticks to its guns, mounting intelligent plays (some new, some translated, some unfairly forgotten, many in their European premiers) without much regard for their mass appeal—although it sometimes scores the odd A-list performer. The resulting experience is often thought-provoking and usually satisfying. It's also well-funded enough to have a clean, modern facility (including a pub, although plenty of

Stalls, Circles & Ice Cream

London theater has its own traditions, which you should be aware of:

◆ Programs are not free; they cost from £2 (for plays) to £5 (for musicals). On top of that, big musicals will also sell a glossy souvenir brochure for £7 to £10.

◆ Some seats are equipped with inexpensive plastic opera glasses, which can be rented for the duration with a 50p or £1 coin.

◆ What North American theaters call "orchestra" seats, London houses call the "stalls." And instead of a "mezzanine," they have a "Dress Circle," and above that, "Upper Circle" or "Royal Circle." If there happens to be a third, topmost level, that is the "balcony," or sometimes, the "gallery." And because many theaters were constructed in a class-obsessed era, there will likely be a separate street entrance for each area.

◆ The break between acts is called an "interval," not "intermission."

◆ The big snack? Ice cream, sold by ushers (or "attendants").

◆ Older theaters are required to deploy the "fire curtain," which seals the stage from the auditorium in the event of flames, once during every performance. It's usually done discreetly during the interval.

◆ A century ago, people were smaller, so there isn't much space in old venues' seats. Leave big bags at the hotel. And ladies, cover your knees, because in the Circles, they will likely be at face-level of the person sitting in front of you.

◆ Londoners generally do not give standing ovations, no matter how brilliant the performance. If you're pleased, applaud more vigorously.

others are nearby) that any theater company would envy. In the summer, it runs a season of scaled-down opera and musicals. The lowest tier costs £6, but when those go, £10 tickets from Monday to Thursday and for Saturday matinees are set aside for students and seniors.

Making just as much of a lower budget, **Arcola Theatre** ★★★ (27 Arcola St., E8; ☎ 020/7503-1646; www.arcolatheatre.com; Mainline rail: Dalston Kingsland), set in a former textiles factory, was founded in 2000 and rose to prominence quickly, regularly impressing critics. They must all have cars because Hackney is not a breeze to reach (it requires a change of Mainline trains or a long, long walk from the Tube). The Arcola's shows, mostly by cool contemporary writers (Adam Rapp, Sam Shepard, and names yet to be in lights), run a month each at the most, keeping the bill brisk. On Tuesdays if there are seats available by 7pm, the theater sponsors "Pay What You Can" sales; arrive with some loose change and an obvious foreign accent. Otherwise, you'll usually pay £12.

New End Theatre (27 New End, NW3; ☎ 0870/033-2733; www.newendtheatre. co.uk; Tube: Hampstead) was built in Hampstead as a mortuary, but since conversion to an 84-seat theater in 1974, it has breathed life into countless world premieres, including some written by Jean Anouilh, Richard Curtis, and Anthony Minghella. Its past talent includes Judi Dench and Emma Thompson.

Reopened in 2006 after a lavish £29.7-million redevelopment, **Roundhouse** ★★ (Chalk Farm Rd., NW1; ☎ 020/7424-9991; www.roundhouse.org.uk; Tube: Chalk Farm), located in a rehabbed 1846 locomotive shed, picks up on the maverick spirit of neighboring Camden with a frisky lineup of innovative theatrical creations such as musical dramas and spectaculars, many of them given a crowd-pleasing, dance-inflected twist. In the 1960s, it was one of London's most important stages. In addition to triumphs from Peter Brook, Nicol Williamson, Helen Mirren, and Tony Richardson; Jimi Hendrix, Pink Floyd, and The Doors played here. It was the place to catch seminal musicals like *Oh! Calcutta!* and *Godspell.* In more recent seasons, it scored with a limited-run appearance by American agitator Michael Moore and the premiere of the funky, kinesthetic *Fuerzabruta,* by the creators of the acrobatic smash *De La Guarda.* Check out its separate events schedule, which often includes student fashion showcases and career advice for artists, all for free or for as little as £1.

For an ethical challenge, try the **Tricycle** ★★ (269 Kilburn High Rd., NW6; ☎ 020/7328-1000; www.tricycle.co.uk; Tube: Kilburn), which evolved from a simple pub theater to a homegrown arts complex (theater, cinema, art gallery, workshop space, cafe) that now specializes in topical and political theater. It mounted the British premieres of *Ain't Misbehavin'* and four August Wilson plays, and its productions of *Kat & the Kings* and *Stones in His Pockets* transferred to the West End and later to Broadway. It often finds a subversive way to make a nuanced political point; famously, one show hashed out West Bank atrocities while cooking aromatic Middle Eastern dishes onstage.

West London, Including Kensington & Notting Hill

The rickety **Gate Theatre** (11 Pembridge Rd., W11; ☎ 020/7229-5387; www.gate theatre.co.uk; Tube: Notting Hill Gate), a black-box, 70-seat space in Notting Hill, puts a premium on fine acting and on producing international work, such as *Tejas Verdas,* about the horrors of Pinochet's Chile, and Eugene O'Neill's rarely mounted, Expressionist *The Emperor Jones.* Its reputation is strong.

You'll find spectacular stuff at the **Lyric Hammersmith** [kids] ★ (Lyric Square, King Street, S6; ☎ 0870/0500-511; www.lyric.co.uk; Tube: Hammersmith), which may look like a fusty Victorian jewel-box theater, but in fact hosts a distinctive mix of multimedia-based shows, avant garde experiments by established writers, and an annual Christmas show to write home about. Its kids shows are its bread and butter. A second, smaller house, the Lyric Studio, is where the wildest stuff is seen. Check its calendar for £9 nights and £7 Studio nights; otherwise, tickets range from £10 to £27 for the main house and £7 to £12 for the Studio.

Back in the 1870s, a Dissenters' chapel on the south side of Sloane Square was converted into a theater, and that space evolved into one of the city's most crucial venues, producing 11 plays by George Bernard Shaw, including the premieres of *Major Barbara* and *Heartbreak House.* Still one of the world's leaders in presenting new plays by rising writers, the prestigious **Royal Court Theatre** ★★ (Sloane Square, SW1; ☎ 020/7565-5000; www.royalcourttheatre.com; Tube: Sloane Square) devotes a hefty portion of its schedule to important premieres from the likes of Tom Stoppard and performances from esteemed actors such as Fiona Shaw. Everything I've ever seen here has been memorable in some way, even if I sometimes felt it could use another draft—but the theater does have a proud tradition of fighting censorship of any kind, so perhaps that stubbornness extends to the authors' willingness to hone their drafts. Among the classics launched here were John Osborne's *Look Back in Anger* and *The Rocky Horror Picture Show,* and past artistic directors include *The Hours* director Stephen Daldry. Investigate upcoming shows before leaving home; since many of its titles catch buzz, the intimate houses can sell out quickly. Seats are just £10 for any play on any Monday evening (shows change often but usually spotlight new talent); get tickets in advance for its downstairs theater, and from 10am on the same day for the upstairs theater, which has unreserved seating. Frequent readings of new plays are also held for £7.50.

The East End

One of London's greatest super ornate old theaters, the **Hackney Empire** ★ (291 Mare St., E8; ☎ 020/8510-4500; www.hackneyempire.co.uk; Mainline rail: Hackney Central or Hackney Downs, or Tube: Bethnal Green, then bus D6, 106 or 253 north) was where, once upon a time, you could catch Charlie Chaplin before he became a superstar. It's still a glitter box brimming with life and applause. Several performance spaces are overseen by an industrious management, so there's always something going on here, be it kids' shows, drama, dance, or comedy— even the occasional karate championship. You could say its glory days as a variety hall are back, which suits me fine, for as long as pleasure palaces like these survive, London's culture will be rich. Tickets generally start around £10.

OTHER AUDIENCE OPTIONS: DIVAS, CONDUCTORS & TV

The West End is a world-class carnival of theatrical delights, but don't let it overshadow London's strong traditions in the other performing arts. Opera and classical music, and to a lesser extent, dance, exert powerful presences on the seasonal calendar. Always check to see if any celebrated international companies are bringing productions to town for a limited run; if they're good enough to warrant an expensive trip across the sea, they'll almost certainly be worth it.

OPERA

Opera's a budget-breaker. Frugal travelers should try the street singers who perform daily at the **Covent Garden Piazza** (Tube: Covent Garden). That's not a joke: Performers are auditioned before being awarded buskers' licenses, so the caliber here is high. Also check to see if there's a touring opera putting down stakes at Sadler's Wells (p. 295). Of course, nothing compares to these institutions:

English National Opera ★★ (The Coliseum, St. Martin's Lane, WC2; ☎ 020/7632-8300; www.eno.org; Tube: Leicester Square). With the Royal Opera entrenched as the country's premium company, the ENO relies on progressive programming (*Nixon in China;* a piece about Muammar Qadhafi)—all sung in English—and the gloriously refurbished London Coliseum theater (topped with a revolving globe) to pull the posh punters. Tickets start around £19, with seats at the sides of the very-high-up balcony (price code P10) starting at £10 on weekdays. In an ongoing "Sky Seats" promotion, 12,000 seats in the Dress Circle, excluding Friday and Saturday nights, are £25 off (reserve at ☎ 0870/160-6059). Students can queue for unsold tickets for £13 with I.D.; the general public pays £30 for the same seats. Once all seats are sold, the ENO releases standing room at the back of the Dress and Upper circles, not the stalls, for £5.

Opera fans don't need to be reminded of the role the **Royal Opera House** ★★ (Bow St., Covent Garden, WC2; ☎ 020/7304-4000; www.royaloperahouse.org.uk; Tube: Covent Garden) plays on the world scene, but outsiders might be surprised at how inviting and attractive its home is. No longer a fusty upper-class enclave, the place changed the way it does business in 1999 after a 30-month renovation; now, instead of being open only to ticketholders, the general public are able to enjoy its cafe and panoramic terrace, as well as (for select performances) hear the music outside when performances begin. The main house, which is shared by the equally prestigious Royal Opera and Royal Ballet, was supplemented with a 400-seat space, the Linbury, for chamber opera and dance, as well as the Clore, a Royal Ballet studio seating 180. Standing room for the biggest productions is £8, and the lousiest seats start at £13 and zoom up to £180 for the stalls. Sniff around for its Travelex Mondays, when 100 tickets cost just £10; seats can be applied for in advance. Students can also pay £10 for unsold tickets but must sign up in advance online to receive e-mail alerts.

DANCE PERFORMANCE

London's dance scene has yet to achieve the vibrancy of New York's or Germany's. That's not to say there's nothing to see; it's just that some of the best terpsichorean productions are put on by visiting companies, not by Londoners. Check The Barbican (p. 294), Roundhouse (p. 299), Sadler's Wells (p. 295), and South Bank Centre (p. 295), which present a cornucopia of performance genres. To find out about one-off performances, check *Time Out*'s "Dance" section.

Laban (Creekside, Greenwich, SW8; ☎ 020/8691-8600; www.laban.org; Tube: Cutty Sark DLR), the lucky tenant of a gleaming new building by the same team that designed the Tate Modern, puts on a mixed bill (£3–£20) from hip-hop to Flamenco, as well as by up-and-comers from its dance school.

The Place ★★★ (17 Duke's Rd., WC1; ☎ 020/7121-1000; www.theplace. org.uk; Tube: Euston) is known for contemporary dance—specifically, both as the home of the Richard Alson Dance Company, the London School of Contemporary Dance, and the host venue of some 100 companies a year from around the world. Prices start at £5 and don't often go higher than £15, and there are no assigned seats.

Royal Ballet ★★ (Bow St., Covent Garden, WC2; ☎ 020/7304-4000; www. royaloperahouse.org.uk; Tube: Covent Garden), known as the country's premier ballet company, caters to classicists and attracts the biggest talents in the dance world. It shares the Royal Opera House with the Royal Opera, which means performances have to be shuffled accordingly. The company often mounts smaller, slightly more experimental work in the building's two smaller performance and rehearsal spaces, the Linbury Studio and the Clore Studio Upstairs.

CLASSICAL MUSIC

With 900 seats, **Cadogan Hall** ★ (5 Sloane Terrace, SW1; ☎ 020/7730-4500; www.cadoganhall.com; Tube: Sloane Square), is a onetime Christian Scientist church now regularly used by the English Chamber Orchestra, the Royal Philharmonic Orchestra, and the BBC Proms, which books it during the summer as a supplement to its concerts at Royal Albert Hall. Tickets are £10 to £35.

Imposing, ornate, and adored by music lovers worldwide, the circular **Royal Albert Hall** ★★★ (Kensington Gore, SW7; ☎ 020/7589-3203; www.royalalbert hall.com; Tube: South Kensington) is one of the few performance arenas on earth where, once they have performed there, artists can truly claim to have made it. During the summer, the BBC Promenade Concerts (the Proms) fill this historic, 5,200-seat hall with classical music, but the rest of the year, the space books a hodgepodge of tours, arena-style musicals, Cirque du Soleil, concerts (the house organ is 21m/70 ft. tall and has 10,000 pipes)—even tennis matches. During summer, RAH's Ignite series of free lunchtime concerts are held most Fridays at noon in its Cafe Consort, but otherwise, whether there are discounted tickets available is up to the promoter of each show. See p. 190 for tour information.

In addition to its lunchtime concerts, **St. Martin-in-the-Fields'** ★★★ (Trafalgar Square, WC2; ☎ 020/7839-8362; www.stmartin-in-the-fields.org; Tube: Charing Cross) evening Concerts by Candlelight (Tues and Thurs–Sat) are popular occasions to flick your Bic to Baroque, chamber, and Early music. Tickets range from £6 to £22, depending on the act and how far back you sit, but the acoustics are terrific, so don't fret about paying less.

Opened in 1901 as a recital hall for the Bechstein piano showroom that was once next door, **Wigmore Hall** ★★ (36 Wigmore St., W1; ☎ 020/7935-2141; www.wigmore-hall.org.uk; Tube: Bond Street) was seized (along with the company) as enemy property in World War I. A nasty start, but it soon reopened as one of the world's great chamber concert halls. Today, it's known for ideal acoustics and a roster of some 400 concerts a year. Outside of summer, it hosts Monday lunchtime concerts that are simulcast on BBC Radio 3. They're a great value at £8 to £10, as opposed to up to £20 for the same seats at night.

Also check out the listings for the Barbican (p. 294), the South Bank Centre (p. 295), and the city's lunchtime concerts (p. 210).

MUSEUMS THAT PARTY

Because so many of London's museums cost nothing to visit, free-entry evenings are not as prominent here as they are in other cities. But that doesn't mean that a few showcases don't know how to jam. Londoners use these occasions to limber up after a long day's work with a glass of wine and some framed eye candy.

Visiting a museum during evening hours is also a smart way to unclog your schedule; wherever possible, it frees up time to see museums or attractions that don't have late hours. The only down side to these events is that some institutions tend to close off less popular galleries. Be sure to give yourself enough time; most museums don't admit patrons 30 to 45 minutes before the posted closing.

Wednesday: The venerable **National Gallery** (Trafalgar Square, WC2; ☎ 020/ 7747-2885; www.nationalgallery.org.uk; Tube: Charing Cross) stays open until 9pm. Some patrons actually take the chance to file past the masterpieces, but many more dally in the bar overlooking Trafalgar Square.

Thursday: The British Museum (Great Russell St., WC1; ☎ 020/7323-8000; www.thebritishmuseum.ac.uk; Tube: Tottenham Court Road or Holborn) keeps its galleries open an extra 3 hours until 8:30pm. The **National Portrait Gallery** (St. Martin's Place, WC2; ☎ 020/7312-2463; www.npg.org.uk; Tube: Leicester Square) keeps its doors unlocked an extra three hours, until 9pm.

Friday: It's the big night! The **Tate Modern** (Bankside, SE1; ☎ 020/7887-8888; www.tate.org.uk/modern; Tube: Southwark or London Bridge) throws light across the Thames all the way until 10pm, and its second-level cafe and panoramic seventh-level restaurant entertains revelers until closing time. **The British Museum** is open until 8:30, and the **National Portrait Gallery** again closes at 9pm. Across town on the last Friday of the month, the **V&A's Friday Lates** (Cromwell Rd., SW7; ☎ 020/7942-2000; www.vam.ac.uk; Tube: South Kensington) throws in funky perks such as guest DJs, fashion shows, and a bar— all to changing themes such as Cuban culture or garden design. And on the first Friday of the month, **Late at Tate Britain** (Millbank, SW1; ☎ 020/7887-8888; www.tate.org.uk/britain; Tube: Pimlico) combines drinks, performances, talks, and concerts with a 10pm closing, about 4 hours past the usual deadline.

Saturday: The **Tate Modern** again posts a 10pm closing.

All week: The **Institute of Contemporary Arts** (The Mall, SW1; ☎ 020/7930-3647; www.ica.org.uk; Tube: Charing Cross) is open until 1am Tuesday to Saturday and 11pm Sunday. On Monday, it's comparatively sleepy, closing at 10:30pm. Many of its most popular talks, performances, and screenings are scheduled for the evening. Its bar stays open, too.

COMEDY CLUBS

London's comedy scene—surprise!—is dominated by Edinburgh's. Each August in the Scottish capital, hordes of wannabe laughmakers head north for the city's famous festival season, where they vie for awards, audiences, and perversely, that shiniest of brass rings, a major London booking. The rest of the year, it seems that half the stages in town are either helping artists groom material for Edinburgh or cashing in on past successes. The fevered competition has created a comedy scene that has less in common with the stand-and-discuss neuroses of New York clubs and more to do with the brittle high concepts of, say, Monty Python or *Little Britain*. All the venues serve food and drink (not included in the ticket price), while shows are usually at 7:30 or 8pm and finish in time for you to catch the Tube home. There's a concentration of venues in the Camden Town/Chalk Farm area.

Amused Moose (Moonlighting, 17 Greek St., W1; Tube: Tottenham Court Road; www.amusedmoose.com; prices are £11 if you bring along a printout of its online show listings; £13 if you forget; or The Progress Bar, 162 Tufnell Park Rd., N7; ☎ 020/7287-3727; Tube: Tufnell Park) has been around long enough for some of its new talent to be famous, and for old talent to validate it with appearances: Screen comics Ricky Gervais, Dave Gorman, and Mackenzie Crook have all performed here. Its banner show is its Saturday night showcase at the Soho pub Moonlighting, but it sometimes books nights at Tufnell Parks' Progress Bar.

Canal Café Theatre ★ (The Bridge House, Delamere Terrace, W2; ☎ 020/7289-6054; www.canalcafetheatre.com; cover £9; Tube: Warwick Avenue) a

The English Channels

At home, TV can suck your schedule dry, but I'm all for watching a little on vacation. TV distills a society's character like nothing else. I can learn more about a place from its soap operas and game shows than I can from a week's worth of newspapers—and I find locals would much rather talk about their favorite programs than the woes of the world. Make a point of tuning into these shows, which occupy an important place in pop culture. Double-check airtimes in the newspaper—they tend to hop around:

Weekdays at 3:30pm, Channel Four: Countdown. This game show for brainiacs was given its due as a couch-potato institution in the 2002 Hugh Grant movie *About a Boy*. Its 30-second ditty, played as contestants solve word and math puzzles, is the U.K. equivalent of the *Jeopardy!* theme. Letter-woman Carol Vorderman has carved a niche as a Mensa-approved entertainer—she even publishes her own line of Sodoku books.

Weekdays at 5:35pm, BBC One: Neighbours, a squeaky-clean suburban "soapie," launched the careers of Kylie Minogue, Guy Pearce, and Natalie Imbruglia. Made in Melbourne, Australia, it's so beloved in Mother England it might as well be British—in fact, the British market is one reason it's still in production. Another bubbly Australian soap, set on the New South Wales seaside, is Home and Away (weekdays at 6pm, Channel Five).

Weekdays at 5pm, Channel Four: Richard & Judy is a chat show emceed by the First Couple of British gab, married Richard Madeley and Judy Finnigan. They're the British version of North America's Regis and Kelly or Australia's Bert Newton—mainstream, reassuring, and attractive to big-name guests who know they'll be treated with kid gloves.

table-cluttered space, has up to 14 shows a week, but its most famous is "NewsRevue" (www.newsrevue.com) a send-up of current events, running since 1979 but updated weekly, that holds the Guinness record for the longest-running live comedy show; it plays Thursday through Sunday.

Chuckle Club ★★ (LSE Bar, Clare Market Building, Houghton St., Aldwych, WC2; ☎ 020/476-1672; www.chuckleclub.com; tickets are £10; Tube: Holborn), held each Saturday at the London School of Economics student union, books genuinely funny comics who share the bill with an equal complement of unknowns. All this despite its deeply unfunny name.

The 400-seat **The Comedy Store** ★★ (1A Oxendon St., SW1; ☎ 0870/0602-340; www.thecomedystore.biz; cover £13–£15; Tube: Leicester Square) was created in 1979 in imitation of clubs popular in New York. It pioneered the alternative movement that elevated Jennifer Saunders, Eddie Izzard, Ben Elton, and *Whose Line Is It Anyway?* to fame, and it's still considered the best place to catch the odd marquee name. Now and then, it's the setting for radio and TV broadcasts, in which case entry is free.

Weekdays, 7, 7:30, or 8:30pm, ITV: Coronation Street, Britain's longest-running soap, and often its top-rated show, has been sudsing along since 1960. "Corrie" is about the goings-on in the fictional industrial town of Weatherfield, near Manchester. William Roache, who plays Ken Barlow, has been on since the start; his character's 1981 wedding drew more viewers than that of Princess Diana and Prince Charles 2 days later.

Weekdays at 7:30pm, BBC One, repeated weekdays at 10pm, BBC Three: EastEnders, on since 1985 and set in the made-up borough of Walford, cashes in on the insular dynamic of life in East London. Its doyenne is pub landlady Peggy Mitchell, played by Barbara Windsor, a 1960s soubrette who looks younger by the year thanks to the knife. The cigarette-addicted, put-upon character of Dot Cotton (now known as Dot Branning) is embraced as a cultural archetype by ironic Brits.

Weekdays, 10:30pm, BBC Two: Newsnight is a current events program hosted by journalism icon Jeremy Paxman.

Mid-May, BBC One: For the **Eurovision Song Contest** (www.eurovision.tv), European countries submit and perform a hokey pop song, and then viewers vote for who was best. This cheesefest, an annual tradition since 1956, is unbelievably popular, with a worldwide audience peaking at one billion, and it started the careers of ABBA and Celine Dion; *Riverdance* was born during the tabulation interval in 1994.

Downstairs at the King's Head ✮ (2 Crouch End Hill, N8; ☎ 020/8340-1028; www.downstairsatthekingshead.com; tickets usually £4–£7; Tube: Finsbury Park) may appear to be an iffy hole in the wall, but in fact it's an admired haunt of well-known comedians who want to try out new stuff, as well as a launch pad for success stories. The best value is "Comedy Try Out Night" Thursdays, when 16 new acts appear (£4).

Hen & Chickens ✮✮✮ (109 St. Paul's Rd., N1; ☎ 020/7704-2001; www.henandchickens.com; cover £6–£12; Mainline rail: Highbury & Islington), a simple room above a pub popular with football fans, used to make its way on new plays, not all of them worthy, but it's been gravitating to comedy, attracting some top-drawer British names (Jimmy Carr, Danny Bhoy).

Jongleurs ✮ (Middle Yard, Camden Lock, Chalk Farm Rd., NW1; ☎ 0870/787-0707; www.jongleurs.com; tickets £15; Tube: Chalk Farm) has 17 locations around the U.K., and so while it brings in names, it also brings in a less discerning, heckle-prone clientele. Meals start at £5.95.

Laughing Horse (☎ 07796/17-11-90; www.laughinghorse.co.uk; cover £4) has roaming shows that spotlight rising (or, sometimes, sinking) performers, which is one reason it puts on one of the cheapest comedy nights in town. Mondays it's in residence at The Blue Posts pub in Soho (18 Kingly St., W1; Tube: Oxford Circus), Tuesdays, it's at the Coach and Horses pub in Soho (1 Great Marlborough St., W1; Tube: Oxford Circus).

Lee Hurst's Back Yard Comedy Club ✪ (231 Cambridge Heath Rd., E2; ☎ 020/7739-3122; www.leehurst.com; £12 in advance, £15 at the door; Tube: Bethnal Green), run by a TV personality, works hard to book comics (four nightly) who know what they're doing. The best night is Thursday, when you get a free curry dinner with the price of admission.

Pleasance Theatre Islington ✪✪ (Carpenters Mews, North Rd., N7; ☎ 020/7609-1800; www.pleasance.co.uk/islington; Tube: Caledonian Rd.; cover £5–£13), with two spaces, has stronger ties than most to Edinburgh; it operates the Scottish festival's chief comedy venue. It also presents some theater.

CINEMA

Hollywood's latest releases show up across the Atlantic anywhere from a few weeks to a couple of months after they've debuted in North America. Increasingly, though, the studios' biggest-budget features premiere in London the same week as they do in Los Angeles, to thwart would-be pirates. Major movie premieres are usually held at one of Leicester Square's giant cinemas, including the Odeon (24-26 Leicester Square, WC2; ☎ 0871/224-4007; www.odeon.co.uk; Tube: Leicester Square), from 1937, the largest cinema in the country, with seating for about 1,700. But tickets for Leicester Square theaters cost an outlandish £12.50. For better prices—in even more historic houses—you'll have to look elsewhere. Because so many handsome old cinemas have survived (although boring mall-style cineplexes are steadily advancing), movie-going can still feel like an event. In most theaters, you even select your seats when you buy your ticket.

After many decades during which the country's studio facilities were either closed or overtaken by international film projects, Britain is slowly learning to accept that its homegrown films are worth attending. *Four Weddings and a Funeral* wasn't a success in the U.K. until its distributor advertised that it had hit number one in America first. The release of *Shallow Grave* in 1994 is considered a watershed because it was one of the first U.K.-bred films in years to earn a profit at home. For more information about movies that are funded and filmed in the United Kingdom, check out the U.K. Film Council (www.ukfilmcouncil.org.uk), the government-backed booster association for the film industry.

One of the oldest houses showing movies in London, Coronet ✪ (103 Notting Hill Gate, W11; ☎ 020/7727-6705; www.coronet.org; Tube: Notting Hill Gate) was built as a small variety house in 1898. In 2004, news came that its owners had sold it to an area church. History buffs despaired of losing this fine institution, done up in rich reds and woods, until the church proudly revealed that it intended to spruce it up and continue operating it as a cinema. The story gets better: Tickets are normally £7, but on Tuesdays, they're half price. The cinema made an appearance in *Notting Hill*, in the scene when Hugh Grant's character wistfully attended a movie starring his estranged girlfriend (Julia Roberts).

One of my favorite ways to spend a Sunday in London is to sack out in front of one of my favorite screens in the world: **The Electric Cinema** ★★★ (191 Portobello Rd., W11; ☎ 020/7908-9696; www.electriccinema.co.uk; Tube: Ladbroke Grove or Notting Hill Gate). The leather seats are softer, deeper, and more private than anything you have at home, and each one is equipped with a footstool, table, and a wine basket—it's a luxurious, romantic way to pass a few hours. The bar in the back of the house sells everything you need, from crudité to booze. Meanwhile, the films, which change daily, hop between first-run and well-received art house movies—nothing too obscure—so if there's nothing worth seeing today, tomorrow is another story. Shockingly, this place stood derelict from 1993 to 2001, and only a fierce campaign saved it. It's an institution now; get seated early for the slightly ribald preview reels, which feature a thumbnail history of the building (built in 1910) and young British stars (like Andrew Lincoln from *Love Actually*) in unbilled cameos. Capacity isn't huge, so to get the best spots (such as the private two-seater sofas in the back), it's wise to book ahead.

Cineasts regard the **National Film Theatre** ★★★ (Belvedere Rd., South Bank, ☎ 020/7928-3232; www.bfi.org.uk/nft; £8.60; Tube: Waterloo), located a stone's throw downriver from the London Eye, as London's best filmhouse. The programming, by the British Film Institute (BFI), is extraordinarily broad and savvy, from classics to mainstream to historic—more than 1,000 titles a year. For example, on a day in a recent July, its three screens unspooled a rare 1924 color film shot by a British road-tripper, Alfred Hitchcock's *Rebecca*, a documentary on teenage songwriters from the 1960s, and the 1974 blood-soaked slasher *It's Alive*. As the country's preeminent archive and exhibitor, it also programs plenty of talks, special previews, and retrospectives—even the occasional free screening.

Thought to be the oldest purpose-built cinema in the U.K., the **Phoenix** ★ (52 High Rd., East Finchley, N2; ☎ 020/8444-6789; www.phoenixcinema.co.uk; Tube: East Finchley) was constructed as the Premier Electric Theatre in 1910; by 1985, despite its handsome Edwardian barrel-vault ceiling, it was nose-to-nose with the wrecker's ball before fans (including director Mike Leigh) rallied. Hollywood is the star here, though plenty of documentaries and Sunday afternoon classics are screened. It also has a liquor license. The £4.50 Monday shows are more than reasonable. Weekend evening tickets are £7.50.

Signified by a marquee of silly, Warhol-esque royal portraits (the Prince of Wales in Dame Edna glasses, the Prince of Wales under an afro), the **Prince Charles Cinema** ★★★ (7 Leicester Place; ☎ 0901/2727-007; www.princecharles cinema.com; 25p per minute; Tube: Leicester Square) may be irreverent about its future monarch, but its respect for film is unquestioned. It shows second-run films at a steep discount (£3 weekday matinees, £4 evenings and weekends, £1 Fridays) and programs a lively slate of classic movies that deserve to be seen on the big screen. Its greatest claim to fame is its family-friendly "Sing-a-Long-a" *The Sound of Music*, a participatory screening of the 1965 classic (p. 216).

Hooray for Bollywood

A 20-minute train ride out of the city will bring you to several thriving Pakistani and Bangladeshi neighborhoods, where Indian-made musicals, called Bollywood films, are the dominant diversion. Many cinemas showing the films are historic 1930s structures that are clinging to life in a tide of advancing redevelopment. Call ahead to ask if the features are subtitled in English. Tickets are £3 to £6 (shows before 5pm are cheaper).

Belle-Vue Cinema (95 High Rd., Willesden Green Library, NW10; ☎ 020/8830-0823; Tube: Willesden Green). It shows a mix of American and Indian film in Northwest London.

Boleyn Cinema (7-11 Barking Rd., Newham, E6; ☎ 020/8471-4884; www.boleyncinema.co.uk; Tube: Upton Park). This 1938 Art Deco house lay derelict in East London for 14 years before re-opening in 1995 as a Hindi venue; it's now said to be the U.K.'s highest-grossing Bollywood cinema.

Himalaya Palace (14 South Rd., Southall; ☎ 020/8813-8844; www.himalayapalacecinema.co.uk; Mainline rail: Southall). Built in 1929 in an ostentatious Chinese temple style, West London's Himalaya Palace languished as a market for 18 years before being restored to film in 2000. It shows Hollywood and Bollywood (London's largest screen for the latter).

Harrow Safari Cinema (Station Rd.; ☎ 020/8426-0303; www.safaricinema.com; Tube: Harrow & Wealdstone). This Northwest London twin-screen cinema specializes in Bollywood.

Open since 1911—it retains much original plasterwork and the proscenium arch—the **Ritzy Picturehouse** ✿ (Brixton Oval, Coldharbour Lane, SW2; ☎ 0870/755-0062; www.picturehouses.co.uk; Tube: Brixton) had some rough times in the '70s, when it was nearly demolished. With the addition of four screens, a cafe, a bar, and state-of-the-art equipment, it's again the neighborhood's pride, and screens everything from mainstream flicks to art films to documentaries. It also stages Q&As with top directors, including Spike Lee and M. Night Shyamalan. Movies cost £3.75 before noon, slightly less than half the evening rate.

DANCE CLUBS, MUSIC CLUBS & THE BAR SCENE

Just as many of London's live music venues don't draw a heavy line between the musical genres they present, no rigid division exists between gig venues and dance venues; in fact, many spaces switch from live music to dance in a single evening. That's one of the things that make the city's nightlife so vibrant, but it's also why it's important to check programming in advance.

Students can often get discounts on entry—as if you needed any more proof that education is valued in England. Don't forget to check the restaurant chapter for top pubs (p. 126); gay and lesbian venues are listed at the end of this chapter.

LIVE MUSIC, INCLUDING JAZZ, POP, FOLK & ROCK

Dozens of theaters and arenas in town book concerts by recognizable names, but it would be fruitless to list them since they're almost all rented by promoters and don't always have something going on. The better advice is to stay on top of who's playing by checking *Time Out* or *New Musical Express (NME)* magazines. Since many big shows sell out months in advance, the best recourse is to book ahead via **See Tickets** (☎ 0871/230-0010; www.seetickets.com); **Stargreen** (☎ 020/7734-8932; www.stargreen.com), which has a small office at 20-21a Argyll St., outside the Oxford Circus Tube station; or **Ticketmaster** (Within the U.K.: ☎ 0870/534; outside the U.K.: ☎ 161/385-3211; www.ticketmaster.co.uk), all of which levy fees but enable you to buy from abroad.

The most important venues post their schedules and link to ticket sellers on their websites. Check out **Bush Hall** (www.bushhallmusic.co.uk); the **Carling Academy Brixton** (www.brixton-academy.co.uk); the **Carling Academy Islington** (www.islington-academy.co.uk); the **Hammersmith Apollo** (sold through www.livenation.co.uk); **Shepherds Bush Empire** (www.shepherds-bush-empire.co.uk); plus the **Electric Ballroom** and **Koko** (see below). **Mean Fiddler** (www.meanfidder.co.uk) controls the bookings at eight city venues, so browse its site, too. Also give the student union at the **University of London** (www.ulu.co.uk) a shot, since the hall books plenty of acts, and it's open to the public.

The most massive venues—the ones where your favorite artist will look like a tiny, bouncing smudge on the far side of 10,000 sweating fans—are the cavernous **Earl's Court Exhibition Centre** (www.eco.co.uk) and the just-rebuilt **Wembley Arena** (www.whatsonwembley.com). The £789-million boondoggle known as the Millennium Dome, on the Thames in East London, mostly shuttered since 2000 after a single year of use, was at press time being rebuilt as an indoor concert arena, possibly Europe's largest, for around 20,000 spectators. Pretentiously renamed **The O₂** (www.theo2.co.uk), it's supposed to re-open in 2007; check ahead to see if it has, and more to the point, whether there have been any takers from the rock world.

You often won't encounter known acts at them, but London also has a few other landmark stages—good for a beery evening out with the locals. At most, you can catch a variety of song styles at the same place from one night to the next.

King's Cross & Camden

For its championing of unsigned artists, **The Bull and Gate** ✭ (298 Kentish Town Rd., NW5; ☎ 020/7093-4820; www.bullandgate.co.uk; cover £5–£6; Tube: Kentish Town), more pub-with-backroom-stage than club, is doomed to fly under the radar jammed with major stages. That means it can charge low covers for a three- or four-act evening.

Particularly midweek, **Dingwalls** ✭ (Middle Yard, NW1; ☎ 020/7267-1577; www.dingwalls.com; cover £5–£15; Tube: Camden Town), an ever-popular house of rock, folk, and acoustic guitar in Camden, often waives its cover before 7pm. How dignified: Audiences may actually sit at tables to enjoy the music.

Any bar that proudly proclaims itself the birthplace of the '70s ditty band Madness would not on the surface seem to be a place you'd want to enter without prior insobriety. But the **Dublin Castle** ✫ (94 Parkway, NW1; ☎ 020/770-0550; www.bugbearbookings.com; cover usually £5; Tube: Camden Town) has street cred. It was the first bar in London to win a late liquor license from the government, so it became an important nightspot. Really no more than a threadbare, greenish pub with a teeny backroom stage, it hosts bands struggling to make it—and a few (Blur, for one) actually have.

Not to be confused with the upscale Electric Cinema, the **Electric Ballroom** ✫✫ (185 Camden High St., NW1; ☎ 020/7485-9006; http://electric-ballroom.co.uk; cover £10–£20; Tube: Camden Town) is one of those dicey, utilitarian halls that never loses the lingering smell of old beer. It has hosted the likes of Sid Vicious, The Clash, and Garbage. Steel yourself for a weeklong roster of punk, goth, industrial, glam, metal, and other genres whose adherents are unlikely to do any more architectural damage to the premises than what's already been done by the ravages of time and neglect. Saturday night is the most accessible, when Shake, a freewheeling disco and '80s event, rolls in. Even though the building is listed (it was the first ballroom in London to replace gas lights with electric, hence its name), Transport for London keeps lobbying to bulldoze it so that it may enlarge the Camden Town Tube station.

Much London nightlife is mired in dance music and the illusion of luxury, but as proof that things are finding their way back, try **Green Note** ✫✫✫ (106 Parkway, NW1; ☎ 020/7485-9899; www.greennote.co.uk; cover £3–£6; closed Mon; Tube: Camden Town) a welcoming vegetarian cafe/bar where acoustic live sets, from folk to jazz, are booked 3 or 4 nights a week. Filled with pillows and upholstered seating, it's a laid-back scene, and prices are sensible (tapas are £2.25–£4). Reservations are suggested if you want to eat in the front room (no meat, all organic), but you can swing in just for the shows.

The prime venue for "names," the intimate **Jazz Café** ✫✫✫ (5-7 Parkway, NW1; ☎ 020/7916-6060; www.jazzcafe.co.uk; cover £10–£25 depending on the act; Tube: Camden Town) keeps the music going from 7pm to 2am, usually in the form of concerts by acts with big followings. There's both standing room and cabaret tables; show up early if you're going for a good position.

Favored by visiting indie bands, **Koko** ✫ (1A Camden Rd., NW1; ☎ 0870/432-5527; www.koko.uk.com; £7 cover; Tube: Mornington Crescent) is a multilevel, 1,500-capacity ballroom that in its former days as a theater saw performances by Charlie Chaplin, and reworked as The Camden Palace in the '70s and '80s, was an epicenter for pop—The Eurythmics, Boy George, and Wham! played their earliest gigs here. Updated and renovated, Koko hosts Club NME on Fridays, a mélange of live bands, guest DJs, a tiered dance floor, and cheap beers. Often, the first 300 people to show up are admitted for free.

If you're not a headbanger, the singer-songwriters at **Water Rats Theatre** ✫✫ (328 Gray's Inn Rd, WC1; ☎ 020/7837-7279; www.plummusic.com; cover £5–£9; Tube: King's Cross St. Pancras) may appeal more than Camden's squalling pubs. Bob Dylan made his U.K. debut in the back room in 1963, and Oasis braved London audiences for the first time here in 1994. It's little wonder, then, why the record-label scouts brave the grime to listen to the new acts, be they alt-country, rock, or hip-hop. You'll find much of the same at an intimate club booked by the same outfit: **The Betsey Trotwood** (56 Farringdon Rd., EC1; ☎ 020/7253-4285; www.plummusic.com; cover £5; Tube: Farringdon).

Islington

The Dublin Castle folks also run the **Hope & Anchor** (207 Upper St., N1; ☎ 020/7354-1312; www.bugbearbookings.com; £5–£6 cover for bands; Tube: Angel), and they apply the same winning, if unexacting, formula here: bands you've never heard of in a guile-free pub setting. Its wee, low-ceilinged cellar space was briefly known for punk bands and for the U.K. debut of Joy Division, but now it's a scruffy but friendly bar where you won't be afraid to spill your beer.

Oxford Street & Soho

Many decades have passed since **The 100 Club** ✸ (100 Oxford St., W1; ☎ 020/7636-0933; www.the100club.co.uk; cover £12–£21, but check its schedule, since 25% discounts are given in advance; Tube: Tottenham Court Road) was a prime hangout for U.S. servicemen homesick for the jazzy sounds of Glenn Miller and his colleagues. In 1976, after passing through an R&B and jazz period which had Louis Armstrong puckering up for audiences, it sponsored the world's first punk festival, and bands like the Sex Pistols—unsigned at the time—took the stage. This red-walled club still can't decide which era to honor, so it careens between punk, swing, R&B, and jazz.

Unlikely as it seems for a chain restaurant, the **Pizza Express** ✸✸ (10 Dean St., W1; ☎ 020/7439-8722; www.pizzaexpress.co.uk/jazzsoho.htm; cover £15–£20; Tube: Tottenham Court Road) in Soho and its sister, **Pizza on the Park** ✸✸ (11 Knightsbridge, SW1; ☎ 020/7235-5273; www.pizzaexpress.com/jazz; cover £15–£20; Tube: Hyde Park Corner), both host casual concerts by acts such as Jamie Cullum, Jacqui Dankworth, and Roy Haynes. Few tourists know that **Ray's Jazz** (113-119 Charing Cross Rd., WC2; ☎ 020/7440-3205; www.foyles.co.uk; free admission; Tube: Tottenham Court Road), a combo record store/cafe, is above the beloved Foyle's bookstore, and fewer know that on many Tuesdays and Thursdays, it gives the gift of free jazz nights.

For more than 45 years, **Ronnie Scott's Jazz Club** (47 Frith St., W1; ☎ 020/7439-0747; www.ronniescotts.co.uk; £25 weekdays, up to £45 for major acts; Tube: Leicester Square) has been the standard bearer in London for smoky, intense, American-style jazz, and it honors a long tradition of pairing visiting U.S. greats with local acts. But the old dive got ritzy. At press time, the 255-seater had just re-opened with higher prices after a £2.1-million renovation, ordered by its new owner. The gavel hasn't yet come down on whether this old-school club has been turned into a shopping mall for music. Entry prices are dotty (and if you want a table, you have to eat—starters hover around a stupefying £12), but it's true that the club draws important names, including Wynton Marsalis, Van Morrison, Tom Waits, and Mark Knopfler. Shows start at around 6:30pm and the main acts take the stage around 9:45pm—good for catching the last Tube home.

Irish and English music is called "roots" here. The postage-stamp sized **12 Bar Club** ✸✸✸ (22-23 Denmark Place, WC2; ☎ 020/7240-2120; www.12bar club.com; cover £3–£7; Tube: Tottenham Court Road) is a central place to find it, booking four acts a night (mostly singer-songwriters), and it costs but £3 to £7 to hear all of them. The adjoining cafe/restaurant is blissfully inexpensive (plated meals top out at £4.50). Enterprise Studios, nearby at 1-6 Denmark Place, is an affiliated space that hosts a Sunday night open-mic night (£3).

The City & Whitechapel

One of those one-stop spots where you can eat, drink, hear music, or peruse art, **The Spitz** ✪✪ (109 Commercial St., Old Spitalfields Market, E1; ☎ 020/7392-9032; www.spitz.co.uk; cover starts at £5 for performances; Tube: Liverpool Street) is characteristic of the creative surge that has swept Spitalfields, giving the once-industrial district a nocturnal personality that attracts clubbers, music lovers, and loungers of every stripe. Acts include world music, rock, blues, and country. The Spitz's multiple personality keeps it from getting unbearably hip with any one crowd and makes it a good destination for the curious dilettante.

Brixton

Plan B (418 Brixton Rd., SW7; ☎ 0870/116-5421; www.plan-brixton.co.uk; cover £5; Tube: Brixton) features a lineup similar to the grungy Water Rats Theatre in King's Cross; it's promoted by the same group. **The Telegraph** ✪ (228 Brixton Hill, SW2; ☎ 020/8678-0777; no cover; Tube: Brixton), a two-level club that introduced The Clash, now ambles along with a lineup including reggae on Thursdays, acoustic and electric bands and DJs on Sundays, and unsigned bands. Roots and reggae fill other nights—after all, it's in the Caribbean neighborhood of Brixton. There's a simple pub-food restaurant too.

DANCE CLUBS

Since the best after-hours fleshpots are scattered across town, making it impossible to end the party without finishing up in a taxi, many tourists end up bailing after the first round of clubbing. The revelers who do go to after-hours clubs are usually in it for the long haul, which is one reason London's deep nights have a reputation as some of the most entrancing and transporting in Europe.

Before you go inside any club, do yourself a favor and consult the maps posted on the nearest bus stop to see which Night Bus (p. 16) you should take home. The Tube shuts down after midnight and stays closed until dawn on weekends, and between those hours, black taxis are not easy to find or catch.

In the club world, cool venues and hot DJs change temperature every month. What's drawing crowds as of this writing may not be worth their time in 6 months. So grab an issue of *Time Out,* which employs journalists so versed in the scene that they seem to write in a secret clubbers' language.

King's Cross & Camden

Okay, so **Canvas** ✪✪ (Bagley's Studios, King's Cross Freight Depot, York Way, N1; ☎ 020/7833-8301; www.rollerdisco.info; cover £10 Thurs and £13 Fri, includes skate rental; Tube: King's Cross) is not exactly a dance club, but it does involve shaking your booty. These Thursday and Friday nights appeal to those sick of or intimidated by the self-important club scene—crowds lace up their roller skates while three rooms spin disco, hip-hop, and house. Needless to say, it's pretty kitschy, so there's no attitude and falling is permitted.

Swinging London, the Sequel

As Bette Midler once quipped, "When it's three o'clock in New York, it's still 1938 in London." She was being snide, but it's true that the 1940s were far too traumatic and transformative for London to completely leave them behind, and young clubbers have rediscovered the hedonistic genre that moved their grandparents: swing. At **Hula Boogie** (South London Pacific, 340 Kennington Rd., SE11; ☎ 020/8672-5972; www.hulaboogie. co.uk; Tube: Kennington or Oval), in a setting that recalls a U.S. Army base in the Pacific, you can unleash your inner jitterbug to the sounds of the '30s, '40s, and '50s. Whenever an obscure dance is called for (the Hand Jive, for instance), the organizers throw in a free 5-minute lesson, and off you go. You can dance from 7pm to midnight for £5, but why oh why is it held only monthly? To tide you over, check for the date and location for the more elaborate roving parties feeding the swing craze: **The Modern Times Club** (www.themoderntimesclub.co.uk; £10–£15), a party where boys and girls dress to the nines, '40s style, and where dance cards are issued before every twirl round the floor; **The Lady Luck Club** (www.lady luckclub.co.uk; £9–£13), a down-and-dirty evocation of a 1950s pulp novel; and **The Virginia Creepers Club** (www.virginiacreepersclub.co.uk; £6), 1950s burlesque with over-the-top glam—think Bettie Page in elevator boots.

The Cross ✪✪✪ (The Arches, 27-31 King's Cross Goods Yard, off York Way, N1; ☎ 020/7837-0828; www.the-cross.co.uk; cover from £10; Tube: King's Cross St. Pancras) has been going strong for many cycles in the ever-changing music world, mostly because it's a pretty cool place to find yourself. Installed in six disused railway arches arranged in a crescent, its exposed brickwork, stone floors, and leather sofas can make a partier feel like a fugitive kingpin or like a Rolling Stone—choose your vibe. Fiction, on Fridays, is its long-running mass-appeal evening, free of VIP sections and attitude; Vertigo, on Sundays, cashes in on the modern Italian club scene and attracts a big crowd.

The three-level multimedia nightclub **Egg** ✪✪ (200 York Way, N7; ☎ 020/ 7609-8364; www.egglondon.net; cover from £12; Tube: King's Cross St. Pancras or Caledonian Rd., or Camden Town) is cracking fun, and gets into just about everything, from house (its specialty), retro, soul classics, and live music. It's super-fashionable, ultra inclusive, and likes it that way. Fridays are Playtime, a popular mixed gay/straight night with a minimum of attitude but a maximum of judgment-free revelry, which books spinners from as far away as San Francisco. Thanks to in-house after-parties, on some weekends it's possible to stay past dawn.

Soho & the West End

For those who don't want to pack it in at 1am, one of London's most central after-hours clubs is **The End** ✪ (18 West Central St., WC1; ☎ 020/7419-9199; www.

Getting Down, Down Under Style

I don't know what it is about Australians in London. In Sydney or Melbourne, they're upstanding members of society, but when they come to Britain—which they do by the thousands, thanks to lenient visa agreements—many party like it's their job. Going a few rounds with a bunch of Aussies has become an integral part of any London nightlife story.

Walkabout (11 Henrietta St., WC2; ☎ 020/7379-5555; www.walkabout. eu.com; Tube: Covent Garden; or 136 Shaftesbury Ave., W1; ☎ 020/7434 0572; Tube: Covent Garden; or Temple Station, Temple Place at Victoria Embankment, WC2; ☎ 020/7395-3690; Tube: Temple; or 56 Upper St., Islington, N1; ☎ 020/7359-2097; Tube: Angel). Aussie bars are becoming as English as pubs, since every sizeable British city now has a few, and they're often heaving with people there to watch satellite feeds of rugby, cricket, football, and my favorite, Australian Rules Football, a strenuous, balletic sport of Olympic proportions. New Zealanders tag along, too (as they do wherever Australians go), and so do South Africans. Even Englishmen frequent these places, although they'll rarely admit to it. Pub grub, including crocodile and kangaroo filets (tacky but fun), is served.

Another Covent Garden pub catering to Aussies, **Belushi's** (9 Russell St., WC2; ☎ 020/7240-3411; www.belushis.com; Tube: Covent Garden), is American-themed (burgers, beers, good music). Though it isn't huge, it's heaving with heaps of antipodeans until midnight most nights.

A Sunday afternoon boozer, **The Church** (The Forum, 9-17 Highgate Rd., NW5; ☎ 020/7284-1001; www.thechurch.co.uk; £6 cover; Tube: Kentish Town), has been wall-to-wall with sweaty bodies leaking alcohol since 1979. It's the quintessential backpacker bash, like the United Nations meets *Animal House*. Held in an intimate former cinema (built in 1934) that by night is a prime venue for rock concerts (check www. meanfiddler.com for its schedule), the party rages from noon to 3:30 pm.

endclub.co.uk; cover £6–£16, weekdays, before midnight, and advance purchase yield the cheaper prices; Tube: Holborn or Tottenham Court Road), which pounds until 3 or 7am, depending on the night, from a festive DJ booth in the center of the dance floor. The crowd is full of out-of-towners intent on having a good time—for those in the West End, your hotel is a sunrise stagger away.

Opium (1a Dean St., W1; ☎ 020/7287-9608; Tube: Piccadilly Circus; cover varies by night) is a sleek venue for world music that attracts a mixed crowd of all interests, singers, and DJs. It's overpriced (some nights cost £12), but central, which means it's often stuffed with visitors from other parts of Great Britain.

The City

You have to take yourself seriously to rank at **Fabric** ✪✪✪ (77a Charterhouse St., EC1; ☎ 020/7336-8898; www.fabriclondon.com; Cover £12–£15; Tube: Farringdon or Barbican) a three-room former butchery by Smithfields meat market where musicheads hack away at beats to find cutting-edge rhythms. If you're a DJ, playing this 2,230-square-meter (24,000-square-ft.) palace is a career zenith. Fridays are the queue-round-the-block FabricLive, when DJ beats blend with live hip-hop and drum and bass, and Saturdays are more about techno, electro, and underground spinners. In Room 1, the groundbreaking Bodysonic dance floor pumps teeth-chattering bass frequencies into the soles of those who dare to move upon it.

One of the city's preeminent venues for live gigs and club nights is the 4.4-hectare (11-acre) Old Truman Brewery, a beer factory that's been redeveloped into a complex of artist spaces and clubs. Its main draw is **93 Feet East** ✪✪ (150 Brick Lane, E1; ☎ 020/7247-3293; www.93feeteast.co.uk; cover £5–£15; Tube: Aldgate East or Liverpool Street), which counts the White Stripes and James Blunt among those who have booked secret gigs or appeared before they got huge. Old-school DJs hang out in the Pink Room (more of a grey-green room, really), but there are lots of stairways, outdoor areas, and dance-floor spaces to explore. Friday and Saturday are the club nights, while Sundays are an intriguing mix of movie screenings and bands. Many people combine a night here with a pilgrimage to the laid-back **Vibe Bar** ✪ (91-95 Brick Lane, E1; ☎ 020/7426-0491; www.vibe-bar.co.uk; free most nights, but £3.50 some weekends after 8:30pm; Tube: Aldgate East or Liverpool Street), a DJ bar with oodles of live acts across the street.

Southwark & Brixton

The largest club in the city, **The Fridge** ✪✪ (1 Town Hall Parada, SW2; ☎ 020/7326-5100; www.fridge.co.uk; cover £8–£20; Tube: Brixton), built in 1914 as the Palladium Picture Playhouse, is a landmark for those who are seriously into hard house, trance, and that zen-like zombie quiver that accompanies them on the dance floor. Its laser-laced longevity typifies the diverse, deeply ingrained aesthetics that makes Brixton an important neighborhood for serious partiers. You get your money's worth, since the party lasts till the Tube starts waking up.

Dance scenesters either love or hate the **Ministry of Sound** ✪ (103 Gaunt St., SE1; ☎ 020/7740-8649; www.ministryofsound.com; cover £10–£15; Tube: Elephant and Castle). As London's first megavenue to successfully export a pseudo-corporate clubbing brand, MoS aggravates many of the hipsters it aims to entrance, but to the layman, it's the setting of fabulous sets, a diverse crowd, and top equipment. Garage bands are what it does best, but plenty of techno, acid house, and virtuosic mixes dazzle the scoffers. Saturday is the peak night; squeeze into the balcony bar and observe the energy gushing from the warehouse-like main floor, called "the box."

GAY & LESBIAN

London has the most varied and vibrant gay and lesbian scene in the world. At last count, the city boasted some 60 bars, 41 dance clubs or club nights, and a dozen saunas—beat that, San Francisco or New York!—but those numbers keep

Drinking in the View

If you're going to deviate from the pub circuit to order an expensive cocktail at a cosmopolitan bar, you might as well do it where there's a view.

Oxo Tower Restaurant, Bar & Brasserie (Bargehouse St., South Bank, SE1; ☎ 020/7803-3888; www.oxotower.co.uk; Tube: Southwark): After work, the penthouse of this affectionately held landmark, once a power station and later a factory for beef-stock cubes, is elbow-to-elbow with media types who are very pleased with themselves. Turn your back to them and enjoy the Thames, eight floors below.

The Trafalgar (2 Spring Gardens, Trafalgar Square, SW1; ☎ 020/7870-2900; www.thetrafalgar.com; Tube: Charing Cross): This outdoor spot's our little secret, since few people seem to know about it. On the seventh-floor Roof Garden of this stone hotel the view takes in The Clock Tower at the Houses of Parliament, the London Eye, and Nelson's Column. Even on a Saturday night, it's never very crowded, which may be unjust, but it makes for a romantic outing for the rest of us.

5th View at Waterstone's (203 Piccadilly; ☎ 020/7851-2400; www.waterstones.com; Tube: Piccadilly Circus): Atop one of the city's best department stores for books, this south-facing cafe takes in Westminster Abbey, Parliament, and Whitehall. Cocktails aren't cheap (£7.50), but they're as cheap as they get for panoramic bars like these.

Ruba Bar (Tooley St., SE1; ☎ 020/3002-4300; www.hilton.co.uk/tower bridge; Tube: London Bridge), at Hilton Tower Bridge hotel, is a business-hotel bar with a difference: a ninth-floor, gratitude-inducing vista including the Tower of London, the Tower Bridge, and the HMS *Belfast*. It's not the hippest spot (its signature cocktail is the Rhubarb Daiquiri), but at least you won't jostle with trendoids.

Vertigo 42 (Tower 42, 25 Old Broad St., EC2; ☎ 020/7877-7842; www.vertigo42.co.uk; Tube: Bank): Because it's atop the tallest building in the City, and every table commands a stellar view of just about everything, this bar deigns to charge £10 for a glass of champagne. That means it's for special occasions. It's most impressive at sundown and at night, but consider the £15 set lunch (soup, salad, dessert), Monday to Friday, when you can see the jumbo jets on their approaches to Heathrow over South London. It doesn't allow kids, and booking is mandatory.

changing since hip venues don't sit still. The scene swells, visitors pour into town, and the music seems to crank a few notches louder when the jolly and inclusive **London Pride** (www.londonpride.org) season rolls along, in late June.

Gay-oriented pursuits have traditionally been centered around Soho, where the bars and clubs take on a festive, anyone-is-welcome flair, but as a mark of a truly integrated city, now nearly every neighborhood has its own pubs, gay nights, and maybe even a small sauna. Where you spend an evening depends on your proclivities and willingness to commute. There aren't usually cover charges unless an event or show is on, when they're about £5 at bars and £11 for clubs.

The monthly magazine *GayTimes* (£3.25; www.gaytimes.co.uk) rounds up the best addresses, but for a clue about events, grab one of two weekly magazines. The racy *Boyz* (www.boyz.co.uk) includes a thorough day-by-day schedule, which also appears on its website. It's distributed for free at many gay bars. The free *QX International* (www.qxmagazine.com), catering more to the club scene, publishes a less comprehensive diary, but it's still useful, and conveniently, you can download a free facsimile of the printed edition every week.

Soho

Thanks to its cobalt-and-steel design, **Barcode** ✯✯ (3-4 Archer St., W1; ☎ 020/ 7734-3342; Tube: Piccadilly Circus), a two-level space on a side street, seems on the surface like a snooty setting, but in reality it attracts a varied crowd of friendly over-25s, and it serves drinks longer than many rivals (until 1am most nights). Its downstairs space does straight-friendly comedy nights on Tuesdays.

Candy Bar (4 Carlisle St., W1; ☎ 020/7494-4041; www.thecandybar.co.uk; Tube: Tottenham Court Road) is one of London's better-known (and only 7-days-a-week) lesbian bars, and given that there aren't too many girl bars in town, it attracts a wide spectrum of types. Later at night, the basement bar opens. The monthly party **Lounge** (www.lounge.uk.net) is another popular lesbian night, but it switches venues so you'll need to make advance plans.

Come six o'clock in summer, Old Compton Street fills with men in boots, pint glasses, and basso conversation, as patrons from **Comptons of Soho** ✯ (51-53 Old Compton St., W1; ☎ 020/7479-7961; Tube: Leicester Square or Piccadilly Circus) and cruisy **Admiral Duncan** ✯ (54 Old Compton St., W1; ☎ 020/7437-5300; Tube: Leicester Square or Piccadilly Circus) overflow and merge into an ongoing block party. Both bars tend to cater to an over-30 crowd and they're light on the attitude.

Friendly Society ✯ (79 Wardour St., W1; ☎ 020/7434-3805; Tube: Leicester Square) is a minimalist basement bar where drinks are almost as strong as the come-ons. Find it down Tisbury Court, an alley between Wardour and Rupert streets (don't worry—it's not scuzzy).

No other dance club in town, gay or straight, comes close to attracting such a pantheon of legendary live performances as **G-A-Y** ✯✯✯ (Astoria, 157 Charing Cross Rd., W1; ☎ 020/7734-6963; www.g-a-y.co.uk; Tube: Tottenham Court Road). Kylie, the Spice Girls, Donna Summer, and of course, Madge, all performed here at the height of their fame, and some have been known to drop by unannounced. The big names visit on Saturdays, when 2,000 chipper young things (many of them bushy-tailed from ecstasy) bop until 4am. (In 2006, the club's setting, the Astoria Theatre, was sold to developers—there are a lot of angry drag queens sounding off about the end of an era—so check ahead to see where the party's moved.) The club's bubblegum-light pre-show hangout, **G-A-Y Bar** ✯✯

(30 Old Compton St., W1; ☎ 020/7494-2756; Tube: Leicester Square), is buzzing most hours of the day with a young, twinkie crowd, who come to chatter and watch videos on the plasma screens. There's a girls' bar, too.

Heaven ✪✪ (The Arches, off Villiers St., WC2; ☎ 020/7930-2020; www. heaven-london.com; £4–£8; Tube: Charing Cross or Embankment) is a big, three-level Saturday night dance blowout, which has been running for ages. Popcorn is its bustling Monday dance night, but Wednesday's Fruit Machine (the British name for a slot machine) is the long-running crowd-pleaser serving up house, pop, and R&B. Bang!!!, the Friday night endeavor, is a '90s-style, pansexual party. None of its nights are groundbreaking; they're simply old-fashioned, straight-friendly, hands-in-the-air dance jams. The independent cabaret-and-karaoke bar **Halfway to Heaven** (7 Duncannon St., WC2; ☎ 020/7321-2791; Tube: Charing Cross), low-key and plain, is so named because it's about halfway between Leicester Square and the Heaven nightclub.

79 CXR ✪✪ (79 Charing Cross Rd., WC1; ☎ 020/7734-0769; Tube: Leicester Square), a contemporary multileveled cruise bar, dark but not sleazy, gets busiest after work; the loft is for socializing and the odd across-the-room flirt.

King's Cross & Camden

A following patronizes**The Black Cap** ✪✪ (171 Camden High St., NW1; ☎ 020/7428-2721; www.theblackcap.com; Tube: Camden Town), a Camden legend, which is shoulder-to-shoulder during its weekend drag and cabaret shows. For those who like it dirty, no other large space in the city can compete with**Central Station— King's Cross** (37 Wharfdale Rd., N1; ☎ 020/7278-3294; Tube: King's Cross St. Pancras) for evenings of full-on, sexually charged pursuits, including nights for lesbians. Fetish nights aren't the only thing going down in cellar cruise spaces.

South of the Thames

Those into rough trade generally have to head south of the Thames, so be prepared to give other riders on the Victoria Line a chuckle if you're heading out in uniform. The ruling pleasure palace in the hood is**Substation South** (9 Brighton Terrace, Brixton, SW9; ☎ 020/7737-2095; Tube: Brixton), which throws a popular boots-and-Levis night on Thursdays. Its popular black music night, Queer Nation, falls on Saturdays. Another well-known leather dive,**The Hoist** (Railway Arch 47c, South Lambeth Road, SE1; ☎ 020/7735-9972; Tube: Vauxhall), on Fridays and Saturdays, has been the set for several pornos and isn't for the faint-hearted.

Saunas

Chariots (www.gaysauna.co.uk) is like the Starbucks of the tub-and-towel set; there are six locations around the city. The largest, with the most space for, er, socializing and sitz baths, are**Waterloo** (101 Lower Marsh St., SE1; ☎ 020/7401-8484; Tube: Waterloo), installed in a warren of atmospheric vaults beneath the railway viaducts and popular with businessmen;**Vauxhall** (Rail Arches, 63-64 Albert Embankment, SE1; ☎ 020/7247-5333; Tube: Vauxhall), again under 19th-century railway arches;**Shoreditch** (1 Fairchild St., EC2; ☎ 020/7247-5333; Tube: Liverpool Street), popular with Whitechapel hipsters and commuters from

Liverpool Street station; and the lower-key **Limehouse** (574 Commercial Rd., E14; ☎ 020/7791-28008; Tube: Limehouse DLR), where you're more likely to meet a genuine East End local. While I would never suggest that skinflints save on a hotel night by crashing at one of these joints (after all, you can't bring luggage), I will submit, with a wink, that you can stay for as long as 12 hours for about £14. **Pleasuredrome Central** (125 Alaska St., SE1; ☎ 020/7633-9194; www.pleasure drome.com; Tube: Waterloo; £13), another under-the-arches, sleekly designed hideaway, never closes, and is one of the few sizable, non-skanky saunas not operated by Chariots.

11 Seven Great Day Trips

Get out of town with few pounds & fewer problems

YOU'VE FLOWN ALL THE WAY TO ENGLAND. IT WOULD BE A SHAME TO MISS seeing some of the sights that make it special—the rolling countryside, the High Streets plied by elderly shoppers, the ageless towns built alongside slow-flowing rivers. You can't get these things in London, but you can sample them in some of the out-of-town places that have played an integral role in the development and culture of London life. Taking an excursion to one of those towns is like getting two experiences for the price of one: You'll see what everyday English life is like, and you'll enjoy world-famous sights such as Windsor Castle, or the quads of Cambridge.

Remember that taking a day trip presents its own "opportunity costs"—for that one day that you're paying to see a single place, you might have been able to see four or five major attractions had you stayed in London. So before you commit to devoting a precious day to heading out of town, carefully weigh how much you really want to see these locations. Are they worth seeing? Absolutely, each for their own reasons. Do you have time? Ah, there's the rub.

Britain has comprehensive transport, but it's not quick as mercury. Because of traffic and a dearth of superhighways, you can expect a 48km (30-mile) trip to take an hour, so a spot that's 129km to 161km (80–100 miles) each way, such as Stonehenge or Bath, will require you to rise at dawn if you want to buy yourself much touring time at all. Going by bus is often less expensive than by rail, but the journey will involve narrow roads. It's an excellent way to see everyday England, but it's inefficient.

I've chosen seven of the most popular day trips out of London and listed them in order of my preference, which has a lot to do with how manageable they are. For every day trip, call or go online before you plan your trip to verify open hours. For a variety of reasons, attractions outside of London sometimes limit their hours, and you'd hate to travel to, say, Windsor Castle and find its gates barred owing to a state visit from the King of Swaziland and his wives.

Although I give highlights for each place—usually more than you could see in a day—it's simply impossible to provide comprehensive guides to seven additional cities in a book about London. So I also provide a tourism information office contact for each city. All of them will be able, for a fee (£3–£4, plus 10% of the room rate), to hook you up with a bed for the night, should you decide, even at the last minute, that you'd rather not trek back to London right away. Many close by 4:30pm, and most charge 30p to 60p for a city map, so before you leave home, download and print the free color maps provided by **Visit Britain** (www.visit britain.com). Museum entry outside of London is between £4 and £6, and colleges and churches charge less than £3, unless otherwise noted.

Saving on Your Excursion's Rail Ticket

Train fares listed in this section are provided as a guideline; National Rail pricing schemes are complicated and unpredictable. The good news is that for all of the destinations served by trains, you can often buy a "same day return" for just a little more than the price of the usual one-way (single) ticket. You just have to return to London the same day you leave it. More money-saving tips:

- Tickets for travel tend to be most expensive on Fridays, when Londoners head out of town for the weekend.
- You can also find incredible deals (up to 70% off) if you happen to be among the first customers to book on a given train departure, but that requires advance planning of several months.
- Prices are highest for tickets with no restrictions, but chances are you won't need to change your itinerary for a day trip, so always spring for the discounted restricted fare.
- If you have a Travelcard for the Underground, it will often enable you to deduct a small amount from your fare to nearer destinations like Windsor. National Rail's phone operators will help you plan routes and hash out your fare questions (☎ 08457/48-49-50 in the U.K., ☎ 011-44-20/7278-5240 from overseas; www.nationalrail.co.uk).
- Sometimes local attractions team up with National Rail to offer discounts on admission if you take the train; ask at the railway box office if deals are on, or check the National Rail website for "offers."

WINDSOR & ETON

You may have had your fill of palaces in London proper, but you haven't seen the best. A fortress and a royal home for more than 900 years, **Windsor Castle** (☎ 020/7766-7304; www.royalcollection.org.uk; Mar–Oct daily 9:45am–5:15pm, earlier winter closing, closed for state visits; £14 adults, £7.50 children 5–16, £12 seniors/students) was expanded by each successive monarch who dwelled in it—more battlements for the warlike ones, more finery for the aesthetes. The resulting immoderate sprawl, which dominates the town from nearly every angle, is the Queen's favorite residence—she weekends here—and its history is richer than that of Buckingham Palace. Windsor, just 20 miles west of London, is no less thronged with tourists and corny souvenir shops, though.

The castle's **State Apartments** are sumptuous enough to be daunting, and a tour through them, available unless there's a state visit, includes entrance to some deeply historic rooms. Around a million people file through every year, so sharpen your elbows. **St George's Chapel,** a Gothic spectacle built by Henry VIII, is the final resting place of 10 monarchs, including Elizabeth II's father (George VI), mother (the Queen Mum), and sister (Princess Margaret). It's safe to assume that this is where she will wind up one day, too. The palace also has a large complement of Her Majesty's priceless art and furniture collection, including the oft-replicated *Charles I in three positions* by Anthony van Dyck (1635–1636, in the

King's Dressing Room); the executed king is buried in the Chapel. In 1992, one fifth of the castle area was engulfed by an accidental fire; the Queen recounted her despair over that, plus the breakup of two of her children's marriages, in her now-famous "annus horribilus" Christmas speech to the nation, and much effort and funding went into putting everything back to the way it was before. In fact, the Queen originally opened Buckingham Palace to visitors to fund the restoration. **St. George's Hall,** one of the repaired areas, is the Queen's chosen room for banquets. Kids love **Queen Mary's Doll's House,** an extravagant toy built in the 1920s with working electricity, elevators, plumbing, and insanely fine details. From October to March, the tour also includes the **Semi-State Apartments,** George IV's private rooms, considered by many to be among the best-preserved Georgian interiors in England. There's also a **Changing the Guard** ceremony at 11am (on alternate days, Mon–Sat, so check the Windsor Castle website).

The Castle is the superstar here, but minor supporting roles are played by the succinctly named **Great Park** adjoining it; the 4.8km (3-mile), pin-straight **Long Walk** that culminates with an equestrian statue of George III; and the museum at **Eton College** (☎ 01753/67-11-77; www.etoncollege.com; £4.50 adults, £3.50 children/seniors/students; 2pm–4:30pm during school term), a short walk over the Thames (which is narrow at this western remove) from the castle. Eton is one of the most exclusive, most unbelievably posh boys' schools in England. Princes Harry and William are alums, known as Old Etonians, as are kings and princes from around the world. **The Guildhall** (High St.; ☎ 01753/74-39-00; free admission), just south of the castle, was where Prince Charles and Camilla Parker-Bowles had a quiet civil marriage in April 2005; it's no St Paul's, where in 1981 Charles wed his first wife, what's-her-name, but it is also the work of Christopher Wren (note its delicate arches). The building was apparently designed without the center columns, which made councilors nervous; Wren threw up some columns but left them an inch shy of the ceiling, just to prove that his architecture was sound.

How to get there: The price difference between transport options is negligible, so because riding the rails is quicker, it's got the edge. **Trains** (☎ 08457/48-49-50; www.nationalrail.co.uk; 38–56 min.; £7) go from Waterloo station to Windsor & Eton Riverside or Paddington to Windsor & Eton Central with a change at Slough. Trains requiring no changes leave twice an hour, and trains requiring a change leave a little more frequently. Or take a coach by **Green Line** (☎ 08706/08-72-61; www.greenline.co.uk; 1 hr. 45 min.; £5 single) numbered 700 or 702 from Hyde Park Corner.

Tourist information: Royal Windsor (Old Booking Hall, Windsor Royal Station; ☎ 01753/74-39-00; www.windsor.gov.uk)

BATH

Easily roamed on foot, Bath, about 161km (100 miles) west of London, is revered as a splendid example of Georgian architecture. The pleasing sandstone hue of its buildings set against the slate-grey British sky, the assiduously planned symmetry of its streets, the illusion that Jane Austen (who lived here from 1800–1805) is taking tea within one of its 18th-century Palladian town houses—Bath's magic comes from its consistent and regal design. No wonder the upper crust of the 1700s found it so fashionable, and no wonder their descendants have not dared

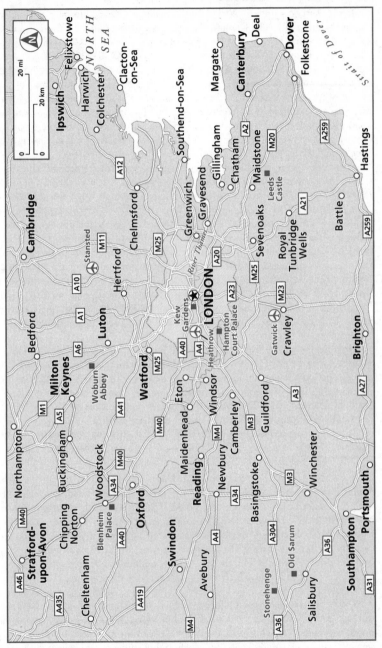

to alter it. And no wonder UNESCO inscribed it as a World Heritage Site—a rarity for an entire city. The Romans were the first to recognize the tourism potential of the natural hot springs, which bubble at a rate of 250,000 gallons a day. The steamy **Roman Baths** (Pump Room, Stall St.; ☎ 01225/47-77-85; www.romanbaths.co.uk; £10 adults, £6 children 6–16, £8.50 students, including a free audio guide; daily 9am–6pm), one of the best-preserved religious spas of that period, were discovered in the late 1800s, and the restoration and accompanying museum are excellent. The Victorians mounted a proud colonnade around the excavation, and water has long been drawn in the adjoining Pump Room; you can drink a glass of the sulfuric stuff if you like, or settle down for a pricey lunch in neoclassical style.

First-time visitors are blown away by the sweep and elegance of The Royal Crescent, a dazzling 30-house development that took 7 seven years to complete, from 1767 to 1775. Its first house is now a period museum, **No. 1 Royal Crescent** (1 Royal Crescent; ☎ 01225/42-81-26; www.bath-preservation-trust.org.uk; £4; Tues–Sun 10:30am–4pm, until 5pm Feb–Oct). Robert Adam put up **Pulteney Bridge,** which crosses the River Avon, in 1773, just as a similar bridge in its shop-lined style, the medieval London Bridge, was crumbling. There are walks along the river, too. Bath also hosts about 20 small museums, including the **Museum of Costume** (The Assembly Rooms, Bennett St.; ☎ 01225/47-71-73; www.museumofcostume.co.uk; £6; daily 11am–5pm, until 6pm Mar–Oct), dedicated to fashion from the late 1500s to today; and the **American Museum in Britain** (Claverton Manor; ☎ 01225/46-05-03; www.americanmuseum.org), devoted to home interiors, applied arts, and folk art from U.S. history.

How to get there: Trains (☎ 08457/48-49-50; www.nationalrail.co.uk; 90 minutes, twice an hr.; £9) leave from Paddington station and let off in Bath Spa, an ugly section of town about 5 minutes' walk from the good stuff. Because they take twice as long and cost nearly twice as much, I don't recommend taking a **National Express** bus (☎ 08705/80-80-80; www.nationalexpress.com; 3½ hr.; £17 single, £18 return), even when special deals are offered.

Tourist information: Visit Bath/Bath Tourist Information Centre (Abbey Chambers, Abbey Churchyard; ☎ 08704/44-64-42; www.visitbath.co.uk).

OXFORD

Whereas the face of London, 92km (57 miles) east, has been forcibly reshaped by the pressures of war, disaster, and commerce, Oxford was made stronger by them. When plague killed townspeople, the colleges snapped up their houses, and when the Reformation cleaned out the churches, the colleges took their land, too. Academies used the extra space to carve out some of the most beautiful college buildings in the world. Here, the reverence for education borders on the ecclesiastical. Yet Oxford is no cloister; it's a decidedly modern city—thriving, sophisticated, and busy.

Wandering the heart of Oxford's cobbled streets and grey stone alleys and ducking into its colleges to soak up their abject loveliness make for a happy afternoon, particularly for fans of architecture. Many of the most iconic building clusters in this city of 140,000 (30,000 of whom are students) are collected together in the center of town, and they were built to house the university's nerve center.

The main research library is the flabbergasting **Bodleian Library** (Broad St.; ☎ 01865/27-72-99; www.bodley.ox.ac.uk; £3.50 tour; daily 9am–5pm), nicknamed "the Bod." It opened in 1602 and has been burrowing under the streets of Oxford, trying to find new places to store its multiplying collection, ever since. The round **Radcliffe Camera** ("Rad Cam"; open via guided tours at the Bodleian) was built in the 1740s to house scientific books alone. It stands on the north side of Radcliffe Square, and on the south is the **University Church of St. Mary** (www.university-church.ox.ac.uk; tower £2; daily 9am–6pm), whose spire provides a top view of the city. Other popular viewpoints are from the octagonal cupola above Sir Christopher Wren's **Sheldonian Theatre** (Broad St.; ☎ 01865/27-72-99; www.sheldon.ox.ac.uk; £1.50; Mon–Sat 10am–12:30 and 2–4:30pm), and from the 22m (74-ft.), rectangular **Carfax Tower** (Carfax; ☎ 01865/79-26-53; price and hour info above), the last remaining chunk of the 13th-century St. Martin's Church, located by the crossroads of the city center. The doors between the inner and outer quadrangles of **Balliol College** (Broad St. and St. Giles; ☎ 01865/27-77-77; www.balliol.ox.ac.uk) still bear scorch marks from where Bloody Mary burned two Protestants alive for refusing to recant. **Magdelen College** (High St.; ☎ 01865/27-60-00; www.magd.ox.ac.uk), pronounced "Maudlin," is one of the largest and most peaceful colleges here; its tower is the city's highest point, and its chapel is carved with breathtaking detail.

Oxford, like Cambridge, is comprised of individual colleges that feed off a central university system. Each of Oxford's 39 colleges has its own campus, tradition, character, and disciplines, although many close their grassy inner sanctums to visitors. The most popular college to visit is **Christ Church** (☎ 01865/28-65-73; www.chch.ox.ac.uk; £4.50; Mon–Sat 9:30am–5:30pm), its interiors loom large in children's literature; it stands in for Hogwarts School in the Harry Potter films, and it was where Lewis Carroll (aka mathematician Charles Dodgson) befriended the little girl for whom he wrote *Alice in Wonderland*. Christ Church is the largest college in Oxford, the site of the cathedral for the local diocese, and its Meadow, still grazed by cattle, is a delightful place to watch boaters (punters) on the rivers Isis and Cherwell.

Offering more than just a pretty facade, **The Ashmolean Museum** (Beaumont St.; ☎ 01865/27-80-00; www.ashmolean.org; free admission; Tues–Sat 10am–5pm and Sun 2–5pm), was founded way back in 1683, literally before anyone knew what the word "museum" actually meant. It houses an important hodgepodge of antiquities and art on par with (but on a smaller scale than) The British Museum, including a lantern carried by Guy Fawkes during the foiled Gunpowder Plot; the Anglo-Saxon Alfred Jewel of gold, enamel, and rock crystal; a Stradivarius violin; and assorted Old Masters paintings. **Modern Art Oxford** (30 Pembroke St.; ☎ 01865/72-27-33; www.modernartoxford.org.uk; free admission; Tues–Sat 10am–5pm; Sun noon–5pm) is a well-respected museum for contemporary works. Hovering somewhere between those two places, the **Pitt River Museum** (Parks Rd.; ☎ 01865/27-09-27; www.prm.ox.ac.uk; free admission; daily noon–4:30pm) offers an oft-freakish blend of folk art and anthropology—think shrunken heads and bundles of poisoned arrows brought back by British explorers over hundreds of years. **The University Museum of Natural History** (Parks Rd.; ☎ 01865/27-29-50; www.oum.ox.ac.uk; free admission; daily noon–5pm) is a Victorian setting for dinosaur bones, fossilized specimens, and the like.

During the school term (mid-Jan to mid-Mar, late Apr to mid-June, Oct to early Dec), some university buildings required for study (libraries, residence halls) are closed, or they only open on Saturdays. At all times of year, watch out for zooming bicyclists; an unwritten law seems to dictate that they own the city.

How to get there: The least expensive, easiest method is by coach, since companies compete with regular buses rolling round the clock. The **Oxford Tube** (☎ 01865/77-22-50; www.oxfordtube.com; 100 min. with no traffic; £12 single, seniors/under 16 £6 single) bus leaves every 12 to 15 minutes from 9:35am to 9:35pm and around every half-hour or hour at all other times, even in the middle of the night. It picks passengers up near the Tube stations at Marble Arch, Victoria, Notting Hill Gate, and Shepherd's Bush. Kids under 12 ride free except on Saturdays. Judging by the way the owners spell their bus line, it seems they weren't educated in the City of Dreaming Spires, but **Oxford Espress** (☎ 01865/78-54-00; www.oxfordbus.co.uk; 100 min. with no traffic; £11 adults, seniors/students £5.50 each way) provides a similarly comfortable coach service (including sockets for mobile phone chargers), but with London stops at Baker Street, Marble Arch, and Victoria. Both coaches drop you off at Gloucester Green, in the Oxford city center. Give rush hours wide berth, since many locals commute to London from these parts. More expensive **trains** (☎ 08457/48-49-50; www.nationalrail.co.uk; 1 hr.; £17 single) go from Paddington station to Oxford, sometimes via Reading.

Tourist information: In addition to selling (yes, selling—not giving) maps and guides, **The Oxford Information Centre** (15-16 Broad St.; ☎ 01865/72-68-71; www.visitoxford.org) offers daily walking tours using accredited guides. Schedules vary, but there's always a daily City and Colleges Tour at 11am and 4pm (£6.50 adults, £3 children under 16). In the summer, it runs evening ghost tours on Friday and Saturday, and on Saturday afternoons, an Inspector Morse Tour attracts sleuths. The Centre also sells self-guided tours that you can download and use with an MP3 player (£5). You can download free maps of the city from Visit Britain (www.visitbritain.com).

CAMBRIDGE

Oxford is a city in its own right, but Cambridge, in the marshes 79km (49 miles) northeast of London, would barely have a pulse without its university. That makes Cambridge manageable. It feels in some ways like a typical English town, with a daily market for crafts and food on its central square, Market Hill. Its best rewards come when you wander through randomly chosen iron gates or along a river path—that's when the inviting little town really opens up. For some reason, the marauding Puritans neglected to smash the 16th-century stained glass windows at **King's College Chapel** (King's Parade; ☎ 01223/33-12-12; www.kings.cam.ac.uk; £3.50; Mon–Fri 9:30am–4:30pm; Sat 9:30am–3:15pm, Sun 1:15pm–2:15pm; extended summer hours) —they probably thought they were just as divine as you will. The chapel's fanned and vaulted ceiling, a work of craftsmanship that stuns even those who care little for such things, was completed at the behest of Henry VII. Its famous choristers sing at services during term time. To the right of the chapel is the Senate House, where every student anxiously converges to read their exam results, posted on its door at graduation time.

Like Oxford, Cambridge's calling card is the elaborate and ancient architecture of its colleges, all of which house students and feed off the central university facilities. Unlike in Oxford, it's easy to venture into the cloistered grounds of many of Cambridge's colleges (the oldest was founded in 1286 after a squabble in Oxford necessitated the establishment of a second educational capital), though doing so usually requires a few quid. The best is **Pembroke College** (☎ 012233/38-10-00; www.pem.cam.ac.uk), the third-oldest in town, distinguished by the oldest gatehouse in Cambridge and by a chapel with an ornate plaster ceiling, which was the first completed work by Christopher Wren (after finishing, the man seemed never to rest again). Unlike many of the colleges, Pembroke never charges visitors a fee to poke around its common areas. In *Chariots of Fire,* sprinters tried to get around the .8-hectare (2-acre) yard of **Trinity College** (☎ 01223/33-84-00; www.trin.cam.ac.uk) in the time it took for its clock to strike 12. Trinity is the largest and most endowed of Cambridge's 31 colleges. Tourists are often told that the wooden **Mathematical Bridge** (1749) spanning the Cam at **Queen's College** (Silver St.; ☎ 01223/33-55-11; www.queens.cam.ac.uk) was constructed using no nails, and when curious students disassembled it to figure out how, they couldn't put it back together without using screws. The college, for the record, is curiously defensive about the accusation, pointing out the original scale model used screws, and saying that anyone who believes this story "cannot have a serious grasp on reality . . . only a pedant could claim that the bridge was originally built without nails." The 12th-century **Round Church** (Bridge and St. John's Sts.; ☎ 01223/31-16-02) is the oldest of four remaining circular churches in England.

Cambridge's storied **Fitzwilliam Museum** (Trumpington St.; ☎ 01223/33-29-00; www.fitzmuseum.cam.ac.uk; free admission; closed Mon) is like London's V&A melded with the Dulwich Picture Gallery: a first-rate neoclassical building full of examples of applied arts and Old Masters that a city 10 times Cambridge's size (108,000) would covet. Here, it's another jewel among many. Mill Lane leads to the River Cam, where you can rent a punting boat for £6 or sit at The Mill pub overlooking the water. (The punting alone will set you apart as a tourist, but if you want to look like a tourist savvy to Cambridge traditions, punt from the back of the boat. In Oxford, they punt from the front.) The meadows along the Cam are known as **The Backs,** and they make for idyllic walks.

The head of Oliver Cromwell, which was impaled outside Westminster Hall in London as a warning against regicide (albeit 3 years after the man died of natural causes), was finally buried within an antechapel (not open to visitors) at Sidney Sussex College in 1960. It's in an unmarked grave, to keep pranksters from pinching the much-abused thing. That's Cambridge in a nutshell: It has many secrets, and history is layered everywhere, but since it's still a working university town, its marvels won't be handed to you the way they are at most tourist sites. You have to wander, wonder, and ask questions.

Keep in mind that colleges aren't open, and authentic street life is at a minimum, outside of term (mid-Jan to mid-Mar, late Apr to mid-June, Oct to early Dec).

How to get there: Nonstop coaches from **National Express** (☎ 08705/80-80-80; www.nationalexpress.com; 2 hours; £10 single) leave hourly from Victoria Coach station; don't get off at Trumpington, but wait for the city center

The Trade-Off with Escorted Tours

Arranging your own day trips using public transportation will almost always be the most cost-effective method, but there are cogent reasons for choosing a guided coach tour. Most have to do with convenience. It's simply quicker to allow someone else to drive you around, making sure you cram a laundry list of major sites into a short time span, and consuming spoon-fed nuggets of information about each place. What you learn won't have much depth, but at least you'll have been.

Problem is, you'll have paid a pretty penny for it: Most tours cost £50 to £60 a day, not including food. I believe you get a richer experience (and one that doesn't have you trooping into gift shops all day), when you do it yourself. But some people desperately want to soak up as many sights as they can, even if it means they skim the surface. For them, here are the two major players in the coach-tour biz, both sold aggressively through the concierges at expensive hotels (who love getting the commissions):

- Gray Line's **Golden Tours** (In the U.K.: ☎ 020/7233-7030, in the U.S.: ☎ 800/548-7083; www.goldentours.co.uk)
- **Evan Evans Tours** (☎ 020/7950-1777; www.evanevans.co.uk)

Better yet are the more affordable **London Walks** (☎ 020/7624-3978; www.walks.com), which runs frequent "Explorer Days" for just £12. These use public transportation and don't include admission fees, but you'll have a local guide every step of the way to show you how it's all done.

---

stop. There are trains, but be warned that Cambridge's station is several miles from the city center, so you will need to call a taxi once you arrive; coaches are the smarter way to travel. If you insist, though, **trains** (☎ 08457/48-49-50; www.nationalrail.co.uk; 45–90 min.; £18 single) run by One Railway take 90 minutes, but the First Capital Connect trains take half that time and leave twice an hour. All depart from Liverpool Street station and stop at Cambridge Station.

Tourist information: Cambridge Visitor Information Centre (The Old Library, Wheeler St.; ☎ 08712/26-80-06; www.visitcambridge.org) sells maps and guides but won't dispense them for free. Cambridge also sells hour-long walking tours on downloadable MP3s (www.tourist-tracks.com; £5). You can download free maps of the city from Visit Britain (www.visitbritain.com).

CANTERBURY

Bath is proper and Salisbury bows to its cathedral, but charming Canterbury, in shape and in spirit, conjures the jumble of a medieval city, battlements and all. St. Augustine established the first cathedral here in 597. Everything is contained within the walled Old City, on the River Stour, in which cars are banned and strolling tangled ageless lanes can absorb you so completely that you forget there are other things to see in town. Its three-towered, steeply priced **Cathedral**

(☎ 01227/76-28-62; www.canterbury-cathedral.org; £6 adults, £4.50 children/ seniors/students; Mon–Fri 9am–5pm, until 6:30pm during summer; varying week-end hours), a UNESCO World Heritage Site, is the mothership for Anglicanism, and it has been drawing sightseers since Henry II's goons stabbed Thomas Becket to death in 1170; the site of the dastardly deed is still a place for reflection. The pilgrims of Chaucer's *Canterbury Tales* told their tales as they made their way here, to pay tribute to his shrine, and plenty of tourist traps still profit off their exploits. The cathedral's undercroft (cellar) is considered to be the finest example from the Norman period left in the country.

Elsewhere in the city, 90km (56 miles) southeast of London in the rolling coun-tryside of Kent, is an excavated portion of the lower-lying Roman town, now the **Canterbury Roman Museum** (Longmarket, Butchery Lane; ☎ 01227/78-55-75; www.canterbury-museums.co.uk; £2.70; Mon–Sat 10am–5pm; varying summer hours). Canterbury is also the home of a university, which gives the old city a notice-able verve and a coziness, to say nothing of funky, student-approved cafes and cloth-ing stores. I love Canterbury, from walking past its old walls, to sipping elderflower cordial in its vegetarian cafes, to discovering Old England around every cobbled corner.

How to get there: Coaches go from Victoria Coach station on **National Express** (☎ 08705/80-80-80; www.nationalexpress.com; 2 hours; £12 single). **Trains** (☎ 08457/48-49-50; www.nationalrail.co.uk; 90 min.; £18 single) go from London Victoria to Canterbury East or from Charing Cross station to Canterbury West. Both stations are equidistant from the town center.

Tourist information: **Canterbury Visitor Centre** (34 St Margaret St.; ☎ 01227/ 37-81-00; www.canterbury.co.uk) is the place to catch walking tours at 2pm daily from Easter through October (☎ 01227/45-97-79; www.canterbury-walks.co.uk; £4.25 adults, £3 children under 12, £3.75 seniors/students).

STONEHENGE & SALISBURY

Construction began about 5,000 years ago on **Stonehenge** (☎ 08703/33-11-81; www.english-heritage.org.uk/stonehenge; £5.90 adults, £3 children, £4.40 sen-iors/students; mid-Mar–mid-May and Sept–mid-Oct daily 9:30am–6pm, Jun–Aug daily 9am–7pm, mid-Oct–mid-March daily 9:30am–4pm), and the first recorded day trips to the megalith were in 1562. Arranged in such a way that it aligns with the rising of the sun during the midsummer solstice, this Neolithic circle of stones is certainly Britain's most important ancient wonder, it's a UNESCO World Heritage Site (together with Avebury, a far less interesting, but still important, line of rocks 39km/24 miles north). Whether its builders, who remain anonymous, worshiped the sun or merely appreciated astronomy is only the beginning of the mystery. We also can only make educated guesses as to how these prehistoric people, using only rudimentary tools, managed to hoist these slabs from Wales to here, and then into place. Even if you don't salivate over such long-ago feats of ingenuity, the distinc-tive profile of the stones, surrounded by empty plains, "henge" earthworks, and hundreds of lumpen burial mounds, will surely be iconic.

To some, Stonehenge is a circle of rocks. If it's raining, it's a damned circle of rocks. But people still ask to go, and if that's their dream, then they should do it.

Just understand that you may not get it, even though the inadequate visitor's center has a few bits about ancient practices and theories on how Stonehenge's arrangement may have evolved over time. You're also not allowed to walk amongst the rocks the way visitors once were; you have to stick to a footpath that curves near the circle but keeps the formation at a safe distance, good for pretty photographs but bad for curiosity. I don't understand the following logic because while respectful tourists like you and me are being kept at arm's length (exception: Clark Griswold, who managed to topple them like dominos in *European Vacation*), the government is planning to plow a tunnel near the precious monument for express car and truck traffic, which many experts predict will cause vibration damage.

The limited experience (a disappointment for many who trudge 129km/80 miles west of London to have it) is why few people see Stonehenge without passing through Bath on the same day. That itinerary is offered by coach tours; putting it together yourself by taking a train to Bath and then finding a bus to the rocks is not ideal because the connections chew up too much time. Salisbury is do-able, though, since trains headed there connect with a bus (see "How to Get There").

Each year from June 20 to 22, people converge upon the stones to celebrate the Summer Solstice. Alternatively, **English Heritage** (☎ 08451/21-28-63; www.english-heritage.org.uk/toursthroughtime; £69 for tours), which controls the site, also runs six popular coach tours each summer that offer the rare chance to walk amongst the stones, as well as a pass through Salisbury to see its famed cathedral. It's smart to book these ahead.

The city of Salisbury is defined and commanded by the soaring 120m (400-ft.) -tall spire of its famous **Salisbury Cathedral** (33 The Close; ☎ 01722/55-51-20; www.salisburycathedral.org.uk; suggested donation of £4; times vary but generally daily 7:15am–6:15pm), built with uncommon efficiency between 1220 and 1258 and barely touched since. This early English Gothic masterpiece is considered by many to be the most breathtaking church in the world. After you've seen it, and lost yourself in gazing at it and sighing, the rest of your time in Salisbury will be contentedly spent walking the city's medieval streets, which were laid in a loose grid and give the city a neat, airy character. It's a lovely town with blissfully little in the way of tourist dreck.

How to get there: Trains don't go directly to Stonehenge; the nearest station is in Salisbury, nearly 16km (10 miles) south. The easiest way to get here is to drive, then. It's located 3.2km (2 miles) west of Amesbury in Wiltshire on the junction of A303 and A344/360. Or take a half-hourly **train** (☎ 08457/48-49-50; www.nationalrail.co.uk; 90 min.; £25 single) from Waterloo station to Salisbury station and from there, bus number 3 from **Wilts & Dorset Buses** (☎ 01722/33-68-55; www.wdbus.co.uk; 45 minutes) to Stonehenge, which from Monday to Saturday leaves four times a day from 11:15am to 2pm, and returns to Salisbury four times between 12:20pm and 3:20pm, with a few extra buses tossed in during the summer; check its website for updated schedules. Sunday service runs less often, so you have to plan this method carefully. On the bright side, this timing enables you to explore Salisbury in the afternoon before heading back to London.

Tourist information: Salisbury and Stonehenge (Fish Row, Salisbury; ☎ 01722/33-49-56; www.visitsalisbury.com).

STRATFORD-UPON-AVON

Stratford-upon-Avon, often described as a "chocolate box" of a town in the Heart of England, doesn't make an ideal day trip from London unless you're willing to make some decisive sacrifices. Not to be confused with Stratford, the up-and-coming multicultural section of East London, Stratford-upon-Avon in Warwickshire, 144km (90 miles) northwest of London, is lily-white and all about the Bard. If he touched it, or if his descendants did, you can bet it's been turned into a tourist attraction. The problem with a trip to Stratford, besides heaving summer crowds, is that its biggest attraction, the highly respected acting company the **Royal Shakespeare Company** (Waterside; ☎ 01789/40-34-44; www.rsc.org.uk), is hard to see on a day trip. The RSC has three theatres in town where it presents as many as three shows a day. Unless you take the train on a matinee day, seeing a show requires an overnight stay. And matinees are frequently booked out by school trips and group tours; if you intend to catch one, you'll need to book about 2 months ahead so you're not shut out. Even if you are, don't sweat it, because the RSC performs steadily in London, too.

The genuine remainders from Shakespeare's day are set upon by Anglophilic coach tourists like dogs upon scraps. The town of 113,000 is, believe it or not, the second-biggest tourist draw in England, after London, so you can imagine how many shops clamor to sell the most miniature thatched cottages and teddy bears in Union Jack tee-shirts. **Shakespeare's Birthplace** (Henley St.; ☎ 01789/20-18-22; www.shakespeare.org.uk; £6.50 joint ticket; Mon–Sat 9am–5pm and Sun 9:30am–5pm, closes earlier in winter) is thought to be the home where the playwright was born, but even if it wasn't—subsequent generations' adoration of the writer have colored historical judgment—it's a good, if heavily restored, example of an upscale Elizabethan house. The locals didn't care for it much until P.T. Barnum tried to buy it and ship it, stone for stone, over to America, and suddenly it became a national treasure. A mile northwest of town, the picturesque thatched **Anne Hathaway's Cottage** (Cottage Lane, Shottery; ☎ 01789/29-21-00; www.shakespeare.org.uk; £5 joint ticket; Mon–Sat 9:30am–5pm, Sun 10am–5pm, hours vary in winter and summer), in a quintessential English garden, is where the playwright's wife lived before she married him, and it dates to the 1400s. You can reach the cottage, a rare window into life 500 years ago, along a public footpath from town. A number of other period houses remain, several of which belonged to husbands of the Bard's kids or grandkids; see them not because you consider them tied to Bill but because you like the Tudor aesthetic.

For all the fragrant gardens and twee, humpbacked cottages, it's easy to forget that in Shakespeare's day, Stratford was a squalid, smelly market town; the roses and friendly hedgehogs were imposed onto the image by later fantasists. That's not to say that Stratford won't fulfill some stereotypes of a pretty English town. Especially in the spring, it's wonderfully inviting. But Stratford's popularity is enhanced by tourist traffic through the villages in the surrounding Cotswolds, which you simply won't be able to see comfortably on a day trip from London.

How to get there: The most direct**trains** (☎ 08457/48-49-50; www.national rail.co.uk; 2¼ hr.; £25 single) go from Marylebone station to Stratford-upon-Avon station. Buses run by **National Express** (☎ 08705/80-80-80; www. nationalexpress.com; 3 hr.; £15 single) take an hour longer, but cost less. Taking the first bus of the morning (8:30am) and the last bus back (5:30pm) only gives you about 6 hours in town, which is do-able but won't enable you to see even a matinee.

Tourist information: **Stratford-upon-Avon Tourist Information Centre** (Bridgefoot; ☎ 08701/60-79-30; www.shakespeare-country.co.uk).

12 The Essentials of Planning

Getting there easily, cheaply, safely & with a fat wallet

FIRST OF ALL, RELAX. GETTING TO LONDON ISN'T AS TRICKY AS IT USED TO be, despite recent security scares. Finding airfare was once the most daunting part, but thanks to the emergence of Web booking, now it's not much harder than finding a cross-country flight. Being ready for the rest (money, electricity, packing) is simply a matter of having the facts.

The only two tools you'll need to get there are a telephone and Web access—and a phone really isn't that necessary. The rest you'll find in this chapter.

WHERE TO FIND TOURIST INFORMATION

Two official information offices, supported by British tax dollars, are set up to help tourists learn what's worth seeing, doing, and eating. **Visit Britain** (☎ 800/462-2748; www.visitbritain.com), the official tourist information bureau for the whole country, has plenty of information to start you off, including consultants you can grill either by telephone or by live Web chat. Its **British Travel Shop** (551 Fifth Ave., Suite 701, New York City, NY, 10176) welcomes walk-in visitors. But **Visit London** (www.visitlondon.com), the city's hip official tourist bureau, possesses the bigger database by far. It's stocked with more information than you'll know what to do with, including special deals, downloadable restaurant guides, and reams of listings for upcoming events (walks, festivals, talks) that you'd never know about otherwise. Visit London doesn't maintain an informational phone line, but it strives to answer all e-mailed questions within 36 hours. Visit London and Visit Britain will both send free information packs to prospective tourists; request those online. I've also found some fun ideas for short events and offbeat days on the commercial weblog the **Londonist** (www.londonist.com).

WHEN TO VISIT

It's always time to visit London. Even though it's approximately at the same latitude of Edmonton, Alberta, the prevailing weather patterns keep London's weather from being extreme in any way. It gets cold in the winter, but rarely snowed in. It gets warm in the summer, but rarely blisteringly so (in fact, most buildings don't even have air-conditioning). The winter months are generally more humid than the summer ones, but experience only slightly more rain.

The principal art season (for theatre, concerts, art shows) falls between September and May, leaving the summer months for festivals and park-going. A few royal attractions, such as the state rooms of Buckingham Palace, are only open in the summer when the Queen decamps to Scotland. In summer, when the weather is warmest and half of Europe takes its annual holiday, the airfares are higher, as are hotel rates (although corporate hotels crank rates much higher than family-owned places tend to), and the queues for most of the tourist attractions, such as the London Eye and the Tower of London, might make you wish you'd come in March. For decent prices and less crowds, I prefer spring and fall—April and October seem to have the best confluence of mild weather, pretty plantings, and tolerable crowds. Prices are lowest in mid-winter, but a number of simpler sights, such as historic houses, sometimes close from November to March (see chapter 5).

The table below charts seasonal weather and price shifts.

	Jan	Feb	Mar	Apr	May	June	July	Aug	Sept	Oct	Nov	Dec
Average Temps ° F	40	40	44	49	55	61	64	64	59	52	46	42
Average Temps ° C	4	4	7	9	13	16	18	18	15	11	8	6
Days of Precipitation (more than 0.25mm)	15	13	11	12	12	11	12	11	13	13	15	15
Avg. hours of sunlight (sunrise to sunset)	8.5	10	12	14	16	16.5	16	14	12	10	8.5	8
Typical transatlantic airfare*	$300 to $430	$300 to $430	$300 to $430	$440 to $520	$500 to $650	$680 to $740	$680 to $740	$680 to $740	$420 to $540	$430 to $500	$360 to $470	$300 to $430

* Vacation holiday periods both at home and in England, such as Christmas or Thanksgiving, can raise prices. These prices don't include tax.

London's Best Annual Events

Festivals and special events are an integral part of London's calendar, and many regular happenings draw tourists from around the world. Find more events at London's city website (www.london.gov.uk/gla/event), at Visit London's site (www.visitlondon.com), and in *Time Out* magazine.

January or Early February
Chinese New Year Festival (☎ 020/7851-6686; www.chinatownchinese.co.uk): In conjunction with the Chinese New Year, the streets around Leicester Square come alive with dragon and lion dances, children's parades, performances, screenings, and fireworks displays.

London International Mime Festival (☎ 020/7637-5661; www.mimefest.co.uk): Not just for silent clowns, but also for funky puppets and Blue Man–style tomfoolery, it's held around town in late January.

February
Great Spitalfields Pancake Race (☎ 020/7375-0441): Held on Shrove Tuesday (usually the last Tues in Feb), this is a race through the streets of Spitalfields by skillet-wielding teams of four, who toss pancakes to each other as they run. Winners receive an engraved fry pan. Spectators get a tale to dine out on.

March
National Science Week (☎ 020/7019-4937; www.the-ba.net): In the second week of March, the scientifically inclined throw a week of talks, shows, and demonstrations to bring kids and adults alike into the fold.

St. Patrick's Day Parade and Festival
(☎ 020/7983-4100): When you're this
close to Dublin and you consider England's
long rivalry with the Emerald Isle, you can
expect lots of raging Irish pride—and lots
of young people using it as an excuse to
get wicked drunk. The city also sponsors
concerts, craft fairs, and kids' activities
promoting Irish culture and heritage. It's
not just about drinking—it just looks that
way. It takes place in the second week of
March.

BADA Antiques and Fine Art Fair (www.
bada-antiques-fair.co.uk): Sponsored in
mid-to-late March by the British Antique
Dealers' Association, it's considered to be
the best in Britain for such collectors.
Some 100 exhibitors move into a mighty
tent in Duke of York's Square, in Chelsea,
for the 7-day sales event, which is
peppered with talks, exhibitions of rarities,
fashion shows, cooking demonstrations,
and wine tastings. Don't expect a bargain
but an education.

Late March or early April
Oxford and Cambridge Boat Race
(www.theboatrace.org): The hugely popular annual event takes less than a half-
hour on the Thames, but the after-party
rollicks into the night. See p. 231.

London Harness Horse Parade
(☎ 01737/64-61-32): On the Monday
after Easter, some 300 horses, donkeys,
and other prancing beasts of burden
promenade through Battersea Park pulling
their various carriages.

April
London Marathon (☎ 020/7902-0200;
www.london-marathon.co.uk): Incongruous as it is to see some 35,000 athletes stagger around town emblazoned
with the logo of the margarine-brand
sponsor, Flora, the Marathon is still a kick
for spectators, and a landmark on the
world running scene. (Hotels around town
tend to fill up ahead of it.) The starter
pistol fires in Greenwich, and the home

stretch is along Birdcage Walk and The
Mall around St James's Park. If you want
to run, apply by the previous October—
and cut out the margarine.

May
Chelsea Flower Show (☎ 020/7834-
4333; www.rhs.org.uk): Tickets go on sale
in November for this lillypalooza, and
they're snapped up quickly. The Royal
Horticultural Society, established in 1804,
which calls itself "a gardening charity dedicated to advancing horticulture and promoting good gardening" (don't you just
love the English?), mounts this celebrated
show for 5 days in late May on the grounds
of the Royal Hospital in Chelsea. The
plants, all raised by champion green
thumbs in a country that knows its flowers,
are sold to attendees on the final day, but
sadly, foreigners aren't usually able to get
their plants past Customs.

June
Beating Retreat (☎ 020/7414-2271):
Drum corps, pipes and drums, and plenty
of bugle calls: This anachronistic twilight
ceremony, held for 3 evenings in early
June at Horse Guards Parade, involves the
salute of the Queen (or another member
of the royal family) and the appearance of
many red-clad marchers. Scholars can
trace its origins back to 1554—so in
other words, it may not signify much, but
for tradition's sake, it's deeply meaningful. It's the nearest relative to the better-
known Trooping the Colour, but without
the crowds. Reserve ahead.

The Royal Academy Summer Exhibition
(www.royalacademy.org.uk): Artists have
been in a frenzy about this blind competition for nearly 240 years. Paintings, sculpture, drawings, architecture—if you can
dream it, you can enter it, and if you're
one of the most talented, your piece is
anointed as the best the country offers
that year. The show is what the Royal
Academy is known for, and although it's
not envelope-pushing, it's a seminal event

in British art culture and shouldn't be missed if you're in town. All the works are for sale, and proceeds fund the Academy's palatial digs for the rest of the year.

Trooping the Colour (☎ 020/7414-2479): Never mind that the Queen was born in April. This is her birthday party, and as a present, she gets the same thing every year: Marching soldiers with big hats. Gee, thanks. Fortunately, the spectacle is extreme, as a sea of redcoats and cavalry swarm over Horse Guards Parade, 41 guns salute, and a flight of Royal Air Force jets slam through the sky overhead. The Queen herself leads the charge, waving politely to her subjects before the riflemen take over in a passive-aggressive show of might. It's the closest thing Britain has to a national day like the Fourth of July, and after such extravagant displays of pomp, no doubt is left that the color has been truly trooped. Held in mid-June, it starts at 10:30am. If you want grandstand seats instead of standing in the free-for-all along the route, you'll need to send a request (tickets are free) by February at the latest to Brigade Major, Headquarters Household Division, Horse Guards, Whitehall, London, SW1A 2AX, United Kingdom. SASEs are required, so you will have to include an International Reply Coupon from your post office so that your return postage is paid. Otherwise, check out the Beating Retreat for a similar, if less elaborate, experience.

London Pride (www.pridelondon.org): A signature event on the world's LGBT calendar, London Pride pulls some 250,000 revelers with an impressive roster of concerts and performances by famous names plus a parade in the center of the city. The gay pride week, co-sponsored by the Mayor's office and a number of vital British corporations (British Airways, Virgin Mobile, and others), also makes for an excellent excuse for some blowout dance parties. Late June.

Wimbledon Championships (☎ 020/8971-2473; www.wimbledon.org): Why watch the Grand Slam to end Grand Slams on television yet again? Check p. 232 for tips on how to net tickets and be one of the 500,000 to witness it in person. Late June to early July.

O2 Wireless Festival (☎ 0871/230-9840; www.O2wirelessfestival.co.uk): Held al fresco in Hyde Park, late in the month. 2006 names included David Gray, James Blunt, and Depeche Mode.

Greenwich and Docklands International Festival (☎ 020/8305-1818; www.festival.org): An ambitious program of free theatrical and musical pieces, many of them developed by artists expressly for the public spaces they're performed in. It's held in late June.

City of London Festival (☎ 020/7377-0540; www.colf.org): Traditional and high-minded classical music concerts held toward the end of the month in some of The City's oldest buildings.

Meltdown (☎ 0870/380-0400; www.rhf.org.uk): An out-of-left-field compendium of contemporary arts held at the end of June at the South Bank Centre, curated each year by a notable such as Patti Smith, Nick Cave, and David Bowie.

The Tower Music Festival (☎ 08708/95-56-66; www.towermusicfestival.co.uk): Major names play the moat of the Tower of London. 2006 acts included James Brown, the Pet Shop Boys, and Dionne Warwick,. Tickets run from £35–£65. It usually spans late June to early July.

June through August

Coin Street Festival (☎ 020/7401-3610; www.coinstreetfestival.org): Held around Southwark and the South Bank, this festival gives various London communities (Cubans, Turks, the elderly) different days devoted just to them. Food, music, dance, and bright colors seem to be the objective, as does finding new excuses to enjoy the embankment on the Thames.

Watch this Space Festival (☎ 020/ 7452-3400; www.nationaltheatre.org. uk): A grab bag of free movies, shows, and concerts in the public space around the Royal National Theatre. Yep, another excuse to strut around along the mighty river.

July

Rise: London United (☎ 020/7983-6554; www.risefestival.org): London's biggest free music festival, which takes over Finsbury Park for a day, promotes cultural diversity and ending racism and presents a mix of hip-hop, indie, jazz, pop, reggae, comedy, and family events.

Clerkenwell Festival and Shoreditch Festival: These modest-sized local festivals, held in mid-July, delve into the traditional culture of each neighborhood: Italian and Roman Catholic for Clerkenwell, and fashionistas for Shoreditch.

The Country Show (☎ 01366/ 72-85-52; www.lambeth.gov.uk): An old-fashioned farm show overtakes Brixton's Brockwell Park (for a single weekend in the middle of July, anyway) with farm animals, jam-making contests, a fun fair, tractor demonstrations, and Punch and Judy puppet shows.

July to September

BBC Promenade Concerts (☎ 020/ 7589-8212; www.bbc.co.uk/proms): The biggest classical music festival of the year, held primarily at the Royal Albert Hall, "the Proms" consists of orchestral concerts for every taste. Seats start at £5.

August

Fruitstock (☎ 020/8600-3177; www. fruitstock.com): Sponsored by a smoothie company, this 2-day festival in Regent's Park is all about free music, a dance tent with a DJ, all-natural food stalls (and plenty of Pimm's), kids' activities, poetry slams, and flopping around on the grass. Pray for good weather.

Great British Beer Festival (www. camra.org.uk): Just like it sounds: more than 450 ales available to try at Earl's Court Exhibition Centre—after all those tastings, you'll be relieved to learn the Tube is within easy reach. It runs 5 days in early August.

Notting Hill Carnival (☎ 0870/059-1111; www.lnhc.org.uk): In August 1958, roving bands of white racists combed the slums of Notting Hill in search of Caribbean-owned businesses to destroy. Two weeks of disgusting race violence, among the worst in London's history, ensued. Resulting community outrage and newly rediscovered cultural pride led to the formation of a new festival, which today is Europe's largest street parade. Originally a party for Trinidanian culture held in a town hall, the Carnival has grown into a powerhouse smorgasbord of cultures spanning the rest of the Caribbean as well as Eastern Europe, South America, and the Indian subcontinent. It attracts some 2 million people during the August Bank Holiday weekend, which includes the last Monday in August. Sunday is kids' day, with scrubbed-down events and activities, but on Monday, the adults take over, costumes get skimpy, floats weave through small streets, and rowdy hordes celebrate into the wee hours.

September

Brick Lane Festival (☎ 020/7655-0906; www.bricklanefestival.com): Inclusive and warm-hearted, this event was established in 1996 as a less intimidating alternative of the Notting Hill Carnival, although it's held a few weeks later, on the second Sunday of September. Some 60,000 arrive to enjoy food, music, performances, a fashion show by resident designers, clowns, and buskers, mostly in the name of honoring the melting pot that the East End has always been.

The Great River Race (☎ 020/ 8398-9057; www.greatriverrace.co.uk): Always over too soon, the Race is the aquatic version of the London Marathon, with rowers vying to beat out 300 other vessels—Chinese dragon boats, Canadian canoes, Viking longboats, and even Hawaiian outriggers—on a morning jaunt from Richmond to the bottom tip of the Isle of Dogs, at Greenwich. It's held on a Saturday in mid-September.

Open House London (☎ 020/7380-0412; www.openhouselondon.org): A blockbuster 2-day architecture-appreciation event that goes down every mid-September. More than 600 buildings, all of them deemed important but normally closed to the public, yawn wide for free tours on a single, hotly anticipated day. Past participants have included the distinctive skyscraper headquarters of Swiss Re (officially "30 St. Mary Axe" but usually called "The Gherkin") and the Mansion House (official residence of the Lord Mayor, completed in 1752). The list of open buildings comes out in August and some require timed tickets, but for most, the line forms at dawn. Open House also organizes walking tours throughout the summer.

The Mayor's Thames Festival (www.thamesfestival.org): In conjunction with the Great River Race, nearly half a million souls attend London's largest free open-air arts festival, which includes more than 250 stalls selling food and crafts, a flotilla of working river boats, circus performers, and antique fireboats, tugs, and sailboats. Sunday sees the Night Carnival, a lavish procession of 2,500 lantern-bearing musicians and dancers crawling along Victoria Embankment (the north bank) from Waterloo Bridge to Blackfriars Bridge, and finished with barge-launched fireworks. It takes place on a mid-September weekend.

Dance Umbrella (☎ 08707/30-14-07; www.danceumbrella.co.uk). One of the world's best dance festivals, with plenty of standing-room seats for as little as £5; it peaks in late September.

Late September to early October
London Fashion Weekend (www.londonfashionweekend.co.uk): It's got nothing on its kin in New York or Milan, but at this brief festival, collections from more than 100 designers are put on sale at deeply discounted prices in the hopes they'll build some buzz.

October
Diwali: One advantage of visiting a multicultural city like London is that it affords you the chance to sample major international holidays in an English-speaking environment. One such treat is Diwali, the Indian "festival of light," when Trafalgar Square is transformed with light displays, floating lanterns, massive models of the elephant god Ganesh, music, dance, and DJs. It's free and held in mid-October.

Origin: The London Craft Fair (www.craftscouncil.org.uk): The Crafts Council, which has organized Europe's biggest crafts fair in the first half of October, has been undergoing some life-threatening reorganization of late, but the plan is to keep the tradition alive. In a purpose-built pavilion in the courtyard of Somerset House on the Thames, a range of disciplines from more than 300 artists are highlighted, from glass to metal, and from furniture to jewelry.

London Film Festival (☎ 020/7928-3535; www.lff.org.uk): An important stop on the world film circuit, it starts at the end of the month and spills into November.

October or November
State Opening of Parliament (www.parliament.uk): There's not much to see in person—just a white-haired monarch zipping in and out of Parliament in a state coach with a cavalry contingent—but the rest is shown on television. Inside, the goings-on aren't much more transparent; Her Royal Highness reads a speech in the House of Lords that she didn't even write (the prime minister did), to kick off the

new season of legislation and establish the ruling party's objectives. She does wear some lush vestments; there's a cavernous room in the Houses of Parliament devoted just to dressing her.

November

Guy Fawkes Night: In 1605, silly old Guy Fawkes tried to assassinate James I and the entire Parliament by blowing them to smithereens in the Gunpowder Plot. Joke's on him: To this day, the Brits celebrate his failure by blowing up *him*. His effigy is thrown on bonfires across the country, fireworks displays rage in the autumn night sky, and more than a few tykes light their first sparklers in honor of the would-be assassin's gruesome execution. Although displays are scattered around town, including at Battersea Park and Alexandra Palace, I suggest getting out of the city for the weekend nearest November 5, also called Bonfire Night, because the countryside is perfumed with the woody aroma of burning leaves on this holiday. If you can't get somewhere cobbled like York or Canterbury, mount Primrose Hill or Hampstead Heath for a view of the fireworks going off around the city.

Lord Mayor's Show (www.lordmayors show.org): What sounds like the world's dullest cable access program is actually a delightfully pompous procession, abut 800 years old, involving some 140 charity floats and 6,000 participants (Pewterers! Basketweavers!) who parade round-trip from Mansion House in The City and head to the Royal Courts of Justice, on the Strand, all to ostensibly show off the newly elected lord mayor to the queen or her representatives. The centerpiece is the preposterously carved and gilt lord mayor's coach, built in 1757—a carriage so extravagant it makes Cinderella's ride look like a skateboard. The procession marks the only time the coach is permitted to venture outside of its air-conditioned garage inside the Museum of London. That's a lot of hubbub for a city official whose role is essentially ceremonial; the mayor of London (currently Ken Livingstone) wields the true power. All that highfaluting strutting is followed by a good old-fashioned fireworks show over the Thames between the Blackfriars and Waterloo bridges. It's held on the second Saturday in November, and it's usually broadcast on TV.

London Jazz Festival (☎ 020/7324-1881; www.serious.org.uk): Some 165 mid-November events attract around 60,000 music fans. Many performances are free.

November

Remembrance Sunday: Another chance to glimpse Her Royal Highness. She and the prime minister, as well as many royals, attend a ceremony at the Cenotaph, in the traffic island of Whitehall, to honor the war dead and wounded, of which Britain has borne more than its share. Those red flowers you'll see everywhere—red petals, black centers—are poppies, the symbol of remembrance in Britain. It takes place on the Sunday nearest November 11.

December

New Year's Eve: London doesn't throw massive street parties—if you want that, Edinburgh's Hogmanay is the place in Britain to be—but Trafalgar Square does host a packed, liquor-free midnight countdown. The next day at noon, some 10,000 participants in the annual New Year's Day Parade (www.londonparade. co.uk) traipse up Whitehall from outside Parliament, head up Regent Street, and hang a left on Piccadilly, winding up by the Green Park Tube stop. Some 500,000 line the route, but four times that number watch it on TV.

Holiday Lights

If you're planning a trip to the city during the affordable period between mid-November and the first week of January, know that:

◆ Oxford and Regent streets around Oxford Circus Tube, plus Carnaby Street just east, are decorated with a series of spectacular illuminated archways; Scrooge may be their electrician, though, since holiday insignia has been usurped by commercialized images such as characters from *The Incredibles*.

◆ Bond Street, befitting its sterling boutiques, goes for a refined white-and-silver lighting motif.

◆ Trafalgar Square hosts a giant Christmas tree, an annual gift from Norway in thanks for helping it out during World War II.

◆ Imagination Design, on South Crescent, Store Street, just east of Tottenham Court Road (Tube: Goodge Street), installs a stunning holiday-themed tableau that stretches up its entire six-story facade.

◆ Harrods on Brompton Road (p. 269) shines so brightly it seems to have been dipped in gold. Stop in for its after-Christmas sale and save some of your own.

ENTRY REQUIREMENTS FOR NON-BRITISH CITIZENS

For tourism, citizens of the United States, Canada, Australia, and New Zealand only need a valid passport to enter Great Britain, and they don't have to pre-arrange visas. You will be asked when you are leaving the country, so it's a good idea (but not a requirement) to have your tickets booked before you land. You should also make sure your passport will be valid for the entirety of your stay.

Visa & Medical Requirements

As of this writing, passport holders from the United States, Canada, Australia, New Zealand, and South Africa do not require visas to enter the United Kingdom as a tourist. The usual permitted stay is 90 days or fewer, although some nationalities are granted stays of up to 6 months. If you plan to work or study, though, you'll need to obtain the correct paperwork. This information may have changed by the time you read this, so check **UK Visas** (www.ukvisas.gov.uk) for the latest rules.

The United Kingdom does not require any special immunizations of its visitors.

GETTING THE BEST AIRFARE TO LONDON

The better question is *when* are they? London is such a popular destination (it's served by more flights from the United States than any other European city) that plenty of airlines are vying to carry you across. Assuming you're not redeeming frequent-flier miles, there are three rules to finding bargains:

1. **For starters, fly on Monday, Tuesday, or Wednesday, when traffic is lightest.** The main London airports serving transoceanic travel are Heathrow (LHR) and Gatwick (LGW). Fly to whichever one yields the best price.

2. **Choose a transatlantic flight that departs after dinner.** This will not only save you another hotel night, since you'll arrive in the morning, but you'll also find lower fares, because business travelers don't favor this timing.

3. **Go off season.** London's weather isn't extreme, so there's really not a no-go month. November through March yield the lowest airfares and hotel rates. Summer prices (June–Sept) can be a steely $600 to $900.

4. **Search for fares on a weekend.** Presumably because fewer business travelers want Saturday flights, many major airlines post lower prices then. You might also save money by booking your seat at 3am. That's because unpaid-for reservations are flushed out of the system at midnight, and prices often sink when the system becomes aware of an increase in supply.

Most times of year, the least expensive way to reach London is with an **air-hotel package,** which combines discounted airfare with discounted nights in a hotel. I swear by them, and smart travelers do, too. The best air-hotel packages invariably cost several hundred dollars less than what you would pay if you booked both of these components separately.

If you find a good air-hotel deal, then your worries about both airfare and lodging will be over, leaving you to plan the real fun. A box introduces you to the major players on p. 38. Remember that the cheapest deals are the ones in which both transatlantic flights fall on Monday, Tuesday, or Wednesday.

Then it's a matter of which airlines you check. **Air India** (☎ 800/223-7776; www.airindia.com), which goes from New York City, is known for sporting consistently cheap prices, such as $300 round-trip tickets outside of summer. These airlines schedule regular flights to London, and many produce e-mail newsletters that might alert you to deep discounts: **Air Canada** (☎ 888/247-2262; www.aircanada.com); **American Airlines** (☎ 800/433-7300; www.aa.com); **British Airways** (☎ 800/247-9297; www.ba.com); **Continental Airlines** (☎ 800/231-0856; www.continental.com); **Delta Air Lines** (☎ 800/241-4141; www.delta.com); **Northwest Airlines** (☎ 800/692-6955; www.nwa.com); **United Airlines** (☎ 800/864-8331; www.united.com); **U.S. Airways** (☎ 800/622-1015; www.usairways.com); **Virgin Atlantic Airways** (☎ 800/821-5438; www.virgin-atlantic.com). The Scottish low-cost carrier **Zoom Airlines** (☎ 866/359-9666; www.flyzoom.com) flies between London and eight major Canadian cities, and at press time, it was gearing up to add New York City and San Francisco from starting prices around £99 each way. The standard on American airlines has tumbled in recent years, and the decline means that the U.K.-based carriers now have a clear advantage. For example, British Airways and Virgin Atlantic are now two of the last transatlantic carriers to honor the longstanding tradition of offering complimentary wine to passengers, a graceful touch that the American carriers have discontinued. So if you find similar prices between carriers, go for the British one—you'll get more respectful treatment for your money.

If you're hitting a wall, use a few online airfare engines or agents (such as **Kayak.com, Orbitz.com, Flightcentre.com, Travelocity.com, Sidestep.com, Qixo.com,** or **Expedia.com**) to search for transatlantic itineraries that allow for one or two stops, since routes that include stops in Paris or Frankfurt (on

Lufthansa or Air France, say) can produce hidden bargains. A famous example is **Icelandair** (☎ 800/223-5500; www.icelandair.com), which since the 1960s has enticed intrepid travelers onto flights to London that stop in Reykjavík long enough for them to take a delicious dip in the famous Blue Lagoon, which is near the airport. That sci-fi cool detour often saves you about $200 off the going non-stop airfare. It flies from six North American cities in summer; fewer in winter. Also look at **Aer Lingus** (☎ 800/474-7424; www.aerlingus.com), which stops in Dublin or Shannon.

Should you require a flight from your home city to the airport from which your transatlantic flight leaves, it's smarter to book with an airline that has a partner agreement with your London-bound airline. That way, if your luggage goes awry on your first leg, or if your first flight is late, your second airline will sort things out. If you fly your first leg on a carrier with no partnerships, such as JetBlue or Southwest, and you're late and miss your London flight, you may be out of luck.

Some travelers are flexible enough to use alternative booking sites such as **Priceline.com**, where buyers name their own price for tickets and hope the airlines take them up on their offer; and **Skyauction.com**, which functions like eBay for tickets. Travelers who plan to head to multiple international cities on their trip should get a free quote for their entire itinerary from **Airtreks** (☎ 877/247-8735; www.airtreks.com), a travel agent that specializes in multi-city tickets. You'll still want to compare its quote with your own fare research, though.

No matter which airline you go with, prepare yourself for taxes, which are usually $100 to $125 from the USA—high for the industry.

If you're a window-seater and you're flying into Heathrow, sit on the right side of the plane and you'll usually get an incredible fly-by of the city on your westerly approach for landing.

BOOKING A PLACE TO STAY

For tips on booking online and bargaining, go to p. 61, and for information on renting an apartment or staying in a private home, go to p. 28.

SWAP, MEET: HOME EXCHANGES

You'd be surprised how many Londoners are dying to visit your own stomping grounds, and if you make contact with the right people, you can swap houses at an agreed-upon time (sometimes simultaneously). It sounds strange, but it tends to work and nothing tends to get stolen because swappers often become good friends. Not just that, but their neighbors tend to go out of their way to show you the coolest parts of their city—the ones that only residents know. You can truly live like a local when you swap homes, and quite a few people end up doing it year after year.

Plenty of exchange clubs exist, and because London's an interesting place, it's pretty well represented in all of them. Which club should you choose? Well, since almost all of them are pitched to specific clientele with their own set of tastes, that's for you to decide. Here are the biggies, in alphabetical order:

Digsville.com (☎ 877/795-1019): For $45 a year, this popular and well-designed site allows users to see photos of their prospective swap and even read feedback from others who have traded with its owner.

Geenee.com (www.geenee.com): A 2006 newcomer, it focuses on just six cities, including London. The owners have visited every flat and rated them with a star system, and members rate each other, eBay-style. Its fee schedule suits people who can't exchange every year: The fee is $75 upon joining, and $120 for the first exchange, but after that, exchanges are free forever.

HomeExchange.com (☎ 800/877-8723): This club of more than 6,000 listings, in business since 1992, breaks searches down by interest, including for seniors, private boaters, long-term stays, and RVs. It costs $50 a year to list.

Homelink.org.uk (☎ 019/6288-6882): Popular with British and Australian travelers (with 13,000 members in 51 countries), this 53-year-old service is also the most expensive, at about $200/year, which includes two printed directories.

Intervac (☎ 800/756-4663; www.intervacus.com): Intervac has been around for half a century, but its old catalog system has migrated to the Web. Its claim to fame is that some 80% of its listings are international (52 countries are represented), which means (as it puts it), "you compete with fewer Americans for overseas properties." Access to all listings is $70 a year.

Swap and Stay (☎ 0870/300-8181; www.swapandstay.com): Another newbie (born March 2006), it requires its properties to be second homes (a vacation property but never time shares). Basically, it's for homes that may sit empty much of the year. The company owners are in England. It's £50 a year.

There are additional exchange sites for special interest groups, designed to provide safe haven for travelers with particular needs. **SabbaticalHomes.com** caters to academics; **Independent Living Institute** (www.independentliving.org) is a free database maintained by a Sweden-based advocacy group for people with disabilities; **HomeAroundtheWorld.com** (☎ 020/7564-3739) is for gays and lesbians and costs £39 for two years; and **SeniorsHomeExchange.com** is for those over 50 and costs $79 for a 3-year listing.

TRAVEL INSURANCE—DO YOU NEED IT?

Yes, you do, principally because you're going abroad. Should something unpleasant befall you, you may need to be flown back home on a stretcher, and no matter how much you beg, you can't save money by coming home as cargo. At the very least, you may need to cancel your trip before you leave, and travel insurance can buffer you from a large financial loss.

But does that mean you need to buy some? Not necessarily—you may already have it. Your existing medical coverage may include an international safety net; ask so you're sure. The credit card you use to make reservations may cover you for cancellation, lost luggage, or trip interruption; again, the only way to be sure is to ask your issuer. Most hotels will issue refunds with enough notice, but a few of the cheap ones won't.

So what else may you want to insure? If your medical coverage and credit cards don't lend a hand, you may want special coverage for **apartment stays,** especially if you've plunked down a deposit, and any **valuables,** since airlines are only required to pay up to $2,500 for lost luggage domestically, less for foreign travel, and not every hotel provides in-room safes.

If you do decide on insurance, you can easily compare available policies by visiting **InsureMyTrip.com.** Or contact one of the following reputable companies:

> **Access America** (☎ 866/807-3982; www.accessamerica.com)
> **CSA Travel Protection** (☎ 800/873-9844; www.csatravelprotection.com)
> **MEDEX** (☎ 800/732-5309; www.medexassist.com)
> **Travel Guard International** (☎ 800/807-3982;www.travelguard.com)
> **Travelex** (☎ 800/228-9792; www.travelex-insurance.com)

TRAVELING FROM LONDON TO OTHER PARTS OF THE UNITED KINGDOM

The British rail system is so comprehensive that many tourists spend weeks on the island without seeing the inside of a car. Considering the high cost of British fuel, rarity of British parking, and narrowness of British streets, having a car is not recommended, but if you are silly enough to do it, make sure you learn how to drive a stick shift before you leave home. Cars with automatic transmissions are inevitably much more expensive than manuals. Driving on the left is easy after a few minutes of pulse-racing acclimation.

RAIL

The original railway builders plowed their stations into the middle of pretty much every town of size, making it easy to see the highlights of the United Kingdom without getting near a car. While the British whine about the declining quality of the service, Americans, Canadians, and Australians will be blown away by the speed and low cost of the system, particularly if you book a month or two ahead. Find tickets to all destinations through **National Rail** (☎ 020/7278-5240; www. nationalrail.co.uk). Make every effort to book as far ahead as possible, since early-bird bookings can yield some marvelous deals, such as £14 for a 4-hour trip to Scotland (although £60–£100 round-trip is more common). It accepts bookings 3 months in advance of travel.

I've never run across a case in which the money you'd pay for a **BritRail pass** (☎ 866/2748-7245; www.britrail.com) is worth it. Tickets bought reasonably in advance will still be cheaper than what you'd pay for the same trips on a pass, and few tourists ride the rails with the near-daily regularity and long distances that would make a pass pay for itself.

BUSES

The least expensive way to get from city to city in Britain is via coach, and because the country's not very big, it rarely takes more than a few hours to reach anyplace. I know lifelong Londoners who have never ventured as near as Scotland because they find the journey—around 5 hours—too cumbersome. **National Express** (☎ 0870/5808-8080; www.nationalexpress.com) is a major carrier with scads of departures, but the best-priced is **Megabus** (☎ 0901/331-0031—it costs 10p a minute to book at www.megabus.com), which serves 36 cities, and charges as little as £1 for early bookings, although £10 to go clear to Edinburgh is a more typical rate. It accepts bookings 2 months ahead. Both coach services depart from Victoria Coach Station, located immediately southwest of Victoria railway station.

A hop-on, hop-off minibus circuit of Scotland is conducted by **MacBackpackers** (☎ 01315/58-99-00; www.macbackpackers.com; from £99), a playful outfit favored by younger travelers. It leaves London every Saturday, returning the next Sunday.

So what's the best place to hear about inexpensive ground tours? Hostels. Drop into one of the places mentioned in the accommodations chapter; most of their lobbies are practically wallpapered with brochures. Don't neglect their bulletin boards, either, since you may catch wind of a shared-ride situation that'll often cost you no more than your share of the gasoline (in England, *petrol*).

COMBO PACKAGES

Some packagers put together dashes to popular European cities (Paris, Amsterdam, Berlin) that include Eurostar/train/air tickets, B&B accommodation for a night or so, and often some sightseeing. Try **Anderson Tours** (☎ 020/7436-9304; www.andersontours.co.uk), check the travel sections of the London papers, and pick up a copy of *TNT* at hostels.

TRAVELING FROM LONDON TO OTHER PARTS OF EUROPE

Not everyone wants to stick around London for their whole vacation. After all, you've flown all that distance, so why not peck around in Europe a little while you're at it? Hop a plane, and you can be in Paris within an hour.

Finding cheap flights poses a slight challenge, since presumably you're not familiar with the European market. But once you know where to look, you'll find some incredible deals, such as £25 one-way to Spain or £30 to Germany—as affordable as coaches, and usually less than trains. Even formerly high-priced airlines such as British Airways now charge low fares.

The so-called no-frills airlines began life by shuttling Londoners to the mass resorts of the Mediterranean, but today, dozens of small-scale carriers fly all over the place (see the box below for more info), including to cities lifelong Europeans have never heard of. And it's useful to learn that because so many Londoners have family in Commonwealth nations such as Australia, New Zealand, and South Africa, flights to those destinations can often be had very cheaply—even when you add in the cost of your transatlantic airfare, it can be cheaper to fly via London to, say, Sydney, than if you flew Down Under from your home airport. The travel pages of London's newspapers as well as *TNT* magazine, dispensed for free at most hostels, are brimming with ads for deals on flights, charter or otherwise.

The big hitch is baggage; if you pack much more than a modest case, you'll get slapped with excess baggage fees. If you'll be returning to London from Europe before flying back home again, consider asking your hotel if you can leave excess luggage behind for a small fee. See p. 350 for more info on this.

Flying from London to Europe, Cheaply

There are literally dozens of no-frills carriers, most of which eschew assigned seating, charge a few pounds for checked luggage, and fly out of London's secondary airports: Luton, Stansted, and Gatwick. The biggest lines are **Ryanair** (☎ 08712/46-00-00 in the U.K. or ☎ 3531/249-7791; www.ryanair.com) and **easyJet** (☎ 08712/44-23-66; www.easyjet.com), both of which start selling tickets to flights for insanely low prices (£3 to Spain) and gradually raise prices to £30 to £50 as more seats are sold. Dozens more smaller carriers specialize in cheap flights to different parts of mainland Europe. You could check prices with each no-frills carrier in turn, but that'd be tedious. Instead, the following websites, which collect prices from multiple carriers, are good starting points. Many of them list last-minute specials, too, in case you have some extra time but can't decide in advance where in Europe you'd like to go. Just remember to look into the visa requirements for the country you'd like to visit—you'd feel really stupid if you bought a ticket you can't use.

These websites focus on the major carriers but not many no-frills airlines: Ebookers.com; Opodo.co.uk; Travelocity.co.uk.

These websites show no-frills carriers (since each one leaves out a few airlines, check them all): Skyscanner.net; Travelsupermarket.com; Gooflight.com; Whichbudget.com; Skylow.com.

EuropeByAir.com (☎ 888/321-4737) sells you $99 vouchers for 150 European destinations that you redeem (one per flight, even connections) at the airport. Taxes of $40 to $80 aren't included, making check-in laborious, and vouchers must be shipped in advance to addresses outside of Europe, so it's not ideal.

Lastminute.com does big business in discounted vacation packages including airfare and hotel. Picture nights at a Red Sea resort, for £219 per person or 4 nights in Venice for £299 per person—that sort of thing.

RAIL

For trips to northwestern Europe, I prefer the train. It's more dignified, since it doesn't require endlessly juggling luggage, enduring airport waiting rooms, and tucking yourself into puny airline seats. As you watch the countryside roll past your window, you get a real sense for how the land fits together. You can stretch your legs whenever you want. Plus, thanks to the opening, in 1994, of the engineering wonder known as the Channel Tunnel, it takes around 3 hours by high-speed train from London to reach the heart of a several major European destinations. Unlike taking a flight, you won't need to set aside extra hours and pounds for trips to and from the airports; you'll get on and off in the heart of each endpoint. You can literally ride the Tube and the Paris Metro in the same day—both before lunch. In fact, you can ride both a black taxi and the loops of Space

Mountain before lunch, since the Eurostar train alights in the middle of Disneyland Resort, just east of Paris. Eurostar links London with Paris, Brussels, Avignon, Lille, and Calais. Book via **Eurostar** (☎ 1233/61-75-75; www. eurostar.com; phone bookings are £5 more) itself or the U.S.-based **Rail Europe** (☎ 888/382-7245; www.raileurope.com), which also sells European rail passes. Check both sites since prices can differ slightly. European trains don't do e-tickets, which means you'll need a paper ticket, so book well before leaving home so they will have time to reach you.

BUSES

A few coach companies also travel to Europe, usually navigating the Channel with an old-fashioned ferry ride. Because of the pressure put on the market by mushrooming no-frills airlines, rates are extremely low. You'll pay as little as £18 from Victoria Coach Station to Paris on **Eurolines** (☎ 08705/14-32-19; www.euro lines.co.uk). Amsterdam or Brussels is £15 with a 7-day advance purchase from **EuroBus Express** (☎ 08706/08-88-06; www.eurobusexpress.net). It can take all day, sunrise to sunset, to reach Paris by this method, so you can imagine what an ordeal it must be to go all the way to Poland or the Czech Republic on a bus, as many cash-strapped Europeans do.

Young, social adventurers should investigate **Busabout** (☎ 020/7950-1661; www.busabout.com), a coach system that follows set loops from London to France and Spain, Italy, and Germany and the Czech Republic. Passengers can hop on and hop off as they please. Some other companies arrange full-on organized tours of Europe's greatest hits—but never for less than you could do independently; choose one only because you'd enjoy having company: **Contiki** (☎ 020/8290-6422; www.contiki.com) is geared toward a party-hearty under-35 crowd, **Budget Expeditions** (☎ 020/8896-1600; www.budgetexpeditions.com) is for social scrimpers, and **Fanatics** (☎ 020/7240-3233; www.thefanatics.com) is for followers of organized sports. Whenever you read a sample itinerary, pay close attention to the departure point; if it's not London (often denoted as "ex. London"), you'll have to find your own way there.

FERRIES

No ferry to Europe sails from London. For those, you'll have to get down to the southern coastal towns of Folkestone and Dover (for France), or Portsmouth (for Spain). Unless you have your own car, it's hard to use the ports of the France-destined lines; most people take them in conjunction with the coach trip booked from London that I just told you about. Some of the bigger players, many sailing the Channel more than a dozen times daily (from £12 each way, 150 min.), are **Seafrance** (☎ 08704/43-16-53; www.seafrance.com) and **P&O Ferries** (☎ 08705/ 98-03-33; www.poferries.com). **Acciona Trasmediterranea** (☎ 08717/20-64-45; www.atferries.com) goes from Portsmouth to Bilbao, Spain, starting at £50 for a 29-hour trip in a four-berth inside cabin. Given the proliferation of low-cost airlines, ferry travel has become an outdated and time-consuming way to travel, and it's mostly used by people who need to transfer cars.

GETTING TO THE AIRPORTS: RAIL IT

Transatlantic flights almost always land at either Heathrow, the world's busiest international airport, or Gatwick, perhaps the most dissed; with a few minor exceptions, the other three airports (Stansted, Luton, and London City) serve flights from Europe, and they're where the cut-rate flyers tend to go. See p. 346 for info on those.

Happily, getting to and from the airports is easy and relatively painless. Every airport offers some kind of rail connection to the central city. You'll rarely have to

Airport Transportation Options
from Central London

Airport	Cost/Avg. time for using Mainline rail	Hours of service	Destinations	Cost/Time for Tube or DLR	Cost/ Avg. time for coach shuttle service	Cost/ Avg. time by taxi
Heathrow (LHR)	Heathrow Express: £15 single, £27 return*/15 minutes OR Heathrow Connect: £9.50 single/30 minutes	5:10am to 11:25pm	Paddington	£4/60 minutes on Piccadilly Line	£10 single, £16 return (www. nationalexpress. com)/50–70 minutes	£51–£55/ 70 minutes
Gatwick (LGW)	Gatwick Express: £14 single, £25 return/30 minutes OR Thameslink: £9/45 minutes	3:30am to 12:30am	Gatwick Express: Victoria; Thameslink: King's Cross Thameslink, Blackfriars, or London Bridge	N/A	£6.60 single, £12 return (www.national express.com)/ 90 minutes	£82/70 minutes
Luton (LTN)	£11.20/60 minutes	5:15am to 12:45am	King's Cross Thameslink, Blackfriars, or London Bridge	N/A	From £2 (www. easybus.com)/ 60 minutes	£75/80 minutes**
Stansted (STN)	£15 single, £25 return/45 minutes	5am to 11:30pm	Liverpool Street	N/A	£10 single, £16 return (www.national express.com)/ 110 minutes	£80/80 minutes
London City (LCY)	N/A	DLR: 5:30am to midnight	N/A	£3/25 minutes on Docklands Light Railway	N/A	£25 to £27/ 20 minutes

£1 less if you book ahead online at www.heathrowexpress.com.

** *As if you'd be daft enough to want a taxi after seeing those prices, these airports don't have ranks for London-bound taxis, so cars must be booked ahead. Check www.london-luton.co.uk and www.stanstedairport.com for a list of their latest approved taxi companies.*

wait more than 20 minutes for the next train on any of these services unless it's very late at night, so you don't have to worry about rushing to catch anything. Railpasses (Senior Railcard, Young Persons Railcard, Family Railcard) are valid for all of these rail routes, but London Underground Travelcards are not; see p. 13 for descriptions of those cards.

The comfy, business-class-level **Heathrow Express** (☎ 08456/00-15-15; www. heathrowexpress.com) zooms to Paddington station every 15 minutes in 15 minutes. Despite its expense, this is one of my routine, surefire splurges, because after a long overseas flight, the last thing I want is to board a Tube train with all my gear. **Heathrow Connect** (☎ 0845/678-6975; www.heathrowconnect.com) is designed to give access to local stations, so it's slower (almost 30 min., since it stops six times), cheaper, uses older carriages, and leaves every half-hour.

Heathrow Express passengers, who arrive at Paddington Station during the morning rush (as transatlantic passengers on overnight flights will) have the benefit of using the station's "taxi sharing" program to reduce the price of an onward taxi trip by a few pounds. Obtain a voucher from the dispatcher at the taxi queue; when there's an accumulation of four or more passengers headed to the same zone, you share a taxi, and tip is included. Otherwise, once you arrive at Paddington, you can hop the Tube system. Keep in mind that if you want to buy the cheapest Travelcard, which is a pass for all-day use, you can only do so after 9:30am.

Gatwick Express (☎ 0845/850-530; www.gatwickexpress.com) runs from Victoria station. You get a £3 discount if you buy a round-trip ticket. You can also get to Gatwick via King's Cross, Blackfriars, or London Bridge stations on First Capital Connect, commonly called **Thameslink** (☎ 08456/76-47-00; www.first capitalconnect.co.uk), in 45 minutes—service ends just after midnight.

The Perils of Early-Bird Fares

Warning: Rail service doesn't start up until around 5am. So don't book any flights that depart at 6am unless you're prepared to a) grab a £45 to £55 hotel room near the airport, such as in an Ibis Hotel or a Premier Travel Inn, or b) splash out on a dawn taxi ride.

On the flip side of that, if you fly into Luton or Stansted late at night, particularly if you have a non-EU passport, you'll suffer through their understaffed immigration checkpoints. I once waited 90 minutes to be cleared from an easyJet flight to Luton, where there was a sole sloth-like officer assigned to process all the passengers without EU passports. He took two coffee breaks in that period, and despite landing with plenty of time, I managed to catch the last bus to London that night as it pulled away; otherwise I'd have been marooned at an airport hotel. The lesson: Avoid Luton or Stansted; or else arrive as early as you can. Heathrow, Gatwick, and London City are better equipped for bearers of foreign passports.

Stansted Express (☎ 08456/00-72-45; www.stanstedexpress.com) runs from Liverpool Street station.

Luton has rail service from the King's Cross Thameslink, Blackfriars, or London Bridge stations by **Thameslink** (☎ 08456/76-47-00, www.firstcapitalconnect.co.uk), but it shuts down after midnight. The correct stop is Luton Airport Parkway Station, which is linked by a free shuttle to the terminals.

City Airport is linked so expediently by the **Docklands Light Railway** that it doesn't require mainline rail service or coach service, so it doesn't have any.

CAR SERVICE

I wouldn't bother. Traffic is too snarled and rail service is too snappy. Besides, the variety of rail and coach connections means that chauffeured rides of any kind are considered a luxury service, and priced accordingly. Pay more than you have to and take longer to get there? If you insist.

PACKING

For your wallet's sake, pack sparingly! I know you've heard that before, but it's really true this time. In 2006, pressed by the government, most of the airlines serving London instituted some laughably strict weight limits. It's not as easy as it used to be to wink your way through the weigh-in. The airlines are desperate for new cash, and they will gleefully charge you for every ounce. In many cases, the conveyor belts at check-in are programmed to halt if they sense a bag over the limit. So you can't avoid thinking about this.

British Airways, for example, which once permitted bags of up to 32 kg (70 pounds), sliced the allowance to a puny **23 kg (50 pounds)**. Now, I don't know about the luggage *you* use for big trips, but mine weighs about 15 pounds before I pack a single stitch. When it comes to carry-ons, you may take on a bag with as much weight as you can lift, safety be damned, but it's got to measure no more than 55cm long by 45cm wide by 25cm deep (22 in. by 18 in. by 10 in.). If you want to bring an extra bag, it'll cost you £60! (Say *what?*). Anything heavier than 32kg (70 pounds), it's said, won't be allowed in the country.

British Airways claims its new system is better because it enables travelers to prepay for extra fees at least 24 hours before they leave home, but that's spin. In truth, it's one more preparation that most of us would rather not be burdened with. And just how do they expect us to weigh our bags again when we're in a hotel, about to return home?

My advice: Plan for souvenirs by starting with lightweight luggage and packing it as far under the weight limit as you can stand. Weigh it on your bathroom scale so you'll have a sense of how much leeway you've got for new purchases.

If you find that you simply must purchase a second suitcase in London, head to the eastern end of Oxford Street (between the Tottenham Court Road and Oxford Street Tube stations), which is lined with ticky-tacky shops selling them at low prices. Many of them also sell plastic-coated, zippered duffels in tartan colors, which are cheap (a few quid) and will see you through the journey home.

Now Playing: Carry On Confusion

During periods when the British government deems the potential terrorist threat to be severe, as it did in the summer of 2006, the list of permitted carry-on items is drastically curtailed. For flights within the U.K. and to Europe, no liquids or gels (except essential medicines and baby foods) were allowed; anything questionable, including toiletries and cosmetics, had to be packed in checked bags. Carry-on bags could also not be larger than 56cm by 45cm by 25cm (22in. by 18in. by 10in.). During tense periods, carry-on items for flights to the U.S. are restricted to travel documents only, but that extreme policy is seldom enforced for long. Requirements change regularly, so keep abreast of the latest rules through the Department for Transport (www.dft.gov.uk) or through your airline.

Despite the fact that these changes result in heavier checked baggage, the airlines, uncharitably, won't budge on their new weight limits. So in addition to making sure your carried items conform, you must be vigilant that your checked baggage is within the limit; otherwise you'll pay penalties.

So what *can* you bring? Basically, clothes, very comfortable walking shoes, prescription medications (keep them in their original, labeled containers and bring signed copies of their **prescriptions** for Customs and emergency use). If you require **syringe-administered medications**, always carry a signed medical prescription.

Pare your toiletries down to the essentials. You're not going to the Congo; you can find staples like toothpaste, contact lens solution, and deodorant everywhere in London—many pharmacies stock the same brands you have at home. Women should bring a minimum of makeup, if they dare; the British don't tend to use very much themselves. Brits are also more likely to wear trousers or slacks than blue jeans. If you plan to go clubbing, pack some fashionable duds—Londoners aren't slouches when it comes to dressing up.

You'll be most comfortable if you dress in clothing that layers well. Even in the depth of winter, London's air can be humid, and sometimes, dressing too warmly can become uncomfortable once you begin to perspire. No matter what the average temperature is (see the box on weather, p. 334), the air can grow cool after the sun sets, so plan for that, too. In the winter, a hat, scarf, and gloves are necessities. A compact umbrella is wise year-round, as is an outer coat that repels water, since you never know when you're going to find yourself out in one of those misty rains that makes the British Isles so lush and green.

Don't bring illegal drugs (duh), and also leave the pepper spray and mace at home; they're banned in the U.K.

MONEY

The British pound (£1), a small, chunky, gold-colored coin, is commonly accepted in vending machines, so you can never have too many in your pocket. It's commonly called a "quid." Like money in America, Canada, and Australia, it's divided into 100 pennies (p)—the plural, "pence," is used to modify amounts over 1p. Pence come in 1p, 2p, 5p, 10p, 20p, and 50p denominations. Patterns on the obverse of the £1 and 50p coins periodically change to commemorate various areas or events. Sometimes you'll see large £2 coins, too.

Bills come in £5, £10, £20, and £50 denominations. Every now and then, you'll receive bills made by the Royal Bank of Scotland as change; don't be troubled, since these are legal tender in London, too.

All prices (except hotels') are listed including tax, so what you see is what you pay. No guesstimating required. I don't know why we don't do it that way at home.

When bringing up prices, always insert the word "pounds": For example, £2.50 would be uttered as "two pounds fifty" but never "two fifty." Another issue of cultural syntax: When asking for change (such as from a taxi driver), it's customary to tell him the amount to keep and not the amount to return to you. For example, to pay him £11 with a £20 bill, don't say, "I'd like £9 back." Say, "Please keep £11." I don't know why. Maybe it sounds more polite.

Every visitor should have several sources for money. Cash is king, as they say (Queen Elizabeth isn't jealous—her face is on all the money anyway), but international exchange complicates its acquisition. Each of the following sources should be considered a part of your toolbox, but weigh the pros and cons of each.

CASH

In the old days, visitors had to bring wads of their home currency or travelers checks and then exchange it, bit by bit, as their trips progressed. Some of them would even obtain a fistful of pounds at their bank before they left home.

These days, because of **ATMs,** carrying unseemly sums of money is no longer necessary or advisable. You can pull pounds out of holes in the wall pretty much whenever you please. Every visitor to Britain should arrive with a working ATM card. But it's still wise to bring enough of your home currency to sustain you for a few days, just in case something goes wrong with your plastic. Store it someplace safe, and don't spend it unless you have to.

Before leaving home, warn your bank that you intend to travel internationally so that it doesn't place a stop on your account when international withdrawals start cropping up. You may also need to adjust your PIN, since English banks require four-digit codes. If you know your PIN as a word, memorize the numerical equivalent, because not all English machines will have letters on their keypads.

Most banks hit you with fees of a few pounds each time you withdraw cash. Your own bank may toss in a small fee of its own (ask ahead to see what its policy is), so gauge for yourself how much you feel comfortable withdrawing at a time to offset that fee. Some banks, such as Citibank, maintain several London branches and do not charge extra withdrawal fees to members of its banks worldwide, so if you have an account with an international bank chain, it'd be smart to use their machines exclusively during your visit. Similarly, ask your bank if it has any reciprocal agreements with any English institutions; as of this writing, Bank of America allowed free withdrawals from Barclays machines.

Before You Leave Home . . .

Here's some basic advice on what to do in the weeks before your flight leaves:

Nuts & Bolts:

- Book a flight and hotel. But you knew that one.
- To ease difficulties in case of theft, make copies of your tickets and passport, one to leave with a friend and one to stash in your luggage. Also consider scanning them and storing the files in a free online e-mail account for easy retrieval on the road.
- Buy the electrical adapters you'll need.
- Warn your bank and credit card lenders that you intend to be using your accounts abroad, and double-check that everything's set up to work properly. While you're at it, jot down their international phone numbers.

Activity Planning:

- If you elect to take the Heathrow Express train, book tickets ahead online (p. 348) and you'll save £1.
- Especially from June through September, reserve the time and date of your visit to the London Eye, Buckingham Palace, Clarence House, Spencer House, the Ceremony of the Keys at the Tower of London, Trooping the Colour, and special exhibitions that require timed tickets (such as at the British Museum).
- If there's a show or concert you have your heart set on catching, book ahead.
- Check the list of major festivals (p. 334) to see if there might be something unexpected you'd like to attend.

Be very quick when using British ATMs. Not just for safety reasons, but because if you fail to retrieve your card within 10 to 15 seconds, many machines will suck it back up again for "security." Should that happen, you'll have to wait until the machine is cracked open under armed guard, which means you won't be able to get your card back for a day or three. It really puts a crimp on your vacation. So grab that ATM card as soon as you see it emerge.

CREDIT CARDS

All of the major credit cards you use at home will work in England, but because of the red tape they stick to vendors, American Express and Diners Club are not as commonly accepted as Visa and Mastercard. British lenders are moving toward a PIN-based system; if a clerk asks you to enter your code but your card doesn't require one, just tell them it's an international card and you don't have a PIN.

Before leaving home, warn your credit card issuer that you intend to travel abroad, otherwise they may place a stop on your account when international charges pop up. Many credit card companies also levy transaction fees of a few percentage points every time you make a charge abroad. Since those companies sometimes bury the fee in the exchange rate, you can't always tell if it's happening. Call your credit card company to ask what its international transaction fee is. One of the few credit card companies that doesn't charge an international fee is **Capital One** (☎ 800/695-5500; www.capitalone.com).

In addition, many vendors charge their own transaction fee (3% is the norm) for many purchases as a way of defraying the cost of dealing with credit card companies; there's no way around this one. Minimum purchases for credit card transactions are also common, and that's also perfectly legal.

Try not to use credit cards to withdraw cash. You'll pay a currency exchange fee, and worse, you'll be charged interest from the moment your money leaves the slot. If your credit card allows for online bill paying through links with your bank account, set up that capability before you leave—at the very least, you can pay off your withdrawals within hours, cutting your losses. Using an ATM card linked to a liquid bank account is far less expensive.

TRAVELERS CHECKS & TRAVELERS CARDS

Now that ATMs are so common and so convenient, fewer and fewer people are using these. They'd be more enticing if banks didn't hit you with fees or padded percentages at both ends—when you buy them, and when you cash them. Still, some old-school travelers feel comfortable using them, and I can't blame them for wanting to feel safe. All the major types—American Express, Visa, Citibank, Thomas Cook—are accepted in London.

Several creditors have come up with **travelers cheque cards,** also called **prepaid cards,** which are essentially debit cards encoded with the amount of money you elect to put on them. They're not linked to your personal bank accounts, they work in ATMs, and should you lose one, you can get your cash back in a matter of hours. If you spend all the money on them, you can call a number and reload the card using your bank account information.

The **American Express** (☎ 888/412-6945; www.americanexpress.com) cheque card costs $15 to open and requires a minimum of $300. But it's hamstrung by the same limitations of using a proper American Express card—not everyone will accept it, and you pay the same high transaction fees that you'd pay if it were a credit card. More establishments take the **Visa TravelMoney** (www.visa.com) version, sold through AAA offices in the United States (☎ 866/339-3378); it costs $10 and keeps a little over 1% of everything you load onto it, plus all the regular international transaction fees. It's not ideal, but it's a relatively safe way to travel with money.

MONEY EXCHANGES

Like travelers checks, changing cash is on the outs, and good riddance, since exchange rates are often usurious. Since ATM withdrawals give much better deals, old-fashioned cambios are few and far between these days, although you'll still find a few upon landing at the airport and around Leicester Square and Piccadilly Circus. If you need to change money, take advantage of the better rates offered by banks during regular banking hours (9:30am–4pm). Money exchange booths are for use only after those hours.

What Do Things Cost?

I usually tell people to think of a price that they'd consider expensive—say, something you'd pay in New York City or Miami Beach—and then turn it into pounds. It's not pretty. You'll find yourself developing a taste for white bread and water. Items are less expensive at supermarkets than at corner stores.

Tube rides in the city center for a day:	£4.90; £4.40 using Oyster
Taxi ride, Bloomsbury to Knightsbridge:	£8
Newspaper:	40p
Tube of toothpaste:	£2.50
Box of tampons:	£2
Package of diapers:	£5–£7
Contact lens solution:	£3.50
Cup of coffee:	£1–£2 (more for lattes and other luxury variations)
Triangle sandwich:	£1–£3.50
Caff breakfast:	£5–£7
Restaurant lunch:	£6 (cheap restaurant), £10 (moderate/expensive joint)
Restaurant dinner:	£8 (cheap place), £14 (moderate/expansive place)
Bottle of wine:	£5–£10
Beer in a bar:	£2.50–£3
Big Mac:	£2
Cocktail in a bar:	£6–£10
Bottle of water:	60p–£1.25
Average museum entrance fee:	£5–£8 (when it's not free)
West End musical ticket:	£50 full price, £25 at TKTS
Movie ticket:	£13 in the West End, £7.50 in the neighborhoods
Walking tour:	£5
Football game:	£30 (and up)
Theatre program:	£2–£5

HEALTH & SAFETY

If you don't feel well and you need the advice of a doctor or a nurse, the national health care system operates a free, 24-hour hotline that can help: **National Health Service Direct** (☎ 0845/4647; www.nhsdirect.co.uk). Citizens of many European countries are entitled to free health care while in Britain (see www.dh.gov.uk/travellers for details), but everyone else is not, although clinics have been known to treat tourists and then look the other way rather than embark upon the odyssey of paperwork required to bill them. Still, for non-EU citizens, I strongly encourage getting health or travel insurance. See p. 343 for info on that.

As for safety, few places in London are unsafe. Some locals are made nervous by a few parts of the East End, but there's not much evidence of random violence to back that up. I don't consider bored teenagers racing cars to be a clear and present danger. Other places that pessimistically might be called sketchy are uniformly distant from the Tube lines, and they only feel tense after dark, when shops close. London is like anyplace; simply be aware of your surroundings and be sensitive to who's around you and you'll do fine. If some drunk tries picking on you, never take the bait. Other than that, you'll find the place to be remarkably peaceful for a city of such enormous size.

The biggest nuisance tourists might encounter—besides tipsy locals—is pickpockets. As chronicled in *Oliver Twist,* London (like all cities of size) is home to a skilled subspecies of crook eager to lift the contents of your wallet or purse without your knowledge. Oxford Street and the Tube are the prime picking grounds. Simply be smart about where you put your cash (I prefer my front pocket), and about who's pressing up close to you. If anyone thrusts a map or a wedge of cardboard in your face, bat it away, since those objects are commonly used to divert attention and hide the act.

I'm almost sorry that I mentioned pickpockets at all because they're not all that common, and now you're going to be worried about them, but honestly—you'll be fine. Just be aware.

If you're truly concerned about theft, consider assembling a "fake" wallet containing a few expired credit cards and a few quid which you can part with in lieu of your real goods. Keep it in an obvious place like your back pocket, and hide the "real" one in a money belt or in your front pocket. By the time a villain realizes they got a decoy wallet, they'll be long gone.

Surveillance is the new British national pastime; there are more closed-circuit TV cameras per person than in any other country. Guns are banned—even on most police officers—so you don't often see the kind of violence taken for granted in the United States. Some male tourists have gotten fleeced for hundreds of pounds at some of the **"hostess bars"** in Soho by failing to understand the exorbitant pricing before they enter. If you do suffer a lapse of judgment and accept the barker's invitation to go into one, understand that if you accept the company of a hostess, you could receive a huge bill that may be exacted by lunkheaded yobs with tattooed fingers and indecipherable accents.

Should you find yourself on the business end of the legal system, you can get advice and referrals to lawyers from **Legal Services Commission** (☎ 020/7759-0000; www.legalservices.co.uk). Victims of crime can receive volunteer legal guidance and emotional fortification from **Victim Support** (☎ 0845/303-0900; www.victimsupport.com). In the unlikely event of a sexual assault, phone the **Rape Crisis Federation** (☎ 01159/00-35-60).

Can I Do That?

Some things that are considered sins back home may lead to legal pleasures in London. Which means they're not sinful as long as you're on British soil! To wit:

- The drinking age is 18. But if you're having your first legit night out in London, take it easy, because beers here have higher alcohol content than in most countries. Start with a pint every 2 hours and see how that does you.
- There are no open container laws. That means you can drink beer in public. Until relatively recently, there were even bars on some Tube platforms.
- You may smoke Cuban cigars. Get them at any tobacconist and puff away. If you're American, though, don't try smuggling them home.
- Absinthe, the brutal quaff nicknamed "The Green Fairy," is available here. Drink yours up because American Customs frowns on it, too.

SPECIAL TYPES OF TRAVELERS
ADVICE FOR FAMILY TRAVELERS

London is a dream for families. Something about it captures kids' imaginations—is it the new-sounding accents, or maybe the talk of princesses, or the tales of people getting their heads lopped off? Maybe the appeal is because so many of the stories kids love, from Roald Dahl to Harry Potter to Peter Pan, take place in London. Whatever it is, children are often captivated by the city's attractions, particularly if they've had a hand in helping the family shape its daily activities.

London attractions are eager to cater to the family market. The kingly treatment starts, at many places, with the so-named **Family Ticket,** which grants a low price for parents and kids entering certain sights together, such as a single price for two adults and up to three kids. Always ask about it, because some box offices neglect to post the prices. Single parents and those with a smaller brood aren't left out, because kids under the age of 5 are almost always admitted for free, and kids under 15 receive hefty discounts off the adult price.

Many museums—and I really, really love this—consider it a badge on honor to offer elaborate **kids' activities,** usually for free or for a pittance. For example, the Natural History Museum lends themed "Explorer Backpacks" equipped with a pith hat, binoculars, pens, paper, and a booklet that engages children under 7 in their visit with simple scavenger hunt activities. Most of the big museums do something similar, and even the smallest exhibitions, such as the Handel House Museum, often offer a nook for coloring, simple hands-on activities, and even a rack of little costumes to try on. I daresay parents will get bored of the museums before their kids do. Perhaps the only place where your very young (under 5) children won't be embraced with open arms is the theatre—many won't admit little ones.

The **Family Railcard** (www.family-railcard.co.uk) is for at least one adult and one child aged 5 to 15, with a maximum of three adults and four kids on one ticket; at least one child must travel with you at all times. It awards adults 33%

off and kids 60% off. Two kids under the age of 5 can travel with an adult for free at all times, even without this card. It's for sale at rail stations.

If you are a **divorced parent** with joint custody of your children, make sure you bring documentation proving that you are entitled to take your kids out of the country; otherwise, Immigration may give you a hard time.

Some resources that offer family-specific travel tips include the **Family Travel Network** (www.familytravelnetwork.com), online since 1995; **Travel with Your Kids** (www.travelwithyourkids.com) specializes in tips for international travel and it also maintains a section just about London's finds. **The Family Travel Files** (www.thefamilytravelfiles.com) rounds up tour operators and packagers geared to families, but its suggestions aren't always the most economical or efficient.

Babysitting: **Top Notch Nannies** (☎ 020/7259-2626; www.topnotchnannies. com) normally brokers child-minders—usually Australians or Eastern Europeans—to wealthy London families, but it also runs a sideline, **Brilliant Babysitters,** which starts with a £10 booking fee and then charges about £7 an hour on weekday evenings and £8 an hour on weekends.

The weekly *Time Out* magazine, on sale wherever you turn in London, includes a section on kids' activities. Of course many events and sights that aren't expressly kid-specific might enchant your offspring, so plumb the other sections, too.

ADVICE FOR STUDENTS

My advice boils down to: Have your I.D. ready to go, and always mention that you're a student, because it'll save you cash. Attractions gladly offer discounts of around 50% for full-time students, but your high school or university identity card may not cut it in a place where clerks have not heard of your school. Before leaving home, obtain some recognized ID such as the **International Student ID Card** (ISIC; www.istc.org) so that there's never a question of your eligibility.

Those under 26 who are not still in school can obtain a **Federation of International Youth Travel Organizations** (FIYTO; www.fiyto.org) card, which performs many of the same tricks as a student discount card. You can get the FIYTO from discount travel sellers and hostelling associations.

Advice for Travelers with Disabilities

London can be very hard going. The city can't seem to strike the right balance between preserving old buildings and making sure they're accessible to all. With the laudable exception of the Docklands Light Railway, only a slim selection of Tube stations offer lift service, and those with plenty of escalators still require passengers to climb several flights of stairs. It's shameful. The situation is so scrambled, and positive changes so slow that you'll need to do a bit of research. For guidance on the transport system's disabled facilities, including free detailed maps, contact **Transport for London Access & Mobility** (☎ 020/7941-4600; www. tfl.gov.uk). On the bright side, most **taxis** are wheelchair accessible; look for the illuminated chair symbol by the "for hire" sign. The government has also set up the **Disabled Persons Transport Advisory Committee** (www.dptac.gov.uk), which supplies transportation information online.

Generally speaking, the more expensive a hotel is, the more likely it is to be wheelchair accessible, but of course, you should always call ahead (as you probably already do anyway) to make sure. Two of the few low-cost lodgings with provisions for guests in wheelchairs are the YHA Thameside and the easyHotel in Kensington, both listed in the "Accommodations" chapter.

Most disabled traveler resources prefer to disseminate their research via the Web or through publications. **Holiday Care** (☎ 020/8760-0072; www.holidaycare. org.uk) is dedicated to providing updated information about the accessibility of attractions, hotels, and transport. **Artsline** (☎ 020/7388-2227; www.artsline.org. uk) helps distribute information about accessible entertainment venues, including which ones have infra-red hearing devices for rental; its database is located at www.artslineonline.com, but it also welcomes calls. Blind or partially sighted travelers will find useful advice from the **Royal National Institute of the Blind** (☎ 020/ 7388-1266; www.rnib.org.uk). **Tourism for All** (☎ 0845/124-9974; www.tourism forall.org.uk) is a charity that passes accessibility information to older travelers as well as to travelers with disabilities.

Two organizations publish guides that may assist in planning: **Access in London** (www.accessproject-phsp.org) is updated about every 7 years—the most recent version is from 2003; and every January, **The Royal Association for Disability and Rehabilitation (RADAR)** (www.radar.org.uk) puts out *Holidays in Britain and Ireland,* a list of 1,500 accessible accommodations and entertainment centers nationwide.

A U.S. agency called **Wheels Up!** (☎ 888/389-4335; www.wheelsup.com) arranges all aspects of a vacation with wheelchair users in mind. The British agency **Can Be Done** (☎ 020/8907-2400; www.canbedone.co.uk) runs tours adapted to disabled travelers.

Wheelchair Travel (☎ 01483/23-76-68; www.wheelchair-travel.co.uk) rents out self-drive and chauffeured chair-accessible vehicles (including ones with hand controls), provides meet-and-greets and day tours, and arranges city sightseeing in vehicles that accommodate up to a dozen people. Car rental runs from £45 a day, but guided services are much more expensive: from £145 for 2 hours.

Once you're in town, the **London Disability Arts Forum** (☎ 020/7739-1133; www.ldaf.org.uk) plans exhibitions and events by and for artists with disabilities.

ADVICE FOR GAY & LESBIAN TRAVELERS

On November 18, 2004, the British government passed the Civil Partnership Act, which allowed gay and lesbian couples the same civil rights afforded to mixed-gender couples, including in matters of inheritance, pensions, and next-of-kin privileges for hospitalizations—basic entitlements still denied to all couples in the United States. That goes a long way toward explaining the culture's prevailing attitude toward same-sex couples, but to London's shame, a few deadly gay bashings have occurred in recent years. These are rare enough to be newsworthy, but it's true that an element of British society can, once full of ale, become belligerent in groups. Particularly in parks at night, be aware of your surroundings and give wide berth to gaggles of drunken lads, who can behave as if they have something to prove.

The website **Queery** (www.queery.org.uk) lists gay and lesbian social events and festivals and is partnered with the **London Gay & Lesbian Switchboard** (☎ 020/ 7837-7324; www.llgs.org.uk), a counseling hotline.

Help for Women Travelers

A true club and not an agency, **Women Welcome Women Worldwide** (☎ 01494/46-54-41; www.womenwelcomewomen.org.uk) is for female travelers and costs $45 a year; at press time, there were more than 535 women registered in the United Kingdom who were eager to meet and host traveling women from around the world. The entire point of the organization is to broaden lives by connecting members with other members from foreign cultures, so if you avail yourself of this group, you'll be seeing London with someone who wants to treat you like a friend and to take an active interest in your experience.

For nightlife planning, the best sources for information (among many less handy glossy lifestyle magazines) are the *Boyz* (www.boyz.co.uk) which publishes a day-by-day schedule on its website. The free *QX International* (www.qxmagazine.com), lets anyone download a free facsimile of its printed edition every week, so you can plot a course through the hotspots while you're still at home. Both publications are distributed for free at many London gay bars.

ADVICE FOR SENIORS

Don't hide your age! Seniors in England are usually classified as those aged 60 and over, and they're privy to all kinds of price breaks, from lower admission prices at museums to a third off rail tickets (but you first have to apply for the **Senior Railcard;** www.senior-railcard.co.uk). If you lived in London, you could get even more, such as free Tube rides forever. How's that for generational respect?

You may hear seniors being referred to as OAPs, which stands for Old Age Pensioners. That acronym is falling out of use, perhaps because it's rare to find a solvent pension fund anymore. Don't be automatically offended if you're also referred to as a "geezer," though—in England, it means a fun-loving (if sometimes rowdy) bloke or dude of any age.

If you're over 50, you can join **AARP** (601 E Street NW, Washington, DC, 24009; ☎ 888/687-2277; www.aarp.org), and wrangle discounts on hotels, airfare, and car rentals. The well-respected **Elderhostel** (☎ 877/426-8056; www.elderhostel.org) runs many classes and programs in London designed to delve into literature, history, the arts, and music. Packages last from a week to a month and include airfare, lodging, and meals.

So if you're of age, brandish that I.D. and strut about like the geezer you are!

STAYING CONNECTED

INTERNET

Getting online in London won't challenge you. Except in the business district of The City, this place is full of international travelers—and therefore, places to get online. If you've brought your laptop, the quest will be easier, since many hotels are wired; rates run from £10 to £20 a day, although £12 is probably the average. Countless Internet cafes and coin-operated kiosks can be found around town. Libraries are reserved for residents, so you can't rely on them.

The most common Internet cafe chain is **easyInternetcafé** (www.easyinternet cafe.com), part of the day-glo empire that brought you easyJet and easyHotel, which operates multileveled spaces filled with row upon row of flat-screen terminals. Rates fluctuate according to how many people are present, but usually hover around £1 for 30 minutes. These places are fairly filthy, understaffed, and crawling with shiftless youth (so keep a close eye on your bags), but they're open until 10pm or midnight and you can usually find a seat. Fifteen locations are around town, with West End locations in Burger King's basement at Piccadilly Circus (46 Regent St., W1; Tube: Piccadilly Circus; 358 Oxford St., W1; Tube: Bond Street; 9-16 Tottenham Court Rd., W1; Tube: Tottenham Court Road; and east of Trafalgar Square 456-459 Strand, WC2; Tube: Charing Cross).

TELEPHONES

Long-distance telephone cards are available at newsagents and post offices, and they bring the per-minute rate for a call to North America to a few pence. Don't use them in your hotel room, since even "free" 0800 calls can cost money there.

The majority of London's **pay phones** are operated by BT (British Telecom). Pay phones on the street accept any coin worth 10p or greater. The minimum cost is 30p, which buys a 15-minute call for local and national numbers. Phones don't give change. Anytime you call a mobile phone in Britain, the fee will be higher (although under the British system there is no fee to *receive* a mobile call). Some pay phones accept credit cards at a premium: 95p per call local and domestic, and £1.20 for international calls or calls to domestic mobile phones. Full charge breakdowns by country and call duration are searchable at **British Telecom** (www. payphones.bt.com/publicpayphones). Stick to payphones on the street if you can, since phones at many pubs and hotels legally jigger their phones to charge at a higher rate—the price must be posted on the phone.

The bigger problem is **mobile phone** service. Apart from renting a phone while you're in London (an undertaking that I wouldn't recommend to the casual visitor), many tourists who have quad- or tri-band mobile phones simply enable the international **roaming** feature of their service. I advise doing this only as an emergency tool or if you have deep pockets, since you'll end up paying as much as $2 per minute, even if you just call another location in London.

What's worse, mobile phone providers such as T-Mobile have a nasty trick up their sleeves: Once they know that your phone is abroad (they're alerted the first time you turn it on, even if you don't make calls), they charge obscene international rates every time someone calls you—even if you don't answer. Even if those callers don't leave a message. Even if your phone's *off.* Tell everyone you know not to call you abroad unless they absolutely have to. Also jot down the time and number of every single call you make, since mobile phone companies are increasingly billing customers for calls they didn't make and then blaming it on bad information sent by the foreign company that handled the call.

If you do have a quad- or tri-band phone that uses the GSM system—and you might without even knowing it—you can buy a cheap pay-as-you-talk phone number from a mobile phone store. For example, **Vodafone** (www.vodafone.com) charges £2 for a SIM card, which you stick in your phone, and then you buy vouchers to load your account with as much money as you think you'll use (no refunds). That will give you a local number, which you can e-mail to everyone back home, that charges local rates (20p–40p per min.), not crazy international

Dial-a-Guide

Local calls start with 020. If the number is close to the center of town, the next number will be 7; otherwise, it will be 8. The main toll-free prefixes are 0800, 0808, and 0500. Numbers starting with 07 are usually for mobile phones and will be charged a higher rate. Numbers starting with 09 and 118 are premium-rate calls that will usually be very expensive (i.e. £1.50 per minute).

From Home:

 ◆ When dialing a number in this book, precede it with your country's international prefix (in the U.S. and Canada, it's 011), add the U.K.'s country code (44), and drop the first zero in the number.

 ◆ You can't reach 0845 or 0870 numbers in Britain from abroad; in those cases, use the Web for information. Whenever possible in this book, I've found a local number that you can reach.

From Britain:

 ◆ Dial 00 first to signal you're making an international call. Then add your destination's country code (Australia: 61; Canada: 1; New Zealand: 64; United States: 1) and last, the area code and number.

 ◆ The main toll-free prefixes are 0800 and 0500.

 ◆ 0845 numbers are charged at a local rate; 0870 at the national rate.

 ◆ If you call a toll-free number located back home, you'll still pay international rates for it.

ones, for your calls. Just remember to call your provider before you leave home and have them "unlock" your phone so that the British SIM card will function in it. That service is usually free. Other U.K. mobile providers with pay-as-you-talk deals, all comparable to Vodafone, include **Orange** (www.orange.co.uk); **T-Mobile** (www.t-mobile.co.uk); and **Virgin Mobile** (www.virginmobile.com).

The English send some 1.035 million text messages a month; they know, as you should, that for quick communications, they're cheaper than a local call.

If you'll be traveling with a laptop and you'll have broadband Web access where you're staying (two big "ifs"), consider downloading a free Internet phone service such as **Skype** (www.skype.com), which will allow free calls to anyone who also has the program, worldwide. Using a USB headset gives you the best call quality (and call privacy), but that's one more thing to pack.

RECOMMENDED BOOKS & FILMS

Lots of movies and books are set in London—too many to count. But the recommendations that follow give a sense of the city's everyday life. The city is the star in these picks, not just a setting.

HISTORY

London: The Biography, by Peter Ackroyd is a doorstop covering every epoch. *The London Compendium,* by Ed Gilnert serves as a street-by-street catalog (maddeningly indexless) of little-known facts. For a witty tour of London oddities by way of the places on its version of the Monopoly board, try *Do Not Pass Go,* by Tim Moore. *The Pax Britannia Trilogy,* by Jan Morris is a three-volume saga of the rise and fall of the British Empire. A *Survey of London, Written in the Year 1598,* by John Stow offers an eyewitness account of the reign of Elizabeth I. Gillian Tindall's *The House by the Thames* spins the story of Southwark's changes by tracing the history of a town house that survived them all. *The London Scene: Six Essays on London Life,* by Virginia Woolf is a quick read in which the writer profiles the city in the early 20th century. *The Subterranean Railway,* by Christian Woolmar details the Tube's tortured creation.

FICTION

Charles Dickens' *Oliver Twist* regards the woes of the Industrial Revolution while his *A Tale of Two Cities* is set in London and Paris in the late 1700s. *The Complete Sherlock Holmes,* by Arthur Conan Doyle proves useful if you want to understand the most elementary Holmsian references. In *The End of the Affair,* Graham Greene captures the psychosis of living in London during the Blitz. *Hangover Square,* by Patrick Hamilton showcases the malaise of the prewar years. Unlike its film adaptation, Nick Hornby's *High Fidelity,* is set in London, and it provides an accurate snapshot of modern city life. *Saturday,* by Ian McEwan, is about a man confronting his views in a post-9/11 city. *London: The Novel,* by Edward Rutherfurd tells the city's tale as an epic saga. *1984,* by George Orwell, was inspired by the writer's post-Blitz malaise in Islington. *253,* by Geoff Ryman is an unusual work tracing the inner thoughts of 253 Londoners as they ride a doomed Bakerloo line train. *White Teeth,* by Zadie Smith offers a comic portrait of the city's modern Asian immigrant families.

FOR KIDS

A Little Princess, by Frances Hodgson Burnett, is a twee but time-proven rags-to-riches tale. *The Story of the Amulet* and *The Story of the Treasure Seekers,* by E. Nesbit collects sassy stories of magic, set in Edwardian London, that cut a pattern for J.K. Rowling's *Harry Potter* series, which is steeped in the British school milieu. *The Mary Poppins* series centers around a practically perfect nanny and some quintessentially West London stories about the upper-middle-class.

MOVIES

Gad-about-town Michael Caine hits on every London lass in *Alfie* (1966). Two young lads fall in love in the gritty Thamesmead project of southeast London in *Beautiful Thing* (1996). Judi Dench plays a wartime burlesque theatre owner (warning: Bob Hoskins naked) in *Mrs. Henderson Presents* (2005). *About a Boy* (2002) features Bayswater, the London Zoo, Regent's Park, and Channel 4's *Countdown*. In *The Elephant Man* (1980), shad Thames, south of Tower Bridge, stands in for darkest Whitechapel. *Four Weddings and a Funeral* (1994) was made at the chapel at Greenwich's Royal Naval College and the South Bank Centre, among other spots. *Withnail & I* (1987) shows Camden Town in the '60s not as a bohemian paradise, but as a bittersweet trap of poverty. *Frenzy* (1972) is a Hitchcock hatchet job filmed mostly around Covent Garden. *The Madness of King George* (1994) was shot around Windsor, Eton, and Syon House. Watch *Notting Hill* (1999) to see Hugh Grant pine in London's swankiest 'hoods. *Secrets and Lies* (1996) showcases an authentic clash of residents of many cultures. *Sliding Doors* (1998) is a clever "what if" fantasy shot all over town. Don't call it stupid; *A Fish Called Wanda* (1988) definitely bears renting. Check out *The Italian Job* (1969) for a car heist classic every Briton can quote.

The ABCs of London

Area Codes See p. 362 for info.

ATMs/Currency Exchange See "Money" on p. 352. The city's main American Express office is at 30-31 Haymarket, SW1; ☎ 020/7484-9610; Tube: Piccadilly Circus.

Business Hours Offices are generally open weekdays between 9 am or 10am to 5pm or 6pm. Some remain open a few hours longer on Thursdays and Fridays. Saturday hours for stores are the same, and Sunday hours for stores are generally noon to 5pm or 6pm. Banks are usually open from 9:30am to 4 or 5pm, with some larger branches open later on Thursdays or for a few hours on Saturday mornings.

Drinking Laws Legal drinking age is 18.

Electricity The current in Britain is 240V AC. Plugs have three squared pins. Foreign appliances operating on lower voltage (those from the U.S., Canada, and Australia use 110-120V AC) will require an adapter and possibly a voltage converter. A few hotels, but not many, will provide a bathroom plug for a simple appliance such as a shaver.

Embassies and Consulates As a capital, London hosts foreign diplomats. Many offices are open only in the morning. **Australia:** Australia House, Strand, WC2B 4LA; ☎ 020/7379-4334; www.uk.embassy.gov.au; Tube: Temple. **Canada:** Canadian High Commission, 38 Grosvenor St., W1K 4AA; ☎ 020/7258-6699; www.canada.org.uk; Tube: Bond Street. **Ireland:** Passport and Visa Office, Montpelier House, 106 Brompton Rd., SW3 1JJ; ☎ 020/7225-7700; http://foreignaffairs.gov.ie; Tube: Knightsbridge. **New Zealand:** New Zealand House, 80 Haymarket, SW1Y 4TQ; ☎ 020/7930-8422; www.nzembassy.com/uk; Tube: Piccadilly Circus. **United States:** 24 Grosvenor Square, W1A 1AE; ☎ 020/7499-9000; www.usembassy.org.uk; Tube: Bond Street; no walk-ups admitted; you must phone ahead for an appointment.

Emergencies The one-stop number for Britain is 999—that's for fire, police, and ambulances. See "Health & Safety" earlier for more info.

Holidays Banks and most businesses close on Christmas Day (Dec 25), Boxing Day (Dec 26). Good Friday and Easter Monday are public holidays. There are three bank holidays, on the first and usually the last Mondays in May (how they fall depends on the year), and the last Monday in August. Museums are generally closed on public holidays but not necessarily on bank holidays.

Hospitals Charing Cross Hospital, Fulham Palace Road, W6; ☎ 020/8846-1234; Tube: Hammersmith; **Chelsea Royal Hospital,** Royal Hospital Road, SW3, ☎ 020/7730-0161; Tube: Sloane Square; **Guy's Hospital,** St. Thomas St., SE1; ☎ 020/7955-5000; Tube: London Bridge; **Soho NHS Walk-In Centre,** 1 Frith St., W1; ☎ 020/7534-6500; Tube: Tottenham Court Road; **St Thomas's Hospital,** Lambeth Palace Road, SE1; ☎ 020/7928-9292; Tube: Lambeth North, Waterloo, or Westminster.

Libraries Library services are not available to nonresidents of London. The main British Library is at 96 Euston Rd., NW1; ☎ 020/7412-7332; www.bl.uk; Tube: King's Cross St. Pancras; Monday, Wednesday to Friday 9:30am to 6pm, Tuesday 9:30am to 8pm, Saturday 9:30am to 5pm, Sunday 11am to 5pm.

Mail At press time, postcards cost 42p to send to Europe and 50p anywhere else. Most letters will cost 50p to 72p, depending on their weight. For price updates, consult www.postoffice.co.uk. Stamps can be purchased at many newsagents, supermarkets, and at any Post Office; most are open 9am to 5:30pm daily, plus 9am to noon Saturdays.

Newspapers and Magazines London offers more publications than one would think a city of its size could support. The broadsheets, ordered from left to right, politically speaking, are: *The Guardian, The Independent, Evening Standard, The Daily Telegraph,* and *The Times.* The salmon-colored *Financial Times* covers business. The tabloids are fluffier and more salacious, and they include *The Sun* (which has published photos of topless "Page Three Girls" since 1970), *The Mirror, Daily Star, The Daily Mail* and *Daily Express;* few of those deliver news as most people would define the term. Most have a weekend or sister publication; *The Guardian's* is called *The Observer. The Sunday News of the World* is notoriously gossipy, as is the muckraking *Sunday People. Time Out* publishes a thorough weekly listing of events and entertainments; new issues go on sale Tuesdays. International publications such as the *International Herald Tribune, Time, Newsweek,* and *USA Today* are widely available. Other popular magazines include *Heat* (celebrity gossip), *Radio Times* (TV listings and celebrity interviews), *Hello!* and *OK!* (fawning celebrity spreads usually planted by publicity agents), *Q* (music and entertainment), and *NME* (music).

Pharmacies Every police station keeps a list of pharmacies that are open 24 hours. Also try **Zafash,** open 24 hours, 233-235 Old Brompton Rd., SW5; ☎ 020/7373 2798; Tube: Earl's Court; and **Bliss,** open 9am to midnight, 5-6 Marble Arch, W1; ☎ 020/7723-6116; Tube: Marble Arch. For nonemergency health advice, call **NHS Direct** at ☎ 0845/4647.

Safety See p. 355 for info.

Smoking Smoking is prohibited in all museums and most restaurants, and plans are afoot to ban it by law in pubs by mid-2007. If in doubt, ask permission.

Taxes All prices, except some hotel tariffs, are listed including taxes.

Telephone Directory Assistance Call ☎ 118-500 or www.bt.com.

Time Zone London is generally 5 hours ahead of New York City and Toronto, 8 hours ahead of Los Angeles, 11 hours behind Auckland, and 9 hours behind Sydney. It is 1 hour behind western continental Europe.

Tipping Waiters should receive 10% to 15% of the bill, unless service is already included—always check the menu or ask your server if service is included because traditions are changing. At pubs, tipping isn't customary unless you receive table service. Taxi drivers should be tipped about 10% of the fare. Service staff at fine hotels should be greased with a pound here and there, but staff at B&Bs and family-run hotels don't expect tips. Bartenders and chambermaids need not be tipped.

Toilets London doesn't have enough of them. Washrooms can be found at any free museum in this guide, any department store, any pub or busy restaurant (although it's polite to buy something), and at Piccadilly Circus and Bank Tube stations. Mainline train stations also have public toilets, some of which may cost 20p to 50p. Also keep an eye out for spray-cleaned, coin-operated (50p) Automatic Public Conveniences, or APCs.

Index

See also Accommodations and Restaurant indexes, below.